D1087511

CLARENDON LAW SERIES

Edited by
TONY HONORÉ AND JOSEPH RAZ

CLARENDON LAW SERIES

The Concept of Law
By H. L. A. HART

An Introduction to the Law of Contract (3rd edition)
By P. S. ATIYAH

Precedent in English Law (3rd edition)
By RUPERT CROSS

Introduction to Roman Law
By BARRY NICHOLAS

Constitutional Theory
By GEOFFREY MARSHALL

Legal Reasoning and Legal Theory
By NEIL MACCORMICK

Natural Law and Natural Rights
By JOHN FINNIS

The Foundations of European Community Law
By T. C. HARTLEY

The Law of Property (2nd edition)
By F. H. LAWSON and BERNARD RUDDEN

An Introduction to the Law of Torts (2nd edition)
By JOHN G. FLEMING

An Introduction to Administrative Law
By PETER CANE

BENTHAM

and the

Common Law Tradition

GERALD J. POSTEMA

CLARENDON PRESS · OXFORD
1986

Oxford University Press, Walton Street, Oxford OX2 6DP

Oxford New York Toronto
Delhi Bombay Calcutta Madras Karachi
Kuala Lumpur Singapore Hong Kong Tokyo
Nairobi Dar es Salaam Cape Town
Melbourne Auckland
and associated companies in
Beirut Berlin Ibadan Nicosia

Oxford is a trade mark of Oxford University Press·

Published in the United States
by Oxford University Press, New York

British Library Cataloguing in Publication Data

Postema, Gerald J.
Bentham and the Common Law tradition.
1. Common law
I. Title
340.5'7'01   K588
ISBN 0-19-825505-5

Library of Congress Cataloging in Publication Data
Postema, Gerald J.
Bentham and the common law tradition.
Bibliography: p.
Includes index.
1. Bentham, Jeremy, 1748–1832.   2. Law—Philosophy.
3. Utilitarianism.   4. Common law.   I. Title.
K334.P67 1986   340.5'7   86–5274
ISBN 0-19-825505-5

Set by Downdell Ltd., Oxford
Printed in Great Britain
at the University Printing House, Oxford
by David Stanford
Printer to the University

TO LINDA AND ALICIA

Preface

[Bentham's writings] are like exploded shells, buried under the ruins
which they have made.

Fitzjames Stephen, Digest of Law of Evidence.

BENTHAM is a pivotal figure in the history of Anglo-American
jurisprudence. He gave both utilitarianism and legal positivism
their first detailed exposition and defence in English, and negotiated
a sophisticated marriage of the two doctrines. But Fitzjames
Stephen's disparaging comment contains more than a grain of
truth. Bentham's most important jurisprudential work has lain
buried under a great rubble. In this rubble we find the ruins of
much of the practice and ideology of the Common Law system he
so mercilessly and effectively attacked, but also a mountain of inaccessible and largely unpublished manuscripts, the remains of a
very long and curiously undisciplined writing career. Spent shells
are buried here, to be sure, but live ones with great explosive potential remain.

Among the potentially most explosive are his early reflections on
the foundations of law and adjudication. They introduce us to a
jurisprudential debate of historic dimensions and fundamental
philosophical significance. Bentham's writings, and the tradition of
debate to which they contribute, raise questions concerning not
only the nature and tasks of law, but also the role of normative
moral-political theory in the construction and defence of conceptions of the nature of law.

The present work is the first part of a larger study of these issues
of philosophical jurisprudence, issues which remain at the centre of
our practice of law. Durkheim observed that 'law reproduces the
principal forms of social solidarity' in a culture.[1] To this we might
add that a culture's available conception (or, as in our culture, conceptions) of the nature of law models, masks, and interacts with
these forms of social solidarity (forms and conceptions of social

---

[1] E. Durkheim, *Division of Labor in Society*, 68.

order and community). The history of a society and of its legal practice, and the history of attempts to understand and conceptualize
them, shape contemporary forms of 'social solidarity', which in
turn shape that practice. Recent debates in Anglo-American philosophical and legal circles concerning the nature and foundations of
law and the forms and limits of judicial reasoning (and theories of
constitutional judicial review) have been decisively shaped by the
history of our legal practice and attempts to understand it. A key
piece of that history was written in seventeenth- and eighteenth-
century Britain at the birth and maturing of its two dominant legal
ideologies: positivism and Common Law theory. The dispute between these two ideologies is not only historically interesting, it is
philosophically fundamental. The terms of our contemporary
debate, the range and nature of the problems both practical and
theoretical needing contemporary solution, were all set in this
period. Perhaps the most powerful witness to the depth and per-
vasiveness of this influence is the utter naturalness to us of these
terms and assumptions. It is difficult for us now to conceive of law
except against the background of these assumptions.

The aim of the following study is to situate these assumptions, to
trace the evolution of the terms of this debate, and thereby to gain
some critical perspective on them. I am convinced that we shall be
able more adequately to address the general philosophical questions that interest us now after we have fully understood the assup-
tions and perceptions that have shaped them and given them life.
For such understanding we must return to this formative period in
the history of our legal culture. While my ultimate aim is critical
and philosophical, the immediate aim of this work is historical and
expository. Thus, save for some very sketchy remarks in 9.4 and
13.2, I have not sought to address directly the philosophical questions raised by the debate between Bentham and the Common
Lawyers, nor have I attempted a full-scale evaluation of the debate
itself. The remarks in 9.4 and 13.2, accordingly, are meant to be no
more than tentative suggestions of the directions a systematic
philosophical investigation might take.

A major theme of this sudy, explored through a number of variations, is the relationship between authority and reason, and more
specifically between individual rational judgment and the law's
claim to authority. Bentham and the Common Lawyers took
sharply different views of this relationship, and had sharply dif-

ferent perceptions of the social problems which gave immediate practical and political urgency to the issue. We shall see how these assumptions and perceptions called forth contrasting conceptions of the nature and fundamental tasks of law.

In Bentham's legal thought this set of problems took shape as the problem of the relationship between a strict direct-utilitarian theory of practical reasoning and a strongly positivist conception of laws as publicly accessible and empirically identifiable authoritative rules with fixed verbal formulations. This problem is most sharply focused in his theory of adjudication, where his ('antinomian') utilitarian practical philosophy and his positivist conception of laws intersect and demand reconciliation. For this reason Bentham's theory of adjudication is the centre-piece of this study.

The most obvious path of reconciliation of utilitarianism and positivism is to interpret Bentham's theory of practical reasoning along indirect- (rule-) utilitarian lines. But this, we shall see, conflicts with some of Bentham's deepest philosophical commitments. His sophisticated attempts to reconcile these two doctrines is intelligible, I shall argue, only if we abandon the received interpretation of his positivism and its philosophical motivation. An alternative interpretation of his theories of law and judicial reasoning is detailed and defended in Parts II and III.

This interpretation differs substantially not only from standard textbook accounts of Bentham's jurisprudence, but also from some recent scholarly work, in particular L. J. Hume's excellent discussion of Bentham's political theory.[2] The differences may dissolve into differences of emphasis, although I suspect some will in fact resist any attempt at simple reconciliation. No doubt the differences are due to the quite different points from which our interpretations begin and the primary theoretical interests that drive them. L. J. Hume is mainly concerned with Bentham's theory of governmental structure, and his focus is on Bentham's mature work on the constitution. I am more concerned with strictly jurisprudential questions and in particular with Bentham's theory of the practical reasoning of judges and citizens under law. Although

---

[2] L. J. Hume, *Bentham and Bureaucracy*, 171–5, 238–43, and *passim*. Because most of Parts II and III were drafted in near final form some years ago, I was not able to take account of L. J. Hume's work in detail without increasing substantially the length of the text. The same is true for two other excellent recent studies of Bentham from which I learnt a great deal: F. Rosen's *Jeremy Bentham and Representative Democracy* and R. Harrison's *Bentham*.

Bentham's work on the *Constitutional Code* is enormously important for my interpretation as well, I start from a study of
Bentham's earliest criticisms of the Common Law tradition, and I
try to construct in detail the context of this jurisprudential debate.
This starting-point is especially useful because it brings to light
general principles and concerns of Bentham's jurisprudential
thought to which he remained committed throughout his life, principles and concerns which are given their most vital statement in
these early (largely unpublished) writings. (It also highlights the important influence of David Hume on Bentham's legal thought and
draws attention to Hume's great but seldom-noticed contributions
to jurisprudence.)

There may be a more comprehensive perspective within which
L. J. Hume's revised standard interpretation and my revisionist interpretation can be reconciled. Perhaps not. Bentham's writings are
so extensive, and were written for so many different occasions,
problems, and audiences, that it is not surprising if attempts to
render the vast rubble of this material into a systematic and
coherent set of theories yield quite different, conflicting, but
equally plausible interpretations. I sought throughout this work an
interpretation of Bentham's jurisprudence which is honest to the
material he left us and to the historical and intellectual context in
which he wrote. But at the same time I sought a philosophical interpretation of the relationship between Bentham and the Common
Law tradition which can genuinely illuminate the underlying philosophical and political issues with which they grappled.

Durham, North Carolina   G.J.P.
July 1985

Acknowledgements

RESEARCH for this work was begun in 1978 under grants from the National Endowment for the Humanities and The American Council of Learned Societies. I am very grateful for their generosity, without which the project in its present form would never have been conceived. A research development grant from the Arts and Sciences Foundation of the University of North Carolina at Chapel Hill enabled me to prepare the manuscript for publication.

Throughout the long gestation of this work I have benefited in many ways from a large number of people, more than I can now name or even recall. Courtesy and co-operation were freely extended to me by all the members and staff of the Bentham project at University College London and the staff of the manuscripts library of the College. They made my several visits not only productive, but also genuinely delightful, experiences. Professor J. H. Burns was a generous and unerring guide through the morass of Bentham manuscripts and helped me greatly to situate Bentham's work historically. John Dinwiddy and Charles Bahmueller helped me at several points. Claire Gobbi was always ready to assist, with grace, intelligence, and charm. Professor H.L.A. Hart read and commented on portions of early drafts, as did Ross Harrison. I benefited greatly from conversations with them. William Twining's encouragement, support, and colleagueship over these years carried me through times when I thought the project was beyond my means. David Lyons taught me the value of both careful textual scholarship and rigorous philosophical reflection on problems of jurisprudence. I hope this work approaches the standards he set for both.

A special word of thanks goes to David Lieberman. Much of the interpretation of Parts II and III was hammered out in conversations with him over the years, and I could not have begun to write Part I without the superb guidance of his own yet unpublished work. He tirelessly read draft after draft. They are much better for it.

My colleagues at Johns Hopkins University and the University of North Carolina at Chapel Hill have generously supported my seemingly interminable work on Bentham. Especially helpful were Stephen Darwall, Richard Flathman, W. D. Falk, and Thomas Hill, Jr., who read portions of the manuscript and gave wise critical advice. I also benefited from the critical comments of Bikhu Parekh and Annette Baier on selected chapters. Claire Miller, Brad Wilson, Carolyn Joines, and Muriel Dyer helped prepare draft after draft, always under impossible deadlines. I am grateful for their cheerful and efficient service.

To my family, Linda Triezenberg Postema and Alicia Sue Postema, I owe a special debt. Pushkin's 'Capricious belles of the *grand monde*' may have redeemed their otherwise 'insupportable conversation' with an occasional brilliant interpretation of Bentham (*Onegin*, Ch. 1, verse xlii), but yet another interpretation of Bentham from me had the opposite effect on dinner-time conversation. Nevertheless, through the years Linda and Alicia have unselfishly supported and encouraged my all-consuming preoccupation and cheerfully indulged my 'insupportable conversation'. While this debt can never be fully repaid, I acknowledge it with joy and dedicate this work to them.

I also wish to thank the following for permission to quote copyrighted material:

The Oxford University Press for passages quoted from Hume's *Treatise of Human Nature* and *Enquiries*.

The Athlone Press, London, for passages drawn from Bentham's *Of Laws in General, Introduction to the Principles of Morals and Legislation*, and *Comment on the Commentaries and Fragment on Government*.

Editors and publishers of *Revue internationale de philosophie* for material which appeared in an article by me in that journal.

Contents

Contents

Abbreviations

(see Bibliography for full references)

BL Add. MSS	Bentham MSS in the British Library.
Bowring	*The Works of Jeremy Bentham. Published under the Superintendence of. . . John Bowring*, 11 vols. *Bowring* i, 161 = vol. 1, p. 161.
CC	J. Bentham, *Constitutional Code* in *Bowring* ix. *CC* 6 = *Bowring* vol. ix, p. 6.
Comm.	W. Blackstone, *Commentaries on the Laws of England.* 1 *Comm.* 68 = vol. 1, p. 68.
Comment	J. Bentham, *A Comment on the Commentaries*, in *A Comment on the Commentaries and A Fragment on Government*, Bentham, *Collected Works. Comment* 119 = p.119.
Enquiry I	D. Hume, *Enquiry Concerning the Human Understanding*, in *Hume's Enquiries. Enquiry I* 44 = *Hume's Enquiries*, p. 44.
Enquiry II	D. Hume, *Enquiry Concerning the Principles of Morals*, in *Hume's Enquiries. Enquiry II* 195 = *Hume's Enquiries*, p. 195.
FG	J. Bentham, *A Fragment on Government* in *A Comment on the Commentaries and A Fragment on Government*, Bentham, *Collected Works. FG* I. 18 = ch. I, para. 18.
IPML	J. Bentham, *An Introduction to the Principles of Morals and Legislation*, Bentham, *Collected Works. IPML* V. 14 = ch. V, para. 14.
IRE	J. Bentham, *Introductory View of the Rationale of Evidence, Bowring* vi.
LNC	T. Hobbes, *Questions Concerning Liberty, Necessity, and Chance*, Hobbes, *English Works* V. *LNC* 50 = Hobbes, *English Works* vol. V, p. 50.
OLG	J. Bentham, *Of Laws in General*, Bentham, *Collected Works. OLG* IV. 2 = ch. IV, para. 2.
PJP	J. Bentham, *Principles of Judicial Procedure, Bowring* ii.
RJE	J. Bentham, *The Rationale of Judicial Evidence, Bowring* vi and vii.
ST	St Thomas Aquinas, *Summa Theologiae. ST* 1a2ae 90. 4 ad 3 = first part of second part, question 90, article 4, reply to objection 3.
UC	Bentham MSS in the University College, London Library. UC lxix, 68 = box 69, p. 68.

Part I
Law, Custom, and Reason

1
Elements of Classical
Common Law Theory

For me it was not Zeus who made that order.
Nor did that Justice who lives with the gods below
   mark out such laws to hold among mankind. . . .
Not now, nor yesterday's, they always live,
   and no one knows their origin in time.

Sophocles, *Antigone.*

CLASSICAL Common Law theory[1] was born at a time when, emerging from feudalism, modern English society and the modern state were taking shape.[2] Political power was increasingly centralized and the ideology of absolutism was making inroads not only on the continent of Europe, but also in England. The Royal Court assumed more and more directive control of society and the economy, and with this development emerged the idea that *law* could be used to control and direct society to serve the ends and goals of the sovereign. Law came to be viewed as the most powerful instrument in the sovereign's repertoire.

Common Law theory arose, in part, in response to the threat of centralized power exercised by those who proposed to *make* law

[1] From the perspective of comparative law, Anglophone legal systems are dominated by 'common law' even today. That is to say, conceptions of law and structures of legal argument typical of Anglophone nations have been decisively influenced by the fact that their legal systems developed not from the Roman, or Civil traditions, but out of English Common Law. Of course, this tradition goes back much farther than the seventeenth century. But it was in the late sixteenth and early seventeenth centuries that a distinctive Common Law jurisprudential *theory* developed. With the term 'classical Common Law theory', then, I wish to pick out a body of thought about the nature of law which begins to take distinctive shape with Coke. It is to be distinguished from contemporary views of Common Law practice and from earlier notions of the law of England—which may have been more directly and explicitly influenced by the natural law tradition (e.g. those of Fortescue, *De Natura Legis Naturae*, or St German, *Doctor and Student*).

[2] For a discussion of the history of this period, see C. Hill, *Intellectual Origins of the English Revolution* and *The Century of Revolution, 1603–1714*; J. A. G. Pocock, *Ancient Constitution*; F. Hayek, *The Constitution of Liberty*, ch. 11.

guided by nothing but their own assessments of the demands of justice, expediency, and the common good. Against the spreading ideology of political absolutism and rationalism, Common Law theory reasserted the medieval idea that law is not something made either by king, Parliament, or judges, but rather is the expression of a deeper reality which is merely discovered and publicly declared by them.[3] It sought to portray legislators and judges as 'not so much the creators of the law as the agents through whom it finds expression'.[4] But Common Law theory gave this medieval doctrine a distinctively historical twist. For the deeper reality manifested in the public statutes and judicial decisons was not a set of universal rational principles, but rather historically evidenced national custom.

1.1 LAW AS IMMEMORIAL CUSTOM

For the *Common Law* of England is nothing else but the *Common Custome* of the Realm . . . it cannot be made or created either by Charter, or by Parliament . . . but being only matter of fact, and consisting in use and practice, it can be recorded and registered no-where but in the memory of the people.

Sir John Davies, *Irish Reports.*

All law in England, according to Common Law theory, either is, or is grounded upon, Common Law; and Common Law is common and immemorial custom, an 'ancient collection of unwritten maxims and customs' (1 *Comm.* 17), recorded in the memory of the people. It is a body of practices, attitudes, conceptions, and patterns of thought, 'handed down by tradition, use, [and] experience' (1 *Comm.* 17). The only way to show that a given rule is a rule of Common Law is to show how it figures regularly in standard legal argument. '[T]he only method of proving, that this or that maxim is a rule of the common law, is by showing that it hath been always the custom to observe it' (1 *Comm.* 68). Such rules *exist* just in so far as they are *used* or relied upon. Therein lies also their *authority*:

---

[3] See Hayek, *Constitution*, 163.

[4] I. Jenkins, *Social Order and the Limits of Law*, 100. Sir John Davies writes in his *Irish Reports* (1612): 'Neither could any one man ever vaunt, that, like *Minos*, *Solon*, or *Lycurgus*, he was the first *Lawgiver* to our Nation: for neither did the King make his own Prerogative, nor the Judges make the *Rules* and *Maximes* of the Law, nor the common subject prescribe and limit the *Liberties* which he injoyeth by the Law', quoted in Pocock, *Ancient Constitution*, 41.

[T]hey are grown into use, and have acquired their binding Power and Force of Laws by a long and immemorial Usage, and by the Strength of Custom and Reception in this Kingdom. The Matters, indeed, and the Substance of those Laws, are in Writing, but the formal and obliging Force and Power of them grows by long Custom and Use.[5]

Not only is Common Law practised, but in the public recognition of, and participation in, this practice over time lies its validity, its 'formal and obliging Force'.

Common Law, then, rests ultimately on general use and acceptance. But the texture of this acceptance is of great importance for the theory. At one point Blackstone says,

in our law the goodness of a custom depends upon its having been used time out of mind; or, in the solemnity of our legal phrase, time whereof the memory of man runneth not to the contrary. This it is that gives it its weight and authority (1*Comm.* 67).

The term 'goodness' in this passage is (perhaps not unintentionally) ambiguous. On the one hand, it surely refers to the *validity*, the legality, the authoritative status, of the rule of custom (see 1 *Comm.* 76). But, on the other hand, it also might refer to the wisdom, justice, or reasonableness of the custom. In fact, three notions—authority/validity, reasonableness, and historical appropriateness—are intimately linked in Common Law theory. The continued practice of the law both manifests and reinforces a general sense of the reasonableness and historical appropriateness of the rules and concepts of Common Law. Let us take a closer look at this nexus of ideas.

First, the conviction of the historical appropriateness of a rule is essential to its authority according to Common Law theory. Since the law exists only in, and is known only through, practice, a rule becomes law or a decision marks a new departure in the law only if it is taken up into the practice of the community. Only time can tell whether a rule becomes a law, because only time—i.e. practice and use over time—validates. However, history as it is conceived here is traditional rather than objective. Time, on this view, is not an empty place-holder for events, or an unseen driving force. It is, rather, a rich tapestry of acts, words, thoughts, and sentiments of a people with whom one identifies, members of 'partnership' across time.

---

[5] Sir Matthew Hale, *A History of the Common Law*, 17. See also Blackstone, 1 *Comm.* 64, 68.

Public action, then, takes on a quasi-ritualistic character. It is a re-enactment of patterns known and recognized through time, reaffirming the continuities binding members of this social partnership.

Although Coke sometimes suggests that it is essential to the authority of any given portion of the law that it be possible to trace *it* back directly to Saxon (or even Roman!) times,[6] the dominant view is that of Hale. It is impossible to trace particular portions of the present body of law back to their origins, Hale maintains, but this is not material, for

the Strength and Obligation, and the formal Nature of a Law, is not upon Account that the Danes, or the Saxons, or the Normans, brought it in with them, but [rather rests upon the fact that] they became Laws, and binding in this Kingdom by Virtue of their being received and approved here.[7]

Because the law is in a constant process of change, adjustment, influence, development, decline, and rebirth, there is no plausible ground for the claim that the law in any single part is identical to the law of the Saxons. Nevertheless, it is the same body of law. The key is not identity of components but a steady *continuity* with the past. Despite the variation over the centuries, we can say with justice that 'they are the same English Laws now that they were six hundred years [ago]', Hale maintains; just as 'the Argonauts Ship was the same when it returned home, as it was when it went out, tho' in the long Voyage it had successive Amendments, and scarce came back with any of its former Materials'.[8] The conviction of the authority of the law is the sense that the rules and practices of the Common Law at present are continuous with the life and the history of the people whose law it is. Law is not only historical, on

---

[6] See D. E. C. Yale, 'Hobbes and Hale on Law, Legislation and the Sovereign', 127 and references at n. 33.

[7] Hale, *History*, 43. This will be important later when we consider Hale's account of the authority of statutory law, below, 1.2.

[8] Hale, *History*, 40. Critics demand, says John Selden, '*When and how began your common laws?* Questionless it is fittest answered by affirming . . . *When there was first a state in that land*, which the common law now governs: Then were natural laws limited for the conveniency of civil society here, and those limitations have been from thence, increased, altered, interpreted, and brought to what now they are; although perhaps, saving the merely immutable part of nature, now, in regard of their first being, they are not otherwise than a ship, that by often mending had no piece of the first materials, or as the house that's so often repaired *ut nihil pristina materia supersit*, which yet, by the civil law, is to be accounted the same still . . .' J. Selden, *Opera* III, quoted in R. Tuck, *Natural Rights Theories*, 84.

this view, but it is immanent in the larger historical process by which the society itself is shaped and transformed.[9]

At the same time, acceptance manifests and is based on a sense of the *reasonableness* of the rules of Common Law. 'Reason is the life of the law,' Coke said, 'nay the Common Law itself is nothing else but Reason.'[10] A. W. B. Simpson summed up the doctrine this way: 'In the common law system no very clear distinction exists between saying that a particular solution to a problem is in accordance with the law, and saying that it is the rational, or fair, or just solution.'[11] We must take care not to misstate the view.[12] The view is not that the rules and provisions of Common Law each uniformly commend themselves to the people as conforming to some independent standards of justice or reasonableness, and for that reason win their approval. Rather, Common Law is seen to be the *expression* or manifestation of commonly shared values and conceptions of reasonableness and the common good. The principles of Common Law are not themselves validated by reason; but they are the products of a process of *reasoning*, fashioned by the exercise of the special, professional intellectual skills of Common Lawyers over time refining and co-ordinating the social habits of a people into a coherent body of rules.[13] In *this* sense, Coke seems to be saying, it is in the nature of law to be reasonable, but at the same time the law, emerging from this unique intellectual process, constitutes the standards by which the community judges the reasonableness or unreasonableness of actions. The visions of good and evil by which a society judges its life and dreams its dreams are drawn from the past and given concrete public expression in its law.[14]

The dimensions of historical continuity and reasonableness are intimately related in the Common Law mind. For the ability of a rule or practice to persist over time depends upon its wisdom being constantly confirmed in the experience of the people. Time and the long experience of a multitude of individuals, confirms the wisdom

---

[9] See esp. Hale, *History*, 40–3.

[10] Sir Edward Coke, I *Institutes*, sect. 21. See also Blackstone, 1 *Comm.* 77.

[11] A. W. B. Simpson, 'The Common Law and Legal Theory', 79. This essay greatly influenced my thinking about Common Law theory.

[12] The points sketched in this paragraph and the next will be discussed at length below, 2.3.

[13] D. E. C. Yale, 'Hobbes and Hale', 125–6.

[14] 'The visions of good and evil, the denominations to be computed—these a society draws from its past and without them it dies.' A. Bickel, *The Morality of Consent*, 24.

and goodness of these ways and values. The happiest nations, Lord Stair maintains, are those 'whose laws have been entered by long custom, wrung out from their debates on particular cases, until it came to the consistence of a fixed and known custom'.[15]

Thus, the validity of a legal standard depends on the public demonstration of its well-tested wisdom. This is one sense of the 'goodness' of custom. But also the wisdom or goodness is implicit, immanent, and apparent only in the fact of long practice. It consists in the rule or practice being accommodated to the 'frame' and 'disposition' of the nation, 'such as by a long Experience and Use is as it were incorporated into their very Temperament, and, in a Manner, become the complection and Constitution of the English Commonwealth'.[16]

The process of accommodation is two-sided. The rules, at first rough and clumsy, are broken in over time, their hard edges smoothed off and softened to fit the contours of community life. At the same time, Hale clearly maintains, participating in the practice described by the rules shapes the dispositions, beliefs, expectations, and attitudes of the people. Thus, what counts as reasonable in large part depends on what can be regarded as continuous with the past history of the people and its law, and what can be regarded as continuous with that past in large part depends on what can be regarded as reasonable projections from laws and arrangements of the past to problems and situations of the present.

Finally, the use and acceptance of the Common Law rests on a *shared* sense of its reasonableness and historical appropriateness. The fact that it is *shared*, mutually recognized, is essential. It is not enough that each member of the community believes that the rules are reasonable, good, or wise; they must also believe that others in the community believe this as well, and that fact is important for their acceptance of the law as reasonable and, in consequence, as valid. This is one reason why the sense of historical continuity is important. For it is only the *public* demonstration of the suitability of the rules over time that qualifies them for status as law. No demonstration of the goodness or wisdom of a rule or practice by any particular person, regardless of his intellectual power, or practical insight, or divine inspiration will suffice. Mansfield, though

---

[15] Stair, *Institutions of the Laws of Scotland* I. 1, 15, quoted by D. N. MacCormick in *Legal Reasoning and Legal Theory*, 58.
[16] Hale, *History*, 30.

perhaps an atypical Common Law judge in the eighteenth century, expressed the typical Common Law view when he said, 'The Common Law of England . . . is only *common* reason or usage . . .'.[17]

The judiciary is a major player in the legal drama as conceived by Common Law theory, yet the role is that of the 'living oracle' of the law (1 *Comm.* 69), an expert witness to it, not its creator. '*Judex est lex loquens*', Coke insisted—the judge is the mouthpiece of a law which transcends the judiciary.[18] Judicial decisions bind the parties to a case, Hale asserts, but

they do not make a Law properly so called . . . yet they have a great Weight and Authority in Expounding, Declaring, and Publishing what the Law of this Kingdom is especially when such Decisions hold a Consonancy and Congruity with Resolutions and Decisions of former Times; and tho' such Decisions are less than a Law, yet they are a greater Evidence thereof than the Opinion of any private Persons, as such, whatsoever.[19]

The office of the judge is not to make, but publicly to expound and declare, the law: *jus dicere* not *jus dare*. In the latter activity they are the recognized authorities. Judicial opinions, expounding and declaring the law, then, are not themselves law but only 'the principal and most authoritative *evidence*, that can be given, of the existence of such a custom as shall form a part of the common law' (1 *Comm.* 69, emphasis added). In the course of reaching and attempting to justify a decision, the judge must seek to formulate the law on the matter in dispute. His opinion must be regarded as the best judgment of one skilled in discovering and formulating such rules of law. The authority and weight of judicial opinions, then, is the authority of an *expert* reporting his or her findings, not the final or formal authority of an official whose saying *makes it so*. (The *holding* has such final authority, but the formulation of the law on which the holding is supposed to rest does not.)

Thus, it is important in classical Common Law theory to distinguish sharply between the law and various *formulations* of its rules.[20] Blackstone states the view clearly: '*the law*, and the *opinion*

---

[17] *Evans* v. *Harrison* (1767), reported in Philip Furneaux, *Letters to the Hon. Mr. Justice Blackstone, concerning His Exposition of the Act of Toleration*, 277, emphasis added. I am indebted to David Lieberman for this reference.

[18] 7 *Coke's Reports* (*Calvin's Case*), quoted in Hayek, *Constitution*, 462.

[19] Hale, *History*, 45. See also Blackstone, 1 *Comm.* 69; 3 *Comm.* 327.

[20] On the distinction between social rules and their formulation see D. Shwayder, *The Stratification of Behaviour*, 240–7.

of the judge, are not always convertible terms, or one and the same thing; since it sometimes may happen that the judge may *mistake* the law' (1 *Comm.* 71). Since mistake is possible, and because new cases often shed new light and call for reformulation of the law, no particular formulation of the law is final, all are corrigible and each judge in deciding each particular case is empowered to reconstruct anew the general thrust of the law (always treating with proper respect, of course, previous judicial formulations). Simpson has captured well this feature of Common Law doctrine.

Formulations of the common law are to be conceived of as similar to grammarians' rules, which both describe linguistic practices and attempt to systematize and order them; such rules serve as guides to proper practice since the proper practice is in part the normal practice; such formulations are inherently corrigible, for it is always possible that they may be improved upon, or require modification as what they describe changes . . . [Thus,] it is a feature of the common law system that there is no way of settling the correct text or formulation of the rules, so that it is inherently impossible to state so much as a single rule in what Pollock called 'any authentic form of words'.[21]

This has two important implications for Common Law theory and practice. First, with regard to theory, Common Law is a form of legal thought and practice which vigorously resists regimentation to a structured system flowing logically from a set of first principles. To represent it as a systematic structure of rules is to distort it; it is to represent as static what is essentially dynamic and constantly shifting. (It is no accident that whereas organic metaphors dominate the writings of Common Lawyers, mechanical metaphors dominate the writings of their positivist critics from Hobbes to Bentham.)

Second, Common Law doctrine allows for a great deal of flexibility in adjudication. First of all, prior decisions and resolutions are binding on the judge only in so far as the prior opinion correctly formulates or articulates the relevant law. It is always open to judges in the future to test the formulation of the rule against the practice of the (legal) community. But this, for the Common Lawyer, is just to test the reasonableness of the earlier formulations of the law. That is, it is to test earlier formulations against the tradition-shaped sense of reasonableness. And since the guiding

<hr/>

[21] Simpson, 'The Common Law and Legal Theory', 94, 89.

assumption is that the Common Law is 'the perfection of reason', to come to the conclusion that some prior formulation of the rule—even if widely followed in the past—is unreasonable, is to discover that it is *not law*, that it was mistakenly believed to be law (1 *Comm.* 71).

Also, secondly, strictly novel cases call for judicial resolution.[22] Common Law theory empowers judges to fashion solutions to novel problems and so empowers them, in effect, to fashion new legal rules, but subject to the constraint that rules to cover new situations must be fashioned out of the materials of the *existing* law. Constrained by consistency with (his or her best judgment of) the general thrust of this body of law, and by recognized forms of institutional argument, the judge seeks a natural extension of the law to the new case. A recent champion of (a revised) Common Law theory expresses the dogma well:

The most powerful engine of change in the common law was, strangely enough, the great 'principle' that like cases should be treated alike. Courts acting on that principle could change the law, indeed make law, without arrogating to themselves undue power because they always seemed to apply past precedents or principles in new ways to situations *made* new by the world around them.[23]

It is *the case*, not the judge, that extends the law. *Judex est lex loquens.*

---

[22] 'There is a Rule in the Common Law, that in *novo casu novum remedium est apponendum . . .*' Lord Ellesmere, quoted by Knafla, *Law and Politics in Jacobean England*, 219. Francis Bacon expressed the same view: 'He that will not apply new remedies must expect new evils: for time is the greatest innovator; and if time of course alter things to the worse, and wisdom and counsel shall not alter them to the better, what shall be the end?' F. Bacon, 'Of Innovations', *Bacon's Essays*, 74. I am indebted to D. Lieberman for this quote.

[23] G. Calabresi, *A Common Law for the Age of Statutes*, 13. This according to G. Calabresi, provides the basis for a strong defence against the objection that judicial innovation is anti-democratic. 'Each judicial decision, at its best', he maintains, 'is meant to represent a reasoned attempt to adapt a past set of decisions to a current problem. It tries to treat like cases alike when what is "alike" changes constantly because of ideological, technological, or even constitutional or statutory change. Common Law rules become dominant slowly over time in response to many separate decisions in real cases by many disparate judges as to what has changed in the underlying framework. . . . At any moment consistency with the fabric can be taken to be a reasonably accurate account of what has evolved from past popular desires, and the judge's task is to do what is needed to accommodate that account to present needs' (ibid. 97).

The favoured device of Common Law judges in the seventeenth and eighteenth centuries for responding to new situations from within the old and established law was the use of legal fictions. So, for example, when significant social and economic changes brought about changes in the characteristic uses of property, judges were called upon to refashion the old feudal law. Its 'forms and delays', says Blackstone, 'were ill suited to that more simple and commercial mode of property which succeeded [it].' But the remedy was not sought from legislative reform of the law. Rather, judges left the old forms 'to languish in obscurity and oblivion' and 'endeavoured by a series of minute contrivances to accommodate such personal actions, as were then in use, to all the most useful purposes of remedial justice'. These now answer well the purpose of speedy and substantial justice. The only difficulty, Blackstone admits, arises from their being fictions. However, 'once we have discovered the proper clew, that labyrinth is easily pervaded;' he says confidently, adding with characteristic eloquence:

Our system of remedial law resembles an old Gothic castle, erected in the days of chivalry, but fitted up for a modern inhabitant. The moated ramparts, the embattled towers, and the trophied halls, are magnificent and venerable, but useless, and therefore neglected. The interior apartments, now accommodated to daily use, are cheerful and commodious, though their approaches may be winding and difficult.[24]

Thus, on this view, Common Law is a dynamic, constantly changing, organic social entity. Old rules die, new rules and practices take their places like new cells replacing old.[25] Change, however, is always incremental, a matter (if I may shift the metaphor) of insensibly altering the fabric of the law by removing a strand here, repairing or reinforcing a strand there, extending a strand from its accustomed place into a new one. In each case, new needs and situations are met by reworking old law, old decisions, old ideas. No general master plan guides the process, no extensive 'new-modelling' of the law is undertaken, but in this incremental way the law is kept in accord with a shared sense of reasonableness

---

[24] All passages quoted in this paragraph are taken from 3 *Comm.* 267–8.

[25] Immediately following the passage invoking the image of the Argonauts' ship (n. 7, above) Hale says the law of England is the same as that of 600 years ago just 'as Titius is the same Man he was forty Years since, tho' Physicians tell us, That in a tract of seven Years, the Body has scarce any of the same material Substance it had before.' Hale, *History*, 40.

and justice in the face of change.[26] Due to the incremental nature of the change, and because it is the work of many over time, significant change is imperceptible and can only be detected after a turn in the course of the development of the law has been taken, and the path of the turning can be traced from the vantage point of history. Maine sums up the classical notion well.

Almost everybody can observe that, when new circumstances arise, we use our old ideas to bring them home to us; it is only afterwards, and sometimes long afterwards, that our ideas are found to have changed. An English Court of Justice is in great part an engine for working out this process. New combinations of circumstances are constantly arising, but in the first instance they are exclusively interpreted according to old legal ideas. A little later lawyers admit that the old ideas are not quite what they were before the new circumstances arose.[27]

This explains the great importance of the sense of history and continuity in Common Law theory. In Blackstone's expository practice to give account of a portion of the law was not to trace it back to *a priori* first principles, but rather to locate it within the living body of law and to trace its historical development. Since law is the accumulation of judgments, decisions, refinements, and adjustments of immemorial custom, to understand the law is to understand the process by which this tradition was built up.[28] Blackstone's *Commentaries* and Hale's *History*, two major classics of Common Law theory, are elegant and powerful expositions, and celebrations, of this process.

[26] This is a distinctively Burkean theme. He says, for example, 'We must obey the great law of change. It is the powerful law of nature, and the means perhaps of its conservation. All we can do, and that human wisdom can do, is to provide that the change shall proceed by insensible degrees. This has all the benefits which may be in change, without any of the inconveniences of mutation. Everything is provided for as it arrives.' E. Burke, *Works* (London, 1854-8) III. 340, quoted in R. Kirk, 'Burke and the Philosophy of Prescription', 380. See also Blackstone, 3 *Comm.* 205-6, 267.

[27] Sir Henry Sumner Maine, *Early History of Institutions*, 230. See also Blackstone: '[F]rom the nature of traditional laws in general; which, being accommodated to the exigencies of the times, suffer by degrees insensible variations in practice: so that, though upon comparison we plainly discern the alteration of the law from what it was five hundred years ago, yet it is impossible to define the precise period in which that alteration accrued, any more than we can discern the changes of the bed of a river, which varies its shores by continual decreases and alluvions' (4 *Comm.* 409).

[28] Pocock, *Ancient Constitution*, 173.

1.2 THE CUSTOMARY FOUNDATIONS OF *LEX SCRIPTA*

An deiser Vorstellung gemessen ist die Erfindung der Gesetzgebung vielleicht die folgenschwerste, die je gemacht worden—folgenschwerer als die des Feuermachens oder des Schiesspulvers—, denn am Starksten von allen hat sie das Schicksal des Menchen in seine Hande gelegt.

B. Rehfeldt, *Die Wurzeln des Rechtes*

Common Law was traditionally denominated '*lex non scripta*', unwritten law. Common Law theory in this way explicitly defined its conception of law in sharp contrast with *written* or enacted law, '*lex scripta*'. The distinction, of course, has little to do with whether or not law is recorded in written documents. Rather, it marks a sharp difference in the modes of existence of, and claims to authority made by, the two kinds of law.[29] Whether written or not, *leges non scriptae* exist in the practice of the community, and are binding in virtue of that fact. They 'have obtain'd their Force by immemorial Usage or Custom', Hale maintains.[30] In contrast, *leges scriptae* are laws existing and regarded as binding, in virtue of being enacted by a recognized legislative body according to recognized formal procedures. Thus, Blackstone points out that portions of canon and civil law are recognized in some English jurisdictions. But this is not in virtue of their being written or enacted, for that would be to recognize a foreign sovereign power, but in virtue of the rules themselves having been 'admitted and received by immemorial usage and custom in some particular cases in some particular courts'.[31]

As the seventeenth and especially the eighteenth centuries progressed, Common Law theory was increasingly pressed to find a place for legislation in its account of English law, for statutory law (and the doctrine of the sovereignty of parliament) took on an ever-widening importance in the political and legal life of the nation. The story of the struggle to find a place for enacted law within Common Law theory is a long and complex one. I shall only touch briefly on a few general considerations which will deepen our understanding of classical Common Law theory.

---

[29] Blackstone, 1 *Comm.* 63–4; Hale, *History*, chs. I, II.
[30] *History*, 3.
[31] 1 *Comm.* 79–80, following Hale, *History*, 18–30.

Enacted law and parliamentary sovereignty

By the seventeenth century the conception of the nature of legislative activity of the sovereign or Parliament had changed. Medieval jurisprudence held that statutes performed, in a more explicit and general way, the same task which occupied the judiciary: namely, declaring, expounding, and making known law which already existed in the traditional practices of the people. To regard a body of persons capable of *creating new* law, through exercise of their own wills, was a radical departure. Law could be seen not merely as the formal and public expression of an existing social (or even natural) order, but as an instrument with which that order could be altered or even recreated. Although many may have regarded this as a great step forward in the social history of mankind, Common Lawyers were deeply sceptical. Coke and Blackstone regarded parliamentary legislation as the sole, or at least major, cause of all that was confused, incoherent, and unjust in the law of England. For Coke, legislative change represented degeneration of the law from its pristine purity in ancient times.[32] Blackstone repeatedly pointed up the radical deficiencies of the statutory law, in contrast to the 'venerable edifices of antiquity'.[33] Hale, who was much less sceptical of legislative innovation,[34] nevertheless argued that explicit law reform should be made incrementally through the courts wherever possible, and never should be attempted on legally foundational or constitutional matters.[35]

There was, no doubt, cause for growing concern about Parliament's exercise of its legislative will as the eighteenth century progressed.[36] But, in the view of Blackstone and his predecessors, the inadequacy of the legislative product was no accident or temporary aberration, it was the inevitable result of features intrinsic to this form of law. First, in the view of Common Law theory, legislation is inevitably the product of a temporary aggregate of arbitrary wills. Since it was thought legislation is the product of will, and not

---

[32] C. M. Gray, Introduction to Hale's *History*, pp. xxiii–xxv.

[33] See, for example, 1 *Comm.* 10–11, 365; 4 *Comm.* 443.

[34] Indeed, Edward I is the hero of Hale's *History* because of his efforts to collect, simplify, and reform ancient law. He called him 'our English Justinian'. See Hale, *History*, chs. VII–VIII, especially 101–5 and Tuck, *Natural Rights Theories*, 133–5.

[35] Hale, *Amendments of Laws*, Hargrave I. 256, 272.

[36] See below, 8.1.

of rational reflection on an existing order independent of will, and since it is validated only by conformity to formal or procedural constraints, there is no guarantee that the individual laws will be reasonable or just. And worse, because the legislative body is a temporary and constantly changing aggregate of disparate wills, unconstrained by any systematic considerations, there is no reason to expect that the legislative product will add up to an internally coherent and reasonable system. Parliament could not be counted upon to submit to the discipline of the Common Law, which forced judges to seek principles for their decisions in the institutional materials and evidence of ancient custom, wherein, according to the theory, could be found a suitable and orderly structure of reason. Legislators, or the sovereign, are fully capable of spinning *law* out of their own 'natural reason', or even arbitrary will. Statutory law, then, unconstrained by the discipline of the 'artificial reason' of the underlying law, threatens the coherence and ultimately the legitimacy of that law itself.

Second, enacted law threatens the very nature of law and the kind of liberty it provides, according to Common Law theory. This concern is most clearly expressed in Blackstone's identification of the concept of sovereign or supreme *power* with *legislative* power. Legislation is essentially an *exercise of power*—the supreme power, according to Blackstone, 'for legislature . . . is the greatest act of superiority that can be exercised by one being over another'.[37] The contrast with Common Law is striking: enacted law is the visible evidence of a supreme exercise of power; judicial decisions, however, are not exercises of power but merely reports of discoveries of an *already existing* prescriptive order. And that order is not created, or imposed from outside the common life of the people, rather it is the *expression of* that life. From this Blackstone concludes that law in this latter form is the structure that makes liberty possible, rather than an order which limits freedom. In this extended sense Common Law can be said to rest on the *consent* of the people. This consent is deeper than agreeing to have other persons represent one in a legislative assembly. It comes from a recog-

---

[37] 1 *Comm.* 46; see also 39–40. Rehfeldt, in the epigraph to this section expresses Blackstone's fear well: The matter of greatest consequence following on the invention of legislation—greater than the discovery of fire and gunpowder—is that the fate of human beings is put in the hand of the strongest. *Die Wurzeln des Rechtes*, 67, quoted in Hayek, *Constitution*, 458.

nition that the rules that govern one's life are *one's own*, they define that life, give it structure and meaning, are already practised and so deeply engrained that they appear to one as purely natural.[38] These evils notwithstanding, Common Law theory could not with credibility deny the growing role of enacted law in English jurisprudence. Nor were there any institutional or historical grounds for asserting the power of judicial review and control of legislation; on the contrary, through this period the doctrine of parliamentary sovereignty gained strength. No institution could plausibly claim competence to sit in judgment on parliamentary legislation. Common Law theory sought through indirect means to confine and rein in the arbitrary beast.

First, it sought to construe the legislative activities of Parliament, as far as possible, as declarative and remedial of ancient Common Law, perhaps enlarging or restricting this ancient custom, but not essentially altering or adding to it.[39] This permitted interpretation and application of statutes according to traditional Common Law categories and subjected potentially wayward legislation indirectly to the discipline of the artificial reason of Common Law. Statute law was seen to operate on and within the principles of Common Law, not altering the substance but regulating the mode of that law.[40] Second, where this strategy seemed to fly in the face of the facts, when statutory law unambiguously marked a new departure, the statutory language was construed narrowly so as to preserve as far as possible the integrity of the underlying Common Law. Behind this strategy was the conviction that formally enacted law can be accepted into the body of English law only to the extent that it can be integrated into Common Law, which was regarded as foundational.

However, Blackstone's *Commentaries* bear witness to the difficulty Common Law theory faced in making coherent sense of the legal and constitutional system of eighteenth-century England (and witness as well to tensions deep in Whig constitutional doctrine). For, while arguing forcefully for the foundational status of customary Common Law, he sought to defend the doctrine of

---

[38] 1 *Comm.* 73–4, 127–8; *History*, 30.

[39] See Blackstone, 1 *Comm.* 85–7; Hale, *History*, 103–5. Hale seems to represent even the great legislative work of Edward the Confessor as a matter of 'settling the law' which, through merger of different peoples into the English nation, had fallen into confusion.

[40] See E. Burke, *Reflections on the Revolution in France*, 105.

Parliamentary sovereignty on Whiggish contractarian grounds. But the doctrines are inconsistent.

Blackstone argued for Parliament's sovereign right to make law from assumptions about the reasons there are for establishing the state. Let me quote the passage in full.

For a state is a collective body, composed of a multitude of individuals, united for their safety and convenience, and intending to act together as one man. If it therefore is to act as one man, it ought to act by one uniform will. But, inasmuch as political communities are made up of many natural persons, each of whom has his particular will and inclination, these several wills cannot by any *natural* union be joined together, or tempered and disposed into a lasting harmony, so as to constitute and produce that one uniform will of the whole. It can therefore be no otherwise produced than by a *political* union; by the consent of all persons to submit their own private wills to the will of one man, or of one or more assemblies of men, to whom the supreme authority is intrusted: and this will of that one man, or assemblage of men, is in different states, according to their different constitutions, understood to be *law* (1 *Comm.* 52, author's emphasis).

This is, of course, a contractarian argument, apparently with more affinity to Hobbes's version than Locke's. Law, created by a body to which all severally pledge their allegiance, is the agent of social unity, that which takes an aggregate of individuals with disparate, conflicting, private wills and inclinations and makes them into *a people, a public, a community.* But also it is assumed that law, to accomplish this task, must be the *product* of the exercise of will of a person or assembly recognized by each and all for the very purpose of putting a permanent end to private conflict and dissensus, and making it possible for the multitude to act as one. I will explore this conception of law and its tasks in Chapter 2. For present purposes I wish merely to isolate a pair of assumptions on which this argument rests: (i) that it is only through *political* union that social union is possible; i.e. without political union behind a sovereign legislator there is no consensus, no binding force, and so, no community; (ii) that the instrument by which political and social union is achieved is the recognition, in the community as a whole, of the validity of rules of law qualified only by their formal legislative pedigree.

Now (ii) is not necessarily inconsistent with recognizing the foundational status of customary Common Law. For it is possible to conceive of the province of legislation as an island (or, perhaps better, an archipelago) existing in the broad sea of customary law.

However, in Blackstone's account (as in Hobbes's) (ii) rests on (i). That is, the plausibility of the argument for a *sovereign* Parliament in Blackstone's understanding of sovereignty, requires the assumption that consensus and community are impossible apart from consensus on the formal qualifications of a legislative sovereign. But this is inconsistent with the claim that customary Common Law is the structure within which enacted law must fit. For Common Law theory assumes *broad consensus* and an already constituted social unity. Common Law decisions do not *create* the social unity, they only confirm, affirm, and maintain it. Common Law is '*Lex Communis Angliae*'[41]—law *of* this English community, springing from and expressing its common life. J. C. Carter, the nineteenth-century American opponent of codification, expressed the Common Law conception in this way. 'Law is not a body of commands imposed upon society from without, either by an individual sovereign or superior, or by a sovereign body constituted by representatives of society itself. It exists at all times as one of the elements of society springing directly from habit and custom.'[42]

Hale on the foundations of enacted law

In Hale we find a more consistent, and indeed a richer and more suggestive, treatment of the relationship between enacted and Common Law. To set the context of Hale's argument we must note that some of the most violent ideological battles of the English Civil War were fought on the field of history. Defenders of the established regime, both its political constitution and its social structure, argued that the constitution and the law were ancient. Coke argued, for example, that in all but inconsiderable parts the law and the constitution had remained *unchanged* since the Saxon era and even before.[43] The regime's opponents, especially radical revolutionaries like the Levellers, directly challenged this historical claim, insisting that history can show that nothing in the present law or constitution resembles the law of the Saxon era, that components of contemporary law can each be traced to particular changes or developments in the law. The ancient constitution is a cruel myth, the Levellers charged, and they argued for a *return to*

---

[41] Hale, *History*, 37.

[42] J. C. Carter, 'The Ideal and the Actual in the Law', 235, quoted in Hayek, *Constitution*, 452.

[43] Gray, Introduction to Hale's *History*, p. xxiii; Hill, *Intellectual Origins*, 56.

the simple justice of the Saxon Common Law.[44] Hale wrote his *History of the Common Law*, in part, to defuse this controversy which had torn apart the nation and threatened the foundations of law, while at the same time defending the idea of the Common Law and the English constitution as ancient and immemorial.

Hale argued that, while the sense of the historical nature of the law and constitution is fundamental, both contending parties had seriously misconstrued the nature of the historical claims made for Common Law.[45] Both sides mistakenly assumed that the historical validity of the Common Law rests on being able to demonstrate, with historical evidence independent of the law and constitution themselves, the precise origins of the law, and its passage through the centuries into the present day. But, Hale insists, this kind of historical knowledge is inaccessible to us. It is simply impossible to give a satisfactory historical account of the origins of our law. Furthermore, against Coke he insisted that it was nonsense to claim that the law has remained unchanged through the centuries. For one of the reasons why it is impossible to trace the law directly back to its actual origins in history is that the law is constantly changing as a result of factors within the law itself. Since laws are by their nature

accommodated to the Conditions, Exigencies and Conveniences of the People, . . . as those Exigencies and Conveniences do insensibly grow upon the People, so many Times grows insensibly a Variation of Laws, especially in a long Tract of Time . . . so that if a Man could at this Day have the Prospects of all the Laws of the Britains . . . it would yet be impossible to say which of them were *New*, and which were *Old*, and the several Seasons and Periods of Time wherein every Law took its Rise and Original (39, 41, author's emphasis).

It is impossible to trace, with any claim to historical accuracy, the origins of any part of our contemporary law, he concludes.

However, it is not true that we have *no* evidence of the immemorial nature of our law. Rather the only evidence we have is *internal* to the law and the constitution themselves. The evidence, he says, is entirely *traditional* (40). That is, the evidence we have of the link between present law and the far reaches of the nation's past is the *present sense or conviction of* this continuity. And herein lies

[44] Pocock, *Ancient Constitution*, 124–7.

[45] Hale, *History*, ch. IV. All pages cited in the text in the remainder of this section are from this work.

the foundation of immemorial Common Law. The mistake both Coke and the Levellers make is to think that the question of *origins* is the essential legitimating matter; however,

Neither was it, or indeed is it much material, which of these is their Original; for 'tis very plain, the Strength and Obligation, and the Formal Nature of a Law, is not upon Account that the Danes, or the Saxons, or the Normans, brought it in with them, but [that] they became Laws, and binding in this Kingdom, by virtue of their being received and approved here (43).

Furthermore, this present acceptance and practice rests on a shared sense of the *continuity* of the law with the past. This requires that it be possible to show, not that the laws are exactly the same as in some distant historical past, but rather that the present laws fit into a public conception of the nation's identity as a people shaped by its collective history. Hale's powerful conception of the historical nature of Common Law is captured evocatively in his metaphor of the Argonauts' ship.[46]

As political polemics, Hale's argument is brilliant, but it has a deeper philosophical significance as well which, I believe, has not been well understood. Hale was not simply trying to give an account of the historical character of Common Law. He was also articulating a view of the role of history in laying the foundations of law. The argument rests on two important assumptions: (i) that law by its nature, and especially the law of England over its history, is and has been in a constant state of flux; and (ii) that, nevertheless, the validity and binding force of the law depends on continuity with the past. How, then, is this continuity to be construed?

Hale clearly rejects the idea that the identity of the law is guaranteed by the identity of the *people* whose law it is, because the people, considered apart from the law, are far from homogeneous (42). Indeed, the identity of the people depends more on the identity of the law than the identity of the law depends on the identity of the people.

Hale also clearly rejects Coke's idea that continuity of the law is due to the identity of present body of law (in substantial portion) with law of the ancient past. We might weaken Coke's claim slightly to suggest that continuity amidst constant change is provided by some stable and fixed *portion* of the law, either substantive or

---

[46] Ibid. 40; see above, p. 6

procedural. But this also is clearly not Hale's view. For all we know, says Hale, *nothing* has escaped the transforming forces of history. This is surely the message of the figure of the Argonaut's ship.

'For all we know'—that is the key. The point is that the *objective* identity of the whole, or of any part of the body of the law over time, i.e. identity that can be confirmed according to criteria independent of the law itself, is *irrelevant*. For all we know, portions—or the whole thing—may be identical, or there may be absolutely *no* single element that is preserved. But that is not the essential matter; what is important is the *conviction of continuity*.

The recent editor of Hale's *History* has suggested that it was Hale's view that, although substantive law may have changed totally over time (whether gradually or in great fits and starts), the basic political frame, the constitutional rules by which all other rules of the system can be authoritatively recognized as binding, have remained the same.[47] Continuity of law is guaranteed, on this interpretation, by the identity through time of what Hart would call the 'rules of recognition'.[48] But this interpretation is inconsistent with Hale's strategy in the *History*. The focus of the historical debate he sought to finesse was essentially *constitutional*; that is, it was the identity of constitutional practice that was precisely at issue between Coke and the Levellers. Hale argued that we have no better external evidence of the identity of our constitution over time, than of any other component of Common Law (40). The materials composing the structural frame of the ship are as likely to have changed as the cabin fixtures. The very point of Hale's argument is that the whole issue of *origins* of laws, including their being traceable to valid lawmaking acts in the past, is irrelevant to the question of validity. What is crucial is present usage, acceptance, and practice of the rules.

Also, this interpretation still insists that the continuity of law is a function of the objectively traceable identity through time of a portion of the law, in this case the formal or constitutional rules giving structure to the law. But Hale does not wish to rest the validity of present rules and practices of law on this ground. For if such objective historical facts were relevant, the failure or inability to produce them would undermine the legitimacy of the law. Hale sought to *sever* the notion of the historicity of law from objective history.

---

[47] Gray, Introduction to Hale's *History*, pp. xxiii, xxvii.
[48] Hart, *Concept of Law*, ch. VI.

What, then, ensures the identity of the Argonaut's ship through all its mutations? Nothing but the shared conviction that it is the same ship that left the port forty years earlier, says Hale; that is, nothing but the present practice of regarding it as the same.

Thus, law rests ultimately, in Hale's view, on an important social fact: the fact of a widely shared conviction and practice of regarding certain rules, regulations, institutions, and procedures—both substantive and formal or constitutional—as historically validated law of the land. This conviction and practice involves treating recognized similarities with the laws and forms and practices of previous times as family resemblances, as commonalities uniting a people over time. This conviction regarding the continuity of law is essential to the present sense of civic identity, in Hale's view. The sense of living a common life, the tie that binds the components of the present social order into a unity, is the shared conviction that this social entity and common life extends backwards and forwards in time like a family, or, as Burke put it, a partnership 'between those who are living, those who are dead, and those who are to be born'.[49] Burke explicitly invokes the spirit of the Common Law tradition when he insists that 'We wished at the period of the Revolution, and do now wish, to derive all we possess *as an inheritance from our forefathers*'.[50] It is in this sense that Common Law reproduces one important form of social solidarity.[51]

This conception of law and its foundations contrasts sharply with the view assumed by Blackstone's argument for parliamentary sovereignty considered earlier. Yet Hale is able to find a place in this theory for legislation, even for a sovereign Parliament. Hale distinguishes in the standard way between written and unwritten law. As we saw above, the distinction marks not two kinds of laws, but rather two modes of existence or validity of laws. Written laws, *leges scriptae*, exist in virtue of valid enactment according to established constitutional rules; unwritten law in virtue of customary acceptance, use, and practice. Hale makes clear that whether a law falls into one class or the other depends *not* on the way in which it was introduced into the body of law, but rather on the *present* basis of its authority. And, he admits that much of what is now considered part of the unwritten Common Law probably first appeared

---

49 Burke, *Reflections*, 194–5.
50 Ibid. 117.
51 E. Durkheim, *Division of Labor in Society*, 68.

as 'Acts of Parliament'. 'Statutes or Acts of Parliament that were made before the Beginning of the Reign of King Richard I and have not since been repealed or altered, either by Contrary Usage, or by subsequent Acts of Parliament, are now Part of the *Lex non Scripta*, being as it were incorporated thereinto, and become Part of the Common Law' (4).

Thus, new rules of law, or shifts in the law, can appear either slowly and incrementally through gradual shifts in practice and the trials of experience, or immediately through legislative enactment. But there is a further process at work which tends either to incorporate such enacted law into the broad course of customary law or to exclude it from the body of law. This process is the same as that by which other rules of custom are incorporated into the law. Either, through continual use, judicial exposition, and interpretation legislated rules are appropriated by and become part of normal practice (7–8), or they lose their status as valid legal standards through 'contrary usage' (4).

In the former instance, after a time enacted law comes to be regarded as valid *not* in virtue of its formal pedigree, but in virtue of its finding its place in the normal practice of the legal community, i.e. in virtue of coming to be regarded as reasonable and an appropriate part of the structure of Common Law. This is a shift in the basis of validity from formal to substantive acceptance of the rules. In neither case is the validity of any particular rule dependent on acceptance of the rule in isolation from the larger body or system of law, but in the former case it is accepted as valid in virtue of conforming to certain formal (constitutional) criteria of enactment, while in the latter in virtue of the fact that it fits into the structure of existing rules and practices. And the latter form of validation unlike the former depends on the substance of the rules themselves.

But this process can have the opposite effect as well: the contrary practice of the court can signal its refusal to 'receive' the legislation as law of the land. On this matter Hale's discussion is sketchier, but we can draw a relatively clear picture from his remarks about the process of appropriation. The validation of enacted law can be undermined by contrary practice in one of two ways. First, since the validity of enacted law rests at the outset on nothing but acceptance of the formal constitutional rules by whose authority it is enacted, and since such constitutional rules are themselves liable to change just like any other rules of the system, the validity of enacted law is threatened by constitutional change *unless* the rules are incorporated into the continuing body of Common Law. This, presumably, was the fate of much parliamentary legislation in the past, now entirely lost to history.[52] Second, Hale suggests that while Parliament (alone) is competent to *make* new law, the legislative product will only be of *limited* legal scope and significance, unless it is incorporated into the Common Law. Without appropriation it can exist, while its constitutional authorizing laws exist, but only as isolated rules, temporary surface disturbances on the legal sea having no deep impact.

If we view Hale's account of the validity of enacted law in this way we can reconcile two otherwise conflicting claims Hale makes frequently throughout the *History*. Hale maintains *both* that the law of England has changed constantly, but gradually and insensibly over long stretches of time,[53] *and* that substantial, even radical, innovations in the law of the land have been produced by Acts of Parliament and sovereign legislative activity.[54] These two claims—which have generated two conflicting interpretations of Hale's jurisprudence[55]—can be reconciled in the following way. As we have seen, Hale maintains that by its nature law accommodates itself to the exigencies and conditions of the people, and that the process is insensible and gradual over a long period of time (39). But this change can be initiated in several different ways: by changes over time in the customs and ways of the people, by judicial decisions and resolutions, and by Acts of Parliament (40). We should recall that judicial decisions cannot make law, so the

---

[52] Hale's view here may be that statutory rules remain valid only as long as the constitutional rules empowering the parliamentary body to create them remain in force, such that when those constitutional power-conferring rules are altered substantially the rules depending on them for validity must find other support, or lose their legal status. But one might object that this condition is too strenuous, for all that is necessary is that the statutory rules be originally enacted under constitutional empowering laws valid at that time, and that there be a general principle that validly enacted statutes remain valid until expressly repealed.

Hale's view, however, is that the latter is, in general, not an option for us. For, he believes, the question of which constitutional laws *were valid* at the time of enactment of the statutes may itself be unanswerable, the answer lost in the clouds of history. But, then, we cannot depend on this source for validation of the statutory law. It is only as good as our collective memory of the specific empowering laws.

[53] Hale *History*, 39; see above, p. 22. See Pocock, *Ancient Constitution*, 170–81.

[54] Hale, *History*, chs. VII–VIII; and Tuck, *Natural Rights Theories*, 133–5.

[55] See nn. 53 and 54, above.

only way in which such decisions can alter the shape of the law is through the rules they stand for being accepted, used, and practised. They *become law* by eventually *becoming custom*. The same is true of enacted law. Although statutes, in one respect, alter the law immediately upon being enacted, yet in another sense they make no impact on the law until they are taken up into the practice of the courts and the community. Thus, there is *insensible change* at the hands of Parliament as well, because whether or not legislated legal innovations actually *have the effect* of altering the shape and direction of the law is something that can be determined only by seeing whether the enacted changes are incorporated into the body of Common Law, and *that* is a process of trial by practice and is not the direct effect of enactment.

If this interpretation is correct, then Hale can be seen to embrace the old notion that law cannot be *made* but can only be announced or declared, without denying a place for legislation in the body of law. For, we might say, Parliament is capable of making new *regulations*, but not *new law*, and the idea of creating from nothing a complete body of law in the form of code would be regarded as absurd.

This account of the foundations of enacted law has two interesting general implications. First, Hale is capable of giving credence to the idea of the legislative sovereignty of Parliament. For no court is competent to invalidate rules properly enacted by Parliament. Yet, for Hale 'Common Law and the Custom of the Realm . . . is the great Substratum' of the law (46). Without finding a place in that substratum, legislation can only be a matter of isolated rules having no *general* impact on the law beyond the narrow application of the statutory language, and, in Hale's view, only resting on the precarious ledge of formal constitutional rules liable to change. Rules incorporated into the law and custom of the realm, in contrast, have their force and authority firmly grounded in their being recognized as components in an organic structure established and confirmed by long use and practice. This leads me to the second implication. For this view provides an account of the persistence and continuity of law through substantial changes in the constitutional and political structure of the community. The law, in Hale's view, has its deepest roots not in the *political frame* or *constitution* of a society, but in its sense of common life. Though the political structure of a community may be an important part of that sense of common life, it is not the whole of it. Acceptance of the *rules of law themselves*, because they fit into a relatively coherent shared picture of the common life of the community, ensures continuity of the law through even radical constitutional changes.

Hale sketches for us, then, a sophisticated conception of law and its foundations. On this view, the immediately evident formal or institutional aspects of law—both legislative bodies and enacted law, and adjudicative bodies and judicial decisions, resolutions, and practices—have their legal significance because they are grounded in an invisible substratum, the custom and practice, the common life, of the community at large. It is this practice which judicial decisions expound, interpret, and declare—and, of course, in doing so, they also shape and alter it. It is also this practice and common life which both confers and substantially limits and controls the exercise of legislative power. Law is like an iceberg, only a portion of it is visible at any particular time, and its nature and scope can never be understood if attention is concentrated upon merely the visible portion.

Common Law theory and the language of politics

Before we proceed, I want to underscore a historical point which has emerged from the preceding discussion. The occasion for, and the character of, Hale's account of the foundations of Common Law make clear that the dispute over the historical claims made for Common Law in the seventeenth century was not merely a jurisprudential dispute. The debate went to the heart of the most pressing and divisive social and political issues of the age.

History and religion—the interpretation of the historical record of the constitution and the interpretation of Scriptures—were the two great political battlegrounds of the century.[56] The political importance of constitutional and national history during this period, as well as the particular interpretation given to them, can be traced directly to the great influence of Common Law thought on the thinking of politically active elements in the society.[57] Common Law was the unifying element in the nation, and its fundamental law. It not only defined social relationships and distributed social

---

[56] See Gray, Introduction to Hale's *History*, p. xx; Pocock, *Ancient Constitution*, ch. II; Hill, *The Century of Revolution*, 149–53. On the political importance of the dispute over interpretation of Scripture, see T. Hobbes, *Behemoth*, esp. pt. I.

[57] Pocock, *Ancient Constitution*, 31.

power, but it also encompassed the basic constitutional law of the land, defining political relations and distributing political power. Common Law was immemorial custom, so the constitution and the relations of power it defined were also regarded as ancient custom. It was inevitable, then, that Common Law concepts, beliefs, attitudes, and prejudices would decisively shape the political language of the time. Pocock has argued that

belief in the antiquity of the common law encouraged belief in the existence of an ancient constitution, reference to which was constantly made, precedents, maxims and principles from which were constantly alleged, and which was constantly asserted to be in some way immune from the king's prerogative action; and discussion in these terms formed one of the century's chief modes of political argument.[58]

But the relations of influence between politics and jurisprudence were reciprocal. Common Law theory surely shaped political discourse, but likewise the great political and social issues of the time shaped the jurisprudential theory. Classical Common Law theory of the seventeenth century was articulated in response to the political and constitutional crisis brought on by the increasing centralization of power and the threat of absolutism. Common Law theory defined the ideological base from which the previously independent Common Law courts sought to challenge the extension of the royal prerogative.[59]

Some historians of the period, most notably Christopher Hill, argue that Common Law was also involved at this time in the widening social and economic struggle. On this reading of English social history, the seventeenth century was a time in which modern commercial society was emerging from its feudal bondage. The propertied class needed some way to break the bonds of ancient feudal tenure while at the same time keeping in check both the forces of absolutism, on the one hand, and the newly emerging democratic forces, on the other. Common Law seemed to provide just the mechanism it needed. For it allowed for substantial reform of the law to meet the new conditions of commercial society without putting into the hands of the king or the Parliament power to remake the social order in its image. And liberalizing of the law

---

[58] Ibid. 46.

[59] Knafla, *Law and Politics*, ch. VII; Hill, *Intellectual Origins*, 257–8; Pocock, *Ancient Constitution*, 52.

could be undertaken, for the most part silently and gradually, at the direction of the men of property, without unleashing more radical revolutionary forces.[60]

And the influence of Common Law theory on political and social issue discourse did not end with the Revolution or the passing of the seventeenth century. Indeed, through the period of Whig dominance in the early- to mid-eighteenth century, ancient constitutionalism was common ground for the old Tory party (having finally abandoned divine right ideology) and the establishment Whigs (who sought to bury their earlier contractarian doctrines in the less revolutionary Common Law doctrine).[61] '[L]egalism . . . pervaded the political thought of England' during the eighteenth century, Sheldon Wolin has observed. 'The dominant tendency was to argue issues like electoral reform, representation, and colonial matters on the basis of law and precedent. The influence of Hardwicke, Mansfield, and Blackstone symbolized the alliance which had sprung up between law and politics.'[62] And towards the end of the century, the Common Law patterns of thought were given new political life in the writings of Burke. 'Our constitution is a prescriptive constitution', he argued;

it is a constitution whose sole authority is, that it has existed time out of mind. . . . Nor was your House of Lords and the prerogatives of the crown settled on any adjudication in favour of natural rights: for they could never be so partitioned. Your king, your lords, your judges, your juries, grand and little, all are prescriptive; and what proves it is the disputes, not yet concluded, and never near becoming so, when any of them first originated. Prescription is the most solid of all titles, not only to property, but, which is to secure that property, to government.[63]

This extension of the language and patterns of thought characteristic of Common Law jurisprudence to political and even social theory can be found in writings well into the nineteenth century, for example in the work of Macaulay and Maine.[64]

[60] See Hill, *Some Intellectual Consequences of the English Revolution*, 29–30, and generally, Hill, *Intellectual Origins*.

[61] See H. T. Dickinson, *Liberty and Property*, esp. chs. 4 and 8, and generally, D. Forbes, *Hume's Philosophical Politics*, ch. 8.

[62] S. Wolin, 'Hume and Conservatism', 253.

[63] E. Burke, 'Speech on the Reform of Representation of the Commons in Parliament' (1782), *Works* VI. 146. See also Burke, *Reflections*, 117–21, 192–5, 281–2.'

[64] Compare Burke, *Reflections*, 177 ff with T. B. Macaulay, *History of England*, ch. X, *Works* ii, 395–6 on the Whigs' use of Common Law patterns of thought to

1.3 REASON AND PRINCIPLE IN COMMON LAW THEORY

> [These maxims articulate] the general dictates of reason which run through the different matters of law and act as its ballast.
>
> Bacon, *Maxims.*

We observed in 1.1 that Common Law theory held that law rests on the twofold foundation of history and reason. In the previous section I tried to clarify the role of history in Common Law theory. I now turn to the role of reason. In Coke, and even in Hale, there is not much difficulty combining these two consistently, because the reason of the law is explicitly recognized as 'artificial reason'— reason *within* the law, we might say. However, in the eighteenth century especially, one finds a considerable reliance on terminology and ideas drawn from natural law theory alongside endorsements of this Cokean doctrine. One of the questions I wish to address in this section is the extent to which natural law theory was actually incorporated into Common Law jurisprudence.

Two conceptions of reason in Common Law theory

In the classical theory of Common Law there is considerable uncertainty and ambiguity concerning the nature of the reason, or reasonability, *of* the law, and the nature and role of reason *in* the law. It is possible to distinguish two conceptions of reason (or reasoning) at work in the theory. Seldom does one find just one or the other expressed, but it is possible to locate in some writers greater emphasis on the one or the other.

One of these, which I shall call the 'particularist' conception, has its roots in Coke's sharp distinction between the ordinary faculty of reason ('natural reason') and the special, 'artificial reason' of the law, a faculty possessed only by a few after long study and experience.[65] According to this conception, the reason of the law is

---

make their case for the Revolution. See Sir Henry Sumner Maine, *Early History*, 230, quoted above p. 13, and generally, Maine, *Popular Government*, esp. Essay III 'The Age of Progress'.

[65] 'Then the king said, that he thought the law was founded upon reason, and that he and others had reason as well as the judges: to which it was answered by me, that true it was, that God had endowed his Majesty with excellent science, and great endowments of nature; but his Majesty was not learned in the laws of his realm of England, and causes which concern the life, or inheritance, or goods, or fortunes of his subjects are not to be decided by natural reason, but by the artificial reason and

entirely concrete and particular, inseparable from the particular situations brought to the law and resolved by it. It is the reason not of rules and principles, but of cases. Thus, the reason of the law is guaranteed, not by any *external* principles or criteria of rationality to which it allegedly conforms, but rather by its own *internal coherence* and *completeness*, by the fact (or rather the presumption) that the myriad of particulars fit together into a coherent whole.

The reason *of* the law consists in the fact that it makes possible a special kind of *reasoning*. Lawyers are 'connoisseurs of cases in point, cognoscenti of matters at hand'.[66] Neither deductive nor inductive, their reasoning is analogical, arguing from particular case to particular case, reflecting 'upon the likenesses and dissimilarities of particular instances either actual or hypothetical, particular to particular—*similia e similibus* as Bracton called it'.[67] Analogy is 'the stuff of law', according to Charles Fried because it is

the only form of reasoning left to the law when general philosophical structures and deductive reasoning give out, overwhelmed by the mass of particular details. Analogy is the application of a trained, disciplined intuition where the manifold of particulars is too extensive to allow our minds to work on it deductively. This is not a denial of reason; on the contrary, it is a civilized attempt to stretch reason as far as it will go.[68]

Hale seems to endorse something like this conception, at least at certain points in his writings. He admits that the laws of England are 'more particular' than laws of other nations, but, he insists, this is desirable because it 'prevents arbitrariness by the judge', and it

judgment of law, which law is an act which requires long study and experience before that a man can attain to the knowledge of it.' Coke, 12 *Coke's Reports*, 63, 65.

[66] C. Geertz, *Local Knowledge*, 168.

[67] R. Stone, 'Ratiocination not Rationalisation', 481.

[68] C. Fried, 'The Artificial Reason of the Law', 57. Roy Stone gives clear expression to this conception of reason and reasoning in Common Law: 'Now what has happened in the history of tortious liability? This case so resembles that, and that another, that a form of action given in each case enables us to make a general statement, a classification. This is trespass. We have a concept derived from the multifarious and varied but curiously associated resembling features. *There is not any universal feature* resembling the form of some ideal entity, nor yet a series of examples each containing its own innate nature serving that end which Aristotle's teleology supposes to be built into everything. It is the ferreting out from particular instances of those resemblances which need not belong to every particular of a kind, but which some bear to others but not necessarily to all, like family resemblances.' Stone, 'Ratiocination', 477–8, emphasis added.

'makes the law more certain and better applicable to the business that comes to be judged by it'. More general laws are, of course, more comprehensive and more easily digested into a system, but 'when they come to particular application, they are of little service, and leave a great latitude to partiality'.[69]

He makes a similar distinction between the reasoning of the moral philosopher and that of the Common Law judge in his attack on Hobbes. The philosopher is capable of tracing logical relations between abstract ideas, but from those ideas no determinate practical solutions can be drawn. For practical situations and the human problems that arise in them are almost infinitely complex and application of abstract notions to these complex situations results only in interminable controversy, for each person applies the concept from his or her own limited perspective. Adequate solutions to such problems must reflect full appreciation of the wide variety of considerations that bear on the situation, and must be sensitive to the impact of the decision on the practical life of the community as a whole. To look to natural reason or general theory for guidance in such situations is to simplify and thus distort the problem and make achievement of an adequate solution unlikely. Thus, the moral philosopher, the person of natural reason, is ill-equipped for this task. Only one who, through long 'observation and experience in Human affaires and Conversation', can with prudence and judgment relate the case at hand to this fund of experience, can be expected to resolve its problems satisfactorily. But, of course, there are few persons alive with such experience and wisdom. The Common Law judge, however, is in the best position to exercise such judgment, not in virtue of his or her *own* experience alone, but in virtue of the fact that the judge works from within the *law*, which is the repository of the experience of the community over the ages. The judge, through long study and practice within this fund of concrete knowledge and experience, is able to situate the dispute or problem at hand in the complex body of experience, and to reason from the particular cases represented there to a solution in the particular case at hand.[70]

The knowledge and the special capacity of judgment or prudence characteristic of the judge are acquired not through study of the

[69] Hale, 'Preface to Rolle's Abridgment', 267.
[70] Hale, 'Reflections on Hobbes' Dialogue', 502–3. I discuss this passage at length below, 2.3.

general principles of some systematic body of knowledge, but only through long years of immersion in the particularity of the law, says Hale. '[M]en are not born Common Lawyers, neither can the bare Exercise of the Faculty of Reason give a man a Sufficient Knowledge of it, but it must be gained by the habituating and accustoming and exercising that Faculty by reading, Study and observation to give a Man a complete Knowledge thereof.'[71] This is a body of law, then, that resists reduction to a system of general principles, i.e. to an economical set of first principles from which the particular rules and decisions of law can (at least in principle) be inferred.[72]

But there is at work in classical Common Law theory another conception of reason which becomes especially important by the mid-eighteenth century. This conception gives reflective reason a much wider scope in the law and portrays the Common Law as a *rational science* based on first principles, or at least potentially transformable into such a science. This conception links reason with general justifying *principles* which are instanced in, and illustrated by, particular decisions and settled rules.

One can find this conception clearly at work in Blackstone's *Commentaries* (sometimes alongside the particularist conception). 'The law of England acts upon general and extensive principles', he maintains (1 *Comm.* 425). Although we normally find no need in daily life to inquire after the reasons or grounds of laws governing our common life and the use and disposal of our property,[73] yet it is possible to consider law 'not only as a matter of practice, but also as a rational science . . . [and] to examine more deeply the rudiments and grounds of these positive constitutions of society' (2

---

[71] Ibid. 505. (I have modernized the spelling in this fragment.)

[72] This is essentially the interpretation of Coke and Hale advanced by Pocock, see *Ancient Constitution*, 35, 171–3, and 'Burke and the Ancient Constitution', 214–22. There is no doubt that this conception can be found in the writings of Coke and Hale, and through them it has found its way into the Common Law tradition. But I am not convinced that it is the *only* view either jurist held of the role of reason in the law. Coke, for example, looked with some favour on Bacon's proposals to systematize and digest the Common Law. He also said regarding Bacon's *Novum Organum*: 'You propose to reconstruct the teaching of wise men and of old. Reconstruct first our laws and justice . . .', quoted in Hill, *Intellectual Origins*, 231, and generally 230–46. Also there is evidence in his *History* and *Amendment of Laws* that Hale was not opposed to attempts to simplify and give systematic structure to the Common Law.

[73] Indeed Blackstone insists that 'it is well if the mass of mankind will obey the laws when made, without scrutinizing too nicely into the reasons of making them' (2 *Comm.* 2).

Comm. 2). At least in part the task of the *Commentaries* was that of 'examining the great outlines of the English law, and tracing them up to their principles' (4 *Comm.* 5).

The study of the principle underlying the law was especially important for students, and future practitioners, of the law. Blackstone attacked the apprenticeship system which exposes young lawyers only to practice, and not to its underlying principles. Not only will such lawyers fail to understand the foundations of their own law, he argues, but they will be ill-equipped for the practice of law except in routine cases. If the student is 'uninstructed in the elements and first principles upon which the rule of practice is founded, the least variation from established precedents will totally distract and bewilder him . . .'. He will be unable to comprehend any arguments drawn 'from the spirit of the laws and the natural foundations of justice' (1 *Comm.* 32). Students must have impressed on them 'the sound maxims of the law of nature, the best and most authentic foundation of human laws' (1 *Comm.* 33).

Nevertheless, Blackstone was somewhat ambivalent about the role of natural law notions in the Common Law of England. On the one hand, one finds appeal to natural law considerations with some frequency in the *Commentaries*—for example, in his defence of the institution of property (2 *Comm.* 1–15) and of the state's right to punish (4 *Comm.* 5–9). Yet, when he took the Bench, he was much less willing to make such appeals and, in fact, was severely critical of those, like the activist Mansfield, who sought to utilize natural law language to introduce considerable innovations in the Common Law.[74] And there is much in the *Commentaries* to support this conservative reaction.[75]

[74] See D. Lieberman, *The Province of Legislation Determined*, 207–9, and opinions of Blackstone cited there.

[75] It is clear this is not standard natural law doctrine. For there is no attempt to make the link between the very general and abstract principles of natural law which he cites, on the one hand, and particular rules and provisions of the Common Law, on the other. In the *Commentaries* Blackstone seems to have accepted Hale's view that the abstract formulas of the moral philosopher need to be filled in by custom and practice. Natural law declares the 'immutable laws' captured by the Justinian precept *Juris praecepta sunt haec, honeste vivere, alterum non laedere, suum cuique tribuere* (1 *Comm.* 40, quoting Justinian, *Institutes* I. i. 3). But it cannot tell us what is to be regarded as 'honest, dishonest, or indifferent', what counts as an injury, or what is each man's due. These matters, as well as the extent and limits of liberty, can be determined only by the law and custom of the realm. See 1 *Comm.* 53.

Blackstone also notes that certain general principles of justice and public policy with a close affinity to traditional principles of natural law frequently figure in

Mansfield was, of course, the most vigorous advocate of this conception of reason in the Common Law among the judiciary in the eighteenth century. The law 'would be a strange Science', he argued,

if it rested solely upon cases; and if after so large an increase of Commerce, Arts and Circumstances accruing, we must go to the time of Richard I to find a Case, and see what is Law. Precedent indeed may serve to fix Principles, which for certainty's sake are not suffered to be shaken, whatever might be the weight of the principle independent of the precedent. But precedent, though it be Evidence of law, is not Law itself; much less the Whole of the Law.[76]

This, in some respects, goes no farther than the view we saw Hale embrace. But Mansfield insisted that the 'law does not consist in particular cases; but in general principles which run through the cases and govern the decision of them'.[77] And this may go farther than Hale would have been inclined to go, especially since Mansfield did not scruple to identify these principles with natural justice, equity, and common reason.[78] As David Lieberman has pointed out, Mansfield's decisions provide some of the most forceful statements of the place of natural law in English jurisprudence in the eighteenth century.[79] It appears that Common Lawyers in the eighteenth century did not refuse to appeal to general notions of justice, convenience, and common good (often framed in the language of natural law) when the particular, black letter resources of the law were found inadequate to the task.

A historical conception of reason

These two conceptions, though distinct, are not entirely incompatible. 'Particularist' reason or intuition is inadequate and

---

Common Law decisions. But even here, the authority of these 'established rules and maxims' rests not on their being derivable from first principles of natural law or reason, but on the same basis as 'established custom', namely on the fact of continued use and acceptance (1 *Comm.* 68).

[76] *Jones* v. *Randall* (1774), in Capel Lofft, *Reports of Cases in the Court of King's Bench*, 385.

[77] *Rust* v. *Cooper* (1774), in Henry Cowper, *Reports of Cases in the Court of King's Bench*, 632.

[78] Law is founded in 'equity, reason, and good sense', *James* v. *Price* (1773), in Lofft, 221. I am indebted to David Lieberman for the passages from Mansfield's opinions cited in this and the previous two notes.

[79] Lieberman, *Province*, 11, 92.

incomplete without guidance from general principles. But the reason of general principles is not a priori, and ahistorical, it is practical and historical; the 'natural law' involved is not external to the tradition, but implicit in it, not socially transcendent, but immanent.

It is possible and desirable, according to the theory, to construct broad general principles of law and with them attempt to capture and explain much of what otherwise would appear to be a confused jumble of unrelated particular rules and decisions yielding no practical conclusion. Yet the principles are uncovered through reflection *on the particular cases*—through experience and the reflection of many on that experience—and not through a priori reasoning. The law, on this view, arises only out of experience, and it is impossible adequately to fashion rules for social life without adequate experience. General rules not yet confirmed by experience, then, must be treated as hypotheses, open-ended proposals, and not as firm and binding law. Thus, the reason which Blackstone, Mansfield, and others believed they saw in the Common Law was reason 'running through the cases', reason in the 'spirit of the laws'. Cases and decisions are not themselves law, but neither are they merely illustrations of some general rational principle the truth and validity of which rests on external grounds. These cases and decisions are the *manifestations* of this reason of the law. General principles—'theory' we might say—are needed in adjudication, but 'theory' is always driven by cases, and not decisions and cases by theory.

The reason involved both in constructing general principles and deciding particular cases is *traditional* reason, that is, reason shaped by the tradition within which it is exercised. It is practical reason exercised within an already constituted, though open-ended, framework. This is still to be distinguished sharply from 'natural reason', i.e. the rational faculty common to all human beings simply in virtue of their humanity, and untutored in the special tradition of the Common Law.

It is this distinction between 'natural reason' and the reason of Common Law which underlies, in part, the opposition of Common Lawyers to the notion of *equity*. In so far as equity has any place in the law, Blackstone insists, it must be identified with the spirit of reason which *runs through the law*, the spirit in which all Common Law judges, if they are doing their job properly, approach the law

(3 *Comm.* 429). But if equity is understood as a body of rational principles which stands in judgment of the law, it must be rejected. One major objection to the court of Chancery was that it purported to make its decisions, often abrogating proper decisions made in Common Law courts, on the basis of nothing more than appeals to 'conscience', and 'natural reason'.

The reason of the Common Law, then, is immanent. But also, because the framework is a historically embodied tradition, it is historical. Blackstone is comfortable with language from natural law theory precisely because he believes that the 'naturalness' and 'reasonableness' of the law is *demonstrated* by experience and its long existence. As Selden argued a century earlier, there may be (or have been) a priori principles of natural law governing the relations amongst men and women, but these principles have been 'limited for the conveniency of civil society here, and those limitations have been from thence, increased, altered, interpreted, and brought to what they are now'.[80] Natural law on this interpretation appears not as a 'higher law' standing in constant judgment on positive human law, but as the light of reason shining through that law. Natural law is best discovered through evolutionary refinement; it 'underlay existing law and must be looked for through it'.[81]

Actually, this reveals a deep ambiguity in Common Law theory, for it is not clear whether Common Law is regarded as itself defining standards of reason and justice in this area of social life (Common Law regarded *as* reason), or whether Common Law is the working out of reason (reason regarded as working *in* and *through* Common Law). Both can be regarded as historicist, but one regards its Common Law standards as autonomous and self-justifying, the other appeals ultimately to a transcendent source of validation. I shall explore this ambiguity in the next chapter.

A 'rational science' of Common Law, then, is possible. But it can never hope neatly to capture within its four corners the rich, living tradition of Common Law. No codification, no reduction of the law to principles without remainder is possible. Principles can, and must, be constructed, but they are always corrigible. And, systematic consistency is not always desirable, for it can be purchased at a price too dear—the price of over-simplification and inflexibility. Even in the present century a Common Lawyer is willing

---

[80] J. Selden, quoted in Tuck, *Natural Rights Theories*, 84; see above, n. 8.
[81] Maine, *Ancient Law*, 45.

to admit that 'The common law is tolerant of much illogicality' at least on the surface, as long as there is 'logic at the root of it'.[82] The law, on this theory, is not to be identified with *either* particular decisions, precedents, and settled rules, *or* with general rules and idealized projections inferred from them (for example, 'the best theory' of such institutional data).[83] If it is possible, then, to capture in a single phrase what law *is*, according to classical Common Law theory, one might say that it is a form of social order manifested in the practice and common life of the nation.

It may be impossible, on this theory, to say precisely what portion of this practice and common life falls within the scope of law and what part falls outside it. But this fuzziness of the concept of law causes the Common Law theorist no great concern, for the conception does not attempt to shut off law from moral and social forces akin to it. Rather it seeks to integrate law into them. There is no sharp conceptual boundary between law and other social phenomena because, on this view, there is no sharp difference between them in the community governed by that law.

[82] Lord Devlin, *Hedley Byrne* v. *Heller* [1964] AC 465 at 516.

[83] As, perhaps Dworkin does in *Taking Rights Seriously*, chs. 3 and 4.

2

Law, Social Union, and Collective Rationality

[W]ithout ideas held in common there is no common action, and without common action there may still be men, but there is no social body.

de Tocqueville, *Democracy in America*.

COMMON Law theory and legal positivism—the two major contenders on the field of British legal theory—emerged as distinctive jurisprudential theories in the seventeenth century, at the birth and early infancy of the modern era. The social and intellectual developments of the period had a decisive impact on terms of the debate between them and on the ways in which they addressed fundamental questions regarding the nature of law. The rise of modern science, the profound intellectual changes brought by the Reformation, and the emergence of commercial society gave new significance to the notion of natural reason and encouraged individuals critically to explore their world, both natural and social. It was also a time of great social and political change and many long-established institutions and traditional ways began to weaken. The strings of the well-tempered medieval universe became untuned. Broad consensus regarding fundamental values and the nature of community seemed to break down and the increasing uncertainty and insecurity generated a widespread sense of moral crisis. Moreover, the exercise of individual natural reason seemed to yield not a more humane, enlightened, and reasonable society, but rather a disjointed, fragmented, and madly conflicted one.

Social theorists generally, and legal theorists especially, implicitly looked to law to establish and maintain threatened social union and to introduce collective order and rationality into what they regarded as the anarchy of private judgment that threatened it. That this was the primary task of law was assumed by both schools of British jurisprudence. However, different conceptions of what constitutes social union or community, and quite different analyses of what could account for the obstacles standing in the way of collectively rational social interaction, produced sharply differing conceptions of the nature of law itself.

In this chapter I begin to explore the philosophical motivations behind Common Law theory and legal positivism. The primary aim is to define more precisely the terms of the debate between these two great jurisprudential traditions. Coke and Hale, the main figures of Chapter 1, will be featured here again; Hobbes appears as their antagonist. However, because both Hobbes and the Common Law theorists substantially reworked a patchwork of political and jurisprudential ideas inherited, at least in part, from the natural law tradition, I have chosen Aquinas's theory for the point of departure of this chapter. It is the most familiar and, I believe, theoretically the most sophisticated discussion of the issues I wish to consider to be found within the natural law tradition.

2.1 AUTHORITY, JUSTICE, AND CO-ORDINATION

> Et ideo cum justitia ordinetur ad alterum, non est circa totam materiam virtutis moralis, sed solum circa exteriores actiones et res, secundum quamdam rationem objecti specialem, prout scilicet secundum eas unus homo alteri coordinatur.
>
> Aquinas, *Summa Theologiae*

Right, according to the *Summa Theologiae*, is an objective, independently existing and discoverable, rational ordering of social behaviour and of relations amongst members of the community (*ST* 2a2ae 57. 1). This ordering is either natural—existing in some sense apart from, and normative for, human artifice and institutions—or it is positive—the product of consensus in the community or of institution by the *princeps* (*ST* 2a2ae 57. 2). Human beings participate in this ordering as *rational* beings, uncovering the rational principles of this ordering and self-consciously directing their actions to accord with it (*ST* 1a2ae 90. 1; 93. 5). 'Right' refers to the objective order; 'law' refers to the precept or ordinance (*rationes ordinatio*) defined with respect to it.[1] Law bears a complex relationship to right: (i) it is descriptive and expressive of

---

[1] *ST* 1a2ae 90. 4. Also: '*lex non est ipsum jus proprie loquendo, sed aliqualis ratio juris*' (*ST* 2a2ae 57. 1 ad 2).

the order of right to the extent that the order is realized in the community; (ii) it prescribes the pursuit and establishment of right; and (iii) it is the primary instrument by which the order is established and maintained.[2]

Human law is a structured body of precepts, addressed to self-guiding rational individuals in a community, directing their efforts to the common good, issuing from recognized authority, and taking a recognized institutional form (*ST* 1a2ae 90. 4; 95–7). Through authority and law, and through them alone, a multitude is made into a people (a community). A 'people is that gathering of a multitude bound together by a consensus as to what is just and by mutual interest', says Aquinas quoting Cicero, adding that the 'notion of a people therefore involves men's mutual exchanges being regulated by just precepts of the law' (*ST* 1a2ae 105. 2). But if the natural order of right is discoverable by exercise of human reason, why do we need positive law to declare and establish it for us? And why are law and authority needed to shape us into a community? To answer these questions we must look more closely at Aquinas's account of human nature and the nature of justice and its role in social life.

Every creature is a goal-seeking being, Aquinas maintains, but this is true of human beings in a special sense. For human beings seek their goals rationally, that is, they self-consciously recognize and select their goals and choose to direct their actions to achieve them. Moreover, human beings are 'made for community', i.e. by nature they are committed to seeking goals *with others*. They want (some of the most important) goals they seek to be shared goals, common to the community. Association with others is a necessary constituent of individual self-fulfilment.[3] Life in a community 'enables man to achieve a plenitude of life; not merely to exist, but to live fully, with all that is necessary to well-being'.[4]

Justice is a virtue of external actions and relations among persons in community. Its aim is the co-ordination of individual actions towards common goals. For, Aquinas maintains, 'it is

---

[2] *ST* 2a2ae 57. 1–2; 79. 1 ad 1; 1a2ae 90. 1–2, 4; 105. 2. On the relations between *jus* and *lex* see T. Gilby's note, *Summa Theologiae* (Blackfriars) v. 37, pp. 2–3 n. c. A similar account of the modes of law is set out in I. Jenkins, *Social Order and the Limits of Law*, ch. V.

[3] See M. Lefebure, Introduction to *Summa Theologiae* (Blackfriars) v. 38, p. xx.

[4] Aquinas, *Commentary on Aristotle's Nicomachean Ethics*, in A. P. D'Entreves, *Aquinas: Selected Political Writings*, 191. See also *ST* 1a 96. 4; 1a2ae 90.2, 3 ad 3; 92, 1 ad 3; 96. 4; 2a2e 26. 3; 58, 5, 9 ad 3; 64.2.

through external actions and things, through which men mutually communicate, that the order of one to another is observed', and not through 'a man's interior feelings'. And since 'it is directed to others, justice consequently is not about the whole field of moral virtue, but only about external deeds and things, and these under a certain specific aspect, namely of the due co-ordination of one person with another' (*ST* 2a2ae 58. 8).

Justice is a virtue of both institutions and individuals. The personal virtue of justice consists in a willing disposition to participate in co-operative schemes and to seek out ways and means by which the pursuit of common goals can be co-ordinated. Authority is the natural and necessary institutional expression of justice as a personal virtue. The task of authority is to ensure success in the co-operative pursuit of common goals by integrating human social efforts which would otherwise be dispersed and fragmented.

Thus, in Aquinas's definition, the *princeps* is he 'who has care of the community' (*ab eo qui curam communitatis habet*, *ST* 1a2ae 90. 4), by which he does not mean that the *princeps* is any more devoted to the common good than his subjects, nor that he is better qualified to discover what in fact are the constituents of common good or natural right. Rather, he means that the *princeps* is one who is uniquely placed effectively to co-ordinate the social interaction of subjects in pursuit of common goals (*ST* 1a 96. 4; 1a2ae 90. 3). Ordering behaviour to the common good belongs only to either the whole people or to the 'vicegerent of the whole people'.[5] For, even in 'a state of innocence' (a community of saints),

many individuals are, as individuals, interested in a variety of ends. One person [in contrast] is interested in one end. So the Philosopher says . . . Whenever a plurality is directed to one object there is always to be found one in authority giving direction (*ST* 1a 96. 4).

That is, even when individual members seek only the common good, different individuals may each prefer, on reasonable grounds, a different combination of the constituents of the common good, or different strategies for achieving the agreed upon goals. The task of authority is to co-ordinate the decisions and ac-

---

[5] *ST* 1a2ae 90. 3. The *princeps* is *personam publicam* in two senses: (i) he acts in behalf of the community (as 'vicegerent'), see Gilby, *Summa* (Blackfriars) v. 28, p. 13 n. c.; and (ii) he manifests the unity of the community (*ST* 2a2ae 57. 2).

tions of the members of the community and thereby the multitude to act rationally as a collective body, a unity.[6]

The principal manifestation of authority, and its primary tool for achieving this task, is positive law and public adjudication within the regime defined by law. Human law is the external articulation both of the inner inclination of each member to seek co-operative interaction with others and of the community's consensus regarding the constituents of the common good and the common way of acting to realize that good (*ST* 1a2ae 105. 2). Thus, the aim of law is not simply to regulate the behaviour of each person, but rather to co-ordinate the activities of all in the community (*ST* 1a2ae 96. 1 ad 2 and 6 ad 3). It does so by defining and declaring publicly a pattern of interactions and reciprocal duties, i.e. a blueprint for the common good.

Thus, despite the accessibility of natural right to human reason, positive law is needed for the following reasons.

1. It must fix standards of behaviour and measures of justice in relations among individuals where natural law and natural right are silent.[7] Natural law consists not only of abstract first principles (*communissima*), according to Aquinas, but also of derivative precepts adjusted where necessary to the special circumstances and character of the society and people concerned (*ST* 1a2ae 94. 4–5; 97). But on some matters calling for social regulation, natural law is silent, at least regarding details. In such cases, positive law is 'derived from' natural law only in the sense that it seeks to implement and make concrete the broad general directives or designs of natural law (*ST* 1a2ae 95. 2). Because natural law lays down only general guide-lines, frequently there will be a number of different *determinationes* of the natural law precepts, on the merits of which reasonable persons may differ widely. Within this range it is more important that there be a common way of acting than that the optimal alternative be adopted. Positive law defines such a common way, and, Aquinas suggests, because its dictates are part of the public knowledge of members of the community, it will succeed

---

6 With St Thomas explicitly in mind, J. Finnis makes this argument for authority in *Natural Law and Natural Rights*, IX. 1.

7 *ST* 2a2ae 57. 2; 60. 5 ad 1; 1a2ae 90. 3; 95. 2. The *locus classicus* of this idea, of course, is Aristotle, *Nicomachean Ethics* V, 7, 1134b 18–24. The notion of the '*adiaphora*'—those things which are 'naturally indifferent' but which must nevertheless be settled one way or another—became, through the Stoics, a commonplace in scholastic jurisprudence.

in co-ordinating social interaction where private proposals are likely to fail. In such cases, actions are good or obligatory because required, not required because good or obligatory (*ST* 2a2ae 57. 23).

2. Despite the accessibility of natural law to human reason, positive law is also needed to declare publicly the requirements of natural law themselves, because the further we move from self-evident first principles, working out their implications for the special social circumstances in which we live, the more we risk error.[8] This means not only that we cannot invest complete confidence in *our own* conclusions drawn from such precepts, but it also means that we cannot *count on others* in the community to arrive at the same results through the exercise of their reason. But since, according to Aquinas, social life is fundamentally co-operative, the rationality of any course of action depends upon assurance that others will do their part in the co-operative scheme of which it is a part, and that requires assurance that we all share (roughly) the same conception of right behaviour. Positive law may not be able to boast of any greater insight into natural right than that available to individuals, but it can publicly define a common way of acting after a bona fide attempt to determine what natural right requires. The argument here does not depend on moral scepticism, nor any deep scepticism regarding the powers of individual reason. It would have the same force if it were true (though not a matter of public knowledge) that most members of the community were capable of discovering on their own the dictates of natural right. The argument rests on the assumption that co-operative interaction necessary for human social life depends heavily on public assurance, and for that law and authority are indispensable.

3. Human beings are naturally inclined to seek the common good and find fulfilment in co-operative endeavours, according to Aquinas, but this natural inclination needs nurturing and training (*ST* 1a2ae 95. 1). Positive law plays an important role here too. Becoming habituated to actions required by law, members of the community 'may come to do of their own accord what earlier they did from fear' (ibid.). The pedagogical resources of positive law, however, are not limited to 'force and fear', for the law itself gives expression to the ideal of co-operative interaction. It is not merely a tool for bringing about a certain transformation in individual conviction and motivation; it embodies that conviction in a publicly

[8] *ST* 1a2ae 91. 3 ad 3; 94. 2, 4–5; 95. 2–3; 2a2ae 60. 5.

recognizable form. Aquinas views law not so much as a (perhaps necessary) limit on individual liberty and achievement of private good, but as an achievement of the social nature of human beings, and a locus of self-fulfilment.[9]

In sum, Aquinas holds that law and authority are public manifestations of the collective life of the people and the means by which the whole people orders collective life (and individual lives) towards achievement of the common good (*ST* 1a2ae 90. 3).

The Thomist view of the relations between individual and collective rationality should now be clear. First, natural right is accessible to natural reason; yet no one can seek to determine the dictates of natural law without consideration of the possibility of co-ordination of social interaction. No argument for a course of action on which, for one reason or another, general consensus could not be assured, could in fact be a course of action in accord with natural right and justice.[10] For right and justice are concerned primarily with patterns of social co-operation for achieving the common good. Thus, arranging matters for the common good, according to Aquinas, is fundamentally a public matter, a matter for which individual members of the community are not fully competent (*ST* 1a2ae 90. 3). It would be a mistake, then, he believes, to leave public matters to private discretion (except in emergency) (*ST* 1a2ae 97. 4). The *princeps*, however, is in a special position. Recognized as competent to speak for the whole people, his proposals will be public and common, and so he can give sufficient assurance that his conception of the dictates of natural law will be generally accepted and followed.

Note, secondly, however, that informal conventions or custom can, in Aquinas's view, perform the same function as the declarations of the *princeps*. 'Although single individuals cannot make laws, yet the whole people can.'[11] In fact, it appears that, for St Thomas, custom is the primary source of law. For the authority to 'order behaviour to the common good' rests first in 'the whole people', and derivatively in the *princeps* (*ST* 1a2ae 90. 3; 97. 3 ad 3). Customs and informal conventions have the force of law because they are the product of the exercise of authority by the whole people

9 See Gilby, Introduction, *Summa* v. 28, p. xxii.

10 Compare D. Regan's 'co-operative utilitarianism', *Utilitarian Co-operation*, chs. 8–12.

11 '[*L*]*icet singulae personae non possint condere legem, tamen totus populus condere legem potest*' (*ST* 1a2ae 97. 3 ad 3, my translation).

and express the common reason of the community. The *princeps* may have a role to play even here, but only as the formal articulator of already established common standards.

Thirdly, there are quite definite limits on the exercise of authority, whether by the *princeps* or by the whole people through custom.[12] There is an objective, rational normative order. The laws of the *princeps* or the people must genuinely seek to set out publicly the principles of this order. To the extent that they deviate, they lose binding force (*ST* 1a2ae 90. 1; 96. 4). And even when the natural law is silent, the silence is not total. It gives *general guidance*; it defines the range of the reasonable. And the directives of authority will bind a reasonable citizen only to the extent that the law falls within the bounds of the reasonable.

2.2 SOVEREIGN COMMANDS AND INDIVIDUAL REASON

> Statutes are not philosophy as is Common Law and other disputable Arts, but are Commands or Prohibitions . . .
>
> Hobbes, *Dialogue.*

The jurisprudence of Hobbes's Dialogue

The problem of reconciling reason and law is sharply focused in the opening pages of Hobbes's unjustly neglected *Dialogue*.[13] After agreeing with Coke that law is right reason, he immediately points out that this creates a serious problem for the authority of law. In fact, this doctrine 'frustrates all the Laws in the World: for upon

---

[12] Custom must be consistent with independent standards of justice and natural law (*ST* 1a2ae 97. 3 ad 1). On Aquinas, and the natural law tradition generally, regarding the doctrine of prescription, see P. Lucas, 'On Edmond Burke's Doctrine of Prescription', 39–43.

[13] T. Hobbes, *A Dialogue between a Philosopher and a Student of the Common Laws*, probably written in the mid- to late-1660's. (See the parallel discussion at *Leviathan* XXVI, 316–17.) Until recently the *Dialogue* was available only in an unsatisfactory edition in Molesworth's *The English Works of Thomas Hobbes*, v. 6. In 1971 J. Cropsey edited a very readable and reliable text. His introduction is helpful, although I believe he is mistaken to claim that the doctrine of the *Dialogue* makes a sharp break from that of *The Leviathan*. Difference of emphasis is evident (very little, for example, is said about the state of nature in the *Dialogue*), but this is easily explained by the fact that Hobbes has quite different objectives in writing the two works. There is some development of the doctrine of sovereign power in the *Dialogue*. Hobbes argues, for example, that the sovereign must secure the assent of Parliament before enacting laws. But this is entirely consistent with *Leviathan* doctrine which holds that the sovereign is above all positive law but is not above the law of nature which binds him to seek the *salus populi*.

this ground any Man, of any Law whatsoever may say it is against Reason, and thereupon make a pretence for his disobedience' (*Dialogue* 54–5). To equate law with reason is to give warrant to each person's judgment of the requirements of reason, and this, in Hobbes's view, is not only dangerous, it is self-contradictory. For '[i]t is not Wisdom, but Authority that makes a Law' (*Dialogue* 55). Law, he insists, is not *philosophy*—its dictates are not indefinitely disputable, nor are its doctrines always open to reformulation and reconsideration. Rather, law consists of commands or prohibitions the contents of which are indisputable (*Dialogue* 69).

Common Law theory, of course, has a ready solution to this dilemma: the reason of the law is not the natural reason of each individual citizen, but rather that 'artificial perfection of Reason' acquired by long study, observation, and experience.[14] But Hobbes immediately rejects this proposal, insisting that 'there is no Reason in Earthly Creatures, but Humane Reason' (*Dialogue* 55). There is nothing special about the reason of lawyers and judges, he insists; it is simply natural reason, which every competent person can exercise, applied to the subject of the laws (*Dialogue* 62). And, he adds, any competent person could master the law (to the extent it can *ever* be mastered) within two months (*Dialogue* 56). This task is easier than Common Lawyers pretended it to be because, Hobbes argues, custom and precedent have no special authority apart from the sovereign's adoption of them.[15]

I deny that any Custome of its own Nature, can amount to the Authority of a Law: For if the Custom be unreasonable, you must with all other Lawyers confess that it is no Law, but ought to be abolished; and if the Custom be reasonable, it is not the Custom, but the Equity [its being in accord with natural reason] that makes it Law (*Dialogue* 96).

Custom (unwritten law), on this view, can claim authority only to the extent that it stands validated by natural reason. Unwritten law, if it claims allegiance at all, is the law of nature, but custom and precedent are not to be numbered among the laws of nature, for 'whatsoever action is against reason, though it be reiterated never so often, or that there be never so many precedents thereof, is still against reason, and therefore not a law of nature' (*Elements* I. 4, 11). The principle of precedent and custom is a childish principle of

---

14 *Dialogue* 55 quoting Coke, I *Institutes*, sect. 138.
15 *Dialogue* 55; *Leviathan* XXVI, 313; *Elements of Law* II. 13, 10 (227).

action, he charges (*Leviathan* XI, 166). Time of itself generates no
warrant to follow precedent (except in so far as it signifies the silent
adoption of the sovereign); indeed, in those cases in which it is
reasonable to have some regard to past practice, it is the more
recent, not the more ancient, usage that reasonably governs our
decision and action (*Dialogue* 97, 142).

But Hobbes sees a more sinister side to Coke's argument.
Through the doctrine of the artificial reason of the law Common
Lawyers have sought to substitute their own opinions for the law of
the land (*Dialogue* 96, 55). This is not only contrary to the fundamental law of England, since the king alone has legislative power,
Hobbes argues (*Dialogue* 55), but it also defeats the basic purposes
of law. For the judgments recorded in precedents are constantly in
conflict; the law supposedly established by them is always unsettled;
and the reasoning of the many judges inevitably is discordant.[16]

Hobbes's solution to the puzzle with which he opens the
Dialogue is to identify law with *neither* the reason of individual
citizens *nor* with some fictitious artificial reason of the law, but
rather with the natural reason of the sovereign. The 'Kings Reason,
when it is publickly upon Advice, and Deliberation declar'd, is that
Anima Legis, and that *Summa Ratio*, and that Equity which all
agree to be the Law of Reason, is all that is, or ever was Law in
England' (*Dialogue* 62). Law, then, is reason—not artificial
reason, but 'the Reason of this our Artificiall Man the Commonwealth, and his Command' (*Leviathan* XXVI, 317).

This brief discussion in the *Dialogue* sketches the outlines of
Hobbes's conception of law. I want to consider now the basic lines
of argument that Hobbes advances for this conception and to draw
out some of its implications.

Subjectivism

Despite the centrality of the notion of 'natural reason' for Hobbes,
he held that all standards of good, virtue, justice, and right reason
are conventional, that outside civil society as he describes it 'there
are no authentical doctrines concerning right and wrong, good and
evil' (*De Cive*, Preface, 98). In fact, it is his radical subjectivism
regarding standards of morals and right reason, rather than his

---

[16] *Dialogue* 84, 89; *Leviathan* XXVI, 317; *Elements* II. 13, 10 (227). Compare
Leviathan XI, 166 with Bentham's argument from 'the paradox of inflexibility'
below, 8.2.

disputed egoism, on which his argument most fundamentally rests. And his account of the nature and rational grounds of morality, law, and the social and political institutions of the commonwealth is decisively shaped by his radical subjectivism.

Subjectivist definitions of 'good' and 'evil' figure prominently in each of Hobbes's major works. In the early *Elements of Law* he says 'Every man by natural passion, calleth that good which pleaseth him for the present, or so far forth as he can foresee; and in like manner, that which displeaseth him, evil.'[17] Nearly twenty years later he writes, more precisely and carefully, but in the same vein, 'The common name for all things that are desired in so far as they are desired, is *good*; and for all things we shun, *evil*.' And from this he draws the obvious relativist implications: 'But since different men desire and shun different things, there must needs be many things that are *good* to some and *evil* to others; so that which is *good* to us is *evil* to our enemies.'[18] Thus, he argued that the absolute and 'metaphysical goodness' on which Bishop Bramhall rested his argument is an idle and illusory notion (*LNC* 192).

This subjectivism infects all terms of moral assessment, all virtues and vices. For the virtues are just good dispositions or manners and vices bad ones, in Hobbes's view. And since 'good and evil are not the same to all, it happens that the same manners are praised by some and condemned by others, that is, are called good by some, evil by others, virtues by some, vices by others.'[19] Thus, in so far as we consider human beings in their natural state (i.e. apart from social conventions and law) we 'can have no moral science because they lack any certain standard against which virtue and vice can be judged and defined' (*De Homine* XIII. 8).

Subjectivism infects Hobbes's conception of reason itself. Practical reason traces the consequences of actions and directs the will to those actions which will achieve that which is desired.[20] But human reasoning is not infallible and so, says Hobbes, we have the notion of 'right reason', that is, the standard by which any

---

[17] *Elements* I. 4, 14; see also *Human Nature* VII. 3.

[18] *De Homine* XI. 4; also *Leviathan* VI 125 and XV, 216.

[19] *De Homine* XIII. 8. In *Behemoth* (58) Hobbes points out that 'several men praise several customs and that which is virtue with one, is blamed by others, and, contrarily, what one calls vice, another calls virtue, as their present affections lead them'.

[20] Those 'actions are most Reasonable, that conduce most to their ends' (*Leviathan* XV, 204).

particular instance of reasoning is assessed and correctness or error determined. Right reason adjudicates disputes regarding 'what is conformable, or disagreeable to Reason, in the actions of common life' (*Leviathan* XV, 216). But, Hobbes apparently assumes, it can successfully do this only if its standards are *accepted* by those in dispute. Where there is no such accepted standard of right reason the disputants 'must by their own accord, *set up for right Reason*, the Reason of some Arbitrator, or Judge, to whose sentence they will both stand' (*Leviathan* V, 111, emphasis added). There is no standard of right reason 'constituted by Nature' (ibid.), for 'this *right reason*, which is the law, is no otherwise certainly right than by our making it so by our approbation of it and voluntary subjection to it' (*LNC* 193). In the state of nature, then, there is no standard of right reason, but only each individual's own reason. However, 'where every man is his own *judge*, there properly is no judge at all; as where every man carveth out his own right, it hath the same effect, as if there were no right at all' (*Elements* I. 4, 6). Thus, Hobbes is committed to the conventionality of right reason, and to the view that in the absence of such conventions there is no standard of right reason.

However, far from counselling despair in the face of such radical subjectivism and relativism, Hobbes turns them to his own use. For, he held, despite the inexhaustible variety of objects of human desire, in the circumstances of human life there will in fact be certain things which any rational person will seek, regardless of what else he or she seeks, because these things will be necessary for the achievement of any other goals. Furthermore, since we all already agree, not only the substance of what accords with reason, but on the fact that it is rational to do that which will secure achievement of one's goals and irrational to do that which will frustrate it, we all also agree that it is perfectly rational to seek these 'necessary goods'. The foremost among these necessary goods, of course, is peace. For, Hobbes argues, no rational person has reason to believe that, in the circumstances in which he or she must live, a state of war will promise anything but perpetual and substantial frustration of his or her goals or desires, whatever they may be. Thus, peace is a necessary condition of achieving or satisfying them.[21]

---

[21] Although this may be true for most human beings, it does not have the universality Hobbes attributes to it. For it rests either on the assumption that every rational person desires self-preservation and shuns death as the greatest evil, or on the assumption that war will stand in the way of satisfaction of any set of desires regardless of their content. But neither of these is universally true.

From this Hobbes concludes that there are universally valid general precepts of reason (laws of nature). They require that peace, and the fulfilment of all conditions necessary for the establishing and maintaining of it, be sought. Given Hobbes's assumptions there is no conflict between his initial assumption of subjectivism and relativism and the claim that there are universally valid general precepts of reason, for the latter are, presumably, principles all rational persons already agree upon (or would if they were to give the subject much thought), each judging by his or her own lights. The main burden of Hobbes's argument is to show that each of us, judging by his or her own lights, will come to the conclusion that the only rational thing to do is to *give up* the right to judge according to our own lights matters of good, virtue, and even what is required by reason. That is, given the enormous diversity of views regarding almost any matter touching common life, to insist upon retaining the right to judge according to one's own lights is ultimately irrational and self-defeating. The only rational thing to do is to entrust completely to the sovereign the right to judge and direct one's life, on the condition that others do so as well. For the state of war can be avoided only if we can establish *common* measures for judging good and evil, justice and injustice, mine and thine, and what is reasonable and unreasonable. But this is never possible, Hobbes argues, as long as we retain the right always to judge by our own lights (which is, in effect, to remain in the state of nature). Even the law of nature fails to provide us with common standards of *behaviour* (in the absence of a coercive power which legislates and enforces them), for they bind one to action only *on the condition* that others act in accord with them (*Leviathan* XV, 215). The only way adequately to secure against the horrors of this state of war is to quit entirely the state of nature, to establish with others a social *union*. Only through the sovereign and his law are social union and common standards possible. Thus, in the notion of social union, and the critical need for it, lies the key to understanding Hobbes's conception of sovereignty and law.

Social union

The only hope for escape from the war of all against all, Hobbes argues, is for all to erect by mutual covenant a sovereign, and thereby 'to conferre all their power and strength upon one Man, or upon one Assembly of men, that may reduce all their Wills, by plurality of voices, unto one Will: which is as much as to say, to

appoint one man, or Assembly of men, to beare their Person'
(*Leviathan* XVII, 227). This solution has *two* essential parts: (i) the
erection of a *common power*, i.e. the creation of a monopoly of
power in the hands of the designated sovereign; and equally
important (ii) the creation of a single will out of the plurality of
wills, i.e. the establishment of *social union*.[22] Union consists in
'including the wills of many in the will of one man, or in the will of
the greatest part of any one number of men' (*Elements* I. 6, 6). But
this cannot be done, Hobbes says in *De Cive*, 'unless every man will
so subject his will to some other one, to wit, either man or council,
that whatsoever his will is in those things which are necessary to the
common peace, it be received for the wills of all men in general,
and of every one in particular' (*De Cive* V. 6). This, Hobbes insists, is
not merely a matter of many wills concurring in the same object,
whether it be the result of a natural convergence of wills in the
single object or convergence brought about artificially through the
agency of a person or body defining a common plan around which
the behaviour of the many is co-ordinated.[23] 'This is more than
Consent, or Concord; it is a *reall Unitie* of them all, in one and the
same Person' (*Leviathan* XVII, 227, emphasis added). Social union
is achieved only when there is a *single* will.

For when there is one will of all men, it is to be esteemed for one person;
and by the word *one*, it is to be known and distinguished from all particular
men, as having its own rights and properties. Insomuch as neither any one
citizen, nor all of them together . . . is to be accounted the city (*De Cive* V. 9).

Hobbes is very clear here. There is unity sufficient for the commonwealth only when there is a will distinguishable from each and
from the aggregate of individual wills, in which single will nevertheless each particular will can properly be said to participate.
Thus, each party in the state of nature must submit his or her will to

---

[22] Already in *Elements* Hobbes seems to realize that these are distinct tasks
(*Elements* I. 6, 6–8), but believes that they are accomplished by one and the same act
of covenanting *with the sovereign* to obey all his commands (*Elements* I. 6, 7). In
De Cive the importance of establishing social union is recognized again, but there
Hobbes suggests that it can be accomplished simply through establishing the common power—each agreeing with each to lay aside the right to resist (*De Cive* V. 4–9).
Not until *Leviathan* does Hobbes address each task separately. It is quite clear there
that he believes social union is not achieved simply by laying aside the right to resist,
for the covenant in the *Leviathan* calls for full *authorization* of the sovereign. On
this notion, see below, p. 54 and generally, D. Gauthier, *Logic of the Leviathan*,
chs. III and IV.
[23] *Leviathan* XVII, 224–6; *De Cive* V. 4–6.

the sovereign's will, and his or her judgement to the sovereign's judgment (*Leviathan* XVII, 227).

The reason for social union in this very strong sense can be gathered from Hobbes's curious contrast of the human social conditions with that of bees.[24] Given their nature, peace, security, and the common good are possible amongst the bees with nothing more than concurrence of wills in a common object. This, says Hobbes, is not sufficient for civil government amongst human beings (*De Cive* V. 5). This is because, first, the passions of human beings are not limited to a narrow and pre-established range, but are in fact capable of indefinite variety (*Leviathan* XI, 160–1). Furthermore, they are inclined to compete for honour, dignity, and pre-eminence. But perhaps most importantly, unlike bees, human beings are at best mutually disinterested. Second, human beings possess the capacity for reason, discernment, and judgment. Far from moderating the socially disintegrating effects of the passions, the possession of natural reason exacerbates them. In these circumstances, distrust amongst human beings in the state of nature will be so great, that even if somehow there were to arise a concurrence of particular wills in a common object or co-ordination of the behaviour around a common plan, there is no reason to expect it to survive and every reason to expect it to break down. Such co-ordination or convergence can reasonably be regarded only as accidental, temporary, and radically unstable.[25]

Of course, it is precisely Hobbes's 'Foole', who says that there is no such thing as justice, who recognizes and proposes to take advantage of this fact. As long as there is assurance that others will do their part in the social bargain, and I can get away with not doing mine, the fool argues, surely it is irrational to forgo such opportunities as justice requires of me. '[E]very mans conservation, and contentment, being committed to his own care, there could be no reason, why every man might not do what he thought conduced thereunto' (*Leviathan* XV, 203). Hobbes's only effective response to the fool, as David Gauthier has argued, is to point out that in the covenant establishing the sovereign he has laid down his right to *govern himself*, to decide for himself what is necessary for his conservation and contentment (except where his life is immediately at

---

24 *Elements* I. 6, 5; *De Cive* V. 5; *Leviathan* XVII, 225–7.
25 *De Cive* V. 4; *Leviathan* XVII, 224–5; XIII *passim*. See G. Kavka 'Hobbes's War of All Against All', and F. S. McNeilly, *Anatomy of the Leviathan*, 159–68. It is here that Hobbes and Hume differ most radically, see below, 3.2.

risk), and has taken the will of the sovereign as *his will*, and the reason and judgment of the sovereign *as his reason* and judgment.[26] To escape from the state of nature, then, one must recognize the radical defectiveness of natural reason and of the right to judge and act according to one's own lights, and take up the reason, judgment, and will of the artificial man.

Social union is the product of the covenant establishing the sovereign, because that covenant consists of *two* parts: (i) mutual agreement of each to lay down his or her natural rights to self-government, i.e. to renounce the natural right to judge what is necessary for one's defence and contentment, and to lay one's strength and wealth at the disposal of the sovereign, and (ii) *authorization* of the sovereign to judge, decide, and to act in one's place (*Leviathan* XVII, 227). *Authorization* is a pivotal notion in the argument of *Leviathan*, for with it Hobbes can explain how the act of one 'artificial' person can properly be taken for the acts of *all* in the commonwealth. In so far as the 'author', or principal, empowers the 'actor', or agent, the agent's actions are directly attributable to the principal, as if the principal acted himself or herself. Thus, the will of the sovereign is a *single will*, distinct from the will of each and of the aggregate, but nevertheless 'representing', and implicating the wills of each.

Hobbes's solution to the problem of the radical insufficiency of individual natural reason, then, is to insist that each individual renounce his or her own right to exercise that faculty and to embrace as his or her own the exercise of that faculty by the sovereign. *Natural* reason is traded for the *conventional* reason of the law and the sovereign's judgment.

[F]or the law is all the right reason we have, and, (though he, as often as it disagreeth with his own reason, deny it), is the infallible rule of moral goodness. The reason whereof is this, that because neither mine nor the Bishop's reason is right reason fit to be a rule of our moral actions, we have therefore set up over ourselves a sovereign governor, and agreed that his laws shall be unto us, whatsoever they be, in the place of right reason, to dictate to us what is really good.[27]

Law and the sovereign's will are right reason, for apart from our agreeing on common standards there is no right reason (each is his

---

[26] D. Gauthier, 'Thomas Hobbes: Moral Theorist', 557–8. See also Gauthier's 'Three Against Justice', 17.

[27] *LNC* 194; see also *Elements* II. 10, 8 and *De Cive* II. 1.

own judge of right reason which is to have no judge at all), and we agree to regard the law as the standard of reason itself.

However, it is important to keep in mind, especially in light of Hobbes's dispute with Coke and the Common Lawyers, that the reason exercised by the sovereign is no different from the natural reason renounced by all of his subjects.

> Would you have every Man to every other Man alledge for Law his own particular Reason? There is not amongst Men an Universal Reason agreed upon in any Nation, besides the Reason of him that hath the Soveraign Power; yet though his Reason be but the Reason of one Man, yet it is set up to supply the place of that Universal Reason (*Dialogue* 67; see also 140).

The sovereign has no special claim to wisdom, insight, or truth. The covenant simply erects the sovereign's garden-variety natural reason as the standard of right reason for the simple reason that there is no other standard or source of reason and his is the only alternative ready to hand.

Reason, commands, and law

From the above argument it follows that not only must the sovereign enforce covenants made between subjects and protect them from internal and external violence, but he must also define common standards of good and evil, virtue and vice, justice and injustice, mine and thine. For

> it belongeth also to the judgment of the same sovereign power, to set forth and make known the common measure by which every man is to know what is his, and what another's; what is good, and what bad, and what he ought to do, and what not, and to command the same to be observed.[28]

Thus, the sovereign's 'right reason' must take the shape of laws and ordinances and public institutions for the authoritative and final adjudication of disputes concerning both civil law and natural law (*Leviathan* XVIII, 234).

From this account of the fundamental task of law we can learn something about the *shape* laws must take, in Hobbes's view. 'A Law is the Command of him, or them that have the Soveraign Power, given to those that be his or their Subjects, declaring Publickly, and plainly what every of them may do, and what they must forbear to do' (*Dialogue* 71). Since sovereign power can only

---

[28] *Elements* II. 1, 10. See also *Elements* II. 1, 13–14, II. 10, 8; *Leviathan* XVII, 234; XXVI, 314; *Dialogue* 72.

be possessed by those who through covenant have undertaken to obey, it follows that 'Law in generall is not Counsell, but Command . . . of him, whose Command is addressed to one formerly obliged to obey him' (*Leviathan* XXVI, 312). Clearly, Hobbes chose his words very carefully here. He expresses a conception of law precisely moulded to fit the special task he assigns to it. Laws are commands of a sovereign addressed to persons already bound to obey, declaring publicly and plainly what must be done or avoided. I shall comment briefly on each of the elements of this definition.

First, regarding publicity and determinacy. This imposes a three-fold condition upon all laws.[29] (*a*) Laws must be recognizable as authentic by suitable public signs. That is, the criteria by which laws are validated must be fully public. (*b*) Likewise, the authority or warrant to issue the law must be established by sufficient public signs. (*c*) What is required by the laws, i.e. their content, must also be plain and determinate. These three conditions are essential, because laws can adequately establish common standards of behaviour, in Hobbes's view, only if their identity, content, and authority are indisputable, and a matter of common public knowledge. Oakeshott puts Hobbes's point this way: 'A law which may be different for each man under "it" is not a law at all but merely a multiplicity of opinions about how the legislator . . . wishes us to behave. There is, in fact no law where there is no *common* authority to declare and interpret it.'[30] If the laws be publicly defined and made known, certainty can be achieved (*Dialogue* 140). Of course, it may not be possible entirely to avoid controversy about the content or authenticity of laws. Thus, the formally defined general rules of law must be applied and adjudicated by institutions empowered to settle finally and authoritatively any remaining disputes (*Leviathan* XXVI, 322–3).

Second, law is the product of the exercise of *authority*. It is the expression of the sovereign's *right* to rule, not merely of his monopoly of coercive power.[31] Imperatives backed by credible

---

[29] *Leviathan* XXVI, 317, 319–20, 331; *Dialogue* 67, 71, 140; *Behemoth* 55, 59.

[30] M. Oakeshott, *Rationalism in Politics*, 281. Recall Hobbes's equation of Common Law with 'philosophy' (*Dialogue* 69). See also *Leviathan* XXVI, 322, *Behemoth* 56, and see esp. *De Cive*, Preface, 98 on the disputatious character of moral philosophy.

[31] Of course, Hobbes comes dangerously close to collapsing this distinction between right and might in his account of commonwealth by acquisition (*Leviathan* XX). In fact, although he preserves a formal and conceptual distinction between them, by insisting that submission to the threat of the conqueror is *voluntary*, this

threats never in themselves count as laws, according to Hobbes, nor does power alone generate obligations. Obligations have their source only in the wills and covenants of those bound by them (*Leviathan* XXI, 268). Mere imperatives backed by threats do not even count as commands.[32] The sovereign's legislative power rests on the covenant establishing the commonwealth, which explicitly authorizes his legislative activity.[33]

Third, law is a command. This is pivotal to Hobbes's conception of law: it is in virtue of this property that laws when publicly identifiable and determinate can hope to perform the task Hobbes assigns to them. Commands are a special kind of imperative. They differ from imperatives of power in which the person in power expects the *threat of evil* to provide reason for compliance with the imperative. They differ from imperatives of counsel or advice in which the counsellor expects independent concerns of the advisee to which the counsellor directs attention to provide reason for compliance. The commander, however, expects that *the expression of his will alone* will be reason enough for the person commanded to comply.

[C]ommanding . . . is that speech by which we signify to another our appetite or desire to have any thing done, or left undone, for reasons contained in the will itself: for it is not properly said, *Sic volo, sic jubeo*, without that other clause, *Stet pro ratione voluntas* . . .[34]

Commands, then, sharply contrast with the other two types of imperative for in the latter cases the person addressed retains his or her right to judge the reasons offered for behaving in the manner set out in the imperative, but in the command, on Hobbes's view, the commander intends the hearer to take the commander's will for his guide to action and not his own.[35] Commands are intended not

---

surely empties the notion of assent of all moral substance. See Gauthier, *Logic of the Leviathan*, 163–4.

[32] *Leviathan* XXV, 302–3. See Bentham's sharply different analysis of commands below, 9.3.

[33] There has been a great deal of debate over whether, on Hobbes's view, *God's* right to rule rests on power alone or also on some kind of consent. But, however we resolve that tangled issue, Hobbes is very clear in the *Leviathan* and subsequent works that the right of the *mortal* sovereign rests solely on consent.

[34] *Human Nature* XIII. 6; see also *Leviathan* XXV, 303; *Elements* II. 8, 6; II. 10, 1–4, and *De Cive* XIV. 1.

[35] See H. L. A. Hart, 'Commands and Authoritative Legal Reasons', in Hart, *Esays on Bentham*, 253.

as invitations to practical deliberation, but as immediate directives to action *precluding* independent practical deliberation on the part of the person commanded.

In light of the argument we considered earlier it is clear why Hobbes should wish to define law in this way. Laws can perform their task of preventing the anarchy of dispute over right and wrong, good and evil, the reasonable and unreasonable, only if they can block all independent exercise of individual judgment and can be put forward as themselves standards of right reason. Laws, in Hobbes's view do not command respect in virtue of their content, i.e. their claim to justice or to express public values. And the hope of achieving concord through general concurrence on substantive rules of law is, he believes, a dangerous illusion (*Elements* II. 1, 13–14). The only road to peace for such a disputatious race is for each to deposit 'his judgment in all controversies in the hands of the sovereign' (*Elements* II. 8, 5).

Thus, Hobbes's definition of law dramatically underscores the fundamental fact that in his commonwealth the subject has laid aside not only his right to use violence, but also his right to govern his actions according to his own discretion and judgment. This right is exercised exclusively, for each citizen, by the sovereign. The sovereign expects the commands he issues to constitute sufficient reasons in themselves for compliance (*Human Nature* XIII. 6).

We are not to conclude from this, of course, that the sovereign is free arbitrarily to make whatever laws he wishes. Hobbes insists, on the contrary, that the sovereign is bound, by the laws of nature and God, to make laws and govern his people for the common good.[36] The sovereign and his laws are capable of *iniquity*, but the covenant effectively removes from the subject competence to stand in judgment over the sovereign and his laws and to hold him to his duty. Against Bishop Bramhall's vigorous argument that surely laws can be cruel and unjust and that we have a duty to oppose them, Hobbes replies,

I think rather that the reason of him that hath sovereign authority, and by whose sword we look to be protected both against war from abroad and injuries at home, *whether it be right or erroneous in itself, ought to stand*

---

[36] *Leviathan* XXX, 376; *Elements* II. 12, 1; *LNC* 176–7. This is the basic theme of the section 'Of Soveraign Power' of the *Dialogue*. Hobbes himself challenges certain laws in this section but they are all laws which purport to put limitations on the sovereign's power.

for right to us that have submitted ourselves thereunto by receiving the protection.[37]

The motto of the just and prudent citizen, according to Hobbes, is to study the laws to know one's duty, but not to dispute their justice.[38] And the conditions of validity of laws must be limited strictly to formal criteria, and must never include matters likely to be controversial, whether matters of morality, religion, or history.

We can conclude this discussion of Hobbes by summarizing the complex relationship between reason (and the law of nature) and positive or civil law. First, civil law provides the sole standard of right reason in the commonwealth. Law *is* right reason. Second, the laws of nature 'contain' the civil law (*Leviathan* XXVI, 314), in the extended sense that the natural reason of each individual (at least once tutored by Hobbes) dictates complete compliance with the laws. 'For nothing is more reasonable than that every Man should obey the Law, which he hath himself assented to' (*Dialogue* 97). The relation between civil and natural law, according to Hobbes, differs sharply from standard natural law doctrine. For Aquinas held that even the *adiaphora* were not entirely unguided by natural law, but rather that natural law's guidance was generic. But for Hobbes the task of the laws of nature is only to persuade us of the reasonableness of *compliance* with the laws, whatever their content. It does not (and must not even attempt) to provide us with reasons in justification of the laws themselves. (The civil laws may, and ideally should, accord with the law of nature in Hobbes's view, but this must not be regarded as a condition of their validity or binding force.)

Thirdly, the civil law 'contains' the laws of nature, for only when the laws of nature are promulgated and enforced by the sovereign do they bind *in foro externo*. When these principles are given precise public content and effectively enforced, 'then are they actually Lawes, and not before' (*Leviathan* XXVI, 314).

Finally, and to return full circle to the debate between Hobbes and Coke, Hobbes insists that where, despite all precautions, the civil law is not obvious, or where it is silent, or where disputes regarding the law of nature itself arise, the courts must look directly to natural reason to guide them (*Leviathan* XXVI, 316, 319). The

---

[37] *LNC* 176, emphasis added; see also *Behemoth* 65.

[38] *Dialogue* 54, 158; see also *Behemoth* 57. Compare this with Bentham's famous motto: 'to obey punctually; to censure freely' (*FG*, Preface, 399). See below, 9.3.

quality most needed in a judge, says Hobbes, is not that he be a good lawyer and know the law well, but rather that he have 'a right understanding of . . . Equity; which [depends] on the goodnesse of a mans own natural Reason, and Meditation' (*Leviathan* XXVI, 328).[39] Where civil law is silent judges must mimic the sovereign.

Summing up his investigation of the relationship between law and reason Hobbes says, 'I Conclude, that Justice fulfils the Law, and Equity Interprets the Law; and amends the Judgments given upon the same Law . . . Equity is a certain perfect Reason that Inter-preteth, and Amendeth the Law Written . . .'. Then, sounding a clear note of irony, he adds, in this 'I depart not much from the Definition of Equity, cited in Sir Edw. Coke . . . though I Construe it a little otherwise than he would have done' (*Dialogue* 101).

2.3   COMMON LAW SCEPTICISM

Reason is too large. Find me a precedent and I will accept it.

James VI and I.

Roots of the strategy of scepticism

Hobbes saw a threat to social order and existing authority in the en-franchisement of individual rational judgment, yet he was too much of a rationalist to reject the sovereignty of natural reason. He sought, rather, to confine and channel it, authorizing its exercise only (except in very special circumstances) by the sovereign and his delegates. Natural reason is the only reason there is, Hobbes insists, but then ruefully adds that this reason is univocal only when one voice speaks. Thus, for the vast majority, the only reasonable course is to be governed by the convention of regarding the reason of the sovereign as right reason itself.

Classical Common Law theory perceived a similar threat, but it regarded the Hobbesian solution as a threat of equal if not greater proportions. Demands made by subjects for a showing of the reasonableness of law and legal authority as a condition of com-

---

[39] The model Hobbes took for adjudication was the Chancery (as it was supposed in theory to function), not the Common Law courts. This is clear already in *Leviathan* XXVI. But this Baconian conception of adjudication is more extensively defended in the *Dialogue*, which was stimulated by Bacon's *Elements of the Common Laws of England*. On the relation between Bacon and Hobbes see J. Cropsey's introduction to the *Dialogue*.

pliance, and claims advanced by king or Parliament extensively to make and remake existing law–both made in the name of natural reason–threatened the foundations of the traditionary order. Classical Common Law theory sought to restore confidence in this traditionary order, to reassert traditionary values and patterns of thought. But it was not enough simply to reassert them in the face of the threat; it had to rise to their defence. It had to make plausible the claim that law is (the embodiment of) reason, while shielding it from radical criticism. It sought to establish the overall reasonableness of the Common Law and so its fundamental authority over subject and sovereign alike, while denying natural reason–whether of king, Parliament, judiciary, or citizen–the right to stand in judgment on it.

The basic strategy of classical Common Law theory was to challenge the competency of individual natural reason. The argument for the fundamental authority of the Common Law was essentially an argument from scepticism.[40] Coke boldly announced this strategy in the *Institutes*: 'the Common Law is nothing else but Reason . . . But this is an artificial perfection of Reason gotten by long study, observation, and experience, and not every mans natural reason . . .'. And, he concludes, 'No man (out of his private reason) ought to be [i.e. regard himself] wiser than the law, which is the perfection of reason' (I *Institutes*, sects. 21, 138).

This text, of course, provided the foil for Hobbes's hostile attack on Common Law theory in the *Dialogue*. In a rich and subtle reply to the *Dialogue*,[41] Hale defends Coke's notion of the 'artificial reason' of Common Law. But it is a refined and moderate scepticism that Hale defends. He allows that there is a fixed and rational order of nature and of the moral affairs of men; and he allows that there is a human faculty of reason by which the reasonableness of this order can be known. But in morals and especially common public affairs 'the objects thereof are more obscure, and not so open to a distinct

---

[40] This is, of course, a familiar conservative strategy, exploited by Burke and his nineteenth-century disciples, and clearly evident in the political theories of, e.g., M. Oakeshott, *Rationalism in Politics* and F. Hayek, *The Constitution of Liberty*.

[41] M. Hale, 'Reflections by the Lrd. Chiefe Justice Hale on Mr. Hobbes His Dialogue of the Lawe'. Hale never published this fragment and must have seen Hobbes's *Dialogue* in MS because he died some six years before its posthumous publication in 1681. See Holdsworth, 500. For a useful discussion of this debate, see D. E. C. Yale, 'Hobbes and Hale on Law, Legislation and the Sovereign'.

and clear discovery . . .'.[42] Furthermore, this faculty is possessed by persons in varying degrees. And even between two equally endowed persons it may be the case that one is more competent in one specialized branch of knowledge than the other.

Law, he insists, is a proper subject for the faculty of reason, and it constitutes a specialized body of knowledge like any other. But its subject-matter–the 'ordering of civil societies . . . [and] measuring of right and wrong, when it comes to particulars'–is much more resistant to rational structuring and certain demonstration than any other subject ('Reflections' 502). This is due, in part, to the great complexity of situations calling for practical judgments, and the radical circumstantial relativity of matters of right and common good ('Reflections' 504). But Hale also blames the radical silence of natural law, or at least the impossibility of achieving any agreement on its requirements beyond the most abstract and empty formulas. In morals, and especially with regard to laws for a community, all men of reason share a general notion of what is just and fit, he admits. But this consensus is immediately lost once we move from abstractions to particulars, even among men of great reason and learning.[43] And further reflection and speculation leads to greater not less dissensus. Casuists, schoolmen, and moral philosophers make the worst judges, 'because they are transported from the ordinary measures of right and wrong by their over-fine speculations, theories, and distinctions above the common staple of human conversations'. But, he continues, 'men of observation and experience in human affairs and conversation between man and man' make the best judges ('Reflections' 503). If we remain at the level of rational speculation, without taking into consideration the vast body of shared knowledge and experience which makes up the 'language' of human affairs, we can only expect perpetual dissensus, uncertainty and insecurity, Hale insists. Common Law is the repository of this accumulated collective experience, the dictionary of this language of human commerce. Only through long immersion in it, grasping not (or not only) its theory, but acquiring

---

[42] 'Reflections' 501. In this and subsequent passages quoted from this work I have modernized spelling and capitalization wherever the changes did not threaten to alter the sense of the passage.

[43] 'Reflections' 503. Blackstone argues that natural law dictates, in the Justinian formula, '*honeste vivere, alterum non laedere, suum cuique tribuere*'. But he insists that we can know what is to be regarded as 'honourable', 'harm', and mine or another's 'own' only through the law (1 *Comm.* 53).

familiar knowledge of its vast particulars, can human affairs be dealt with justly and reasonably. Thus, against Hobbes he concludes, 'men are not born Common Lawyers, neither can the bare exercise of the faculty of reason give a man sufficient knowledge of it, but it must be gained by the habituating and accustoming and exercising that faculty by reading, study, and observation . . .' ('Reflections' 505).

Despite its subtlety, Hale's sceptical case for the authority of Common Law reveals a deep ambiguity at the foundations of classical Common Law theory.[44] It is possible to distinguish three quite different versions of scepticism that may underlie Common Law theory, and three different conceptions of the relationship between law and reason, although the Common Law tradition never clearly distinguishes them. The aim of this section is simply to articulate as clearly as possible each of these conceptions. I will not attempt definitively to say which is the genuine or preferred version, from the point of view of Common Law theory. I suspect there is no basis for making such a judgment with any confidence. Because Hale's discussion suggests, to some extent, each of them, I will treat it as my text, but I will also draw freely from other sources where necessary.

Wisdom of the ages

Looking back on his four-volume outline of the Common Law and its development, Blackstone remarks with evident satisfaction that 'the fundamental maxims and rules of the law . . . have been and are everyday improving, and are frought with the accumulated wisdom of ages' (1 *Comm.* 442). Here Blackstone echoes the most prominent defence of the classical Common Law conception of law. On this view, the authority of the law rests ultimately on its justice and reasonableness, but the witness to this fact, and its strongest demonstration, lies in its very age, its persistence, and continuity over great reaches of time. This is a presumption allegedly strong enough to defeat the contrary judgment of any particular individual. It is reasonable for me, says Hale,

to prefer a law by which a kingdom hath been happily governed four or five hundred years than to adventure the happiness and peace of a kingdom

---

[44] This ambiguity is evident also in subsequent conservative political theories built on the same foundation. See references in n. 40, above, especially Hayek, chs. 2–4.

upon some theory of my own though I am better acquainted with the reasonableness of my own theory than with that law ('Reflections' 504).

We must defer to the greater wisdom of the long-established law. This deference is due ancient law not because our ancestors were individually any wiser than we, but because no individual or even entire generation can match the experience and wisdom accumulated over countless generations and reposited in the law. Law is the great textbook of civil experience recording the products of continuous experiments with civil arrangements. Considered apart from this vast reservoir of experience, says Coke,

we are but of yesterday . . . our days upon the earth are but as a shadow in respect of the old ancient days and times past, wherein the laws have been by the wisdom of the most excellent men, in many successions of ages, by long and continual experience, (the trial of light and truth) fined and refined.[45]

The argument seems to rest on two related claims. First, it is argued that the law has been subjected to 'the trial of light and truth' and has been constantly, though incrementally, readjusted to the complexities of civil life and the common good. The perfection of any art, it is argued, is the product of time and this is no less true of the art of fashioning a body of law to fit a nation and its needs.[46] Time, 'the wisest thing in the inferior world . . . as it discovers day after day new inconveniences, so it doth successively apply new remedies'.[47] Second, it is claimed that, for the fashioning of civil arrangements, there is no alternative to the test of time and history; in particular, no single person or generation, however sagacious and far-seeing, can hope to match the record of history. '[L]ong and iterated experience . . . is the wisest expedient among mankind', Hale insists, because it 'discovers those defects . . . which no wit of man could either at once foresee or aptly remedy' ('Reflections' 505). History is the only available laboratory for law and civil arrangements.

Now, too much, perhaps, can be made of these claims, but they have a certain degree of plausibility. To attempt to fashion anew a

---

[45] Coke, 'Calvin's Case', 7 *Coke's Reports*, quoted in Pocock, *Ancient Constitution*, 35.

[46] 'But, as it is said of every Art or Science which is brought to perfection, *Per varios usus Artem experientia fecit*; so may it properly be said of our Law, *Per varios usus Legem experientia fecit*. Long experience, and many trials of what was best for the common good, did make the *Common Law*.' Sir John Davies, *Irish Reports*, Preface, quoted in Pocock, *Ancient Constitution*, 41.

[47] M. Hale, *Amendment of Laws*, in Hargrave's *Tracts*, v. I. 254.

body of law without benefit of the lessons of the past is very likely to fail. The argument sounds a certain cautionary note, one which, as we shall see, is not lost on even a radical legal reformer like Bentham. But as yet it yields no general scepticism of natural reason, but only a caution not to put too much stock in a priori civic schemes.

However, classical Common Law theory[48] wishes to draw a much stronger, twofold conclusion. It concludes, first, that long continuance of a law is conclusive proof of its basic wisdom and reasonableness (though minor adjustments may be needed). Second, from the claim that law is the product of history and the accumulated wisdom of generations, it concludes that no individual or contemporary group is in a position to assess its reasonableness; that the reasons of the law are beyond the ken of any single person or generation.

Clearly, the first conclusion depends for its plausibility on the second, for *at best* past experience provides us with a clearly defeasible *presumption* of the wisdom of a law. Why could not the trials of a body of law over the years demonstrate to an historically sensitive observer that it just cannot do the job? Common Law theory wishes to block such challenges. This is the aim of the second conclusion. But this conclusion goes well beyond the argument given for it. For it is one (perfectly plausible) thing to say that the experience of any individual or generation is limited and needs to be supplemented by the widest range of experience available. But it is quite another thing to insist that the limitation of experience is, or brings with it, a limitation on our ability rationally to take in and self-consciously to learn from this experience. The argument we have thus far considered does not deny, and in fact implicitly relies on, the possibility of the present generation or qualified members of it, taking in, getting a full grasp of, and then applying the accumulated experience of the past. But learning from the past also involves learning that time changes things, not just marginally but substantially, such that arrangements suitable in the past may turn out to be radically unsuited to altered conditions. Thus, it seems that from the very historical vantage-point prepared for us by the law we may be in a position to find the law as it exists wanting. However, classical Common Law theory will have

---

[48] Or at least some of its apologists; Hale is perhaps the most moderate of the group, continually issuing cautions but recognizing the need at times for substantial and extensive reform of the law. See, e.g., his discussion of law reform in *Amendment of Laws*, conveniently excerpted in E. Howard's, *Matthew Hale*, ch. XV.

none of this: 'No man (out of his private reason) ought to be wiser than the Law, which is the perfection of reason', Coke insists (I *Institutes*, sect. 138).

Thus, if confidence in individual natural reason is effectively to be shaken, a new argument needs to be advanced. There are resources for such an argument within the Common Law tradition, but they are only suggestive and the tradition is not clear about the directions in which the suggestions should be developed. Nevertheless, much can be learned about the tradition by tracing out these suggestions, even if in the end we are unable definitively to assign one of the views, to the exclusion of the others, to the foundations of the theory.

Collective wisdom

Perhaps a clue to deeper argument involved here lies in the fact that the traditionalism at the core of Common Law theory rests on a particular, though incompletely articulated, conception of community. It is a *Gemeinschaftlich*, traditionary conception of society, in which the law is regarded as the repository of tradition and a (if not the) primary bond of the community. It is regarded not so much as the sole device for keeping the community from flying apart (as Hobbes regarded it), but as that through which members participate in, and in virtue of which they feel a part of, the community.

This *Gemeinschaftlich* conception of community is associated with a social conception of reason or knowledge. Knowledge, or wisdom, on this view, is essentially a collective product and a collective possession. 'We are afraid to put men to live and trade each on his own private stock of reason,' Burke explains, 'because we suspect that this stock in each man is small, and that the individuals would do better to avail themselves of the general bank and capital of nations, and of ages.'[49] An individual exercises reason and gains wisdom to the extent that he or she thinks and acts within the structures of collective wisdom. It may be useful for some purposes to construct general theories of the practices and traditions of the community, but they will always be abstract and incomplete and the insight they can yield will be limited. The 'bank' of collective wisdom, our common capital, is available to one not through general theories *of* our collective life and its traditions, but through gaining full facility *with* it. This, perhaps, can explain why Hale thought a person with a full working knowledge of the specifics of Common Law and custom,

---

[49] E. Burke, *Reflections on the Revolution in France*, 183.

and thereby acquainted directly and in the concrete with 'the common staple' of 'human affairs and conversation between man and man' makes a better judge of civic right than the philosopher or theologian ('Reflections' 503).

For the purpose of capturing this notion of practical judgment within given structure of traditions, Burke in the late eighteenth century rehabilitated the term 'prejudice' from the Englightenment's scrap-heap.[50] Prejudice is not blind, unthinking bias, but rather untaught intuition, preconceived and not fully self-conscious opinion and attitude, learned (or better, acquired) through participation in the traditions and common life of the community.[51] Individual rational judgment apart from all such prejudice is impossible, since reason can be exercised only *within* a rich, given context of beliefs, concepts, aims, and attitudes. The wise and prudent person, on the occasion of reflection on one or another such prejudice, seeks not to explode it, when it initially appears ungrounded, but rather seeks to uncover its latent wisdom.[52] Custom and precedent, we might say, are the juridical forms which 'prejudice' takes.[53]

But this notion of collective wisdom, and by extension the idea of the Common Law as the repository of the collective wisdom of the English nation, admits of two quite different interpretations. These can be seen if we look again at the structure of the argument we considered above. Note first that, although the 'wisdom of ages' argument put history at its centre, the argument was not historicist. That is, while it was argued that wise, just, and reasonable civic arrangements could be discovered only through long experience, the validation of judgments of wisdom, justice, or reasonableness did not depend on this historical connection. The argument presupposed that there are *ahistorical* standards validating these judgments, though they are *discovered* only through long experience. Now it is in part this implicit assumption that leads, as we saw above, to the

---

[50] Gadamer, who also develops an anti-rationalist, collective, and tradition-bound conception of reason, has also recently tried to rehabilitate the notion of 'prejudice', though without explicit reference to Burke. See H. G. Gadamer, *Wahrheit und Methode*, 261–5, 269; *Philosophical Hermeneutics*, 9, 28, and the editor's introduction, pp. xii–xxvii; and 'The Problem of Historical Consciousness', 103–60, esp. 106–13, 137. See also Peirce, *Philosophical Writings of Peirce*, 229.

[51] This is also echoed in Wittgenstein's doctrine that a language game is accessible to a learner only if he is willing to 'trust something'. See *On Certainty*, para. 509.

[52] Burke, *Reflections*, 183. This seems to be the dominant strategy of Blackstone's *Commentaries*.

[53] See E. Halévy, *The Growth of Philosophic Radicalism*, 159, 162; and Burke, 'Speech on Reform of Representation', *Works* VII. 94–5.

inadequacy of the argument for the sceptical purposes it was supposed to serve. Individuals learn the principles of common good or justice in the schoolhouse of history, but once they are well tutored, they can use the principles they have acquired critically to assess the products of history, in particular, the law. This conclusion can be blocked only if, either (i) the validating principles are unavailable in principle to individual reason, or (ii) there are no further, more fundamental validating principles beyond the deliverances of historical tradition. Corresponding to each of these possibilities is an interpretation of the notion of collective wisdom. Only the first, however, is consistent with the main thrust of the 'wisdom of ages' approach. Let us consider that interpretation first.

The basic idea is most easily conveyed if we consider a theological version of the collective wisdom notion. On this view, there is a divinely ordained moral order, but this is revealed only through the historically developed traditions of the community. Individuals may be able self-consciously and reflectively to grasp bits of this divine plan, but it is grasped in its totality only collectively in the living traditions and practices in which we as individuals participate. Thus, there are, on this view, standards by which the justice and goodness of our laws and ways can be demonstrated, but they are not accessible to any single individual or generation. The existence of our laws, then, is proof of their goodness.

And once this theological version is articulated it is clear that there could be a parallel non-theological version. There are rational standards of goodness, reason, and justice, it might be argued, but they are accessible only to us *in community*. 'The individual is foolish', says Burke, and 'the multitude, for the moment, is foolish, when they act without deliberation; but the species is wise, and, when time is given to it, as a species it almost always acts right.'[54]

Both versions of this argument seem to give a historical, communal twist to the familiar Thomist natural law doctrine. No longer is the law of nature accessible to individual human reason (or individuals in co-operation with other individuals), even in principle, except through participation in the historical evolution of one's community's practices and traditions.

This argument sets out an interpretation of Coke's doctrine that Common Law is the perfection of reason, which is historical with-

[54] Burke, 'Speech on Reform of Representation', 95.

out being historicist, and which, if sound, effectively meets the challenge of contrary private assessments and interpretations of the law. But the argument faces an obvious problem. It is not so much an argument as a statement of faith. By its own terms it cannot demonstrate the wisdom of the laws to us for we are *ex hypothesi* incompetent so to judge. It can only implore us to *believe* them wise and just.

It is not clear to me that any writer in the classical Common Law tradition, other than Burke at its fringes,[55] embraced this argument. Blackstone may have implicitly relied on something like it to make his marriage of natural law and Common Law ideas work, but he never explicitly sets out the argument. Hale, in the 'Reflections', as we have seen, believes that there is an objective, rational moral order accessible to us in some sense, but that it is beyond the grasp of individual natural reason except in its most abstract form. And he does suggest that we can come much closer to ordering our lives and interaction in accord with this order by immersion in the Common Law, the repository of 'human conversation'. But it is not at all clear he would endorse fully the 'historical natural law' conception this argument suggests.

Much of the difficulty in deciding this question stems from the fact that classical Common Law theorists did not clearly distinguish this strong version of the 'wisdom of ages' argument from the weaker version of that argument we considered earlier, on the one hand, and a quite different conception of collective wisdom, incompatible with the 'wisdom of ages' argument, on the other hand. Without, then, resolving the question of whether the Common Law tradition is committed to this strong version of the 'wisdom of ages' argument, let me turn to a second, different strain of argument linking reason and Common Law which draws more heavily on the conception of community on which the theory seems to rest.

Community practice constitutive of reason

One problem with attributing the above notion of collective wisdom to the Common Law tradition is that it rests on the assumption of some transcendent source of validation, an assumption which seems at odds with the strong 'this-worldly' empiricism

---

[55] For an interpretation along these lines see R. Kirk, 'Burke and the Philosophy of Prescription', and S. Wolin, 'Hume and Conservatism', 253–4.

of the tradition. And there are in the tradition suggestions of a quite different notion of collective wisdom which explicitly rejects any hint of transcendent validation. It is the idea that reason itself—or at any rate, the sort of practical reason called for in human civic affairs—is essentially social, that the collective wisdom reposited in the historically evolved Common Law provides the context within which alone the exercise of civic practical reason is possible. On this view, we look in vain for a source of validation of Common Law, for Common Law is, in a special sense, self-validating.

Hale seems to hint at this view when he insists in the 'Reflections' that practical moral and civic affairs can be ordered adequately only by the exercise of the prudence[56] of the judge, who, through his immersion in the concrete details of the Common Law, is fluent in the common language of human affairs and conversation. The philosopher and theologian are not qualified for this task, recall, because they seek to elaborate and articulate notions of the 'just and fit . . . common to all men of reason' *apart* from this staple; 'they are transported from the ordinary measures of right and wrong by their overfine speculations, theories, and distinctions above the common staple of human conversations' ('Reflections' 502, 503). The suggestion is that *juris*prudence is not an enterprise of rational discovery of general, governing principles, but rather the enterprise of making judgments from a grasp of the concrete relations and arrangements woven into the fabric of common life. 'Human conversation' is a powerful metaphor for a complex of continuous relations and interactions made possible and meaningful by a background of shared understandings, and common and public meanings. Authorities articulate measures of the just and the fit needed for the regulation and ordering of civil societies, but they defend them in terms defined by this assumed background. Thus, the background is understood not as a constraint on what is feasible, but as constitutive of what is reasonable.

One gets a similar suggestion from Hale's *History of the Common Law of England*. There he states that the Common Law judge looking for a 'rule of decision' goes first to the settled Common Law and custom of the realm, second to authorities and decisions in the past on the same or like cases, and finally to 'the Reason of the Thing

---

[56] I have in mind here 'prudence' in the old-fashioned sense, i.e. as a translation of the Aristotelian notion of *phronesis*.

itself' (*History* 46). But the idea here is not the Hobbesian one that once the formal sources of law run out the judge is entitled to appeal to his unaided natural reason. Hale argues, rather, that the judge who appeals to 'the reason of the thing itself' goes back again to the law and custom, and the human 'conversation' on which they rest, and by sensitive judgment and analogy works to the solution of the case before him. '[T]he *common* Reason of the Thing', he stresses, is his only guide (ibid., emphasis added). To illustrate, he considers interpretation of deeds or covenants. Here the judge, conversant with the concrete commerce of the parties (which is shaped by the existing law and customs), is better able to carry out this task than 'a bare grave Grammarian or Logician, or other prudent Men' (ibid.). For what is desired in such a case is not a finding of what the words of the document mean in some abstract sense (if there is such), but rather understanding of it in light of the relations that characteristically obtain between parties like those before the bar.[57] The reason of the thing itself can only be found in the *common reason* of the concrete situation, illuminated by the Common Law, Hale clearly assumes, because the law is the repository of community experience and in it the judge can find a case 'either in Point or agreeing in Reason or Analogy with the case in question' (ibid.). That is, for a solution in novel or unregulated cases the judge looks to the same resources of experience and common sense, of shared understandings and common ways, as those which informed past decisions and settled rules and can be presumed to underlie the ordinary interactions of members of the community. Common reason is, we might say, juridical common sense.

The notion of Common Law as immemorial custom offers us a lens through which we can take a look at this notion of collective wisdom or common reason. In Chapter 1 we noted the importance to Common Law theory of the sense of the historical dimension of law. But it is curious that this historical sense, especially in Hale's discussion, is taken to be invulnerable, or at any rate indifferent, to 'objective' historical investigation. Hale insists that the origins of the Common Law are no longer recoverable. But, he argues, even if they were recoverable, those facts would be irrelevant to the historical foundations of the Common Law (see above, 1.1).

---

[57] Compare L. Fuller's discussion of the 'customary' foundations of contract law in 'Law and Human Interaction'.

It is not easy to say with full confidence precisely what this comes to, but two points seem to stand out. First, the history at issue here is history expressive of the community's sense of identity. History, in this view, situates individuals in the society, relates them to their fellows, by directing each to a received, recognized, and shared collective past. The essential characteristic of this sense of history is its intersubjectivity. The 'objective' details of the past, are, then, less important than the broad conception of community which is communicated by widely shared beliefs about its past. Second, while it is in some ways legitimated *by* this sense of historical continuity, the law is itself involved in the creation and preservation of this sense of a common past. Part of the message of Hale's *History* seems to be that this is *our* (i.e. the English people's) past, *because* it is the past recorded and preserved for us *in our Common Law*. One might say that the processes and practices of Common Law, on this view, define a kind of secular public ritual. The metaphor can easily be abused, but it captures the important idea that engaging in practices used 'time out of mind' is significant to participants, not because their actions simply reiterate age-old routines, but because these actions, like ritual acts,[58] *re-enact* traditional patterns and give them a sense of continuity with the past. Thus, they are reminded of, or taught anew, truths about links with their 'consociates'[59] which they might otherwise overlook. Common Law, on this view, defines a common past and, thus, a common point of orientation for the present—a common world around which a community can form.

The Common Law, then, not only defines a framework for social interaction, a set of rules and arrangements facilitating the orderly pursuit of private aims and purposes, but it also publicly articulates the social context within which the pursuit of such aims takes on meaning. It is the reservoir of traditional ways and common experience, and it provides the arena in which the shared structures of experience publicly unfold.

The conception of collective wisdom now under consideration is sometimes expressed by classical Common Law writers in terms of liberty or even consent. For example, Blackstone asserts that 'in-

[58] See I. Scheffler, 'Ritual and Reference', 433–6.

[59] I take this term from A. Schutz, *The Problem of Social Reality*, 17–18, although my use of it is broader than his, for with it I want to capture the Burkean idea of a 'partnership' across *both* time and space (Burke, *Reflections*, 194–5) without the quasi-mystical connotations Burke gives it.

deed it is one of the characteristic marks of English liberty, that our common law depends upon custom; which carries this internal evidence of freedom along with it, that it probably was introduced by the voluntary consent of the people.'[60] This 'internal evidence' is simply the fact that custom could be established only through the reciprocal adjustments of persons involved responding to *their* needs in the circumstances *they* faced. The claim is not that custom always arises from some sort of freely entered bargain. In fact, the notion of liberty (and the related notion of consent) used here is not strictly individual or private liberty. It is, rather, a notion of *civic liberty*—liberty of the polis—to which a notion of individual liberty is related derivatively. Individuals enjoy this liberty in so far as they participate in structures characterized by civic liberty. The essential idea is that the laws and institutions of Common Law are not *imposed* upon citizens of England (either by some foreign power or by arbitrary parliamentary legislation)[61], but are in fact expressive of the nature and will of the people themselves. Arising from custom, and confirmed by long continuance, the Common Law is 'incorporated into [the] very Temperament [of the people, and has] become the Complection and Constitution of the English Commonwealth'.[62]

It appears, then, that the notions of consent and liberty at work here have no strong voluntarist connotations. The central idea here is not that of will or choice, or of conditional agreement, but of *identification*. We are free because the laws by which we are governed are *ours*, we are told. Ours, not because we *own* it, or

---

[60] 1 *Comm.* 74; see also Hale, 'Reflections' 505.

[61] Blackstone points out, in the sentences opening the paragraph from which the passage above was taken, that Rome '*in the times of its liberty*' also paid 'great regard to custom', since it recognized that assent might be granted 'by a uniform course of acting accordingly' as well as by 'suffrage'. But this time of liberty was past, he insists, when all law-making power was concentrated in the hands of the emperor and Rome came to be ruled by imperial decree. See 1 *Comm.* 73–4, also 1 *Comm.* 127.

[62] Hale, *History*, 30. English law, says Sir John Davies, is 'so framed and fitted to the nature and disposition of this people, as we may properly say it is connatural to the Nation, so as it cannot possibly be ruled by any other Law. This Law therefore doth demonstrate the strength of wit and reason and self-sufficiency which hath been always in the People of this Land, which have made their own Laws out of their wisedome and experience, (like a silk-worm that formeth all her web out of her self onely) . . .' *Irish Reports*, Preface, quoted in Pocock, *Ancient Constitution*, 33–4. See also Blackstone 1 *Comm.* 17–20 and 4 *Comm.* 407–43 for similar sentiments.

dominate it, or have the power to turn it to our own use and purposes; but ours because we feel entirely at home with it, see it as an
integral part of daily life, and participate fully in it. Consent is not
the basis of laws of the community, nor the means by which they
are created, but rather an expression or recognition of one's participation in community.[63] To participate in a practice, on this
view, is not merely to comply with its requirements, or even to do
so thinking correctly that one ought to comply with them (for that
can be true of a visitor merely doing in Rome as the Romans do); it
is further to see oneself in partnership with consociates in the practice, jointly regarding its norms as binding. Thus, it cannot be the
mere conformity of actions of the members of community to the
requirements of custom that is 'internal evidence of this freedom',
but their continual *use* of it, recognition of it as constitutive of *their
own* social relations, and *participation* in its practices.[64]

Furthermore, long-established customary ways give better
evidence of the true choice of the nation because they represent the
deeper, more permanent and deliberate determinations of the community as a whole, than the arbitrary wishes of some temporary
majority.[65] And, the implication is, individuals are truly free when
this 'birthright' is secured to them,[66] and they can fully participate
in it.

We are now in a better position to understand what is meant by
the claim that Common Law is common reason, and in virtue of

[63] For a recent discussion of this notion of consent see S. Cavell, *The Claim of Reason*, 23-8.

[64] It is, of course, an open question whether this is an accurate description of the attitudes of the English people in the eighteenth century, as Blackstone maintains. Bentham, we shall see (8.2), regarded it as a giant fraud.

[65] Burke, intentionally invoking a traditional Common Law theme, clearly articulates this notion of consent. He argues that the presumption 'in favour of any settled scheme of government . . . that has long existed and flourished under it' is a better presumption than even 'the *choice* of a nation' and 'far better than any sud-den and temporary arrangement by actual election'. This is because, he explains, 'a nation is not an idea only of local extent and individual momentary aggregation, but it is an idea of continuity which extends in time as well as in numbers and in space. And this is a choice not of one day or one set of people, not a tumultuary and giddy choice; it is a deliberate election of ages and of generations; it is a constitution made by what is ten thousand times better than choice; it is made by the peculiar cir-cumstances, occasions, tempers, dispositions, and moral, civil, and social habitudes of the people, which disclose themselves only in a long space of time' (Burke, 'Speech on Reform of Representation', 100). This idea is echoed by G. Calabresi in his recent defence of a common law theory of statutory revision, *A Common Law for the Age of Statutes*, 97-8.

[66] See Blackstone, 1 *Comm.* 128; 4 *Comm.* 443.

that is self-justifying. First of all, to justify any particular judgment, to demonstrate its wisdom or goodness, according to this
view, involves no appeal to transcendent or independent standards
of reason, but only a showing that the proposed arrangement is, or
comfortably fits into, a common way of life. '[T]he only method of
proving, that this or that maxim is a rule of the common law,'
Blackstone reminds us, 'is by showing that it hath been always the
custom to observe it' (1 *Comm.* 68). Now, this does not restrict us
to routinized repetition of past actions, for novel situations may
call for creative decisions. But to make decisions in such cases is to
exercise an essentially social capacity. That is, it is to judge what I
know others in the community would regard as reasonable and fitting (where their recognizing the reasonableness is in part reciprocally dependent on their recognition that I would so regard it).
These judgments can be made with confidence (though they are not
infallible), not because one is a good predictor of their behaviour,
or has special insight into their secret consciousness, but simply
because one understands at a concrete level the common life in
which we all participate. Just as to learn to speak a language is to
develop the social competence to produce and to recognize creative
uses of language,[67] so too to become fluent in the language of
'human affairs and conversation' is to acquire the social capacity to
make judgments that even in novel cases one can be confident will
elicit recognition and acceptance as appropriate from the community. There is nothing mysterious or metaphysical in this notion
of a social capacity. It simply rests on the idea that some practices,
and the beliefs and attitudes blended into an interpretation of
them, are entirely common.

Secondly, from the point of view of participants, the norms and
requirements of the practices are largely *transparent*—they are the
lens *through which* civic experience is viewed—they are not themselves objects of reflection or scrutiny. They define the background
against which judgments of justice, wisdom, reasonableness are
made. Questions about *their* justice, wisdom, or reasonableness
simply do not arise (for participants taking this view of the practice).
'They *are*, and nothing more; this is what constitutes the awareness
of . . . [the] relationship [of participants] to them' Hegel points out

---

[67] On this see R. Brandom, 'Freedom and Constraint by Norms', 194–5, and J.
Rosenberg, *Linguistic Representation*, 3.

in his brilliant description of this traditionary point of view.[68] This 'disposition consists just in sticking steadfastly to what is right, and abstaining from all attempts to move or shake it, or derive it'. For example, that 'something *is* the property of another, this is fundamental; I have not to argue about it . . . I have to think neither of making laws nor of testing them.' In fact, 'such thinking on my part would upset that relation'. For

if I inquire after their origin and confine them to the point whence they arose, then I have transcended them; for now it is I who am the universal and *they* are the conditioned and limited. If they are supposed to be validated by *my* insight, then I have already denied their unshakeable, intrinsic being, and regard them as something which, for me, is perhaps true, but also is perhaps not true.

Reason, on this view, is necessarily *internal* to the tradition. Critical reflection and even challenge to aspects of the tradition are possible within it, but such a critic can only question whether some part of the practice fits with the practice as a whole. There simply is no position from which one can challenge the reasonableness of the tradition itself. There are, on this view, no extra-traditional rational standards. And since, according to classical Common Law theory, the law is the repository of this tradition and the arena in which it publicly unfolds, radical challenge to it cannot get off the ground. It is in this respect that the traditionary conception of collective wisdom and reason is sceptical.

This is not the place critically to assess this account of the reasonableness and legitimacy of Common Law. But it is worth pointing out one difficulty facing the argument which might explain why classical Common Law theory never sharply distinguished between it and some version of the 'wisdom of the ages' argument. Consider again Hegel's description of the traditionary mind. The strength of the traditionary position comes from the shared sense in the community of the transparency of the tradition, its utter naturalness and obviousness. To challenge traditionary ways (like challenging common sense)[69] is nearly unthinkable. It is the unspoken test of reasonableness. What sense could be given to the demand to test it?

---

[68] G. W. F. Hegel, *The Phenomenology of Spirit*, para. 437, p. 261. All subsequent quotations in this paragraph are taken from para. 437 of the *Phenomenology*.

[69] For an illuminating discussion of this mind-set see C. Geertz, 'Common Sense as a Cultural System', in Geertz, *Local Knowledge*, 73–93.

But this, its greatest strength, is turned against it once the traditionary conception is itself enlisted in the service of political argument. Once articulated *as an argument*, interlocutors are invited to reflect on it, to treat it as a valid object of critical scrutiny. The very act of making the argument invites us to regard the tradition as something which, in Hegel's phrase, is perhaps true, but also is perhaps not true. Moreover, once it becomes necessary to *convince* people that tradition must be regarded in the traditionary way, it becomes clear that they no longer regard tradition in that way. 'How do you keep the boys down on the farm once they've seen Paris?' It was for this reason, that Hegel, greatly attracted to the sense of integration, harmony, and community in traditionary societies, nevertheless thought them largely unrecoverable once the Enlightenment and the drive for individual liberty penetrated into the modern mind.[70]

Conventionalism

The traditionary conception of Common Law requires a certain naïve innocence which, once lost, cannot be regained. Hale seems to have been aware of this in his critique of Hobbes. In fact, in this remarkable fragment Hale briefly suggests a third line of defence of Coke's doctrine of the artificial reason of Common Law which combines elements from both the Hobbesian and traditionary conceptions of law. Hale does not seek, in this argument, to deny to reasonable persons a position from which the merits and demerits of Common Law might be weighed. Rather he wished to show that, from the same perspective from which such critical scrutiny can be launched, it can be shown that there is good reason to accept the requirements of law as fully binding, even when the rules cannot commend themselves to our reason.

To begin, consider again the feature of modern social life which concerned Hobbes and classical Common Law theory alike, namely that even reasonable persons exercising their best judgment constantly come up with widely differing views about how civic affairs

---

[70] Compare Graham Wallas's observations on Burke's conservative strategy: 'Burke was sincerely convinced that men's power of political reasoning was so utterly inadequate to their task that all his life long he urged the English nation to follow prescription, to obey, that is to say, on principle their habitual political impulses. But the deliberate following of prescription which Burke advocated was something different, because it was the result of choice, from the uncalculated loyalty of the past. Those who have eaten of the tree of knowledge cannot forget.' *Human Nature in Politics* 182–3, quoted in Kirk, 'Burke', 380.

should be ordered. In such circumstances, says Hale, 'Though a certain and determinate law may have some mischiefs in relation to particulars, . . . [such a law] is preferable before that arbitrary and uncertain rule which men miscall the law of reason' ('Reflections' 503).

There is, on this view, a perspective, albeit limited, outside the boundaries of the tradition itself from which the reasonableness of *compliance* with the tradition can be demonstrated. The argument, clearly, is that which we have already seen, in different versions, in Aquinas and Hobbes. If social interaction is to be possible, there must be some common way of acting around which interaction can be co-ordinated. In the absence of agreement on the independent merits of possible alternatives we are forced to accept that pattern which we can be most assured others on whom the success of our action depends will accept and follow. The most important property of laws, Hale argues, is that they are *certain* and *settled*. Thus,

though perchance at first the makers of them saw reason to pitch upon this institution rather than an other, yet in things thus settled it is not necessary that the reasons of the institution should be evident unto us. It is sufficient that they are instituted laws that give a certainty to us, and it is reasonable for us to observe them though the particular reason of the institution appear not ('Reflections' 505).

Hale boldly admits that it may be impossible to reconstruct a substantive rationale for much of the ancient law. But that does not undermine it, he insists, for its legitimacy rests not on its intrinsic merits, but on the simple fact that *it does the job* of defining a clear and settled rule of action and thus promises successfully to co-ordinate social interaction.

How, then, does this view differ in substance from that of Hobbes? Setting aside the potentially great differences between their conceptions of human nature and of community, the immediate difference lies in Hale's claim that it is not the legislative activity of the sovereign or his (judicial) delegates that can best fulfil this task, but the adjudicative activity of the prudent Common Law judge who is well acquainted with human affairs and conversation. That is, Hale in this argument relies on the traditionary conception to the extent that he believes that greater success in co-ordination of social interaction can be achieved through the careful, interstitial working out of shared understandings of common ways and practices, than through explicit creation of new rules and laws from the detached position of the sovereign legislator. The task of co-ordinating social interaction—not only between citizens, but also between citizens and the judiciary—is inescapably contextual. Argument from analogy to familiar past cases or incidents or general features of shared social life is more likely to succeed, he insists, than creating a new rule which itself needs interpretation before it can efficiently guide action.

This line of argument, perhaps, is too sketchy for us to be able to assess it, but it is possible to see how it departs from the earlier arguments we have considered. This argument, like both the wisdom of ages and the traditionary arguments, is 'sceptical' in the sense that it seeks to deflect or undermine the force of challenges to the reason, goodness, or justice of substantive doctrines of Common Law. But it allows much wider scope for individual rational judgment ('natural reason') than either of the other lines of argument do. It does not declare natural reason incompetent to assess the law. It does not assume that the law meets standards of justice which are beyond our comprehension; but neither does it deny that there is a position from which intelligible questions about the reasonableness of the laws can be raised and discussed. On the contrary, it assumes the competence of individuals rationally to assess their social situation and take a general view of the law and its role in that situation. It advances, rather, a much more pragmatic argument for Common Law. The most basic reason for compliance with the law lies simply in the fact that *it works*, it does the job of public ordering that needs to be done. And Common Law does this better than the Hobbesian alternative, because only it is close enough to the resources of common belief and experience in which alone, Hale believes, solutions to problems of civic ordering can be found.

Hale only suggests this line of argument in a few places in his 'Reflections', and he never develops it in detail. It is, nevertheless, an emerging theme in the Common Law tradition, which became increasingly important as the eighteenth century progressed, especially in the face of pressing demand for a reasoned defence of authority which did not rely on appeals to transcendent reason. Whether or not he directly drew inspiration from the arguments of

Hale, Hume's theory of law and justice, first set out some seventy years after Hale's fragment was written, develops Hale's suggestions into a sophisticated defence of the Common Law conception. We shall complete our discussion of pre-Benthamite British legal theory with a detailed look at Hume's jurisprudence in the next chapter.

3

Hume's Jurisprudence:
Law, Justice, and Human Nature

> After this convention, concerning the abstinence from the possessions of others, is enter'd into . . . there immediately arise the ideas of justice and injustice; as also those of *property, right,* and *obligation.* The latter are altogether unintelligible without first understanding the former.
>
> Hume, Treatise.

LONG admired and much discussed by moral philosophers, Hume's theory of justice has largely been ignored by legal theorists. But it is as natural to read Hume's account of justice as a discussion of fundamental issues in jurisprudence as it is to regard it as part of a larger theory of the virtues. And the contribution it makes to jurisprudence is, in my view, at least as great as its contribution to moral philosophy. This should not be surprising, since Hume wrote from within a tradition in which moral philosophy embraced jurisprudence as an important component.[1]

Situating Hume's discussion in the tradition of British legal theory will be doubly beneficial. Not only are Hume's theory and the arguments for it thereby clarified, but in return they illuminate the jurisprudential landscape stretching back to Coke and forward to Bentham, Burke, and the nineteenth century. Hume, in fact, is pivotal in the development of British legal theory. In an intellectual *tour de force* he blends elements from Hobbes, Hale, and his own epistemology, into an account of law and its foundations which simultaneously deepens and revolutionizes the Common Law tradition.[2]

---

[1] See D. D. Raphael, 'Hume and Adam Smith on Justice and Utility', 97.

[2] Burke, of course, transformed the Common Law tradition into a potent political credo for the nineteenth century, and it is his idiosyncratic reading of that tradition that had the greater historical impact, but it is Hume's version of the tradition which is the more philosophically coherent and satisfying.

Furthermore, Hume's reflections on justice and law shaped Bentham's perception of the problems of jurisprudence and his struggle to solve them, although he rarely acknowledges his debt to Hume in this respect.[3] Surely, Blackstone was the more immediate and persistent force agitating Bentham's thinking about law and adjudication, but Hume's influence was the more profound and lasting. Repeatedly, especially in Bentham's early formative years, his formulation of problems regarding the foundations, nature, and basic tasks of law, as well as strategies for solving them, are silently shaped by Hume. Bentham's theory of law is uniquely his own, but he could not have developed it without Hume's help. The importance of Hume for the larger narrative of this book requires that we take a careful and detailed look at Hume's jurisprudence.

3.1 LAW AND JUSTICE

Our property is nothing but those goods, whose constant possession is establish'd by the laws of society; that is, by the laws of justice.

Hume, *Treatise.*

Before I proceed to the details of Hume's theory, a few more words should be said about its credentials as a theory of law and its relationship to the Common Law tradition.

Justice as a juridical notion

A view widely held among English-speaking jurists locates law somewhere between social rules and critical morality—or, in an older terminology, between positive morality and natural law. The task of a jurisprudential theory, on this view, is to give an account

---

[3] The young Bentham acknowledged generally his intellectual debt to Hume in the *Fragment on Government* claiming that his reading of Hume's *Treatise* halted the aimless 'wanderings of a raw but well-intentioned mind', and set the course for his lifelong 'researches after moral truth'. Encountering for the first time Hume's thesis that all virtue is grounded in utility, Bentham reports, he felt as if scales had fallen from his eyes (*FG* I. 36, n. v.). Hume's influence is clearly evident in those passages in which Bentham invokes Hume's authority against contract theories of political obligation (*FG* I. 36) or the often muddled distinction between 'is' and 'ought' (e.g. *Bowring* v, 320; *Bowring* viii, 128; *RJE, Bowring* vi, 230 n. *). Also Humean terminology (though perhaps not doctrine) is pervasive throughout Bentham's reflections on language, knowledge, and ontology. (See Postema, 'Fact, Fiction, and Law', 45–54.) Hume's discussion of justice, however, is rarely mentioned explicitly; nevertheless, we shall see in ch. 5 how deeply Bentham was influenced by this discussion.

of the nature of law, and a precise location of law between these two poles, distinguishing it from, and relating it to, both. On these assumptions it is difficult to characterize Hume's theory of justice. Is it a theory of morality or of law? of positive morality or critical morality? of social custom or of formal law? These questions arise because justice, the virtue on which all others depend in one way or another according to Hume, is, for him, essentially a matter of conventional social rules, but rules which have features which jurists often associate with law and not with 'pre-legal' social rules or custom.[4]

It is tempting to try to force Hume's account of justice to either one pole or the other. On the one hand, one might say that Hume is not concerned with law at all, that he is concerned, rather, with morality—in particular, with the virtues of interpersonal justice and promise-keeping. Law, on this reading, appears late in his discussion, with the rise of government and its formal institutions of adjudication, enforcement, and legislation (*Treatise* III, ii, vii–x). On the other hand, one might argue that Hume is not talking about justice at all, and so not about any recognized *moral* virtue, since his account of the virtue of justice *presupposes* established positive rules, whereas justice is a supra-legal notion, defining standards by which such positive rules are to be judged.

Both responses are unfortunate. They simplify and distort the rich, multi-layered texture of Hume's analysis, and force us to choose between conceptual categories which Hume sought to bridge. They both assume a sharp distinction between justice and law, but Hume, like Hobbes, regarded justice as an essentially *juridical* notion, a concept that cannot be separated from the concept of law. (Frequently Hume uses 'rules of property', 'laws of society', and 'laws of justice' interchangeably.) The first proposal above overlooks the fact that Hume in the *Treatise* is writing moral philosophy and jurisprudence simultaneously. One important objective of *Treatise* III ii is to give an account of justice, fidelity, allegiance, and chastity as virtues *of individuals*,[5] as the

---

4 Compare, for example, H. Hart, *The Concept of Law*, ch. V, sect. 3, with the discussion below (4.2) of the techniques by which conventions 'fix all questions with regard to justice' (*Enquiry II* 286).

5 Justice is a virtue only of individuals, it is not a virtue of institutions, laws, systems of property, or the like. To regard justice as a virtue of these institutions would be to suggest that they are conceivable apart from justice, a thesis Hume rejects (*Treatise* 490–1).

foundation for his account of the natural virtues. And this account presupposes and is entirely dependent upon his account of certain basic social institutions and conventions.

Justice *is*, for Hume, a juridical virtue and thus is inseparable from law, but the second proposed reading of Hume's intentions carries over too much from Hobbes into this feature of Hume's theory. For Hobbes, the sovereign—i.e. legislative will and government enforcement—is established first; law and justice are products of this legislative will. Hobbes intended his account of law as a clear alternative to the conception advanced by Common Law theory. His model is statutory, not customary or common, law. Hume's account, in contrast, owes much more to the Common Law tradition: law is a development from and is always intimately tied up with the basic structuring conventions and customs of a community. And law is as much involved in the defining of the basic institutions of justice as it is in their interpretation and enforcement by formal governmental institutions. To make this clear we need to look at the progression of Hume's discussion in *Treatise* III, ii from property to centralized government.

From property to public works: historical and analytic dimensions

Treatise III, ii tells the story of the gradual emergence of modern society and of the modern state fully equipped with formal institutions for the making, enforcing, and interpreting of law and for planning and administering projects for the public good. The ordering of Hume's discussion is determined by his overlapping theoretical objectives. His discussion radiates from a core on which all the rest progressively depends. This dependence is evident in the fact that the structure of argument for property provides a model for each of the subsequent discussions. But the dependence goes deeper. Hume's account is a genetic one: institutions are built upon institutions. The need for each arises from the defects in the institutions of the previous stage—defects which, paradoxically, are due largely to the success of these institutions. The needs are defined and met at one stage, then refined to give rise to new problems and needs. I will sketch very briefly this progression.

The basic conditions for social intercourse are established by the institution of property, according to Hume. Social cooperation and productive combination of efforts beyond the narrow circle of the family are thereby made possible. But as commerce (that is, trade, and interaction generally) expands a need arises for a method by which strangers, lacking the regular and intimate contact which breeds trust, can bind themselves to actions at a distance (*Treatise* 519–20). Out of this need arises the convention of promising (and formal contract). Making a promise, on Hume's account, is a special, relatively formal, method of undertaking obligations to others, one in which the use of language and formalized devices plays a crucial role *(Treatise* 515–20). Annette Baier points out that the special role of promise, among the sources of obligation, for Hume, is to enable cooperation among strangers, and to extend that cooperation to future actions and distant goods and property.[6] Thus, the convention of promising in Hume's view shares a good deal with what we would recognize as the institution of contract. Promising extends the convention of property and consent by providing (i) security that the rights transferred by consent *are recognized as* so transferred, and (ii) a form whereby conditions can be attached to consent.[7]

With this convention in place, Hume believes the basic structure of society is settled. Basic social relations are defined, a framework for social interaction is settled, and means for modifying them is put at the disposal of the members of the community. But this success again creates problems, for now the economy can expand, society can grow and become more refined. But in such 'large and polished societies' there arises a need for the formal and authoritative administration of justice (*Treatise* 543). This is a complex development and the various strands woven into the fabric of government must be isolated.

First, the need arises for institutionalized forms of enforcement of the rules of justice already instituted. As societies grow, the impact of any one individual's actions increasingly tends to extend beyond one's immediate grasp. Also, the proportion of the members of the society with whom one has little or no direct contact increases. This tends to distort our perceptions of the consequences of our actions. Whereas in the narrow circle of the neighborhood, the necessity of self-restraint is evident upon the

---

6 A. Baier, 'Promises', 181. In an earlier draft she wrote, 'Promise is an artifice for treating the remote as if it were contiguous—for treating the stranger as a trustworthy intimate, for treating the future as if it were present, treating the distant as if it were close, the general as if it were specific and individual, the absent as if it were present.'

7 Baier, 'Truth and Superstition', 17.

least reflection, this becomes less evident now. 'The consequences of every breach of equity seem to lie very remote, and are not able to counterbalance any immediate advantage, that may be reap'd from it' (*Treatise* 535). They are, however, no less real for being remote, Hume insists. And since we are all subject to this weakness of foresight, it is likely that violations of justice will be frequent. This sets up a further problem, for even when I do perceive the remote consequences of my action I have an incentive to violate the rules of justice, since I have no assurance that my fellows far distant from me, of whom I personally know very little, will be able or willing to resist this weakness which I recognize in myself. We have an 'assurance problem' of significant proportions. The solution, says Hume, is for us to agree to the institution of an agency for the enforcement of justice. Magistrates then remedy 'the narrowness of soul, which makes [one] prefer the present to the remote', while 'constrain[ing] others to a like regularity' (*Treatise* 537).

Similarly, growth of the society and the increasing distance between people and the inevitable partiality of persons to their own interests unconstrained by other natural sentiments or benevolence, strain the bonds of shared understanding of the rules of justice. This calls for institutions for the authoritative interpretation of these rules (*Treatise* 538). The need for judicial articulation and determination of the law is a sign of a degree of (or at least the threat of) disintegration of the shared understanding on which the conventions of justice rest.

The task of civil law, says Hume, is to 'fix all the questions with regard to justice' in large and polished societies (*Enquiry II* 286). This involves not only adjudicating differences of interpretation of existing standards, but also filling in the details which existing custom and convention have left incomplete (*Treatise* 513; *Enquiry II* 196). This calls for more or less explicit rule-making and fashioning of social arrangements which then 'extend, restrain, modify, and alter' the existing conventions of property (*Enquiry II* 196). The picture Hume suggests is that of established conventions of justice serving well enough the needs of the community in their crude and rough way for a time, but as commerce expands, and the need for refinement of the rules increases, new conventions are explicitly created.[8]

---

[8] For a systematic discussion of such uses of law see Postema, 'Coordination and Convention at the Foundations of Law', 182–97. Forbes points out that,

Finally, Hume argues that government aids us further in advancing our own collective projects by helping plan and co-ordinate public works projects which would be too difficult to undertake relying only on informal methods of co-ordination (*Treatise* 538–9). In this discussion of the progression from property to public works, historical and analytic objectives go hand in hand. Hume believed that the sequence he describes reproduces (at least roughly) the actual development of modern civilized societies. And he clearly held that societies could exist at levels requiring no magistrates or other institutions (cf. *History* I, 52), and perhaps even without the practice of promising (*Treatise* 540–1).[9]

The key feature in this analysis is the nature and direction of dependency. The sequence Hume describes is not a sequence of institutions transforming and transcending earlier ones; rather, later stages *preserve* and *build upon* earlier ones. Later institutions are impossible, perhaps even unintelligible, without the institutions of the prior stages. In contrast with Hart's well-known discussion, which gives a hypothetical account of the transition from a pre-legal society to a society with a fully fledged legal system,[10] Hume gives us a detailed description of the architecture of a modern legal system, storey by storey, pointing out all its essential components and noting their dependencies and interrelationships. Thus, custom and the relations of property (and social relations generally) which it defines are the core structuring elements in Hume's jurisprudence around which all the other refinements and artifices of law are

according to Hume, the appearance of the legislator presupposes a certain level of economic development and of civilization (D. Forbes, *Hume's Philosophical Politics*, 316). Hume does not state explicitly whether the source of such legislation would be the judiciary or some explicitly recognized legislative body. But it appears that *initially* law-applying institutions would be the primary fashioners of new rules, for the first formal institution of government to appear, according to Hume, is that of magistracy. Formal legislative bodies come later in his account.

[9] However, Hume (*Essays* 116–19) gives a slightly different picture in which, at a primitive stage of social development, a 'barbarous monarchy' takes the place of the convention of justice and establishes some semblance of order. This administration governs with absolute discretion and without any general laws or rules. And later in the same essay he says: 'law, the source of all security and happiness, arises late in any government, and is the slow product of order and of liberty' (125). Thus, Hume seems to allow for the possibility of a form of *government* prior to the development of any general rules regarding property. Compare this with Hume's description of 'civilized monarchy' the power of which is in theory no less absolute, but which governs within the limits of general custom, example, and a sense of its own interest. (*Essays* 126)

[10] Hart, *The Concept of Law*, 89–96.

built. The laws of 'civil' as well as 'natural' justice 'are built on the very same foundation of human convention' (*Treatise* 543).[11]

Hume and Common Law theory

A major thesis of this chapter is that Hume's theory of justice is plausibly and profitably seen as a revision and extension of some basic themes of Common Law jurisprudence. I do not, however, wish to overstate this claim. I do not claim that Hume self-consciously worked within the English Common Law tradition. His legal training, which was substantial,[12] would have been largely in Scots law, not English Common Law, and there is much evidence of this influence in his writings.[13] Nevertheless, Hume shares with Common Law jurists a number of basic views, and this fact warrants treating Hume's jurisprudence, for our purposes, as a development of the Common Law tradition.

Like Common Law jurists, Hume traced the roots of modern civil law to common custom and tradition. Law and political authority are the products of countless hands over many generations working and reworking traditional materials handed down to them.

Did one generation of men go off the stage at once, and another succeed, as is the case with silkworms and butterflies, the new race, if they had sense enough to choose their government, which surely is never the case with

---

[11] Thus, what Hume calls 'laws of nature' (i.e. duties and rights existing prior to formal recognition by magistrates) are thoroughly *conventional*. And, just as according to Common Law theory the law decided and articulated in the courts is merely a refinement of the common custom of the land, so too 'civil law' according to Hume is an extension and refinement, through the activities of magistrates, of 'natural' conventional justice. Thus, the distinction between 'laws of nature' and 'civil laws' in Hume parallels the Common Law distinction between the custom of the realm (without regard paid to its recognition by the courts) and the Common Law (i.e. that custom as recognized and enforced by the courts). It does not reproduce the distinction between unwritten and written (or statutory) law.

[12] Hume read law between 1725 and 1729. Also the literary society to which he belonged during this time included the advocate and jurist (and kinsman) Henry Home of Kames, who was fifteen years his senior. E. C. Mossner, *The Life of David Hume*, 52–65. According to Mossner, 'Hume's legal knowledge both theoretical and practical was not inconsiderable. . . . Of theoretical jurisprudence, Hume was a master' (55). On the legal thought of the period, see P. Stein, 'Law and Society in Eighteenth-Century Scottish Thought'.

[13] There is, of course, much use of Roman law in the *Treatise* (504–13) and *Enquiry II* (192–204, 303–11). Also, Paul Lucas argues that Hume follows Scots law in his emphasis on the doctrine of prescription as a basis for his account of authority and justice. P. Lucas, 'Burke's Doctrine of Prescription', 60.

men, might voluntarily, and by general consent, establish their own form of civil polity, without any regard to the laws or precedents which prevailed among their ancestors. But as human society is in perpetual flux, one man every hour going out of the world, another coming into it, it is necessary, in order to preserve stability in government, that the new brood should conform themselves to the established constitution, and nearly follow the path which their fathers, treading in the footsteps of theirs, had marked out to them (*Essays* 463).

Civil society is a community of overlapping generations extending backwards and forwards in time. Traditions and customs bind it together and give it stability. This does not preclude change or improvement of the laws, Hume points out, for '[s]ome innovations must necessarily have place in every human institution' (ibid.). But these must be interstitial—'violent innovations no individual is entitled to make' (ibid.)—and subject to the constant refinement of testing their acceptance as part of the customs of the community. '[T]hey are even dangerous to be attempted by the legislature; more ill than good is ever to be expected from them . . .'[14] These sentiments are familiar, of course; we have met them, in one version or another, in Coke, Hale, Blackstone, and the other Common Lawyers.

Similarly, history, or at least the sense of the 'antiquity' of the law and constitution, is, for Hume, the richest and most important source of their legitimacy. 'Antiquity always begets the opinion of right.'[15] Yet here Hume seems to echo the more sensitive and sophisticated constitutional theory of Hale,[16] rather than the cruder Coke-inspired doctrine of 'ancient constitutionalism' which enjoyed a resurgence in the 'Country' party during the mid-eighteenth century. Like Hale, Hume argues that it is absurd to think that the present political constitution can be traced back to pre-Norman times. England has seen several different constitutions during its history.[17] What is most fundamental to legitimacy, for Hume, as

[14] *Essays* 463; see also *Essays* 116, 125, 499. Compare Bentham's contrary view below, 6.2.

[15] *Essays* 30; see also 456, 499.

[16] Hume was much influenced by Hale's *History of the Common Law* (Forbes, *Hume's Philosophical Politics*, 316). A clear example of this is Hume's assessment of Edward I (*History* II, 141 ff). Hume's *History* was motivated by much the same concern to cut through the debate about the 'ancient constitution'. See, for Hale: above, 1.2, for Hume: D. Miller, *Philosophy and Ideology in Hume's Political Thought*, 166–8 and Forbes, 260–307.

[17] See Hume, *History* IV, 354–5, esp. at 355 n.: 'The English constitution, like all others, has been in a state of continual fluctuation.'

for Hale, is not the constitution's being traceable back to ancient times, but the fact of its *present* wide *acceptance*. 'In each of these successive alterations, the only rule of government which is intelligible or carries any authority, is the established practice of the age, and the maxims of administration, which are at that time prevalent and universally assented to.'[18] A sense of antiquity is important for this acceptance. But it is not the objective fact of the constitution's antiquity that is important, but rather the fact that the constitution is *commonly regarded as* immemorial. This is not an expression of political cynicism; it is merely the (pragmatic conservative) view that the most important thing for society is that lines of authority be absolutely clear, settled, and matters of common knowledge. 'In the particular exercises of power,' says Hume, 'the question ought never to be forgotten, *What is best*? But in the general distribution of power among the several members of a constitution, there can seldom be admitted any other question, than *What is established*?' (*History* IV, 354). A shared sense of the antiquity of the law is important for this purpose because it increases the 'salience' of the existing constitution.[19] Although this is expressed in Humean terminology, this doctrine of the constitution and political authority has a clear pedigree in Hale's influential *History of the Common Law*. Hume may not have self-consciously followed Hale or the other Common Law jurists when he constructed his theory of justice, but it is clear that he was constructing a general philosophical theory to support doctrines he shared with them.

3.2   HUMAN NATURE AND THE ARTIFICE OF JUSTICE

[Man is] the creature of the universe, who has the most ardent desire for society, and is fitted for it by the most advantage.

Hume, *Treatise*.

The artifice of justice

The sense of justice, according to Hume, is an artificial virtue—artificial, not because it is arbitrary or capricious, but

---

[18] Hume, *History* II, 525; see also *History* II, 518–25; *History* III, 212; *History* IV, 354–5, 367–8; *History* V, 128, 544–5; *Essays* 495 n. 2, 499; *Treatise* 546–7. Compare Hale, *History*, 17, ch. IV generally, and above, 1.2.

[19] This is the upshot of *Treatise* 508–9, 556, and 566.

because it depends for its existence on human education, reflection, and invention (*Treatise* 484; *Enquiry II* 307). The sense of justice presupposes the existence of a system of established social rules invented or constructed (in one sense of that word) by a species capable of reflecting on what experience reveals as the necessary conditions of existence, and of adjusting and fixing beliefs, intentions, and natural passions to ensure that these conditions are met.

Human existence, beyond absolutely the most primitive, is wholly dependent upon broad patterns of social interaction and co-operation. 'Human nature cannot by any means subsist, without the association of individuals', claims Hume (*Enquiry II* 206). The solitary human being, lacking sufficient power, skill, and knowledge, could not withstand the slightest misfortune, and so looks to join forces with others in mutually beneficial co-operative efforts. 'By the conjunction of forces, our power is augmented: By the partition of employments, our ability encreases: And by mutual succour we are less expos'd to fortune and accidents' (*Treatise* 485). These forces driving toward survival combine with natural social appetites uniting men, women, and offspring in the family to bring people together in social union. However, due to the scarcity of necessary material goods and the vulnerability and instability of possession, co-operative efforts and social union are subject to powerful, centrifugal forces of individual selfishness and family-confined generosity. Human nature and the circumstances of human life put people in constant competition for scarce material resources and each person is naturally impelled to acquire as much as possible, paying no heed to claims of possession.

In Hume's view, the chief advantage of society, as well as the most fundamental condition of its survival, lies in securing and expanding the stock of material goods for individual enjoyment and thereby establishing conditions for productive and mutually beneficial co-operation. The foremost threat to social co-operation essential to human survival and improvement is the perpetual violent challenge to the stability and certainty of possession of material goods. It is only through the invention of a scheme of fixed general rules, binding upon all members of the community, and stabilizing and securing possession and use of property, that this challenge is met. Reflecting on this lesson of nature and experience, human beings are led with little difficulty to see that their own interests are individually and collectively best served 'by a convention enter'd into by all the members of society . . . for the distinction of property, and for the stability of possession' (*Treatise* 489, 491). The 'several interested passions', then, 'adjust themselves after such a manner as to concur in some system of conduct' (*Treatise* 529). The origin of justice, Hume concludes, lies in the self-correction of the interested passions, upon the promptings of observation, reflection, and judgment.[20]

In the following sections I will consider in detail Hume's account of the genesis of justice, but first I want to look more carefully at the circumstances which make a scheme of rules of justice both necessary and possible.

Human nature and the 'state of nature'

The conventions of justice, on Hume's account, arise amongst individuals in a primitive, 'wild [and] uncultivated' (*Treatise* 486) condition, whose dominant motivations issue from the interested passions. This cannot fail to suggest a Hobbesian conception of human nature and strategy of argument. However, although Hume's strategy parallels that of Hobbes to some extent, his conception of human nature and the circumstances creating the need for justice stand in sharp contrast with Hobbesian doctrine.

Hume admits readily that justice is 'the cautious, jealous virtue' (*Enquiry II* 184).[21] But he does not embrace Hobbes's radically individualist picture of human nature. On the contrary, Hume conceives human nature as basically social, even in the fictitious 'state of nature'.[22] Hume uses the fiction of a 'state of nature' as an analytical device to help isolate the factors that combine to generate the structuring institutions of society, and to display the funda-

---

[20] *Treatise* 489; see also *Essay* 466–7. On the rise of the 'principle of countervailing passions' and Hume's role in it see A. O. Hirschman, *The Passions and the Interests*, Pt. I.

[21] 'Justice, the virtue of the self-interested, is the virtue that curbs self-interest', D. Gauthier, 'Three Against Justice', 11.

[22] 'Hume's awareness of man's social interdependence is so striking a feature of his thought, in the *Treatise* especially, that it would be nearer the mark to say that for him society is the "natural unit".' (Forbes, *Hume's Philosophical Politics*, 105). The thesis advanced in this section is too large to be dealt with adequately here. Others, on whom I have relied, have developed parts of the interpretation in greater detail. See Forbes, ch. 4; Miller, *Philosophy and Ideology*, chs. 1 and 4; and especially several papers by Baier, including 'Hume on Fixing and Adjusting in Nature and Artifice', 'Helping Hume to "Complete the Union"', 'Promises, Promises, Promises'.

mental human needs to which these institutions answer.[23] But he clearly maintains that the needs in question are inescapably social. Indeed, it is the essential sociality of human beings that both creates the need for the artifice of justice and makes possible its invention and establishment. It is impossible to ground justice in benevolence, Hume clearly argues.[24] Nevertheless, justice has its roots in the fundamentally social nature of human beings. If a purely solitary life for humans were possible, the need for justice would never arise (*Enquiry II* 191–2).

'Man, born in a family, is compelled to maintain society from necessity, from natural inclination, and from habit.'[25] Surely, Hume insists, we participate in social interaction automatically, instinctively, without giving it a thought. It is a matter of habit; we don't know any other way to live—'being born in a family'. Moreover, we actually long for companionship, feel genuine disinterested tenderness and affection for others, desire their good, and seek to achieve it. And this desire can be traced to something deep in human nature, a kind of natural necessity.

Our essential sociality appears at three distinct levels: action, sentiment, and thought. First, because of the unavoidable scarcity of material goods on which human survival and improvement depends, the actions (and decision-making) of human beings are radically interdependent.

> The mutual dependence of men is so great in all societies that scarce any human action is entirely complete in itself, or is performed without some reference to the actions of others, which are requisite to make it answer fully the intention of the agent (*Enquiry I* 89).

Action in a material environment shared with others making demands upon it as well unavoidably involves *social interaction*. And 'as men extend their dealings, and render their intercourse with others more complicated, they always comprehend, in their schemes of life, a greater variety of voluntary actions, which they expect, from the proper motives, to co-operate with their own'

---

[23] *Treatise* 493–4. For a very suggestive critique of Hume's method, see A. Ferguson, *Essay on the History of Civil Society* Pt. 1, sect. i.

[24] In this respect Hume differs sharply from Hutcheson, from whom he derived much inspiration. See Raphael, 'Hume and Adam Smith', 89–90. For a recent discussion of the relationship between Hume and Hutcheson, see D. F. Norton, *David Hume: Common Sense Moralist*.

[25] *Essays* 35. 'The propensity to company and society is strong in all rational creatures' (*Essays* 207).

(ibid.). As Schelling points out, social interaction is characteristically a matter of people responding to an environment consisting of other people responding to their environment, which itself includes responses of the first group.[26] Hume's point is important if we are to understand the genesis of the convention of justice. To be sure, the outcome of any individual's action is affected by what others do (or choose). But that is not all, for that is true as well about the interaction between an individual and nature. (My staying dry depends both on my choice—whether or not to carry an umbrella— and on the weather.) The important feature of social interaction is that what one person chooses depends upon what one expects others to choose, and what they choose (and so, what one can expect them to choose) depends on what they can expect one to choose. 'Reference to the actions of others' is necessary if one's own action is to 'answer fully [one's] intentions'. Few human actions are complete in themselves. In this sense, human action is unavoidably interdependent.

Second, this interdependence of action can be traced to an even deeper psychological interdependence. The doctrine of sympathy is central, not only to Hume's moral philosophy, but also to his account of the passions and, as we shall see shortly, his theory of knowledge and judgment. Against Hobbes, Hume insists that human beings are often moved by a disinterested natural inclination to seek the company and conversation of others (*Treatise* 363, 489). But this is not just one passion or inclination among others. It is, in Hume's view, psychologically fundamental. Sympathy, 'the easy communication of sentiments from one thinking being to another' (*Treatise* 363), is essential to the explanation of almost every passion and sentiment Hume considers, and issues from a deep human need.

Human desire, abstracted from its social context is inconceivable, Hume maintains. 'We can form no wish, which has not a reference to society.' Nor would such desires 'have any force, were we to abstract entirely from the thoughts and sentiments of others' (*Treatise* 363). The reason for this is that 'the minds of men are mirrors to one another' (*Treatise* 365). Our passions, sentiments, and even opinions are mutually reflected, iterated, 'reverberated' (ibid.) in the minds of others, and individual self-consciousness is dependent upon the recognition of others. In itself

[26] T. Schelling, *Micromotives and Macrobehavior*, 14.

the individual mind is incapable of gaining a sufficiently coherent or stable conception of itself. Adorno captures one side of this thought when he writes, 'a human being becomes human at all by imitating other human beings'.[27] But he ignores the essential Humean point that there must be *reflection*, 'reverberation', of the recognition. The human self, according to Hume, depends on the reflection and confirmation in another rational and thinking being like itself in whom it can find itself and to whom it can communicate all the actions of its mind (*Treatise* 353, 363).

Thus, one's sense of self and sense of one's worth is not epistemologically privileged; one's judgments and evaluations, in Hume's view, must be 'seconded by the opinions and sentiments of others'.[28] We seek the good opinion of others, says Hume in the *Dissertation on the Passions*, in order both to fix and to confirm our opinions of ourselves (II. 10). Duncan Forbes points out that, for Hume, 'Our individuality is not "given" [by nature], but is a product of social experience.'[29] We learn about ourselves through commerce and communication with others. Self-reflection, on this view, is simply a matter of viewing oneself from the perspective of others. And this capacity is both a basic necessity of human life and a necessary component of virtue.[30]

This communication with others is necessary not only for a general sense of self, but also for the intelligibility of one's particular passions and sentiments. 'Hatred, resentment, esteem, love, courage, mirth and melancholy; all these passions I feel more from communication than from my own natural temper and disposition' (*Treatise* 317). Hume's view seems to be that immediate experience of one's sentiments and inner feelings, uninterpreted by custom

[27] *Minima Moralia*, 154, quoted in S. Lovibond, *Realism and Imagination in Ethics*, 105 n. 1.

[28] *Treatise* 316. Cf. *Treatise* 303: 'Men always consider the sentiments of others in their judgments of themselves.' On the public nature of character on Hume's view, see Baier, 'Truth and Superstition', n. 13.

[29] Forbes, 106. On Hume's view, sympathy 'brings the thoughts and feelings and activities of different persons into unison, before they ever understand the grounds of their community with each other' (105–6, quoting C. W. Hendel, *Studies in the Philosophy of David Hume*, 264).

[30] 'By our continual and earnest pursuit of a character, a name, a reputation in the world, we bring our own deportment and conduct frequently in review, and consider how they appear in the eyes of those who approach and regard us. This constant habit of surveying ourselves, as it were, in reflection, keeps alive all the sentiments of right and wrong, and begets, in noble natures, a certain reverence for themselves as well as others, which is the surest guardian of every virtue' (*Enquiry II* 276).

and practice, is irregular and not fully intelligible (*Treatise* 293–4, 580–3). For

> if a person full-grown, and of the same nature with ourselves, were on a sudden transported into our world, he wou'd be very much embarrass'd with every object, and wou'd not readily find what degree of love or hatred, pride or humility, or any other passion he ought to attribute to it (*Treatise* 293–4).

Apart from the agreement or confirmation of the thoughts and sentiments of others, we do not know how we (ought to) feel. '[C]ustom and practice . . . have settled the just value of every thing . . . and guide us, by means of general establish'd maxims, in the proportions we ought to observe in preferring one object to another.'[31] (The 'ought' here is clearly not meant to carry any moral weight; Hume means it simply in the sense of what is appropriate in the circumstances.) To identify a certain sentiment as, say, a feeling of pride, is to associate the feeling with a certain pattern of feelings, beliefs, and behaviour which pattern agrees with the response of most other persons in the community to similar situations, and which would be regarded as appropriate responses to that type of situation.[32]

The need for reflection and confirmation of one's feelings issues from a deeper need for stability and consistency in one's life and one's view of oneself. We 'find so many contradictions to our sentiments in society and conversation', Hume ruefully observes, 'and such an uncertainty from the incessant changes of our situation' (*Treatise* 583), that we need some shared common point of view towards which we can orient our immediate experience. This drive for regularity and stability not only forces one to regiment one's feelings to some steady policy, but it also requires that that policy or rule be a common and public one. One must abandon the idiosyncratic irregularity of one's private experiences for the

---

[31] *Treatise* 293. 'Particular customs and manners alter the usefulness of qualities: they also alter their merits' (*Enquiry II* 241). See also 'A Dialogue', 237, and Forbes, 108–9.

[32] Hume *may* be making the psychological point that we need affirmation of our feelings by others, but the texts suggest the stronger, *conceptual* point that conformity to customary patterns is a logical requirement of experiencing particular passions. The parallel with Wittgenstein at this point is striking. See *Philosophical Investigations*, sects. 138–242 generally, and 242 ff applying the general argument to the problem of private sensations. (I follow here S. Kripke's recent illuminating reading in *Wittgenstein on Rules*, 86–113.)

stability of a common, public point of view which alone makes conversation and communication possible. Just as we correct immediate perceptual experience by reference to a common point of view, so too we correct our sentiments to conform to the customs and practices which constitute our common life (*Treatise* 581–3). And it is to this principle of sympathy and the deep psychological need for coherence that we should appeal in order to explain 'the great uniformity we may observe in the humours and turn of thinking of those of the same nation', rather than to climate or geography as others have suggested (*Treatise* 316–17; *Essays* 208–9).

Sympathy, clearly, is not simply to be identified with fellow-feeling or other-regarding concern. Indeed, this psychological principle, which establishes a necessary link between an individual and the community, is essential for Hume's account of nearly all of the passions whether they be interested, positively other-regarding, or negatively other-regarding.[33] Whatever 'passions we may be actuated by; pride, ambition, avarice, curiosity, revenge or lust; the soul or animating principle of them all is sympathy' (*Treatise* 363).

Perhaps the most interesting implication of this view (at least as concerns Hume's relation to Hobbes)—an implication which Hume does not hesitate to draw in his political writings—is that even the sentiment of *interest* is dependent on communication and the opinion of others. 'It may further be said, that, though men be much governed by interest, yet even interest itself, and all human affairs, are entirely governed by *opinion*' (*Essays* 51). It is not entirely clear what Hume has in mind here. He could be making the simple point that often what I believe to be in my interest—just like my opinions about most other matters—is influenced by the opinions of others. But I suspect he intends something stronger: that what counts as being within the range of 'one's interest' (i.e. one's *conception* of the boundaries of one's interest) depends on standards or notions inherited from general 'opinion'. In any case, he makes clear, in the *Essays* that when it comes to political matters, the force of arguments of self-interest *presuppose* the influence of opinion of public good and legitimacy (*Essays* 30–1).

---

[33] See e.g., *Treatise* II, i, v; and II, ii, v–ix. Ferguson seconds this view. See Ferguson, *Essay* Pt. I, sects. ii–iii, and *Principles of Moral and Political Science*, v. I, 34. For 'to be in society, he points out, is simply "the physical state of the species" and men agree and quarrel, are selfish and anti-social or the opposite in society'. Forbes, 'Introduction' to Ferguson, *Essay*, p. xvi.

The social dependency of human individuals goes even deeper than this on Hume's view. For just as no wish or desire is conceivable abstracted from the thoughts and sentiments of others in society, so too no thought or judgment, no claim of knowledge or warranted belief, can be made without implicit reference to custom or opinion. In Hume's view, society is necessary not only for understanding oneself, but also for even the most rudimentary understanding of one's environment.

The sceptical arguments of *Treatise*, Part I yield a paradox for Hume: since they demonstrate the severe limitations of reason, they show that most of our natural beliefs on which all of common life depends can be given no rational foundation, yet it seems insane to reject them. Hume's 'sceptical solution' to this paradox reveals that Hume sought to limit transcendent, a priori (and essentially solipsistic) reason to make way for custom and 'the reasonings of common life'.[34] It is 'custom to which I attribute all belief and reasoning' (*Treatise* 115). Custom, the principle of weight and authority equal to reason itself (*Enquiry I* 41), is 'the great guide of life'.[35] It alone

renders our experience useful to us . . . Without the influence of custom, we should be entirely ignorant of every matter of fact beyond what is immediately present to the memory and senses. We should never know how to adjust means to ends, or to employ our natural powers in the production of any effect. There would be an end at once of all action, as well as of the chief part of speculation (*Enquiry I* 44–5).

Custom and opinion are 'natural prepossessions'—i.e. common judgments which do not themselves rest on reason or evidence, but are that against which reasonings and evidence are assessed, and in terms of which actions are conceived and judged as eligible or ineligible.[36] The 'general rules' and 'maxims' which densely populate Hume's epistemology are not private policies, or even universal

---

[34] *Enquiry I* 41; Kripke illuminates the similarities between Hume's solution and Wittgenstein's sceptical solution to his own parallel sceptical paradox, Kripke, *Wittgenstein*, 62–71.

[35] Cf. *History* III, 192, 'custom and precedent . . . [is] the principle by which men are almost wholly governed in their actions and opinions'. Also: 'Habits, more than reason, we find in everything to be the governing principle of mankind', *History* V, 159.

[36] See *Essays* 487–8; *History* IV, 290. 'When a man is prepossessed with a high notion of his rank and character in the creation, he will naturally endeavour to act up to it, and will scorn to do a base or vicious action which might sink him below

human dispositions (or at least not *just* that). They are constituents of *social practices*, defining a common point of view on a shared world.[37] As Annette Baier points out, what Hume calls 'habit' or 'custom' is what, after Wittgenstein, we might regard as 'norm-recognizing and correction-sensitive participation in a form of life, or practice'.[38]

Natural belief and judgment result from the operation of the 'imagination', which in Hume's view is a kind of instinct or sentiment (*Enquiry I* 46–9) working with an inherited fund of prepossessions. Thus, opinions and judgments, like passions, are subject to the 're-verberations' of sympathy.[39] Not only our passions, but also our beliefs, call for confirmation and reflection from other rational beings. It is our natural affection, indeed deep need, for *conversation* as well as company that demands that our beliefs and judgments conform to the common point of view defined by custom (*Treatise* 489, 581–3).

Human nature and justice

This conception of human nature is central to Hume's account of the genesis of justice. Human sociality makes justice both necessary and possible. First, the need for justice arises from severe and disastrous competition for scarce resources among persons whose motivation, under necessitous circumstances, is dominated by 'avidity', the 'insatiable, perpetual, and universal' desire to acquire 'goods and possessions for ourselves and our nearest friends' (*Treatise* 491–2). But this avidity is the product of limited benevolence and the selfish desire for riches and power. The basis of benevolence in sympathy is, no doubt, clear, but Hume's doctrine of sympathy also explains to some extent the natural limits of benevolence. The need for a mirror of one's own mind may well be

that figure which he makes in his own imagination' (*Essays* 82). At some points Hume uses the terms 'prepossession' and 'prejudice' interchangeably (anticipating Burke, see above, 2.3). See *Essays* 487–8, 495 n. 2, 573–4; *History* III, 210–12.

[37] Cf. H. Putnam's 'institutionalized inductions', *Reason, Truth, and History*, 106–7.

[38] Baier, 'Promises', 176–7.

[39] In the *Dissertation on the Passions* Hume says, 'Our opinions of all kinds are strongly affected by society and sympathy, and it is almost impossible for us to support any principle or sentiment, against the universal consent of every one' (152). This same view is frequently expressed in the *Treatise*, e.g. at 115 ff, 293–4, 316–21, 365, 583, 592.

fully satisfied by having at hand one's family and close friends.[40]
There seems no obvious need to extend the scope of one's attention
to the entire community; indeed, to the extent that competition for
survival is inevitable, the principle of sympathy is likely to induce a
rather fierce partiality for those in the inner circle necessary for
one's own sense of identity.[41] (This can, perhaps, be moderated by
reflection on the fact that one's relations to others are subject to
fluctuation such that 'a man, that lies at a distance from us, may,
in a little time, become a familiar acquaintance' (*Treatise* 581).
But this requires more careful reflection than many people engage
in.)

In addition to benevolence, the peculiar power—the 'insatiable,
perpetual, and universal' power—of the drive for material goods,
which Hume regards as the force most destructive of society, is best
explained, according to Hume, by recalling its origin in sympathy.
Nothing 'can give us an esteem for power and riches, and a contempt for meanness and poverty, except the principle of *sympathy*,
by which we enter into the sentiments of the rich and poor, and par-
take of their pleasure and uneasiness' (*Treatise* 362). The desire for
wealth and power is Hume's favourite example of how the mirroring and nesting of sentiments can actually cause a reverberation:
The possessor of riches experiences the initial pleasure and satisfaction in the riches; this is, then, reflected in the sympathy of the
beholder who experiences pleasure and esteem; this, in turn causes
a secondary satisfaction in the possessor arising from the love and
esteem he acquires by the possession of them. This satisfaction,
which 'is nothing but a second reflexion of that original pleasure,
which proceeded from him', according to Hume, 'becomes one of
the principal recommendations of riches, and is the chief reason,
why we either desire them for ourselves, or esteem them in others'
(*Treatise* 365).

[40] 'He will still be miserable, till you give him some one person at least, with
whom he may share his happiness' (*Treatise* 363). Moreover, the 'public' needed to
confirm one's judgment of character (especially one's own) may be restricted to a
select few 'who have a connexion' with one (*Treatise* 591; also 602, 605).

[41] Hume's analysis of the psychological sources of political factionalism rests on
the above account of human sociality: 'When men act in a faction, they are apt,
without shame or remorse, to neglect all the ties of honour and morality, in order to
serve their party; and yet, when a faction is formed upon a point of right or principle,
there is no occasion where men discover a greater obstinacy, and a more determined
sense of justice and equity. The same social disposition of mankind is the cause of
these contradictory appearances' (*Essays* 30).

However, in the natural sociality of human beings also lie the seeds of the resolution of the problem posed by unrestrained avidity. First, even in the 'state of nature' human beings are born into families (*Enquiry II* 190), which for Hume are *Ur-* societies. In this *Ur*-society, restraints establishing order, preserving peace, and making cooperation within the family possible, are *naturally* imposed (*Treatise* 486). Given this education into the custom of self-restraint in the interest of the larger unit of which one is a part, only the slightest reflection on this experience will lead persons to see the advantage in extending this solution to the society at large, says Hume. The conventions of justice are merely the extensions of solutions to co-ordination problems from the micro-social context to the macro-social.[42] The experience of solving such problems in the family provides a salient precedent for solution of similar problems at the macro-social level.

Of course, the solution can work only if the sense of advantage is widely shared in the community; that is, only if a sense of 'common interest' develops (see below, 4.1). But the capacity of the human mind to reflect and enhance the beliefs, intentions, and sentiments of others, which is the underlying force of human sociality, makes possible the development and reinforcement of just that sort of mutually referential belief and intention. This does not make the achievement of co-ordination through agreement upon a set of conventional rules of justice inevitable, but it does provide a crucial element without which agreement could never be achieved.

3.3   THE TASK OF JUSTICE

[T]he convention for the distinction of property, and for the stability of possession, is of all circumstances the most necessary to the establishment of human society . . .

Hume, *Treatise.*

Material conditions of social life and the task of justice

In order rightly to understand Hume's view of the distinctive task of justice, and his reasons for identifying justice with the laws of property (and contract), we need to distinguish Hume's generic account of the task of justice from his specific interpretation of that

---

[42] *Treatise* 486, 489, 492–3; *Enquiry II* 192.

generic task. In its most *generic* form, the task of justice is to establish and preserve the most basic conditions of social life. It guarantees peace, order, and stability, and defines the framework within which mutually supportive and productive co-operation becomes possible (*Treatise* 485). By 'establishing a good correspondence among men' (*Treatise* 526), justice makes possible the intercourse and social condition of human beings (*Enquiry II* 186). Thus, all social interaction (beyond the immediate family) depends on the framework of justice.

But in Hume's view, the social fundament is material, that is, economic.[43] More precisely, Hume's substantive view is that social order and stability, and thus the possibility of all social intercourse, rest on the foundation of stable possession of material goods. As 'the principal disturbance in society arises from those goods, which we call external, and from their looseness and easy transition from one person to another . . . the stability of possession, is of all circumstances the most necessary to the establishment of human society' (*Treatise* 489, 491). Thus the *specific* task of the convention of justice is to partition existing and future material goods among members of the community and to determine appropriate conditions of acquisition, use, and transfer.

To this extent, then, Hume identifies justice with rules defining property. However, although rules for possession and use of material goods are fundamental for Hume, it would be a mistake to regard justice as solely concerned with property thus narrowly construed. It is the social role of property to underwrite and structure all social relations, positions, and conditions. Given this social function of property, justice must be construed more broadly to embrace all basic social relations. Rules of property encompass more than merely the proper methods of acquisition, possession, and conveyance of land, moveables, or other valuables in a society. At bottom, property rights are personal rights. They define a broad set of relations between man and man, between man and woman and child, and between individuals and their society. Justice, so understood, defines a *social* constitution, the 'fundamental law' of a society.[44] Viewing property in this way Hume simply reflects the dominant Common Law view. Feudal law, and the modern Com-

---

[43] *Treatise* 486; *Enquiry II* 183–92. See Forbes, 86 ff.

[44] It is clear that the 'fundamental law' Hume speaks of at *Treatise* 561 is not restricted to matters of the political constitution. Hume says there are no predeter-

mon Law which developed out of it and which structured British society, was in origin and basic outline a law of property.

But what reason does Hume have for assigning this fundamental social role to property? Are not rules prohibiting and punishing violence to the person at least as important for social order and stability? Don't we fear as much (even more) for our lives as for our possessions when ordinary social controls break down?[45] In jurisprudential terms: is not the penal law at least as fundamental as the civil law?

On the social priority of property Hume is very clear. The 'convention for the distinction of property, and for the stability of possession, is of all circumstances the most necessary to the establishment of human society . . .'. Once it is established, 'there remains little or nothing to be done towards settling a perfect harmony and concord' (*Treatise* 491). Rules defining crimes and punishing violence to the person may still be needed to some extent, but only as auxiliaries. The primary task of social ordering is performed by rules of property.

Hume's explicit argument for this view is not very convincing. He distinguishes three different species of goods which the interested passions seek: internal satisfaction of our minds, external advantages of our bodies, and the enjoyment of material goods. But we cannot be deprived of the first, Hume maintains, and the second 'may be ravish'd from us' but doing so is of no advantage to the person who so deprives us. It is only in possession of our material goods, then, that we are exposed to significant violence at the hands of others (*Treatise* 487–8).

But surely this argument rests on a false premiss. Although the advantage gained by our attacker *may* not equal the suffering we experience as victims, and what the attacker gains is somewhat altered in the transfer, nevertheless, it surely does not follow that there is no advantage or gain for the attacker. For example, enslavement and other forms of coerced labour may yield great gains and little or no 'alteration' and 'loss' in the sense Hume has in mind. Similarly, there may be considerable gain in killing another, or

mined limits to what might be included in a society's view of its fundamental law. The notion of fundamental law then is that of the basic structuring law of a society. Hume's treatment of the political constitution is self-consciously patterned after his account of property; see *Treatise* 555–6.

[45] See J. Harrison, *Hume's Theory of Justice*, 42, 60.

physically disabling him, in order to eliminate him from competition.[46] (Whereas Hobbes always had a sharp sense of this nastier side of human nature, Hume seems to refuse to recognize it.)

However, there is a somewhat more plausible argument implicit in these remarks. In Hume's view, the directly anti-social passions, e.g. malice, are not very strong in human nature and 'tho' pernicious, they operate only by intervals' (*Treatise* 491). So, very seldom will sheer malicious pleasure motivate such violence. Furthermore, although selfishness, and the interested passions generally, are more powerful (perhaps even dominant) in human nature, they are socially destructive only when material survival is uncertain, Hume claims. It is the threat to the basic conditions of human life itself that makes the radical insecurity of the state of nature so savage and fearsome. But once material conditions are stabilized, survival is assured, and the foundations of material improvement laid, Hume believes, there is little occasion for socially destructive behaviour.[47] Each person comes to realize that socially destructive, selfish behaviour makes the agent unfit for society in the eyes of the community, and so is directly and radically self-defeating (*Treatise* 492, *Enquiry II* 283). Competitive urges can then be directed into socially beneficial channels and even vanity can be 'esteem'd a social passion, and a bond of union among men' (*Treatise* 491).

As we saw in 3.1, Hume was clearly aware of the limits of the self-enforcing capabilities of such arrangements. But this should not obscure the fact that, for Hume, the functionally basic task of law is that of establishing the rules of property and with them the basic framework of social relations in the community. This is not a

---

[46] Annette Baier pointed out the possibility to me.

[47] Hume seems to share a view here with Bentham (see below, 11.3) and many other writers of the century that the main cause of competition, conflict, violence, and, more generally, of narrow self-preference lies in material scarcity, and that a more refined nature and a spirit of co-operation is ushered in by civilized commercial culture. Ferguson, however, correctly points out that the opposite is often the case. 'Men are so far from valuing society on account of its mere external conveniences, that they are commonly most attached where those conveniences are least frequent . . . Affection operates with the greatest force, where it meets with the greatest difficulties . . . [But] in a commercial state . . . man is sometimes found a detached and a solitary being: he has found an object which sets him in competition with his fellow-creatures, and he deals with them as he does with his cattle and his soil, for the sake of the profits they bring. The mighty engine which we suppose to have formed society, only tends to set its members at variance' (*Essay* Pt. I, Sect. iii).

matter of establishing institutions for the regulation of behaviour; rather, the job of the rules of justice is *to constitute a people*, to make a community out of an aggregate of socially inclined but ununified individuals. The call for enforcement only comes at a later stage of social development when the self-enforcing capabilities of the union are overtaxed. And at that point coercive enforcement of the rules is needed, not to define the obligations or to create the primary reasons for conforming to them, but to underwrite independently grounded obligations.

Moreover, for Hume, the first thing needed to constitute a people is the definition of *property* rights, not the definition of offences against the person. Murder, he says is impossible 'without statutes, and maxims, and *an idea of justice and honour*' (*Enquiry II* 210–11, emphasis added). The point, I think, is not (just) that an action can be, legally speaking, a murder only if there are legal rules defining the offence, and the action falls within the scope of the rules. Rather, it is that a collective programme to combat violence to the person is impossible unless the collective body, the community, is constituted. Such an effort calls for co-ordination, not only in prosecution of the crime, but also in identifying the action as a crime. (There can be as much discord regarding what counts as unjustified violence against the person, as there can about what counts as one's property.) But such co-ordination is possible only after the basic constitutive relations among persons in the group are defined. This is a task, in Hume's view, only for laws of justice, that is, for laws of property.

Justice and rules

The sole contribution of justice to public, as well as private, good lies in guaranteeing the stability of possession. And stability is achieved only by restraining human partiality and avidity by general and inflexible rules, says Hume. Property must be stable, and must be fixed by general rules, he insists (*Treatise* 497).

Yet, Hume admits, the connection between justice and utility (both public and private) is 'somewhat singular' (ibid.). Sometimes it takes great penetration and experience to see the utility of inflexible adherence to the rules of justice (*Essays* 116–17). For, although the rules are adopted to serve this end, 'it is impossible for them to prevent all particular hardships, or make beneficial consequences result from every individual case' (*Enquiry II* 305). In fact, justice may well call for actions which are contrary not only to private interests, but also to the public interest (*Treatise* 497, 532).

The singularity of the relation between public utility and the virtue of justice is due to the close link between justice and rules. We should note five related properties of justice.

1. Justice is not concerned merely with any single type of action that might be captured under a single rule or principle. It is concerned, rather, with a *scheme* or *system* of rules, and thus with a complex set of interlocking actions, among individuals (*Treatise* 497). The benefit arises not from each individual act regarded apart from the system, but rather 'from the whole scheme or system concurred in by the whole, or the greater part of the society' (*Enquiry II* 304).

2. The rules of justice must be predetermined. Possession is not to be decided case by case according to what the utilities of the particular case seem to dictate, for case by case determination according to utility can only increase uncertainty. (As we shall see shortly, such case by case determination according to utility may not even be possible.) Predetermined patterns, on the other hand, are certain and reliable.

3. The rules must be quite general in scope. Again, to maximize certainty, the rules must be insensitive to widely varying circumstances of social life.

All the laws of nature, which regulate property, as well as all civil laws, are general, and regard alone some essential circumstances of the case, without taking into consideration the characters, situations, and connexions of the person concerned, or any particular consequences which may result from the determination of these laws in any particular case which offers (*Enquiry II* 305).

4. Similarly, they must be rigidly and inflexibly applied. The 'laws of justice [are] perfectly inflexible' (*Treatise* 532), for flexibility would undermine the certainty which is their *raison d'être* (*Treatise* 502). One might say that the special value of justice, for Hume, lies precisely in the *insensitivity* of rules to the demands of utility in particular circumstances. This is not to say that exceptions to the rules may never be found, but, unless justice itself has in the circumstances become pointless,[48] the exceptions are allowed only

---

[48] At *Essays* 474–5 Hume criticizes the Tory doctrine of passive obedience, arguing that there are times when violation of the general rule of allegiance is justifiable. But the cases which he mentions are extreme, e.g. where the institutions of govern-

when they can be formulated in general terms and appropriately fitted into the scheme of rules (*Treatise* 551). Thus, Hume leaves no room, at this level in any case, for the traditional Aristotelian doctrine of equity, i.e. the notion of reason correcting the injustice of the application of the rule in the particular case while recognizing and affirming the justice of the general rule.

5. Finally, the rules of justice must be public, a matter of common knowledge. For stability comes not only from knowing what one must do, but also from the firm assurance that one can count on others doing their part in the co-operative scheme, the success of which depends on each doing his or her part (*Treatise* 489).

Thus, although from the restricted perspective of a particular action and its apparent utility or disutility justice may seem pernicious—opposed to the good of the individual and society alike—Hume is confident that, from a more enlarged view (*Enquiry II* 305), 'this momentary ill is amply compensated by the steady prosecution of the rule' (*Treatise* 497). I will consider below (4.3) whether there are adequate grounds for this confidence.

Justice and utility

Looking back at Hume's argument from the perspective of Bentham's utilitarianism, the connection between justice and public utility which Hume explores is 'somewhat singular' in another respect. If, in the first case, the singularity was due to the special character of the virtue of *justice*, in this case it is due to the nature of *utility* as Hume conceives of it. Bentham complained that Hume's use of the notion of utility was 'altogether vague' (UC xiv. 317; *IPML* I. 1, n.a.), and failed to distinguish various species of public usefulness. To overcome this imprecision and vagueness Bentham proposed a dual refinement of the Humean conception of utility: (i) the terms 'utility' and 'disutility' were tied to concrete, determinate real entities, viz. pleasure and pain (and aggregates of them), and (ii) the utilitarian norm was defined in terms of maximizing the net total utility so understood.

Now, there is no doubt that Hume often uses 'public utility' to mean little more than 'that which is generally useful or beneficial'.

ment and society itself are directly threatened with extinction. In such cases, Hume admits, *fiat justitia ruat coelum* surely is self-defeating. But he is quite willing to sacrifice public good in the name of justice in less extreme and self-defeat-threatening situations.

But Bentham failed to see that, especially in his discussion of justice, Hume used a more sophisticated and precise notion of utility, albeit one which is decidedly not utilitarian.[49] For, whereas a utilitarian of Bentham's stripe would argue for the acceptability of convention on the grounds that its general adoption would maximize net total utility, Hume's argument appeals to a notion of *mutual expected advantage*. On Hume's view, a scheme of rules has public utility if and only if *each party* in the group governed by the scheme may reasonably expect to gain from general compliance with it. For justice is the product of redirected self-interest.[50]

We might note one important consequence of Hume's reliance on this notion of utility for his account of justice. The task of justice, according to Hume, is to minimize, and where necessary to adjudicate, the pervasive conflicts of interest that arise regarding possession of scarce material goods. Now a utilitarian might also recognize the value of a scheme of rules for prior determination of issues of rightful possession, and insist that conflicts arising after the convention is established appeal first to the rules of the convention for resolution. However, the utilitarian has resources within the background theory (i.e. in the principle of utility itself) to adjudicate the dispute between conflicting private interests should the convention prove to be inadequate in some way. That is, the utilitarian conception of public utility provides a determinate (though ideal) decision-procedure for adjudicating conflicts of interest. In this respect the utilitarian approach contrasts sharply with Hume's. In the latter's view, *there is no* ideal rational principle to which parties can appeal for resolution of conflicts of private interest. Resolution is possible only by appeal to the positive rules of the convention, respect for which will be mutually advantageous over the long run. Mutual advantage, then, underwrites the scheme of positive rules, but there is no resolution possible by appeal to that underwriting notion. Public utility attaches only to the scheme of rules, and the latter alone provides the basis for resolution of conflicts of private interest. Utility, on Hume's understanding, like

---

[49] See Hart, 'Introduction' to Bentham's *IPML* (1982), pp. xlii–xliii; K. Haakonssen, *The Science of a Legislator*, 40; Miller, *Philosophy and Ideology*, 74–5.

[50] D. Gauthier, 'David Hume, Contractarian', 17. Textual evidence for this interpretation of Hume's notion of utility is offered in sect. IV of Gauthier's paper. For reasons to resist Gauthier's classification of Hume as a contractarian, see Baier, 'Truth and Superstition', n. 15.

many of the requirements of justice and right for Aquinas (see above, 2.1), presupposes co-operative acceptance of and actions on common public standards.

Thus far justice has been characterized only in broadly formal terms, but it would be a mistake to think that justice, according to Hume, is a purely formal notion, the virtue of 'rule-abidingness'.[51] Justice is a substantive moral virtue, for Hume, but it does not presuppose a set of ideal principles or rational norms ('natural laws') which can be identified, even in outline, apart from the practices and rules of a particular community. Rather, it is only '[a]fter this convention, concerning abstinence from the possessions of others, is enter'd into, and every one has acquir'd a stability in his possessions' that the ideas of justice and injustice arise. 'The latter are altogether unintelligible without first understanding the former' (*Treatise* 490). Justice *conceptually presupposes* a convention established in and generally accepted by the community. It is time now for us to explore Hume's reasons for thinking this and for thinking that such a convention could arise amongst self-seeking individuals in a 'state of nature'.

[51] Harrison, 29–30.

4

Hume's Jurisprudence: Common Law Conventionalism

'Tis interest which gives the general instinct: but 'tis custom which gives the particular direction.

Hume, Treatise.

JUSTICE is addressed to the problems arising from the inevitable interdependence of human social behaviour. The sole virtue of justice lies in co-ordinating this social interaction. Its necessity lies in the disastrous consequences of failure to co-ordinate it. The special genius of Hume's account of justice lies in his realization of the fact that in this necessity, and the strategic interdependence of social behaviour, also lies the possibility of success.

The problem, as Hume sees it, is to explain how, from the interested passions alone, general concurrence in a scheme of rules for mutual benefit might arise. Hume's explanation involves giving an account of the strategic situation facing each of the parties in the group and a description of the processes of self-adjustment of belief, intention, and sentiment which result from recognition of this situation. Hume's argument proceeds in two stages (although his discussion obscures this fact): in the first he explains the emergence of a sense of common interest (4.1 below); in the second he explains how this convention is made specific (4.2 below).

4.1 THE ORIGIN OF JUSTICE: STRUCTURE OF THE ARGUMENT

When this common sense of interest is mutually express'd, and is known to both, it produces a suitable resolution and behaviour.

Hume, Treatise.

The emergence of a sense of common interest

A sense of common interest arises out of a gradual appreciation by members of a group of the situation facing them, and the adjust-

ment of belief and intention that result from this appreciation.[1] The
process begins with the alteration of certain beliefs regarding
private interest and advantage.

When therefore men have had experience enough to observe, that whatever
may be the consequence of any single act of justice, perform'd by a single
person, yet the whole system of actions concurr'd in by the whole society, is
infinitely advantageous to the whole, and to every part; it is not long before
justice and property take place (*Treatise* 497–8).

'Upon the least reflection' (*Treatise* 492) one sees the advantage of
restraint on the pursuit of one's interest. And with but a little more
thought one will come to see that this is true of others as well. One
is then inclined to express this to others and the generalized belief is
confirmed and deepened ('reverberated') through recognition of
other parties' expressions of the same thought. Thus, what 'each
man feels in his own breast' he also 'remarks in his fellows'
(*Enquiry II* 306). And from individual reflection on private advantage comes a shared, reciprocally expressed, sense of common interest in a general scheme of mutual restraint.

This leads naturally to the next and crucial stage: the adjustment
of intentions.

I observe, that it will be for my interest to leave another in the possession of
his goods, *provided* he will act in the same manner with regard to me. He is
sensible of a like interest in the regulation of his conduct . . . Every member
of society is sensible of this interest: Every one expresses this sense to his
fellows, along with the resolution he has taken of squaring his actions by it,
on condition that others will do the same (*Treatise* 490, 498, author's
emphasis).

On reflection one recognizes that mutual advantage is possible only
if there is concurrence in a general scheme, and on this basis one expresses and recognizes in others, a willingness to participate in such
a scheme. This resolve is not solitary—the intentions are mutually
referential and mutually dependent (a second 'reverberation').
'When this common sense of interest is mutually express'd, and is
known to both, it produces a suitable resolution *and behaviour*'
(*Treatise* 490, emphasis added).

---

[1] For the discussion which follows I learned a great deal from A. Baier's 'Hume
on Fixing and Adjusting'.

An apparent gap in Hume's argument

The conclusion Hume draws here—that from mutual expression of *willingness* to participate in a co-operative scheme there follows immediately *behaviour* in accord with such a scheme—moves too quickly. Up to this point Hume has offered an acute analysis of the strategic situation facing individuals in a hypothetical state of nature. This, however, would not automatically issue in action on the part of any individual, for co-ordination of the actions of the parties depends on there *being* already in existence a general scheme of action on which the mutually interdependent expectations can focus. Each has resolved to participate, conditional on participation of the others, in a general scheme *should* one exist. But we have not yet been given any reason to think one does exist. Hume gives us a classic description of a 'co-ordination problem'.[2] Conventions—actual regularities of behaviour, patterns of co-ordinated, interdependent actions, arising within this kind of strategic situation—are *solutions* to such problems. In the circumstances Hume describes, and given what is at stake if co-ordination were to fail, almost any regularity will do if there is general concurrence in it. But there must be such a scheme already in practice, or co-ordination may not be achieved.

This problem is masked by the ambiguity of Hume's description of the mutually referential intentions which the parties form.[3] In some places Hume describes them as conditional intentions formulated prior to action, where the antecedent of the conditional ('provided others concur in the scheme') must be satisfied (or one must be reasonably assured of its satisfaction) before one undertakes the action. 'Every one', Hume says, 'expresses this sense to his fellows, along with the resolution he has taken of squaring his actions by it, on condition that others will do the same' (*Treatise* 498). Whereas, in other passages he describes them as complex intentions-in-action, which are not conditional, but rather involve suppositions or expectations as to the behaviour of others. For example, at *Treatise* 490 he says, 'the actions of each of us have a reference to those of the other, and are perform'd upon the supposition, that something is to be perform'd on the other part'.

[2] See E. Ullmann-Margalit, *The Emergence of Norms*, ch. 3, drawing on the ground-breaking work by T. Schelling, *The Strategy of Conflict*. See also D. Lewis, *Convention*.

[3] Baier, 'Hume on Fixing and Adjusting', 23–5.

How can Hume bridge this gap? Hume might have assumed that the circumstances in which the parties find themselves would be such that conditional intentions automatically resolve themselves into choice and action. This may be what Hume has in mind when he says that once the mutually referential intentions are formed, 'No more is requisite to induce any one of them to perform an act of justice, who has the first opportunity' (*Treatise* 498). But what would the circumstances have to be like for this automatic resolution to occur?

To answer this question we should note first that there is a concrete, practical difference between the two kinds of intentions mentioned above *only if* there is some degree of uncertainty felt by any of the parties regarding the decisions and actions of others in the group. Assuming for present purposes that the parties are perfectly rational and fully understand their strategic situation, this uncertainty will be due only to ambiguity in the strategic environment of the parties. Ambiguity obtains if and only if it is commonly known that there are at least two available general patterns of actions which would successfully co-ordinate the behaviour of the parties. Now, it is usually stipulated that a 'proper' co-ordination problem has the property of ambiguity, but one can easily see that a degenerate (because 'unproblematic') co-ordination problem is one in which there is available only *one possible* pattern of actions which would successfully co-ordinate the behaviour of the parties. For example, only one pattern of actions for the members of the group might be physically or psychologically possible, or, given their available knowledge, conceivable. Stated more generally, a situation lacking ambiguity would be one in which no member of the group would seriously disprefer general conformity to a particular regularity of behaviour, call it R, to general conformity to any other conceivable regularity, R*, if that member could unilaterally bring about general conformity to R*.[4] If, following Hume's lead, we may refer to regularities which provide solutions to co-ordination problems as 'conventions', then we might call the convention achieved in this degenerate case a *dominant* convention,[5] because the choice of the pattern is dominant from the point

---

[4] The important criticisms by M. Gilbert ('Game Theory and *Convention*') of Lewis's 'non-triviality' condition are avoided here because the notion of *ambiguity* does not depend directly on the technical, game-theoretic definition of co-ordination-equilibria.   [5] Gauthier, 'David Hume, Contractarian', 7–8.

of view of each party. Now, if there were a dominant choice available in the strategic environment Hume describes, then the conditional intentions would nearly automatically (by a very small, and rationally dictated, step) be transformed into intentions-in-action. A dominant convention would result.

However, it is important to distinguish dominant conventions from *stable* conventions. A convention is stable if and only if conformity to a particular regularity is not strongly dispreferred to non-conformity, *given* general conformity to that regularity.[6] A stable convention is self-perpetuating. But, as one can see from the definition, stability is a property of *established* conventions. They presuppose common knowledge of general concurrence in the established regularity.

Now, we might ask, could it be that the convention of justice that is straightaway produced, as Hume claims, is a dominant convention? This could be so only if one of two conditions obtained. Either he believed that there is no ambiguity (in the special sense defined above) in the strategic situation facing the parties, or he has confused dominance with stability. The former is surely not consistent with Hume's view of the situation, for Hume is keen to stress the radical ambiguity in the strategic situation.[7] And the latter explanation is only slightly more plausible. For although it is easy to confuse stability with dominance, it is clear that Hume does not regard the conventions of justice as inherently stable. The rationale for establishing magistrates and the apparatus of government rests on the assumption of the inevitable instability of conventions of justice (*Treatise* 534–8). Furthermore, an explanation which does not attribute a major confusion to Hume is preferable, if one is available. I believe there is.

Shifting perspectives on the 'agreement'

We can understand Hume's discussion of the reciprocal intentions comprising the sense of common interest in a quite different way, one which sheds light on some otherwise puzzling aspects of Hume's argument for justice. The ambiguity in Hume's description of reciprocal intentions may be due to the fact that Hume shifts

---

6 Ibid. 8.

7 *Treatise* 506–7 n. See also *Treatise* 488 where Hume seems to follow Hobbes (in *Leviathan* 120: 'But whatsoever is the object of any mans Appetite or Desire; that is it which he for his part calleth *Good*'). The argument of *Treatise* III, ii, iii clearly rests on the assumption of radical ambiguity, see below, 4.2.

back and forth without warning between two different perspectives on the 'agreement' which constitutes the convention of justice. *Both* of these perspectives, I shall argue, are important for the success of Hume's argument.

First, one might regard Hume's argument thus far as a hypothetical and schematic reconstruction of how conventions regarding property (timelessly) arise. From this perspective, the advantage of the convention is viewed *prospectively*—great benefit is seen for each party, and for all, *if* a scheme can be found. Thus, from this perspective, the conditional intentions are yet to be focused on a single pattern of behaviour. If the condition of ambiguity in the strategic situation obtains, then there is, strictly speaking, a gap in Hume's argument between the formation of the conditional intentions in the sense of common interest and the establishment of the convention of justice. But this gap is not long left unbridged. Hume merely plays it down at this point in his exposition. He suggests that the step left to be taken is a small one to which the contribution of reasoning and calculation will be slight. Once the conditional intentions are formed, he says, the sense of common interest carries one, in concurrence with others, into the general plan (*Enquiry II* 306). The process, by which the parties are thus carried, of course, is yet to be specified. This is the topic of the next section of the *Treatise* (III, ii, iii). Thus, what appears in the section presently under consideration (*Treatise* III, ii, ii) is not an unbridged gap in Hume's argument, but a somewhat telescoped argument, to which he returns later.

This first suggested reading of Hume's argument takes the mutually referential intentions of the parties to be conditional intentions. But it is possible to define a different perspective on the agreement by focusing on the mutually referential intentions-in-action, i.e. those intentions arising in the actions themselves which rest on suppositions of conforming behaviour on the part of other members of the group. Hume seems to rely on the fact that we learn the advantages of justice from reflection on our *experience* of acts of justice and injustice, i.e. experience of acts of conforming to an established general pattern of restraint (*Treatise* 498, 490). Perhaps, Hume is not begging the question of how the convention is in fact established, but rather taking a *retrospective* view of established patterns of social interaction, not being concerned for the time being with how they might be achieved in the first instance.

Such a retrospective view is not concerned with the creation or explicit *construction* of conventions of justice, but with setting out the reasons which *now* exist for continued *compliance* with them. So it is in reflection on a scheme already in existence—reflection to which Hume invites us—that we see its incomparable advantages. What gives us reason to act according to an established convention or custom is that doing one's part according to the scheme reinforces by example a practice which in fact solves the co-ordination problem (a set of such problems) the group faces.

To make this argument work Hume does not need to assume that the conditions of 'dominance' obtain in the strategic situation, but only the conditions of (relative) 'stability'. That is, Hume does not need to assume that the existing pattern is one which each individual in the group would choose as the pattern in which all concur if he or she were able to choose for the group. He need only assume that each clearly prefers general conformity to the pattern to general nonconformity. The existing pattern (however it evolved) may be regarded as a solution to a *genuine* co-ordination problem characterized not only by interdependence and a shared preference for co-operation over failure of co-operation, but also by genuine ambiguity (if we ignore the fact of general concurrence).

Thus, Hume argues that reflection on the experience of the instability caused by injustice—disconformity with the existing pattern—leads one to see the advantages of co-operation and conformity. This leads one to form a resolution not only to conform *if* others do, but to conform *on the supposition* and *expectation* that they *do and will*. And in a Humean community this supposition is simply, we might say, a matter of common sense. For the *common interest* one notices is apparent in the common situation which all face. And from long experience of 'commerce' and 'conversation' in the community one knows that when one recognizes this common interest in one's own breast, one thereby also remarks it in one's fellows (*Enquiry II* 306). The convention, and the sense of common interest on which it rests, are 'prepossessions'—part of the common world.

It is now clear why Hume insists that this convention is not a promise or contract or product of consent (*Treatise* 490; *Enquiry II* 306). What Cavell says of Wittgenstein's notion of 'agreement in judgments' is equally applicable to the sort of 'agreement' involved in Humean conventions: 'the idea of agreement here is not that of coming to or arriving at an agreement on a given occasion, but of be-

ing in agreement throughout, being in harmony like pitches or tones
... [being] mutually *attuned* from top to bottom'.[8]

We have, then, two different understandings of Hume's argument. But these readings are not incompatible. They sketch out not two different arguments, but rather two perspectives on the same argument.[9] The prospective point of view is strictly analytical, setting out the structural features of the strategic situation, and to that extent it is abstracted from concrete historical factors; whereas the retrospective argument takes the point of view of a concrete individual in historical circumstances. Moreover, the retrospective argument presupposes the analytical structure of the prospective. The reason why following the established practice carries with it the advantage of public and individual utility has little or nothing to do with the intrinsic merits of that particular scheme of rules. The reason lies solely in the fact that *it exists*, and since it is already in existence and a matter of public knowledge *it works*, i.e. it solves the co-ordination problem the group faces. Thus, neither the intrinsic merits, nor the historical origin of the pattern are relevant to accounting *now*, retrospectively, for the rational appeal of conformity to that particular pattern. The mere fact that it exists, i.e. that it is an established pattern which focuses concretely the expectations of all the parties involved, when understood against the background of the general argument for the necessity of a general scheme, is sufficient to explain its rational force. The retrospective argument is persuasive because it is a special instance of the analytical structure of the prospective argument. In this respect Hume's account of justice is a sophisticated generalization of Common Law conventionalism (see 2.3).

Historical evolution of the convention

We have not yet done justice to Hume's argument, however, for he, like the Common Law jurists, was keen to emphasize the historical evolution of the convention of justice. This convention (like conventions of language and measures of exchange), 'arises gradually, and acquires force by a slow progression, and by our repeated experience of the inconveniences of transgressing it' (*Treatise* 490). The reflections involved in the emergence of the sense of common interest are

---

[8] S. Cavell, *The Claim of Reason*, 32.
[9] That Hume wishes to embrace both perspectives is clear from *Treatise* 490, 498, 503.

not formed at once, but 'in fact arise insensibly and by degrees' (*Treatise* 503).

This, however, is not incompatible with the portrait of Hume's argument I have sketched above. It adds important historical detail, helping to explain the *existence* of the established pattern of interaction presupposed by the retrospective argument.

The process of evolution Hume hints at here is a complex mix of spontaneous and undeliberate co-operative action, retrospective reflection, prospective deliberation and design, all iterated many times over through a long period of time and involving several generations, with the result, perhaps not fully intended, of establishing a community-wide practice. Imagine small groups of individuals—for example, families or groups of close friends—which encounter problems co-ordinating their interaction (respecting possession of material goods). Perhaps without anyone fully realizing that they face a particular problem, and without their deliberating about possible solutions, there emerges spontaneously a pattern of co-operative action. In such a case, individual intentions will fit together into a scheme or system, but they will emerge in the action, rather than *prior to it.*[10] The advantage of this pattern might then be acknowledged, retrospectively, and perhaps conditional intentions actually formed. As the range of social interaction expands, individual members of the larger groups, again facing similar problems of co-ordination, build on this experience. Solutions in microsocial situations yield 'precedents' for solutions to problems of macro-social interaction. In some cases, even in larger groups, a pattern might emerge spontaneously or 'by accident'. Or, if the strategic conditions are favourable, and there already exists a tightly integrated network of mutually referential conditional intentions, it may be enough for an individual, through unilateral action, to initiate a new pattern.[11]

Thus, Hume suggests, from a combination of a large number of such smaller interactions there could arise a community-wide scheme. Although the scheme is 'artificial' and in one sense 'constructed', i.e. evolving from reason, reflection, and design, it may not have been the product of any single design, the object of any

[10] Baier, 'Hume on Fixing and Adjusting', 24.

[11] This is a clear case in which 'No more is requisite to induce any one of them [the members of the group] to perform an act of justice, who has the first opportunity', which act 'becomes an example to others' (*Treatise* 498).

collective decision or action. Indeed, Hume thinks this would be very unlikely.[12] (Hume would have agreed fully with Ferguson when he wrote that it is precisely due to the fact that 'men, in general, are essentially disposed to occupy themselves in forming projects and schemes' that social institutions and the progress of civilization are not products of any single project or scheme.[13]) However, the rational force of the demand for conformity does depend on each person's taking a view of the whole scheme; for it is only on the general view that the advantages of conformity to the practice will emerge.[14]

For if it be allowed (what is, indeed, evident) that the particular consequences of a particular act of justice may be hurtful to the public as well as to individuals; it follows that every man, in embracing that virtue, must have an eye to the whole plan or system, and must expect the concurrence of his fellows in the same conduct and behaviour (*Enquiry II* 306).

Thus, the explanation of the existence of the scheme is entirely dependent on the history of its evolution. However, the history alone does not yield the *rationale* for the scheme; for that, both history and the analytic structure, which requires a synoptic eye, are essential.

The tension here between Hume's emphasis on the *historical* nature of the constitutive institutions of society, on the one hand, and his use of an *ahistorical*, analytical device to describe the dynamics of that development, on the other hand, echoes a tension

---

12 In the *History*, Hume takes pains to point out 'the great mixture of accident, which commonly concurs with a small ingredient of wisdom and foresight, in erecting the complicated fabric of the most perfect government' (II, 525). See also *History* IV, 368. Cf. R. Hardin, *Collective Action*: 'In the static analysis of choice, one simply checks the costs and benefits of alternative actions and then determines which action is best. In the dynamic analysis, the fundamental problem often is to explain how the costs and benefits have come to be what they are. For this reason, to see that a convention "works" and to understand how it is maintained may be easy. To explain how it arose may be beyond our capacity, because it may have arisen out of a series of accidental choices, insights, and interactions too numerous for anyone to know, and mostly unpredictable even though each seems explicable in hindsight' (190–1).

13 Ferguson, *Essay* Pt. III. sect. ii.

14 In this respect, Hume differs from the earlier social contract tradition represented by Grotius and Pufendorf. Hume appears more 'rationalist' than the social contract tradition he criticizes for this very fault. See Forbes, 28. 'Reason', in the extended sense in which Hume sometimes uses the term, is, he says, 'nothing but a general and a calm passion, which takes a comprehensive and a distant view of its object' (*Dissertation* 161).

we sensed earlier between the doctrine of the essentially social nature of human beings and Hume's use of the device of the fictitious state of nature and its assumption of pre-social individuals. This tension is real, but it yields no paradox or contradictions for Hume. It represents two sides of the same reality which Hume sought to explore. Neither can be jettisoned without distortion.

4.2 THE ORIGIN OF JUSTICE: DEFINING THE RULES

Habits, more than reason, we find in everything to be the governing principle of mankind.

Hume, *History.*

Hume's analytic strategy

Having discussed the origin of justice, Hume turns in the *Treatise* to consider the 'rules which determine property' (*Treatise* III, ii, iii). Some readers have thought this signals a shift in Hume's discussion from an attempt to *justify* (to show reasonable) the artifice of justice (property) to an attempt to give an empirical and historical *explanation* of the specific rules of property which we find in most civilized legal systems.[15] Indeed, a central theme of this section of the *Treaise* is that for most of the positive rules of property known to Roman and Scots Law no specific rational warrant can be found. The principles of first possession, prescription, accession, or succession can be traced only to the operation of human 'imagination' and 'fancy'. 'What possessions are assigned to particular persons; this is . . . often determined by very frivolous views and considerations' (*Enquiry II* 309 n.).

But this reading of Hume's intentions at this point in the argument is mistaken. Hume makes very clear his objective at the outset of the section (*Treatise* 503). Recognizing that there is a historical story to tell about the birth and maturing of each of the components of the convention of justice in particular communities, he nevertheless adopts for his purposes in the ensuing discussion the fiction of a group of people convening to determine *de novo* the rules of their institution of property. That is, Hume here explicitly takes up the prospective, analytic perspective on the argument for justice we noted above. The fiction of a people emerging from a state of nature makes this analytic argument possible. As we have

15 J. Harrison, *Hume's Theory of Justice*, 86.

seen, this is not meant to supplant the historical explanation which might be given for the rules of property. Rather, the analytical discussion is needed to clarify the necessary structure of that development, to bring to light the dynamic forces which drive it, and to connect it with the general rationale he has already outlined.

Hume, then, seeks a *justification* of the rules of property, not merely a historical explanation; or rather, he seeks an explanation which reveals the rationality of the concrete, historically evolved institutions of property with which we are familiar. This is not to say that Hume believes that the specific principles of property with which we are familiar are themselves capable of rational defence apart from the historical circumstances of their evolution. In fact, we shall see that Hume's argument relies heavily on the claim that they cannot be given independent rational defence. Though they are 'without sufficient reason', the principles 'justly become sufficient reason[s]' for conforming to a certain pattern of social behaviour. Hume's strategy is to set out a justification for *following* certain rules, a key component of which is the difficulty of providing a rational justification of the rules *themselves*. Thus, Hume develops one important theme running through Hale's 'conventionalist' defence of Common Law (see 2.3).

It is important to keep in mind, that although the present discussion represents the second stage in Hume's account of the origin of justice, we are not concerned with a *second convention* which parties in the hypothetical state of nature must agree upon. Rather, we are invited to consider the *same* convention more concretely described.

In this connection it is instructive to note that Hume's account of the origin of government exactly parallels his account of property. First he sets out the grounds for the convention establishing government, then in a subsequent section he raises the question how the government is actually constituted (to whom is allegiance owed?). And there he explicitly states that 'the same convention, which establishes government, will also determine the persons who are to govern, and will remove all doubt and ambiguity in this particular. . . . The same promise, then, which binds them to obedience, ties them down to a particular person' (*Treatise* 554). This is equally true of the convention of property. Although Hume sometimes calls the framework of expressed reciprocal intentions (the birth of which we witnessed earlier) a 'general convention', nevertheless, strictly speaking (from the analytic perspective here adopted) the convention does not exist. There simply is *no* agreement until there is agreement *on specific rules* which solve the co-ordination problem facing the parties in the state of nature. The sense of common interest, even agreement upon the general principle that possession must be stable, 'can never serve to any purpose, while it remains in such general terms' (*Treatise* 502–3). We need agreement upon, and general concurrence with, particular rules distinguishing *mine* from *thine*.

If this is so, why does Hume sharply distinguish the two stages of his analysis? He does it, I believe, to point up his conviction that the utility, both public and private, of a scheme of rules of property depends almost entirely on there being general concurrence in *some scheme or other*, and not on the details of the scheme itself.[16]

That *there be* a separation of distinction of possessions, and that this separation be *steady and constant*; this is absolutely required by the interests of society, and hence the origin of justice and property. What possessions are assigned to particular persons; this is, generally speaking, pretty indifferent; and is often determined by very frivolous views and considerations (*Enquiry II* 309 n., emphasis added).

The guiding theme of Hume's entire argument for property, as for government, is that it is 'interest which gives the general instinct; but 'tis custom which gives the particular direction' (*Treatise* 556).

Imagination fixing the rules of justice

There is an interesting similarity at this point between Hume's strategy and that of Hobbes. For Hobbes, the only escape from the radical uncertainty of standards of social behaviour and the conflict that inevitably followed in train was general agreement upon an all-powerful sovereign, who was empowered to make and enforce social standards. The sovereign will define the standards of justice. In Hobbes's view, reason called for compliance with standards of social behaviour with which others in the community can be counted upon to comply. Given the extreme undesirability of the state of nature, compliance with any set of rules the sovereign creates will be preferable to plunging back into the state of nature.

Thus, Hobbes separates justification of compliance with the law from justification of the laws themselves through the device of a

---

[16] See also Baier, 'Hume on Fixing and Adjusting', 26.

contract establishing the sovereign who is given free rein to legislate. Hume achieves the same objective while regarding the rules themselves as the object of 'agreement'. Hume's theory differs from Hobbes's not only in respect of the sort of 'agreement' involved, but also because Hume succeeds in developing an account of justice (and law) which stresses the 'artificiality' of its principles without making them products of the legislative will of any particular person (or even of any group). Thus, Hume can give an account of justice and law that does not presuppose centralized government as Hobbes's does.

But Hume's account of human nature and his description of the state of nature differ sharply from Hobbes's. What, then accounts for Hume's relative indifference to the content of the rules of property? To answer this question we need to return to the hypothetical scene of the birth of the convention of justice sketched in 4.1.

Upon reflection the parties remarked to themselves and to each other on the need, in the absence of restraints on individual self-aggrandizement, for stable and certain possession of material goods—the only hope for individual survival against the elements, as well as the well-spring of all improvement in human life. This shared conviction produced a shared and mutually expressed willingness to participate in any scheme for stabilizing possession, on the condition that others also participate. This sense of common interest is not just an abstract recognition that such agreement would be a good thing, but a present, genuine, and lively willingness to do one's part in such a scheme. In light of what is at stake, each of the parties is poised on the edge of agreement. But since the willingness is conditional, the agreement will be achieved only if there is a single, commonly acknowledged focus for their agreement.[17]

---

[17] There is an interesting parallel here (though not an exact analogy) to Hobbes's notion that in the state of nature the laws of nature bind only *in foro interno* (that is, in effect, conditional upon assurance that others will also comply with them). The important difference between these notions is that, whereas for Hume the lack of assurance is due to uncertainty about which amongst a number of different possible rules others are likely to choose to follow (the problem of ambiguity), for Hobbes there are strong incentives in the situation not to comply with the rules, even when they are clear and unambiguous. Thus, for Hobbes, given the radical instability of any agreement, there is always reason not to comply *in anticipation*, if advantage can thereby be gained. In game-theoretic terms, Hume regards the strategic situation which the parties face as a *co-ordination* problem, while Hobbes sees it as a *prisoner's dilemma* situation.

The reason why agreement is not automatic is that there may be *several* regularities of behaviour for the group which could co-ordinate its efforts. Why not simply choose the optimal one? Because we have no reason to believe that the regularity regarded as optimal by one party is the same as that regarded as optimal by all (or a lion's share) of the other parties. Indeed, experience teaches us, Hume argues, that we can expect there to be almost as many different views of which of the candidates is optimal as there are viable candidates. This is true, in Hume's view, whether we understand 'optimal' in terms of private benefit or usefulness (who can benefit most from the range of material goods available for distribution, *Treatise* 502), public interest (which distribution would benefit most the community as a whole, *Treatise* 555), natural benevolent sentiments (*Treatise* 581–3, 591), individual moral merit or virtue (*Treatise* 502; *Enquiry II* 192–3), or equality (*Enquiry II* 193–4). Indeed, any principle *recommended on its merits* is bound to fail, says Hume.[18] He is confident that any rule 'which, in speculation, may seem the most advantageous to society, may yet be found, in practice, totally pernicious and destructive' (*Enquiry II* 193).

Although his objections to the various substantive proposals he considers vary somewhat in detail, the problems each such proposal faces are reducible to two general heads.[19] (*a*) There is no settled or agreed upon content for the principles. That is, there is agreement

[18] 'If any other rule than established practice be followed, faction and dissention must multiply without end' (*History* IV, 355). A recurring theme of the *History* is the confusion and social disruption caused by appeals to principles which purport to rest for validation not on established practice ('prepossessions') but on independent reason, natural law, or revelation. See *History* III, 210–12; IV, 354–5; v, 94–6, 544–5; *Essays* 487–8, 499–500, 573–4.

[19] This is true for public utility as well as the other principles Hume mentions, despite some of the language of *Enquiry II*. *Enquiry II* 195–6 clearly recognizes the limits of public utility in this respect. Also, in the *Treatise* Hume argues, 'The private interest of every one is different; and tho' the public interest in itself be always one and the same, yet it becomes the source of as great dissentions, by reason of the different opinions of particular persons concerning it' (555). The potential for dissensus over utility is due not only to partiality, or to the difficulties of getting unbiased data on individual benefits and losses, or of doing the calculations correctly (problems which worried Bentham later). It is due also to the notion of utility Hume is working with (see above, 3.3). Since utility = mutual expected advantage, and since that can be calculated only upon the assumption that some regularity of behaviour has been achieved, differences among individuals over the common good may arise because people may favour one regularity over another on the implicit assumption that agreement on the regularity had been (or could easily be) achieved.

on the truth or validity of the principle only if it is virtually emptied of all content. But it is useless at the abstract level, and to make the principle any more concrete invites an indefinite number of different and conflicting interpretations.[20] So either the principle is useless (as a solution to the problem the parties face, it represents only a lateral move at the same level of generality), or it produces 'an infinite confusion in human society' (*Treatise* 532). Alter- — natively, (*b*) the principle requires continual readjustment of the distribution of goods in order to keep the distribution in line with the dictates of the principle. Relative moral merit, ability to benefit from possession, relative quantities of goods possessed—all of these constantly change with the decisions and actions of recipients and the winds of fortune. But rules thus fickle and changing could never produce the stability and constancy which are, in Hume's view, the *raison d'être* of rules of justice.[21] The task of the conventions of justice is 'to cut off all occasions of discord and contention' (*Treatise* 502). These principles, however, invite it.

This radical dissensus regarding all likely candidates for rationally grounded principles of distribution can be traced to what Hume regards as an inescapable fact of human nature: the severe partiality (*Treatise* 488-9, 532) and myopia (*Treatise* 555, 581) of the private perspective of any human individual.[22] And these limits of the private perspective deeply infect an individual's rationality and natural sentiments. However, for Hume, the curse of partiality and myopia can be broken. Salvation for human beings lies in their ability to adjust and redirect their beliefs, sentiments, and judgments to accord with a common, collective perspective.

[E]very particular person's pleasure and interest being different, 'tis impossible men cou'd ever agree in their sentiments and judgments, unless they chose some common point of view, from which they might survey their object, and which might cause it to appear the same to all of them (*Treatise* 591).

[20] Clearly, Hume has in mind familiar appeals to vague and excessively abstract principles of 'natural law' (see *Treatise* 526-7). Recall Hale's 'Reflections', 503 (above, 2.3).

[21] *Treatise* 502, 532-3, 555; *Enquiry II* 194.

[22] By 'private perspective' I mean the perspective (including perceptions, sentiments, interests, and passions) of a person which is in some sense logically prior, in Hume's view, to the common point of view to which human beings adjust their own perspective. (For example, the immediate appearance of distant objects being smaller than objects nearer to us, which appearance is then 'corrected', *Treatise* 603.) It should not be inferred from this that Hume regards 'privacy' as the *natural* condition of human beings.

Social intercourse, commerce between persons, even the most limited and primitive communication between human beings, would not be possible without such adjustment.

But, Hume believes, this common perspective is not a given, a brute natural fact about our world. It is a collective human *achievement*, an 'artifice' if you will, of monumental importance. And its persistence is not guaranteed. On the contrary, Hume seems to think that in some respects our common life and perspective are fragile. Thus, 'fanatics'—those 'sublime theorists', whether religious or political—who threaten the common life with their insistence upon reconstruction of the community on the pattern of some proposed general principle with alleged divine or rational authority, must be regarded as 'common robbers'. Such threats to the commonwealth are justly treated with 'the severest discipline' (*Enquiry II* 193).

Despite the utter failure of reason to solve the problem of co-ordination, hopes for agreement amongst the parties are not dashed. Quite to the contrary, Hume believes success was never more likely. For what reason could never accomplish, 'imagination' and 'fancy' can accomplish without great effort. Here again we see Hume dramatically pointing up the limits of a priori, transcendental (or at least *asocial*) reason, only to make way for the ordinary reasonings of common life. Reason and interest give 'the general instinct' and bring the parties to the brink of agreement, 'but 'tis custom which gives the particular direction' (*Treatise* 556).

Imagination is engaged in the following way. With the parties poised on the edge of agreement, aware of both the ambiguity in the strategic situation and the radical unsuitability of any proposal advanced on its merits, the parties only need something to engage their attention (*Treatise* 505, 512 n.). They need only some salient feature or property of one of the many possible rules which isolates it from the other candidates, which is obvious to each party, and which is known to be obvious to each of them. Successful co-ordination (that is, 'agreement') can be achieved in the type of situation Hume carefully describes if there is one rule or regularity which publicly stands out from the others, and the parties can read the same message in the common situation. The feature which makes a candidate rule salient need not be anything of deep significance. The 'slight connexions', seemingly 'arbitrary and capricious analogies', and 'very frivolous views and considerations', (*Enquiry*

II 195–6, 210, 309), will be sufficient in the circumstances to focus attention, so long as they are 'the most obvious and remarkable' (*Treatise* 508 n.).[23] It is just such salience, he argues, that marks out occupation, prescription, succession, and the other rules of property (and parallel rules regarding political legitimacy) as appropriate 'determinations' of property.[24]

The task of the rules of justice, and likewise of municipal law, is 'to cut off all occasions of discord and contention' (*Treatise* 502; *Enquiry II* 286), i.e. to define a framework for social interaction regarding matters on which there may be wide dissensus on the merits. The technique, Hume suggests, is to *treat as* having *normative* significance certain publicly accessible and determinate *natural facts*. 'In all these cases, and particularly that of accession, there is first a *natural* union betwixt the idea of the person and that of the object, and afterwards a new and *moral* union produc'd by that right or property, which we ascribe to the person' (*Treatise* 510 n., author's emphasis). The normative significance of these natural facts is a product of convention or law. It is essentially artificial (*Treatise* 514–16).

This technique is essential for the facilitation of voluntary transfer of property, and is the device by which actions and words can now have (or can be taken socially to have) binding effect in the future and at a distance, as in promising (and in contractual relations). The technique, in Hume's view, reaches a high degree of refinement in modern (and even ancient Roman) law. The refinement may reach a point where the formalities of law appear no different from the mumbo-jumbo of religious ceremony and superstition (*Enquiry II* 198–9). But there is no essential difference between these legal formalities and the more familiar techniques of transfer of property and formal giving of one's word (*Treatise* 515–16, 524).

---

23 Cf. L. Fuller, 'Human Interaction and the Law': 'where A and B have become familiar with a practice obtaining between C and D, A is likely to adopt this pattern in his actions towards B, not simply or necessarily because it has any special aptness for their situation, but because he knows B will understand the meaning of his behaviour and will know how to react to it' (228).

24 'The advantages which result from a parliamentary title, preferably to an hereditary one, though they are great, are too refined ever to enter into the conception of the vulgar. The bulk of mankind would never allow them to be sufficient for committing what would be regarded as an injustice to the Prince. They must be supported by some gross, popular, and familiar topics; and wise men, though convinced of their force, would reject them in compliance with the weakness and prejudices of the people' (*Essays* 495 n. 2).

This *technique* is the key to the solution of the problems facing parties in the hypothetical state of nature prior to the creation of the conventions of property. Rules of this convention, like rules of modern law, cannot allow their identification, or application to depend on the indefinitely variable and idiosyncratic moral considerations. This fact is dramatically evident, to Hume, in civil adjudication which forces judges to decide matters in an all-or-nothing fashion even when prudence or equity would induce them 'to strike a medium, and divide the difference betwixt the parties' (*Treatise* 531). But this feature of modern adjudication is merely an instance of the more basic fact that *justice* defines rights and duties that admit of no degrees, that either apply or do not apply, and are not susceptible of gradation, as are, characteristically, all matters of virtue and vice which such rights and duties are supposed to adjudicate (*Treatise* 529–30). Institutionalized adjudication in sophisticated legal systems simply refines a feature shared with less formal practices or systems of norms.[25]

The ground of hope for success of this general technique is the same throughout the range of its use as well. Not only must the natural facts that are selected for normative significance be publicly accessible, and so recognizable by all, and known to be so. But also, and most importantly, they must be abstracted from the matters around which controversy and dissensus swirl. They can be regarded by all parties, regardless of their position on the merits, as *neutral* to the underlying debate and so each can reasonably expect them to operate in an impartial fashion.[26]

Imagination and reason

It is important to understand clearly the role of reason, and its limits, in the situation Hume describes. First, regarding the limits of reason: we must note that reason will never get the parties over the gap created by conditional intentions, even if we add salience to the parties' stock of common knowledge.[27] For reason will lead each party only to form new *conditional* intentions, the antecedents

---

[25] This gives us further reason to think that Hume's theory of justice was intended as a jurisprudential as well as a moral theory.

[26] See, e.g., *Treatise* 537–8 where Hume argues that the neutrality of all magistrates and officials guarantees the success of their adjudicative and legislative efforts.

[27] The thoughts in the next two paragraphs were stimulated by M. Gilbert's 'Some Limitations of Rationality'. See also Hardin, *Collective Action*, 159.

of which must be fulfilled before the consequents can be detached and issue in decision and action.

Suppose that, amongst all the candidate rules for determining property, rule R* stands out as unique in some way. Suppose that this is obvious to each party, and even that each 'expresses this sense to his fellows'. Nevertheless, each party still must face the question, what must I do? Which rule shall I choose? The only rational thing to do, of course, is to choose R* *on the condition that the others do*. To choose R* unilaterally, without expectation that the others will do so would not be rational. But will the others choose R*? Since we assume that they are in relevant respects like me, and if one considers only their reasoning, I must conclude that they will reason just as I have and will resolve to *choose* R* *conditionally* as well. Obviously, we have made no progress. And no help lies in further 'reverberations' alone, i.e. in further replications of the reasoning of others and theirs of mine. On the road to agreement, reason has hit a slick patch and can only spin its wheels. No further progress is possible.[28]

Our only hope is that imagination is practical, that it is capable of moving us to action. We can break out of the cycle of reiterated conditional intentions only if we have some basis for the belief that, reason aside, the other parties will choose to follow R*. The inclination so to choose cannot be rational, at least in the sense we have been using this term all along. It must be an arational impulse or inclination. Thus, Humean co-ordination problems can be solved only if it is true, as a matter of psychological fact about human beings, and widely known to be true, that they are inclined (at least to some extent, and at least where rational considerations are equally balanced) to follow the promptings of imagination. (If, for example, human beings were, on the contrary, highly counter-suggestive or instinctively nonconformist, noticing others are inclined to choose

---

28 The argument above holds not only for new co-ordination problems, but also for problems which have established patterns or conventions as solutions. Suppose there is an established precedent for solution to a recurring co-ordination problem. Why follow the precedent in the next case given the existence of the regularity in the past? Absent information about *arational* inclinations of the other parties, it would be rational for me to decide to go on as before, conditional on others doing so, and they, being rational, would choose the same. This nesting of conditional intentions can be broken only if there is public knowledge of a tendency on the part of most of us to do as we have done before. Since all the resources of 'reverberation' are available, this tendency need not be very great, but the ball can get rolling *only* with a push from an arational source. (Or, at least this seems to be the view to which Hume is committed.)

R* might direct one against it.)[29] The truth of such assumptions aside, that such a view about human nature is distinctively Humean is clear. Indeed, Hume delights in pointing out against his rationalist opponents the influence of such non-rational factors in human psychology. The basic need for confirmation by others, and the laws of association, give Hume all the warrant he believes he needs to support this conviction.

Salience, then is a product of what Hume calls 'imagination', not reason. But we must take care to understand this faculty of imagination. In Hume's usage, the term 'imagination' does not refer simply to a brute fact about the psychological tendencies of individual human minds.[30] Imagination succeeds where reason fails not only because it is practical, but also because it is *social*. Imagination would not do the job if it were merely a fact about human psychology that, in the circumstances, R* would be regarded as unique among candidate rules. Salience cannot be a 'private' fact; it must be public if it is to focus attention and detach conditional intentions. The 'impact on the mind' of some otherwise frivolous consideration has the desired effect only if it is confirmed (or can reasonably be expected to be confirmed) by similar experiences in others. Imagination works to solve Humean co-ordination problems only because each party can read the same message in the common situation. Each must be confident that his or her response is not idiosyncratic. The reports of imagination, on Hume's view then, are more like linguistic intuitions (sensing proper and improper usage) than sense data. Imagination is a *social* capacity (see above, 2.3).

But none of this warrants the conclusion that *following* imagination is *irrational*.[31] Hume gives three reasons for resisting this conclusion. First, the fact that the rules of justice proposed by imagination (and the inclination to follow them when salient) cannot themselves be shown to be rational does not in any way undermine their authority. There is no need to fear, Hume assures us,

that our attachment to this law will diminish upon account of the seeming frivolousness of those interests, by which it is determin'd. The impulse of the mind is deriv'd from a very strong interest; and those other more minute interests serve only to direct the motion, without adding any thing to it, or diminishing from it (*Treatise* 556).

29 Gilbert, 'Limitations', 20.
30 *Pace* Harrison, 84.   31 *Pace* Harrison, 86–9.

The rationale for compliance lies not in the rule itself, but in the strategic social context, and the problem for which it provides the solution. All the reason one needs for complying with a co-operative scheme has already been spelled out, and would be fully appreciated by the parties. 'Frivolous' considerations merely *focus* that rational and motivational energy, as it were, on a specific pattern of action. Thus, the 'strategic context' can transform otherwise rationally indifferent or even irrational considerations into rationally compelling ones. This explains, says Hume, how a former judicial decision, 'though given itself without any sufficient reason, justly becomes a sufficient reason for a new decision' (*Enquiry II* 308). The key is to shift justification of decision or action from justification *of the rule* on which one acts to justification of *following the rule*.

Second, Hume points out a further reason and motive for compliance created by achieving a solution to the co-ordination problem faced by the parties.[32] In addition to the public harm done (and the harm done to long-range self-interest of the agent) by failure to conform, injury to other individuals may well be done. Once the specific rules of the convention have been fixed, the mutually referential intentions are transformed into *expectations*, on which the parties act. The actions of each 'have a reference to those of . . . other[s], and are perform'd upon the supposition, that something is to be perform'd on the other part' (*Treatise* 490). To violate the rules of the convention, is to fail to do one's part, and inevitably to defeat the expectations on which others legitimately relied (*Enquiry II*, 310–11).

Third, the model for the operation of imagination in this context which Hume constantly uses is that of legal reasoning, especially argument from analogy. But it is a mistake, I believe, to regard this as an implicit criticism of legal reasoning.[33] In fact, we can learn from Hume's use of this model something more about his understanding of the faculty of imagination. Hume surely is anxious to point out, against the intuitionists and rationalists, that there is no *fact of the matter* outside of the practice of legal reasoning and the body of commonly recognized legal doctrine that warrants the claim that the instant case lies closer to precedent case A than to precedent

---

[32] For an argument for compliance with Humean conventions along similar lines see Postema, 'Coordination and Convention', 179–82.

[33] Again, *pace* Harrison, 91–2.

case B. Nevertheless, it would be equally wrong to say that such judgments of analogy are merely subjective, idiosyncratic, or arbitrary. Among those learned in the law, Hume suggests, such judgments are open to critical scrutiny. That is, it is possible, *from within the practice*, to discriminate in many (if not all) cases between valid and invalid claims of analogy (or at least between more and less plausible assertions of analogy). But this is consistent with and illuminates his use of the notion of imagination (at least in the contexts we are considering).

We might say, then, that the capacity of imagination at work in novel cases in discovering analogies and disanalogies to past precedent is more like the capacity to formulate novel sentences which a community of speakers of the language can recognize as appropriate, than either the intuition of some truth in a mind-independent reality, or the mere psychological disposition blindly to respond to certain external stimuli. Since this capacity fits no standard model of reason advanced by Hume's opponents, he is unwilling to attribute it to reason proper. Nevertheless, it is akin to the reasonings of common experience which, Hume believed, his sceptical arguments saved from the excess of rationalist philosophy.

It would be a mistake to label judgments of analogy, and more generally, the deliverances of imagination, as 'irrational' or unwarranted; for they may well be fully warranted, but only within the practice of which they are a part, and the practice may be capable of no further justification. This suggests Wittgenstein's thought that 'to use a word without a justification [*ohne Rechfertigung*] does not mean to use it wrongfully [*zu Unrecht*]'.[34]

But, of course, Hume does not leave the matter here. For he situates the exercise of 'imagination' within a larger strategic social context and this enables him to demonstrate the reasonableness of complying with the deliverances of this social capacity. It yields a rational *justification* where none seemed possible.[35] He has, in

---

[34] L. Wittgenstein, *Philosophical Investigations*, sect. 289. I follow Kripke, *Wittgenstein on Rules*, 74, 86–8.

[35] This strategy is still attractive to social theorists. Cf. Hardin: 'one could reasonably explain a large part of the group-oriented collective action in advanced, diffuse nations as contract by convention. . . . Such an explanation is important, not least because it makes comprehensible much activity that might seem to defy the narrow rationality of self-interest. However, it may do so in part by fitting modest, even surprisingly modest, degrees of extrarational behaviour into a larger and largely rational social context. The extrarational behaviour may do no more than serve as the catalyst to initiate and perhaps establish a contract by convention, which can then be sustained without further extrarational support' (155–6). But keep in mind n. 28, above.

effect, united two of the three themes underlying Common Law theory (2.3)—'common reason' traditionalism and pragmatic conventionalism—into a single coherent theory of law and authority. And, like Common Law theory, he sought to expose the emptiness and pretensions of 'natural reason' and appeals to 'private judgment' (what he calls 'reason in a strict sense' at *Dissertation* 162), in order to make room for the 'ordinary reasonings of common life', reasoning dependent upon the 'prepossessions' and 'prejudices' of common life. Those who seek to escape the limits of this 'common reason' in private judgment and independent reason will find, Hume insists, that either they have merely substituted one set of prejudices for another,[36] or they discover, along the lines we have just sketched out, that the greatest wisdom lies in complying with and not disturbing these common opinions.[37] The problem with Hobbes's political theory, Hume complains, is that, despite his brilliant analysis of the problems of modern social life, he still sought a solution in 'natural reason'.

Hobbes's politics are fitted only to promote tyranny, and his ethics to encourage licentiousness. Though an enemy to religion he partakes nothing of the spirit of scepticism; but is as positive and dogmatical as if human reason, and his reason in particular, could attain a thorough conviction in these subjects (*History* VI, 153).

Hume's self-professed scepticism led him, like Common Law jurists before him, to the view that the only solution to the paradoxes of private rationality, which Hobbes exposed so clearly and the events of the previous century underscored so emphatically, was to subordinate private rational judgment to the *collective rationality* of common opinion and established practice.

To the extent that his argument is sound, Hume succeeds in providing both an *explanatory* and *justificatory* account of law and authority which makes no appeal to external natural laws or independently discoverable rational principles. The principles in terms of which we can consider the reasonableness of compliance

---

36 'They fancied, that they were exercising their judgment, while [in fact] they [merely] opposed, to the prejudices of ancient authority, more powerful prejudices of another kind' (*History* III, 211).

37 'Or should a man be able, by his superior wisdom, to get entirely above such prepossessions, he would soon, by means of the same wisdom, again bring himself down to them for the sake of society, whose welfare he would perceive to be intimately connected with them. Far from endeavouring to undeceive the people in this particular, he would cherish such sentiments of reverence to their princes, as requisite to preserve a due subordination in society' (*Essays* 488).

with existing tradition and practice—principles of private and of public utility—are dependent, ultimately, on tradition and practice for their content, and thus provide no firm basis for a radical critique of the practice, or for proposals for its radical reform.

> To tamper, therefore, in this affair, or try experiments merely upon the credit of supposed argument and philosophy, can never be the part of a wise magistrate, who will bear a reverence to what carries the marks of age; and though he may attempt some improvements for the public good, yet will he adjust his innovations as much as possible to the ancient fabric, and preserve entire the chief pillars and supports of the constitution (*Essays* 499).

4.3　ANSWERING THE SENSIBLE KNAVE

> [H]e, it may perhaps be thought, conducts himself with most wisdom, who observes the general rule, and takes advantage of all the exceptions.
>
> Hume, Enquiry II.

As a bridge to the concerns of the rest of this book, I wish to conclude this discussion of Hume's jurisprudence by considering a problem facing Hume's argument for justice which, we shall see, becomes a central theme of Bentham's jurisprudence. It is the problem of the rationality of 'perfectly inflexible' rules of justice.

Hume maintains that justice serves *both* private and public good, it does so because it secures stability and certainty of possession (and, more generally, reliability of social interaction) which is absolutely necessary if social co-operation is to be achieved. Essential to such stability and certainty is the (nearly) absolutely inflexible compliance with, and enforcement of, the rules of justice. But why such inflexibility? Is it not conceivable that there will be situations in which private or public good is clearly sacrificed in complying with the rules of justice?

Hume, of course, must allow for such divergence because the possibility of it is assumed by his argument for the artificiality of justice. The motivation to do justice cannot be reduced to the natural sentiments (either interested or disinterested), Hume argues, because such sentiments operate on a case by case basis and would be repelled by actions which promise sacrifice of public (or private) good, whereas justice sometimes demands precisely such actions (*Treatise* 480–3, 495–7; *Enquiry II* 303–5). But it would be a grave mistake to conclude that doing justice in such cases is contrary to the individual's or the public's good, he insists. The *appearance* of conflict arises from the fact that we tend to assess the act in question in isolation from the general scheme of rules, i.e. the complex system or pattern of social interaction extended over time, within which the action takes place. Thus, while *in isolation* the action may seem contrary to utility, it will be seen in fact to contribute substantially to public good, when properly assessed *within* the context of the practice (*Treatise* 497).

Hume's focus on the utility of actions in a practice—i.e. in a context of a complexly interrelated pattern of actions, structured and facilitated by a set of publicly known and shared rules—is crucial for his case, and for the development of utilitarian social and political thought. As we shall see, it plays a major role in Bentham's thought. However, noting the utility of practices is not sufficient for Hume's argument for the rationality of compliance with justice to succeed.[38]

Gauthier has pointed out with justification that, whereas Hobbes sought to overcome the limits of individual rationality by redirecting *reason* into conventional channels (law becomes the only standard of reason), Hume seeks to overcome similar limitations through redirection of *interests*.[39] But the only hope of accomplishing this lies in appeal to the interested passions themselves (*Treatise* 492). (The interested passions may be assisted here by reason, of course.) For this strategy to succeed it must be possible to show to the sceptic (Hume's sensible knave, for example, *Enquiry II* 282)

[38] It must be kept in mind that the question here is not, What *now* motivates (most) people to comply with the rules of justice? (And surely it is not the question: How can we get an evil person to change his mind?) On this question Hume is very clear. To the extent that there is any motivation beyond mere habit (*Enquiry II* 203), the most common motivation, and perhaps even the strongest, is a sense of duty or justice (*Treatise* 481, 544; *Enquiry II* 283). But, of course, such explanations presuppose the existence of conventions of justice, *and* the rationality of complying with them. (Similarly, appeals to education 'in probity and honour', and the devices of politicians (*Treatise* 500–1; *Enquiry II* 203), and even appeals to enforcement by law (*Treatise* 534–7), presuppose the existence and rationality of compliance with the rules of justice, *pace* Harrison, 51.) The question, rather, is: Is it rational for an individual to participate in the formation of the practice of justice and is it rational for such a person also to comply with the rules of the practice thus established? Answers to these questions 'first determined us' to comply, says Hume, though other motives may (later) have surpassed them in 'dignity or force' (*Enquiry II* 203; *Treatise* 544).

[39] Gauthier, 'Three Against Justice', 23. See also Hirshman, 25–6.

that his or her self-interest is consistently served, when viewed properly over the long-run. Hume clearly admits that if the proposed restraints on the interested passions in fact were contrary to them, they 'cou'd never be enter'd into, nor maintain'd'. Hume intends to show that such restraints are 'only contrary to their heedless and impetuous movement' (*Treatise* 489).

But could not our sensible knave respond to Hume's argument as follows? 'I fully recognize the advantage both for the public and for myself of there being a set of rules and of general conformity to them. But why should I follow them in every case, rather than follow them whenever it is in my interest to do so? Of course, I will have to take precautions to ensure that others believe I am following the rules even when I am not, and I must be careful not to mistake cases of short-run sacrifice of advantage for cases of genuine long-run sacrifice. But why should I think that that commits me to following exceptionless rules?' Hume draws a compelling portrait of this sensible knave himself:

And though it is allowed that, without a regard to property, no society could subsist; yet according to the imperfect way in which human affairs are conducted, a sensible knave, in particular incidents, may think that an act of iniquity or infidelity will make a considerable addition to his fortune, without causing any considerable breach in the social union and confederacy. That *honesty is the best policy*, may be a good general rule, but is liable to many exceptions; and he, it may perhaps be thought, conducts himself with most wisdom, who observes the general rule, and takes advantage of all the exceptions (*Enquiry II* 282–3).

Before we turn to Hume's attempt to answer the sensible knave we should note that there is no escaping this problem by appealing to benevolent sentiments or concern for the public welfare. For an exactly symmetrical case can be made for the public utility of there being general conformity with the conventions of justice, while allowing that there are cases in which public good is best served in the circumstances by violating the rules—perhaps in secret, but violating them nevertheless (see *Treatise* 481). The parallel to the sensible knave of the *Enquiry II*, is the 'man of merit, of a beneficent disposition' who has reason to wish 'that with regard to [a] single act, the laws of justice were for a moment suspended in the universe' (*Treatise* 497). This, we shall see, is precisely the concern that drives Bentham's search for a utilitarian theory of adjudication.

The usual response Hume gives to the knave is that he has failed properly to count all the costs of his actions. For if he were to count these costs, he would clearly see that momentary loss 'is amply compensated by the steady prosecution of the rule, and by the peace and order, which it establishes in society'.[40] But if this reply goes beyond the earlier point that we must consider the act not in isolation, but in the context of the practice, then Hume must show us *how* the knave's loss of fortune is fully compensated. If Hume does not do this, he has simply reiterated the claim which the knave effectively has challenged, viz. that it is always in his long-run self-interest to conform to the rules of justice. It is not enough for Hume to point out the advantages of general conformity with the rules.

There are three lines open to Hume to support this claim. First, Hume might maintain that because actions in such a practice are intricately linked, and success depends not simply on one's own action but on the co-ordinated actions of all the other members of the community, it is reasonable to believe that every violation of the rules genuinely threatens the very survival of the system and thereby of society. (The 'vault' analogy (*Enquiry II* 305) suggests this line of argument.) Thus, although as societies expand, and the social bonds stretch to embrace more and more people and more and more situations, and the impact of any single act on the structure tends to fade from one's view, the impact nevertheless is real. So real, in fact, that any act in violation of the laws of justice jeopardizes the entire structure.

Now, since the rules presently under discussion are rules defining the 'social constitution' of a community—its 'fundamental law', as it were—the seriousness of violations in particular cases is a bit more plausible. The rules of justice define the basic ground rules for all interaction and intercourse in society. Flexibility, then, may be allowable, perhaps even desirable, as we move out toward the periphery, it may be argued; but that is possible only if the constitutional core is stable, and guaranteed to be so. This conclusion, while not uncontroversial, is a good deal more plausible than the same claim made about an arbitrary set of social rules governing possession of material goods, abstracted from consideration of the social role of the rules. Nevertheless, Hume has seriously overstated his case. Society is remarkably resilient. It has a great capacity

---

[40] *Treatise* 497; see also *History* V, 329.

to rebound from violations of even its most fundamental and widely shared principles. This is, indeed, a very thin reed on which to rest his entire case for justice.

Hume seems to admit as much: 'Some extraordinary circumstances may happen, in which a man finds interests to be more promoted by fraud or rapine, than hurt by the breach which his injustice makes in the social union' (*Essays* 35–6). And in the *Enquiry II*, immediately after sketching his portrait of the sensible knave, Hume confesses that, 'if a man think that this reasoning much requires an answer, it would be a little difficult to find any which will to him appear satisfactory and convincing' (283). Hume is slightly disingenuous here, for surely the knave's 'reasonings' must be answered, if Hume's case for justice is to succeed.[41]

But Hume has a second option open to him. He argues that such exceptions are permissible only if they themselves could be formulated into a general rule and incorporated into the system of justice (*Treatise* 551–2). Similarly, he sometimes argues that, despite the immediate and apparent losses, the agent is better off complying with the existing set of rules, since the only alternatives are general compliance with *some* other set of rules and general noncompliance. But normally an individual can not unilaterally shift general compliance to another set of rules and general noncompliance is clearly out.

All general laws are attended with inconveniences, when applied to particular cases; and it requires great 'penetration and experience, both to perceive that these inconveniences are fewer than what result from full discretionary powers in every magistrate, and also discern what general laws are, upon the whole, attended with fewest inconveniences' (*Essays* 116).

This reply, however, simply misses the point of the knave's, (and beneficent person's) objections. They do not call for alteration of the rules; indeed, their arguments are consistent with the conviction that, as a set of general rules for general compliance, the existing rules are the best conceivable. They call to our attention cases in which it seems rational 'to suspend the laws of justice for a moment'. They raise the prospect of equity—or the analogue of equity in the knave's case—correcting the law which is unjust only due to its generality, a correction limited to the special case at hand and not made a generalized exception to the offending rule.[42]

---

[41] B. Stroud, *Hume*, 215.
[42] See, e.g., Aquinas, *ST* 1a2ae 96, 6.

Perhaps Hume would appeal to his conception of utility (above, p. 108) to support the following response: The knave's argument makes the mistake of assessing the utility of *actions*, whereas only rules may be assessed in that way. The utility of actions can be assessed only indirectly through assessment of rules under which they fall. This reading would explain Hume's insistence on formulating exceptions in general terms so as to fit into the general scheme of justice. Also he would no longer have to hold that each act of injustice threatens the survival of the convention, for it is possible for individual actions within the practice to be causally independent such that the long-run benefits of 'the steady prosecution of the rules' are unaffected by the defection from the practice by any particular action.

However, it is unclear whether Hume would have put his argument in these terms. The indirect-utilitarian argument turns on the distinction between assessments of *rules* and assessments of *actions*, but a key feature of Hume's conception of public utility was that it was tied to *actual* as opposed to *ideal rules*. But nothing, then, prevents one from considering the utility of an *action*, *given* general compliance with an established scheme of rules. Even if Hume himself would have embraced this argument, it is clear that it could not succeed in answering the knave. The argument *assumes* that the knave may consider only rules (or general conformity to them) and not individual actions. Hume's special notion of utility as mutual expected advantage does not support this assumption.

A third tack combining elements of the first two is left to Hume. He claims that the violation of a rule of justice in any particular case threatens the survival of the entire convention. What would have to be true for this claim to be plausible? Why, in particular, does Hume suppose that the only alternative to general conformity is general *disconformity* (conformity to no regularity)? Amongst the most important conditions are: (*a*) Actions of parties to the convention must be tightly locked in patterns of interdependence such that what each does depends greatly on what every one else can be expected to do. (*b*) The convention must be quasi-unstable, that is, although *given* the conformity of all the others no party may strongly disprefer conformity himself or herself; nevertheless, conformity is dispreferred in the *absence* of sufficient *assurance* of general conformity. And (*c*) violations of the rules of the convention must be public. Under these conditions, any violation will be

known and is likely to undermine confidence of others in the conformity of their fellows, which insecurity is likely to mushroom
with the inevitable 'reverberations' around the community. And
since the convention is the solution to a co-ordination problem, the
only hope for general conformity to some other regularity is that
the community can co-ordinate their choices around it, but the confidence needed in the reliability of others necessary to succeed in
such co-ordination will have been eroded.

There is no doubt that the above three conditions are consistent
with the social situation at the birth of the conventions of justice
which Hume describes, and the success of social interaction within
such a practice is likely to enhance those conditions. For interdependence will surely increase as 'commerce' made possible by
justice increases; also as society expands the distance between individuals increases and with it natural bonds of trust are weakened.
The success of justice makes artificial methods of assurance that
others will do their part increasingly necessary. For, I am liable to
'be the cully of my integrity, if I alone shou'd impose on myself a
severe restraint amidst the licentiousness of others' (*Treatise* 535).

In these circumstances, Hume argues in effect that the only way
in which the knave's strategy—to take advantage of those particular circumstances in which, given the general conformity of
others, his private fortune can be advanced by injustice—can succeed is for him to keep both his action and his intentions (his
general policy) from public knowledge. (This is the knave's only
option since the other conditions are not within his unilateral control.) He must give every appearance of adopting the strategy of
always following the rules of justice, while secretly harbouring his
own 'selfish' policy, to do justice only when it suits his overall
advantage.

Now Hume's argument is that this strategy is bound to fail.
Why? Because, says Hume, 'a little reflection' shows anyone that
'selfishness and confin'd generosity, acting at their liberty, totally
incapacitate them for society' (*Treatise* 499). One is made fit for
society only through redirection of the interested passions into a
fully fledged disposition to justice.[43] Furthermore, such knaves,
'with all their pretended cunning and abilities', are likely sooner or
later to betray their own maxims, 'whence they can never extricate

---

[43] *Treatise* 499; Gauthier, 'Three Against Justice', 24.

themselves, without a total loss of reputation, and the forfeiture of all future trust and confidence with mankind' (*Enquiry II* 283). But this seems to beg the question. For, it seems, fitness for society depends on the willingness of others to put trust and confidence in one, but that depends only on the *appearance*, not on the *reality*, of one's commitment to justice. Similarly, the knave might agree that knavery is not for everyone, since it takes a special cunning and skill. But there is no reason to believe that discovery is inevitable for everyone. Isn't such a belief just a pious hope?

No, says Hume, and the reason lies in his view of human nature. It is a basic human need, according to Hume, which calls for reflection and confirmation of one's soul in the souls of others. To cut oneself off from others is to cut oneself off *from oneself*, for it is only in the mirror of the souls of others that one finds one's own identity. The pleasures and satisfactions of conversation and intercourse are essential to human life. But the knave's strategy requires for success just the sort of 'privacy' that makes such intercourse impossible. For a central governing principle of one's life must be scrupulously kept from public knowledge. One's real, true perspective must be kept private. Thus, a truly successful strategy of deception effectively cuts oneself off from the community in which alone one can find the confirmation essential to one's own happiness. Were the knave to be 'ever so . . . successful', he would be 'in the end, the greatest dupe', having 'sacrificed the invaluable enjoyment of a character, . . . for the acquisition of worthless toys and gewgaws' (*Enquiry II* 283). Thus, the knave makes himself fit for society in the eyes of the community, only to make himself entirely unfit for (i.e. unable to enjoy) society in reality. Because this is a prospect unlikely to be seriously entertained by any human being, Hume is confident that any knave will be found out. No knave could keep his cover indefinitely. Thus, Hume seems to think that the knave's proposal is both self-defeating and practically impossible. From which it does not follow that the knave might in some situations wish the rules of justice were suspended in the universe for just that moment. It is perfectly conceivable that there will be such cases, but there is no way to take advantage of them systematically.

This intriguing argument is open to (at least) one serious objection of which Hume himself seems to be aware. The argument rests heavily on the need for mirroring of oneself in the minds of others.

But, this need could be met by social contacts limited to only portions of the community, perhaps including only one's family and
one's circle. But justice calls for self-restraint regarding the possessions of *all* members of the community. The present argument
does not show that it is in the knave's interest to follow the dictates
of justice in those cases in which injustice will be undetected and
the victims are psychologically distant, as it were. Hume has
available to him a twofold reply. First,[44] recall the general truth, according to Hume, that our relations to others fluctuate greatly; that
'a man, that lies at a distance from us, may, in a little time, become
a familiar acquaintance' (*Treatise* 581). Intimates can become
estranged, and this is as likely to happen to the knave as to anyone
else. But the knave's estranged intimate will know of his duplicity
and may have reason to make it public knowledge. Only if the
knave's circle of associates is securely permanent can the strategy
succeed. Thus, the knave has reason to expand the circle he treats
with respect according to the rules of justice.

Second, for the rest of us, Hume points out that custom and
habit move us to follow the rules in all instances, even those in
which the contribution to private (or public) good is not obvious
and may not even be paid. Regularly, the rules of justice not only
make it easier for one to do so, but also one develops an inclination
to behave in this way (*Treatise* 422). We come to do justice 'as a
rule', and it is a common observation running through the *Treatise*
and *Enquiries* that general rules often carry us beyond the principle
and reason from which they first arise.[45]

Thus, Hume seems to argue that human nature is such that
individual behaviour is inevitably governed by general policies,
rules, customs, and habits. The careful, discriminating, always
calculating reason which the knave and beneficent person must rely
on is just not available to human beings. The alternative to following justice 'as a rule' is following some other *general* policy, and
clearly it is better to follow rules to which others conform than to
follow private rules of one's own making. Thus, in this case, as in
the case of the determination of the rules of property, although this
tendency to be governed by custom is not itself rationally defensible, it is rational for the rules of justice to be 'perfectly inflexible',

[44] I am indebted to Annette Baier for this thought.
[45] *Treatise* 499, 551; *Enquiry II* 207. Generally see *Treatise* 293–4, 362, 371, 374,
598; and *Essays* 37.

given this fact of human nature. Although it is quite conceivable that there are cases in which it would be better, in that instance, to suspend the rules of justice, it is impossible, given human nature, systematically to recognize and exploit them. The problem arises because the general rules of justice appear to be inefficient. Public utility, for example, might better be served if there were some way in which the stability and certainty of public rules of justice could be maintained while at the same time allowing for them to be suspended when they genuinely work inconvenience. But the only way that can be accomplished, according to Hume, is for the community to co-ordinate their decisions and actions around a different set of public general rules which allow for the exception. But, of course, the cases at issue are just those which do not lend themselves to that sort of treatment. And so, Hume concludes, the proposals of the knave and the beneficent person are practically infeasible, and it would be irrational to seek to implement them.

Despite its obvious interest, I will not attempt to assess this argument. I have spelled it out in detail because it reveals yet another place in which Hume seeks to exploit the 'non-rational' elements in human nature, and because the problem is one to which we shall return frequently in our discussion of Bentham's maturing theory of adjudication. Indeed, one major objective of Bentham's theories of law and adjudication is to marry the advantages of both the stability of fixed general rules and the flexibility of 'equity' which Hume has here so vigorously rejected.

Part II

Bentham's Critique
of Common Law:
The Roots of Positivism

5

Utilitarian Justice and the Tasks of Law

Justice (that is utility in so far as it consists in observation of Justice) depends upon expectation and expectation follows the finger of the law . . .

Bentham, UC lxx(a).21.

A central theme running through all of Bentham's jurisprudential writing is the conflict between the demand for stability and certainty of law and the need for flexibility in adjudication. Keenly aware of the utility, indeed necessity, of relatively fixed general rules for social conduct, Bentham nevertheless regarded the principle of utility as the sole and sovereign rational decision principle. Thus, he insisted that judges must be free to respond to the constantly varying demands of utility in particular cases. The complex history of the development of Bentham's theories of law and adjudication is the history of a series of increasingly sophisticated attempts to solve this central problem of utilitarian political and legal theory.

This history begins to unfold in, and is largely shaped by, Bentham's early reflections on justice, utility, and Common Law adjudication. In these early writings, Bentham defines the basic terms of the conflict, surveys with remarkable insight the issues at stake, and proposes a unique utilitarian solution for his native Common Law system. His almost immediate dissatisfaction with this solution set him on a course of increasingly deeper reflections on the nature of law and adjudication which eventuated in a complex and sophisticated jurisprudential theory only a small part of which is presented in his classic treatise, *Of Laws in General*. However, in abandoning his initial solution, he did not abandon the principles underlying his early argument, rather he came to the firm conviction that no Common Law system, even a substantially revised and reformed one, could adequately satisfy these principles.

Thus, these early reflections underlie the development of his mature jurisprudential theory.

My discussion of these early writings will proceed in two stages. First, Chapter 5 sets out in a quite general form the problems and issues around which Bentham's jurisprudence developed. It begins with a look at his early reflections on justice, rules, and utility, and then traces Bentham's shaping of these early ideas into structuring elements of his developing theory of law. This discussion will fix the basic direction of Bentham's thought and uncover an important guiding assumption regarding the central aim or task of law. Second, Chapter 6 focuses these themes more precisely on the Common Law and Bentham's attempt to make coherent sense of this institution in terms of the principles and categories discussed in Chapter 5.

5.1   JUSTICE, UTILITY, AND EXPECTATIONS

> The principle of natural rights admits of no compromise. Instead of rights talk of expectation.
>
> Bentham, UC xxix. 6.

J. S. Mill once remarked that, when it came to jurisprudence, Bentham found the battering-ram more useful than the builder's trowel.[1] This surely does not do justice to the careful and sophisticated analyses of jurisprudential concepts in *Of Laws in General*, for example; but it is an accurate description of Bentham's usual treatment of central moral notions. A contemporary critic captured with reasonable accuracy Bentham's reductionist method when he said,

Mr Bentham maintains, that in all cases we ought to disregard the presumptions arising from moral approbation, and, by a resolute and scrupulous analyis, to get at the naked utility upon which it is founded; and then, by the application of his new moral arithmetic, to determine its quantity, its composition, and its value; and, according to the result of this investigation to regulate our moral approbation for the future.[2]

No moral concept suffers more at Bentham's hand than the concept of justice. There is no sustained, mature analysis of this notion

[1] J. S. Mill, 'Austin on Jurisprudence', 159.
[2] Francis Jeffrey, writing in the *Edinburgh Review* IV (1804), quoted in J. Steintrager, *Bentham*, 13.

to match that of Mill's discussion in *Utilitarianism*.[3] Seldom willing to take the notion seriously, he was most inclined to respond to talk of justice in an entirely polemical fashion, dismissing it summarily as, at best, innocently vague and potentially obscurantist, but more often a mask for social antipathy and malevolence.[4]

If justice be admitted in the character of an independent subject of love, where shall we stop—what limit can there be to the number of these objects? To justice must we not add in like manner Equity—right reason— legitimacy and so on. The catalogue of these supposed innate and universal objects of love, may it not be various in the various languages some or all of them—may it not, in a word, vary with the language? (UC cvi. 401).

Bentham's early utilitarian conception of justice

It is all the more remarkable, then, that we should find amongst his earliest discussions of law a sketch for an essay on justice. Opening this sketch, he remarks that systematic reflection on law and legislation must begin with determination of the 'import' of, and relations between, the two fundamental notions of political theory: justice and utility. 'Perhaps there is not a topic in the whole field of political disquisition more universally nor frequently applicable than this nor on which it more behooves men to have their ideas settled' (UC lxx(a). 17). Our ideas, however, are often 'fluctuating', and even when settled, they often betray inadequate understanding. Especially troubling, according to Bentham, is the common view that justice and utility are in direct and constant conflict. What is even more troubling is the fact that, despite the attractions of utility, the popular favourite in this conflict is justice.

Why is justice more highly regarded than utility? he asks. Because, in popular opinion, the demands of justice are clear, determinate, easy to discover and to observe, and to determine whether others are observing; thus, they promise greater security. Justice sets a fixed and inflexible standard, while the demands of utility, it is believed, are unpredictable and constantly changing with the changing circumstances. 'Justice feigns a rule ready fixed

---

[3] J. S. Mill, *Utilitarianism*, ch. V. A thorough discussion and persuasive interpretation of Mill's theory of justice can be found in several recent papers by D. Lyons, especially, 'Human Rights and the General Welfare', 'Mill's Theory of Justice', and 'Benevolence and Justice in Mill'. A germ of Mill's analysis of justice can be seen in some relatively late remarks of Bentham on justice. See below, pp. 156-8.

[4] See, for example, *IPML* X. 40 n. b[2]; *CC* 123; and UC xiv. 103-7.

and established. Utility recognizes the rule as yet to seek. . . . Utility is spoken of as something that will yield—Justice as an inflexible line—something that will break rather than bend. Utility as applicable to many measures at a time and these opposite—Justice . . . as applicable to but one' (UC lxx(a). 17, 18).

In this characterization of the alleged conflict between justice and utility Bentham clearly echoes Hume. Justice does not define a standard against which laws can be measured, rather it *presupposes* the existence of established rules and laws (or, as we shall see shortly, of legitimate expectations). Bentham naturally associates justice with law, and the administration of it. The conflict between justice and utility is the conflict between adherence to established rules and the violation (or setting aside) of a rule in order to secure a clear advantage in a particular case. But, of course, the conflict set up in this way admits of a utilitarian solution. Rather than reject the general characterization of either justice or utility, Bentham argues that what makes justice an attractive political ideal is the utility of secure and determinate public rules themselves. This argument is haltingly expressed in this early essay:

It was sufficiently understood that it was justice, that is the keeping [of] the chain of analogies . . . unbroken, that kept the stock of happiness for the time being together: any decision or act therefore by which it should be manifest that [the] chain was intentionally/knowingly broken (viz.: broken in the instance in question with such circumstances as indicated a disposition to break in an indefinite number . . . [of] future instances) would have the effect of making it appear as if the whole stock was in danger. . . . A much greater, because indefinite[,] defulcation of happiness [is thereby] threatened than the utility of any particular measure assignable could make an addition. Justice . . . being superior in utility to utility itself (UC lxx(a). 18).

A reasonably clear argument is discernible through the tortured style of this passage. It is only when utility is mistakenly restricted to immediate expediency that a deep conflict between justice and utility can be seen to arise, says Bentham. Justice demands adherence to established rules in the face of arguments from immediate utility to the contrary: but a careful accounting of the relevant utilities yields the same conclusion, he insists. For, intentionally setting aside an established rule (in circumstances indicating a disposition on the part of the official to do so in the future) is likely to cause greater insecurity and so loss of happiness, than can ever be gained by alteration of the unsatisfactory rule. Narrowly restricting utility to immediate advantage yields the paradox that justice emerges superior in utility to utility itself. There is no deep conflict, he concludes, between justice and utility, broadly and properly construed. (However, Bentham seemed aware even here that the conflict is not entirely eliminated, for he restricts the argument to cases in which there is in the official action some indication of a general disposition to ignore the laws. It is not clear how important at this point this restriction is for Bentham.)

There is no conflict between these two fundamental notions because, in the relevant contexts, the two principles yield the same prescriptions. But what accounts for this harmony? Bentham's answer differs significantly from familiar attempts to reconcile justice and utility in Mill and Sidgwick and from Hume's account discussed earlier. Justice, he insists, in so far as it is an intelligible standard, simply focuses on a particular *species* of utilities, *and* because this species of utilities is, in the contexts in question, likely to be of overriding importance, the dictates of justice are also very likely to be the dictates of the principle of utility itself.

Following his favoured 'bifurcation method', Bentham distinguishes 'original utility' from 'utility derived from expectations' (I shall call this 'expectation utility').[5] The distinction is intended to define two exclusive and jointly exhaustive classes of utility. Expectation utilities depend causally on beliefs regarding likely future behaviour of public officials or private persons. The class of original utilities includes all utilities which do not depend on such beliefs. However, the utilities Bentham has in mind are those linked to the fulfilment or disappointment of expectations regarding only certain future events. Bentham's notion has little in common with the modern decision-theoretic notion of expected utility. His notion is concerned not with the proper utilitarian assessment of alternative future states of affairs in light of their relative probabilities. It focuses, rather, on certain *sources* of utilities. Expectation utilities derive from two main sources: (i) habits, customs, or promises (and more generally, the patterns of behaviour of other persons), and (ii) law deriving from statute or from the custom of officials, beliefs corresponding to which he calls 'opinion[s] of praejudication'.[6] Thus, expectation utilities are those which have their origins in beliefs regarding the likely behaviour of persons, private or official, in

5 UC lxx(a). 20; UC xcvi. 74; UC lxxii. 1; *Comment* 231.
6 UC lxx(a). 19; UC xcvi. 74; *Comment* 231.

virtue of established practices, habits, customs, or the general rules (and in some cases the absence of them) which govern their behaviour. Excluded from the class at this point are expectations regarding utility-producing natural events.[7] Now Bentham links justice directly with expectation utilities. 'Utility [is] twofold: 1. original, 2. derived from expectation. The term justice . . . [is a] substitute for (or dependent on) the term utility in the latter sense.'[8] Thus, justice, in so far as it is an intelligible political notion demands following established rules, practices and patterns of behaviour which rest for their ultimate authority not on their intrinsic merit or utility, but on the expectations they engender and protect. For example, in a related manuscript Bentham considers the so-called law of nations (which, he says, ought properly to be called 'the Morality of Nations') the practices of which depend greatly for their utility upon interlocking expectations.

There is a custom among European nations that a vessel approaching to a fort belonging to another nation shall salute it with a certain number of guns. Now certain and plain it is, that in the producing of a certain quantity of noise and smoke there can be no original utility: and yet utility there is. Why? because it [the salute] is expected.

And he notes that this explains the great importance of, and reason for dispute over, the history of relations among nations.

Selden and Grotius had their dispute concerning the dominion of certain laws. They compiled Histories upon Histories to show the exercise of it . . . Why? but that they both perceived that if one party had been used a certain number of times to make use of it along with others, he would reckon upon and expect the being suffered to do so still . . . [and] that these several facts if admitted would serve at once as grounds of such an expectation (considered as probable) and as indices of it (considered as actual) (UC lxxii. 1).

The example here is international custom, but the most common example, and the model for Bentham, as for Hume before him, was the law of property.

---

[7] At this stage in Bentham's thinking there is some ambiguity regarding a third source of expectations. At UC lxx(a). 19 he includes 'opinion of original utility' along with the other two. But in a closely related manuscript he dismisses this idea as a mistake. Expectation determined by 'expediency', he insists, falls properly into the category of original utility (UC xcvi. 74), but he does not say why this is so. The view in UC lxx(a). 19 prevails, however, as we shall see below in 5.2, at least when the expectation takes the form of 'alarm'. A decade or so later 'sentiment of utility' is clearly included among the sources of 'natural expectations' in his *Civil Code*, *Bowring*, i, 323, and plays an important role there.

[8] UC xcvi. 74; see also UC lxx(a). 19, 20, 21.

The conduct of Justice in deciding the right to an article of property in dispute between two parties is governed by two considerations. . . . 1. To consider the parties themselves, it ought to bestow the article in question upon the one of them whose expectation of having it is the strongest. 2. To consider the public, it ought to bestow . . . it upon that one of the parties on whom the public . . . expects most strongly to see it bestowed (UC lxix. 238).

Thus, Bentham, like Hume, closely associates justice with conventional arrangements of general rules and practices which structure, underwrite, and seek to protect expectations essential to social interaction. Justice is both a product and protector of expectations. However, Bentham's account differs from Hume's in two important respects.

First, despite the close association between justice, rules, and utility, it is clear that on Bentham's utilitarian account of justice, justice is not to be identified with conformity with established rules. Justice, for Bentham, is first of all a matter of respecting expectation utilities, and only derivatively is it a matter of following rules. How far is it true, as Blackstone claims, that justice is dependent upon law? Bentham asks. 'Thus far: Where Justice (that is utility in so far as it consists in the observation of Justice) depends upon Expectation and Expectation follows the finger of the law . . .'[9] Justice consists in following the law where following maximizes respect for expectation utilities. Although conformity may maximize expectation utility in most cases, it may not do so in all cases. Once we recognize the connection between expectations and justice, we can perceive 'why certain exceptions [to established rules] may be made in some cases, without injuring or detracting from a rule of Natural Justice'. And in some cases considerations of original utility may provide, in part, the warrant for the exception, 'because a manifest tho' less general utility in those particular cases may carry expectation with it' (UC lxx(a). 19). That is, where original utility seems to counsel setting aside or altering an established rule, expectations may not be seriously disappointed, indeed they may call for the decision, if the utility of the novel decision is sufficiently 'manifest' (i.e. publicly recognized). It is not the amount of utility that is important here, but rather the assurance of common public knowledge of the utility. (This, of course, is most likely to occur, for example, in cases in which great disutility would

[9] UC lxx(a). 21 citing Blackstone, 1 *Comm.* 55.

be caused by following the rule.) Established rules have a justified claim on official attention, independent of their original utility merits, only because they provide a focus for public expectations.

Second, the expectations on which Bentham focuses, and justice which seeks to protect them, are given a distinctively utilitarian interpretation. The demands of justice are to be taken seriously because and only because they concern a *species* of utility, and this species is distinguished from original utility, not in terms of its nature, but in terms of its *source*. Nothing in Bentham's conception of utility, (unlike Hume's, see above, 3.3) prevents combining expectation utilities and original utilities in a single calculation. They are directly commensurable. Their claim to special attention in the contexts in which justice is an important concern lies in the fact that, on Bentham's view, they are of overriding utilitarian weight and importance.

Thus, Bentham is not arguing for a *principled* restriction of official attention to consideration of expectation utilities, to the exclusion of all other potentially relevant utilities. His utilitarian theory of justice does not mark a departure from the direct-utilitarian view that the principle of utility is always the sovereign decision principle. Tied to expectations is a *species* of utilities which, in Bentham's view, are especially weighty in contexts of official decision-making, and this is why they tend to override relevant original utilities. But there is no reason to believe that they will do so in every case. Neither does respect for expectations dictate uncompromising adherence to rules. As we have seen, Bentham follows Hume in reckoning the language of justice and rights as the language of inflexibility. 'Justice feigns a rule ready fixed and established', an inflexible rule that allows no prudent bending (UC lxx(a). 17, 18). Despite the usefulness of such language, Bentham insists ultimately on the more 'yielding' language of utility and expectations. 'The principle of natural rights admits of no compromise,' he complains in a critique of the French Declaration; 'instead of rights talk of expectations' (UD xxix. 6).

Bentham has harsh words for the intellectual indolence of lawyers and judges caused by the doctrines of justice and precedent.

When lawyers persist in giving to their maxims an authority original, without exception, and without appeal, the most salutary of them turn, upon many occasions, poisonous. There is not one of them which should be established without a standing proviso tacked to it in favor of utility. There is not one of them of which some higher reason cannot be given, so far as it is reasonable, which higher reason ultimately is utility . . . [The lawyer's attitude] comes of getting certain maxims by rote and applying them undeviatingly as if they were *sui juris* without enquiring whether they may not be suspended by a utility superior to their utility (UC li(a). 31, 32).

There is implicit here a decisive repudiation of the Humean doctrine that the human mind is governed throughout the largest part of its operation by custom and habit (*Enquiry I* 44). Hume, we may recall, not only observed, but put at the centre of his jurisprudence (and his philosophy in general) the fact that human beings 'are mightily addicted to *general rules*, and that we often carry our maxims beyond those reasons, which first induc'd us to establish them' (*Treatise* 551). Bentham, for his part, accepts that the human mind is frequently afflicted with this malady,[10] and adds that this is especially true of minds trained in the Common Law. But he takes this to be a major intellectual failure, the product of personal indolence and sinister social forces. Thus, Bentham's 'rationalism' is apparent already at this early stage in his career. It takes the practical effect here of demanding that where there are good utilitarian reasons for a rule or maxim, the judge must penetrate through to them and treat them as his ultimate reasons for decision and action, and thus regard them as open to qualification by appeal to greater utility in particular cases. There is no inclination in Bentham, then, to counsel officials to ignore or overlook any relevant utilitarian considerations in their deliberations. Justice and utility are not in deep conflict, in Bentham's view, because justice properly understood is *reducible to* utility.

Utility: 'the ruler and decider of all things'

Out of bits and pieces, largely from later writings, it is possible to sketch out a second line of analysis of justice which is not identical to Bentham's early account. He never makes an effort to choose between the two, perhaps because he believed they were equivalent or at least compatible, perhaps because he thought it didn't really matter once it can be shown that justice is reducible to utility, and perhaps for both reasons. The alternative account is interesting, however, not for the role it plays in his jurisprudential theory (it

[10] See, e.g. *IRE, Bowring* vi, 14 n *.

plays no such role), but because it seems to anticipate J. S. Mill's analysis advanced over forty years later in *Utilitarianism*.

In the *Deontology* Bentham sets out to show that all virtues are reducible to (or 'modifications of') either prudence or benevolence. Justice, he maintains, is nothing more than benevolence under particular circumstances (UC xiv. 227). Often, even in his later writings, the circumstances he has in mind are those in which the utilities are predominantly tied to 'fixed expectancy' (*Bowring* iii, 388 n.∗; *Bowring* v, 277). However, occasionally he ties justice more directly to rules. For example, a late (1818) entry in his commonplace book includes the following germ of an analysis of justice: 'Justice is beneficence: in the cases in which the non-performance of it is considered as punished, or punishable by the force of one or other of the several sanctions: principally the political, including the legal, and the moral or popular' (*Bowring* x, 511). On this account, acts of justice are those special cases of beneficence which are in fact enforced by sanction from some authoritative source, typically through establishing and enforcing rules. Similarly, in papers penned some ten years earlier, Bentham observes that to say an act is required by a dictate of justice is not simply to say that one ought to perform the act, but also that non-compliance will be punished (UC lxxxii. 142). The clearest statement of this line of analysis can be found in materials from the last few years of Bentham's life. 'By Love of Justice', he writes in 1829, 'is meant regard for human happiness considered as promoted by observance of fixed rules, especially rules laid down by authority of government . . .' (UC cvi. 397). This analysis is spelled out in slightly more detail in his *Article on Utilitarianism*. Here he distinguishes his conceptual analysis—his account of what assumptions are made by those who use the term 'justice'—from his substantive utilitarian conception of justice.

In and by the employment given to the word justice two assumptions are implicitly contained: . . . [1] that by competent authority the general rule of action has been laid down: . . . [and 2] that whatsoever be meant by rectitude and propriety this rule is itself . . . a right and proper one (UC xiv. 382).

He then adds his utilitarian account of what would make such a rule 'right and proper':

If then so it be that the rule thus exhibited in the character of a maxim or dictate of justice is the same which on this same occasion would be found to be a dictate or say precept emanating from the greatest happiness principle, then . . . the dictate or say precept . . . may be said to be a dictate of justice.[11]

Several features of the development of this account deserve comment. First, Bentham insists throughout that the link between justice and utility is forged by the concept of fixed general rules or laws. Justice is essentially a juridical concept. But his understanding of the nature of this link shifts. In so far as justice is identified with respect for fixed expectations, the link to rules is close but entirely contingent, as we noted above. As he develops his alternative account he tightens the connection between justice and rules by *identifying*, as Hume did, justice with *established rules* (which nevertheless must meet the condition of serving general happiness). The link between justice and expectations is still maintained, however, because established rules tend to focus and confirm, and so to *fix*, expectation.

This stage in Bentham's analysis is ambiguous, however. The ambiguity is not one to which Hume's account was subject. Because of Hume's conception of utility, it is difficult to pry established, working general rules apart from their utility. As we noticed in Chapter 3, Hume's notion of utility does not provide a basis for judging rules themselves in the abstract. If the rules work at all, they serve the public good, and only in the most extreme cases can there be reasons of utility to warrant setting aside established rules in favour of some alternative rules. Bentham's conception of utility, however, does allow assessment of alternative feasible sets of rules in terms of their respective contribution to the overall well-being of the community. And this makes his account of justice here ambiguous. For it is not clear what the relationship is between the two conditions in his analysis of justice (*established* rules, and rules *which meet the test of utility*). It is not clear on which of these two conditions he wished to place emphasis when they conflict.

The ambiguity is cleared up in his last proposal. Like J. S. Mill, Bentham defines justice in terms of a certain kind of *ideal* rule—viz. the best, right, or proper rule which could be authoritatively adopted and enforced. This is part of his *analysis* of the concept of justice. When I say, then, that the activities of some government officials violate a dictate of justice, on this account, I

---

[11] Ibid. Bentham seems to offer a similar analysis of non-legal rights, see Hart 'Natural Rights: Bentham and John Stuart Mill' in Hart, *Essays on Bentham*, 88–9.

do not imply that officials violated an already established rule, but rather that there is a rule or principle which can be rationally defended, which rule could and ought to be authoritatively established in law or the political constitution. His utilitarian version of justice fits easily into this analysis, for only argument from overall utility can provide the rational grounding for a dictate of justice thus understood. (The parallel to Mill's strategy here is striking, though, of course, Bentham gives only the barest sketch of the account which Mill worked out in much greater detail.)

This sketch of an analysis of justice is interesting for both historical and for general philosophical reasons. Philosophically it is interesting because it seems to anticipate recent attempts to develop indirect- or rule-utilitarian accounts of central moral notions. However, the analysis played no important role in Bentham's moral, political, or legal theory. In fact, immediately after proposing his analysis Bentham himself dismissed it as inadequate or at least as providing no reason to take the notion of justice seriously for theoretical purposes. 'Vague, obscure and little satisfactory as the incomplete explanation of the word justice must as yet be confessed to be this is all that can yet be done towards rendering the import attached to it clear and determinate' (UC xiv. 382). Although it may be possible to continue in the direction Bentham here suggests to develop a credible indirect-utilitarian moral or political theory, Bentham himself was never inclined to do so. Quite to the contrary, he insisted throughout his life that the sole fundamental, and always applicable decision principle is the principle of utility. The problem with taking the analysis of justice seriously, Bentham holds, is that it may give people the idea that there is really something in the notion of justice, understood as in some sense independent of utility, as if it were a moral notion with an independent claim on our attention and deliberation. Bentham fought hard throughout his writings against such a tendency.

The principle of utility is 'the only principle the observance of which affords any promise of being conducive to the maximum of the quantity of happiness in the community . . .' and any proposition 'exhibiting to view any other word or phrase in the character of an appellation of any other ultimate end in view is little . . . better than a self contradictory one' (UC xiv. 388).

Thus, despite the interest of his alternative analysis of justice, for his legal and political theory Bentham relied heavily on his early, strictly reductionist analysis, but with a noteworthy shift of terminology. In the place of 'justice' he put his 'disappointment prevention principle'. This principle, to which he gives broad scope in his jurisprudence, nevertheless is always and *on each occasion* to be followed only because to follow it is to follow the principle of utility. The principle of utility, Bentham insists, is the 'principium generalissimum', *species* of which can be distinguished for ease of understanding and application to different areas of the law (UC xcvi. 75). Thus, in a characteristic passage Bentham maintains that whenever a matter of distribution of property or other benefit is in question, the property or benefit should be given to that party who will experience the greatest disappointment upon not receiving it. To emphasize the pervasive presence of the background principle of utility he adds one exception: when, by any different disposition, happiness in greater quantity, probability taken into account, will be produced (*Pannomial Fragments, Bowring* iii, 212; also BL Add Mss 33,550 fo. 14.) (To this he adds the procedural constraint that the burden of providing that any case calls for the exception lies on the party who stands to benefit from the exception if granted.) For Bentham the principle of utility is both '$\pi\alpha\nu\tau\omega\varkappa\varrho\dot{\alpha}\tau\omega\varsigma$' (the ruler of all things) and '$\pi\alpha\nu\tau\alpha\pi\omega\varkappa\varrho\iota\tau\dot{\eta}\varsigma$' (the decider of all things) (UC xcvi. 73). It is not only the ultimate evaluative principle, it is the sole sovereign *decision principle*.

5.2 HUMAN NATURE AND THE FOUNDATIONS OF JURISPRUDENCE

> . . . it is by means of [expectation] that the successive moments which compose the duration of life . . . become parts of a continuous whole.
>
> Bentham, *Civil Code.*

I have argued that, despite some late suggestions to the contrary, it would be a mistake to understand the special place assigned to respect for expectations along indirect-utilitarian lines. But, then, the importance for Bentham's legal theory and the great weight he assigns expectation utilities are puzzling. Why give expectation utilities such prominence? Our attempt to answer this question will uncover two assumptions which implicitly drive much of Bentham's jurisprudential thought.

The priority of expectations

First, note that Bentham's discussion of utilitarian deliberation is implicitly restricted to legal and quasi-legal contexts. The great weight Bentham assigns to expectation-utilities can be explained in part by the assumption he makes regarding the primary task and social role of law. In Bentham's theory, law plays the social role that Hume assigns to property. Its task is to lay the foundations of society, to *constitute* a people. Like Hume, Bentham believes this involves focusing the expectations of members of the group, making possible the social interaction necessary for survival, improvement, and happiness. It is not surprising, then, that expectations should figure prominently in utilitarian deliberation of officials. Moreover, law and legal officials are in a nearly unique position dramatically to affect, shape, secure, or undermine expectations on a community-wide scale. The extent to which individuals can influence expectations, either positively or negatively, will vary greatly with the circumstances and the positions of the agents in question. But the impact of law and decisions of its officials on expectations is more nearly constant.

The assumptions on which the above explanation of Bentham's view of expectation utilities rests depart from the standard understanding of Bentham's positivist jurisprudence[12] and stand in need of justification. I will undertake that task in the following section of this chapter, and additional evidence will be brought to light in subsequent chapters. But in this section, I want to discuss a second assumption on which Bentham's assignment of overriding importance to expectation utilities rests.

The philosophical basis of this assignment is laid in the early theoretical part of Bentham's work on the civil code (to which he turned in the 1780s). The capacities and sentiments involved in expectations are, he maintains, fundamental to human life (*Bowring* i, 308). Security of expectations is a necessary condition of achieving anything beyond momentary happiness; indeed, it is necessary if recognizably *human* life is to be possible. In a remarkable passage in his *Principles of the Civil Code* he writes,

In order to form a clear idea of the whole extent which ought to be given to the principle of security, it is necessary to consider, that man is not like the brutes, limited to the present time, either in enjoyment or suffering, but

[12] See, e.g., L. J. Hume, *Bentham and Bureaucracy*, esp. ch. 2 and 238–41.

that he is susceptible of pleasure and pain by anticipation, and that it is not enough to guard him against an actual loss, but also to guarantee to him, as much as possible, his possessions against future losses. The idea of his security must be prolonged to him throughout the whole vista that his imagination can measure (ibid.).

The product of 'this disposition to look forward, which has so marked an influence upon the condition of man' is *expectation*. The powers of imagination and foresight, and the sensibility of anticipation, enable human beings to live not only in the discrete present moment, but also in the continuous flow of the present into the future through plans, fears, and expectations. This marks a distinctive difference in the condition of human beings as compared to that of all other sentient beings. Human well-being consists not only in the good of the moment and the *actual* security of future good, but also in the security of the individuals' expectations regarding the future. This, in Bentham's view, is not just one more source of pleasure and pain alongside all the others. This disposition has a deeper significance for human beings which makes security of expectation a matter of primary utilitarian importance.

It is by means [of expectation] that we are enabled to form a general plan of conduct; it is by means of this, that the successive moments which compose the duration of life are not like insulated and independent points, but become parts of a continuous whole. Expectation is a chain which unites our present and our future existence, and passes beyond ourselves to the generations which follow us. The sensibility of the individual is prolonged through all the links of this chain (ibid.).

This is, of course, the barest sketch of an argument, but something like the following seems to be suggested. Because of the disposition of expectation, human beings are capable of *both* planning, structuring, shaping the future *and*, even more deeply, projecting themselves into that future. Without a secure, reasonably predictable future, such activities would be difficult, perhaps impossible, and surely pointless. But these activities are of enormous value to us, first of all in the sheer delight of exercising these capacities and bringing to completion our own plans and projects. But their value and importance to us runs deeper, for only through such activities can we as individuals shape our own identity, and ensure our personal continuity over time. Thus, without security of expectations, we experience both the frustration of curtailment of our liberty to plan for the future and to carry out these plans, and the deeper pain of personal discontinuity, of alienation from our past and future. And, Bentham suggests, a sense of personal continuity and coherence is essential to any individual's conception of happiness beyond that restricted to the pleasures and sufferings of the immediate moment. Thus, it appears that security of expectations is a kind of 'primary good' for Bentham (like the social bases of self-respect for Rawls). It is a necessary condition of any person's well-being regardless of what the components of that well-being might be. Given this understanding of the importance, as a matter of psychological fact, of security of expectations for individual human well-being, it is not surprising that Bentham should believe that expectation-utilities bear great practical weight in utilitarian deliberation.

Security, reason, and human nature

Perhaps we may interrupt the development of the main theme of this chapter briefly to make some observations of a quite general sort about Bentham's view of human nature. The observations of this subsection are important if we are rightly to understand the underlying aims of Bentham's legal and political theory and so they fit the broad objectives of this ground-laying chapter.

If we keep in mind the above explanation of Bentham's reckoning of the utilitarian significance of security and expectations, it is possible to gain some insight into his view of human nature. It can help us restore balance to a widely held but misleading interpretation of this view. Douglas Long has recently advanced this interpretation in a compelling form[13] and I shall use his discussion to focus our reflections here.

It is tempting to contrast Bentham's view of human nature with the picture we get from J. S. Mill, especially in *On Liberty*. For Mill, the human individual is a dynamic, spontaneous, self-creative being with a future of unbounded potential. In sharp contrast, Bentham's conception, says Long, is that of a passive receptor of pleasures and pains responding to its environment in a mechanical pattern of attraction and aversion. For Mill, liberty is essential for human development because it breaks the social tyranny which enslaves and threatens to choke off the soul. Individual liberty opens up, for a self-creative being, a boundless and uncharted future. Whereas for Bentham, liberty is essentially a matter of

[13] D. Long, *Bentham on Liberty*, see esp. 18, 23–5, 82, 115–8, 147–9, 207–20.

security, of protection from a hostile environment. The great value of liberty, and of law which makes it possible, lies in fixing the future, making it determinate secure, predictable. It enables individuals to carry out their nature-dictated and limited goals with reasonable efficiency. Bentham's negative conception of liberty, says Long, is simply a reflection of his negative and essentially passive (even, in the literal sense, reactionary) conception of the self. The most utopian vision that Bentham permits himself is one in which the law is fixed, clear to all, and efficiently adjudicated and effectively enforced, where the boundaries of action, rights and privileges—both private and public—are known and known to be respected (UC cxlii. 200; *Bowring* i, 193–4). This is, surely, in Marx's contemptuous phrase, the utopia of a 'modern English shopkeeper'.[14]

No doubt there is much truth in this sketch of Bentham's view of human nature. Surely, there is nothing romantic in Bentham's view, no celebration of the dynamic and self-creative potential of human beings which preoccupied later nineteenth-century theorists from Mill to Marx. On Bentham's account, human nature is cautious, prudent, even timorous. But the above sketch of that account has the truth of a caricature; it represents part of the view as the whole. This is so in at least two respects.

First, the emphasis on security in Bentham's jurisprudential writings is unmistakable and enormously important, but this should not be taken to *exclude* or deny the loftier, more self-directed and even spontaneous aspects of human nature. Rather, Bentham focuses his attention upon those factors which, in his view, are absolute preconditions for human life of any description. Security is a, or perhaps *the*, 'primary good', according to Bentham. It should be no surprise, then, that security should be the main focus of his jurisprudence, especially given his convictions concerning the primary *task* of law. The utopia Bentham sketches is a limited utopia precisely because it is a vision of the perfection *of law*. 'The perfection *of the law* will be at its *acme*', Bentham predicts, 'and the condition of mankind *as far as depends upon the law* will be at its optimum' when the conditions he spells out are met (UC cxlii. 200, emphasis added). This view is limited not by the boundaries of human nature so much as by what reasonably can be

---

[14] K. Marx, *Capital* I. 609–10.

expected from the law. The task of law (for Bentham, the most important social task to be performed) is to lay the foundations of social coherence and stability, which are essential for personal coherence. Personal coherence is not the whole of human happiness, but it is its *sine qua non*. It is unfair, then, I think, to derive from this set of concerns a full theory of human nature. Bentham does not *deny* that there are further dimensions of the human self not comprehended in the limited view he has adopted, he simply—and for obvious theoretical reasons—ignores them. And as we shall see later, Bentham's emphasis on the stability and determinacy of law is designed precisely to make possible the flexibility in adjudication which the Humean account of justice and law thought impossible.

Second, the above sketch represents Bentham as a true son of the Enlightenment in so far as he was determined to rest his legal and political theory on a true and empirically based 'science of man'. But it mistakes both the model and the thrust of this science. Long and others make a good deal of Newton as the model for Bentham's science of man, the suggestion being that the account of human nature Bentham sought was mechanistic and crudely materialist. He was interested only, wrote Hazlitt, in 'reducing law to a system, and the mind of man to a machine'.[15] Bentham was much impressed, surely, with Newton's achievement, and often fancied himself as the Newton of the moral sciences.[16] But it was Newton's determination to base all his conclusions on observation and experiment (UC c. 135; UC xiv. 365) and his success in giving a systematic structure to the science of physics that Bentham most admired. Bentham believed that there are general truths about human nature and behaviour in society which could also be observed (though not proven by experiment—UC c. 135) and systematically structured into a science. But it is less clear that Bentham took Newton's theory of mechanics as a model for explanation of human behaviour, and even less that it shaped his conception of the basic elements of human nature. Indeed, in so far as Bentham's general philosophical method had a model, it was that of Linneaus and the early systematic work in the biological sciences, in which organization, and classification (what Bentham called 'methodi-

---

15 W. Hazlitt, *The Spirit of the Age*, 2.
16 See Long, *Bentham on Liberty*, 16. See UC clvii. 32.

zation') was the key to rational understanding (UC xxvii. 140–1, 144, 154, 164–5).[17]

More importantly, concentration on Newtonian mechanics overlooks the extent to which Bentham was committed to the Enlightenment objective of freeing individual reason and judgment from what Kant called its 'self-incurred tutelage'—man's inability to make use of his understanding without direction from another.[18] Peter Gay correctly observes that Bentham was the 'arch-*philosophe*, who took eighteenth-century radical ideas into the nineteenth'.[19] Already in his earliest writings, Bentham quite deliberately placed his work squarely within this tradition. The Preface to his *Fragment on Government* sounds a clarion call to Enlightenment rationalism applied to jurisprudence and 'the moral sciences' generally. His target in the *Fragment* and his *Comment on the Commentaries* was Blackstone and the confused mixture of natural law and Common Law ideology found in Blackstone's *Commentaries*. This work, he believed, brought to light the cause of a 'national torpidity' which inculcated submission to authority, not so much *in conduct*—a form of submission he thought essential to social life—'but *in judgment*, which is a source of ignorance and stupidity' (*Comment* 346). His aim, in these works, and throughout his life, was to emancipate 'the judicial faculties' of the public from the shackles in which the established legal and political tradition had bound it.[20] Out of sinister motives, these forces fostered superstition—ungrounded opinion based on fear or delusion—and prejudice—the refusal to evaluate one's judgments and opinions in light of some external standard, and to call one's loyalties to moral accounting.[21] Although Bentham liked to see himself as the Newton of the moral sciences, he also prided himself in being the Luther of

---

[17] *FG*, Preface, p. 418; *Bowring* viii, 124–6, 269–70; Steintrager, *Bentham*, 22 and the UC manuscripts referred to there in n. 7.

[18] I. Kant, 'What is Englightenment?' 3. Kant goes on: '*Sapere aude!* Have courage to use your reason!—That is the motto of the enlightenment' (ibid.). Bentham selected the following passage from Persius' *Satires* for the motto of his *Comment on the Commentaries*: '. . . *Veteres avias tibi de pulmone revello*' ('I pluck the old wives' tales out of your head [lit. 'lung']').

[19] P. Gay, *The Englightenment: An Interpretation*, vol. 1, p. xiii; quoted in Long, *Bentham on Liberty*, 20.

[20] *Comment* 349. In his *Autobiography*, J. S. Mill acknowledged that Bentham 'had always identified deference to authority with mental slavery and repression of individual thought'. See *Early Draft of J. S. Mill's Autobiography*, 188, and generally, B. Friedman, 'An Introduction to Mill's Theory of Authority'.

[21] See J. Austin, *Province*, 299.

jurisprudence (*RJE*, *Bowring* vii, 270 n.). He declared the birth-right of every Englishman to be, not the right of property, but 'the right of private judgment'; on this 'everything that an Englishman holds dear' is based (*FG*, Preface, p. 406).

In support of his account of Bentham's conception of human nature Long takes a passage from an important set of manuscripts written around the time of the composition of the *Fragment*. In it Bentham maintains that one is self-governed when one's motive for action is not pain resulting from the will of another person, but pleasure or pain from the power of inanimate or irrational bodies, or of the parts of one's own body (UC lxix. 55). Commenting on this passage Long says, 'Liberty is here already conceived of, not as an expression of a dynamic self, but as subjection to the hedonistic dictates of the sensory organism in a world of potentially dangerous "inanimate or irrational bodies". "Self-government" means not self-expression or self-development, but self-defence.'[22]

But another interpretation of this passage is possible, one which stresses the enlightenment-rationalist rather than the mechanistic elements of the passage. If we keep in mind the Hobbesian doc-trine, of which Bentham was well aware, that submission to the will of another involves deference both in conduct and in judgment (see above, 2.2.) then 'self-government' here must be understood in terms of rational self-direction, that is, action on one's own judg-ment of the reasons there are for acting in one way rather than another. To be sure, there is no hint here or anywhere in Bentham's writings of the expressive, self-creative aspects of the human self. Bentham is, in this respect a rationalist, not a romantic. The world is rationally ordered, and human beings in virtue of their individual rational faculties are capable of participating in it. Liberty, security, and enlightenment are important precisely because they make it possible for each person to take his or her responsible place in that ordered universe.

But Long is correct to point out that this is a static human universe. The rational self Bentham pictures is capable of rational direction of action but only upon a set of ends and aims, desires and aversions, bestowed by nature upon it. 'Sense, which is the basis of every idea,' says Bentham, is also the basis of every enjoy-ment, 'and unless man's whole nature be new modelled, so long as

---

[22] Long, *Bentham on Liberty*, 18.

man remains man the stock of sense . . . never can encrease' (UC cxlii. 200).

Absent from this, Bentham's most utopian, picture is any sense of the plasticity of human nature or the openness of the human future. He has 'not made sufficient allowance for the varieties of human nature, and the caprices and irregularities of the human will', Hazlitt complains. He has 'bound volatile Hermes' and 'struck the whole mass of fancy, prejudice, passion, sense, whim, with his petrific, leaden mace . . .'.[23] Absent also is any suggestion of the self's involvement in the shaping, or the assessment, of nature's package of aims and desires.

Absent, finally, is any awareness of the human desire or capacity to join with others in defining and carrying out a conception of the common good or shared values. For Bentham, conflicting conceptions of individual or common good are merely different arrangements of uniform human interests—and more often different views of the most efficient means of satisfying these interests. Political struggle, purged of superstition and the corruption of 'the principle of sympathy and antipathy', is transformed into debate over technical means of resolving competing interests. There is no need for more fundamental political debate because the basic terms of resolution exist already in the uniformity of human interests. Bentham never recognized the possibility of deeply conflicting conceptions of good or justice or the direction of social life, which reflect potentially incompatible ways of viewing and valuing social life. Nor did he have any sense of the value of a people's forging for themselves a common conception of justice or common good.

Bentham's idea of the self is that of a rationally self-directed individual, prudently adjusting his actions and plans to the realities of his environment, but always thinking and judging for himself. If this ideal is to be put within reach of each individual in society, Bentham thought, two conditions must be met: (i) personal security and social coherence, the necessary conditions of personal coherence (which alone makes rational self-direction possible), must be put on a firm foundation; and (ii) forces, both social and intellectual, which enslave the mind and judgment must be destroyed. Bentham's commitment to securing these two conditions shaped the broad goals of both his jurisprudence and political theory.

[23] Hazlitt, *Spirit of the Age*, 5.

5.3   SECURITY AND THE FUNDAMENTAL TASK OF LAW

> The law does not tell a man what he should do to accomplish specific
> ends set by the lawgiver; it furnishes him with base lines against
> which to organize his life with his fellows.
>
> L. Fuller, 'Human Interaction and the Law.'

Once Bentham succeeded in showing, to his satisfaction, that justice properly understood does not conflict with utility, and that all intelligible talk of justice can be reduced to talk of utility under a special description, he almost entirely dropped the term 'justice' from his theoretical vocabulary. Except for very occasional (although not in themselves uninteresting) comments in his later writings, the term does not appear again, and the notion plays no significant theoretical role in his jurisprudence.

This is not the case, however, for the concepts he developed for use in his early analysis of justice. These carry an increasingly heavy load in his developing theory. The most important of these is the notion of *expectations*, although it is quickly merged with the slightly broader concept of *security*, which is made to do all the theoretical work of justice, and much more. From the late 1770s and early 1780s onwards, security is the primary focus of his utilitarian theory of law, and the first deputy of his sovereign principle of utility. In this section I trace the career of this concept and through it uncover Bentham's assumptions regarding the fundamental social tasks of law.

In this section I shall try to show, contrary to the common reading, that Bentham did not hold that the primary function of law is social discipline and 'social control'. The centrality of the notion of sovereignty and especially of command in his jurisprudence cannot be denied, nor can the prominence of the model of the criminal law in his analysis of the formal, logical structure of law. But I will argue that these are best understood against a quite different conceptual and normative background than is commonly assumed. Bentham's conception of law, I shall begin to argue here, is far less manipulative and 'managerial' than is standardly assumed. In fact, it comes reasonably close to the 'interactive' and 'facilitating' conception championed by Lon Fuller.[24]

[24] L. Fuller, 'Human Interaction and the Law', and *The Morality of Law, passim.* By 'managerial direction' Fuller has in mind the kind of bureaucratic rationality which manipulates behaviour through general rules and directives im-

Security: objective and subjective elements

The complexity of Bentham's concept of security can be seen by starting with its simplest element, modelled by familiar features of the criminal law, and then adding to it one by one the other components to fill out the concept.

We begin again with the distinction between original utility and expectation utility. In his earliest writings Bentham illustrates the distinction by drawing examples from the criminal law and law of property. If a law is justified, he asserts in the *Comment*, it must be seen to serve utility, 'either original, or derived from expectation'. So, for example, a law prohibiting assault is grounded on original utility. 'For whether a man expects to be safe from beating or does not, beating is at all events a pain to him.' The disutility with which the law concerns itself in no way depends on the beliefs or expectations of the victim or others. In contrast, the disutility caused by theft can only be explained by reference to the expectations of the owner, the expectation to retain possession indefinitely.[25]

Now, Bentham assumes here and consistently throughout his career that expectations are the only utilitarily relevant considerations in the context of property and private law generally. 'Expectation is the basis of every proprietary right', he insists. This alone 'affords whatever reason there can be for giving [alt.: adjudging] a thing to one man rather than another' (UC xxix. 6). But Bentham also recognizes the important role of expectations in law protecting the physical integrity of the person. Physical assault, for instance, tends to cause not only the original disutility of physical suffering on the part of the victim, but also fear and apprehension on the part of the public generally. These expectations are not the product of any single act, but rather a function of the system of rules (or lack, or inadequacy of, such a system).[26] Thus, there is a strong

posed from the top of some hierarchically structured enterprise, rules usually designed to serve ends of those who issue the rules, or at least ends not shared by the subordinates whose behaviour is manipulated by them.

[25] *Comment* 231; also UC lxx(a). 19, 20. Precisely this difference in utilitarian foundations, Bentham claims, explains why certain laws must be the same in all societies, while others vary greatly from society to society. The former laws, resting in a substantial way on original utility, depend on largely invariant features of human nature, whereas the latter depend on expectations and these, in turn, on potentially widely variable beliefs, experience, prejudices, attitudes, and practices.

[26] This is made clear in R. Nozick's sophisticated discussion of similar issues in *Anarchy, State and Utopia*, ch. 4. See also Postema, 'Nozick on Liberty'.

case for treating the utilities associated with them as a species of expectation utilities alongside those we discussed earlier.

In *IPML* Bentham creates a special category to capture this species of utilities. In Chapter XII he distinguishes between the *primary* and the *secondary* mischief of a criminal offence. The primary mischief is the original disutility caused by the offence, suffered by an assignable individual or set of them. The secondary mischief, however, 'extends itself either over the whole community or over some other multitude of unassignable individuals' (*IPML* XII. 3). That is, the harm done by assault, for example, is both a private harm and a *public* harm.[27] According to Bentham, this public harm is composed of two elements: alarm and danger (*IPML* XII. 5–13). Danger is the *actual* likelihood of similar offences occurring as a result of not taking available steps to punish the offence in question. Alarm consists in the pain and apprehension of suffering, the expectation of harm, experienced by the public at large. Both the primary mischief (original disutility) and the danger may be regarded as objective harms, in the sense that they are not dependent upon the beliefs or expectations of those who suffer them. But the secondary mischief—alarm—involves also an important subjective component which is expectation-dependent. It is also worth keeping in mind here that the labels 'primary' and 'secondary' are not intended to suggest priority of utilitarian significance, but rather a *logical* priority. They are first-order and second-order disutilities in the sense that the second-order mischief of danger (or alarm) requires for its explication the notion of the first-order mischief. (Indeed, we shall see shortly that Bentham tends to give utilitarian priority to matters of second-order harm, especially alarm.)

We are now in a position to introduce the notion of security. To do so, consider first Bentham's view of the relation between liberty and law.[28] Following Hobbes, Bentham defines liberty as 'neither more nor less than the absence of coercion'. The idea of liberty is 'purely negative'. 'When a person is neither constrained nor restrained with respect to an act . . . he is said with respect to that act to be free, to be at *liberty*' (UC lxix. 44, author's emphasis). It would be absurd to say that law produces or creates liberty, says Bentham, for all law can do is constrain or restrain actions of people

---

[27] Hume also recognized both of these, see *Enquiry II* 310–11.
[28] For a detailed and very useful discussion see Long, *Bentham on Liberty*.

and that infringes liberty. Liberty is an entirely natural condition. The only thing law can do is to *secure* some range of liberty for some collection of individuals by constraining other actions which may interfere with the liberty.

[Liberty] is not anything produced by law. It exists without law and not by means of law. It is not producible at all by law, but in the case where its opposite *coercion* has been produced [by law] before. That which under the name of Liberty is so much magnified, as invaluable, the unrivalled work of Law, is not *liberty*, but *security* (UC lxix. 44).

Bentham's point here is that the rhetoric of liberty rests on a fundamental confusion: it preaches the incomparable value of liberty and praises law as its source as well as its guardian. But it is not liberty that we seek; it is security, for it is only security that can be the product of law.

The contrast between liberty and security reveals an important property of Bentham's notion of security. Whereas liberty is an entirely objective notion, it is the state of *actually being free* from restriction and constraint, security involves an essentially subjective element. Liberty, even liberty of considerable extent, is possible without security, Bentham observes, but this is the liberty 'possessed by Hottentots and Patagonians', and it is much less valuable than the liberty secured by law—'the possession which is the pride of Englishmen' (UC lxix. 55). That is, unsecured liberty is of little value. What we need (for coherence in our own lives) is a reasonable basis for predicting our own individual futures, and this comes not from the mere possession, but from the *sure knowledge*, of that liberty. Security itself is a source of liberty, then, for without assurance of no interference in one's activities, one may be inclined not to engage in them. (Insecurity has what American lawyers would call a 'chilling effect' on action.) Thus, contrary to Bentham's original claim, law can be seen to *produce* liberty. Yes, he replies, but only *indirectly* and through the direct production of security. And this only reinforces the main point. The task of law is not to create liberty, but to maximize security.

Thus, the notion of security embraces both first- and second-order concerns identified in *IPML*.[29] Moreover, the previous paragraph

[29] In his later writings, this thesis is expressed in the following terms. Security is the immediate subordinate end to the all-comprehensive end of government: the greatest happiness of the greatest number. This end or goal generates two principles: the 'positive-pain-prevention principle' (applying to all matters of 'objective' harm

suggests that Bentham regards the subjective, expectation-dependent component of security to be of greater importance, in the context of law, then the other, objective components. This suggestion is reinforced by comments Bentham makes in *IPML*. For example, he believes that very few, if any, 'self-regarding offences' (i.e. actions the alleged disutility of which is suffered entirely by the agent) are justified on utilitarian grounds. His reason is that, even if such actions produce primary mischief (which he regards as uncertain), they produce no *secondary* mischief, no alarm, and so no public harm (*IPML* XVI. 64, pp. 277–8). And, in consequence, they are not proper concerns of the law. The law, it seems, must restrict its focus to those concerns with a substantial *public* component.

Security: 'the principal object of the laws'

Thus far we have seen security, especially in its subjective aspects, at work both in property law and in criminal law protecting the integrity of the person. However, this concept plays an even more fundamental role in Bentham's jurisprudence. For Bentham, security is the principal object of law *in general* and in every branch.[30] The full implications of this assumption will be traced out in the remainder of this chapter and over the next several chapters.

First, consider again the proposition that law can only produce security and not liberty, and that it does so through limiting other liberties (e.g. constraining and coercing others not to interfere with certain actions of mine). This poses a problem for a race that seeks as a *sine qua non* of all happiness the good of security. For law itself presents a serious danger and represents a serious source of insecurity. 'It is not enough for me', Bentham admits, 'that I am at liberty as against you. It is not enough that I am secured from being constrained or restrained by you. My happiness may be as effectively destroyed by my being constrained or restrained by the Law . . .' (UC lxix. 55). It looks as if security in one quarter can be purchased only at the price of insecurity in another. But the fact that law is itself, in several different ways, a source of insecurity creates no genuine paradox in Bentham's view. For what we can reason-

that may be the concern of the law), and the 'disappointment-prevention principle' (which takes over for 'justice' on Bentham's early analysis). See *Pannomial Fragments, Bowring* iii, 211–12.

[30] *CC* 11; *Civil Code, Bowring* i, 307, and generally 322–6; *Pannomial Fragments, Bowring* iii, 211–13; and *Bowring* ii, 269–70.

ably hope for is not perfect security, but *maximal* security, and that may require that we sacrifice security at some points in order to gain a greater and compensating security at some other point. Thus, the insecurity-causing features of law produce not a refutation of this view of the relation between law and security (for, outside of law security is virtually impossible), but a new set of problems for his account of law.

The most obvious source of such law-generated insecurity lies in the potential abuse of the power of coercion lodged in the government, but there are other equally troubling sources. Security is a function not simply of the effectiveness of enforcement, but also of the clarity of the definition of permitted and prohibited actions. Insecurity may arise, then, (i) from the fact that it is not clear to what extent *others* may or may not interfere with one's own liberty; (ii) from the fact that it is unclear to what extent *one* may interfere with the liberty of others without calling down the coercive force of the law upon one; (iii) from uncertainty about the scope and limits of the powers of officials to restrict one's own liberty either in the particular case, or in general by means of some rule or law, and (iv) from the fact that it is unclear who is to count as an official authorized coercively to interfere with one and what is to count as an authentic general rule authorizing such interference.

Thus, the problem of law-related or law-generated insecurity is not simply the ancient problem, *Quis custodiet ipsos custodes*? It is also the problem of determining *who* those guardians are, under what conditions they are authorized to exercise their power, and how that power is to be exercised. For the purpose of minimizing the several insecurities noticed above the device of coercion, now directed against officials rather than private persons, is surely insufficient. What is needed is clear definition of the limits of liberty, and of the scope, limits, and authenticating conditions of official power. Thus, in addition to a device for enforcing constraints there must be a device for defining a framework of rights, powers, duties, responsibilities, and other relationships. Security is the focal concern of *all* these activities both 'penal' and 'distributive'. The latter includes both civil law (*'droit distributif privé'*—UC xcix. 34) and constitutional law (*'droit distributif politique'*—UC xxxii. 130).

Second, we have seen that, as Bentham's thought developed, 'security' replaced 'justice' in his theoretical vocabulary, while the concept of respect for established expectations retained its centrality. In his early discussion Bentham seemed to follow the standard view of Hume, Smith, and others in the mid-eighteenth century, identifying justice with arrangements for the definition, stability, and protection of *property*. Adam Smith, for example, maintained that 'The first and chief design of every system of government is to maintain justice; to prevent the members of society from encroaching on one another's property, or seizing what is not their own. The design here is to give each one the secure and peaceable possession of his own property.'[31] However, there are in Bentham's identification of justice with respect for expectation utilities the seeds of a broader application. By the early 1780s, when he turns to matters of the civil code, he still writes that expectation is the basis of every 'proprietary' right, but property is broadened to encompass all the proper objects of concern of the civil law.[32] Under the law of property, 'in its most extensive sense', he maintains later, 'may be included all objects of general desire' (UC xiv. 366; see also 382). He criticizes Locke for limiting his view to property in its narrowest designation—viz. 'matter of wealth'. Locke overlooks, 'so many other valuable subject matters of possession, namely power, reputation, condition in life . . . and exemption from pain in all the several shapes in which either body or mind is the seat of it . . . possessions giving security to which is among the functions and cares of justice' (UC xiv. 392). Bentham anticipates the modern tendency to regard *all* rights secured to an individual by law as 'a species of normative property belonging to the right holder . . .'[33] Among the general classes of objects of security that Bentham recognizes are wealth, reputation, personal integrity (of mind and body), power, rank, and condition in life.[34] In Bentham's view, all forms of social interaction available to human beings except political relationships and institutions fall under the concept of property.

The following picture of the social function of law emerges from this discussion. The principal object of law is to provide security

[31] A Smith, *Lectures on Jurisprudence*, 6.

[32] See *Civil Code, Bowring* i, 307–8. 'Security depends on the care taken to save from disturbance the current of Expectations' (UC xxxii. 2). A few years later Bentham wrote, 'Keep the current of expectations inviolate: in these words are contained the great landmark of the civil code . . .'. (UC xxix. 6).

[33] H. L. A. Hart, 'Legal Rights', in *Essays on Bentham*, 185. Bentham's criticism of Locke is unfair, see *Second Treatise*, para. 123.

[34] See, e.g., *Pannomial Fragments, Bowring* iii, 213, 225; *CC* 11; UC xiv. 392.

for every citizen in the relations each bears to other citizens and to governmental authorities. On the public or constitutional level, this requires securing citizens against unwarranted encroachment from government. On the private level, it calls for securing expectations throughout the whole range of possible social relations. In both cases the task, as Bentham sees it, is twofold. First, rights, duties, and powers, must be defined and 'distributed', and practices and conventions established. The law must spin out the great web of social relationships, the basic framework of social interaction. This framework defines the base lines against which citizens may organize their lives. The law determines the *social* reality within which individual lives are lived out, and ends and purposes are pursued, on analogy with the determination of the *physical* environment by laws of physical nature. (The crucial disanalogy between them, of course, is that the former are artificial.) Second, this framework must be 'given execution and effect'; that is, it must be applied and enforced. This second task comprises two sub-tasks: (i) that of fine-tuning and adjusting the general framework through adjudication, and (ii) maintaining it through enforcement. Bentham assigns this task of enforcement for both private and public (constitutional) law to the penal law. The other tasks are assigned to 'distributive law' (civil or constitutional).

Furthermore, this assignment of tasks also suggests a kind of functional priority: the *primary* social task of law is that of defining social and political relationships. Penal law, supplying motivation through threat of punishment, is seen as auxiliary. Thus, the fundamental task of law is not to bend citizens to the sovereign's will through the coercive mechanisms at its disposal,[35] but to define, settle and secure a social reality which makes possible the pursuit of individual aims, purposes, and plans of life. The law's task is not only, or even primarily, regulative (though there are, of course, regulative tasks to perform), rather it is fundamentally *constitutive*. The sovereign lawgiver 'is not the master of the dispositions of the human heart: he is only their interpreter and their servant. The goodness of his laws depends upon their conformity to the general *expectation*' (*Civil Code, Bowring* i, 322).

Civil v. penal: logical and functional distinctions
But at this point we must take up directly an important challenge to this interpretation of assumptions underlying Bentham's

[35] L. J. Hume, *Bentham and Bureaucracy*, 241.

jurisprudence. My interpretation, it might be objected, flies in the face of obvious and central doctrines of Bentham's jurisprudence, in particular: (i) the logically basic role of the concepts of command and sovereignty in his definition of law[36] and (ii) the centrality of the concept of *offence* for any systematic, rationally structured code of laws.[37] That is, the criminal law is not plausibly regarded as merely an auxiliary in Bentham's jurisprudence; it is rather, the *model* on which all law is conceived, the kind of law to which all other forms of law must be reduced. The theoretical priority given to the concept of command entails (i) that laws must be seen as essentially directive, or mandatory, such that all legal relations can be reduced to species of duties or the negation of duties; (ii) that laws must be seen as the imposition of will by a superior upon an inferior which implies both that laws impose requirements upon action which effectively preempt individual judgment and that the laws themselves direct action to the ends and purposes of the lawgiver, not the subject; and (iii) that the notion of sanction is logically essential, the notion of an unsanctioned law is a kind of absurdity.

It would be absurd, of course, to deny that the notion of command is central to Bentham's definition of law. But there is good reason to question whether Bentham understands the notion in the (essentially Hobbesian) way assumed by this objection. I will consider this issue later (9.3). Nor do I wish to deny, more generally, that Bentham takes the notion of a mandatory norm as conceptually basic to his account of the notion of *a* law, and of a complete and integral system of *laws*. Nor shall I deny that Bentham assigns a certain priority to the penal law. Perhaps the strongest statement to this effect can be seen in his

---

[36] The *locus classicus* of this view, of course, is *OLG* I and II. But the view is reiterated often throughout his writings. For example, UC lxix. 70–5; *IPML*, Concluding Note; *FG* I. 12 n. o; *Pannomial Fragments, Bowring* iii, 217, 223.

[37] 'Does not the idea of *an offence* govern everything in matters of law?' (*General View, Bowring* iii, 163). See also *Pannomial Fragments, Bowring* iii, 213; *IPML* XVI and Concluding Note, paras. 15–23; and Hume, *Bentham and Bureaucracy*, 242–3. At *Bowring* iii, 161 Bentham seems to express the same view: 'If a legislator have given a complete description of all the acts which he is desirous should be regarded as *offences*, he will have formed a complete collection of the laws: he has referred everything to the penal code.' But note that he continues: 'If he have established all the obligations of the citizens, all the rights created by those obligations, and the circumstances which shall cause those rights to begin and end, he will again have formed an entire code: but here he will have referred everything to the civil code.'

General View of a Complete Code of Laws:

Penal laws . . . are those alone which follow in a regular train, and form a complete whole. What are called civil laws, are only detached fragments belonging in common also to the penal laws. . . . [Only from the matter of penal law is it] possible to construct the principal portion of the edifice of the laws. It is proper, therefore, to take the penal law, which alone embraces all, as the foundation of all the other divisions of the law.[38]

But the objection which draws attention to these doctrines is insufficiently sensitive to the subtleties of Bentham's legal theory and to the way in which he weaves conceptual and normative elements together into a coherent whole. There is, in fact, a most compelling interpretation of the doctrines and claims to which this objection adverts which is entirely consistent with the view I have sketched above.

The key to this interpretation lies in understanding the peculiar way Bentham draws the distinction between civil and penal law and his motivation for drawing the distinction in this way. Our story begins with the severe theoretical crisis in early 1780 which brought to a halt Bentham's attempt to complete his *Introduction to the Principles*.[39] Abruptly he put off publication of the text (most of which was already printed) 'when, in the investigation of some flaws [he] had discovered, he found himself unexpectedly entangled in an unsuspected corner of the metaphysical maze . . .' from which he could not easily extricate himself (*IPML*, Preface, p. 1). The difficulties forced him to face questions which took him to what he saw as the logical and philosophical core of jurisprudence:

Wherein consisted the identity and *completeness* of a law? What the distinction, and where the separation, between *a penal* and a *civil* law? What the distinction, and where the separation, between the *penal* and *other branches* of *the law* (*IPML*, Preface, p. 8, author's emphasis).

If Bentham's objective in the writing of *IPML* was simply that of laying the conceptual and normative bases for the criminal law, this explanation of his refusal to publish his first seventeen chapters is puzzling and inadequate. Why should such questions of general jurisprudence, especially the abstract and 'metaphysical' question

---

[38] *Bowring* iii, 163. See *OLG* XIX. 2: 'But the civil branch of each law . . . is but the *complement* of the penal . . .' Also *OLG* App. E, p. 306.

[39] For a detailed account of this crisis see the Editor's Introduction to *OLG*, pp. xxxi–xxxv.

of the proper principles of individuation of laws, threaten to under-mine the substantial work already done to put criminal justice on a firm utilitarian basis? And why should the distinction between penal and civil law be crucial for the success of that project?

Bentham's explanation makes better sense if his objective went beyond merely developing a defensible theory of criminal justice. Indeed, this was the case, for he wished his work to 'serve for an in-troduction to the principles of legislation *in general* as well as to the penal branch in particular' (*OLG*, App. E, pp. 305–6, emphasis added). The crisis which forced Bentham to explore the logical rela-tions between civil and penal laws, and the principles by which laws are individuated and systematically related, was brought on by his increasing awareness that 'criminal' or 'penal' elements can be found in each traditional branch of law, including the civil and con-stitutional; and that the simple model of the penal law with which he had been working did not easily accommodate the distribu-tional and definitional tasks of civil law which he came to see were of considerable importance.[40]

At the end of his investigation in his *Introduction to the Prin-ciples* he turned his attention to the question of the 'limits of the penal branch of jurisprudence' (*IPML* XVII). First, he considered the problems of marking the boundaries between law and private ethics. Then he turned to the task of distinguishing various *branches* of law. This went smoothly until he tried to distinguish *penal* from *civil* jurisprudence (*IPML* XVII. 29). How are the con-cerns of the latter branch related to the penal branch? he asked. How is the penal 'code' related to the civil 'code'? Can the concerns of property law, contract law, family law, and the law of master and servant—which in effect he had addressed earlier under the aspect of 'justice' and respect for expectations—be adequately accommo-dated within a model of law which takes the concept of *offences* as the central organizing concept (see *IPML* XVI)? He had already, before beginning work on the *Introduction to the Principles*, recognized to some extent the quite different tasks of both 'private' and constitutional law (UC lxix. 148). But it was not until later that he realized the full theoretical implications of recognizing these as important tasks of law. This forced a crisis because Bentham feared, for a time at least, that the entire theoretical structure he had erected would have to be dismantled and reconstructed on

---

[40] See Long, *Bentham on Liberty*, ch. 9.

some other basis. Douglas Long observes that 'One of the most important themes in *Of Laws in General* is the development of Bentham's awareness that this additional function of law, which defines the civil law as distinct from the penal, also renders that distinction fundamental to the structure of a complete code of laws . . .'.[41] (This is correct, with only one minor qualification: from *IPML* XVII. 29 one can infer that probably Bentham was already aware of the importance of this functional difference before he launched full force into the *études* which now make up *Of Laws in General*.)[42]

One possible approach to the problem Bentham uncovered here would have been to recognize a second distinct logical type of law or norm alongside that of the mandatory norm modelled upon commands. This, of course, is the familiar tack advocated by Hart in his criticism of Austin and Bentham.[43] But Bentham did not elect this approach. He was anxious to develop a simple, unified, and conceptually lean account of the logical structure of laws, and so refused to multiply logical types of law when leaner alternatives appeared open to him.

His philosophical strategy, brilliant even if ultimately unsuccessful, was twofold. First, he modified his basic model of a legal norm in two respects.

1. He allowed not only for commands, and so mandatory norms, but also for permissions. This called for the construction of a 'logic of the will' (deontic logic) which carefully and brilliantly mapped out the logical relations among most of the important deontic notions needed in his jurisprudence. The result of these researches was a modified account of law—an 'imperatival' rather than a simple 'command' theory[44]—which made room for a second type of law without adding to his original conceptual base anything more than the logical operator, negation. A permission was defined as the negation of a command. With this notion, Bentham was able to construct, to his satisfaction, an analysis of legal powers as specially targeted, exception-creating permissions within the scope

---

[41] Ibid. 157.

[42] The editors of OLG maintain that *IPML* XVII. 29 could not have been written later than Nov. 1780 (*OLG*, p. xxxii). The manuscripts for *OLG* (UC lxxxiii(a) and (b)) were written between 1780 and 1782.

[43] H. L. A. Hart, *Concept of Law*, ch. III and 238–40 and Hart, 'Legal Powers', in, *Essays on Bentham*.

[44] See generally, D. Lyons, *In the Interest of the Governed*, Pt. II.

of a general mandatory rule.[45] Bentham argued vigorously that with this conceptual equipment a large part of what is 'distributed' by both civil and constitutional law can be analysed as parts of laws. No new *kind* of law need be recognized.

2. But this technique alone did not find a place for all those laws which comprise civil law as ordinarily understood. In particular, it did not yet account for laws which set out to delineate the conditions under which persons qualify for, acquire, lose, or transfer the duties, rights, powers, and privileges of law. That is, Bentham needed to explain not only what it is to *have* legal ownership, for example, but also how one acquires title, and how the laws defining such matters fit into his conceptual scheme. These 'expository' laws were accommodated within the above model as merely that part of one (or more) general mandatory laws which *defines* (and qualifies) the offence (that is, the act which the mandatory norm prohibits). Thus, the law of contracts regarding the rendering of private services can be understood in the following way. There is a general rule prohibiting any individual from obliging another to render him any service. To this general rule there is the exception: that one may do so, if the person obliged to render service consents or contracts to do so. This opens the door, says Bentham, to an enormous body of 'circumstantiative' material concerning *inter alia* 'What contracts the law adopts and holds for good: what construction it puts upon them: what it looks upon as performance of them: which stipulations it looks upon as implied in such as are expressed: what others it imposes on him in consideration of a change of interest brought about by subsequent events', and so on (*OLG*, App. G [Corrigenda]).

Thus, Bentham's researches into the logic of the will and into the notion of a complete and integral law led him to the conclusion that the distinction between penal and civil law is not best represented as a distinction between two irreducibly distinct *kinds* of law, but as a distinction between two different parts of the same laws.[46] Every complete law has a penal element—a mandatory or imperative

---

[45] See, for example, *OLG* XVI. 10–13 generally Hart, 'Legal Powers'.

[46] It is a little surprising that Bentham, after allegedly wrestling long and hard with this problem, hit on a solution which is strikingly similar to Blackstone's. Blackstone divides his *Commentaries*, and so the subject matter of the common law, into rights (private and public) and wrongs (also private and public), insisting, however, that every complete legal rule includes *both* the definition of a right and the specification of a wrong (= offence plus sanction or remedy). See 3 *Comm.* 2 and 119.

part, plus a 'comminative' or sanction-threatening part—and a civil element—which embraces all its 'expository', 'qualificative', and permission-creating matter (*OLG* XVI).

This reduced all law to the model of a much expanded and qualified command. But the second essential part of Bentham's strategy was to distinguish sharply between the *logical structure* of laws and their *social functions*. Thus, for Bentham, the labels 'civil' and 'penal' do not designate different *kinds* of laws, but they do embrace different essential *tasks* performed by the law. The civil part of the law performs the definitional, distributional, and ultimately constitutive tasks; the penal part performs the regulative task. 'A civil law is that which establishes a right; a penal law is that which, in consequence of the establishment of a right by the civil law, directs the punishment in a certain manner of him who violates it.'[47] Between the two parts of the law (the two 'codes') there is 'a most intimate connection'; they interpenetrate each other at all points. Penal law would be incomplete, indeed incomprehensible, without the civil aspect; the civil code, as a matter of fact, would be virtually impotent without the penal.[48]

Despite this intimacy, Bentham frequently speaks of one or the other as if it enjoys some kind of priority. As we have already noted, Bentham sometimes assigns priority to the penal law. J. Raz, expressing a common criticism of Bentham and positivist legal theory generally, charges that Bentham, 'by concentrating on the criminal law, tended to emphasize the primary [social] function of prohibiting undesirable behaviour and to overlook the other functions' which law may serve.[49] Raz cites the following passage from Bentham's *General View* to support his charge:

. . . the penal code ought to precede the civil code, and the constitutional code, &c. In the first, the legislator exhibits himself to every individual; he permits, he commands, he prohibits; he traces for every one the rules of his conduct; he uses the language of a father and a master. In the other codes, he has less to do with commandments than with regulations and explanations,

[47] *General View, Bowring* iii, 160. See also *CC* 8, 11–12, 23.
[48] Long, *Bentham on Liberty*, 151, following UC xcvi. 102–3. But he could also have cited *CC* 12: 'Of the matter of the penal code, the designation made is not complete until a designation has been made of all the sorts of acts which, by it, are dealt with in the character of offences. Of the matter of the civil code, the efficiency would be throughout as nothing, were not the several acts by which the distributions made by it are violated, dealt with on the footing of offences.'
[49] J. Raz, 'On the Functions of Law', 303.

which do not so clearly address themselves to everybody, and which are not equally interesting to those concerned . . . (*Bowring* iii, 161).

But this passage gives no support to Raz's thesis. Bentham assigns priority to the penal code here, but it is of priority in the arrangement of codes for public promulagation only that he is speaking in this passage. It comes in partial answer to the question, 'In what order should the different parts which compose a complete code of legislation be arranged?' (*Bowring* iii, 161). Bentham is not at all concerned with any functional priority here.

There are other passages, one especially in *General View* which I quoted earlier (at note 38) which seems to give stronger support to Raz's thesis. But all the passages cited in note 38 can be seen to express the view that penal law has a kind of *logical* priority. 'The matter of the civil code is *in its form* little else but a sort of exposition of the terms employed in the commands delivered by the penal code' (*CC* 12, emphasis added). 'The [civil law] does not include the [penal], but the second implicitly includes the first. Say to the judges, "*You shall punish thieves*", and a prohibition of stealing is clearly intimated. In this point of view, the penal code would be sufficient for all purposes' (*Bowring* iii, 160).[50] But 'the point of view' Bentham has in mind here is the logical one; the implicit analogy is to an analytic truth the consequent of which is contained implicitly in the antecedent. 'Criminal Jurisprudence concerning possessions supposes a distribution already made of them by Civil Jurisprudence' (UC xcvi. 102–3). But nothing follows from this regarding the relative priority of *social* functions.

Indeed, when he explicitly considers the social functions of the law, Bentham claims priority for the civil code. With regard to the generic end of security, 'the principal and leading operation' which the law must take up is that of defining the class of offences, and to that end developing all the 'expository matter' necessary for the civil code (*CC* 11–12). It is by this means only that 'the law . . . afford[s] the means of knowing what is each man's property' (*CC* 12). Bentham even suggests that, were it not for the temptations to which men are in general subject, this definition of relations might be sufficient (ibid.). But because of the inescapable need for enforcement of the framework of legal relations, obligations, rights, and

[50] Actually on the next page Bentham suggests that a complete statement of the law could be made from the vantage point of the civil law. See the passage quoted above, n. 37.

powers defined by distributional law, penal laws must always be appended. The penal law is a kind of physician to the body politic (*CC* 23). It cannot *produce* health in the body, but it can protect it, and through preventive medicine ward off some of the most serious maladies to which it may be subject. The task of penal law is to 'give execution and effect' to the civil or constitutional law.[51]

With relation to the civil code . . . the matter of the penal code is but a means. By the arrangements contained in the civil code, so many directive rules are furnished; what the penal code does, is but to furnish sanctions, by which provision is made for the observance of those directive rules (*CC* 12).

Far from overlooking the facilitating and arranging—indeed, the constituting—functions which law may serve, Bentham gives them pride of place. Thus, we may conclude that, for Bentham, law is not simply an instrument through which power is wielded and behaviour regulated, it is, more fundamentally, a principle of order by which social reality is constituted.

5.4 EXPECTATIONS AND THE GENESIS OF LAW

Law is the most splendid triumph of humanity over itself.

Bentham, *Civil Code.*

We may conclude from the above discussion that, despite Bentham's preoccupation with reform of the criminal law in his early, formative years, his jurisprudence (even at that time) had a broader focus. Security, to be sure, was for Bentham the primary aim of law, but 'security' encompassed both the *protection* of individuals from harm, and, in the first instance, the definition and construction of those social roles and relations which make social life possible. This latter function, we have seen, shapes and directs the protective, regulative and enforcement activities of the law.

Over the course of the next several chapters, and especially in Chapter 8, I will show that this assumption about the primary tasks of law underlies not only his view of what constitutes *good law* (from a utilitarian point of view), but also his theory of the *nature*

---

[51] *CC* 23. This language is standardly used by Bentham to express functional subordination. See especially his discussion of the functional relationship between procedural and substantive law, UC xcvi. 74–5 and *PJP*, *Bowring* ii, 6, discussed below in 10.1.

of law itself. In this concluding section I shall begin the argument for this conclusion by considering Bentham's brief account of what Hume would call 'the origins' of law. (This account parallels in interesting ways Hume's account of the origins of justice, but also in equally interesting ways parts company with it.) This discussion, I believe, will deepen our understanding of Bentham's assumptions about the relationships that obtain among security, expectations, and the nature of law. Subsequent chapters will discuss in detail arguments of Bentham which rest implicitly or explicitly on these assumptions.

In the early chapters of his *Civil Code* we have fragments of a 'logical' or 'conjectural history' of law.[52] In this account the rise of the institution of property plays a central role. One is immediately reminded of Hume's discussion. And indeed, Bentham's discussion is almost unintelligible, and surely hopelessly incomplete, without background setting and argument supplied by Hume's much more fully developed account. Bentham in his discussion makes explicit what we found implicit in Hume's theory of justice. For Bentham, property is essentially a legal notion; property and law are inseparable. 'Property and law are born and die together. Before the laws, there was no property: take away the laws, all property ceases' (*Civil Code, Bowring* i, 309). The notion of property is a fiction, says Bentham.[53] There can be no such thing as 'natural property'. Property is an artificial, conventional relation between a person, a thing, and other persons. Going beyond this Humean claim Bentham insists that 'property is entirely the *creature* of law' (*Bowring* i, 308). Thus, the origins of property *just are* the origins of law. With 'the slightest agreement among . . . savages reciprocally to respect each other's booty' history records 'the introduction of a principle, to which you can only give the name of law' (*Bowring* i, 308–9).

But, we must not import more of Hume's theory into Bentham's account than is warranted. For Hume the origins of law can be traced to the origins of the institution of property. Although property is the foundation for all other social relations (to determine the conventions regarding property is to determine, ultimately, all the

---

[52] Bentham also makes use of this device for analysing language, exhibiting thereby its underlying aims and the relations among its parts. See UC cii. 269–81 and *Essay on Language, Bowring* viii, esp. 322–3.

[53] *Bowring* i, 308. Compare Hume, *Treatise* 515, 527.

basic social relations), nevertheless, it is clear that Hume *starts out* with the problem of the distribution and security of (in Bentham's jargon) 'matters of wealth'. However, Bentham insists at the outset on a wider notion of property which embraces *all* basic social relations.[54] Thus, he addresses *directly* the question of the origins of the 'social constitution', whereas Hume addresses it *indirectly*. Hume's account of the 'social constitution' depends on empirical assumptions about the centrality of control of 'matters of wealth' which Bentham does not need to make. This allows Bentham's account to be more general than Hume's.

Nevertheless, the traditional notion of property does exert its influence on Bentham's account. For his *analysis* of the variety of social relations and conditions about which private law concerns itself is modelled directly upon that notion. The legal relations defined by the civil part of law are essentially *proprietary* in character. Thus, the notion of a domestic state or condition ('condition in life': for example, master, parent, or wife) is that of 'an ideal base about which are ranged rights and duties, and sometimes incapacities' which are linked to (put in the possession of) an individual by a certain 'investitive event with respect to the possession of that state'.[55] Because of the analytical importance of the traditional notion of property for Bentham's account, and because material-economic conditions figure prominently in his discussion of the hypothetical 'pre-legal' state, Bentham develops his account primarily with a focus on material property.

Like Hume, Bentham begins his discussion with a description of the social and psychological conditions, and the basic human needs associated with them, to which law responds. For this Bentham makes use of the familiar heuristic device of a hypothetical 'savage' or 'pre-legal' condition. Without security ('the distinctive mark of civilization'), the human condition is one of extreme scarcity and a constant, unrelenting and inevitably losing struggle against nature for mere survival (*Bowring* i, 307). This has direct psychological consequences, in Bentham's view. It 'destroys . . . the gentlest sentiments of nature', putting human beings in direct and deadly

---

[54] See above, p. 174. At *Bowring* i, 308 Bentham makes clear that the potential range of the principle of security to which law must be directed is not restricted to security of material possession, but rather 'must be prolonged to one throughout the whole vista that one's imagination can measure'.

[55] *General View, Bowring* iii, 192; see also UC xxxiii, 60.

conflict.[56] 'Like the most ferocious beasts, men pursue men, that they may feed on one another' (ibid.). The material basis of sympathy, goodwill, and co-operation does not exist, and each person is thrown into a cruel struggle with both nature and other human beings. At the same time natural limitations of human reason and sentiment exacerbate these conditions. The natural aversion to labour and an irrational preference for the present ('lack of foresight')[57] are characteristic of human beings in this uncivilized condition. As a result, there is little incentive to invest painful labour in the present in order to reap greater benefits in the future, both because of one's own natural inertia and because there is no assurance that others will not take advantage of one's own foresight and self-sacrifice.

Thus, severe natural conditions and basic human needs make joining for survival essential, but those conditions, and the natural limitations of sentiment and reason make such co-operative combination difficult. Security of possession will go a long way towards solving this problem, Bentham maintains, for it will make co-operation possible, and, with forces united, the niggardly hand of nature can be forced to open. Also it will eliminate those material conditions which cause destructive competition and undermine the 'social' sentiments. Furthermore, property overcomes the aversion to labour, by assuring one's enjoyment of its fruits, and thereby making attractive the prospect of eventually profitable labour (*Bowring* i, 307–8).

But, Bentham observes, recognition of the utility of stable and secure possession is not enough. Natural feeling alone cannot produce such security. The armies of the idle and impatient will always threaten to take advantage of those inclined, out of natural feelings, to labour for their own good or to respect the fruits of the labours of others. The only hope is to secure possession and stability artificially at the hand of law. 'Law alone has been able to create a fixed and durable possession which deserves the name of Property. The law alone could accustom men to submit to the yoke of foresight . . . it alone could encourage them in labour' (*Bowring* i, 307). Thus, law, the product of human will and invention, 'is the most splendid triumph of humanity over itself' (*Bowring* i, 309).

---

[56] On Bentham's view of the effect of material conditions on human sentiments see below, 11.3.

[57] *Bowring* i, 307, 309.

To see how, in Bentham's view, the law accomplishes this we need to introduce the notion of expectations, which, Bentham complains, jurists have almost entirely ignored but which is essential to jurisprudence.[58] The idea of property just is the idea of established expectations, says Bentham (*Bowring* i, 308). This expectation consists in the 'persuasion of power to derive certain advantages' from some object. But this expectation is entirely the work of the law: 'It is the law alone which allows me to forget my natural weakness: it is from the law alone that I can enclose a field and give myself to its cultivation, in the distant hope of the harvest' (ibid.). Of course, the law does not make me any stronger, but what it does is assure me that my efforts now can be expected to pay off *for me* in the future. The expectation does not regard *my own* efforts or nature, but the actions of *other people* around me.

But do not expectations with regard to one's physical possessions already exist independent of the law; could they not exist in the 'savage', natural state? Yes they may, and typically will, exist in such a state, Bentham replies, but they will be exceedingly weak: 'A feeble and momentary expectation only results from time to time, from purely physical circumstances.' But law gives birth to new and substantial bonds of expectation. The law amplifies feeble natural expectations (*Bowring* i, 309; UC xxix. 8).

Bentham's argument here is exceedingly sketchy. There is nothing like the carefully developed analytical structure one finds in Hume's *Treatise*. We might ask, for example, why do expectations play such an important role here? Why doesn't the lawgiver seek to distribute property so as to maximize utility? How exactly does law fit in? How, in particular, does it amplify expectations? There is, however, more than a faint suggestion of the Humean framework in the above discussion. If we were to superimpose Bentham's sketchy argument here on the rich background of Hume's account, much that is otherwise entirely mysterious is made reasonably clear. Because Bentham's conception of law is modelled on explicitly legislated rules, rather than custom, law inevitably enters the picture as a *deus ex machina*. Nevertheless, its

[58] 'The views of jurists must have been extremely confused, since they have paid no particular attention to a sentiment so fundamental in human life: the word expectation is scarcely to be found in their vocabulary; and argument can scarcely be found in their works, founded upon this principle. They have followed it, without doubt, in many instances, but it has been from instinct, and not from reason' (*Bowring* i, 308).

role and nature are made clearer by viewing it against the Humean background.

Bentham gives a rudimentary description of a co-ordination problem (or at least an assurance problem) which arises from conditions similar to those set out by Hume. In particular, parties in the 'savage' state come to recognize the need 'reciprocally to respect each others' booty'. And, 'the slightest agreement' yields an arrangement which is at least law-like, albeit unstable. What is more, it is clear from his description of the situation of the parties, and discussion later, that the most important thing, from the point of view of each party, is that there be *some* agreement, *some* arrangement *or other*, for respect of possession. It is less important, especially at this stage, what that arrangement looks like. Thus, the first and most important argument for the rules of actual possession and prescription is that they are simple, 'natural', and most likely to focus attention (*Bowring* i, 327). Bentham observes that 'There is nothing more diversified than the condition of property in America, England, Hungary, and Russia: in the first country the cultivator is proprietor; in the second he is a farmer; in the third he is attached to the soil; in the fourth he is a slave' (*Bowring* i, 311). Nevertheless, 'the supreme principle of security', which governs 'original distribution' as well as determination of title within an established system of property (*Bowring* v, 266), 'directs the preservation of all these distributions, how different soever their natures, and though they do not produce the same amount of happiness' (*Bowring* i, 311). The only apparent way to reconcile this with Bentham's utilitarianism is to assume that Bentham has in mind a situation in all essential respects like the co-ordination problem Hume sets out in his discussion.

Bentham suggests two possible ways in which the law secures possession and expectations. First, it creates expectations in the absence of any already existing conventions or agreements (*Bowring* i, 323), by creating a set of clear, accessible, public rules on which all can focus. Second, where expectations already exist—whether 'natural' or the product of some earlier agreement, custom, or usage (*Bowring* i, 323)—the law underwrites them by making them more public, and clarifying, codifying, and enforcing them. In this way the law amplifies expectations, transforming 'that which was only a thread in a state of nature' into 'a cable, so to speak, in a state of society' (*Bowring* i, 309). The task of law, especially the 'civil' part of law, then, is to 'make liquid' the rights and powers and possessions of individuals, which outside of law would be entirely inchoate (*OLG* XVIII. 14)—to make real, tangible, accessible, and so useful, what is otherwise unreal, indeterminate, useless.

We may say, then that for Bentham, as for Hume, the primary task of law is that of co-ordinating social interaction at the most basic level of social life, thereby making social life possible. This explicates, in part, the Benthamite doctrine that security is the principal object of the law. It also explains why Bentham assigned functional priority to the 'civil' dimension of law.

Despite the parallels between Hume and Bentham on the 'origins' of law, there are two important respects in which Bentham's account differs from Hume's. First, although both regard law as the artificial product of human invention, Hume insisted upon the essentially *customary* foundations of law. For Hume the conventions of law develop informally as the result of the actions and interaction of many individuals over time. Legislation, on Hume's view, is a late comer on the legal scene. Bentham in contrast was never[59] inclined to conceive of law in any way except as the expression of will of a sovereign lawgiver. He seems to acknowledge the existence of custom and usage in the *Civil Code* (*Bowring* i, 323) and he discusses custom extensively in the *Comment* (see below, Chapter 7), but custom never counts as *law* unless it is 'legalized', i.e. recognized and 'adopted' by the lawgiver. Consequently, it is in a more restricted sense that Bentham's discussion here is an account of the 'origins' of law. There is nothing in Bentham's account corresponding to the *historical* dimension of Hume's account. Bentham's is entirely 'analytical' or 'hypothetical' (Bentham would say 'conjectural' or 'logical'). The device of the primitive state is entirely heuristic, designed to display clearly the range of human individual and social needs to which the artifice of law is designed to respond.

Second, Bentham, unlike Hume, held that *once* a stable framework of social relations *is established* and expectations fixed upon it (and upon the processes by which it is defined), it is possible to alter, reform, and revise it better to meet the demands of maximal general welfare (*Bowring* i, 323-6). The only condition is that expectations must never be seriously shaken (*Bowring* i, 309, 322). The expectations, and the scheme of rules and practices which focus them, are

---

[59] The only place in Bentham's entire corpus that I can recall a contrary suggestion is the passage from *Bowring* i, 308-9, quoted above, p. 184.

not as fragile in Bentham's view as they are in Hume's. And the law itself is capable of shaping them (and not just articulating and codifying the rules and practices already in existence). Consequently, Bentham was willing to argue, for example, that it is possible to revise and reform the system of property, while giving due respect to established expectations, so as to achieve a more nearly equal distribution of wealth (*Bowring* i, 312–16). Equality must never be sought at the expense of security, he insists (*Bowring* i, 303), but it may—indeed, for good utilitarian reasons it *must*—be sought to the extent possible within a stable and secure framework of law.

The implications of this account of the 'origins' or foundations of law must still be drawn out. With this general discussion of some of the central notions of Bentham's jurisprudence now completed we can take up this task. I will begin the story with an account of Bentham's lifelong struggle with the theory and practice of his native Common Law system.

6

Bentham as a Common Law
Revisionist

[L]aw itself is only beneficence acting by rule.

Burke, *Reflections.*

THE history of Bentham's thought recapitulates its logical structure. This is especially true of his theories of law and adjudication. The first decade of his adult life (1770–82) was the most fertile and creative period of his life. In his earliest writings on these topics one finds the most fundamental ideas of the theories set out. They are schematic and abstract, to be sure, but they are already intelligible and powerful enough to define the structure and mark out the path of development of his mature theory. The history of his jurisprudential writings from that point onwards is the story of the unfolding of these seminal ideas into increasingly more concrete and determinate shape. They are enriched, articulated, and developed; but *they* drive the development. Seldom are they substantially altered or revised. The career of these theories resembles the career of a Hegelian *Idea*—though, no doubt, the philosopher of Queen Square Place, who never entertained an Idealist thought in his life, would shudder at the comparison.

In the previous chapter we looked at one set of such seminal ideas and traced part way the path of their development. In this chapter we encounter the same concerns and issues again, but this time focused by the special problems of adjudication within a legal system dominated by decisional law. We shall see how Bentham fashions for himself the basic principles of his discussion of justice. Considering the strictly juridical concept of justice which Bentham entertained, it is not surprising that he would move easily from a discussion of the relation between justice and utility to a discussion of adjudication. Indeed, in the remark (discussed at the outset of the previous chapter) that justice requires 'the chain of analogies' to be maintained (UC lxx(a). 18), the implied context is clearly that of Common Law adjudication. And the manuscript fragment from which the discussion of this chapter begins is contemporaneous with the essay on justice and utility, contains much of the same language, and was probably intended for the same work.[1]

Bentham's hatred of English Common Law, of course, is legendary, and had already fully matured in his demolition of Blackstone's *Commentaries* in the *Comment* of 1774–5. The suggestion, then, that Bentham at any point in his career considered a revisionist *account of* Common Law, as opposed to a radical 'deconstruction' of it, is likely to strike many readers as implausible. Thus, a few words about the subject of this chapter are in order.

In the materials we shall consider Bentham clearly assumes a context of non-statutory decisional law. Although he discusses issues of statutory interpretation and adjudication under the shadow of statutory law, he is primarily concerned here with the special problems of adjudication within (as he called it) 'judge-made' law. No defence of familiar Common Law *theory* or practice is attempted, however. Rather he tries to articulate for himself the principles and minimal conditions which such a practice of adjudication must meet. Once these principles and conditions were made clear, Bentham was convinced that no system of law remotely resembling his native Common Law could possibly meet the conditions. I shall look carefully at Bentham's arguments for this conclusion in Chapter 8. In this chapter I will outline the principles and the conception of law on which those arguments depend. This is, then, a 'revisionist' account of Common Law adjudication not in the sense that he advances the account in the hope of preserving the institution, perhaps through reform, but only in the sense that it is from reflections upon the practice of adjudication within a decisional law system that his thoughts on the nature of law and adjudication arise.

6.1 THE CASE FOR *STARE DECISIS*

[The] line of analogy must be neither bent nor broken.

Bentham, UC lxiii. 49.

Revealing the special, heterodox focus of his account, Bentham opens the discussion not with an analysis of the nature of custom

---

[1] 'Law Common v. Statute', UC lxiii. 49–50. It is this fragment, probably, which is referred to in the 'list of heads' for the 'Introd.' in UC xcvi. 73, 74 where the essay-fragment 'Justice v. Utility' is also listed. On the similarity of language see below, n. 19.

and how it is judicially recognized, articulated, and applied, but rather with the concept of *judicial precedent* and the nature and scope of its authority. In an early fragment entitled 'Law Common v. Statute' (UC lxiii. 49–50), Bentham points out that 'Judges cannot make any exception to a rule of Law, but what are deducible from some other—although it may happen that the rule beneficial upon the whole is so only *ex majori parte*, and not as to those exceptions'. Echoing his discussion of justice, he insists that 'the line of analogy be neither bent nor broken'. Law, like justice—or perhaps we should say justice in the administration of the law—requires that established rules or precedents be followed even when there are good reasons of utility—Bentham talks of 'convenience' here—calling for an exception. This signals, although it does not in itself state, a doctrine of strict adherence to precedent. Exceptions may be legitimate, as are decisions in novel cases (cases not directly covered by existing laws and precedents). But legitimacy is not to be determined by considerations of utility or convenience, but by projections from the body of existing precedents. Exceptions are legitimate when they 'are deducible from some other' rule of law. In novel cases, argument must proceed by way of *analogy* to existing law (UC lxiii. 49). Though the judge states a new law, this must be, as much as possible, derived from the pattern of the old law (*Comment* 197).

In a contemporaneous manuscript Bentham states 'There are two reasons for the utility of this maxim' of *stare decisis*: (i) 'the check to the Judges . . .' and (ii) 'that men may have a certain rule to guide them and know what they have to expect'.[2] This is expanded in 'Law Common v. Statute'. It is necessary that the line of analogy be strictly followed, he argues,

First to keep the judge from assuming the province of the Legislator, which he would do if he were governed solely by considerations of convenience: whereby that province would pass into other hands than are intended.

Secondly, that those who are to act in any new case may be better able to conjecture beforehand what is likely to be the decision, and to order their conduct accordingly (UC lxiii. 49).

---

[2] UC l. 124. This is in a batch of manuscripts, probably of very early date, concerned largely with matters of procedure and evidence, though some material also deals with punishment and the theory of offences. The general heading for this entire batch is 'Certainty'. It is the fragmentary and somewhat primitive discussions of offences, as well as the style of writing and use of paper, that suggest a very early date for the manuscripts. Thus it is very likely to be contemporaneous with the sketch-essays 'Justice v. Utility' and 'Law Common v. Statute'.

These arguments are familiar fare in legal theory. One can find them, for example, set out in almost the same words in Blackstone:

For it is an established rule to abide by former precedents, where the same point comes again in litigation: as well to keep the scale of justice even and steady, and not liable to waver with every new judge's opinion; as also because the law in that case being solemnly declared and determined, what before was uncertain, and perhaps indifferent, is now become a permanent rule, which it is not in the breast of any subsequent judge to alter or vary from according to his private sentiments (1 *Comm.* 69). For though in many other countries every thing is left in the breast of the judge to determine, yet with us he is only to *declare* and *pronounce*, not to *make* or *new-model*, the law (3 *Comm.* 327, author's emphasis).[3]

However, Blackstone's arguments are embedded in a larger theory which radically affects their scope and thrust. As we have seen, according to orthodox Common Law theory judges are bound, not to past decisions, but to the rules and principles implicit in them. The decisions themselves do not·constitute the law, nor are their general pronouncements (dicta) regarded as legislative. As Hale and Blackstone following him insist, the past decisions of the court over time constitute only the *best evidence* of the law. And a rule implicit in a past decision is binding because its *use* in that decision indicates that the rule is part of the common legal tradition on which the courts draw for justification of their decisions. Thus, as we noted in Chapter 1, the formulation of any rule of Common Law is always corrigible, even when the rule is formulated explicitly in the opinion of a precedent case. As Blackstone put it, '*the law*, and *the opinion of the judge*, are not always convertible terms, or one and the same thing; since it sometimes may happen that the judge may *mistake* the law' (1 *Comm.* 71, author's emphasis).

The consequence of this doctrine is that, although the judge, according to Blackstone, is 'sworn' to decide, 'not according to his own private judgement, but according to the known laws and customs of the land' (1 *Comm.* 69), nevertheless, he is not bound to any past articulation of that law, never absolutely bound to follow a previous decision, and always free to test it against his tradition-

---

[3] Compare also Paley, writing a decade or so after Bentham: 'Deference to prior decisions is founded upon two reasons: first, that the discretion of judges may be bound down by positive rules; and secondly, that the subject upon every occasion, in which his legal interest is concerned, may know how to act and what to expect.' W. Paley, *Moral and Political Philosophy*, 508.

shaped judgment of its reasonableness.[4] This is not inconsistent with the model of the judge as discoverer of, and spokesman for, the law and custom of the land, nor is it inconsistent with the doctrine of precedent defended earlier; rather, this view is intrinsic to that doctrine. For on Common Law theory, established law rests on and derives its authority form a shared sense of its reasonableness. So Willes J. expressed orthodox Common Law theory when he wrote, '[p]rivate justice, moral fitness and public convenience, when applied to a new subject, make common law without precedent, much more when received and approved by usage'.[5]

Bentham's case for *stare decisis* sharply contrasts with the Blackstonian approach. While defending strict adherence to precedent, Bentham delivers a hammer-blow to the traditionalist view of Common Law which Blackstone faithfully echoes. 'Why should decisions be uniform?' Bentham asks. 'Why should succeeding ones be such as to appear the natural and expected consequences of those preceding them? Not because it *ought to have been* established, but because it is established' (*Comment* 197 n. c). This is because '[t]he deference that is due to the determination of former judgments is due not to their wisdom, but to their authority: not in compliment to dead men's vanity, but in concern for the welfare of the living' (*Comment* 196). Not only is the traditionalist doctrine misdirected in attributing (perhaps hidden) wisdom to past decisions, according to Bentham, but also it rests on the clearly false assumption that our predecessors were somehow *wiser* than we. 'For my part,' Bentham confidently states, 'I know not that we owe any such deference to former times' (*Comment* 203). We certainly have no reason to regard our predecessors as wiser, and in many cases we have substantial reason to believe them to have been less wise (*Comment* 196, 203). But all this, he says, is beside the point. For, whether the law in the past rested on good reasons or not, and whether that reason has now ceased or not, is irrelevant to the *only* sufficient grounds we *now*

---

[4] Blackstone, 1 *Comm.* 69–71. See R. Cross, *Precedent in English Law*, 28. Cross quotes a somewhat more extreme version of this doctrine from the mid-nineteenth century: 'You are not bound by any rule of law which you may lay down, if upon a subsequent occasion you should find reason to differ from that rule; that is, that this House, like every court of justice, possesses an inherent power to correct an error into which it may have fallen.' Lord St Leonards, *Bright* v. *Hutton*, 3 HLC 343 at 388, quoted in Cross, 23.

[5] *Millar* v. *Taylor* (1769) 4 Burr. 2303 at 2312, quoted by Cross, *Precedent*, 26.

have for adhering to it,[6] viz. 'its being a *standing*, an established' rule. Its being 'reasonable or not reasonable', is 'comparatively but a trifling difference'.[7]

But why shouldn't the reasonableness of the past decision be relevant? Why is the mere fact of the rule's being established sufficient warrant to follow it, even when doing so conflicts with obvious utility or convenience? The reason is set out in his early analysis of justice. In 'Law Common v. Statute' Bentham, explaining the rationale for his doctrine of *stare decisis*, draws directly upon that analysis:

> The course of expectation was fixed by the general rule which was formed without recourse to those exceptions: instance after instance has happened to confirm the rule before the case that (consistently with independent utility) called for the exception—people acquire a persuasion that any case that shall come within the aspect of the rule will be governed by it . . . [and] they act accordingly. . . . This is the expectation [which] was made up before the case calling for the exception was foreseen, it is now too late to alter it after the act has happened (UC lxiii. 49).

The doctrine of expectations underlies Bentham's call for strict adherence to precedent. 'The reason that pleads for the uniformity of decisions, is the same that pleads with equal force for their notoriety . . . [viz.] that public expectation may know what course it has to take' (*Comment* 196).

The notion of expectation is pivotal for the development of Bentham's theory of adjudication, for it allows him to work out his views in two directions: (i) with it he develops a 'conventionalist' account of the nature and limits of adjudication within a Common Law system,[8] while (ii) situating the entire theory comfortably within his direct utilitarian theory of practical reasoning. In the next section we will follow Bentham as he attempts to work out the first part of his emerging theory of adjudication, and in 6.3 we will

[6] See *Comment* 114–15, 203.

[7] *FG*, Preface, p. 409 n. p, author's emphasis. For a more recent, American statement of the same view consider the following from Justice Brandeis: '*Stare decisis* is usually the wise policy, because in most matters it is more important that the applicable rule of law be settled than that it be settled right.' *Burnet* v. *Coronado Oil and Gas Co.* 285 US 393, 406–7 (1932) (dissenting opinion). Richard Hyland called this passage to my attention.

[8] In this respect, Bentham can be seen to advance and develop the 'conventionalist' theory of Common Law which was adumbrated by Hale and set out in detail by Hume. See above, chs. 2–4.

consider the utilitarian interpretation he gives to the conventionalist conception of Common Law.

6.2 CONVENTIONS AND THE LIMITS OF JUDICIAL LEGISLATION

[No] degree of wisdom . . . can render it expedient for a judge. . . to depart from pre-established rules.

Bentham, UC lxix. 6.

Bentham's doctrine of *stare decisis* requires adherence to established precedent not only when, the rule being beneficial on the whole, nevertheless utility calls for an exception in a particular case, but also when the rule itself seems arbitrary or unreasonable (*Comment* 204–5). Bentham even goes so far as to say, 'I could wish to see it established by those magistrates as an inviolable maxim and in the minutest article, *to improve nothing*: to relish, nay to thirst after improvement, but *to fetch* it ever and only *from its proper source*' (UC xxvii. 91, emphasis added). The 'proper source' obviously is the legislature. 'Nothing can be of greater importance than that the provinces of the Judge and the Legislator should be kept distinct. Better were it for the law [to] remain as it is at present, with all its numerous imperfections on its head than to receive amendment at their hands' (UC clix. 263).

This is a startling assertion coming from the pen of one of the severest critics of eighteenth-century British legal system who sought radical reform of the law from the very outset of his career. It is also puzzling in another respect. For Bentham's view of the proper origins of law reform was historically anomalous. Conservative elements in eighteenth-century Britain embraced the Common Law doctrine that the law was the embodiment of justice and reason and, where it needed readjustment, this should occur incrementally and at the hands of the men of the law who know it best, the judiciary. In contrast, progressives, who recognized the arbitrariness, barbarity, complexity, and sheer cumbersomeness of the Common Law, and who sought progressive reform to meet the needs of the rapidly emerging commercial society (think, for example, of Mansfield or Kames), also held that such reform was only possible through the agency of the courts. It was a commonplace among both the conservatives (like Blackstone) and the progressives (like

Kames) that Parliament was a hopelessly inept body from which could be expected only greater confusion.[9] Why, then, should Bentham, 'the great questioner of all things established',[10] press the established Common Law doctrine even farther than defenders of that doctrine would be willing to go? There may be several explanations for this anomaly. I will consider in detail only one of them here.

Why may we not seek judicial improvement of the law? The general form of Bentham's argument is familiar already from our study of Hume, and we found it again, in a revised form, in Bentham's early analysis of justice. Even when the existing rule is repugnant to utility Bentham insists upon the necessity (the manuscript original term is 'utility') of adhering to it, at least in so far as judicial alteration of the law is concerned (*Comment* 204). The utility of the scheme as a whole is put in jeopardy by judicial legislation because expectations are defeated. A judge must 'never think in his judicial capacity of mending [the existing rules of law]. The expectation of men is that such rules whatever they may be as have been conformed to in time past, such will be conformed to in time future. This expectation is disappointed when any one of these rules is violated by an opposite one being set up in its stead' (UC lxix. 6). Thus, says Bentham, 'partial good' is purchased at the price of 'universal evil' (*Comment* 223–4). The judge, sensitive to the evil or disutility worked by the established rule in the particular case before the bench, will be inclined to make an exception to the rule in this case, without attending sufficiently to the insecurity he or she introduces, thus undermining the confidence of the public in the regularity and predictability of the law. The reason why 'a new resolution made in the teeth of an old-established rule' is mischievous, he argues in the Preface to *A Fragment on Government*, is that

it puts men's expectations universally to a fault, and shakes whatever confidence they may have in the stability of any rules of Law, reasonable or not reasonable: that stability on which every thing that is valuable to a man depends. Beneficial be it in ever so high a degree to the party in whose favour it is made, the benefit it is of to *him* can never be so great as to

---

[9] See generally D. Lieberman, *The Province of Legislation Determined*.

[10] J. S. Mill, 'Bentham', in *Collected Works* X. 78. See, e.g., Bentham's attack on Blackstone's and Common Lawyers' attitudes toward innovation in *Comment*, App. F and the two Prefaces to *FG*.

outweigh the mischief it is of to the community at large. Make the best of it, it is general evil for the sake of partial good. It is what Lord Bacon calls setting the whole house on fire, in order to roast one man's eggs (*FG*, p. 409 n. p).

This argument, however, is puzzling in two respects. First, it seems to run together three different sets of distinctions: (i) that between the utilities of the individual parties and the utilities of the community as a whole, (ii) that between the utilities of the particular case and utility of the steady prosecution of the entire system of rules, and (iii) that between original utility and expectation utility. The ambiguity between (ii) and (iii) is also found in another version of the argument from which Bentham concludes that no 'degree of wisdom, or of probity, however consummate, . . . can render it expedient for a judge to make a sacrifice of utility *concatenate* to *insulate*: in other words to depart from pre-established rules' (UC lxix. 6). (In the margin Bentham proposes as synonyms of 'insulated utility': 'particular, simple, separate, independent'.) But in the present context these different distinctions may come down to the same thing (at least roughly and in general, and enough to make the conclusion plausible). For the issue turns on the alleged mischief of introducing a new rule in the place of an old and established one which, by hypothesis, is repugnant to utility. Expectations, which largely 'follow the finger of law' would be focused on the established rule, thus the utility which conflicts with it will be predominantly original utility. Moreover, since the case in Common Law adjudication is shaped entirely by the parties, the benefits may reasonably be thought to be enjoyed largely by the winning party (and any persons in similar situations in the future once the new rule is established). The community as a whole may also gain, but it is not unreasonable to think that these benefits in most such cases will be proportionately much less significant. Whereas the costs of setting aside the established rule will be borne not only by the losing party but by the community as a whole, because, in Bentham's view, by setting aside a single rule the stability of the entire scheme of rules is threatened. Departure from established precedent, perhaps

adds to the pleasure of a part of the community: viz. those who are favoured by the obligation which it tends to establish or enforce, but [it] adds [also] to the pain of the whole of the community, those persons among the rest, by putting them in fear of seeing themselves contrary to their expectations deprived of what they had been accustomed to as their expected rights and subjected to unexpected duties (UC lxix. 199).

Thus, 'partial' or 'insulated utility' to a small set of beneficiaries is offset by the 'general' disutility of the threat to the law itself.

This, then, looks very much like the argument for the utility of 'justice' we saw in 5.1 , and it is not implausible if we accept with Bentham the assumption that in such circumstances at least expectation utilities will be, as a matter of fact, overridingly weighty. But this leads to a second puzzle. For Bentham is concerned here with (utilitarian) correction and improvement of existing law by replacing 'standing rules' with new and allegedly better rules. (This is *not* simply a matter of 'equitable' correction of particular rules—that is, correcting in the particular case for defects due to inevitable and necessary 'generality', which correction requires no corresponding correction of the rule itself.) Bentham is concerned with law*making*. However, he clearly holds in the passages we have considered that the arguments do not apply to Parliamentary lawmaking, to new statutes introduced by a legislature, even though, he admits, almost all new statutory law contravenes some standing rule and so upsets expectations.[11] Thus, Bentham's argument here cannot be explained simply in terms of the overriding weight he is inclined to assign to expectations in legal contexts. There is something special about attempting to set aside old rules and establish new ones—that is, something special about legislation—when performed by a judge 'in his *judicial capacity*'. There is something peculiar in the *role* or *office* of the judge (or at least of the judge in a Common Law system) which makes judicial legislation inevitably result in partial good at the price of universal evil.

But it is also clear that the problem lies not in the judge, his training, or the information available to him.

Not that a man being a Judge is the less fit for a Legislator: on the contrary no man so likely to be fit as he. No man who has such good opportunities of being acquainted with the details of those imperfections of the law which want correcting. '*Tis the provinces/functions that should be distinct and not the persons.* The same person who acting by establishing a rule in the character of a Legislator shall do eminent service, shall *by establishing the same rule* in the capacity of a Judge do infinte mischief (UC clix. 263, emphasis added).

[11] See *FG*, 409 n. p; UC lxiii. 49–50; UC clix. 263.

Improvement or reform of the law must not originate from the bench, argues Bentham, because judicial activity of that sort involves a deep confusion of function. The problem lies not in judges exercising legislative power, but rather in their doing so *in the course of adjudicating particular cases.*[12] Of course, within the context of a Common Law system of adjudication it is difficult to distinguish in practice between setting aside an established rule in a particular case, on the one hand, and making a rule for future cases, on the other, because the new decision (or its rationale) is supposed to *become law.* And so, the only way to block judicial *legislation* is to insist that the judge adhere strictly to established rules.

It is now clear that the two basic reasons Bentham cites for his doctrine of *stare decisis*[13]—stability and security, and the sharp separation of the adjudicative and legislative functions—are directly related. Bentham's argument for the separation of function depends on something about the link between community expectations and stability of the law, on the one hand, and the institutional positions of the judge and the legislator, on the other.

Before we look at this argument we should distinguish it from other familiar arguments for the separation of legislative and adjudicative functions. First, Bentham's argument does not rest on the familiar observation that the Court is 'undemocratic' (or at least 'anti-majoritarian'). Of course, in its most familiar guise,[14] this is not a utilitarian argument at all, but it would not be difficult to

---

[12] Salmond distinguishes between judges making law by formulating and declaring it through '*dicta*', which he regards as 'legislative', and making law *by applying it*, which he regards as adjudicative. He observes that the former, 'judicial declaration unaccompanied by judicial application', is 'not of binding authority'. J. Salmond, *Jurisprudence*, 223-4. Just such lawmaking through adjudication is Bentham's target. Part of his concern is captured by Shapiro: 'Clearly, where judicial lawmaking occurs, adversary proceedings are something of a facade. If the judge is consciously seeking to formulate general rules for future application, his considerations must range far beyond the immediate clash of interests of the two parties. That is the message of the "Brandeis brief", with its parade of "legislative" facts, that is, facts about the general social conditions as opposed to the immediate facts of the dispute. Such briefs are open acknowledgement by bench and bar that the parties are essentially an example or sample of the social reality to be legislated upon rather than disputants whose conflict is to be resolved.' M. Shapiro, *Courts*, 34-5.   [13] UC lxiii. 49; UC 1. 124; see above, p. 193.

[14] For example, the argument that, since judges are not democratically elected, and the judicial process does not allow full public participation, judicial legislation/ activism is a violation of the democratic right of citizens to participate meaningfully in the creation of laws that govern their activities and limit their liberties.

construct a utilitarian version of it, especially if we were to identify, as Bentham was prone to do, 'the greatest happiness of the greatest number' with the outcomes of majoritarian political procedures. However, rarely in this period of his life does one find any suggestion of his argument.[15] Even in his later, radical democratic period he was not much inclined to adopt it. And, in any case it is clearly not the argument relied on here.

Secondly, in the period under consideration Bentham begins to develop an argument that comes to play a central role in his later campaign for codification. He argues that only the legislator (more properly, the code-writer) can take a sufficiently general view of the entire field of action and of law needed for rational and effective legislating. Louis Jaffe expressed part of what Bentham had in mind when he said, 'The question may be asked whether there is not an essential conflict of attitude between the task of adjudication and [that of] long-range planning. The former may be thought to intensify the sense of the particular . . .'.[16] But Bentham's concern goes beyond this, for it is a call for *radical* law reform. It is only the codifier—equipped with the conceptual and theoretical tools Bentham himself forged—that can survey the entire field of action and propose sweeping and radical reform for the defects of existing law.[17] That is, in his later argument, Bentham's concern was to reject the 'incrementalism' of Blackstone and the Common Lawyers generally.[18] Judicial reform, on this argument, can only at best do 'partial good' while leaving untouched and exacerbating the more general and radical evil. However, despite the importance of this argument in his later work, this is not the argument—not the sense of 'partial good' and 'universal evil'—that Bentham has in mind in the present context.

In these early manuscripts we find a different, and in many ways more interesting argument. In 'Law Common v. Statute' Bentham

[15] In the *Comment* at one point Bentham suggests that 'the common reason', or 'the reason of the majority of the people who use their reason about the matter' is more likely to be represented by 'that of many hundred men chosen the greater part of them by the people' (speaking now of England), than by 'that of four men, appointed by the Crown' (*Comment* 159; see also 223). (Also, Bentham seems to argue on some such grounds against judicial review of legislation, see *FG* IV. 30–3.) But cf. *OLG* XIX. 6 for a quite different assessment of the 'common reason' of the Parliament.

[16] L. Jaffe, *Judicial Control of Administrative Action*, 51.

[17] See *OLG* XIX, *A General View of the Complete Code of Laws, Bowring* iii. 155–210, and below, ch. 12.

[18] See R. Posner, 'Blackstone and Bentham', 594–6.

notes that even in novel cases judges are bound to decide only by appeal to analogy to established rules and past decisions, and not by appeal to utility or convenience. He defends this restriction on the ground that under it 'those who are to act in any new case may be better able to conjecture beforehand what is likely to be the decision, and to order their conduct accordingly' (UC lxiii. 49). Analogy, he maintains, is 'more easily agreed upon' than utility.

To judge whether such a rule which is proposed as being like another rule, is so, a man has but to compare the rules themselves. To judge whether it be in itself right, he has a variety of other circumstances to consider, which presenting themselves in different numbers and differently upon different persons . . . make this a task much more difficult than [the] former (UC lxiii. 49).

Utilitarian calculation, he argues here, is much more complex than argument from analogy, its complexity being a function of both the larger number and the unbounded variety of considerations that must be weighed as well as of the fact that these considerations tend in some cases to appear different to different observers. Thus, people are more likely to come to agree on analogy than on utility.[19]

But why should that fact, if it is a fact, be important here? Should not the relevant consideration for a utilitarian be whether the calculation of utilities is *correct*? Not, I think, in the sorts of situation Bentham seems to have in mind. The utility of rule-governed social interaction often depends largely on the predictable pattern of behaviour which the rules define. In such cases, the utility of one or another course of action depends largely on its being agreed upon (recall Hume). But in novel cases citizens and (secondarily) officials face a special problem of co-ordination. One person's decision regarding future action may depend largely on the decisions and actions of many others, but their actions depend in turn on his. Sufficiently public rules might serve to focus expectations of all the affected parties and so co-ordinate their interaction, but in the absence of such rules the parties seem to be left to their own individual devices. In such circumstances, appeal to analogy, Bentham claims, is much more likely to yield agreement

---

[19] Bentham's language here immediately recalls 'Justice v. Utility'. With UC lxx(a). 17, 18 (above, p. 150) compare the following: 'It is not always that the line of analogy ordered [?] is that of utility. The former is straight and inflexible, the latter takes on throughout the inflexions from the influences of the circumstances it meets within its course' (UC lxiii. 49).

on a desirable pattern of interaction (or rule), and thus succeed in co-ordinating that interaction, than direct appeals to utility.[20] Therefore, established rules of law, and analogies naturally drawn from them, provide a focus for public expectations. From them citizens can, with some reliability, predict the decisions of judges and the behaviour of their fellow citizens.

It is worth noting that this conclusion squares with an argument we considered in 5.1. There we saw Bentham maintain that sometimes it is precisely the superior utility of one course of action which carries expectations with it; so that appeal to original utility may require setting aside an established rule, but without defeating expectations. These two arguments are consistent because the argument for setting aside established rules rests not on the fact that the preferred alternative in fact *maximizes* utility, but on the fact that the utility in question is *manifest*. Where the utility is sufficiently clear and public, it, rather than analogy, may provide the best focus for the convergence of expectations. And since the concerns of justice, and of proper adjudication lie, according to Bentham, with co-ordinating judicial activity with public expectation (with what is 'more easily agreed upon'), appeal to manifest utility in these circumstances, entirely satisfies these concerns.[21]

But Bentham goes on in the passage from 'Law Common v. Statute' to consider an objection. For if what is said is correct, then it seems to provide equally good reason for blocking the *legislator's* appeal to utilities as it does for blocking *judicial* appeal to them. To this objection Bentham mysteriously replies that it does not apply with the same force to legislators, because judges are more likely than the legislators to be 'mistaken (i.e. [to] disagree with the majority) in their notions of the utility of the alternatives' (UC lxiii. 49). But, again, we may ask why is the judge more liable to

---

[20] Note the parallel to Hume's account of the rational force of analogy, *Enquiry* II 308 and above, 4.2.

[21] Also see below, pp. 213–14 and the discussion of UC lxix. 238–9. Later Bentham tends to minimize the scruples he has in these early manuscripts about the public salience of utilitarian considerations. A more common view is that expressed in the *Civil Code*. There he argues that the best way to ensure that laws are 'consistent'—by which he means not only logically consistent with each other, but also systematically coherent and 'naturally conformable to the general expectation', such that 'every analogous law is, so to speak, presumed beforehand'—is to ensure that the law is in accord with utility. 'It is only possible to make laws truly consistent, by *following the principle of utility*. This is the general point of union for all expectations' (*Bowring* i. 323, 324, author's emphasis). See also *CC* 509.

utilitarian error than the legislator? The key to the solution of the puzzle seems to lie in Bentham's equation of utilitarian error with 'disagreeing with the majority'. Implicit in the argument above is a contrast between the conditions under which the legislator effectively makes law and those necessary for 'judicial law-making'. Roughly, on his view, co-ordination with the expectations of the public ('majority') is essential for successful judicial rule-making, but this is much more difficult for judicial than it is for legislative rule-making. The problem is not that the judge is more likely than the legislator to make mistakes with regard to the *actual* proper balance of utilities, but rather that, given the indeterminacy of utilitarian calculation, and the likelihood of different perceptions of the relevant utilities, the judge's determination of the *right* (i.e. utilitarianly correct) course of action may not square with that of the public (indeed, there may be no unanimity amongst the members of the community regarding the proper balance of utilities). Thus utility does not provide a sufficiently reliable focus of public expectations, whereas expectations naturally converge on 'analogy'—i.e. on settled rules of law and projections from them into novel or exceptional cases. While the legislator is capable of making law *de novo* because as a matter of fact the expression of his will *is taken as law*—that is, the expression of his will is itself a focus of expectations—the judge is able to make his choice of a rule *law* only by showing that it *already is law*. The judge's declaration of a rule as law can only be effective if it comes to be regarded as such by the community, and that is not guaranteed. The only way in which he can guarantee it is for him to show that the rule is rightly projected by analogy from existing law.[22]

The assumption seems to be that for something to become law it is necessary that it come to be *regarded as* law. This is not difficult in the case of statutory law because there is already a practice of recognizing the product of parliamentary action as law. There is no such practice, Bentham maintains, with regard to the activities of the judiciary within ordinary Common Law practice at least. Thus, judicial rule-making faces a special sort of co-ordination problem. If the judge were merely to follow his best judgment as to the balance of utilities in a particular case, he would fail to take expectations into account, but in a special way. He may, in fact, be correct about the proper balance of utilities, and yet, because he

[22] See UC lxix. 6 and below, pp. 206–7

does not carry public expectation with him, defeat those expectations. The utility of the rule depends on its being *taken as*—having the force of—law; so if he is unable to win acceptance of the rule, his decision is capable at best of doing only partial good. The decision produces only 'insulated', 'individual' utility at best and threatens to set fire to the whole house just to roast one man's eggs.

This interpretation is confirmed and the argument further developed in another early manuscript. Bentham begins by supposing a case in which 'the new anomalous rule [is] in itself more conformable to utility than that which would have been the regular one. Still as things stand it is probable that all things considered the decision would be less conformable to utility' (UC lxix. 6). This is not because the judge has done his utilitarian sums wrong, but because merely doing utilitarian sums 'right' will not guarantee that the rule will become law. The utilitarian gains, however, depend on the optimal rules actually being regarded as law. There are two problems here, both crucial. Such a decision will not be conformable to utility, first,

> because it cannot but be doubtful whether *succeeding judges* will be most swayed by the *insulated* (particular, simple, separate, independent) utility of the new rule or by the *concatenated* utility of the old which it supersedes. Consequently, it is doubtful whether the rule which it is designed to establish will in fact be established. If it be not, the particular mischief stands entirely uncompensated.
>
> Secondly, it is yet more doubtful which of the rules the *public* will *expect* the succeeding judges shall be swayed by (UC lxix. 6, author's emphasis).

The main and most important point of this passage is that judicial decisions intended to have 'legislative' effect depend for this effect upon concurrence by both the body of active judges and the public. A new rule may be singularly attractive on utilitarian grounds, but the superior utility of the new rule depends on its attaining the status of a rule of law. 'At length, if the new rule be received and adhered to for a certain length of time and by a certain number of Judges, it takes its seat among the rules that are established' (UC lxix. 6). But there is nothing the judge, alone and in the course of adjudication, can do to ensure that the rule will be regarded as law. Its becoming law depends on (i) his fellow judges also recognizing the superior utility of the new rule *and* recognizing that the long-range utility of adopting and following the rule outweighs the immediate disutility of defeating expectations focused around the old rule; and (ii) on the people, at least the people most likely in the future to be affected by the rule change, anticipating that the succeeding judges will decide in this way. But, of course, it is clear that the determination of the judges depends on the expectations of the people, and so the decision and expectations of the judge in the instant case is reciprocally dependent on the decisions and expectations of both the rest of the judiciary and of the public. This is a classic example of a co-ordination problem. Thus, effective, law-establishing adjudication under standard conditions in a Common Law system, requires not (only) that the judge get his utilitarian sums right, but (more importantly) that he co-ordinate his decision-activities with the expectations of both the public and his colleagues on the bench.[23]

On the whole, this task of co-ordinating is difficult. Sometimes, when the utility is 'manifest', it will provide a proper ground for judicial decision,[24] but in most cases successful co-ordination is possible only by appeals to precedent and rule naturally projectable from the body of settled law.[25] Thus, no 'degree of wisdom . . . can render it expedient for a judge . . . to depart from pre-established rules' (UC lxix. 6).

Bentham presses the argument a step further and in a direction which embodies implicitly a deep criticism of accepted Common Law theory. Doing 'novel justice', he argues, under a Common Law system produces 'all the effects of injustice' (UC lxix. 6). This

[23] For a more systematic discussion of this condition see my 'Coordination and Convention', 186–94.

[24] UC lxx(a). 19. In the manuscript under discussion Bentham mentions this 'salience' condition along with two other conditions. 'The mischief of departure' from established rules, he says, 'is less in proportion first as the departure is less wide[,] secondly as the insulate utility produced is more signal. Thirdly, as the reputation of the judge for probity and knowledge [or: understanding] is more acknowledged, and consequently his opinion more likely to pass into a rule, and be adopted by succeeding judges' (UC lxix. 6). This third condition is also a 'salience' condition, since it consists in the acknowledged reputation of probity etc. and not the *fact* of probity.

[25] See also the following intriguing argument in *Civil Code*. Bentham says that the requirement of publicity of laws which follows from the principle of respect for established expectations entails not only the formal condition of promulgation, but also certain constraints on the *content* of the laws. For 'there are some laws naturally more easily understood than others; such are, laws conformable to expectations already formed; laws which repose upon *natural* expectations. This natural expectation, this expectation produced by early habit, may be founded upon superstition, upon a hurtful prejudice, or upon a sentiment of utility: this is of no importance; the law which is conformed to it maintains its place in the mind without effort . . .' (*Bowring* i, 323).

is because fashioning new rules of law under Common Law is 'necessarily', by the very nature of the process, *retrospective*. And in this respect Common Law rule-making differs significantly from statutory lawmaking.

A Decision of Common Law upon a new point never seems to have set up *de novo* the general rule that may be deduced [i.e. inferred] from it. It supposes that contrary to the truth that rule to have been set up already. It supposes therefore that the rule ought always to have been conformed to (UC lxix. 6).

This is very compressed, but the argument seems to be that the only way in which new rules can be introduced in a Common Law system is for the judges to *pretend* that the rules are not new at all, but rather implicit in the existing law, and so already part of the custom of the land. We see now that Bentham is not merely relying here on Common Law dogma, but he is reporting the alleged fact that judges in the Common Law system can only hope to achieve the co-ordination necessary for giving their decisions legislative effect if they can show convincingly that their 'new' rule is in fact not new at all. But the price of such success is that the parties must be assumed to have *already known* this law and have already adjusted their behaviour to it, or at least they *ought to* have. Thus, the new rule is discovered to *have been* already binding. The creation of law is inevitably and inescapably retrospective, because the fact of newly creating the law in the case at hand can be admitted only upon pain of failing to make it law!

This, says Bentham, is worse than despotism. For the despot exercises arbitrary power through individual commands. But although the despot may do great injustice, he cannot do the *kind* of injustice which the legislating Common Law judge does. The despot is not capable of the injustice of retrospective lawmaking, precisely because there are no generally held expectations that the despot's decisions will be 'restricted to that conformity to any before established circumjacent rules to which the [judge] is restricted' (UC lxix. 6).

In fact, the judge 'does much more mischief in his function as a Judge . . . than he would if [he were] lawfully invested with despotic power'. Because, if he were invested with that power, he would be enabled to 'and naturally would prevent the mischief resulting from the retrospective operation of his power'. However, in the circumstances, 'this is what acting as a judge, he can have no pretence for doing' (UC lxix. 6). That is, the despot, unconstrained by pre-existing rules, and expectations of the community that he will follow them, can decide each case on its individual merits alone. Furthermore, if expectations to some extent are likely to be generated, he can take steps to prevent them from arising, or prevent their disappointment, or compensate the resulting loss, or at the very least take the defeat of such expectations into account in his deliberations. But the judge is effectively barred from such remedies. He is faced with the dilemma: either he admits that he is engaged in lawmaking and thereby fails to do so, or he must merely adjudicate the particular case at hand and pretend that he is not making new law and so ignore, or deny the existence of, expectations he surely will defeat. To admit that he is disappointing expectations would be to admit that he is not in fact deciding according to pre-existing law, but rather according to his assessment of the merits of a new rule. But he is barred that move on pain of public inconsistency and failure to bring into existence the law he seeks, in fact, to create.

The alternative, of course, is openly to admit that judges make law, that is, to establish the practice of recognizing the dictates of the *judiciary* as as much law-creative as the declarations of the legislator. But this public consistency in Common Law practice is purchased at the price of radical instability of the law. Once judges are empowered in this way to legislate, Bentham argues, it is impossible to distinguish their legislating from their adjudicating, and no decision can be regarded as established. But in a legal system consisting largely of judge-made law this is disastrous, for then no rule is established, no rule can be depended upon. The judge becomes a 'despot' deciding each case on its merits. There is only one possible solution to this radical uncertainty once the fact of judicial legislation is publicly recognized: adopt a rigid requirement of *stare decisis*. In order for there to be *any* stability, any degree of predictability, past decisions must be adhered to for no other reason than the fact that they were decided. Only in this way can expectations of the public be sufficiently focused to allow the law to achieve its primary task of defining a stable framework for social interaction.

(British legal history seems to have confirmed, to some extent, Bentham's a priori argument. For once the traditional, declaratory theory of Common Law was seen to be a mask for the pervasive fact of judicial legislation—once it became second nature to call the rules of Common Law 'judge-made law'—a process which began in the eighteenth century culminating in the London Street Tramways decision in the 1890s—it was no longer possible to leave judges uncontrolled in the exercise of this legislative power. Thus, the strict doctrine of precedent was the natural product of the shift in view of the activity of judges under Common Law from that of Coke, Hale, and Blackstone to that of Bentham and Austin.)

Bentham's argument, then, seems to be the following. The primary and most important function of a system of laws is that of securing community expectations. Its greatest utility lies in defining a stable framework of publicly recognized rules which provide a focus for expectations regarding the behaviour of both citizens and officials. In a Common Law system, rules and standards of law must be extracted from the actions and decisions of judges and the validity and effectiveness of such rules depend on their being widely recognized or acknowledged by the public. Given such a system, the law can adequately perform its fundamental utilitarian task only if judges forswear the temptation to introduce new rules or make exceptions to established rules (without guarantees that other judges and the public in general will come to the same view), even when original utility seems to demand it.

6.3 UTILITY AND COMMON LAW ADJUDICATION

The ground of all legal decisions is expediency, real or supposed.

Bentham, *Comment.*

The originality and interest of Bentham's theory of Common Law adjudication lies not in his linking of precedent to considerations of certainty and predictability of law. This is common fare in legal theory, and it was already so in the eighteenth century. The interest lies, rather, in his insights into the interdependence of official and public expectations in adjudication, and in his attempt to integrate the argument for *stare decisis* into his general utilitarian practical philosophy. What is distinctive of Bentham's theory is its attempt to weave the doctrine of precedent into the fabric of an essentially direct-utilitarian conception of practical decision-making. We have seen evidence of this commitment to the sovereignty of the principle of utility in Chapter 5. It is also clear in his early writings on Common Law.

Bentham insists that judges ensure that their decisions conform to precedent and to analogies reasonably projectable from precedent, and holds that these rules have practical force only in virtue of the expectations associated with them. But he insists further that judicial deliberation considers only these expectations (or rather the expectation utilities), and should be concerned with the rules and prior decisions *only in so far as* they in fact focus public expectations.

> The business of the Judge is to keep the distribution of valuables and of rewards and punishments in the course of expectation: conformable to what the expectation of men concerning them is, or if apprized of the circumstances of each case, as he is, he supposed *would be*. To do that he is to put himself in their place, and to pronounce from such lights, and from such lights only, as can appear to them (*Comment* 197 n. c).

Two important claims are made in this passage: (i) that judicial business is ultimately that of making decisions on the balance of expectations, and (ii) that to determine where that balance lies he is to put himself in the places of each of the parties affected by the decision. This is a theme which runs through Bentham's discussions of adjudication throughout his life, regardless of whether the context of judicial decision is Common Law, statute, or code.[26] A fuller statement of this view can be found in the early 'Preparatory Principles' manuscripts (UC lxix. 238-9). The argument is worth extended discussion.

To illustrate his point Bentham considers a case of a title dispute. In deciding the right to an article of property, Bentham claims, the resolution of the dispute is determined by two sets of considerations: (i) the balance of expectations of the parties to the dispute, and (ii) the balance of expectations of the public at large (or, rather, expectations of that portion of the public which is likely to hear of the decision). The settled rules provide evidence of, and perhaps the primary focus for, public and individual expectations. But it is the expectations on which the decision must rest. That is, he holds that *both* the decision is correct only when it accords with the balance of expectations in the case, *and* the judge must base his decision on his understanding of just this balance of expectations.

---

[26] This suggestion can be found as early as the early 1770s (UC lxx(a). 19) and as late as 1829-31 (*Bowring* iv, 388, 312); see also UC lxxxvi. 39; UC lxxxi. 124-5; UC cxiv. 222, 236; *Bowring* iii, 212.

Bentham gives the process of deliberation a distinctively utilitarian interpretation. The weight of expectations is not to be assessed in terms of the strength of the *arguments* for title from existing rules that can be given, but rather by determining the subjective *intensity* of the expectations. The question the judge must consider is not (at least not ultimately) which party has offered the weightiest *reasons* drawn from the law for according him title, but rather 'in which of the two parties the expectation of having a thing is the strongest' (UC lxix. 238).

The stronger a man's expectation is of having a thing the stronger is his disappointment . . . if he fail to have it: in other words the greater is the pain of the disappointment . . . [Thus,] more good will issue upon the whole from giving it to him whose expectation is the strongest (UC lxix. 239; see also UC lxx(a). 20).

To this he adds, in the fragment 'Justice v. Utility', that 'the great advantage of the doctrine of Expectation is that it presents all along a certain matter of fact, on which the opinion pronounced in any instance that such a thing is right or wrong, is equity or is not equity, is founded' (UC lxx(a). 22).

But, he observes, this gives rise to a problem: how is the strength of expectations to be measured? The most obvious method is to question each person likely to be affected by the decision. But Bentham rejects this method, and not just because it would be enormously time-consuming. He argues, rather, that once it is known that the judge's decision will be influenced by his perception of the strength of the expectations of the parties, it will be recognized by all concerned that it is in the interest of each party to exaggerate the intensity of his expectations when interrogated by the judge. Thus, the judge cannot hope to obtain an accurate measurement of expectation intensity in this way. There are, as it were, transaction costs which tend to distort the calculations.

What then has the judge to do? [Bentham asks.] He must put himself in the place of both: of the parties and also of the public (to measure the strength of his own expectation). He supposes himself first in the situation of one of the parties; then in that of the other. He observes in which of the situations his own expectations would be strongest, and that party in whose situation he finds his expectation to be the strongest is the party in whose favour he determines (UC lxix. 238).

The judge determines which expectations are strongest, then, by determining which expectations *he* would have were he in the respective positions of all the parties affected.[27] On this basis he can locate the balance of expectations and make his decision.

But this method itself is open to a serious objection. The judge's subjective experience upon projecting himself into the situations of the parties can be taken as a reasonably reliable measure of the intensity of the expectations of the parties and the public only if the 'expectation-reactions' of persons in the society are the same, or at least homogeneous. But what reason have we to assume this? Bentham does not deny that such reactions may vary widely over the population in a society, neither does he claim that the judge has no way of telling when this may be the case (nothing in Bentham's argument here depends on the assumption of the radical inaccessibility of the subjective experience of other minds to us). Rather, he argues that although the judge may accurately intuit such divergence, it is not possible *publicly* to *verify* this intuition and so the judges may not treat such differences as relevant for the purposes of his decision.

The reasons which a man could find for supposing one man's temperament more sanguine than another's must be founded on ocular . . . inspection and that in a variety of situations and for a length of time. Such reasons are in their nature incommunicable . . . These appearances then being indescribable, the Judge could have no means of satisfying the public of the existence of them on the supposed existence of which he should think to ground his decision. So that it would not be in his power to give the public any stronger reason for supposing him to have grounded his decision on these considerations, than they could have for supposing it grounded on considerations of his own favourite interest . . . (UC lxix. 238–9).

Appeals to such intuitions are objectionable, on Bentham's view, not because the decision is likely to be wrong or arbitrary, but because the intuitions are by their nature incommunicable, and because it is often difficult for the public to distinguish appeals to intuition from prejudice or bias.[28] (We might add, it is often difficult for the person making the judgment to make that distinc-

---

[27] There is a parallel to R. Hare's 'role-shift' test in *Freedom and Reason*, 86–111. But even more interesting is Bentham's explicit admission that this test is plausible only on the assumption of a basic uniformity of human desires and interests. Bentham, it seems, is more willing to acknowledge the underlying assumptions of his utilitarianism than are at least some contemporary utilitarians.

[28] Compare this with R. Dworkin, *Taking Rights Seriously*, 162–3.

tion as well.) If these intuitions do not allow of public demonstration, then they must, for these purposes, be ignored. Bentham clearly assumes here that adjudication must be a process of *public* deliberation and demonstration. Although the principle of expectations governs every decision, for a decision to be correct, it is not enough that it *be*, in fact, in accord with that principle, but it must be possible to *show* publicly that it is. Or more precisely, judicial decision *is not* correct according to the utilitarian standard, unless it can be publicly *shown to be* correct according to that standard.

From this Bentham concludes that, for the purposes of judicial decision-making, people are to be considered roughly similar in their 'expectation-reactions', and the 'role-shift' method is the most reliable way of measuring intensity of expectations. And since in the present context, expectation utilities are normally the weightiest, and often the only, utilities involved (UC lxx(a). 19), Bentham's proposal is equivalent to requiring judges to balance the relevant utilitarian considerations. In a manuscript headed 'Laws and Decisions—Calculations they ought to be grounded on', Bentham explicitly interprets the expectation balancing as *utility* balancing. He maintains that, when it must be decided which of two claims of title to some piece of property to recognize, the judge must show that the happiness of the community as a whole, including the happiness of the two parties in contention, will be maximized by the determination of title he proposes.

The ratio of the number that represents the balance of pleasure accruing to the society in the case of its being given to Titius, to the number that represents the balance of pleasure accruing in the case of its being given to Sempronius, will represent the chance that the act of our . . . judge has for being conformable to utility (UC lxix. 198).

This link to utilitarian balancing is also clear in the following passage from Bentham's *Comment*:

How have stood the stocks of Pain and Pleasure upon such a disposition of things as the determination in question is calculated to bring on? This is the question, stated indeed in the most general and comprehensive terms, which a Judge ought to put to him[self] upon the occasion of every fresh case. The answer it cannot be expected should be given here. To give the answer would be at once to delineate the whole scheme of what ought to be the Common Law. Let it suffice just to hint, that the answer ought to be the summing up the several pains and pleasures that are certain or probable to happen upon each side of the alternative that is proposed (*Comment* 199).

Bentham claims not only that the principle of utility alone must be used as a standard against which past rules of law must be tested (already a departure from strict *stare decisis*), but also that the judge must make his decision on the balance of utilities *in each case*. And it is clear from this passage that he does not restrict judicial attention to expectation utilities,[29] although they, of course, will predominate. Thus, proper judicial reasoning must penetrate *through* the screen of established rules, to the utilitarian concerns underlying conformity to them. Powerful utilitarian arguments require judicial conformity to precedent, but the sole judicial decision principle is still the principle of utility.

We might ask, however, does this not undermine the doctrine of *stare decisis*? Bentham considers this objection:

[H]ard, then, it will be said, and novel is the task you have set to Judges. Nice . . . the test you have set up of a well-formed judgment. [But] where is the judge whose practice shall abide it?

To which he replies,

it will be proper to observe that in general the line of uniformity is the line of utility. That the road to utility lies in the beaten track of precedent; . . . the more steadily they adhere to [precedent, the more] do they discharge the duties/business of their function (UC lxix. 199).

There is no conflict, he insists, between his requirement that the judge decide each case on its utilitarian merits and the doctrine of *stare decisis*, because both generate the same results. There is, in effect, an extensional equivalence obtaining between the two doctrines. Not content to leave the matter here, however, he insists further that his account is not only prescriptive—requiring judges to appeal to utility in each case—but also properly descriptive of the actual practice of (the best) judges.

Many a grave Magistrate who judges causes as the Clubman before St. Dunstans sounded the horn and who like Mons. Jourdain in the play has been talking prose all his life time without knowing a syllable of the matter, may well be surprised, perhaps, at this account of what he has been doing, but let him reflect a while and then answer whether it is not a just one.[30]

---

[29] In the manuscript margin alongside this passage Bentham writes 'Original Utility' (*Comment* 197 n. 1).

[30] UC lxix. 199. Bentham makes similar claims for his hedonic calculus. Recognizing that it is an idealized model of practical deliberation, he insists nevertheless that it is exemplified in ordinary practice: 'Nor is this a novel and

The extensional equivalence between the dictates of *stare decisis* and the dictates of utility is no mere accident, since any judge, fully self-conscious of his decision-making activity, would have to admit that he in fact followed precisely the procedure Bentham describes and recommends, although perhaps he would not readily admit that publicly. The doctrine of *stare decisis*, then, does not describe actual judicial deliberation (*that* is determined only by utility), but it does issue a sort of public guarantee, and so (Bentham hopes) provides an adequate focus for public expectations to which, then, the utilitarian judge must direct his deliberation.

Although he soon calls for the complete abandonment of Common Law, we can see in this early account of Common Law adjudication some of the central features of his mature theory. In particular, we see here an (admittedly strained) attempt to unite his deep commitment to the sovereignty of the principle of utility with his recognition of the need for a device which can focus public expectations in a way that public knowledge of the practice of direct appeal to utility cannot. Within a legal system dominated by judge-made law, the doctrine of strict *stare decisis* alone holds out hope for successful performance of this central task of law. *If* it is to answer 'in any even the most imperfect degree' the purposes of law (*OLG* XV. 9), Bentham insists, Common Law must be governed by a strict and unbending doctrine of *stare decisis*. But the costs of such a system, assessed in terms of its radical inflexibility and its inability, despite all efforts, to provide suitably determinate, predictable legal standards,[31] are so great in Bentham's view that he came to the firm conviction that Common Law must be completely scuttled and replaced with a system of law which is radically different in basic conception, form, and content.

In the passage I quoted at the opening of 6.2 Bentham says first, 'I could wish to see [the maxim for all judges] established . . . to improve nothing'. But he immediately realizes that this wish is premature. 'Yet I doubt whether things may be yet ripe for the establishment of such a maxim: till the whole structure be cleared by

unwarranted, any more than it is a useless theory. In all this there is nothing but what the practice of mankind, wheresoever they have a clear view of their own interest, is perfectly conformable to' (*IPML* IV. 8).

[31] Bentham claims that under Common Law people acquire expectations that a rule articulated in a past case will be applied to future cases as well, and then act accordingly. But he adds, ironically, 'that is, they would *if they knew the rule*' (UC lxiii. 49, emphasis added).

such a general and systematical revision, as all minds will look up to as arduous, and weak minds will start from as chimerical' (UC xxvii. 91). Before law can hope to perform, with even minimal success, its defining tasks, it needs to be radically recast. This 'general and systematical revision' of the law, we learn from *Of Laws in General*, calls for reforms of the conception of law itself, of the way in which law and legal relations are conceived. 'If you want good laws, burn those you have and make new ones', said Voltaire.[32] Bentham, the self-confessed disciple of Voltaire,[33] would take this revolutionary thought one large step further: if you want law at all, burn what now passes for law and construct anew from its ashes 'real law'. However, although Bentham abandoned Common Law, he did not abandon the principles and themes articulated in this attempt to come to terms with the practice of Common Law adjudication. They reappear and are further refined and expanded both in his criticism of Common Law theory and practice and in his development of an alternative theory of law.

[32] Voltaire, *Dictionaire Philosophique*, s.v. 'Loi'.
[33] See Bentham's (unsent) letter to Voltaire, Nov. 1776, *Correspondence I*, 367–8.

7

Custom, Rules, and Sovereignty

[T]he authority of the sovereign is founded or at least in a great
degree influenced by custom and disposition.

Bentham, *Of Laws In General.*

THE basic outlines of Bentham's positivist theory of law are very
familiar. Law is a (systematically arranged) set of commands backed
by threats all of which commands can be traced directly or indirectly
to a common source in the legislative acts of a sovereign whose
sovereignty rests on the habit of obedience of the bulk of the community. This nutshell summary of Bentham's doctrine, while
accurate as far as it goes, masks a theory of great complexity, a
theory the nature and complexity of which has not been fully
appreciated.

   L. J. Hume gives a clear statement of the most widely accepted
view of Bentham's theory of law.[1] He rightly points out that the
key notions in Bentham's theory of law and of political society are
command and *sovereignty*. Bentham's legal and political thinking
was entirely 'dominated by the categories of the [modern] sovereign
state' (67). Bentham equates 'political society' with the 'state of
government' which is hierarchically divided into governors and
subjects. 'As in the modern state, the relationship between governors and subjects was direct and the power or authority of the
governors fell on all subjects alike' (63). Bentham tells us in the
Fragment that this power though not infinite is nevertheless indefinite—no limits can be set on it. It is exercised exclusively through
explicit or implicit (tacit) commands. And the power to issue these
commands rests on nothing more than the habit of the people to
obey them. Political society, according to L. J. Hume's Bentham,
is *constituted* by this regime of will and (passive) obedience. And
they not only provide the foundation of such society for Bentham,

---

[1] L. J. Hume, *Bentham and Bureaucracy*, 62–7. Parenthetical references in the
next two pages will be to this work. For criticism of Hume's account of Bentham on
sovereignty see F. Rosen, *Jeremy Bentham and Representative Democracy*, 234–42.

but they shape its character, since the key social relationships of rights and duties are created by them (63).

These propositions, L. J. Hume notes, appear in a section of the *Fragment* setting out Bentham's definitions of basic terms of his analysis. But they constitute more than terminological stipulations: they represent Bentham's fundamental beliefs about political society. In particular,

they expressed a belief that will and obedience—not the tacit adoption and acceptance of socially–created norms and values—constituted the bonds holding a society together. And they represented rights and duties as the products of will, as sustained by sanctions and as therefore depending on the existence of a sovereign to create and maintain them (64).

Not only did Bentham fail to recognize the role of 'socially-created norms and values', according to Hume, but also his individualist psychology and theory of motives made it impossible to account for the social habits and customs which structure and underwrite social institutions (65). These motives 'did not supply any ordering principle independently of the sovereign's law, although the sovereign's law might exploit them in the interests of order' (65–6). Thus, 'at the point where it was most important that he should give an account of habit or custom', namely, in explication of the pivotal notion of the *habit of obedience*, Bentham 'evaded the issue and left it unresolved' (66).

Some of this is correct, at least as far as it goes. But some of Hume's claims are, I believe, quite mistaken and the total picture of Bentham's account of law and political society which emerges is distorted. Hume, like many commentators and critics, has failed to distinguish different theoretical levels at which Bentham worked and different polemical purposes motivating the various statements and arguments he makes throughout his writings. The result is a reading of Bentham's intentions and the theoretical claims they generate which is insensitive to the subtlety and breadth of his theory. Bentham's theoretical motivations are obscured and the basic character and thrust of his theory is distorted.

I have indirectly challenged part of this standard interpretation in Chapter 5. In this chapter I want to take a further step in correcting this distortion, and at the same time prepare the ground for our discussion of Bentham's critique of Common Law theory and practice in the next chapter. The focus of this chapter will be on

Bentham's account of custom and customary rules, and his theory of sovereignty. I shall try to show that Bentham has a relatively sophisticated account of custom on which, in fact, a quite subtle and powerful account of the foundations of law rests.

7.1 CUSTOM AND RULES

[Customs are] general observations . . . inferred, in way of abstraction, from these same particular facts, and expressed in the form of rules.

Bentham, UC xxxi. 88–9

Commentators have paid little attention to Bentham's account of custom largely because he never sets it out in detail in any one place. The most extensive discussion can be found in the *Comment*, but even there his remarks are scattered and incomplete. Although I focus attention primarily on the *Comment*, I will also range some distance from it to construct as completely as possible Bentham's view of custom.

Behavioural regularities

We speak of customs of both individuals and groups, Bentham maintains, but in each case we refer to a regularity of behaviour, a series of actions among which a similarity is observable (*Comment* 181, 303; UC lxix. 71–2). To this generic statement Bentham appends several distinctions.

First, he distinguishes two classes of custom in terms of the parties involved in the practice. Custom *in pays* is a regularity in the behaviour of the people, whether of the society generally or some localized portion of it. Custom *in foro* is judicial custom (*Comment* 182, 308–9). Whereas the former could conceivably involve almost any kind of social behaviour or integrated course of action, the latter is limited by Bentham to either adjudicative decisions, particular commands to parties pursuant to such decisions, or actions in execution of them.[2]

Second, Bentham distinguishes two classes of custom according to their respective origins. Customary regularities of behaviour arise either spontaneously or from some form of legal compulsion

---

[2] See, e.g., UC lxiii. 49; UC lxx(a). 19, *Comment* 218 (decision); UC lxix. 110, 115, 144, 151 (command); UC lxix. 151, UC xxxi. 88–9 (punishment).

(*Comment* 234–5, 332–3). The former he calls 'originally spontaneous custom'. The latter he often calls 'legalized custom', but he also uses the latter term to mark a different distinction, so I will refer to it as 'law-produced custom'. This latter kind of custom, in essence, is simply any regularity of behaviour, any structure or order in social behaviour, produced either by explicit general command or statute law, or (implicitly) by judicial decision. Bentham is keen to make the point that this is at best a bastardized form of custom, since it amounts to nothing more than the expected response of obedience to an effective law or judicial mandate. In particular, he is anxious to point out that such customs cannot be said with any plausibility to be customs 'of the people', or rules or patterns of behaviour to which their practice manifests their 'consent'.[3]

Third, Bentham distinguishes between customs that are 'legalized' and those that are not.[4] Legalized custom is customary behaviour made binding or obligatory by some act of law, where an act is made binding by making the agent liable to punishment for failing to perform the act. Customary behaviour may be legalized either by an Act of Parliament or through judicial recognition. The more interesting and much more common method is that of judicial recognition (or adoption) of the custom. Bentham occasionally suggests that a single judicial act of punishing the non-observance of some customary rule is sufficient to make the customary behaviour legally binding. But he observes that this single judicial act can have this effect only if it occurs in the context of a more general practice of enforcing customs of the sort. For only in such cases can one infer from the single act that the custom will be enforced, i.e. that the behaviour is binding for the future (*Comment* 218). That is, a legalized custom, whether *in pays* or *in foro*, presupposes a custom *in foro*. Judicial custom can both create and

---

[3] At *Comment* 234–5 Bentham argues that the so-called 'particular customs' of Common Law, i.e. localized customs recognized as legal even though inconsistent with the general rule of Common Law, are regarded as genuine custom and 'immemorial' only because Blackstone and others have confused 'originally spontaneous custom' with customs actually produced by local judicatories which Common Law courts now refuse to recognize. At *Comment* 221–3 and 332–3 Bentham argues that whereas there may be *some* sense in which originally spontaneous custom could be said to represent the consent of the people—since they are rules practised by the people over a long period of time—nevertheless almost all custom *in pays* now a part of Common Law is *law-produced*, and there is *no* basis for regarding it as manifesting the consent of the people. See below, 8.2.

[4] *Comment* 182–3, 308; UC lxx(a). 7.

legalize customary behaviour *in pays*. But in each case, prior to the judicial act the behaviour in question is *not obligatory*, on Bentham's view.

Now if Bentham had left the matter here we would have to conclude that his account of custom is extremely crude. For one thing, Bentham seems to treat the customs of a group or community as on a par with the 'customs' or personal policies of an individual. But this overlooks some very important differences between them. An individual's customs—what one 'does as a rule'—may be entirely idiosyncratic in the dual sense of being unique to one and entirely private. At one end such customs shade off into personal policies or strategies for meeting personal goals; at the other end they shade off into mere habit. In the latter case, to say 'that's what I do as a rule' is just to say 'that's what I've done in the past', perhaps suggesting in addition that I'm likely to do so in future.

Some group or social customs *may* be of this sort, but typically group customs involve more than mere habitual coincidence of behaviour. They involve an *inter*personal, interactional element. The fact that others behave in complementary ways, that one (perhaps not entirely self-consciously) expects others to do so, and that they in turn expect one to conform, are not irrelevant to one's reason for conforming to some recognized regular pattern. In fact, these facts form part of the reason one has for so behaving (although it is seldom necessary to rehearse this reason to oneself before acting). Furthermore, social or group customs are to some extent prescriptive. Not only is this the way people (including oneself) *have* behaved, and are likely to behave in future, but also it is the way one *ought to* behave—in *some* cases we might even say that it is the way one is obligated to behave—at least until a reason of some weight can be brought forward against doing so.

But Bentham's account of custom seems to ignore these rather simple and obvious features of custom. Custom is identified only with a set of 'exterior' acts which appears to exhibit a certain regularity (UC lxix. 71–2). This impression is reinforced by Bentham's doctrine of 'legalized custom'. Sometimes, in order to emphasize the sharp difference between custom and law, between mere custom and custom made into law, he maintains that talk of mere custom is simply talk of an assemblage of actions in the past having no reference to the future (*Comment* 181), or if there is some implication for the future, it is only that one is likely to behave in the same way in the future. It is only with the introduction of law, and in particular with the introduction of punishment, he maintains, that the idea of obligation enters the picture.

However, the appearance here, for which Bentham is entirely responsible, is nevertheless deceiving. His account of custom is nearly as sophisticated as Hume's, though for reasons partly polemical and partly metaphysical he does not allow himself language to express his view clearly or persuasively.

Rules as inferential entities

What we have thus far is not Bentham's full and considered account of custom, but only the bare bones of such an account. To begin the process of putting flesh on these bones we need to introduce the notion of a rule or maxim. Typically Bentham restricts the term 'custom' to the set of *actions* themselves among which some pattern or order is apparent. (*Occasionally*, he uses the term to refer to the regularity or pattern itself.) But the rule or maxim is 'the proposition announcing' the course of action (*Comment* 304). That is, 'custom' refers to the actions, 'rule' and 'maxim' refer to a proposition. In the case of a rule concerning some customary course of conduct the rule has three important properties: it is (i) a *general* proposition, which simultaneously (ii) describes the course of conduct (it expresses the 'idea' of that course of conduct), and (iii) prescribes behaviour in accord with the pattern. It is in this dual sense of *capturing/describing* and *prescribing* that the rule 'announces' the course of conduct. Thus, the rule of some custom sets out not only what is or has been the case, but also what *shall be* the case (*Comment* 185, 190–1, 303–4). A rule is a proposition which either directs the active faculty or guides the intellectual faculty (*Pannomial Fragments, Bowring* iii, 215). A rule (or 'dictate') purports to state *reasons* an agent has for acting in a certain way. So, for example, Bentham maintains, of 'the only sort of reason that deserves the name', (i.e. a dictate of utility) that it *is not* a law, 'but it *is* a reason for a law, as it is for any other *article of conduct*' (UC lxix. 72). It may be the 'ground' of a law or an action, i.e. 'it may be that consideration which *determines* those, whose concern it is, to make a law: as any act of the judgment may be that which serves to determine any act of the will' (UC lxix. 73). Similarly, the rules of custom *in foro* are general assertive propositions assumed as grounds of the particular decisions and commands made by judges (UC lxix. 119).

There is one last feature of rules, according to Bentham, which decisively influences his view of custom and Common Law. Rules are essentially subjective. Suppose I am advised by a friend to act in a certain way, or suppose the law directs me to do so, and, after considering the advice or the command, I act accordingly. In each case, Bentham maintains, 'in doing it I make the Law [or advice] a *rule* to act by' (*Comment* 40). My friend may offer me (his opinion regarding my) reasons for acting in that way, and the law may set out a public directive obliging me to act in that way, but in choosing to act on the advice or in accord with the law I *make* the advice or law *a rule* for my action.

Here the notion of rule is used to express the idea that my action was the product of self-directed choice or decision, as opposed to being the product of strictly external compulsion, and Bentham is anxious to capture this important idea. But he also regards rules as subjective for another reason.

Rules are prescriptive propositions purporting to set out reasons for acting. Now reasons, on Bentham's view, are *facts*, but rules or dictates, even when correct or accurate statements of facts, are merely expressions of *opinion* about them. So, for example, 'a dictate of utility is but someone's opinion that there is utility in a certain mode of conduct' (UC lxix. 72). Similarly, a rule or maxim regarding some customary behaviour is 'a general proposition serving to express some observation made by him that utters it, concerning the coincidence of . . . Judicial usages in some point of view'; 'a proposition containing the opinion of him who is the author of it' (*Comment* 190, 185). Whereas a custom is made only by those involved in it (e.g. a custom *in foro* can be made only by judges), says Bentham, the (or rather *a*) rule of the custom can be made by *anyone*, though the rule or maxim 'becomes current' i.e. widely accepted, 'according to the apparent truth and importance of it, or the credit of him who utters it' (*Comment* 191). Thus, rules (unlike laws, as we shall see in Chapter 8) have no *public*, external existence like the acts constituting the custom. They exist only as *ideas*, and ideas in Bentham's ontology are always the subjective possession *of someone* or other.[5] By saying that such rules are mere opinion Bentham does not wish to imply that all opinions are equally accurate or authoritative. But he does mean to suggest that they are private or subjective, not themselves publicly accessible, and

[5] See UC lxix. 151 and generally Postema, 'Fact, Fictions, and the Law', sect. II.

perhaps also that there will always be a very wide range within which accuracy will be entirely indeterminate.

Unlike the concrete, publicly accessible acts comprising the custom, rules of the custom are arrived at by inference, not by observation. Rules are 'inferential' or 'conjectural' entities (UC lxix. 164), drawn by 'induction' or 'abstraction' from the observed course of actions comprising the custom. Bentham's discussion of this process of construction is usually limited to rules of custom *in foro* (that is, rules of Common Law), but the account can easily be generalized to cover custom *in pays* as well. Suppose a judge, then, were faced with a case not directly covered by any existing statutory law. The judge is forced to decide on the basis of such a 'rule as shall appear to be the just expression of the judicial practice in like cases' (UC c. 98). First, he must survey all the cases that bear close analogy to the case before him and note the decisions made in each of the cases. Then he must consider what rule would justify the line of decisions and cover the instant case as well. Finally, he would apply that rule to the facts of the instant case and announce his decision on this basis.[6]

Although the custom in this case is custom *in foro* and the rule is constructed by a judge, the process of constructing ('conjecturing') rules can be utilized by anyone. Indeed, since customs *in foro* are practices of judges in deciding the affairs and conduct of citizens (i.e. they are customs which either create anew, or legalize, customs *in pays*), citizens who are likely to be affected by judicial practice will want to construct such rules in order to determine where their legal rights and obligations lie.

In summary, then, custom more broadly conceived consists of a collection of particular acts exhibiting a certain uniformity plus 'general observations, deduced or inferred, in the way of abstraction, from these same particular facts, and expressed in the form of Rules' (UC xxxi. 88–9). But we cannot conclude our discussion of Bentham's theory of custom here, for we still need some explanation of the prescriptive character of customary rules.

---

[6] Brief accounts of the process are scattered throughout Bentham's writings, but the clearest and most complete brief statement can be found at *RJE, Bowring* vi, 552 which I follow here. See also UC lxx(a). 7, 19; UC lxix. 115, 119, 151, 188; *Comment* 331–2; *OLG* XV. 2; *General View, Bowring* iii, 157; *PJP, Bowring* ii, 155.

Expectations and the prescriptive character of custom

In Bentham's view, 'propositions' are prescriptive in either of two ways: (i) as expressing some species of command (or more generally, imperation—*OLG* X) backed explicit or implicitly by threat of some sort of sanction, or (ii) as a statement of reasons one has for acting in a certain way (UC lxix. 72–3). But customary rules do not seem to fit either pattern. It is possible, of course, that it is Bentham's view that such propositions merely *purport* to set out reasons or express commands, whereas in fact all they do is express the speaker's approbation or disapprobation of some action. This is the case with dictates of natural law, according to Bentham.[7] But this is not Bentham's view of customary rules. Many, if not all of them are rightly regarded as prescriptive in some sense. But, then, they must be related to one or the other of the two categories of 'propositions' above.

The most prominent suggestion in the *Comment* reduces customary rules to a species of command, 'quasi-command' he later called them.[8] Since the rules are formulations of the judicial practice of punishing behaviour regarded as offensive, the reasons might be regarded as residing in the implicit prospect of punishment for non-compliance with rules that can be constructed from judicial practice (*Comment* 185; UC lxix. 98, 119, 151). This account, though adequate as far as it goes (for Bentham's purposes), is nevertheless incomplete and misleading. It is incomplete because it accounts only for those customs (largely customs *in pays*) which are 'legalized'. It fails to account for the prescriptivity of non-legalized custom, either custom *in pays* or *in foro*. Now Bentham clearly maintains that non-legalized custom is not *obligatory*, but it is clear also that the notion of obligation here is Bentham's standard notion of legal obligation—i.e. of a command backed by a threat of sanction. We can conclude that such customs are not *legally* binding, for they are legally binding only if one is liable to suffer some sanction for failure to comply. Nevertheless, they may still be binding, or reason-giving, in some other respect.

In most cases it would not be plausible to claim that conformity with customary rules is required by considerations of original utility. This leaves as the only remaining candidate in Bentham's scheme of

---

[7] UC lxix. 102, 142, 148. See below, 8.2.
[8] *FG* I. 12 n. o; *Pannomial Fragments*, *Bowring* iii, 223.

things the initially most likely one, viz. expectation utilities. And indeed Bentham's view is that the prescriptive force of custom lies in expectations. They generate sufficient reasons for acting, but, Bentham makes clear, they do not generate *obligations*, which wait upon official recognition of the custom and punishment of non-compliance (UC lxx(a). 7). Customs shape (and are shaped by) expectations and it is often only for this reason that there is sufficient justification for legalizing custom *in pays* (*Comment* 231-4). 'The ground of all [proper] legal decisions is expediency, real or supposed. One ground of expediency is popular expectation: one ground of expectation is, past usage' (*Comment* 306 n. c).

As we have seen in the previous chapter, this is precisely the case Bentham makes for rules of custom *in foro*. Citizens, observing the actions of judges, formulate a general rule, i.e. construct an idea of a course or pattern of official conduct, which is further confirmed by subsequent judicial decisions. This fixes the expectations of the citizen-observers which in turn produce a uniformity in their behaviour, a custom *in pays* (UC lxiii. 49; UC lxix. 143). Once these expectations are fixed judges are bound to respect them and act accordingly. It is precisely because the course of past judicial decisions can, at least to some extent, fix the expectations of the people that the judges must abide by such customary rules even when original utility might dictate a quite different decision.

This link between custom and expectations is essential for the prescriptive force of custom *in pays* also (see UC lxx(a). 19). This is clear from Bentham's extended discussion of Blackstone's Common Law rules for legitimating particular customs (*Comment* 235-51). At each important point Bentham insists on testing Blackstone's rules against 'the doctrine of expectations'. If it conformed to this doctrine, he accepted it; if it seemed to conflict with it he rejected it. The assumption throughout is that custom *in pays* has prescriptive force just to the extent that it arises out of and focuses expectations.

We also noted in 5.1 another passage in which this doctrine of Bentham's is relied on. The so-called law of nations, Bentham there maintains, is composed of treaties, agreements, and customs. And often the rules of international law consist of nothing more than the interlocking expectations of nations based on past practice (UC lxxii.1). But there is an even more interesting example discussed in greater detail in the *Comment* (334-5).

Bentham considers an example of an 'originally spontaneous custom' *in pays* which is subsequently 'legalized' by Common Law. It is the 'Custom of the Realm', says Bentham, that carriers should make good the loss or damage done to goods entrusted to them for transport, and the law now obliges them to do so. But it is not improbable that at some earlier time the law did not require this of carriers, though it was their custom nevertheless to do so. They were not at that time *obliged* 'by the political Sanction' to do so. None the less, the reluctant carrier may well have been determined to do so—not by the law, but by considerations of what is called natural justice enforced by the moral sanction (*Comment* 334). 'Natural justice' no doubt refers in this case to consideration of expectations.[9] Since the carrier was entrusted with the goods, was likely to profit from this trust, and since the owner was incapable of taking care of them while the carrier had it in his power to do so, the owner expected the carrier to do so, and the carrier 'was sensible it was expected of him, and prepared himself accordingly'. Thus, 'it seemed reasonable [that the] Carrier should be answerable' for the damage or loss. Furthermore, since it was reasonable he should be held liable, 'he had reason to think that if he did not, he should be thought to have acted unjustly' and consequently lose to some extent 'the good will of his acquaintances'. Thus, says Bentham, 'actuated by these or similar considerations, for a certain time Carriers were in the habit upon a loss or damage happening to the goods they carried, to make amends' (*Comment* 334).

In this example, Bentham's view is reasonably clear. The prescriptive force of custom rests first of all on the legitimate expectations it creates. The owner had reason to expect care to be taken, and the carrier recognized this and adjusted his behaviour accordingly. On this basis he could reasonably be expected to compensate damage done to the goods entrusted to him. This gave him reason to compensate the loss. But further he could also see that others, including the owner, would with good reason regard his refusal to compensate the loss as unjust, and on this basis refuse to trade with him in future, thereby 'enforcing' the requirements of 'natural justice' with the 'moral sanction'.

This example is important for several reasons. First, it locates the prescriptive force of non-legalized custom squarely in expectations. Second, although the 'moral sanction' is invoked by Bentham, it is

9 UC lxx(a). 19–20 and above, 5.1.

clear that he recognizes an 'internal' aspect of this sanction. The carrier has reason to fear the loss of the goodwill of his potential customers because he realizes they *have good reason* to regard his behaviour as unjust; and they refuse him their good offices *for the reason that* he violated rules they regarded as reasonable and just.[10] Third, the expectations Bentham considers in this example are clearly interdependent. The expectations arise out of social inter-action which is mutually dependent.

Custom, for Bentham, we can now see, is not merely a matter of uniformity of 'exterior' actions, a matter of mere coincidence of habits of people. Rather, it is essentially *interactional*. The carrier's 'habit' arises out of the framework of mutually acknowledged expectations. This interactional, or interdependent, character of customs is not always clearly brought out by Bentham, but it is a mistake to saddle him with a cruder view which ignores this essential property. Bentham's sensitivity to this aspect of custom, especially in the context of Common Law adjudication, was clearly evident in the materials discussed in the previous chapter. There we noticed that proper Common Law adjudication takes place, according to Bentham, in a complex network of interdependent relations and ex-pectations involving judges and citizens. The rules (of custom *in foro* is this case) are shaped by and derive their force from this network of interdependent expectations.

Thus, we have here an account of customary rules which accounts for their ontological status, and their prescriptive force, and ex-plains how they are transformed into rules of law. This account quite clearly departs significantly (and quite intentionally) from the conception of it current in traditionalist Common Law theory. But it is a serious attempt to give an account which is faithful to the phenomena within the limits of Bentham's ontology and general conceptual scheme. It is not entirely complete or adequate as it stands, but it builds on the foundation laid earlier by Hume and raises an important question Hume never directly considered: what is the relationship between the general normative proposition formulating the practice of a group and the actual behaviour of members of the group engaging in the practice? This question will concern Bentham increasingly as he considers the adequacy of the conceptual structure of Common Law theory.

---

[10] We will have a good deal more to say about this 'internal' aspect of the moral sanction in 11.5, below.

Bentham's account of custom clearly implies that one can legitimately speak of customary *rules* (for there is indeed something over and above the mere aggregate of 'exterior' acts); however, these are not rules of *law*.[11] Customary rules may 'determine' (prescribe or call for) certain actions, and 'ground' decisions, but they do not make such actions or decisions *obligatory* or *legally* binding. The rules fall short of law; in precisely what respects they fall short, according to Bentham, is a matter we will take up in earnest in Chapter 8.

7.2 THE ROLE OF SOVEREIGNTY IN POSITIVIST LEGAL THEORY

> [The] ideas of orders, obedience, habits, and threats do not include, and cannot by their combination yield the idea of a rule, without which we cannot hope to elucidate even the most elementary forms of law.
>
> H. L. A. Hart, *Concept of Law.*

With Bentham's general account of custom in hand we can turn to the pivotal notion in Bentham's theory of law, the doctrine of sovereignty. Most of the rest of this chapter will be devoted to tracing the development of this doctrine in Bentham's writing. But before we can do that with any profit we need to make clear a number of general features of the doctrine and its role in positivist (and in particular, Bentham's) jurisprudential theory.

Theoretical functions of the doctrine of sovereignty

The most striking fact about the doctrine of sovereignty is its extraordinary versatility. It is employed by Bentham (and Austin) to perform a very large number of different theoretical tasks. The apparent simplicity and versatility greatly attracted Bentham of course, but they also provide a fertile source of misunderstanding. The concept of sovereignty utilized in political theory provides a basis for identifying and distinguishing autonomous political communities. (An integral and independent political community is one in which the person or body which enjoys the habit of obedience from the community habitually obeys no other power. Bentham, it turns out, is not especially interested in this use of the notion.) In

---

[11] '*Rules*? yes, say I: *Rules of Law*? No.' (*Bowring* iv, 484.)

constitutional theory it locates the supreme governmental power in the legislative branch. In jurisprudential theory it guarantees the efficacy of law and provides a principle for systematically relating all components of a legal system. (Two different laws belong to the same legal system if and only if they can be traced to a common source.) And this provides a criterion by which the identity of legal systems can be determined.

But most important for my purposes here is the fact that the concept of sovereignty purports to define criteria of validity of laws, i.e. criteria by which the identity and authenticity of laws within a legal system can be determined. Here especially it is important to distinguish quite different, though related, theoretical claims which the classical doctrine of sovereignty implicitly makes. To separate these claims a few general distinctions must be introduced. Criteria of validity are the structural elements of a body of law, the glue which keeps it together as an integral unit. Such criteria have an 'ontological' function: they define conditions which entities—rules, principles, norms, commands, acts—must meet for them to *be* authentic legal entities in a given legal system. That is, they define conditions which a rule, for example, must meet for it to count as a law (as opposed to a personal policy or principle of morality) of a given legal system (as opposed to some other legal system). In addition, such criteria may also be assigned the 'epistemic' function of defining tests by which authentic rules, principles, or act-in-law can be identified and distinguished from inauthentic or spurious rules and the like.[12] Now, if one may say, simplifying greatly, that criteria of validity could be captured by a set of rules, then we can distinguish two sets of questions or claims about these rules: (i) one might discuss the *content* of the criteria, i.e. the conditions of validity that alleged legal norms or acts must meet, and (ii) one might consider the mode of existence, the authority, or the grounds of the criteria themselves.

The doctrine of sovereignty has something to say on each of these points and different things at different levels of generality. First of all, it sets out criteria which are designed to perform simultaneously *both* 'ontological' *and* 'epistemic' tasks. Second, it has something to say about the ground or mode of existence of the criteria: they exist simply as matters of social fact. In particular,

---

[12] J. Coleman distinguishes these two functions (using slightly different terminology) in 'Negative and Positive Positivism', 141.

these must be facts about the habits of obedience of the bulk of the community. Third, it also requires that the *content* of the rules be defined solely in terms of publicly accessible, social facts. In particular, they must be facts about the *legislative* actions of the sovereign or of parties to whom the sovereign has delegated law-making power. Although these claims fit together systematically in Bentham's jurisprudential theory, it is important to keep in mind that they are distinct claims. And Bentham was aware of the differences amongst them, at least to the extent that he perceived that the third set of claims does not follow from the second, and that he needed a separate argument to establish them.[13]

Thus, according to the doctrine of sovereignty, a rule is valid in a given legal system if and only if it can be traced back ultimately to an exercise of sovereign legislative power which is the common source of all other laws in the system, where the sovereign's position or power is constituted by the habit of the people generally of obeying laws issuing from this source. However, a problem immediately arises at this point: how can the mere fact of compliance with orders or commands, even if it is compliance on the part of a large number or members of the community, transform a person's expression of will into *law*? Contemporary critics often charge that the doctrine of sovereignty confuses the notion of the *efficacy* of a legal system with the idea of the *validity* of its component laws. Efficacy may be a *condition* of validity, but it is not to be equated with it. This problem generates two questions which will guide the ensuing discussion of the development of Bentham's jurisprudential concept of sovereignty: (*a*) What exactly is the relationship between the social facts of habitual obedience and the sovereign's exercise of legislative power? And (*b*) What exactly is the nature of this habit of obedience? Before we turn to the development of this concept in Bentham's thought I want to sharpen these questions a little.

Habit of obedience: mechanical v. interactional models

Consider the first question. On Bentham's view, a law is valid in virtue of its issuing directly or indirectly from a valid exercise of lawmaking power—of the 'power or imperation' (*OLG* IX, especially 8–9). But the power of imperation is a *normative* power,

---

[13] The theoretical problems touched on here are discussed in a more systematic way in my 'Coordination and Convention'.

the power to issue valid commands or permissions, to invest persons with certain rights and powers or to divest persons of them. It is the power to make it the case that what one says or does has *legal effect* (*IPML* XVII. 22; *Comment* 92). Although this power, in Bentham's view, may *rest on* the ability physically to manipulate persons or things (*OLG* XI. 11 and n. h), it is not to be identified with this power. It is a different *kind* of power: it indirectly involves a power to direct the behaviour of persons, but it does so *through* the exercise of the power to issue valid imperations.

Now Bentham has a sophisticated analysis of normative or legal powers in *Of Laws in General*.[14] But it is clear from this account that such powers are entirely the work of law: they are created by (and exist entirely in virtue of) either certain legal permissions or by conditions on the scope or application of certain other laws defining rights, powers, duties or the like. This seems to create a problem for Bentham, for on his view laws exist only as the *product* of the exercise of sovereign legislative power, but it appears that the exercise of such power presupposes the existence of at least one law, viz. that which confers legislative power on the sovereign. Bentham, then, seems to be faced with a dilemma: either he accepts that there are some laws which are not the products of the legislative will of the sovereign (and then we need some account of their existence and validity), or he denies that there are such laws with the result that his account flies in the face of the facts.[15]

Now, Bentham might reply here that this sovereign power is constituted by the habit of obedience of the people. '[O]f the power of the sovereign himself the constituent cause is the submission and obedience of the people' (*OLG* XI. 11 n. h, p. 139). But this just introduces the original puzzle again. What does Bentham mean by 'constituent cause' of the sovereign's (imperational) power?

---

[14] For a detailed discussion see H. L. A. Hart, 'Legal Powers', in Hart, *Essays on Bentham*. This is a very helpful account, but I disagree with his account of Bentham on investitive and divestitive powers. Hart maintains that they, like other powers of imperation, are created by permission-granting laws. But Bentham's view is that they are created by making the application of general rules of law (granting rights or other powers, or imposing duties) to certain persons *conditional* upon the performance of certain well-defined public acts by persons said to have the investitive or divestitive powers. See *OLG*, App. B and *General View*, *Bowring* iii, 186–90.

[15] Hart observes, for example, that legislative power is characteristically conferred, and often limited, by law in many legal systems ('Legal Powers', 218). More generally on the problem of the limits of sovereignty see Hart, 'Sovereignty and Legally Limited Government', in *Essays on Bentham*.

It is tempting to find a clue in an obscure passage of the *Introduction to the Principles* uncovered by J. Burns. 'Sovereign power', says Bentham,

is exercised either by rule or without rule: in the latter case it may be termed *autocratic*: in the former case it is divided into two branches, the *legislative* and the *executive*. In either case, where the designation of the person by whom the power is to be possessed, depends . . . in any sort upon the will of another person, the latter possesses an *investitive* power . . . with regard to the power in question.[16]

Now this passage suggests that there may be some party 'behind' the sovereign which can choose to confer or not to confer sovereign power on a person or legislative body. Could this party be the people themselves, and could their submission to the expressed will of the sovereign be the way in which supreme legislative power is conferred on the sovereign?

As we shall see below, Bentham later in his career develops a view which may at first be confused with this. But even if he held the view here attributed to him it does not solve our problem. For it *presupposes* a division of sovereign power and a power of investment, and these presuppose laws or rules (or something of that sort) that distribute this power and create the power of investment. At best, this can explain how sovereign power is vested in one person or body of persons in the community rather than another, but it does not yet explain how popular submission and obedience *constitute* the sovereign's power.

Hart surely is right that this matter will remain entirely mysterious if we regard such submission (as he and most critics do) as nothing more than the mere regularity of behaviour of the people in compliance with the sovereign's expressed will, compliance which is more or less mechanically triggered by the sovereign's command. Hart argues, of course, that we can avoid this mystery at the foundations of law if we replace the mere *habit* of personal *obedience* to the sovereign with general *acceptance* of certain fundamental, 'constitutional' rules, acceptance which is manifested in the practice of legal officials at the very least and perhaps also of a substantial portion of the populace.[17] That is, Hart insists that what lies at the foundations of law is not a habit of personal

---

[16] *IPML* XVI. 54 (p. 263); see J. Burns, 'Bentham on Sovereignty', 138.
[17] Hart, 'Legal Powers', 216–19, *Concept of Law*, chs. IV and VI, and 'Sovereignty', 238.

obedience, but rather the acceptance of a customary rule defining criteria of validity of laws of the system. Bentham's doctrine of sovereignty cannot capture this notion and so, he concludes, it must fail as an account of the foundations of law.[18]

As a criticism of Austin, this may be entirely just, but directed against Bentham its justice is much less clear. There is some evidence that Bentham may have held a mechanical conception of the disposition to pay obedience. For example, explicitly following Filmer, Bentham traces the origin of this disposition to the structure of authority in the family. Rejecting Lockean and Rousseauan notions of natural equality, Bentham insists that inequality of power is a natural and inevitable fact of the human condition. We are born subject to the authority of our fathers, and in the family we 'are trained into' the disposition to obey. 'Once formed nothing is easier than to transfer it from one object to another.'[19] This suggests that the disposition to obey is programmed into us very early. In political society, the focus changes but the mechanism is the same. The response of obedience is tripped by appropriate stimuli from a new source, the sovereign. Thus, his power is 'caused' by, consists in, his ability to trip this response when he desires.

However, there is reason to question this picture of Bentham's doctrine of the habit of obedience. First, this habit cannot consist merely in compliance with the laws and commands issuing from the sovereign. It is crucial to Bentham's account that the complaint behaviour be a response *of obedience* to the expressed will of the sovereign. That is, compliance with the law is forthcoming, at least in part, *for the reason that* subjects recognize that the laws issue from the sovereign. But this implies that the disposition to obey involves, at the very least, certain intentional elements, in particular the belief that the behaviour in question is *a proper response* to the sovereign's declarations.

---

[18] Hart, *Concept of Law*, 78.

[19] UC c. 109, and 104–13 generally. See also UC xxv. 10–15; UC lxxxvii(a). 69, 70; *FG* I. 13 n. p; *FG* I. 16. It should be noted here that Hume held a view similar to this (see *Treatise* 486) and insisted that habit forms the solid basis of all government: 'Habit soon consolidates what other principles of human nature had imperfectly founded, and men, once accustomed to obedience, never think of departing from that path in which they and their ancestors have constantly trod' ('Of the Origin of Government', in Hume, *Essays,* 37). But Hume saw no inconsistency in holding these views while advancing a theory that establishes law and government solidly on custom and convention. See above, 3.1

Second, the terminology Bentham uses to describe or refer to the social facts at the foundations of law is not constant. Frequently, he talks about a *habit* of obedience, which entails the existence of a large number of acts of obedience in the past. But he seems to prefer to talk of 'the *disposition* to pay obedience'. As Hart has recently pointed out, this disposition might be settled, not by a long habitual course of actions in the past, but by a settled *intention* to obey a certain class of legislative commands.[20] Now, Bentham clearly allows that the disposition in question might rest on 'the will of one moment which the will of any other moment may revoke' (*Pannomial Fragments, Bowring* iii, 219), so it may be possible in Bentham's view for the disposition to rest on such an intention without the backing of a regular practice. But he has in mind here the extraordinary case of sovereignty based on contract. In the usual course of events, the disposition arises from a general practice of obedience, but that does not rule out such intentional elements. The question that will concern us is, What is the relationship between the internal or intentional aspects of this disposition and the pattern of actions in the past?

A third reason for questioning the mechanical model lies in the fact that Bentham was willing to use the term 'habit' to refer to participation in *customary* practices (*Comment* 234). And such behaviour may depend on (or originate in) a complex network of reciprocal expectations of the behaviour of others participating in the same practice. That is, Bentham's usage of the terms 'habit' and 'disposition' does not exclude the possibility that habitual behaviour is consciously 'interactional', known to be interdependent and engaged in at least partly for that reason.

But if we regard the disposition to obey as 'interactional' then there is some hope that we can develop a somewhat more plausible conception of the foundations of law. On the mechanical model of the habit of obedience, sovereignty is a relation between the sovereign and each member of the community regarded individually. Each subject is disposed (or, perhaps, not disposed) to obey the sovereign regardless of the actions of any other subjects. But on the 'interactional' model the disposition to obey can only be understood in collective terms. For a command to *count as* law, it is not enough that the person addressed be moved by the command to act in compliance with it, it is also necessary that the command be

[20] Hart, 'Sovereignty', 236.

regarded generally, and known by each person addressed by it to be regarded generally, as authoritative law (see above, pp. 205–7). Thus, on this interpretation the disposition to obey is a complex one, depending on one's beliefs and expectations regarding the behaviour and attitudes of most of the other members of the community.

It is my thesis that the interactional model is the more accurate representation of Bentham's notion of the disposition to obey, and that Bentham held that law rests at its foundations on a complex custom or practice of recognizing certain expressions of will as authentic laws. This custom generates the 'constitutional' rules which define the powers of the sovereign (as well as potentially limit these powers). In turn, this practice itself can be shaped by the exercise of the sovereign legislative power it confers, and so can be seen as, in part, issuing from the sovereign, though ultimately it rests on the practice of the people. The task of the next section is to substantiate this thesis.

7.3 DEVELOPMENT OF BENTHAM'S DOCTRINE OF SOVEREIGNTY

Now by a sovereign I mean any person or assemblage of persons to whose will a whole political community are (no matter on what account) supposed to be in a disposition to pay obedience: and that in preference to the will of any other person.

Bentham, *Of Laws in General.*

This classic statement of the doctrine of sovereignty is found at the opening of the second chapter of *Of Laws in General.* However, to get a clear and complete picture of Bentham's doctrine we need go to writings prior to *OLG*: to the *Fragment on Government* and to unpublished work contemporaneous with it, and some even earlier.[21]

The seed-bed of the doctrine of sovereignty

In an early sketch entitled 'What a Law is', Bentham maintains that it is important to fashion a concept of law which captures both its

---

[21] For a reading of Bentham's doctrine of sovereignty which stresses the continuity of the doctrine from *FG* to *CC*, see F. Rosen, *Bentham and Representative Democracy*, ch. III.

'nature' (i.e. substance or contents) and its conditions of authenticity (UC lxx(a). 4). 'The notion of a law is compleat', he asserts, 'when it embraces its source or origination, its matter, and its form' (UC lxx(a). 5). The 'matter' of a law is its content or ends; its 'form' is its logical structure. The notion of the *origin* of a law 'includes the description of the persons and the solemnities: of the persons who are to make it; and of the circumstances they must place themselves in before and while they make it' (UC lxx(a). 5). This part of the notion of law addresses the issue of its authority or authenticity (ibid.). Thus, to determine the authenticity of any law it must be possible to trace it to its origin. That origin must meet two kinds of criteria: (i) criteria regarding the status of those purporting to make the law, and (ii) criteria regarding the manner in which it is made. The latter criteria concern what Bentham calls 'formalities': that is, 'those transactions or other circumstances extrinsic to the law itself, on which depends, whether it shall be taken to have issued from the source from which in itself it purports to have issued' (UC lxix. 74). Bentham takes pains here to stress that the authority of a law is not tied in any way to an assessment of its content or the ends to which it is directed. 'The authenticity of a law is a question exterior to, and independent of, that of its content' (UC lxx(a). 4). To know its authenticity it is sufficient to know by whom and in what manner it was made (ibid.).

Criteria of validity, then, have the following general features: (i) they concern only matters of 'pedigree' and not matters of content of the laws; (ii) they specify *who* are empowered to make laws and the manner in which they are to be made, and (iii) the formalities— the recipes for producing authentic law—they define are needed to ensure *public recognition* of the laws as authentic. One interesting implication of this view, which Bentham does not explicitly draw here, is that since lawmaking must follow a recipe, it is possible for a party who is empowered to legislate to fail to do so if that party fails to follow the recipe. Like all formalities, in Bentham's view, they constitute *de facto limitations* on the exercise of legitimate power.[22]

In this short sketch Bentham does not say much about the grounds or authority of these criteria themselves. But he gives an intriguing hint. He says that a law made by him or some other private individual could not be authentic, 'because the nations are

---

[22] See *OLG* XI. 21–7 and *RJE, Bowring* vi, 508–25.

not in the habit of obedience to laws of my making' (UC lxx(a). 4). This may be the earliest appearance (early 1770s probably) of the notion of the habit of obedience in Bentham's writings. And it is noteworthy that it appears, not in a definition of *sovereignty*, but in a more general discussion of criteria of legal validity. It is unclear from this brief suggestion whether Bentham held the habit of obedience to be the *basis* for the criteria of validity he sets out, or that the habit should be *included among* the criteria themselves. But it is clear that, although the motivation to comply with any law is supplied by the lawmaker in the threat of sanction, it is not this threat that authenticates the command. The authority of the law rests not on the ability to coerce but on meeting conditions of validity which are related in some way to a general habit of obedience of the populace.

These themes reappear and are developed further in a later essay (probably written sometime between 1774 and 1776) of the same title: 'What a Law Is'. Laws are commands, Bentham maintains, but they are distinguished from other commands by reference to their sources, substance, and formalities (UC lxix. 74). Again, authenticity is defined in terms of the two familiar elements of pedigree: 'A Law is authentic in its original, when it is the Will of the accustomed lawgiver or lawgivers expressed with the accustomed formalities' (UC lxix. 87).

Further insight into the nature and social role of these criteria is given in the next paragraph. 'The use of these formalities', he says,

is first to make it sure that the commands in the Law are in fact what were meant to be given by accustomed parties, secondly that they have had . proper opportunities to form the opinions by which those commands have been determined, [and] thirdly to make it appear that they are so to those who are to obey them (UC lxix. 87).

It is clear that the central task of criteria of validity is to provide a public and common basis for distinguishing laws from pretenders to that status, distinguishing the authentic from the spurious. The 'epistemic' function is central to Bentham's account. It is not enough that the commands addressed to the people are, in fact, the (considered) commands of the empowered lawgiver, it must publicly *appear* to be so to those who must obey them.[23] (We might add here, from observations made earlier, that this is important not only for

[23] Thus, 'ceremonies of authentication' are necessary. They are 'employed as signs for the purpose of making known to the people that such or such a discourse is expressive of the will of the legislator' (*OLG* X, p. 126 n. 12).

those who must obey the laws, but also for those who must apply, enforce, and adjudicate disputes arising under them. See above, 6.2.)

In addition Bentham suggests here (though he does not develop the thought) that the formalities ensure that lawmakers have the opportunity (and perhaps, depending on the nature of the form- alities, *are forced*) to consider carefully whatever warrant there is for making the law. Since the formalities give public assurance of this, they may thereby increase the 'legitimacy' of the legislative product.

Nothing much is said about the basis on which these criteria rest, except that the lawgiver and the formalities are 'accustomed'. There is, however, one passage later in the same set of manuscripts which, despite its ambiguity, needs to be considered here. In a dis- cussion which parallels Chapter I of the *Fragment* (especially *FG* I. 9) Bentham asserts: 'The obedience paid to any *particular* Law rests ultimately on a circumstance extrinsic to all Laws, a *general habit of obedience*. A habit of executing upon all occasions and in all points commands of some one person at least or body of persons in the state' (UC lxix. 204). This difficult passage can be given several different readings. It will be instructive to note the most plausible of them. The first sentence introduces two contrasts. The first is between the (implicit) immediate basis of obedience and the 'ultimate' basis. The point of the contrast, I believe, is to abstract from the subject's immediate motive of fear of sanction to focus on a different feature of compliance with the law. This is implied by Bentham's claim that he wishes to focus on 'a cir- cumstance extrinsic to all laws'. This abstracts from the particular *content* of laws, to be sure, but it abstracts also from a feature intrinsic to all particular laws, namely that they (explicitly or im- plicitly) threaten some evil upon non-compliance. Bentham wishes to focus attention on a feature which is not a property of any par- ticular law, but on which obedience to any particular law rests: the general habit of obedience, not to any particular laws, since they may change, but to the will of the sovereign lawmaker.

This much is relatively clear, but the intriguing ambiguity lies in deciding whose *general* habit Bentham refers to. Three possibilities suggest themselves, each of which gives a different interpretation of the relationship between an individual citizen's obedience to a par- ticular law and the general habit of obedience. First, the general habit may be that of the individual citizen whose obedience to the particular law is referred to at the opening of the passage. On this reading the habit of obedience is simply a one-to-one relationship between the subject addressed by the law and the sovereign. Bentham could be saying that to understand the command of the sovereign as a *law* we must look beyond the citizen's immediate response to the threat of evil to his or her more general habit of submitting to whatever issues from the sovereign.

This, however, is not a very plausible reading of Bentham's remarks for two reasons. First, Bentham clearly holds that what qualifies the commands of the sovereign as laws is the fact that they are obeyed generally by the community at large. The habit of a single individual to do whatever another person requires of him or her does not qualify the commands of that person as law, though we may rightly say that the one person has the other in his or her power. Second, Bentham clearly does not hold that the sovereign's command counts as law only if the person addressed habitually obeys the sovereign. For the person obligated under law may well be moved *only* by consideration of the evil likely to be suffered for non-compliance. These two points suggest that, for Bentham, obedience in any particular case (even the obedience of the other-wise unwilling) does not rest simply on a natural inequality of power. The sovereign's power is *socially constituted*—artificial rather than natural.[24]

A second interpretation takes the general habit of obedience of the passage to be that of the bulk of people in the community. But this again permits two different readings, depending on how we are to understand the claim that obedience in the particular case 'rests ultimately on' the more general habit. One possibility, suggested by Hart, is that the power of the sovereign to force unwilling compli-ance in particular cases rests not on any natural superiority but on the establishment in the society of general attitudes of submission and obedience.[25] The idea is that the sovereign is capable of com-manding *others* to enforce his command against the recalcitrant citizen. So his ability to command any particular subject depends on his ability to direct the behaviour of others and that ability is constituted by their general disposition to submission.

There is no doubt that something like this idea is at work in Bentham's theory of law. The efficacy of law in Bentham's view

[24] See Hart, 'Sovereignty', 222.   [25] Ibid.

surely rests on some such power. But it is not clear how this relates to the conditions of authenticity we have considered above, nor is it a reading forced by the passage above. A second reading is possible which shows greater promise of connecting up these matters of habit of obedience with the earlier discussion of the conditions of validity.

For Bentham might be saying here that obedience in a particular case (coercive sanction aside for the time being), depends on the individual citizen addressed by the command recognizing that it is an authentic command. He or she may be willing ('disposed') to comply with the law, but whose commands are to *count as* law is a matter he or she can determine only by looking to the general dispositions of the people in the community. Thus, the individual's disposition to obey depends on the disposition of the populace in general. And this is true of the bulk of the members of the community. That is to say, the disposition to obey, on this' reading, takes on a distinctively interdependent or 'interactional' character. This would explain why formalities, 'ceremonies of authentication', and the like, are so important, for they are ways of assuring each individual that certain rules or commands are rules others are likely to follow. They are the commands with which the bulk of the community are disposed to comply.

This is to view the question of obedience from the perspective of the citizen, but we can also look at it from the point of view of the lawmaker. The lawmaker wishes to order or direct social behaviour in a certain way. He or she cannot do so by sheer force of will or coercive power. Sovereign power consists in the ability to issue commands recognized as authoritative, and that depends on meeting conditions which are publicly recognized as necessary for the commands or rules from any person to count *as law* and so as proper objects of the disposition to obey.

The kind of interdependence uncovered here is the same sort of interdependence between the source and the subjects of legal rules which we considered in 6.2. There we saw that, in order for their decisions to take on the force of general rules of law, judges had to focus expectations of both the people and the rest of the judiciary. The criteria for recognizing the rules as authoritative are different here—they are concerned with explicit legislative activity of a recognized lawmaker—but the structure of the social situation is very similar. This, then, is not a far-fetched reading of this passage, though it is not the only possible one.[26] If we turn to the *Fragment on Government* we can find confirmation for this 'interaction' interpretation.

Sovereignty in the Fragment on Government

F. C. Montague rightly observed that the scope and intent of the *Fragment* 'may best be expressed by calling it an essay on sovereignty'.[27] Bentham's discussion of sovereignty in *OLG* explicitly relies on this work, especially *FG* IV which is addressed to the issue of possible limits on sovereign power. But before we look at the details of Bentham's argument important for my present purposes, it would be helpful to set out the main objectives of the argument of Chapter IV of the *Fragment*.

The chapter is explicitly concerned with two general questions and implicitly with a third. (*a*) On what basis does the sovereign's right to make law rest (and more generally on what does the authority of law rest)? (*b*) Can there be limits on the supreme legislative power? The implicit question is (*c*) on what does the obligation to obey the law rest? Now Blackstone maintains that answers to (*a*) and (*c*) are to be found in the idea of a social contract. But he also maintains in answer to (*b*) that it is a necessary truth that in every legal system there is a supreme, *absolute,* and *unlimited* legislative power (1 *Comm.* 49). Bentham wants to show this answer to (*b*) to be simply false. Limited sovereignty is not only conceivable, he insists, but we can point to clear historical examples of it. Furthermore, he argues, it is inconsistent with the main thrust

[26] Another interpretation is suggested by the passage. The 'general habit of obedience' could refer to habits of the *courts.* This is strongly suggested by the language of the second sentence of the passage. It is a habit of *executing* the commands of some person, says Bentham, and this is language which Bentham usually reserves for the activities of courts or other law-applying officials. (For example, he maintains that the primary end of the law of adjudicative procedure is 'to give execution and effect' to the substantive law, see *PJP, Bowring* ii, 6.) Bentham's claim in the passage under consideration could be interpreted, then, to maintain that any individual's obedience to a particular law (whether from the motive of fear of the sanction or from the disposition to obey the authentic commands of the sovereign) depends on the general habits of judges of recognizing and enforcing sovereign commands. See Hart, 'Sovereignty', 234–9, for a discussion of this interpretation of the 'habit of obedience', and a critique of Bentham's doctrine interpreted in this way.

The suggestion is intriguing, but I have found no confirmation of this reading elsewhere in Bentham. To my knowledge, wherever Bentham speaks of the disposition to obey he has in mind that of the people at large.

[27] F. C. Montague, in the introduction to his edition of the *Fragment on Government*, 59.

of the contract doctrine and with that part of natural law ideology that Blackstone embraces elsewhere in Book 1 of the *Commentaries*. Both of these doctrines are committed to the view that there are a priori theoretical limits to the legislative authority of the sovereign, such that if these limits are violated the legislative product is said to be 'void', 'invalid', or even 'not law'. Bentham is also anxious to attack this doctrine. He, then, advances two main theses in this chapter: (i) that there are no a priori theoretical limits on sovereign power; (ii) that nevertheless, it is possible for sovereign power to be limited. In the course of arguing these two theses he puts forward and argues two additional theses: (iii) that the 'right' of sovereignty rests on the general disposition of the populace to obey, which is the key to the *validity* of laws, and (iv) that the question whether one ought to obey the law is a different matter to be determined only by calculations of utility.[28]

The pivotal passage for our purposes is *FG* IV. 23. There Bentham maintains that in the absence of a 'common signal' marking the 'juncture for general resistance', the supreme governor's authority is indefinite. And since whether or not there is such a signal in any community is strictly a contingent fact—its existence can be derived from no general moral or conceptual truth—it follows that there are no theoretical limits that can be placed on sovereign authority. On the other hand, sovereign power is not by necessity unlimited. It may be limited, for example, by 'express convention', precisely because the convention defines such a common signal. I shall consider first Bentham's account of these possible, contingent limits of sovereign power, and then look briefly at his defence of the claim that there are no a priori theoretical limits.

To explain the possibility of limits on sovereign power we need to return to the foundations of that power. 'By what is it that any degree of *power* (meaning *political power*) is established?' Bentham asks. 'It is neither more nor less . . . than a habit of, and disposition to obedience: *habit*, speaking with respect to *past* acts; *disposition*, with respect to *future*' (*FG* IV. 35, author's emphasis). This is the social fact that underlies all sovereign power and, thus, all law. But the disposition admits of indefinite variation, both regarding to

---

[28] In the *Fragment* Bentham calls this a question of 'obligation'. (We might call it a question of *political* as opposed to *legal* obligation.) But this is an uncharacteristic use of the term for Bentham. He almost always reserves it for sanction-backed requirements on action. See *Pannomial Fragments, Bowring* iii, 217, for example.

whom or what it is directed and regarding its scope and limits. 'This disposition . . . is as easy . . . to conceive as being absent with regard to one sort of acts; as present with regard to another' (*FG* IV. 35). So it is easy to account for observed historical cases of limited sovereignty.[29] The limits are determined by a limited disposition to obey. Bentham's main thesis, then, is that if we wish to discover the conditions of validity of laws in a particular community, if we wish to discover both who are empowered to make laws and the recipes they must follow to enact valid law (which may also include *substantive* limits), we must look to the general disposition of the community to obey.

But Bentham has more to say about the nature of this disposition. The first clue comes in the following passage: 'For a body then, which is in other respects supreme, to be conceived as being with respect to a certain sort of acts, limited, all that is necessary is, that this sort of acts be in its description distinguishable from every other' (*FG* IV. 35). That is, an essential condition of limiting the disposition to obey is that the boundaries be capable of sharp definition. The reason for this comes from Bentham's earlier argument that there can be limits to the sovereign's power, only if there is a '*common* signal alike conspicuous and perceptible to all' (*FG* IV. 22) by which the fact of the sovereign's having transgressed the limits of his power is made public. But this entails that not only must the boundaries of sovereign power be sharply defined, but the definition must be fully public such that the sovereign's respect or violation of them can be a clear matter of common knowledge. Now the 'express conventions' that exist among federated sovereignties to which Bentham draws attention are just such common signals. 'By means of a convention then', he says, 'we are furnished with that common signal which, in other cases, we despaired of finding' (*FG* IV. 36). That is, the sign which neither the natural law theory, nor even his utilitarian principle could supply, is here provided by the convention. For

[a] certain act is in the instrument of convention specified, with respect to which the government is therein precluded from issuing a law to a certain effect. . . . The issuing then of such a law (the sense of it, and likewise the sense of that part of the convention which provides against it being supposed clear) is a fact notorious and visible to all (*FG* IV. 36).

---

[29] Bentham gives several examples of limited sovereignties in *FG* IV. 34 and *OLG* II. 1 n. b.

And in this case the disposition to obey can confine itself within the defined bounds. Within the bounds, the subject population is prepared to obey whatever laws are made by the sovereigns, 'beyond them the subject is no more prepared to obey the governing body of his own state, than that of any other' (ibid.).

Now this discussion clearly presupposes the interactional account of the disposition to obey which I suggested a few pages earlier. First of all, we need such an account to explain the necessity of a 'common signal' for defining the limits of the disposition. Bentham clearly maintains that qualifications of the sovereign, and the limits of its power, must be matters of *public* knowledge. It is not enough that the sovereign's will is authenticated in some way to each citizen individually; it is necessary, further, that the authentication be *common knowledge*. That is, whether or not the mandates of a certain group of persons qualify as law is a fact about the *collective* and *interdependent* behaviour (and attitudes) of the members of the society.

This is confirmed by the language Bentham chooses to define the concept of sovereignty in *OLG*. The sovereign is one 'to whose will a whole community are . . . *supposed to be* in a disposition to pay obedience' (*OLG* II. 1, emphasis added). Bentham repeats this formula almost verbatim from the definition of sovereignty he gives in *FG* I. 10, which is witness to the fact that Bentham has, as always, carefully chosen his words. It is not enough that members of the community are in fact disposed to pay obedience to the will of some person or body of persons, it is essential that they (also) *be supposed* (generally and widely believed) to do so.[30]

Bentham's use of the notion of a common signal recalls a similar use in the *Comment* in the context of customary practices. He gives the example of the co-ordinated use of a common pasture on a manor, in which the Lord's putting out his cattle to graze on the commons was a signal to tenants to do so as well (*Comment* 243). This

---

[30] Jolowicz, following Pollock, took Bentham's choice of words here seriously (unlike most of Bentham's critics). They preferred Austin's language, which makes sovereignty 'purely a matter of fact', to Bentham's 'ambiguous' definition, but they did so on the basis of a misunderstanding of Bentham's use of the term 'supposed'. In contrast with Austin, who made sovereignty turn simply on the presence or absence of the *actual fact* of habitual obedience, Bentham, Jolowicz objected, introduces 'an element of law into the matter' and so makes his definition of law circular. H. F. Jolowicz, *Lectures on Jurisprudence*, 104–5. But clearly, in the present context Bentham intended no such legal connotations, and this is consistent with usage one finds throughout his writings.

suggests strongly that talk of a common signal defining the limits of the disposition to obey clearly suggests that the disposition itself is customary, indeed interactional in character. For a law is valid only if it enjoys (or can be expected to enjoy) widespread compliance, but it can be expected to receive such compliance only if each recognizes the rule of law as having been issued from 'the accustomed person' according to 'the accustomed manner' and only within the accustomed limits.

This interactional account of the disposition provides a much more plausible explanation of the potentially indefinite variations which the disposition admits, than the 'mechanical' model usually attributed to Bentham. If the habit of obedience were learned or programmed in early in life, say in the experience of natural authority in the family, it would be reasonable to expect a largely uniform and fairly simple form of the habit to emerge in the political community. But this is not Bentham's view of the disposition to obey. This suggests that he had a much more sophisticated view of the dynamics involved than the rather too crude mechanical model.

This interpretation of the doctrine of sovereignty is further confirmed by a close look at his defence of the claim that there are no a priori, theoretical limits to sovereign authority, i.e. no limits which can be deduced from general rational principles. The argument focuses explicitly on natural law theory, but there is also implicit in it an argument against the theory of 'tacit consent' on which Blackstone rests his theory of sovereignty.

Natural law theory purports to set out an account which simultaneously defines criteria of validity of laws (and so, in part, accounts for the foundations and limits of sovereign authority), and determines what makes a law good, just, or proper, and in consequence determines the limits of political obligation. Now Bentham believes natural law theory is incapable of succeeding in either of these tasks, but he focuses mainly on its difficulties regarding the former.

The main strategy of natural law theory is to include *within* the criteria of validity of a law considerations regarding the moral status—the justice, expediency, or other merit—of the laws. This is understandable, since the theory attempts to set out the conditions under which it is rational or morally obligatory for us to obey the law. But it cannot succeed, Bentham insists. For the standards of natural law are so vague that either they are entirely indeterminate and useless as criteria by which to judge particular laws, or they are relatively specific and determinate but highly controversial and unlikely to be widely accepted. As a result natural law theory (like the notion of 'tacit consent') cannot define 'the juncture of resistance' in sufficiently *public* terms.

This, however, is a problem not only for natural law and consent theories. It is also a problem, he admits here, for his own utilitarian theory of obligation. It is only by calculation of the utilities of one's act that one determines whether one must comply with the law or not. 'It is the principle of *utility*, accurately apprehended and steadily applied, that affords the only clue to guide a man through these straits' (*FG* IV. 20). Only the balance of utilities can determine the extent and limits of one's duty to obey the law. But the principle of utility, though more determinate than natural law principles and indeed the only rational practical principle, does not itself define a sufficiently public standard. It does not itself yield a *common* sign by which the limits of obedience can be known. It can, at best, define for '*each man in particular* the juncture for resistance' (*FG* IV. 21, emphasis added). That is, although the principle of utility (unlike the standards of natural law) provides a rational and determinate basis for political obligation, it cannot provide assurance that when resistance is rational or obligatory for *one* person it is at the same time, with regard to the same law, rational *for everyone* else.

Now this creates no serious difficulty for utilitarian theory, but it completely undermines natural law theory. For natural law theory insists that its standards for the *assessment* of the laws in terms of their moral status are simultaneously standards of *validity* of the laws; the principle of utility makes no such claim. But the question of individual obligation to obey a given law and the question of that law's validity—its status *as a law*—are two different questions, Bentham insists. The former is a question which one must put to oneself and decide on the basis of one's best judgment (in Bentham's view, best judgment of the balance of utilities). But the latter is essentially a matter of *public criteria*, of what one can reasonably expect other members of the society to (think and) do. Thus, whether an individual has compelling reasons (even if they are moral reasons) for disobeying a given law is not necessarily or directly relevant to the question of that law's validity. What is relevant to that latter question is whether one has reason to expect general resistance to the law. And *that*, unlike either natural justice or maximal community happiness, depends on there being a common sign, a publicly recognized limit to the sovereign's authority.

Again, we must conclude that the disposition to obey cannot be regarded as a fact about only the relationship between the sovereign and each member of society individually. It is essentially an interactional, interdependent affair. What one has an obligation to do may or may not depend on what others think or do, but whether something counts as a valid law necessarily depends on one's disposition to recognize it, which disposition depends on the expectation that *most others* in the community will or do also recognize it, where their recognition depends in part on the expectation that one will (or does) recognize it.

Bentham argues that no a priori, theoretical limits can be placed on the extent of sovereign authority. In particular, we cannot deduce such limits from some general normative political theory defining what counts as good, just, or proper law. Limits are possible. But they must be determined by looking to the social facts of co-ordinated recognition of the legislative activity of the sovereign in each particular legal community. I want to make two observations about this doctrine before we leave the *Fragment*. First, although Bentham suggests elsewhere that considerations regarding the moral status of the content or ends of the law may not be included among the criteria of *validity* of laws, the argument he advances in *Fragment* IV commits him to a somewhat weaker and more interesting conclusion. For what he argues there is that the criteria must be sufficiently *public*. This rules out morally substantive criteria wherever those criteria are themselves controversial, not widely shared, or the like. Thus, we cannot derive criteria of validity from a priori moral or political theories, for these theories cannot be shown to be universally accepted. But this does not rule out the possibility that *in some particular* legal community the limits on the sovereign's power are in part morally substantive. If the criteria by which the community is disposed to assess the laws are sufficiently public, determinate, and widely shared, then they may well serve the purpose.[31] Indeed, Bentham is *committed* to

[31] Hayek attacks legal positivism for advancing the doctrine of absolute legislative power of the sovereign. Against this view he insists that sovereignty depends on allegiance which in turn depends on the sovereign meeting certain expectations which the subjects hold regarding the sovereign's exercise of its power. 'The power

recognizing this possibility by the insistent 'empiricism' of his definition of sovereignty. If the content of the criteria of validity can be determined, as Bentham maintains, only by going to the societies in question and *looking* (or rather constructing the criteria from the general practice of obedience), then what the content will be cannot be settled ahead of time, either in favour of natural law or of positivism.

This leads me to my second observation. Despite his strictures against natural law theory trying to deduce criteria of validity a priori (or at least putting a priori limits on what can or cannot appear among the criteria), Bentham imposes one important a priori limit of his own: the criteria of validity of laws must be criteria of the validity of *the products of legislation*. Of course, this limitation is entirely natural given the way in which Bentham (following Blackstone at this point in the *Commentaries*) formulates the issue of validity. But it is not difficult to formulate the question of criteria of validity of laws more broadly—indeed, we have already seen that Bentham himself did so elsewhere. So the question must be raised here whether Bentham's restriction of criteria of validity in this way is simply arbitrary, or whether he can give satisfactory defense of it.

Leges in principem

Of Laws in General extends and deepens the doctrine of sovereignty of the *Fragment* in two important respects. First, Bentham explicitly extends the scope of possible 'exceptions' to the doctrine of unlimited sovereign power. In a long and important footnote (*OLG* II. 1 n. b) he draws attention not only to federative arrangements among sovereignties (e.g. The Netherlands) but also to constitutional arrangements dividing power *within* a single state[32] and even substantive

of the legislator', he maintains, 'thus rests on a common opinion about certain attributes which the law he produces ought to possess, and his will can obtain the support of opinion only if its expression possesses these attributes.' F. A. Hayek, *Law, Legislation, and Liberty*, I, 92. Clearly, Bentham could fully accept this view, as long as it is advanced as a contingent claim about the content of criteria of sovereignty an investigator is likely to find in a given legal system. Thus, also, Bentham could accept Hume's discussion of 'fundamental law' (see *Treatise*, 563–4 and above, 3.3) as a contingent fact about, say, British law, or any legal system. What he would reject is the claim that these conditions are logically *necessary* for there to be law in a community.

[32] Bentham's example is the Roman Republic to which Hume called attention in his essay 'On Some Remarkable Customs', quoted in Hart's 'Sovereignty', 227.

limitations (for example, on legislation interfering with religious practices). In a later chapter he considers the possibility of power divided in such a way that the supreme legislative (or executive) power is located in one body while another body has the power to judge and punish the supreme power upon public accusation (*OLG* VI. 19 n. n). He declares his opposition to such an arrangement on grounds of expediency and stability, and also (partly for those reasons) regards it as unlikely. Nevertheless, there is no general theoretical bar to such an arrangement. It is surely possible, says Bentham,

for every distribution as well as every limitation of power is possible that is conceivable. The power of the governor is constituted by the obedience of the governed: but the obedience of the governed is susceptible of every modification of which human conduct is susceptible: and the rules which mark it out, of every diversity which can be clearly described by words (ibid.).

This is Bentham's most latitudinarian statement of the doctrine. Any limitation on sovereign power is *in principle* possible, as long as the limit can be sharply focused, because the disposition to obey is indefinitely mutable. The details of these matters, he adds, belong to *constitutional law*. Thus, from what appeared at first in *FG* to be a single, rather rare exception to the unlimited power of the sovereign is opened up to embrace the whole of constitutional law. And from this point on Bentham treats the matter of the foundations of law, as well as the matter of the division of and limits on sovereign power in the state, under the head of constitutional law or '*droit politique*'.[33]

This leads us to the second respect in which *OLG* builds on the theoretical foundations laid in the *Fragment*. *FG* IV discusses possible limits on sovereign power, but Bentham does not regard these as *legal* constraints. Actions of the sovereign transgressing acknowledged limits cannot be considered 'illegal' though they may properly be termed 'unconstitutional' (UC lxix. 200). This view is forcefully advanced again in *OLG*:

In the definition that hath just been given of a legal mandate it follows that the mandate of the sovereign be it what it will, cannot be illegal: it may be cruel; it may be impolitic; it may even be unconstitutional . . . but it would be perverting language and confounding ideas to call it *illegal* (*OLG* I. 8, author's emphasis).

---

[33] UC xxxiii. 92, 79; see J. H. Burns, 'Bentham on Sovereignty', 143–5.

However, it would be a mistake to conclude from this, with Austin, that limits on the sovereign must be relegated to constraints of 'positive morality'.[34] For, whereas Bentham is anxious to distinguish rules defining limits from all other laws of a legal system, yet he clearly regards them as having something of the character of law, and in any case are quite different in character and function from rules of positive morality. And in *OLG* Bentham shows how such rules can actually be traced, in part, to the sovereign's own legislative activity.

Mandates issuing from the sovereign and restricting the exercise of its power are of two sorts, says Bentham.[35] The first are mere concessions or privileges which the sovereign may make to individuals or to the people as a whole. These clearly bind the sovereign only as moral commitments and have their force, in Bentham's view, only from the 'moral sanction'. They are best regarded as *promises* made by the sovereign to the people, and are on a par with international treaties. There is another group of mandates limiting the sovereign, matters of constitutional law or '*leges in principem*'.[36] Laws *in populum* are addressed to and govern the people; *leges in principem* are addressed to and are meant to govern the sovereign power in the state, and thus they 'stand upon a very different footing' (*OLG* VI. 15).

Such laws can be addressed either to the sovereign from whom they emanate (*pacta regalia*), or to future sovereigns ('recommendatory mandates'), or to both (*OLG* VI. 16). It is especially through Bentham's discussion of recommendatory mandates that his view of the foundations of *leges in principem* emerges most clearly.

For the sake of simplicity consider two successive sovereigns, Rex I and Rex II. Presumably Rex I had reasons for issuing the restrictions on the exercise of his power, but what reason has Rex II to follow them upon succeeding Rex I? Bentham's answer is, in effect, that it is a condition of Rex II's legitimacy, that is, of the sovereign power being vested in him, that he publicly acknowledge

---

[34] J. Austin, *Province*, 254.

[35] Burns notes this difference in 'Bentham on Sovereignty', 142. Throughout this section I have been stimulated by Burns's ground-breaking work, but I am especially indebted to him for drawing my attention to Bentham's important discussion of *leges in principem*.

[36] Strictly speaking '*leges in principem*' refers to laws addressed to 'the prince'. However, it is clear that Bentham uses this term more broadly to cover much of what we would include under constitutional law. See *OLG* X, p. 109; UC xxxiii. 79; UC c. 64 and Burns, 'Bentham on Sovereignty', 144.

these mandates as binding on him. The passage warrants quotation in full:

In most instances therefore it will have happened that upon any change taking place in the sovereignty such adoption [of Rex I's mandates] shall have taken place: it will have become customary for [Rex II] so to do: the people, influenced partly by the force of habit and partly by the consideration of the expediency of such adoption, will be expecting it as a thing of course: and this expectation will add again to the motives which tend to produce such effect in any given instance (*OLG* VI. 17).

Of course, he adds in a footnote, such adoption by Rex II is not inevitable. Indeed, smooth transition of sovereignty is a rather recent political phenomenon. Often in the past, whether the declarations of will of one sovereign would persist after the decease of that sovereign was a very uncertain matter, because (presumably) the underlying expectations and customs were not fully formed. However, Bentham concludes,

So great . . . is the influence of all these causes [mentioned above] when taken together, that in any tolerably well settled government the successor is as much expected to abide by the covenants of his predecessor as by any covenants of his own. . . . This expectation may even become so strong, as to equal the expectation which is entertained of the prevalence of that disposition to obedience on the part of the people by which the sovereignty *de facto* is constituted: insomuch that the observance of the covenant on the one part shall be looked upon as a condition *sine qua non* to the obedience that is to be paid on the other (ibid.).

Bentham clearly states here that the footing on which such *leges in principem* rest is not, like that of *leges in populum*, that they issue from the sovereign, but rather that they have been absorbed into the customary rules which define the conditions of sovereignty itself. Having first issued from the sovereign, they have taken on a different character. They have focused the expectations of the people which shape their interdependent disposition to pay obedience and have been incorporated into it as informal customary constraints. Bentham goes on to say, uncharacteristically, that *actual* adoption under these conditions may not be necessary since Rex II *will be deemed* to have adopted them and will be held accountable in accord with them.

This adds a new element to the basic model of sovereignty and its limits set out in the *Fragment*. For, not only can customary arrangements determine the limits of sovereign power by defining the conditions under which such power is vested in a particular sovereign person or body of persons and under which that power is exercised, but also it appears that the sovereign is able in certain circumstances to modify these customary limits and rules. It is easy to see how to extend this account to Rex I's *pacta regalia*, but, of course, whether in fact they succeed in focusing expectations and so become customs (as opposed to merely moral constraints) is a contingent matter.

The theory is developed further in Bentham's discussion of 'declaratory' or 'reiterative' mandates in Chapter X of *OLG*. Bentham recognizes that there may be laws which simply restate laws which already exist in some form or other (*OLG* X, § iii). These are most frequently employed, says Bentham, where the 'primordial law' takes the form of custom (*OLG* X, p. 104). And a case in point is law *in principem*. Except in the very rare cases in which sovereignty rests on explicit original contract,

the authority of the sovereign is founded or at least in a great degree influenced by custom and disposition: on a habit of commanding on one side, accompanied by a habit of obeying on the other: and more immediately on the one part in a disposition on the one part to expect obedience, on the other part in the disposition to pay it, according to the course of that custom from whence the disposition takes its rise. In such cases the force and efficacy of the law may depend in a considerable degree on the existence and efficacy, real or supposed, of some customs to which it is or pretends to be conformable. When therefore a law *in principem* is established having custom for its foundation, the appealing to that custom is a sort of step taken towards the ensuring the observance of it (*OLG* X, p. 109).

This important passage is remarkable for several reasons. First of all, it provides a clear and sophisticated statement of the 'interactional' understanding of the disposition of obedience. Sovereignty rests on a complex set of interdependent relationships among citizens, and, as clearly stated here, between citizens collectively and the sovereign. The 'habit of commanding' is dependent upon or constituted by the sovereign's 'disposition . . . to expect obedience'; and the disposition to obedience depends on expectations regarding the exercise of the sovereign power. *Both* are shaped by 'that custom from whence the disposition takes its rise'.[37] Law rests

---

[37] In *Pannomial Fragments*, Bentham says that the disposition to obey derives either from habit or from convention. He identifies the latter with the will, and by

for its foundations and authority on a complex custom or practice which encompasses the behaviour, attitudes, and expectations of both the citizens in the community and those who exercise sovereign power. The foundation of law consists in the state of mind and expectation of both subjects and sovereign, and the relations of interdependence obtaining between them.[38]

Second, we also learn from this passage that declarations of the sovereign not only create new or modify existing constitutional custom, but they can also from time to time declare or codify that custom or parts of it. Such laws bind the sovereign who issues them in just the same way that Rex I's recommendatory mandates bind Rex II, viz. as conditions of his holding and exercising sovereign power.[39]

From this discussion of *leges in principem* a conception of the foundations of law emerges which is even richer than that implicit in the *Fragment*. The force and authority of law depend on a general disposition in the population to obey. But that disposition is matched by dispositions on the part of the rulers and lawmakers. The disposition rests on an intersecting network of mutual expectations among subjects and between the sovereign and the subjects collectively. These expectations tend to be focused into more or less stable patterns of behaviour and choice which take on the character of custom or practice. But the custom has a precise focus. It is concerned not with particular types of actions, but rather with conditions *laws* must meet if they are to count as laws, i.e. with criteria of validity of laws. This practice may simply exist informally in the background of law, receiving no explicit formulation. But it is also capable, at least in part, of explicit formulation, modification, and limitation. In this way it is possible for the constitutive customary

implication the social contract. Of habit he says, it is 'the result of a system of conduct of which the commencement is lost in the abyss of time' (*Bowring* iii, 219). The echo of Common Law doctrine here is striking—it could not have escaped Bentham's notice.

[38] See *Principles of International Law, Bowring* ii, 541–2.

[39] Hart, in 'Sovereignty', 233, puzzles over a passage in *OLG* in which Bentham suggests that the point at which obedience is withheld might 'be settled by law as well as by an inward determination' (*OLG* II. 1 n. b). Hart claims that there is nothing in Bentham's theory of law that would allow him to say this, but Hart tentatively suggests (at 235), without offering any textual evidence in support, that Bentham *may* have been referring to the *practice of the courts* in enforcing the laws of the sovereign. But the activities of the sovereign uncovered here and earlier offer, to my mind, a more plausible explanation of what Bentham may have had in mind.

practice (the constitutional practice) to make its way into the actual body of formal law.[40] The sovereign can settle matters which, prior to its declaration, were not fully settled. Thus, it is possible to find in some legal systems a (perhaps substantial) portion of constitutive custom codified in a written constitution or set of constitutional documents. But this 'law' is clearly of a quite different character from the other laws of the system. It is different both because it is *presupposed* by all other law—it defines conditions which all other laws must meet to qualify as members of the legal system in question—and because it does not exist simply in virtue of having been issued by the sovereign. The explicitly formulated constitutional laws do not constitute the full reality of the 'law behind the law'.

It is little wonder, then, that Bentham was reluctant to regard sovereign actions in violation of these constitutional limits as *illegal*. He insisted that in a 'strict and proper sense' only laws *in populum* are laws, and actions contrary to them illegal. Rather, he insists, *leges in principem* or constitutional laws are 'transcendent laws' (*OLG* VI. 15), lying beyond and supplying the foundations for ordinary laws. These rules (or more precisely customary practices) are of a quite different nature, calling for a different analysis and having a different mode of existence, as Hart latter recognized. Nevertheless, because of their special role in the legal system, and their special concern with conditions of validity of laws, they cannot properly be regarded merely as validity of laws, they cannot properly be regarded merely as informal social practices or matters of positive morality.

Hart v. Bentham

By this time the similarities between Bentham's doctrine of sovereignty as I have interpreted it and Hart's familiar account of the foundations of a legal system should be obvious. But some important differences should be noted. First, there is no inclination on Bentham's part, as there is at times in Hart, to speak of a legal system resting on *a* (*single*) rule of recognition. Lying at the foundations of law, the 'constituent cause' of sovereign power, in Bentham's view, is a complex network of social interactions, expectations, and regularities which tends to congeal in different ways at different times, which can be codified in part, but which is characteristically open-ended and shifting.

[40] See Bentham's two examples at *OLG* X, pp. 109–10.

Second, and more important, the range of participants in the practice is potentially narrower in Hart's theory. For Bentham the constitutional practice is the product of the interaction and inter-dependent expectations of the people as a whole (and the rulers), whereas for Hart, although the practice *may* be that wide, all that is necessary is that there be a coherent practice of the *law-applying institutions* of the community. There are corresponding advantages and disadvantages of each approach. The problem Bentham faces is the easy confusion of efficacy of (mere general compliance with) the law with its *validity*. Hart's theory, of course, allows for a clear distinction between these because the essential practice is that of in-stitutions which *apply* the law *to others*; we don't have to look to the conforming behaviour of the people subject to the law. But Bentham does have the equipment to make this distinction. For behaviour constituting mere compliance with the law differs from behaviour constituting a customary practice, as he understands it. There is an essential intentional, or what Hart would call 'internal', aspect to the practice for which Bentham gives a quite plausible in-itial account. On the other hand, Hart's theory in the eyes of many critics has too narrowly confined the foundations of law to the practice of the courts, when it seems that not only efficacy but the very validity of law seems to rest importantly on a wider popular conventional basis than he allows.[41]

Third, Bentham is much clearer than Hart about the inter-dependency between rulers and the ruled. The customary prac-tice constituting the criteria of legal validity is a practice of both and arises out of the need to co-ordinate the expectations of both.

Finally, Hart distinguishes much more sharply than Bentham does between conditions of validity and conditions of legality. Often Bentham regards the limitations on sovereign power as a kind of *duty*, such that violations of them constitute a kind of *wrong done* to the people, rather than failure to create valid law. And he often speaks of the 'enforcement' of, for example, *pacta regalia* by the moral sanction. In Hart's view, Bentham's account of the limitations on government (legal or not) fails because he insists on forcing these limitations into the wrong logical category. Whereas such limitations in fact define *disabilities*, Bentham's

---

[41] See, e.g., J. Lucas, 'The Phenomenon of Law', 94.

imperational theory of law forced him to construe them as *obligations*.[42]

But this criticism does not go as deep as it seems. Bentham understood this distinction and had the conceptual equipment to take account of it in a sophisticated and plausible, if not ultimately satisfactory way (see 7.2). But it is not an easy distinction always to keep in mind and Bentham often either ignores it or simply loses grasp of it. However, some of the cases in which he speaks of the moral sanction enforcing *leges in principem* are quite consistent with an account which is sensitive to the two different logical categories to which Hart draws our attention. Bentham's analysis of normative powers supplies the terms needed for an analysis of the sovereign power of imperation. That power is created by a general rule (or network of rules), resting on a customary basis. (It consists of some combination of mandates and permissions the details of which need not worry us here.) The essential feature of this set of rules is that it defines conditions that must be met by any party who is to possess and exercise the power. That is, it defines investitive and divestitive conditions. Now these conditions can take an indefinite variety of forms, but wherever there are such conditions they, in effect, define limitations on the imperational power of the sovereign. Now some investitive conditions create investitive power in others (likewise for divestitive conditions). But the rules may also confer investitive or divestive significance on natural events. (An example of this is the rule of succession in a hereditary monarch which makes transfer of sovereign power turn on the natural events of birth and death.) It is also conceivable that the actions of the sovereign could be regarded as divestitive events. Certain actions performed by the sovereign could then be regarded, according to the constitutive practice of the community, as having the legal effect of invalidating the legislative activity of the sovereign. This would be true, for example, if the sovereign attempted to legislate on matters of religious practice.

Thus, we can fit Bentham's theory of limitations on sovereignty into his theory of normative powers. And so it is possible clearly to distinguish in theory the invalidity of a sovereign act from its being liable to moral sanction. However, Bentham invites confusion by referring to the social-psychological basis on which both the constitutional practice and the moral sanction rest as 'dispositions'. But it is

---

[42] Hart, 'Sovereignty', 241–2.

clear that they are quite different dispositions. The former is a disposition to recognize the expressions of will of a person or body of persons as law and to comply with them on condition that others in the community also do so. The latter rests on the sentiments and is a disposition to express dissatisfaction and discontent with the actions of the sovereign, and, correlatively, the disposition of the sovereign to feel shame and to view 'in the light of punishment' the discontent expressed by members of the public.[43] Now, these two are not unrelated in Bentham's view. In fact, the disposition involved in the moral sanction, when given public expression is likely to generate the expectations which may congeal into custom over time.[44] But they are clearly different dispositions.

Bentham may in some cases still confuse the limitations on sovereign authority with obligations enforced by the moral sanction, but in some cases in which he refers to the moral sanction in this context there may be no confusion at all. Two explanations are possible. First, in some cases *leges in principem* begin their lives merely as sovereign concessions or promises, and only later work their way into constitutional practice. Thus, whatever force such limitations may have prior to acquiring constitutional status, as it were, will have to be attributed to the moral sanction. Second, although it is possible in principle to distinguish duties from disabilities, in practice they often go hand in hand. For example, a man who attempts to marry a woman while still married to another woman both fails to bring about a valid second marriage and violates a moral if not legal duty. It is not hard to find similar examples amongst constitutional limitations on legislative power. For example, constitutional immunities protecting individual rights impose disabilities on the legislature. But violations of provisions of a Bill of Rights are not only regarded as constitutionally void but also as morally reprehensible. It is not at all implausible for Bentham to believe that many limitations on the sovereign power will also be 'corroborated' by obligations on the sovereign backed by the moral sanction.

Hart's criticism of Bentham's theory on this score at least is not warranted. Bentham can be charged with insufficient care and a certain degree of confusion and inconsistency in his discussion of these matters, but without much difficulty it would be possible to

---

[43] *Influence of Place and Time*, 108.
[44] Ibid. 132.

construct out of the materials Bentham provides us a consistent account of the foundations of law not far distant from Hart's own, and in some respects more plausible.

Divided sovereignty and democratic theory

One final development of Bentham's doctrine of sovereignty must be noted because it has important implications for the scope and character of Bentham's general theory of sovereignty. Soon after writing *OLG* Bentham turned his attention more directly to issues of constitutional law. There he divided sovereignty functionally into two parts: the 'sovereign constituent power' and the 'sovereign efficient power'.[45] The former is the power a person or body of persons has to vest the sovereign efficient power in some other party. The latter involves all governmental power, including the legislative, executive, and adjudicative power. Now it is this distinction which is given elaborate development later in Bentham's monumental work on the *Constitutional Code* (*CC* 9, 46). There he develops a democratic theory of government in which the 'supreme constitutive power' is located by the constitution in the people generally. His preferred constitution formally defines the investitive and divestitive powers in terms of elections and popular recall on the basis of universal manhood suffrage (and, in addition, less formally through his 'Public Opinion Tribunal'). The people, then, are sovereign on this theory, or rather they possess and are able to exercise *a share* of sovereign power. The Parliament, the officials of the executive and the civil service, and the judges and officials of the adjudicative branch, all exercise other parts of the sovereign power, power which is vested directly (or in some cases indirectly) in them by the people.

Now Hart maintains that this later doctrine represents a radical departure not only from Bentham's earlier doctrine of sovereignty, but also from his earlier theory of law.

The concept of popular sovereignty as developed in the *Constitutional Code* is therefore not only a quite different concept from that which enters into Bentham's discussion of the possibility of limited sovereignty but involves a quite different theory of law. This is because the constitution which confers on the electors the 'supreme constitutive authority' is,

[45] UC clxx. 47, 174. These manuscripts were composed about 1788, some six to eight years after the writing of *OLG*. However, there are hints of this distinction earlier. See *OLG* VI. 15 n. 1 and *IPML* XVI. 54 (p. 263).

according to Bentham, law though it does not derive its status from any sovereign or any command but from the fact that it is 'generally acknowledged to be in force'.[46]

But, if my interpretation of Bentham's doctrine of sovereignty and its limitations is reasonably accurate, then this is a mistake. The democratic theory of sovereignty in the *Constitutional Code* is a natural extension of the earlier doctrine and perfectly consistent with the theory of law presupposed there.

Note that the theory of government developed in the *Constitutional Code* is a *normative* political theory. Bentham is there setting out his view of the best (utilitarian) structure for government. He is not discussing the general *jurisprudential* issue of the foundations of law for *any* system. He advances here a political theory within the context of, and using the conceptual tools provided by, his broader jurisprudential theory. Now according to that general theory (i) sovereignty may be limited in indefinitely many different ways, and (ii) sovereign power can be functionally distinguished in theory into constitutive, legislative, and operative (executive/adjudicative) power. As a matter of general jurisprudential theory it is an open and empirical question just how the power thus distinguished in theory is actually distributed in any given political community. In particular, the *constitutive* power can rest in the hands of quite different persons or groups, or in the hands of no persons whatsoever (as in a monarchy). Democratic political theory calls for locating that constitutive power in the hands of the people generally. And so democratic constitutional law would distribute this power to the people, for example, through formal mechanisms for election and recall of government officials.

We can discuss such constitutional arrangements and others in the abstract, and make proposals for the implementation of one or another such scheme. This is precisely the enterprise in which Bentham's *Constitutional Code* is engaged. But if this code were to be genuine constitutional *law* in a state, the constitutional code would have to be transformed into constitutional *practice*. That is, a constitution exists only if it is practised, that is, only to the extent, as Bentham says, that 'it is generally acknowledged to be in force'. This constitutional practice may be substantially codified, and in the sense we have discussed before it can be regarded as 'law', that is, 'transcendent law'.

[46] Hart, 'Sovereignty', 228–9, quoting *CC* 9.

There is nothing, then, in this later development of Bentham's doctrine of sovereignty to jeopardize either his theory of law or his earlier theory of sovereignty. In fact, this later doctrine explicitly rests on that earlier doctrine.

It appears, then, that Bentham—like Hart and like Bentham's Common Law predecessors—holds that the foundations of law rest firmly on custom or convention. But, of course, he differs sharply with Common Law theory about the content of these conventions. Like Hart, he insists they do not consist in acceptance of some indefinitely specified set of *substantive* legal or constitutional standards, but rather in certain morally neutral, formality- (or 'pedigree'-) defined criteria of validity. More specifically than Hart, he insists further that they be defined in terms of a common legislative origin for all laws. The task of the next two chapters is to explore Bentham's reasons for insisting on this '*strong positivist*' conception of law.

8

Plucking Off the Mask of Mystery

Law shews itself in a mask.

Bentham, *Comment.*

HAVING found the prospect of practising law repugnant, the young
Bentham sought some other channel for his intellectual energies.
His reading of Enlightenment social theory and criticism provided
both the channel and a challenge. '[I]f philosophers would be of
use to the world,' wrote Helvetius, 'they should survey objects
from the same point of view as the legislator.' For 'morality is
evidently no more than a frivolous science, unless blended with
policy and legislation'.[1] Through Helvetius Bentham discovered his
'genius for legislation'[2] and turned almost immediately to a project
he titled *Elements of Critical Jurisprudence* or *Principles of Legal
Policy*.[3] Following the continental pattern, Bentham's social
criticism and call for law reform took shape as a proposal for a fully
rational, systematic science of legislation, the immediate focus of
which was criminal jurisprudence.[4]

8.1 LAW IN EIGHTEENTH-CENTURY ENGLAND

The life of the Common Law has been in the unceasing abuse of its
elementary ideas.

Milsom, *Historical Foundations of the Common Law.*

It is not surprising that Bentham's drive for reform of law and
legislation should take this focus since English penal law in the

---

[1] C. Helvetius, *De l'esprit*, 81. I am indebted to David Lieberman for pointing
out this passage to me.

[2] Bentham retells the story of this self-discovery in *Bowring* x, 27. See also his
letter to Forster (Apr./May 1778), *Correspondence* II,99.

[3] See the Editor's Introduction to *IPML* (1970), pp. xxxvii–xxxviii. The history of
some of the most important early manuscripts is told briefly in D. Long, *Bentham
on Liberty*, pp. xi–xiv.

[4] D. Lieberman, *The Province of Legislation*, 281. See Bentham's letter to
Voltaire (Nov. 1776), *Correspondence* I, 367. By 1775 or 1776 the previous work,

eighteenth century was barbaric and the object of criticism across a wide political spectrum.[5] Eighteenth-century Britain saw an enormous increase in criminal legislation, especially capital statutes, mostly for crimes against property.[6] Parliamentary action was rash, unsystematic, and blindly reactionary, both in the sense that the statutes were designed to protect the ruling social hierarchy against perceived threats from the masses, and in the sense that they reacted episodically and violently to each newly perceived threat in all its particularity. The reactionary nature of contemporary criminal legislation was bitingly satirized by the young Bentham:

> The country squire who has had his turnips stolen, goes to work and gets a bloody law against stealing turnips. It exceeds the utmost stretch of his comprehension to conceive that the next year the same catastrophe may happen to his potatoes. For the two general rules . . . in modern British legislation are: never to move a finger till your passions are inflamed, nor ever to look further than your nose.[7]

By mid-century, the criminal law was a hodge-podge of confusion and inconsistency.[8] English law published a 'dreadful catalogue' of capital crimes, including 'transgressions which scarcely deserve corporal punishment' while it omitted 'enormities of the most atrocious kind'.[9] The presumption of knowledge of the criminal law embodied in the maxim 'ignorance of the law is no excuse' was a cruel joke for all but a very few who could afford legal advice. Indeed, Bentham insisted that the presumption should be the opposite: 'the presumption is always so strong that an Offender knew nothing of the matter' (UC lxxix. 69). 'Men [are] ruined for

'Principles of Legal Policy', was recast as 'Crit[ique] [of] Jur[isprudence] Crim[inal]', see UC cxl. 14. But there is a substantial batch of manuscript material dating from 1773 and maybe earlier on matters of criminal jurisprudence. See UC xcvi; UC cxliii. 1–75; UC lxix. 1–56; and Long, *Bentham on Liberty*, pp. xii.

[5] For the social history of the next few pages I am primarily indebted to the fine recent study by D. Lieberman, *Province,* esp. ch. 10. The locus classicus, of course, is L. Radzinowicz's *History of English Criminal Law* I, pts. 1–3. See also E. P. Thompson, *Whigs and Hunters*; D. Hay *et al., Albion's Fatal Tree*, esp. Hay's own piece, 'Property, Authority, and the Criminal Law'; and H. T. Dickinson, *Liberty and Property*, ch. 4, esp. 159–62.

[6] Hay, 'Property, Authority', 18; Radzinowicz, *Criminal Law* I. 4.

[7] UC cxl. 92, quoted in Lieberman, *Province*, 267.

[8] For example, although it was a felony to damage the bridges of Brantford or Blackfriars, the same damage to the London or Westminster bridges carried the death penalty. To steal a sheep or horse, or pick man's pocket of a few pence, were capital crimes, whereas the attempt to take one's father's life was merely a misdemeanour. Lieberman, *Province*, 269.

[9] Ibid., quoting Romilly, *Observations*.

not knowing what they are neither enabled nor permitted to learn' (UC xxvii. 172).

But not only was the law absurd and unknowable, it was savage. It breathed 'too much the Spirit of *Draco*'s' law, 'all degrees of offence being confounded and all proportion of punishment destroyed'.[10] Hanging was the universal solution, the pervasive threat. But it was selectively applied. Because Parliament legislated the death penalty indiscriminately, and often allowed most crimes against property affecting the gentry particularly to be tried by summary conviction,[11] local magistrates determined for themselves when the full penalty of the law should be exacted and when 'mercy' could be shown.[12] This regime of selective terror further tightened the discipline and control of the propertied élite over the rest of the populace. The savage law was not only unknowable, but it in effect put complete legal power in the hands of those who could control local justice to deal as they wished with any threats to their property or their control.

Some, like Paley, actually praised this legislative policy for its 'delicacy and circumspection'.[13] But many attacked it as barbarous. Among these critics one finds *both* Bentham and Blackstone—an 'unlikely partnership', as Lieberman points out.[14] But it was a limited partnership, the limitations of which can be seen in the distinct sources of worry underlying their respective critiques of parliamentary criminal law. For Blackstone, criminal statutes with all their inconsistency, rashness, complexity, and inhumanity were merely the most glaring symptoms of a deeper disease which threatened the law itself: the irresponsible exercise of parliamentary sovereignty.[15] Although in theory it was sovereign, Parliament could exercise its legislative power in contempt of the Common Law, according to Blackstone, only at the price of ineffectiveness and ultimate breakdown of the law itself. Blackstone saw the irrational excesses of criminal legislation as a threat to the integrity of Common Law, and thereby to the legal system as a whole.

The contrast with Bentham's analysis of the social and jurisprudential disease could not be sharper. Bentham recognized the primitive, contradictory, myopic character of parliamentary legislation.

---

[10] O. Ruffhead, *Statutes* I. xxi, quoted in Lieberman, 272.

[11] Dickinson, *Liberty and Property*, 162.

[12] See Hay, 'Property, Authority'.

[13] Hay, 25-6, quoting W. Paley, *Principles of Moral and Political Philosophy*, Bk. VI, ch. 2.

[14] Lieberman, *Province*, 266.   [15] Lieberman, *Province*, ch. 2.

But he saw this not as a deep or ineradicable defect but rather explained it in terms of the infancy of the 'art and science of legisation' to the maturing of which he turned his considerable intellectual energy. The defects of criminal legislation had deeper roots for Bentham in the Common Law system which Blackstone defended against parliamentary intrusion. *This* was the social cancer, of which recent criminal legislation was merely a symptom. The defects of legislative drafting can be corrected, but 'the cobweb of ancient barbarism',[16] which, according to Swift, was capable of 'catching small flies, but let wasps and hornets break through', had to be destroyed. The technique of control by terror and enforced ignorance had its roots in very nature of the Common Law, in Bentham's view, and it had two major consequences: it reduced the population to abject subordination and it made possible the oppression and depredation of the people by sinister interests cloaked by the law.

Indeed, by the mid-eighteenth century English Common Law had grown into a complex thicket of technical rules, antiquated concepts, and mysterious procedures. Having developed from a bundle of special writs stretched and contracted by analogy, fiction, and liberal interpretation, substantive rules of law were complex, particular, often hidden, and resisted incorporation into a general theory or statement of the law. Developing from the writ system, English law became 'a series of discrete causes of action, each surrounded by its own judicial lore, statutory interventions, and customary modes of professional practice'.[17] No one—not even Blackstone—pretended such a complex body of traditional practices could be reduced to a set of rational principles comprehensible to those not steeped in the tradition. '[The] various rights and duties of the various classes of mankind', wrote Bentham, 'were jumbled together into one immense and unsorted heap' (UC xxvii. 172). Even present-day defenders of the Common Law admit that it 'is more like a muddle than a system';[18] or, as Bentham insisted, 'a labyrinth without a clew' (UC xxvii. 172).

[16] Bentham's letter to the Gazeteer (1770), see D. Baumgardt, *Bentham and the Ethics of Today*, 22.   [17] M. Shapiro, *Courts*, 93.

[18] A. W. B. Simpson, 'Common Law and Legal Theory', 99. Christopher Hill shows that these problems had emerged already by the late sixteenth century. 'The resulting confusion, as many observers argued, created a paradise for the dishonest lawyer.' C. Hill, *Intellectual Origins of the English Revolution*, 227. See, ibid., 228-9, for passages from sixteenth-century critics of the Common Law, esp. the Common Law judiciary.

This body of law owed something to parliamentary legislation, something to judicial rule-making, and a great deal to lawyers and 'conveyancers' specializing in wills and land transfers. 'The conveyancers were so successful', Shapiro observes, 'that soon only they understood the law they had made, and later no one, including them, understood the whole of it.'[19] This law, then, was largely the product of the legal corporation: 'Judge & Co.' as Bentham called it. This gave Common Law and Common Law judges uncommon independence, but it was achieved at the price of inevitable corruption and universal ignorance of the law among the people. Between the law and the litigant was erected a terrifying barrier of procedure, technicalities, and officials, which could be overcome and even manipulated, but only if one had the time and the money.[20] Thus, a large portion of the population was excluded entirely from the benefit of use of the law and denied its protection—the same portion of the population that was terrorized by it. The techniques of manipulation of ignorance, complexity, and selective terror for sinister ends, evident in recent parliamentary legislation, could not be seen, according to Bentham, as mere aberrations of an essentially rational system of law. Rather, they comprised the latest expected chapter in a saga that had been written over the centuries. If society was to see any improvement, its law must be reformed; if its law was to be reformed it must be burned to the ground and rebuilt according to a new and rational pattern. This is the interpretation Bentham gave to the Helvetian challenge.

In Chapter 6 we observed that there was implicit in Bentham's argument for a strict doctrine of *stare decisis* the germ of a radical critique of traditional Common Law. It is the aim of the present chapter to set out the main elements of this critique.

8.2 CRITIQUE OF COMMON LAW PERFORMANCE

Veteres avias tibi de pulmone revello

Persius, *Satires* (motto of Bentham's *Comment*).

Bentham frequently called attention to the barbarity, inhumanity, and inefficiency of contemporary English law, especially criminal law, but he saved his severest criticism for the system of Common

[19] Shapiro, *Courts*, 94. See also Lieberman, *Province*, ch. 8, esp. 201–2.
[20] See R. Graveson, 'The Restless Spirit of English Law', 102.

Law which spawned and nurtured these laws. This criticism of Common Law is generously spread throughout Bentham's writings. Slight variations are detectable, but a persistent general pattern can be seen through all the writings. The attack is aimed roughly at two different flanks of the Common Law: first, the discrepancies, even inconsistencies, between Common Law theory and its practice or performance; second, the alleged incoherence of the theory itself. In this section I will consider the first line of attack, and turn to the second in 8.3, below.

Bentham's driving aim in his critique of Blackstone, as indeed in his jurisprudential writings generally, was 'to pluck the mask of Mystery from the face of Jurisprudence'.[21] Over the centuries a myth had been constructed around the practice of the courts to legitimize their activities. This myth had been newly outfitted in the finest literary style by Blackstone, the most recent high-priest of the cult of Common Law (*Bowring* iv, 483). Bentham sought to 'demythologize' the Common Law, to set this myth against the realities of life of most people subject to this form of law and to show up the glaring inconsistencies between theory and performance. The objective of this demythologizing was not simply to clear the way for a more realistic account of the workings of Common Law, but also to expose the extent to which this myth had been manipulated by the corrupt and sinister interests of the legal élite and those in whose service they worked.

Natural law and private opinion

The legitimizing myth of Common Law in the eighteenth century rested on two foundations (see 1.1). (*a*) The Common Law was regarded as the expression of the immemorial custom and practice of the people. This practice was declared from time to time, articulated, and given legal shape by the courts. But their task was merely to make more public and concrete what already exists in the traditions and patterns of thought and action in the community. Consequently, this law rested on the *consent* of the people in the deepest sense, for this assent manifested itself not in the transitory expression of momentary will but in the persistent practice over

---

[21] *FG*, Preface, p. 410. 'Nothing is more important than to dissipate the air of mystery which the unnecessary use of many technical words and forms [in Common Law] has spread over the whole subject' (UC xxvii. 91). See also *Comment* 124 and H. L. A. Hart, 'The Demystification of the Law', in Hart, *Essays on Bentham*.

time, a time no single person or generation could trace out. And (*b*) at the same time (perhaps in virtue of the above) Common Law was guided by and embodied the law of a rational Nature. Natural law or natural justice upheld the law and corrected custom and practice, for it was only the practice that could be regarded as reasonable and true that constituted the foundation of Common Law.

Bentham relentlessly attacked both parts of this Common Law myth. The attack on the myth of natural law is familiar and need not detain us.[22] According to Bentham, to appeal to 'natural law', or to 'reason' or to the 'reasonableness' or 'unreasonableness' of some practice or rule, is to appeal to a chimera. It cannot be construed as an appeal to some independent, public standard or principle of judgment, for there is no such standard. Rather, it is only the expression of private opinion, or more often simply private sentiment, *disguised as* appeal to a public standard.[23] 'What is called the Law of Nature is neither a Precept nor a Sanction, but the mere opinion of men self-constituted into Legislators' (UC lxix. 109). Thus,

When a man disapproves of a mode of conduct considered independently of any actual System of Jurisprudence he says there is a Law of Nature against it. . . . If he cannot tell why he disapproves of it he begins talking of a Rule of Right, a Fitness of Things, a Moral Sense or some other imaginary standard which howsoever varied in description, is from first to last nothing but his own private opinion in disguise.[24]

The appeal to 'reason' (as used in contexts Bentham is now considering) has the same function: to mask reliance on nothing more than unsubstantiated private sentiment. The 'fallacy' here 'consists in supposing [the words 'reason' and 'reasonable'] to stand for something that is fixed and certain, and that all men are agreed about, and that it could be told by certain indications independent of opinion, whether a given course of conduct was reasonable or otherwise' (*Comment* 159). *Reason*, however, (as it is in fact used in these contexts) is radically *relative*. What is meant by the claim

[22] For a more extensive discussion see Lieberman, *Province*, ch. 11.

[23] For a recent version of this same argument see J. Ely, *Democracy and Distrust*, ch. 3.

[24] UC lxix. 102. This obviously anticipates the attack on the 'principle of caprice', or the 'principle of sympathy and antipathy', in *IPML* II. See also UC lxix. 71-2, 106; UC lxx(a). 23; and similar objections to judicial use of the notion of 'policy' in *RJE, Bowring* vii, 310-11.

that some regulation is 'unreasonable'? Nothing more, Bentham claims, than that the speaker disapproves of it, that it is contrary to his or her reason:

Now what is [it] to be most evidently contrary to reason? . . . Let others answer as they please; for my part I will speak plainly, and confess that with me to be most evidently contrary to reason, is to be most evidently contrary to my reason, i.e. to what I like. Perhaps I might go farther and add, apprehending it at the same time to be contrary to what would be liked by others, being in a situation to be apprized of the circumstances that are in the case. But the most prompt and perhaps the most usual translation of the phrase 'contrary to reason', is 'contrary to what I like' (*Comment* 197–8).

One can detect the influence of both Hobbes and Hume in this passage. The radical subjectivism of reason echoes Hobbes, and the possibility of introducing some control by submitting persons to the same set of facts and hoping for the same reaction of sentiment suggests Hume. But Bentham sees no solution in the Humean move, for even if there were some sort of agreement, this would be entirely fortuitous and the most slender reed upon which to rest the security and certainty of law. Of course, Bentham parts company with Hobbes too, for the relativity and indeterminacy of appeals to reason is, for the most part, eliminated when the eminently rational principle of utility is made the basis of appeal. 'Had our Author again instead of reason said utility, he would have said something. He would have referred us for a foundation for our judgment, to something distinct from that judgment itself. He would have referred us to calculation founded upon matter of fact.'[25]

The only determinate, concrete content that can be given to natural law or reason is entirely private and subjective because of the abstractness of these notions (*Comment* 15–17). They offer no public shared standards for assessment of rules, laws, actions, or decisions. This has two disastrous consequences for law and adjudication. (*a*) Justification of judicial decisions is removed entirely from the public arena. Judicial decisions resting on appeals to natural law or reason rest entirely on private sentiment or whim. And (*b*) this opens the door wide for corruption and the manipulation by sinister interests of those who are subject to law. These themes will be sounded repeatedly throughout his critique of Common Law.

---

[25] *Comment* 199; see also *RJE*, Bowring vii, 310–11.

The pestilential breath of fiction

They can be seen in full dress in Bentham's persistent and bitter attack on the Common Law's use of legal fictions. Blackstone praised fictions as the life-blood of the law, the source of its flexibility and infinite capacity for controlled adaptability to new and changing circumstances. According to the standard view, fictions enabled judges to observe ancient forms laid down by time-honoured precedent while bringing about changes in the law demanded by altered social, economic, and political conditions.[26]

But for Bentham legal fictions symbolized all that was corrupt in Common Law. 'Fictions', he complains, '*never were* useful: the general mischief they did by the example of usurpation surpassed the benefits of the particular provision. By doing partial good in that exceptionable way they hindered its being done in no way that was unexceptionable.'[27] It is an especially fecund mischief done by fictions. First, 'Fictions keep the law as to its intellection imprecise, unapprehensible, and suspected . . . [and] to its notion fluctuating [and] contradictory' (UC xxvii. 88). Common Law was a thicket of complex technicalities, fictions, and forms. For example, the Common Law of descent of property 'is so complicated . . . ; it admits distinctions so singular; the previous decisions, which serve to regulate it, are so subtilized, that not only is it impossible for simple good sense to presume them, it is also difficult for it to comprehend them. It is a study profound as that of the most abstract sciences: it belongs only to a small number of privileged men' (*Bowring* ii, 323–4). And even they are forced to specialize because 'no one lawyer pretends to understand the whole' (*Bowring* i, 324; *Comment* 46). Bentham readily agrees with Coke that the reason of the Common Law is 'artificial reason', though Bentham prefers to call it 'technical', i.e. 'absurd and dishonest'.[28]

[26] See Blackstone, 3 *Comm.* 267–8. At 3 *Comm.* 43 Blackstone suggests that fictions facilitate equitable correction of laws unjust due to their generality. For criticism of this use of fictions see Harrison, *Bentham*, 30.

[27] UC xxvii. 88, author's emphasis. Recall Bentham's discussion of judicial improvement of the law, above, 6.2.

[28] *Bowring* iv, 498; 'Ask a lawyer What is Common Law? it is more than he can tell. But he is certain that it is the perfection of reason. For Lord Coke has told him so; and a thousand compilers have repeated it after Lord Coke. . . . He knows not (very well) what Common Law is: however, he knows what it is not: or rather what is not *it*: which is always something. "Whatever is not Reason is not Law." . . . What Reason? What, this man's reason, or that man's reason, or my reason? Oh no, nothing like it—a particular sort of reason—a sort made on purpose—a legal

And the device of fiction-making spreads the cancer of inscrutability through the entire body of the law, 'even [in] those parts where they (themselves) are not to be found'. The law is like 'the lying boy in the Fable: The abuses of language though not perpetual are yet so frequent and their existence so notorious, that when any part of language presents itself men can never think themselves in security' (UC xxvii. 91). Throughout the whole body of the law 'there is no such thing as trusting to the obvious import of those words and forms'; for all one knows, they may have been given an import totally different if not contrary to the obvious one (ibid., see UC lxx(a). 35).

Thus, law is entirely inaccessible to all but the professional élite. Far from guaranteeing security, Common Law systematically undermines it: wherever there is Common Law, 'security is an empty name' (*CC* 196). Only a very few can ferret out even the most basic outlines of the law, and even they are likely, in the process, to create more doubts than they settle. 'Unwritten law' cannot possess the quality of certainty. 'The citizen can find no part of it, cannot take it for his guide; he is reduced to consultations—he assembles the lawyers—he collects as many opinions as his fortune will permit; and all this ruinous procedure often serves only to create new doubts' (*General View, Bowring* iii, 206; see also *Bowring* v, 235).

This is all damning enough, for it makes it impossible for Common Law to focus and guide expectations, and consequently to perform with even minimal adequacy its primary function of securing expectation. But the mischief which Bentham sees in this device goes even deeper, for legitimating the widespread use of fictions grants a general 'mendacity-licence' to the judiciary.[29] This has three further undesirable consequences. First, it buys 'flexibility' of the ancient Common Law at the price of making completely private and idiosyncratic and judicial process of deliberation and decision. That is, the excessive technicality and artificiality of the language of the law makes it impossible to frame judicial opinions in terms that can be grasped and assessed by the public. Bentham's attack on mendacity is in no way moralizing. Mendacity is objectionable precisely because it takes the process of judicial decision-making

reason. The Common Law of Common Lawyers is according to Reason: but it is legal Reason' (UC lxiii. 50). Here, of course, Bentham follows Hobbes, see 2.2, above.

[29] *Bowring* v, 13, 452; *RJE, Bowring* vii, 263–70.

entirely out of the public arena. The public justification offered for the decision is not the actual justification, or at least is not always the actual justification; and as a result we can never know when to take the judiciary at its word. So the technique of fictions, like that of appeal to 'natural law', is objectionable because it makes impossible the fully public justification of judicial decisions, which we saw in Chapter 6 is an essential characteristic of proper adjudication. The door is opened wide to judicial arbitrariness, bias, and caprice.

Second, the use of fictions produces 'a general debility . . . in the understanding of the deluded people' (*FG*, App. p. 511). Evidence of this debility is the fact that they have come to accept that falsehood is a necessary instrument of justice.

A third, even more sinister consequence follows on this. For fictions are 'lies, devised by judges to serve as instruments of, and cloaks to, injustice' (*Bowring* iv, 498). Injustice here takes the form, first, of judicial usurpation of legislative power not constitutionally given it (*FG*, App. p. 509). This would be serious enough if it were not for the fact that such power inevitably brings with it corruption and the unlimited opportunity to prey upon those who are unprotected (*CC* 75). And 'the more prostrate that debility, the more flagrant the ulterior degree of depredation and oppression, to which they might thus be brought to submit' (*FG*, App. p. 511). Fictions of the poet are harmless and produce amusement; fictions of the priest and lawyer are pernicious and produce tyranny. 'By the priest and the lawyer, in whatsoever shape fiction has been employed, it has had for its object or effect, or both, to deceive, and, by deception, to govern, and, by governing, to promote the interest, real or supposed, of the party addressing, at the expense of the party addressed' (*Bowring* viii, 199).

Given the pattern of development of the Common Law, judges are dependent upon the lawyers for fashioning the forms and instruments of the law and for maintaining a coherent body of rules, and the lawyers and conveyancers are dependent upon the courts to give effect to their endlessly complex devices. The result was the emergence of an autonomous guild—'partnership' Bentham calls it —'having for its object the extracting, on joint account, and for joint benefit, out of the pockets of the people, in the largest quantity possible, the produce of the industry of the people.'[30] Because the rights and duties of the people are hopelessly obscure, and

---

[30] *FG*, Preface to 2nd ed., p. 509. See also *RJE*, *Bowring* vii, 199–214; *Bowring* iv, 489, 504, 537–8; *CC* 194.

known only to the legal monopoly (*OLG* XV. 6), they, the people, are at the mercy of the legal profession. They can neither protect themselves against injury, avail themselves of their rights, nor fulfil their duties. Thus, 'while the rights we are bid to be grateful for are mere illusions, the punishments we are made to undergo are sad realities' (*Justice Petition, Bowring* v, 546). The great masses of persons without adequate means were thus put absolutely at the mercy of those with means who could manipulate the law and the profession to their own ends.[31] This is the cruellest tyranny of the Common Law, a tyranny not suffered even by slaves in the American South, Bentham charges (*Bowring* v, 547). *Contra* Blackstone, who praised the complexity and technicality of the Common Law as the great protectors of English liberty, the envy of the European continent,[32] Bentham presses the charge that precisely these characteristics provide the most fundamental threat to that liberty.

Against this background, Bentham finds it very easy to explode the myths of Common Law legitimacy. Far from existing 'from time immemorial', all the examples Blackstone cites of fundamental rules of Common Law can be shown, says Bentham, to have had their beginning in either some proper legislative act of a constitutionally empowered legislative body or in the autocratic and unconstitutional act of legislation of some judge or series of judges (*Comment* 165-80, 332-3). This, plus the fact of the widespread use of the device of fictions and appeals to 'natural law', 'reason', and the like, puts the lie to the Common Law dogma that judges never make law but only declare it (UC xxvii. 90). If we wash the history of Common Law with the acid of reality we will see that it could not exist except for the constant creative, though absolutely unauthorized, actions of the judiciary. Quite literally, Common Law is *nothing* if it is not *Judge-made*.[33]

But, then, *if* Common Law is a matter of custom or practice at all, it is the artificial custom of the professional law élite, the legal

[31] Perronet Thompson writes in the *Westminster Review* (1829) (based on the draft prepared by Bentham): 'If a poor man injures the rich, the law is instantly at his heels; the injuries of the rich towards the poor are always inflicted *by* the law. And to enable the rich to do this to any extent that may be practicable or prudent, there is clearly only one postulate required, which is, that the rich shall make the law.' P. Thompson, 'The 'Greatest Happiness' Principle', reproduced in J. Lively and J. Rees, *Utilitarian Logic and Politics*, 137.

[32] 1 *Comm.* 327-8, 423-4, 265-8.

[33] This, of course, is a pervasive theme in Bentham's writing. A sampling of the passages in which this is discussed is the following: *Pannomial Fragments, Bowring* iii, 223-4, 227; *Bowring* iv, 483-5; *Justice Petition, Bowring* v, 546; *RJE, Bowring* vii, 539 n. *; *CC* 8.

partnership, Judge & Co. The custom of the Common Law is not 'custom *in pays*' but strictly 'custom *in foro*', born of illegitimate partners and nurtured in corruption. What degree of pretence could possibly sustain the belief that the enormously complicated, technical, and artificial concepts, rules, and forms of Common Law reflect the traditions, customs, and practices of the people? The suggestion, Bentham thinks, would be comic, were it not tragic in its consequences.

From this Bentham concludes that there can be absolutely no substance to the idea that Common Law rests for its legitimacy on the consent of the people. The law cannot be seen as the formal expression of the common practices of the people, so all that is left is to see the behaviour of the people in conformity to the law as the product of the law itself and the punishment threatened for the breach of it. But to call this 'assent' to the laws is a cruel joke and an 'abusive application of the term "assent"', for it conflates coerced compliance with spontaneous obedience (*Comment* 221).

Actually, there are *two* problems here. First, the attempt to ground the legitimacy of the law, and the obligation to comply with it, on consent must fail. For the Common Law is neither made by the people subject to it nor can they be said to have consented to it. But secondly, there is no way in which an ordinary person could rationally submit to the law. In light of the radical obscurity of the law the only possibility open to the ordinary person is blind, passive, and inevitably haphazard obedience. Rational compliance, upon the basis of an understanding of the law and its rationale, is impossible for almost every person in society. Thus, not only does Common Law expose the mass of people in society to depredation at the hands of the professional law élite and those they serve, but it also removes from them any possibility of responsible, intelligent citizenship. Social order is maintained through terror, manipulation of ignorance, and abject subordination of the masses, not through the exercise of rational and responsible citizenship—citizens freely censuring the law by their own lights while obeying punctually (*FG*, Preface, p. 399).

Dog law

The second of the two charges mentioned in the previous paragraph is made most forcefully in Bentham's attack on the essentially retrospective character of Common Law (UC lxix. 6; *Justice Petition*,

Bowring v, 546). Because we have considered this charge in 6.2 we can be brief here. Common Law is a collection of judge-made laws; 'on each occasion, the rule to which a judge gives the force of law, is one which, on this very occasion, he makes out of his own head' (*Bowring* v, 546). But judges succeed in making laws, says Bentham, only if they can convince other judges and (most of the people who are affected by it) that they are *not* doing so. Common Law judges, then, are forced to regard the parties as bound by laws which they could not have known and to which they could not have conformed their behaviour prior to the judicial ruling. The retrospective character of Common Law is not simply a problem of abuse of discretion to which Common Law adjudication is, for some reason, specially prone. It is, rather, a disease endemic to the kind of legal ordering Common Law is: Common Law is 'by its very essence' restrospective.

In addition to the practical contradiction and duplicity Bentham believes he had uncovered here, he had three other important objections to the *ex post facto* lawmaking of Common Law. First, such laws or rulings, of course, defeat expectations of the parties in the particular cases at hand. Moreover, he argues (at UC lxix. 6) that Common Law ideology makes it impossible for the judge to take steps to prevent, alleviate, or compensate the losses this brings about. Second, more seriously yet from Bentham's perspective, are the general, systemic consequences of a form of law which works largely in a retrospective fashion. Much more serious than the defeat of particular expectations and the unfairness done to individuals (which after all can be compensated or even overridden in particular cases)[34] is the damage done to the *system* of law itself, for

---

[34] See UC lxix. 199. In what is probably an early manuscript Bentham discusses the conditions under which retrospective *legislation* may be justified. He sets down the maxim that such a law is justified if it appears that the mischief of the act made penal is greater than the mischief of the example of the law (UC lxiii. 34). 'Appears' is important; it does not mean 'seems', but rather 'is publicly seen or believed to be'. (There is a similar usage in the following passage of *PJP*, *Bowring* ii, 21: 'In point of utility, apparent justice is everything; real justice, abstractedly from apparent justice, is a useless abstraction, not worth pursuing, and supposing it contrary to apparent justice, such as ought not to be pursued.') The point seems to be that the primary evil of retrospective laws (like the good of 'justice') lies in their relation to public security. But Bentham goes on to say that retrospective laws may be justified if, for example, they make it publicly known that one cannot take advantage of loopholes in the law to the detriment of society, with the proviso that the good of this public example not be outweighed by the increased likelihood of the abuse of retrospective laws (UC lxiii. 34).

the primary and overriding virtue of law, security, is almost entirely undermined. 'The mischief of the example of the [retrospective] Law consists in the *idea* of insecurity, the form of apprehension, which it serves to spread among the people' (UC lxiii. 34). It is the *system* of rule by retrospective law, of judicial decisions ungoverned by publicly ascertainable rules, to which he objects, and this system is objectionable because it causes *general* alarm and insecurity. The *public* cost of such a regime, not the unfairness to individuals, or violation of individual rights, is the more serious concern for Bentham.

There is a third, perhaps even deeper objection. Under a regime of retrospective law, in which one first learns of the crime by being punished for it (*OLG* XIII. 1–2; UC lxix. 159), rational and responsible obedience is effectively ruled out. Common Law achieves a sort of social order, Bentham argues, but it does so by treating human beings like brute beasts—the order of Common Law is the discipline of brutes. 'Dog law', he calls it.

When your dog does anything you want to break him of, you wait till he does it, and then beat him for it. This is the way you make laws for your dog: and this is the way the judges make law for you and me. They won't tell a man beforehand what it is he *should not do* . . . they lie by till he has done something which they say he should not *have done*, and then they hang him for it (*Bowring* v, 235).

Obedience to laws and social order generally is obtained not by addressing the understanding or even the will of individual citizens, but rather only by playing upon their blind fear (*Essay on Promulgation, Bowring* i, 161). 'To be governed by Statute Law belongs only to men. By Common Law it is that even Beasts are governed. A mode of government that is fit only for Beast and for them fully, because incapable of better.'[35] The central theme, rather obliquely expressed here, is that law must take a shape in which the structure or order it creates and maintains is one which is fit for human habitation and in particular one in which, while order is maintained, individual rational judgment is given free rein. The deep criticism underlying all the others in the *Comment*, and the theme of the *Fragment*, is that Common Law in multifarious ways seeks to 'torpedo' rational individual judgment and to foster submission to authority, in conduct *and judgment*, based on ignorance and

[35] UC lxix. 151; see also UC lxix. 163; *OLG* XIII. 2; *RJE, Bowring* vi, 519–20.

stupidity *(Comment* App. F, 346). Thus, again, Bentham argues that Common Law, far from liberating, actually enslaves and tyrannizes, but it is a tyranny not of action (or action alone) but of the *mind* and *judgment*.

Dead men's thoughts

Bentham plays a variation on the above theme in his satirical attack on the use of precedent in Common Law.

> It is a maxim among these lawyers that whatever had been done before may legally be done again, and therefore they take special care to record all the decisions (formerly) made against common justice and the general reason of mankind. These, under the name of precedents, they produce as authorities to justify the most iniquitous opinions, and the judges never fail of decreeing accordingly.[36]

This from the pen of Swift, not Bentham, but it is echoed by Bentham:

> '*Whatever is, is right*—(whatever is—that is to say, whatever, by men in the situation in question, has been done)—being tacitly assumed as a postulate, —the rectitude of doing the same thing, on any and every subsequent occasion deemed a similar one, is stated and acted upon, as a necessary consequence. This is called *following precedents* (*CC* 322).

Precedent, he charges, perpetuates error, injustice, and evil. Any form of iniquity is ripe for its support; 'it will serve to support any act howsoever maleficent' (UC cii. 120), 'and many an error by the same example will rush into the state'.[37]

But even when the original decision is arguably not in error, following precedent produces mischief, Bentham claims. For it perpetuates patterns and practices, rules and regulations, fitted for an earlier and probably much different time. '[T]he more antique the precedent—that is to say, the more barbarous, inexperienced, and prejudice-led the race of men, by and among whom the precedent was set:—the more unlike that same *past* state of things . . . is the *present* state of things' (*CC* 323). Lawyers know dead men's thoughts too well[38] and pay no attention to the thoughts and well-

---

[36] J. Swift, *Gulliver's Travels*, Bk. 4, ch. 5.
[37] Shakespeare, *Merchant of Venice*, IV. i.
[38]   The Lawyers, Bob, know too much.
         They are chums of the books of old John Marshall.
         They know it all, what a dead hand wrote,

being of the living (*Comment* 196). Indeed, argues Bentham, 'the fruit of a too superstitious respect for antiquity is the inscrutable tangle of complexity and obscurity' of the Common Law of his day (*Civil Code, Bowring* i, 324).

However, the most serious complaint Bentham has against a system based on the principle of precedent is that precedent becomes 'an avowed substitute for reason' (*Bowring* x, 511). 'Mechanical judicature' is substituted for 'mental judicature'. Rational reflection, guided by a refined sense of the sufferings to which human beings can be subjected, is replaced by blind imitation: judges, 'by opulence rendered indolent, and by indolence and self-indulgence doomed to ignorance, follow their leaders,—as sheep follow sheep, and geese geese' (*CC* 322). He satirically calls the principle of precedent 'the sheep and goose principle'.[39] What Bentham pointed out earlier as a virtue (of sorts) of 'analogy'—its inflexibility, its unwillingness to bend, its refusal to 'take on . . . inflexions from the influences of circumstances' (UC lxiii. 49; UC lxx(a). 18)—is now branded its greatest vice. Not only is precedent in any particular case insensitive to the genuine merits of the case, but it also 'propagate[s] mental imbecility' because it requires 'the minimum of thought and discernment [and] so of reflection and labour'.[40]

Thus, again Common Law is the efficient cause of stupid conformity, but in this case not conformity of citizens obeying the law, but of officials and judges in adjudicating disputes arising under it.

The paradox of inflexibility

But now we seem to have caught Bentham up in a contradiction in his own criticism of Common Law. For we have seen that he objects *both* that Common Law is excessively rigid *and* arbitrarily flexible and indeterminate, that Common Law adjudication involves *both* mindless imitation *and* judicial manipulation of

> A stiff dead hand and its knuckles crumbling,
> The bones of the fingers a thin white ash.
> The lawyers know a dead man's thoughts too well.

C. Sandburg, 'The Lawyers Know Too Much', in *Smoke and Steel*, 85. David Luban brought this poem to my attention.

[39] UC lxxxi. 126; UC cxiv. 222; UC cii. 120; UC xxxi. 94–5, 141; BL Add. MSS 33,551, fo. 87.

[40] UC cii. 120. See also *CC* 322 and UC li(a). 31–2.

fictions and abstract formulas of 'natural law', and the like, governed only by judicial whim and sinister interest.[41]

This, however, is not a contradiction in Bentham's critique of Common Law. Rather, Bentham here is displaying what he takes to be contradictions deep in the practice of Common Law itself. This separates Bentham's criticism of the practice of Common Law from the steady stream of criticism directed against it since the late sixteenth century. In particular, although the late eighteenth century saw the emergence of rigid formalism in the practice of the courts,[42] it was not this extreme rigidity and glorification of technicality alone which drew his fire. The defects in Common Law, in Bentham's view, went much deeper. Because it could not satisfactorily reconcile the conflicting demands of general security and the need for flexibility in adjudication, it was doomed to swing, pendulum-like, between the opposite poles of arbitrariness and rigidity. The only available device for introducing some degree of stabilty and certainty into an otherwise unstable and indeterminate system of law is a strict principle of *stare decisis*; but this, paradoxically, produces not less, but more opportunity for arbitrariness and ultimately less accountability. This is 'the paradox of inflexibility', as I shall call it. It will be instructive to trace out the argument behind this criticism even though it will go over some of the ground already covered in the preceding pages, because it will put those various arguments and objections into a general framework and make Bentham's overall view clearer.

The argument may be easiest to grasp if we see it developing in three distinct stages.[43] In the first stage, Bentham begins by noting the indeterminateness and arbitrariness of Common Law adjudication along lines we considered in the preceding section. He argues that judicial decision, in the absence of some strict doctrine of precedent, even if individually reasonable and justified, cannot begin to serve the goal of security which is the basic function of law. 'It is only in as far as subsequent decisions are rendered comformable to the rules that are fairly to be drawn from prior decision that such prior decisions can answer, in any even the most imperfect

---

[41] This seems to be the charge made by Graveson, 'Restless Spirit of English Law', 106, 107; and by S. Letwin, *Pursuit of Certainty*, 164.

[42] See Lieberman, *Province*, ch. 8.

[43] The argument, or substantial portions of it, can be found in many places, esp. in Bentham's later works, but the two clearest statements of the argument can be found in *OLG* XV. 9-12 and *Justice Petition, Bowring* v, 478.

degree, the purpose of a law.'[44] We saw in 6.1 that, for Bentham, the only solution to the arbitrariness and insecurity of judicial decision in the absence of publicly known statutory rules is to introduce a strict regime of *stare decisis*. With this principle firmly entrenched, we can move to the second stage of the argument which traces the consequences of establishing this principle in Common Law adjudication.

The unfortunate but inevitable consequence of *stare decisis* is *ridigity* in the decision-making process. The aetiology of this disease is set out in a remarkable, though puzzling, passage from *Of Laws in General* which I shall quote at length.

One other capital imperfection [of Common Law is] . . . the *unaccommodatingness* of its rules. Every decision that is given is spun out of some vague maxim, conceived in general terms without exceptions, and without any regard to times and circumstances. . . . Even when it aims at utility, which perhaps is now and then, it either falls short of the mark or overshoots it. A sort of testimony in recognition of this truth is contained in the magnificent and well-known adage, *fiat justitia ruat coelum*. . . . Hence the hardness of heart which is a sort of endemical disease of lawyers where that part of the law which is in the customary form is predominant in the system. Mischief being almost their incessant occupation, and the greatest merits they can attain being the firmness with which they persevere in the task of doing partial evil for the sake of that universal good which consists in steady adherence to established rules, a judge thus circumstanced is obliged to divest himself of that anxious sensibility, which is one of the most useful as well as amiable qualities of the legislator (*OLG* XV. 12 n. 1).

Rigidity—the *fiat justitia* mentality—is occasioned by the necessity of continually doing partial evil in order to preserve the greater good of security and uniformity. Faced with the task of trying to secure expectations to some extent, the practical judgment and ordinary human sympathies atrophy.

Familiarized with the prospect of all those miseries which are attendant on poverty, disappointment, and disgrace, accustomed even to heap those miseries on the heads of those by whom he knows them to be unmerited, he eases himself by habit of the concern which the prospect of them would produce in an unexperienced mind (ibid.).

---

[44] *OLG* XV. 9. Also: 'In general they are expected to tread in one another's steps: and in the degree, in which this so indispensable habit is conformed to, depends altogether such feeble and even vacillating degree of security, as it is in the power of judge-made law to afford' (*Bowring* v, 478).

That is, he gradually loses the sense of sympathy and concern which such miseries would cause in lay persons unused to witnessing suffering, 'just as a man whose trade is in blood becomes insensible to the sufferings which accompany the stroke of death' (ibid.). This deadening of ordinary human sympathy, loss of focus of practical judgment, is not absolutely unavoidable in any particular person. But, he maintains,

It must be no common share of humanity that can induce him, nor any common share of wisdom that can enable him to keep this rigour within the bounds presented by utility, and the necessary regard to uniformity of decisions. By men of ordinary mould the dictates of utility in these circumstances may easily be lost sight of altogether: and a precedent the most absurd and mischievous conformed to with as much tranquillity as an equally apposite precedent of a complexion the most reasonable and salutary (*OLG* XV. 12 n. i).

There is, in this remarkable passage, deep insight into the effects of institutional structures and their roles on the psychological roots of moral and practical judgment.[45] But this atrophying of human sentiment and judgment is not inevitable, except in an institution like Common Law.[46]

He gives three reasons for this claim. First, he suggests that judges become insensitive to the misery and injustice done by administering the law, because the law they administer is itself unjust. They administer it none the less because they believe (rightly, in Bentham's view) that the greater good of uniformity and security requires overlooking injustice done in particular cases. This, though important, is not sufficient to distinguish Common Law from other forms of law which may be equally unjust. Thus, secondly, he points out that the problem with Common Law is that there is no way effectively to correct the injustices. Without the tools of the legislator, the legislative solutions the Common Law judge seeks to construct will never be adequate. They can neither be sufficiently broad in scope, nor sufficiently precise in formulation. The judge has neither the authority nor the power to construct

---

[45] See also the powerful satirical description of the typical professional attitude at *RJE, Bowring* vi, 206.

[46] Would this not be as likely for adjudicators under statute or code law? Bentham admits that it may, but he also insists that it is possible to combat it. Indeed, his struggle to fashion an adequate theory of adjudication is driven by precisely this challenge. See below, chs. 10–12.

adequate solutions. The partial good he does within some limited context always risks the much greater evil of undermining the stability of the law (*Justice Petition, Bowring* v, 478).

But these are not the fundamental problems. For even if the law were relatively just, the problem lies in the fact that the judge is charged with *both* tasks of protecting the security and certainty of the law—since there is no other effective source of legal rules—*and* at the same time maintaining some sensitivity to the demands of justice and particular utility of each case. Given this task, and the importance of providing for security, the judge is forced to ignore the miseries caused by such rules in particular cases. Doing so he becomes increasingly insensitive to those utilities, and soon loses sight of them altogether. Consequently, when utility in fact calls for an exception to the established rules, or the overruling of an unjust rule, the judge has neither the sympathetic insight, nor the practical wisdom to recognize the need nor the power to take appropriate action.

The jurisprudence of Common Law becomes 'mechanical'. The norms of the craft, perhaps once rightly introduced to serve proper goals or the common good, take on significance to the members of the class independent of their instrumental value. Lawyers and judges tend to apply their rules and maxims 'undeviatingly as if they were *sui juris* without inquiring whether they may not be suspended by an utility superior to their utility' (UC li(a). 32). The ends of the craft (the ends of the law) are entirely lost sight of, and the means come to be valued for their own sake. To an extent this is natural and inevitable in almost any profession, but this development takes an especially sinister turn amongst professionals within the Common Law system. For the rules have their origin in the devices and decisions of the profession-assisted courts. They inevitably serve the sinister interests of the guild. Turning technicalities into first principles, means into ends, is *due to* sinister interests of the guild, perhaps, but it is not merely a self-serving device. It is done to *legitimize* the activities, not only to the public, but also to themselves. This is a kind of self-deception.

It is important to keep in mind that Bentham is not arguing here that in the cases in question the judge's decision to follow precedent rather than answer the call of utility is mistaken. The problem, rather, is that the judge makes what may be the right decision for the wrong reasons, or more commonly for *no reasons whatsoever.*

It is a blind, and thoughtless, as well as heartless form of adjudication. But this leads us to the third stage of the argument. For despite this rigidity—or rather, precisely because of it—there arise great pressures from the public and from within the law itself to reintroduce some degree of flexibility in to the law. '[W]hen at length the eyes of the public have to a certain degree opened, the evil which has been the result of [judges] thus treading in one another's steps . . . has become so palpable and grossly mischievous . . . not only allowance but applause has been bestowed on a departure' (*Bowring* v, 478).

Here enter the devices of legal fictions, abstract and contentless notions of 'natural law', 'equity', 'reasonableness', 'policy', and Latinized principles like '*contra bonos mores*' and the like. These devices introduce flexibility into the law, but at an enormous price, the price of mendacity and, more seriously, of removing judicial deliberation and decision-making from the public arena. No fixed standard can escape the poison thus introduced into the body of law, every use of an established rule can be perverted to achieve the end desired by the judge. The door is opened wide to arbitrariness, bias, and caprice—not to mention the full effect of sinister interest.

But the threat of arbitrariness is now intensified many fold by the fact that these devices—strict adherence to precedent and manipulation of vague notions and creation of fictions—exist side-by-side, equally available tools for the judge to use in any particular case. 'Then it is', concludes Bentham, 'that the judge finds himself at perfect liberty to give or to refuse impunity to the murderer, at pleasure: if he refuses it, liberality is his word: if he give it, *stare decisis*' (*Bowring* v, 478). This is complete arbitrariness, 'arbitrariness to a degree of perfection'. For the judge 'without danger either of punishment at the hands of the law, or so much as censure at the hands of public opinion, . . . can give success to plaintiff or to defendant, according as he happens to feel inclined. Such is the case where, within his reach, he sees two opposite sources of decision, from either of which he can draw at pleasure' (*Bowring* v, 478). The 'fountain of justice' from which Common Law, according to Mansfield, draws its rules and thereby 'works itself pure'[47] is poisoned. In an ironic reversal of Mansfield's metaphor Bentham insists that the supreme principle of Common

---

[47] William Murray (later Lord Mansfield), argument for the plaintiff in *Omychund* v. *Barker* (1744), quoted in Lieberman, *Province*, 238.

Law is 'the double fountain principle'.[48] The judge is not the passive conduit for justice and mercy, he is 'a conjuror, who, to the great astonishment of the spectators, draws from the same fountain bitter waters, or sweet' (*Civil Code, Bowring* i, 326). He can never lose, for if he abides strictly by precedent, he is praised for his 'principled stand', and if he sets it aside he is praised for his 'liberality'. That is, given the structure and pressures within Common Law judges can decide first to whom they wish to see the case go and then find a convenient label to put a legal face on this private and idiosyncratic decision. Furthermore, because this is the product of structural features deep in the institution of Common Law adjudication itself, 'this dilemma . . . occur[s] at every turn' (*OLG* XV. 9). And the result is arbitrariness 'to any degree of perfection'.

We have come full circle, then, to complete the paradox of inflexibility: in order to introduce some modicum of stability and security in the legal system, and to avoid the arbitrariness and unpredictability of each judge deciding according to his own lights, *stare decisis* must be introduced. But the device is self-defeating, because it breeds even greater arbitrariness. The original arbitrariness was, at least, known and publicly acknowledged. The arbitrariness resulting from the operation of the double fountain principle is painted over with pretence of either rigorous, disciplined adherence to principle, or liberal sensitivity to continuing changes in circumstances and the progress of society and the law. This is the perennial debate between the 'Liberalists' (rallying around Mansfield) and the 'Rigourists' (rallying around Lord Camden). But this debate, says Bentham, is a *bogus* debate.[49] Given Common Law—not only as it happens to be, but as it is *by nature*—in all but the most

---

[48] The following may have been Bentham's inspiration:

> Two urns by Jove's high throne have ever stood,
> The source of evil one, and one of good;
> From thence the cups of mortal men he fills,
> Blessings to these, to those distributes ills.

Pope, *Homer's Iliad*, 24, v. 663. Compare Bentham's rendering: 'A sort of vase has been seen, from which, at command wine, either of one colour or another, has been made to flow. From this emblem the name of the *double fountain* principle has been given' (*Bowring* v, 478). See also UC lxxxi. 110; *Judicial Establishment, Bowring* iv, 360; *Codification Proposal, Bowring* iv, 542; *Civil Code, Bowring* i, 325–6; *RJE, Bowring* vii, 308–9, 339; *Scotch Reform, Bowring* v, 14; *Comment* 199–200; and *OLG* XV. 9.

[49] *IRE, Bowring* vi, 145–8; *Lord Brougham Displayed, Bowring* v, 558.

mundane and ordinary cases there is as good reason for following established precedent as there is for setting aside the law and deciding on the particular utilities of the case.[50] It is pointless to take sides in this debate. It is as irresolvable under Common Law as it is inevitable. What is needed, Bentham insists, is not to take sides, but rather to alter the fundamental terms of the debate; i.e. to eliminate Common Law entirely and replace it with a system which can hope properly to resolve the conflict between certainty and flexibility.

8.3 CRITIQUE OF COMMON LAW THEORY

[Of] the interpretation of laws . . . there is no end; comments beget comments, and explications make new matter for explications . . .

Locke, *Essay.*

The severe defects of Common Law surveyed above—its injustice, indeterminacy, arbitrariness, and inevitable corruption—have their roots, in the view of Bentham, in the very nature of this conception of social ordering. Injustice, uncertainty, confusions, and corruption are possible, and in his day were all too evident, properties of statutory law as well, but these defects, Bentham insisted, are only 'accidental' and can be removed through rational, systematic reform with special attention paid to advancement of the 'science of legislation'.[51] The defects of Common Law, however, are ineradicable because essential (*RJE, Bowring* vii, 309–10 ; UC lxix. 188). Common Law is nothing more than a fiction, 'a thing merely imaginary' (*Comment* 119). It is a phantom as unreal as the gold mountain, but infinitely more sinister because it is the creation of a legal élite designed to serve its own corrupt interests and lust for power. This attack on the essence of Common Law and its theory is the focus of the remainder of this chapter.

The dilemma of Common Law theory

We noticed in Chapters 1 and 2 that Common Law theory in the eighteenth century, especially in its Blackstonian version, embraced

---

[50] *Book of Fallacies, Bowring* ii, 395 n.

[51] Most of Bentham's jurisprudential writings were designed to contribute directly or indirectly to the perfection of this science. This includes, for example, the more general studies in *IPML,* and *OLG,* and the more specific work on legislation drafting and related matters, e.g. *General View, Bowring* iii, 206–10, UC c. 34–86 ('*Projet forme*'), 90–5, and *Nomography, Bowring* iii, 233–83.

much of the language, if not the underlying substance, of natural law jurisprudence. In the previous section we watched Bentham dismantle all claims Common Law might have made to rest on some transcendent 'reason' or natural law. One part of Bentham's attack on Common Law theory, then, has already been explored. But there was also another strain in Common Law theory, both more fundamental and historically more important, viz. its portrayal of Common Law as the respository and guardian of the ancient custom of the land. It is the conception of Common Law as customary law which is the focus of the attack we shall consider now. It is the claim that Common Law custom—essentially 'custom *in foro*'—is *law* that Bentham regards as an incoherent fiction.

The easiest way to expose the fraud and incoherence of Common Law theory, says Bentham, is to ask to be shown *a* (rule of) Common Law. If Common Law actually provides a body of law, it must be possible to isolate *one* such genuine law for inspection (*Bowring* iv, 483). But this simply cannot be done. The Common Law jurist faces a dilemma: either point to legally authoritative entities, which, however, turn out not to be laws at all; or point to propositions that could pass as laws but they cannot be authoritative, and so again fail to qualify as laws (*OLG* XV. 11).

The argument that Bentham utilizes to construct this dilemma depends on the account of custom which we explored in 7.1.[52] Common Law is customary law. It consists not of written signs expressive of the will of a legislator, but rather it consists of an assemblage of particular judicial acts and commands which, in virtue of the more extensive interpretation which people are disposed to put on them, have 'somewhat of the effect of general laws' (*OLG* XIII. 2; *Comment* 119, 331). These are authoritative public commands, but they are commands concerning *particular* individual acts and their force is spent on the particular parties (UC lxix. 115; *Comment* 95). Moreover, there is no verbal discourse involved—or rather, whatever is capable of being properly formulated into an 'assemblage of signs' is only particular (*OLG* XIII. 2). But judicial acts alone cannot serve as law, for 'what there is of law in the case must be general, applicable to an indefinite multitude of individ-

---

[52] The clearest and most complete statements of the argument can be found in *OLG* XIII, various passages in the *Comment*, and UC lxix. 151. I will rely directly on these. But see also *CC* 8; *RJE, Bowring* vi, 552; *Pannomial Fragments, Bowring* iii, 223–4.

uals not then assignable'.[53] Laws must be general propositions. 'To serve as ingredients in a system of Law we must have not ideas of individual items of conduct, but ideas of sorts of articles of conduct' (UC lxix. 151). But how are these general propositions to be determined? According to Common Law theory, this is done by a process of extrapolation, which Bentham professes to find mysterious and 'metaphysical'.

But let the case be delineated ever so exactly, it is still but that individual case that is delineated: to make a rule that can serve for cases yet to come, a new process must be carried on: the historian [reporting the decision of the prior case] must give place to the metaphysician; and a general rule must be created by abstraction out of this particular proceeding (OLG XV. 2).

Thus, it is only by 'abstraction' or 'induction' that particular actions and orders of judges are given 'somewhat the effect of general laws'. Though statute laws are 'actual', Common Law rules are 'inferential' (UC lxix. 164) consisting of rules 'as shall appear to be the just expression of judicial practice in like cases'. (See above, 7.1.)

But such rules must be *formulated by* someone. Who is authorized to do so? Here, Bentham argues, Common Law theory faces a dilemma for if someone is authorized he or she becomes a *legislator*,[54] and thus 'it is not, then, an affair of common law, but of statute' (UC lxix. 151). Moreover, if anyone is so authorized, *everyone* is, which is absurd. But if no one is authorized, then *there are no* general rules and so *no law.*

From this loose and general view of what is called Common Law it is manifest how difficult it is to say what it is. . . . It exists not in any certain form of words: the acts it is founded on are acts of authority: but the words in which they are expressed are yours, are mine, are anyone's (UC lxix. 151).

Of course, to say that there is no authoritative statement of the law is not to say that all statements of law are equally useful. A judge's conclusions will naturally carry more weight than those of a common man. But that is because he

---

[53] *OLG* XIII. 2; *Comment* 331; UC lxix. 119; UC lxx(a).7.

[54] Compare J. C. Gray, who quotes the famous aphorism of Bishop Hoadley (1717): 'Whoever hath an absolute authority to interpret any written or spoken laws, it is he who is truly the Law-giver to all intents and purposes, and not the person who first wrote or spoke them'. And then adds: '*a fortiori*, whoever hath an absolute authority not only to interpret the Law, but to say what the Law is, is truly the Lawgiver'. *Nature and Sources of Law*, 102.

will naturally be supposed more likely to form such conclusions as shall be the same with those formed relative to the same matter by others that are Judges. His character of Judge is a certificate of his possessing a certain degree [of] experience and discernment, and in short a habit of thinking analogous to that of his brethren (*Comment* 331).

The judge's statement of a rule of law in a given case is no more *authoritative* than anyone else's, but it is *more reliable* as a barometer of the thinking on the bench and so of likely decisions in the future.

We can restate the dilemma of Common Law theory as follows: if a proposition of Common Law is authoritative, it is only particular, and hence not law; but if it purports to be a statement of a general rule of law, it cannot be authoritive, and hence, again, it is not law (*OLG* XV. 11). 'The common account of Common Law is that it is a Law only not written: just the reverse of this is the truth: It is something written; but only that something is not Law' (UC lxix. 120).

Common Law theory is incoherent, Bentham concludes. It may be a theory of something (mysterious and 'metaphysical'), but whatever it is it cannot be *law*. Common Law is *no-law*, a sheer fiction. 'As a System of general rules, the Common Law is a thing merely imaginary' (*Comment* 119). This conclusion, of course, has the ring of paradox, but that is not entirely unintentional. Like Proudhon's 'Property is theft!' Bentham's paradoxical conclusion was designed to upset and confuse ordinary jurisprudential categories. But while Bentham's argument is rhetorically powerful, it is nevertheless puzzling. It deserves a closer look.

Private rules and public laws

Bentham appears to set out his argument as an internal critique of Common Law theory. On that theory judges are not empowered to make law, the only *authoritative* pronouncements they are empowered to make are decisions in application of pre-existing law, and these are restricted in their legal force to the parties in the case. Any more general pronouncement can be regarded as corrigible, open to challenge. No general formulation of the rule of law in any case can be regarded as finally authoritative. But then we must conclude, says Bentham, that there simply is no such thing as law under the Common Law system. For surely, legal rules must be general and authoritative, and since there are no such rules, there cannot be law. And since there are no laws under such a regime, all judicial decisions are little more than unauthorized exercises of power.

Clearly, this argument turns on a very important premiss: law consists of *authoritative general* propositions of law (rules). Now there is, surely, an interpretation of this premiss which Common Lawyers would immediately reject, but Blackstone and other Common Lawyers would be willing to agree that in some sense law is made up of general rules, and perhaps even that they must be authoritative (though the interpretation of this condition is likely to be a matter of contention). But if we adopt the Common Law interpretation of these claims, it appears that the conclusion Bentham draws does not follow. For from the fact that judges do not make law, and that their statements regarding Common Law rules are always corrigible, it does not follow that there are no such rules. To draw this conclusion Bentham needs the further premiss: if a rule is an authoritative legal rule, then it must be given an explicit, fixed, verbal formulation. (This can be regarded either as an additional assumption of the argument or as an implication of Bentham's notion of what counts as authoritiative.) Only with some such premiss as this can we drive Common Law theory into absurdity. However, it is obvious from our discussion of the theory in 1.1, that this assumption asserts precisely what Common Law theory is anxious to *reject*. Rules of Common Law are constructed from existing popular or judicial practice, but there is no fixed canonical verbal formulation of them.

Bentham's argument, then, can succeed only if it imports an assumption from outside Common Law theory, an assumption which seems remarkably close to (or derived from) Bentham's own alternative theory of law. The argument seems seriously to risk begging the question against Common Law theory. Of course, Common Law does not meet Bentham's standards of what is to count as law, but that is because he takes the statute as his model, and Common Law makes no pretence of modelling its component rules on statute law. Bentham's argument can escape the charge of simply, and rather too obviously, begging the question against Common Law theory only if he can provide some more general argument for his assumption, an argument which does not directly rely on his positivist conception of a law but from which that conception can be seen to follow. This, of course, entails that

Bentham's argument loses its character as an internal critique of Common Law theory, but it may yield an argument of some interest none the less.

The argument, of course, is not hard to find. We have explored the basic outlines of it in the preceding three chapters. The argument appeals to Bentham's conception of the fundamental tasks or functions of law, and the first theorem of the doctrine: that for law adequately to perform its primary tasks it must be fully public, certain, and both its content and its authority (validity) uncontestable (or as nearly so as is possible). It is for this reason that a law must always be

a [piece of] discourse—conceived mostly in *general*, and always in *determinate* words—expressive of the *will* of some person or persons, to whom, on the occasion, and in relation to the subject in question, whether by habit or express engagement, the members of the community to which it is addressed are disposed to pay obedience (*Bowring* viii, 94).

This argument can be found frequently throughout Bentham's writings. One characteristic formulation is the following.

A rule of Law must be predicated of some certain assemblage of words—It never can be predicated of a bare assemblage of naked ideas. It is words only that can be spoken of as binding: because it is words alone that are producible with certainty when occasion comes for any individual to be bound.[55]

In Bentham's view, the greatest virtue of a rule of law (at least with respect to its form) is that it be public, determinate, and as a result certain and predictable in its application. Only under these conditions, so the argument goes, can it be said to be binding, because only under these conditions could it effectively guide action. The 'inferential' rules of Common Law can only be, at the very most, each individual's interpretation or construction of the practice.

From a set of *data* like these a law is to be extracted by every man who can fancy that he is able: by each man perhaps a different law: and these then are the *monades* [sic] which meeting together constitute the rules which taken together constitute . . . the common or customary law.[56]

[55] *Comment* 259 n. a; see also *RJE, Bowring* vi, 552.
[56] *OLG* XV. 11. Statute law, in contrast, 'mark[s] out the line of the subject's conduct by visible directions, instead of turning him loose into the wilds of perpetual conjecture' (*Comment* 95; see also 118–19).

Common or customary law consists of rules of some sort, Bentham allows, but they cannot be rules *of law* because they cannot begin to perform adequately the fundamental and necessary *functions of law*. For rules of Common Law are essentially and unavoidably matters of private conjecture, not publicly identifiable standards. They are 'monads' in a social universe which do not converge, but at best only overlap accidentally and unpredictably. 'Whether in any case [the rule] of the pleader shall happen to be the same with that of the Judge is a matter of cross and pile.'[57] This indeterminacy has the further consequence of judicial arbitrariness:

Uncertainty . . . is at its maximum, in the case where the same rule of action has no determinate set of words belonging to it. . . . In this case, on each individual occasion, the rule of action, by which the fate of the suit or cause . . . of the parties litigant is determined, is the arbitrary will of the Judge, made known, in the same individual occasion, for the first time.[58]

This, at the very least, delivers the ordinary citizen into the hands of the legal élite. 'Rules which are laid down in determinate words, may . . . be understood without art. Rules which, not being laid down in determinate words, can scarcely with propriety be said to exist, cannot be understood . . . without art' (*RJE, Bowring* vii, 197).

This is not to say that statute law is not without its problems. 'It is true', Bentham admits, 'that the same ideas may not present themselves to all men's minds upon the appearance of the same signs.' Nevertheless, in the case of statutory law there is 'always a common standard which all men acknowledge, and all men are ready to resort to' (UC lxix. 188). There is, then, some common public object around which interpretations can focus, and this, Bentham maintains, imposes a considerable constraint on the extent of conjecture and interpretation.

But it might be objected that Bentham has overstated the problems of the indeterminacy of content of Common Law rules. There are, after all, recognized treatises which set out the rules of

---

[57] That is, pure chance (*Comment* 210). Common Law, says Bentham, is nothing more than 'jurisprudence', *jus*, not *lex* (OLG XIII. 3). The contrast Bentham intends here is not that between *justice* and law, but that between *theoretical* propositions *about* law which are based merely on conjecture and are mere matters of opinion, and authoritative, valid statements *of* law. Recall here Hobbes's claim: 'Statutes are not philosophy as is the Common Law'. *Dialogue* 69.

[58] BL Add. MSS 33,549, fo. 17.

Common Law in reasonably concrete and determinate language. To this Bentham replies that, even if treatises give determinate formulations of legal principles in some cases (a claim of which Bentham is sceptical), they introduce a new source of indeterminacy. For there are many such treatises and they frequently conflict and there is no more agreement about the relative authority of the treatises than there is about the content of the rules to be conjectured from judicial practice without the aid of the treatises.[59] Thus, the rules of Common Law are indeterminate with regards to their *content* and, even where there seems to be a relatively determinate rule, its *authority* is entirely unsettled. It is

a misfortune peculiar to Common Law . . . that the signs [of the laws] themselves are not established (or generally agreed upon). No person can settle within himself, much less can any two persons settle with one another what collection it is, what book contains that standard . . . [that] all men are ready to abide by (UC lxix. 188).

But the problem of the indeterminacy of the authority of the rules of Common Law goes even deeper, according to Bentham. Common Law theory, especially in Blackstone's version, maintains that the validity of a rule of law depends, in part, on a shared sense of the rule's justice or reasonableness. But this confuses the question of the authenticity of laws with their merit.

[F]or as to *unwritten* institutions [rules and principles of Common Law], as there is no such thing as any certain symbol by which their authority is attested, their validity, how deeply rooted soever, is what we see challenged without remorse. [This is a] radical weakness, interwoven into the very constitution of all *un*written Law (*FG*, Preface, p. 402 n. e, author's emphasis).

In Common Law there is 'no certain symbol' by which the validity of a law can be authoritatively established and publicly attested. So when one challenges the merit, the reasonableness, or the expediency of the law, one at the same time 'sets oneself to contest the right' (ibid). This in Bentham's view has two disastrous consequences. First, the legal status of propositions is always open to challenge and, by the nature of the case, cannot be authoritatively and finally settled. Substantive matters are always contestable, we can never reach anything more than temporary coincidence of

[59] *Comment* 207–10; *OLG* XV.

opinion. Morally and politically substantive matters, as we have seen, are divisive and we can expect little agreement. Furthermore, even if we could get full public support of the sole rational and fully determinate standard for such assessment, the principle of utility, we would still not have a sufficiently public standard by which to assess *validity*.[60] Thus, the authority of propositions of law under a Common Law system must be radically indeterminate.

Second, there is a reverse effect which is, in Bentham's view, equally disastrous. Because there is no way of distinguishing challenges to the rule and challenges to 'its right', i.e. its validity, there is strong pressure not to question, challenge, or censure the laws *at all*. This abject fear of any sort of rational challenge of the law is evident on every page of Blackstone's *Commentaries*, Bentham charges.[61] The fear of undermining the authority of the laws in general stifles all inclination to question the reason or justice or expediency of any particular law. This has the further result of blocking all movements for the reform or improvement of the law. But worst of all, it has the effect of forcing all citizens into blind and passive obedience. In a system which confuses legality with justice, validity with reason, and in which, consequently, there is no way to signal the force and direction of challenge, there is no room for the exercise of responsible and critical judgment and choice. In such a system, the call to obedience is a call to abject and mindless acquiescence. Through its 'silent method' of reacting *post facto* to what are then judged undesirable actions, the Common Law can achieve 'somewhat the effect of general law'.[62] A certain degree of order and regularity in social behaviour can be achieved. But this is 'a mode of Government that is fit only for Beasts' (UC lxix. 151).

Thus, it is not enough, in Bentham's view, to ensure that the rules of law themselves are expressed in some determinate and publicly accessible form. For the *authenticity* of the rules must be equally uncontested. So the criteria by which the rules are determined to be valid must be defined in terms of publicly accessible, fully deter-

[60] See 7.3 ('Sovereignty in the *Fragment on Government*').

[61] *FG*, Preface pp. 402–3; *Comment* 346–7.

[62] UC lxix. 154; also *OLG* XIII. 2. 'There is no mode of conduct producible by command, but what is equally producible without command. Hence it is easy to understand how the same effect that is produced by Statute Law, that is by command, may be produced by Common Law, that is by a course of punishing without command' (UC lxix. 147). See also UC lxix. 151.

minate marks or conditions. 'What the subject sees, he may perhaps obey: what he does not see he cannot obey. What he must see is the Will of the legislator when it is intelligibly expressed' (*Comment* 139–40). So, once again, written law, law meeting the conditions of Bentham's strong positivist conception of law, fills the bill where Common Law dismally fails. 'Written law has a certain manifest foundation', Bentham argues.

There is a legislator—there is a will—there is an expression of that will, a known period of its birth. Unwritten law possesses none of these qualities: its origin is unknown; it goes on continually increasing—it can never be finished; it is continually altering without observation.[63]

From this sketch it is clear that the assumptions underlying Bentham's critique of Common Law theory are precisely those we encountered in his critique of Common Law practice. His argument for the claim that Common Law is sheer fiction is that it is completely incapable of serving the fundamental tasks of law. Where we need clear, determinate, public rules, the content and authenticity of which are beyond contest, Common Law offers us only endlessly contestable, constantly fluctuating rules and criteria of validity. The primary task of law is to focus expectations, co-ordinate social interaction on a broad scale and more particularly, to use Hume's words, 'to cut off all occasions of discord and contention' (*Treatise* 502). For this task Common Law is clearly unsuitable, in Bentham's view, whereas a form of law on the model of (a properly structured and systematic) statute law is well suited (*Bowring* iv, 480, 483 ff). Common Law must be rejected not because it is not in *some* sense or other a kind of 'law', but because, due to its radical indeterminacy and inability to supply adequate public standards, it cannot even minimally serve the basic ends of law.

The theory of fictions

An important objection to the above argument must be considered here. One might object that I have too quickly concluded that Bentham's critique of Common Law theory rests on the same considerations and arguments on which he based his critique of Common Law practice. For there is another argument for the same conclusion that can be drawn exclusively from his general philo-

---

[63] *General View, Bowring* iii, 206; see also UC lxiii. 49–50; *Comment* 120; *RJE, Bowring* vi, 552.

sophical views, in particular his theory of fictions. Bentham's strong positivist conception of law, which insists that criteria of validity be defined solely in terms of empirical facts, regardless of its utilitarian merits, is the product of his radically empiricist-nominalist ontology and epistemology, it might be argued. On Bentham's theory of fictions, only commands and sanctions and habits of aggregates of people can be regarded as real. These alone can qualify as the materials out of which a legal system can be constructed. On this view, the problem with Common Law is not that it is not real *law*, but that it is, strictly speaking, *no real entity whatsoever*. We must, on this interpretation, take Bentham's charge seriously: Common Law rules are *unreal*, existing merely as the fictitious projections of the mind from some real entities with which they are constantly confused. At best on Bentham's view, the argument continues, such rules are *ideas* in my mind, or yours, or the judge's. Bentham's positivism, on this interpretation, is the direct product of his (normatively neutral) ontology.[64]

No doubt Bentham's theory of fictions shaped his criticism of Common Law and his theory of law generally (as it did almost every doctrine he advanced). Clearly, the account of custom set out in 7.1 above is much influenced by that theory. However, a close look at the theory of fictions will reveal that it could not have independently generated Bentham's positivist theory of law. At crucial points Bentham had to rely on the kind of normative considerations I have uncovered above.

This is not the place to give an exposition of Bentham's complex theory of fictions.[65] I will only give a very brief sketch of a few of the central claims to prepare the way for my argument. Fictitious entities are logical constructions out of real entities (or rather, out of ideas of real entities), or out of other fictions ultimately anchored to real entities. These constructions are formed into hierarchies, the formation of which is directed by the principles of

---

[64] Dworkin makes this charge generally against positivists, see *Taking Rights Seriously*, 348, and discussion of it in D. Lyons, 'Moral Aspects of Legal Theory', 242–3.

[65] Recent Bentham scholarship has rightfully paid much attention to the role of Bentham's theory of fictions in his legal, moral, and political theories. See J. Steintrager, *Bentham*, ch. I; Long, *Bentham on Liberty*, 38–9, and *passim.*; L. J. Hume, *Bentham and Bureaucracy*, 58–62, 190, 247, and *passim.*; and especially R. Harrison, *Bentham*, chs. II and III. However, my argument in the text rests on an interpretation that departs at several points from the more widely accepted reading of this theory. See my 'Facts, Fictions, and Law', esp. sect. II.

'systematic arrangement' and 'methodization'. Bentham does not make altogether clear just what he takes to be the ontologically primitive entities for this construction, but on one very prominent version he includes only material objects ('substances'), impressions (or sensations), and ideas. Out of these, we can construct all (or most of) the rest of the entities that populate our folk ontology. Bentham is quite aware that his primitive ontology (his set of 'real entities') is extremely restricted—so restricted, in fact, that without fictions all but the most primitive thought and communication about, and rational interactions with, our world would be impossible. Thus, fictions are potentially misleading but nevertheless *indispensable*. The aim of the theory of fictions was not to provide a rationale for the elimination of entities from our folk ontology or their concepts from our conceptual scheme, but rather to *regiment* this essential intellectual device: to define a method whereby the range of legitimate application and use of the concepts could be precisely determined. Consequently, it is important to distinguish between those fictions which are necessary (because useful for organizing our thought about and manipulation of the world around us for our own needs), and those which are useless and can be eliminated without loss. The latter include both *innocuous* fictions which may even give pleasure (the fictions of poets) and *pernicious* fictions which are used for sinister purposes (the fictions of priests, in Bentham's example).

Now Bentham relegates *legal* fictions and especially the fiction of Common Law, to this latter category (*Bowring* viii. 199). It is an unnecessary fiction which must be purged from our political and jurisprudential thinking. However, there is nothing in the theory of fictions itself, i.e. in the basic ontology or the principles of construction or methodization, which can be relied on to draw the line between necessary and pernicious fictions. That determination is entirely pragmatic (utilitarian). Rights, obligations, powers, title, and a host of other such legal 'entities' are also fictitious. But Bentham recognizes that they are essential for any adequate theory of law, and so provides an analysis of them in terms anchored eventually to real entities. They are then qualified for use in the theory. And we know their proper boundaries so that we are not misled into drawing unwarranted implications from their use. Clearly, then, Bentham could not rest his *rejection* of fictitious Common Law simply on his theory of fictions.

As a matter of fact, as we have seen, Bentham did offer an analysis of customary (and *a fortiori* Common Law) rules in terms that rescue them from the conceptual junk-heap. Customary rules, then, have a bona fide ontological status alongside rights, obligations, and the like. The problem with Common Law rules is not that they are fictions, but that they are *doubly fictitious*.[66] They not only purport to be real *entities*, but also (and this is their crime) they pass themselves off *as law*. Common Law rules are simply customary rules masquerading as law. Common Law is a counterfeit, a pretender (*Bowring* iv, 483), and thus pernicious.

According to Blackstone, the law is not to be identified with either the particular decisions of the courts or any particular person's formulation of the rule of the decision. It is rather the ideal projection from this evidence. It is an objective 'entity' about which citizens and judges may have opinions, and *of which* the various statements are formulations. But this is just pernicious nonsense, says Bentham. Common Law *purports* to provide common, public general rules, but all it can show us are particular decisions, and private opinions.

The Common Law, in order to make it the fitter for adoration, was to be turned into an abstruse and invisible quiddity . . . [L]ike certain tyrants of the earth, [it] was never to shew itself in public: like them it was to make its existence perceivable only by means of its delegates . . . [T]he Oracles were not the words of the Pythia that spake them, but her words were the evidence of an *Apollo* whose oracles they were (*Comment* 195).

Such things could never qualify as law, nor could they do so even if 'demythologized'. There is, of course, a strong and important criticism of Common Law in this, but it depends heavily on considerations external to the theory of fictions. In particular, it depends on an account of the essential functions and tasks of law and the most efficient means of carrying them out.

There is further reason for thinking that Bentham's rejection of Common Law as fiction was motivated by concerns beyond his underlying ontological and epistemological views. On Bentham's analysis, the 'rules' of customary or Common Law, in so far as they can be said to exist, exist only as purely *subjective ideas* in the minds of individuals. But Bentham was not forced by his theory of

[66] Compare here Bentham's view that probabilities are 'doubly fictitious' (*Bowring* viii, 211); see my 'Facts, Fictions, and Law', 55.

fictions to give this account. Within this theory Bentham has the resources to construct a much more sympathetic account of Common Law which, while consistent with his basic ontology, could allow a significant degree of intersubjectivity and of critical assessment on rational grounds of individual expressions of 'opinion' about what the rule of a practice is. This is clear from Bentham's analysis of probabilities.[67] Although he starts out with an analysis of probability statements which appears radically subjectivist, a closer look reveals a quite different picture. Probability statements, or assessments of the 'probative force' of evidence for some principal fact, involve more than the expression of the speaker's current state of mind. They also implicitly appeal to a complex fact about how (or how much) the evidence *would* incline the speaker to embrace the principal fact when both are considered under certain appropriate conditions. This approach, though surely not entirely satisfactory in the view of Common Law theory, would nevertheless allow Bentham to capture a good deal of what that theory wishes to claim for this particular form of law, in a language derived directly from Bentham's spare ontology. Indeed, occasionally there are suggestions in Bentham's discussion that he would not reject such an account of customary rules. Recall that he holds that the rule of some custom *in foro* is that which shall appear to be the '*just expression* of judicial practice in like cases'.[68] Any particular formulation of the rule expresses the speaker's opinion of this matter, but it is an opinion *about* the best or just expression of this practice, which is subject to some degree of intersubjective assessment, or so Bentham here seems to suggest. But even if Bentham did seriously advance such an analysis, he would still press his objection against Common Law. For what motivates his rejection of Common Law is not that it does not have adequate ontological status, but that it cannot adequately meet conditions set for *laws*, conditions which are determined not by his theory of fictions but by his view of the underlying functions and tasks of law. Thus, under his preferred analysis, or even under this more sophisticated one, Bentham would maintain that the 'rules' of Common Law cannot be sufficiently public and determinate for the purposes for which we have need of law.

---

[67] See 'Facts, Fictions, and Law', and references cited there.
[68] UC c. 98; see also *Comment* 197–8.

There are two further sets of reasons for circumspection about attributing to the theory of fictions a dominant role in the shaping of Bentham's positivism. First, frequently Bentham asserts that, whereas Common Law is pure fiction, statute law is *real law* (see, for example, *Comment* 119-20). But his considered view, frequently expressed, is that only the logically complete, integral legal rule, the rule which is an integral part of a systematically arranged and rationally ordered set of codes of law, is real law. (See UC lxix. 94, 98; *IPML*, Concluding Note, 2; *Pannomial Fragments, Bowring* iii, 216.) But Bentham is quite aware of the fact that this is an ideal construct: 'Statutes are such as we find them, Laws are such as we may conceive them' (UC xcvi. 85). No such laws existed in his day, and arguably none exists today. Furthermore, the principles determining this ideal structure are heavily dependent upon Bentham's general views regarding the utilitarian tasks of law. (See below, 12.3.) Clearly, the notion of 'real' here, to which statutes only approximate (and for which Common Law rules do not even qualify), is not an ontological notion at all.

Second, suppose Bentham got his way and the law of England was transformed into his ideal 'pannomion'—consisting of complete and integral expressions of the will of the sovereign, etc. Even in this case, despite Bentham's language to the contrary, the individual laws in such a code could not be regarded as *real entities* on the criteria spelled out by Bentham's theory of fictions. For according to those principles, what is real are only the written marks or uttered sounds. But, clearly, *they* are not the laws. They are *expressions* of the laws (or of the will of the sovereign). For them to take on significance as laws we need to relate them to a large number of complex and intersecting social practices: first, to give the marks or sounds expressive or linguistic significance ('meaning' in some language); second, to give these *words* or *sentences* significance as *laws*. Now, it may have been Bentham's conviction and hope that these practices themselves could be understood ultimately in terms of real entities. But it is quite clear that they are *fictions* and the written or spoken expressions dependent on them must also, then, be fictions. Written laws are no more real entities, on Bentham's criteria, than are customary rules. There is, in Bentham's view, a sense in which statutory laws are 'more real' than Common Law rules: they are less 'conjectural', more public. But this is not a sense of 'real' that gets funded by his theory of fictions.

Bentham's critique of Common Law is of special interest because in that criticism we find clearly manifested the considerations and arguments that moved him to his positivist conception of law. We have seen in this chapter that this radical critique of both the practice and the theory of Common Law rests on the same set of principles and arguments, drawn from his social and political theory, in particular his conception of the primary tasks and functions of law, and the best or most efficient means of serving them. Thus, Bentham's defence of his conception of the *nature* of law rests not on normatively neutral, analytical or conceptual considerations, but on his analysis of fundamental human and social needs and the ways in which law can be used to meet them. Jurisprudence draws directly on political theory. His is a distinctively utilitarian positivism.

9

Utilitarian Positivism

> No great improvements in the lot of mankind are possible, until a
> great change takes place in the fundamental constitution of their
> modes of thought.
>
> J. S. Mill, *Autobiography.*

WE have seen that Bentham rejects Common Law and custom as
fictions, but what is fictitious about them is their claim to be bona
fida *legal rules.* He does not deny that such social phenomena
could, or ever did, exist; neither does he deny that they could be
said to consist of *rules* in some sense. But he does insist that they
could never constitute *laws.* To consider them laws is to fall into
confusion. We have seen that Bentham's arguments against Common Law theory rest at crucial points on his assumptions regarding
the proper utilitarian functions of law and the features that a
system of legal rules must possess if it is adequately to serve those
functions.

One might legitimately ask at this point just how this jurisprudential strategy differs from the discredited strategy of the natural
lawyer who refuses to recognize a rule *as a law*, no matter how well
established in a legal system, if it fails the test of justice. Bentham
seems to have violated his own most basic positivist principle, that
of confusing what *ought to be* with what *is.* One reviewer of Bentham's *Of Laws in General* makes precisely this charge.[1] Bentham,
he maintains, attempted to undertake a strictly 'empirical investigation of the facts to which the term "law" pointed . . . He sought
to establish a purely sociological theory of law', unencumbered by
the fictions and moralizing of earlier natural law theory. On this
interpretation, Austin's dictum to the effect that 'the existence of
the law is one thing, its merit or demerit another'[2]—a dictum
Bentham clearly would have endorsed—is the cornerstone of the
positivist theory of law. But, then, if the argument of the preceding

---

[1] K. Olivecrona, 'The Will of the Sovereign', 107–8.
[2] J. Austin, *The Province of Jurisprudence Determined*, 184.

chapter is correct, we must conclude that Bentham violated his own fundamental distinction, and thereby undermined his entire positivist project.

No less a Bentham scholar than Professor Hart is inclined to take a similar, though somewhat more moderate, view. Hart, in his recent *Essays on Bentham*, praises Bentham for avoiding the mistake made by Hobbes and other social theorists of defining 'our terms in legal or political theory as to make the practical conclusions which we favour follow from them'. In contrast, the 'terms that Bentham uses to define law are all flatly descriptive and normatively neutral'.[3] This, he writes, is the 'healthy centre' of Bentham's legal positivism and his most important legacy. However, complains Professor Hart, 'at important points [Bentham's] utilitarianism gets in the way of his analytical vision'.[4] In Hart's view, these are unfortunate, though consequential, theoretical slips. But the damage, if the criticism is correct, is much more extensive than Hart admits. For the criticism rocks Bentham's theory of law at its foundations. That theory would not only be problematic in matters of detail, but it would be incoherent at its core.

In this chapter I will defend Bentham against this criticism which, I believe, rests on two mistakes. First, it seriously misunderstands Bentham's theoretical motivations; second, it rests on a mistaken view of the jurisprudential enterprise generally. The distinction between law as it is and law as it ought to be—as well as that between the 'expositor' and the 'censor'—are indeed important elements *of* his theory, but they are not foundational *to* it. His positivist theory of *laws* is one part of a more general theory of *law* which is explicitly grounded on his utilitarian social and political theory. In the first three sections of this chapter I shall argue that Bentham's reliance on normative considerations in his criticism of Common Law theory and his argument for his positivist theory of law, would not be regarded *by him* as a mistake, but rather as an essential part of the programme he set for himself at the outset of his career. In the concluding section I shall argue that this programme—despite some misgivings I have about its execution—is not incoherent, but in fact rests on a more plausible understanding

---

[3] H. L. A. Hart, *Essays on Bentham*, 28.
[4] Ibid. 162.

of the jurisprudential enterprise than that inherited from Austin and Analytical Jurisprudence.

9.1 THE EXPOSITOR, THE CENSOR, AND UNIVERSAL JURISPRUDENCE

I have built solely on the foundation of utility.

Bentham, Letter to Voltaire (1776).

We may begin with Bentham's familiar distinction between the 'expositor' of the law and its 'censor'. Bentham frequently praised Hume for exposing the confusion of what ought to be with what is the case. This was, in Bentham's view, the 'most important discovery in moral philosophy',[5] and he relies on it directly to mark out his distinction between the expositor and the censor.

To the province of the *Expositor* it belongs to explain to us what, as he supposes, the Law *is*: to that of the *Censor*, to observe to us what he thinks it *ought to be*. The former, therefore, is principally occupied in stating, or in inquiring after *facts*: the latter, in discussing *reasons*. . . . To the *Expositor* it belongs to shew what the *Legislator* and his underworkman the *Judge* have done *already*: to the *Censor* it belongs to suggest what the Legislator *ought* to do *in future* (*FG*, Preface, p. 397, author's emphasis).

It is tempting to interpret this passage as stating a special case of the more general distinction between facts and values which Bentham is implicitly endorsing. However, contrary to the views of many readers of Bentham, I believe this is a mistaken interpretation of Bentham's intentions.

As we have seen in the previous chapter, it was very important in Bentham's view to distinguish sharply the questions of the justice or merit of a law from the question of its existence or validity. Both natural law and Common Law theories muddy this distinction, with different results. Natural law makes justice a condition of validity and so introduces radical uncertainty into determination of the content and authenticity of laws. Common Law confuses what is established with what is just or reasonable and thus blocks all occasion for critical assessment and challenge of existing law. It is the latter fault that most concerns Bentham in the Preface to the

---

[5] UC c. 5; see also *Bowring* viii, 128 n *; *Bowring* v, 320; *RJE, Bowring* vi, 240 n *.

Fragment and motivates the above formulation of the distinction between the expositor and the censor.[6]

The problem with Blackstone's *exposition* of the Common Law, Bentham argues, is that it seeks silently to *legitimize* the laws through doctrinal exegesis. The mere fact that a practice has existed for a long period of time is sufficient to warrant praise from Blackstone for its wisdom and goodness. This is hopeless obscurantism and 'ancestor-worship', Bentham charges. There may be good reasons for following established practices, but they are reasons of expediency (expectation utility) and have absolutely nothing to do with the alleged wisdom of our ancestors (*Comment* 196). The result of Blackstone's confusion which worries Bentham most in the *Fragment* Preface is that it simply shuts down all avenues for criticism and censure of the law. But, in order to make censure possible without threatening at the same time the entire system of law, it is not enough to recognize the logical difference between stating a fact and making a criticism or recommendation. For the 'facts' of the existing law, according to the Common Law conception, are inextricably tied up with matters of moral and practical judgment. The problem of the *Commentaries*, on Bentham's analysis, lies not in Blackstone's intellectual failure or dishonesty, but in the conception of law he set out to expound. The way to ensure clear separation of exposition and censure is to separate conditions of validity from assessments of merit, and that is to call for a radical change in the way in which legal practice is understood —a change which will inevitably alter the practice.

The distinction between *is* and *ought*, then, is sharply drawn, but within a very specific context: discussion of the validity, content, and merit of particular laws. And it is motivated by a very specific set of normative considerations. We must take care then not to generalize this distinction between expositor and censor without explicit warrant. There is, in fact, textual evidence to show that Bentham was inclined to restrict the sharp distinction between these two functions to the context just spelled out.

In the *Introduction to the Principles*, for example, the distinction between expositor and censor appears in conjunction with a further

---

[6] David Lyons argues that the positivists' 'separation thesis' rests not on a logical or conceptual insight but on a moral judgment ('Founders and Foundations of Legal Positivism', 730–2). Bentham's theory gives historical support for this claim, although the moral judgment on which Bentham rests his theory is different from the one Lyons attributes to the positivists.

distinction between *local* and *universal* jurisprudence (*IPML* XVII. 21, 24). Local jurisprudence concerns itself with the *substance* or *content* of the law of a particular jurisdiction. Universal jurisprudence, in contrast, is concerned with matters of legal 'form'— features that may be shared by laws in (nearly) all legal systems. Bentham contrasts universal jurisprudence with 'censorial jurisprudence'. The former is concerned with the form laws must take, the latter with the substance of laws, i.e. with content the laws *ought* to have. This seems to be a distinction not in terms of *function* (the one concerned with the *is* the other with the *ought* of laws), but rather one of *subject matter*, universal jurisprudence serving *both* local and censorial jurisprudence.

This is confirmed by a closer look at what Bentham regarded as the province of universal jurisprudence. Bentham conceived his two major works on jurisprudence, *IPML* and *OLG*, as general statements of the first principles of censorial and universal jurisprudence, respectively.[7] But he included in the latter category more than merely the analysis of central legal concepts. Its task was to 'form a sort of universal anatomy of the entire body of the law' (*OLG*, App. E, p. 308 n. 1), to produce a comprehensive plan for law, 'complete in all its branches, considered in respect of its *form*; in other words, in respect of its method and terminology' (*IPML*, Preface, p. 6). Within this charge fell not only definition or regimentation of concepts (e.g. of law, obligation, rights, power, liberties, title, etc.), but also determination of principles of individuation and standards of completeness of laws, determination of the essential features and relations among the various parts of a law, principles for the arrangement of material in a public code suitable for public instruction, as well as principles of legislative drafting. The objective of universal jurisprudence was nothing

---

[7] In his retrospective view of these two works in *OLG* XIX. 2 Bentham relates the previous eighteen chapters of *OLG* (referred to here as a single chapter) to the long Chapter XVI of *IPML* ('Division of Offences') as follows: 'Take this chapter then and the preceding one [*IPML* XVI], lay them together and we have, such as it is, a complete and pretty detailed plan of a complete body of the laws. The former chapter, taking the lead, gave an idea of the nature, purport and *substance* or matter of the laws: the business of the present has been to give an idea of the *form* into which it might be proper that substance should be cast: of the expressions or shapes of discourse with which it seems necessary that the several laws as determined by the principles contained in the preceding chapter, should as it were be clothed, in order that the true nature and mutual connections of those laws might be made apparent, and of the order in which it seemed most convenient those masses should be arranged.'

short of providing the conceptual framework, the terminology, and all the technical machinery required by the censor or, more precisely, by the drafter of a complete code of laws.

And it is clear that for this monumental task, as well as that of censorial jurisprudence, the fundamental guide for Bentham was the principle of utility. In an unsent letter to Voltaire (November 1776), for example, Bentham described his early work on law (and more importantly the motivations for his researches into jurisprudence). 'The object of it', he wrote, 'is to trace out a new model for the Laws. . . . To ascertain what the Laws ought to be, *in form and tenor as well as in matter.*' And he boasts that his inspiration had been, not Hale or Coke, nor Grotius or Pufendorf, but Helvetius, Beccaria, and Voltaire himself. And, he adds, 'I have built solely on the foundation of utility'.[8]

Similarly, the Preface of *IPML* lists titles of ten projected works on legal topics the publication of which would fulfil Bentham's designs for a complete critical and expository view of the law. These include works on principles of legislation regarding civil, penal, procedural, constitutional, and international law, and principles of political economy, and finance. The subject of the tenth would be universal jurisprudence. Commenting on the list Bentham says, these ten parts, *each* of which 'exhibit what appear [to Bentham] *the dictates of utility* in every line', provide the materials for construction of a complete code of laws (*IPML*, p. 7, emphasis added). Thus, it appears the dictates of utility are as important to the subject matter of universal jurisprudence as to censorial.

These passages express the aims and objectives of the young Bentham about to put jurisprudence on the map of science. But the same view is expressed in the works on universal jurisprudence themselves. The inquiries with which the entire *Of Laws in General* was taken up were calculated only to be of use to the lawmaker or sovereign who is moved to construct the body of law according to the direction of the principle of utility (*OLG* III. 2). 'The fundamental principle which is the basis of the system of laws here sketched out is the principle of utility', Bentham asserts in his concluding, retrospective chapter.[9] And to Lord Ashburton he readily admits that 'a work of law upon [the model developed in *OLG*] is virtually a project of reformation . . . and that every title

[8] Bentham, *Correspondence* I, 367, emphasis added.
[9] *OLG* XIX. 5; see also *Bowring* iv, 480.

of it may be considered as a proposal for the alteration of the laws at present in force in so far as they differ from the model of supposed perfection which it is the design of such title to exhibit' (*OLG*, App. E, p. 310).

Thus, while Bentham insists on a sharp distinction between is and ought, validity and merit, and the functions of expositor and censor at the level of particular laws, his distinction is much less sharp at other levels, especially at the level of general reflection on the nature and proper form of laws. And this should not be surprising, since the need for a sharp distinction between the validity and merit of laws arose, in Bentham's view, from consideration of the proper functions of law and a conception of society which it was to serve.

9.2 NEW FOUNDATIONS FOR LAW

The object of it is to trace out a new model for the laws . . .

Bentham, Letter to Voltaire (1776).

Very early in his study of law Bentham became convinced of the evils of the English legal system—its injustice, its anachronistic and tottering institutions and forms, and its gross inefficiency. He traced these evils not to political or economic conditions, but to the characteristic *forms* and *methods* of Common Law. In his view, Common Law failed both as a structure of laws and as a form of adjudication. It failed as a system of legal rules because such propositions of law as could be extrapolated from judicial practice were nothing more than one person's interpretation or construction of that practice, and these constructions, in the happiest of circumstances, at best overlap with the interpretations others put on the same practice. Law is, under Common Law, essentially and unavoidably a matter of private conjecture, not a set of publicly identifiable standards. An institution of this sort, according to Bentham, cannot begin adequately to serve the functions of defining a social order and broad-scale co-ordinating of social interaction which Bentham's social and political theory set for it; nor can it guarantee full publicity and accountability of official decisions. Common Law fails as a form of adjudication because it must try to maintain some security of expectations, but with the inevitable result of encouraging simultaneously both rigidity in and arbitrariness of judicial decision-making. The basic problem, Bentham came to see, is that under Common Law the functions of *law* and of *adjudication* are confused. Judges are required both to secure expectations and to adjudicate particular disputes. In Bentham's view they cannot avoid failing at both tasks.

Moreover, the professionalization of the law, and the mystery and hocum it needed to preserve its autonomy and power, radically alienated people from the law, and thereby, in Bentham's view, from an important part of themselves. For it put insuperable obstacles in the way of enlightened, rational, and responsible participation in social and political life.

This was not always true of customary law, according to Bentham. Before the appearance of written law, legal rules issuing explicitly from a recognized legislative power, there were structured political communities (*Comment* 118–19). And people in 'states' (as Bentham calls them) were governed by customary law—'though probably not under any such name as Law' (ibid.). This regime of particular commands and 'unauthoritative', conjectural rules constructed from them worked reasonably, at least passably, well. In fact, the system was clearly beneficial in comparison to even earlier arrangements which provided case-by-case decision on the merits as the only method of resolving disputes and maintaining social order. The restriction of official decisions to precedent produced stability, certainty, and the past decisions gave guidance for behaviour in the community.[10] At the time, Bentham allows, the practice of customary law was 'a vast improvement over the previous barbarous condition' (*Bowring* iv, 490). It was beneficial because the community was small and homogeneous, and so, we may infer, the potential for radical indeterminacy of and conflict over the rules of such governing law was not fulfilled. Convergence of interpretation of the practice of people or courts was not merely accidental; people had some reason to expect it.[11] Also, in those communities, Bentham claims, 'the public mind was not ripe enough for the formation of a general rule of action covering the whole field of action' (UC xxx. 60).

But society grew in size and sophistication. It became more enlightened and civilized. The 'silent method' of governing could no longer efficiently carry out the tasks of law. Explicit general

[10] *Bowring* iv, 490; *RJE, Bowring* vii, 310 n. 1; *Comment* 119; UC xxx. 60–2.
[11] *Bowring* iv, 490; UC lxix. 154 and (less clearly) 147.

commands were needed (UC lxix. 147, 154). The certainty and continuity of custom broke down and there arose the need for a centralized, systematic, and fully public structure of law. The conditions which created the problem—the expansion of society and the stretching of the bonds of custom—also gave birth to all that was needed for its solution: the capacities of the human mind were expanded greatly and the conditions were made ripe for the enlightenment of the public. Time was, customary law was useful, even positively beneficial. 'Time was:—but that time is now at least at an end.' Now 'the times are ripe for the making of real law' (*Bowring* iv. 490). Thus, the concept of law itself can be historically dated. It arose when the social need arose for a fixed, public body of rules issuing from a centralized source (*Comment* 118–19). The term 'law' 'was invented . . . to denote a general Command of Public Government', Bentham asserts (UC lxix. 142).

Thus, Bentham clearly was aware of the historical relativity of his conception of law. His critique of Common Law and his passionate defence of his alternative conception are both grounded on an awareness of the unique needs of emerging modern society and a radically different conception of social relations. The breakdown of close-knit, homogeneous societies, adequately governed by custom and relations of personal trust, and with their loss the loss as well of shared standards for the assessment of individual and collective behaviour, created the need for a new social structure which could harness and turn to general benefit the energies released by the emerging commercial society. Also emerging at the same time was a new conception of society. No longer plausible, he believed, was the notion of society as a community bound together by personal loyalties and shared traditions, working toward collective goals. In its place arose the conception of a pluralistic, individualistic society bound by agreement—or the perceived need—to abide by certain rules of the game which organized and co-ordinated otherwise chaotic activity of individuals in pursuit of individually defined goals.

Bentham's critique of Common Law is essentially a detailed accounting of the failures of this form of law to meet the needs of modern society. Mere reform of this 'Gothic castle'[12] was not enough in view of its radical deficiencies. What was needed in

---

[12] See Blackstone 3 *Comm.* 267–8.

Bentham's view was a complete and radical reconstruction. Common Law had to be replaced with an entirely new form of law designed anew to meet the new conditions. Standing in the way of success of this programme of transformation were, of course, political inertia and the opposition of those whose 'sinister interests' were well served by the corrupt institution. But on Bentham's analysis, the sources of resistance were to be found deeper in, or at the very least were decisively shaped by, the characteristic patterns of thought, the central concepts, and even the language of Common Law. The grievance lay in the very currency of Common Law language, Bentham charged (*Comment* 345).

But this was a potent source of resistance, for, as we saw in Chapter 1, Common Law theory was not just a jurisprudential theory, and the framework of beliefs and attitudes which it shaped had a role to play in British society and politics outside the courts of Westminster. Common Law theory was a framework of political ideas and principles, a political ideology dominant throughout the first half of the eighteenth century. Thus Bentham's attack on Common Law was not, and could not have been regarded at the time as merely a detached philosophical assessment of a jurisprudential theory. It was a direct challenge to the ruling political ideology. And Bentham was surely aware of this.[13] The 'profound conceits' strewn throughout the *Commentaries* are in no way peculiar to Blackstone, Bentham observes. '[T]hey are an inheritance derived to him from his predecessors . . . the patrimony of a great part of the profession: and through their means of a still greater part of the world at large' (*Comment* 344). Bentham saw himself as carrying on the tradition of radical social criticism established by Voltaire, Helvetius, and the other Enlightenment critics on the continent. As L. J. Hume observes, 'he became a jurist because he believed, with a long line of earlier thinkers, that law and jurisprudence provided the key to politics and social relations and to the solution of their problems'.[14] But he had a special reason for this belief: the dominant jurisprudential theory was also the ruling political ideology, an ideology which in his view shackled, rather than liberated, human reason. Shrouded in mystery and tradition-worship, it was pathologically opposed to reform (*FG*,

---

[13] See, e.g., the two prefaces to *FG*, esp. the second, *FG*, p. 508; and *Comment*, App. F.

[14] *Bentham and Bureaucracy*, 57.

Preface, p. 394), and it induced and perpetuated mental slavery of the people.[15]

Thus, in Bentham's view, reconstruction of the law had to start with radical reconstruction of the categories within which law was conceived and the language with which we discuss law. Common Law *theory* and the whole framework of beliefs and attitudes associated with it had to be destroyed and replaced with a radically new conception of law. 'My primary aim', he announced in the *Comment*, 'is the emancipating [of the] judicial faculties [of members of the public] from those shackles in which it is the tendency of [Blackstone's] instruction to hold them bound' (*Comment* 349). Bentham's attack was not restricted to Blackstone, but was directed against the whole system of thought, the dominant way of conceiving of law,[16] which in Hazlitt's words represented 'that sort of tyranny . . . that is enshrined in traditions, in laws, in usages, in the outward symbols of power, in the very idioms of language'.[17]

To this end Bentham sought to shift the paradigm of law away from the customary rules and practices of Common Law to the sharper lines of statute law and its idealization, the code. Bentham was very conscious of the fact that he was engaged in an attempt to shift the paradigm conception of law. This is evident from his letter to Ashburton (quoted at the close of 9.1, above). After describing the subject matter of *OLG* in outline he concludes:

Your Lordship will easily perceive that a work of law upon this plan is virtually a project of reformation addressed to any nation to the circumstances of which it is meant to be applied, and that every title of it may be considered as a proposal for the alteration of the laws at present in force in so far as they differ from the model of supposed perfection which it is the design of such title to exhibit. . . . It is evident that the plan as far as it went could in a certain sense be the destruction of the *customary* or as it is so uncharacteristically termed by us, the *common* law; since whatever goes at present under that name would either be abrogated or *homologated* as the Flemish writers call it, that is expressed in assignable authoritative terms and thereby converted into the form of statute law.[18]

---

[15] '[T]he hydrophobia of innovation tends to enervate the energies of the human mind' (*Comment* 346). Bowring reports that Bentham wrote the following words in his own copy of *FG*: 'This was the very first publication by which men at large were invited to break loose from the trammels of authority and ancestor-wisdom on the field of law' (*Bowring* i, 260).

[16] See D. Baumgardt, *Bentham and the Ethics of Today*, 22.

[17] W. Hazlitt, *Political Essays*, 12.

[18] *OLG*, App. E, p. 310. See also *OLG* XV. 3 n. a, and esp. *Comment* 119.

Departing from the view announced earlier, Bentham admits in a manuscript from the mid-1770's that 'the idea of Law has never been precisely settled . . .'. But he insists that his business 'is therefore not to remind the reader what *is* meant by a Law: for no one entire thing is as yet meant by a Law; but to declare what shall be meant by a Law . . . [i.e.] what in my judgment *may* conveniently be meant by it in future'.[19] This term, in his judgment, must be limited so as to apply only to complete and integral units in a rationally structured code. But this departs even from the usage in which he often indulges, usage which identifies law with *statutes*. He confesses: 'I cannot say that a statute is not a Law: for if I did, usage would contradict me. But this I say, that it does not correspond to the idea I would wish to have exclusively annexed to the word Law' (UC lxix. 98).

Bentham regarded his attack on Common Law as falling in the great Enlightenment tradition of rational challenge of established institutions. He challenged this legal and social establishment as Newton and Galileo (and Luther) attacked the metaphysics of the Schools and the Church, seeking to free human beings from unreasoned submission to authority. Like the great critics of the Church and religion who sought to undermine its value and authority by shifting the paradigm of 'reason' and 'knowledge' and defining religion as 'unscientific', so Bentham sought to break the grip of tradition by shifting the paradigm of law and law-related reason. The guiding objective of *OLG*, and of universal jurisprudence in general, was to 'lay the foundation for the plan of the complete body of laws supposing it to be constructed *ab origine*' (*OLG* XIX. 1).

9.3 SOURCES OF BENTHAM'S POSITIVISM

[E]xcess in scepticism is less unmanly than excess in deference to authority: reason may profit by the former; it is stifled by the latter.

Lord Kames, *The Common and Statute Law of Scotland.*

It is time now to take a retrospective look at the development of Bentham's positivist conception of law. I will not attempt a detailed summary, rather, I want to draw together themes we have

---

[19] UC lxix. 86, 89, author's emphasis. Bentham's motto was: Don't argue over the import of words, fix it (*OLG*, App. D, p. 303 n. f).

considered at length in previous chapters to illustrate in broad strokes the impact of Bentham's normative social and political views of his thoughts about the nature of law.

Bentham, Hobbes, and Hume

A useful place to begin is to consider the relationship between Bentham and the tradition of British legal theory which we traced in Part I. But we can be brief about this, since we have already considered in detail Bentham's critique of the traditionalist Common Law doctrine. It remains now to sketch out the extent to which Bentham followed, and the extent to which he departed from, the approach and theoretical positions of Hobbes and Hume.

Like all the other jurists we have considered, Bentham's reflections on the nature and structure of law were shaped by assumptions about the social conditions within which law as a formal institution arises and the tasks which it must assume. Although he borrowed much from Hobbes, Hume still clung largely to the Common Law conception of community and the role of law in it. In a community of common goals with a heritage of shared traditions which makes pursuit of such goals possible and meaningful, law is not only a co-ordinator of the traffic of social interaction, it is also expressive of the common values and commitments bonding the community together. Law, on this view, is endogenous, the matrix of social life and continuous with it.

Bentham, following Hobbes, rejected this conception of law and of community on which it rests. The Common Law conception of society, in Bentham's view, was both descriptively false and politically objectionable. It was false because the commonality and sense of shared traditions it assumed no longer existed. It was objectionable because appeals to such traditions disguised the concentration of power in the hands of the ruling professional élite. It was a conception of law and society that was ultimately authoritarian. In its place Bentham proposed a conception of a community of individuals bound by loyalty to clear public rules, rather than common goals and shared traditions. Law, on this view, is a set of common rules. They are mutually recognized, but they may not be endogenous to the community, since there may be nothing truly common in the community from which they can arise. Rather, they are exogenous, an external framework of rules fixed and public, which makes social life possible. They are not necessarily imposed from above. Ideally, they are the product of a negotiated compromise, actual or hypothetical, amongst conflicting individual goals and interests. They define a *modus operandi* of social interaction to which citizens are loyal because of the ability of the rules to co-ordinate that interaction, not because of their intrinsic appeal. Law is, then, a necessary condition of social life, introducing order and co-ordination into the chaos of the pursuit of individual aims. But it does not participate in that life. Rather than defining a common conception of public good it defines boundaries for the pursuit of individual good and facilities for the orderly private alteration of those boundaries.

The task of law, according to Bentham, is to define anew, to establish, and then to sustain, a social and political order and framework for broad-scale social interaction. Like Hobbes, Bentham identified law with legislation, the general commands of an increasingly centralized public authority. Bentham conceived of law as the *cause* of social order or regularity, not merely a description of, or prescription for it (UC lxix. 142, 99, 102). Thus, he believed, law cannot properly be seen as the expression of something 'deeper'—either some deeper nature, or some deeper moral principles—for the very reason that we can no longer count on the universal acceptance of these notions of nature or natural law. If law is to succeed in establishing and maintaining a social order, it must be capable of wearing its validity publicly on its face. In this respect, although he borrows a great deal from Hume, he departs decisively from him. Hume regarded the appearance of formalized law, legislation, and centralized governmental functions, as merely the next stage in growth *based on* and only further *assisting* an already established conventional order. Bentham sees a much more radical break. On Bentham's analysis of modern society, law can achieve its ends and serve adequately its primary tasks only if its content and authority can be established without any need to rely upon investigation into either moral or traditional historical (or theological) matters. The key to its success was to cut its ties clearly from such matters which, in his view, were inevitably contentious, and at the very least were not sufficiently public, to supply the needed public assurance of general compliance. Furthermore, Bentham was not as hopeful as Hume that Common Law could perform the task they both regarded as important. Bentham charged that the radical professionalization of Common Law had not only made it unsuitable for the task of providing a framework of public rules, but it had corrupted it to its roots. No solutions to the problems of modern society were to be found in revising and reforming Common Law.

While Bentham accepted much of Hobbes's conception of law, he objected to its authoritarian features. This dissatisfaction had two sources. First, he analysed the nature of the social problem facing law differently from Hobbes. Social instability, in Bentham's view, was the product of a lack of assurance and the absence of fully public standards, not the more radical deficiencies of Hobbes's state of nature. What was needed was not a set of rules to *replace* individual practical rationality in social contexts, but rules to focus (and sometimes establish) expectations. Thus, *publicity* and *authenticity* are the keys to legal validity, not the absolute authority of Hobbes's law. Second, throughout his legal and political writings Bentham sought not to confine or restrict individual practical reasoning, but to free it up. Although he correctly perceived the problems of public and collective rationality which both Hobbes and Hume had brilliantly analysed, nevertheless he sought a legal and political theory which solved these problems while leaving to the individual full scope for the exercise of his or her rational powers. Bentham was never as sceptical of individual practical rationality as Hume or Hobbes. I shall return to this point shortly.

Now it is clear why Bentham was attracted to statutory law and the command as paradigms of his conception of law. First of all, with the notion of command Bentham could capture the *artificial* character of law. Law conceived as command could not be regarded as some mysterious, unalterable fact of nature, as Common Law theorists often tried to portray it. To conceive of law as command invites the questions *who* issued it? and *when*? and with what authority? Law is clearly portrayed as an artificial creation of human society. The paradigm captures the related important idea that law is not just descriptive of social order, but is its 'cause'—not an expression of some deeper reality, but the *instrument* by which the social relations necessary for human life are constituted and sustained. This has important implications for Bentham. For once this view is adopted, no existing system of law and legal relations can be protected as sacred. All law, social relations, and institutions, are opened to critical assessment, challenge, and reform. According to Bentham, only on such a view can we gain both a proper appreciation of the enormous value of law and social institutions and a perspective sufficiently sharp and critical to recognize their defects and mount efforts to improve them.

An essential condition of this sort of rational and critical appreciation of law and social institutions is the ability to distinguish clearly for private reflection and public debate between the existence, validity, and content of law, and the focus of one's obedience, on the one hand, and the justice, expediency, or merit of the law, on the other. The notion of command permits the formulation of clear, public, and non-contentious criteria of validity. Validity can be understood simply in terms of *authentic* expressions of will, that is, commands (or other imperations) from a publicly recognized source issued according to 'formalities' which make clear to all the fact that the command is authentic. Thus, Bentham combines both 'ontological' and 'epistemic' functions of criteria of validity in a single set of criteria (see above, 7.2). In fact, the 'epistemic' function drives his positivist conception of validity, for the social problem which calls for law, on his view, is at bottom an epistemic one: the problem of making certain rules and standards of conduct a matter of public, common knowledge. The notion of command also allows him to settle problems of the determinacy of content. Commands are forms of discourse, communication, so it is entirely natural to regard them as expressed in a language regimented to some canonical formulation.

Finally, this conception of law allowed Bentham to formulate in a precise and theoretically fruitful way questions about the logical relations among laws and to develop principles defining the systematic structure of a body of laws. In order to undertake these investigations, laws had to be conceived as propositions of some sort, regimented to some canonical verbal formulation, and questions of their authority and validity relegated to matters other than their internal relations. Bentham sought in *Of Laws in General* to formulate 'a sort of universal anatomy of the entire body of the law whatsoever considered nakedly as a collection of expressions of will, abstraction being made of the propriety of the volitions so expressed' (*OLG*, App. E, p. 308 n. 1).

Conceptual revision and utilitarian practical reasoning

There is one further source of Bentham's positivist theory of law which we have not yet considered. The full importance of it will not become clear until we have a chance to explore Bentham's mature theory of adjudication and its role in a code-dominated legal system (the task of Part III, especially Chapters 12 and 13.1). Nevertheless, already in Chapters 5 and 6 we have seen the depth of Bentham's commitment to what I called 'the sovereignty of the principle of utility' for all practical reasoning. It would be useful here to consider the impact which this direct-utilitarian view of practical reasoning had on Bentham's reflections on the nature of law. Thus, the argument we shall consider draws more heavily on Bentham's utilitarian theory of practical reasoning, than on the concerns of his social and political theory which have occupied our attention thus far, although the concerns that emerge here lie very close to the surface in those other areas of his thought as well.

In Chapter 7 we observed that Bentham was quite willing to recognize the existence of bona fide customary rules, and the prescriptive force of (most) customs and practices. (The account of this prescriptive force of customs drew on his earlier utilitarian account of justice as respect for expectation utilities.) But we also saw that he refused to regard these rules as *legal* rules, and their prescriptive force as amounting to (legal) *obligation*. We shall see below, especially in 13.1, that Bentham's insistence on the principle of utility as the sole decision principle for all rational agents (even judges)—that is, his conception of the essentially uniform character of practical reasoning—led him to adopt a conception of legal rules quite different from what we have come to expect from positivist legal theory. These features of his view are consistent with a pattern of analysis and argument which pervades his legal and political theory. I shall briefly sketch this pattern and then illustrate it with three examples now familiar to us.

To begin we must recall that Bentham sought to construct a theory of law and government which was comprehensive, systematic, and relentlessly rationalist. Every aspect of the theory had to be precisely defined and demonstrably rationally grounded. Likewise, every aspect of society, government, and law had to be left open to the critical scrutiny of any rational person on the basis of the clear, public standards defined by the theoretical framework. However, he came to believe very early that ordinary patterns of thought and prevailing theories could not be relied upon to provide materials for this purpose, for more often than not they put obstacles in the way of rational, critical thought about law and society. Conspicuous among the obstacles of thought and practice were notions or principles which sought to block, confine, or restrain individuals in their exercise of their own critical rational powers. Consideration of the merits of institutions, or official practices, or of individual actions, was hampered by a thick veil of authority, tradition, and principle. Common Law theory and practice, of course, was the greatest offender here. Its ideology, as well as its corrupt practice, fostered mindless submission to authority. Bentham is quite clear in his formulation of this, in his view, most damning charge. He objects *not* to 'submission in behaviour which is the mother of peace: but [to] submission of *judgment* which is the mother of stupidity' (*Comment* 346 n. 1, emphasis added). The deep evil of Common Law is that it denies individuals 'the right of private judgment' which is, he forcefully adds, 'that basis of everything that an Englishman holds dear' (*FG*, Preface, p. 406). This ultimate form of tyranny struck its roots into the human mind and clings 'round the human understanding like a nightshade'.[20]

Thus, Bentham would not countenance the alienation of the right of individual judgment. He became suspicious of any attempts to exclude from an individual's repertory for rational deliberation considerations which were clearly relevant. He relentlessly exposed all attempts to crib and confine the exercise of individual rational powers and sought to eliminate all notions that appeared to do so from the universe of discourse of practical philosophy.

It is not surprising, then, that frequently we have encountered the following pattern of argument. Bentham considers for potential use in his own theory a conception in ordinary use, or part of a powerful or influential theory. He observes that as ordinarily understood, it is either 'inflexible', 'allows no compromise', or is in some other way 'peremptory'. His response is either thoroughly to discredit the notion or to refashion it in such a way as to make it suitable for his purposes, with little regard for the distance he must drive the notion from ordinary usage to achieve this end. Consequently, whenever Bentham encountered conceptual materials essential for his theory which, in ordinary usage, introduced discontinuities into the essentially smooth topography of direct-utilitarian practical reasoning Bentham subjected them to a form of rational reconstruction which purged them of their exclusionary or peremptory character. Bentham seldom engaged in strictly conceptual or

[20] Hazlitt, *Political Essays*, 12.

linguistic analysis. As Mill and other contemporaries were quick to notice,[21] Bentham had little patience with such analyses. Rather than linguistic analyses, he sought substantive, working definitions or conceptions to which he assigned definite theoretical tasks. To illustrate this pattern let us look briefly at his early analysis of justice, his positivist account of rights and obligations, and his notion of command and its place in his theory of laws.

Justice. Consider first his early account of justice. Bentham observed that, as ordinarily understood, justice is associated with stable, fixed, and determinate standards of public conduct, whereas utility is associated with constantly fluctuating assessments at the mercy of changing circumstances: 'Utility is spoken of as something that will yield—justice as an inflexible line—something that will break rather than bend. Utility as applicable to many measures at a time and these opposite—Justice . . . as applicable to but one' (UC lxx(a). 17, 18). This stability is achieved by justice by excluding from practical deliberation the otherwise relevant considerations of the consequences of acting on the dictates of justice. In the extreme, we are called upon to do justice, though the heavens may fall. Bentham rejected this exclusionary or peremptory notion of justice, but he recognized the value of stability. This called for a reconstruction rather than a rejection of the concept of justice. Justice, Bentham held, is not to be identified with considerations essentially different from and conflicting with utility, but rather with an especially important *species of* utilities, viz. expectation utilities. In those contexts in which the virtue of justice is ordinarily thought to be controlling it will also be true, Bentham argued, that expectation utilities will be especially weighty. But consideration of expectation utilities does not block consideration of other relevant utilities which may call for contrary decisions or policies. They are to be considered alongside expectation utilities according to the usual utilitarian process of deliberation. Concerns of justice, properly understood, then, are in no way peremptory. *'Fiat justitia ruat coelum'* is not a rational principle, though it may be implied by justice ordinarily understood. If it is, then so much the worse for the ordinary conception of justice. The only rational conception of justice is that which reduces justice to a species of utility.

[21] See the observations of Mill and the writer in the *Edinburgh Review* quoted in the opening of Chapter 5. The manifesto for Bentham's unconditionally rationalist approach to legal and political theory can be found in the Preface of *FG*. See also UC xcvi. 60–71, published as App. F to the *Comment.*

Rights. Bentham's treatment of rights reveals a more complex and subtle strategy at work. First, all talk of extra-legal rights (moral rights, natural rights) is either rejected out of hand (as 'nonsense on stilts') or reduced to species of utilities in the manner (and even the language) of his analysis of justice. For example, he argues that talk of such rights is objectionable precisely because it 'admits of no compromise'. It absolutely excludes from practical political deliberation considerations which are clearly relevant to rational decision and action. Its peremptory character is irrational and obscurantist, and so he proposed: 'Instead of rights, talk of expectations' (UC xxix. 6). Similarly, for talk of natural rights against the government Bentham insisted that we substitute talk of 'securities against misrule'.[22] Thus, for the task of critically assessing and reconstructing basic political institutions we are best off abandoning the language of rights altogether, replacing it with explicitly utilitarian notions of security and expectations.

But Bentham realized that he could not do away with the concept of rights, and the correlative concept of obligation, entirely, for these are key building-blocks of any theory of law. Thus, he needed an analysis of legal rights and obligations which would meet his theoretical needs. His positivist analysis of these concepts is very familiar, so I can be brief. Rights are defined in terms of obligations. There are two species of rights: (i) 'naked rights', rights one has to do or have something just in case one has no obligation to refrain from doing it or to give it up; and (ii) 'vested rights', rights to do or have something just in case someone else has an obligation not to interfere with one's enjoyment of it (*Pannomial Fragments, Bowring* iii, 217–19). Rights, then, are benefits conferred or secured by obligations, and one has an obligation only if one is likely to suffer in some way if one fails to act in the prescribed way. More specifically, one has an obligation to ϕ, according to Bentham, just in case there is a rule (i.e. an authoritative command) directing one to ϕ and providing that if one fails to ϕ one is likely to suffer evil.[23] Rights, then, are benefits protected by coercive legal commands.

---

[22] *Securities Against Misrule, Bowring* viii, 557. For general discussions of Bentham's attack on the doctrine of natural rights see W. Twining, 'The Contemporary Significance of Bentham's *Anarchical Fallacies*', and Hart's 'Natural Rights: Bentham and John Stuart Mill', in his *Essays on Bentham*.

[23] This somewhat awkward statement of the analysis is designed to incorporate two essential elements of Bentham's account in one statement: (i) the necessary (and

This analysis of the concepts of obligation and rights is open to familiar objections. It has often been pointed out that it fails to capture the ways these notions are normally used by officials and subjects of the law. It reverses the conceptual relationship between obligation and sanction; for, as ordinarily understood, a sanction is imposed because (for the reason that) the obligation has been violated, rather than the obligation consisting in liability to suffering the sanction. Moreover, one who asserts that a person has an obligation is not making a prediction, or setting out some fact, about a future coercive response to his or her behaviour. Rather, one is assessing a certain kind of behaviour of the person, or saying something about the existence of reasons for that behaviour. This set of criticisms is often summed up by saying that Bentham's analysis fails to capture the 'normativity' of statements of obligation. 'Such statements', writes Hart, 'are not historical or factual statements describing the past, present or future actions, attitudes or beliefs of either subjects or officials of the legal system, but statements of what individuals legally must or must not do . . .'[24]

One might also raise a slightly different, but related, objection. David Lyons has argued that while rejecting moral (extra-legal) rights, utilitarians like Bentham and Mill have tried to accommodate genuine legal rights within utilitarian political theory.[25] Legal rights, according to this utilitarian view, are in themselves morally neutral (they lack normative force); but when such rights (or the institutions of which they are constituent parts) are morally justified, they are genuine rights invested with the moral force of rights. But this view is incoherent, says Lyons. Neither Bentham nor any other utilitarian can successfully accommodate genuine legal rights in a utilitarian political or legal theory. This is because if they are genuine rights, they must have the 'moral force' characteristic of rights and that consists of the power to exclude from practical con-

widely recognized) predictive element (see *Pannomial Fragments*, *Bowring* iii, 217; *FG* V. 7 n. c); and (ii) the equally important (though seldom recognized) requirement that the evil suffered upon disobeying the command is provided for by the command (see *IPML* III. 4, and Concluding Note, para. 6; *OLG* XI. 11, 12). Hart ably defends this interpretation of Bentham's 'mixed theory' of obligation in *Essays on Bentham*, 127–43.

[24] Hart, ibid. 144. See also P. M. S. Hacker, 'Sanction Theories of Duty', 131–70.

[25] Lyons, 'Utility and Rights', 107–38.

sideration a range of direct-utilitarian arguments regarding the exercise or interference with rights. However, Lyons argues,

utilitarian arguments for institutional design (the arguments that utilitarians might use in favor of establishing or maintaining certain legal rights) do not logically or morally exclude direct utilitarian arguments concerning the exercise of, or interference with, such rights. As a consequence, evaluation of conduct from a utilitarian standpoint is dominated by direct utilitarian arguments and therefore ignores the moral force of justified legal rights.[26]

This leads to incoherence, says Lyons, because the utilitarian insists, on utilitarian grounds, on including rights in his legal theory the moral force of which is ruled out by his utilitarianism.

Now the 'moral force' of rights, on which Lyons rests his argument, is their alleged peremptory character, precisely the property which troubled Bentham so much. Rights, understood according to Lyons (and, we may suppose, ordinary opinion), introduce discontinuities and exclusions into the essentially smooth and undifferentiated topography of utilitarian practical reasoning. Bentham fully recognized this feature of the ordinary conception of rights (whether legal or natural/moral). However, the charge of incoherence cannot be laid at his door.[27] For, although he sought to incorporate rights and obligations into his utilitarian legal theory, he did not attempt to incorporate these notions as ordinarily conceived. His analysis clearly has no room for this alleged peremptory moral or normative force of rights. And this does not seem to be an oversight on Bentham's part. Far from regarding this as a fault of his analysis of rights and obligations, Bentham would regard this as one of its virtues. It is the ordinary conception of rights, insisting as it does on this exclusionary property, that stands in need of revision. His positivist account of these notions is proposed as a substitute for the ordinary conception, a reconstruction of the ordinary notion, purged of (for Bentham) the insupportable assumption that

[26] Ibid. 110.

[27] In an aside Lyons says that Bentham never squarely faced this issue of the moral force of rights justified on utilitarian grounds. Bentham assumed, he says, 'either that, once the rules are justified, they must be followed; or else that particular cases simply cannot arise such that the justified rules require one thing and the direct application of the utilitarian standard to those cases requires another' (ibid. 125). It should be clear from the above discussion, from Chapter 5 onwards, however, that this is far from true. Indeed, it would be more accurate to say that from the outset of his career in the 1770s Bentham was obsessed with this problem.

rights and obligations introduce discontinuities into the process of practical reasoning. The 'normativity' of claims about rights or obligations is captured to the extent rationally possible, according to Bentham, by the notions of command or directive plus sanction. But neither directives nor sanctions introduce any new *kinds* of practical reasons, nor do they operate as 'exclusionary reasons' blocking appeal to other relevant considerations. Rather, they introduce new or additional reasons for acting in prescribed ways. But these are reasons of essentially the same sort, and subject to the same utilitarian operations as other practical reasons one might have. On Bentham's account, legal rules (and their progeny, rights and obligations) do not alter the structure of practical reasoning under law, they merely add new reasons.

It appears, again, that Bentham's underlying commitment to a direct-utilitarian theory of practical reasoning led him to appropriate concepts essential for his legal and political theory from our ordinary conceptual repertory, and to reconstruct them along distinctively positivistic lines. A positivist analysis of legal standards is called for not only by the utilitarian tasks of co-ordinating social interaction and securing expectations, but also by his utilitarian conception of practical reasoning. The former is guaranteed by the fact that both the content and the validity of positivist legal standards are to be determined by criteria concerned with certain matters of determinate social facts and not concerned with the moral quality of the rules. The latter is guaranteed by the fact that such legal standards may introduce relevant considerations into the practical reasoning of officials and subjects governed by the laws, but these considerations will not be in any way peremptory.

Commands. Finally, Bentham's direct-utilitarian programme of conceptual reconstruction can also explain an otherwise puzzling feature of his positivist definition of law. On Bentham's definition, laws are a species of command, but Hart has recently pointed out that Bentham's analysis of commands is problematic. According to Bentham, a command is the expression of a volition (intention, or 'wish') regarding the conduct of others.[28] But in addition to this

---

[28] 'What a Law is', UC lxix. 70–1; *OLG* I, XIII. Hart, *Essays on Bentham*, 242–55 criticizes Bentham's analysis of commands on the grounds that he fails to grasp the distinction between *expressing* a sentiment or intention and *stating* that one *has* the sentiment or intention. This criticism, I believe, is unfair and based on a mistaken reading of Bentham's philosophical doctrine that all language is a sign of thought (*Bowring* viii, 329). See my 'Facts, Fictions, and Law', esp. 55–7.

psychological dimension of commands, there is a social dimension. For commands are only a species of wish distinguished from other species in terms of the *social relations of power* between the person expressing the wish and the person to whom the wish is directed. A command is a wish of a person superior in power to another regarding the action of the inferior.[29]

Hart argues that this analysis of commands is inadequate at least for the reason that it fails to take account of the fact that 'where a command is sincere the commander intends the expression of this intention to function as at least part of the hearer's reasons for doing the act in question'.[30] Hobbes captures better the concept of command, Hart claims, when he says 'Command is when a man saith do this or do not do this yet without expecting any other reason than the will of him that saith it.'[31] In Hart's view, Hobbes grasped, as Bentham failed to do, that the commander intends that his intention regarding the other person's action be taken by that person *as itself* a reason for so acting, to the exclusion of deliberation of his own regarding the reasons there may be for doing what he is commanded to do. The command, Hart maintains,

is intended to preclude or cut off any independent deliberation by the hearer of the merits pro and con of doing the act. The commander's expression of will therefore is not intended to function within the hearer's deliberations as a reason for doing the act, not even as the strongest or dominant reason, for that would presuppose that independent deliberation was to go on, whereas the commander intends to cut off or exclude it.[32]

Commands, properly understood, says Hart, are meant to be peremptory in just this way.

Hobbes, it seems, displayed a subtler grasp of the concept than Bentham, *if* Bentham sought to give an analysis of the ordinary concept.[33] But it is a little surprising that Bentham, a careful student

---

[29] 'What a Law Is', UC lxix. 144; see also *Pannomial Fragments, Bowring* iii, 223. Hart does not take notice of this important component of Bentham's account of commands.

[30] Hart, *Essays on Bentham*, 252.

[31] Hobbes, *Leviathan* XXV.

[32] Hart, *Essays on Bentham*, 253. This point is even stronger than Hobbes's, for it seems to say that the command cannot operate as both a peremptory reason excluding other considerations *and* a positive reason for action. But, surely, that is what Hobbes intends in the passage above.

[33] And assuming Hart is correct. For criticism of this analysis of commands (and implicitly of authority) see J. Raz, 'Authority and Justification', 7.

of Hobbes, should have advanced an analysis so clearly inferior to Hobbes's own account. It is more plausible to think that Bentham explicitly rejects this Hobbesian analysis of commands, and the ordinary notion, if Hobbes was right. This does not seem arbitrary, if we keep in mind the underlying utilitarian motivation of his positivist theory of laws. For Hobbes, the peremptory character of legal standards was essential, for on his understanding of the fundamental tasks of law, it was essential that laws (sovereign commands) replace the self-defeating attempts at rational decision-making by individuals with the peremptory demands of the sovereign. Bentham had adopted a different conception of the basic social problem to which law is addressed and the fundamental task of the law, as a result. Furthermore, Bentham did not have the radical fear of individual rational decision-making that Hobbes and Common Law jurists had. On the contrary, as we have seen, he regarded any attempt to shackle or confine the critical and deliberative rational powers of individuals as intolerable manipulation of will by will. His ideal was, rather, direction of the understanding by the understanding (see below pp. 368–70). He sought a view of law which could ensure submission of conduct to the social order without requiring submission of judgment (*Comment* 346), and which could hope to secure compliance not by way of mindless obedience, but through allegiance based on conviction (*FG*, Preface, pp. 399–400). Law could not be conceived along Hobbesian lines without threatening this underlying ideal.

Law, then, on Bentham's view, is a command. But no expression of will regarding the actions of others in itself yields any reason to act. If commands give reason, it is because there is always the probability of suffering a sanction for failing to comply, or because there are independent utilitarian reasons for performing the prescribed act. Law, on this conception, must be capable of addressing those who, for various reasons, are motivated to act in ways that maximize the welfare of the community. That is, law must be conceived in such a way that rational obedience is possible. Of course, it is a grave mistake to expect all people to be motivated by beneficence, and so there must always be sanctions. But, even here, laws do not seek to block normal rational deliberative processes of human beings. They do not seek to remove from the subject the prerogative of deliberation and decision on the merits. They merely address additional, perhaps compelling, reasons for complying.

Now, one might object at this point that Bentham's analysis has gone too far, even for his own purposes. For he seems to assume, with Hart and Hobbes, that any account of commands and authority that recognizes the 'exclusionary' character of appeals to authority requires surrender of individual judgment. But, one might object, this is a mistake, for what concerns the commander or person in authority is not what the person addressed thinks, but how that person *acts*. And clearly that is Bentham's concern here too (see *Comment* 346). So commands and authoritative directives do not preclude deliberation, or critical evaluation or assessment of them or of the basis of the claimed authority. They only preclude *acting* on these deliberations.[34]

The alternative analysis of commands and authority suggested in this objection, I suspect, would not appeal to Bentham. For it still divorces action from rational deliberation. But Bentham sought to secure submission of conduct (rather than judgment) through direction of *reasons to* the 'understanding', rather than excluding them from the scope of its competence. These reasons are primarily the reasons of the laws themselves, and supplementally the reasons added by the sanctions. Thus, if we assume that the concept of authority must be defined in terms of some form of exclusion or peremptoriness, then Bentham might be said to have erected a conception of law which *rejects* the notion of authority and rests solely on the notions of reasons and sanctions. It is clearly a reductionist account of law, but one with a normative, rather than conceptual or metaphysical motivation.

If this is right, then it is Austin, not Bentham, who introduced Hobbesian authoritarianism into classical positivism. Austin seems to embrace Bentham's enlightenment rationalism in its utilitarian dress. But, unlike Bentham, he allows that only an intellectual élite can be safely permitted to be guided in their deliberations and decisions by the principle of utility.[35] Citizens simply are incapable of such an effort, and so, may not act on utilitarian considerations (even though these considerations are the appropriate standards for assessment of actions). They must act, rather, on authority; that is, on rules which are in fact dictated by utility, but are not known by the citizens to be so, or at least are not acted on for that reason. The

---

[34] Ibid. 7.
[35] J. Austin, *The Province of Jurisprudence Determined*, Lecture III. See R. B. Friedman, 'An Introduction to Mill's Theory of Authority'.

bulk of the population must accept on faith the deliverances of the utilitarian élite. Austin, it seems, is closer to the Common Law tradition than would first appear. For this approach differs in motivation from the traditionalist Common Law approach only in the substitution of the wisdom of the utilitarian élite for the wisdom of the ages. Both define authorities which no individual citizen is regarded as competent to challenge. This departs radically from both the letter and the spirit of Bentham's utilitarian positivism.

9.4 NORMATIVE DIMENSIONS OF JURISPRUDENCE

You sober people who feel well armed against passion and fantasies . . . You call yourselves realists and hint that the world really is the way it appears to you . . . you are still burdened with those estimates of things that have their origin in the passions and loves of former centuries.

Nietzsche, *The Gay Science.*

Lon Fuller observed many years ago that, unlike Austin and the Analytic Jurists after him, Hobbes openly defended his positivist conception of law on normative political grounds.[36] It is evident from our study of British legal theory from Hobbes to Bentham that Hobbes was not unique in this respect. We encountered general accounts or theories of the *nature* of law, and even *definitions* of law, but in each case they were not exercises in a priori metaphysics or conceptual analysis but were firmly grounded in reflection on familiar legal practice and its point and on the appropriate tasks or functions of law in society. This might have been expected from theorists in the Common Law tradition which took pride in blurring the distinction between the descriptive and the normative, but it is initially surprising to find it also in Hobbes and even more surprising in Bentham. But the evidence is overwhelming that, despite their insistence that the criteria for identification of *laws* be purged of all moral or evaluative conditions, they never sought to defend an account of the *nature of law* by appeal solely to morally neutral social facts, or a priori conceptual or linguistic analysis. Bentham's radical linguistic revisionism is clearly incompatible with the suggestion that he simply sought a definition of the ordinary concept of law. In fact, he believed that there was no one thing generally

[36] Lon L. Fuller, *The Law in Quest of Itself*, 28, 75.

meant by the term 'law' (UC lxix. 86). But it would be a mistake to regard his as merely a stipulative definition of law, useful for the purposes to which he sought to put it. For he did not regard himself as merely offering a *different* conception of law from Blackstone's; he saw his as a superior *rival*. The Common Law conception *distorted* the law and legal practice. Again and again we saw Bentham pointing to the facts of this practice and of judicial reasoning to support his charge of distortion at the hands of Common Law theorists, and to support his own contentions about proper judicial decision making. Bentham's stipulative definition of law—if that's what it is—rides piggy-back on a deep substantive *theory* of law and its practice. In this one respect all the jurists we have discussed seem to have agreed, although obviously they offered sharply contrasting theories.

This account of the work of Bentham and his Common Law opponents is confirmed by Sir Henry Maine. Maine's theory of social institutions led him to conclude that in pre-modern societies traditional history (like that at the core of Common Law theory) was essential for the understanding and legitimation of law, but that it is a mark of emerging modern societies and political structures that history of that sort was no longer essential. Appeal to sovereignty and formally validated statutory law replaced appeal to history and tradition in the identification and legitimation of law. Thus, Maine argued, by completely divorcing law from traditionary history, the two great modern geniuses of legal thought, Hobbes and Bentham, became the greatest historians of their day. While they

failed to see a great deal which can only be explained by the help of history, they saw a great deal which even in our day is imperfectly seen by those who, so to speak, let themselves drift with history. Sovereignty and Law, regarded as facts, had only gradually assumed a shape in which they answered to the conception formed by Hobbes [and] Bentham . . . , but the correspondence really did exist by their time and was tending constantly to become more perfect.[37]

On Maine's reading of the history of the period, the conflict between the Common Law and positivist conceptions of law reflected

---

[37] Sir Henry Maine, *Lectures on the Early History of Institutions*, 396–7. Maine adds Austin to this list, but I agree with Fuller (*Quest*, Lecture I) that the motivation behind Austin's jurisprudence was quite different. Despite Bentham's contribution to what he called 'Universal Jurisprudence', Austin was the first major English-speaking Analytic Jurist.

rival views of a practice in transition. Each had a right, to some extent, to claim that their own theory better captured the nature and foundations of legal practice. However, Common Law sought to block the spread of what they regarded as distorting influences that threatened the integrity of that practice, while the positivists seized upon the new developments as the pivot around which to shape a new conception of the nature and point of that practice.

Fuller complained that something happened between Hobbes and Austin that drove positivism to hide its normative origins like an unpleasant family secret. But it looks as if this embarrassment within the positivist family arose much later, in fact in the generation sired by Bentham himself. It is a matter of dispute whether we should view Austin as a wayward child setting modern jurisprudence on a sterile and confused path, or rather as the spokesman for a positivism philosophically come of age—come of age, because the earlier position seemed incoherent, or at least in deep tension and unclear about its own identity.

The latter has been the dominant view for over a century, at least in English-speaking nations. Jules Coleman argued recently, for example, that

Legal positivism makes a conceptual, or analytic claim about law, and that claim should not be confused with programmatic or normative interests certain positivists, especially Bentham, might have had. Ironically, to hold otherwise is to build into the conceptual account of law a particular normative theory of law; it is to infuse morality, or the way law ought to be, into the concept of law (or account of the way law is). In other words, the argument for ascribing certain tenets to positivism in virtue of the positivist's normative ideal of law is to commit the very mistake positivism is so intent on drawing attention to and rectifying.[38]

Coleman, like Olivecrona, would convict Bentham of internal inconsistency. But even if Bentham intended to construct a theory of law on normative grounds one might press the objection, as David Lyons has, that the enterprise itself rests on a logical error. For, he argues, conceptual analysis is always logically prior to evaluation. Before we can know what a good X would be, or what sort of Xs there are, we need to know what it is to be an X. Disagreement over what laws are just or wise or what rights we have *presupposes*

---

[38] J. Coleman, 'Negative and Positive Positivism', 147.

agreement about what it is to be a law or to have a right.[39] Although the relevant concepts may change over time, at any point in time there must be 'sufficiently determinate and relatively stable criteria of application based on common usage' if normative discussion and dispute can be carried on at all. Bentham, it seems, went wrong because he tried to do two different things at the same time: 'He tried to lay the conceptual groundwork for a system of social control that he thought would be maximally useful to create and maintain. At the same time, he tried to reveal the conceptual foundations of an existing system of social control, namely law.'[40] In fact, Lyons concludes, Bentham's project of conceptual revision *presupposes* the sharp distinction between analysis and evaluation, because that project requires comparison of the relative utility of alternative conceptual schemes, and requires first the accurate identification and analysis of the existing set of concepts.[41]

Now, I do not think Bentham always kept clearly before his mind the difference between developing an account of the nature of law (inevitably drawing upon normative or evaluative considerations)—an account of law *as it is*—on the one hand, and arguing for a set of concepts it would be useful to adopt in order to make law more useful to us, on the other. Some of the textual evidence discussed above is at least ambiguous on this score. His account of the nature of law would probably have been different, and to my mind more plausible, if he had paid more attention to the distinction. It would be a mistake, however, to follow these critics of Bentham in condemning the entire enterprise as internally inconsistent and logically incoherent. I do not accept Bentham's theory of law, but I am largely in sympathy with his conception of the jurisprudential enterprise. In the remainder of this chapter I wish to say a few words in defence of this conception. The issues are rather larger than can be adequately addressed in a work such as this, but I hope to indicate the direction in which a defence of what we might call 'normative jurisprudence' might go.[42]

Note, first, that there is no internal inconsistency involved in Bentham's insisting *on normative grounds* (even *exclusively* on

[39] Lyons, 'Founders and Foundations of Legal Positivism', 727–9.

[40] Ibid. 729.

[41] Ibid. 729–30.

[42] In different ways, and with quite different results, this question has recently been addressed by Raz in 'The Problem about the Nature of Law', R. Dworkin, in 'Law as Interpretation', and D. Lyons, 'Moral Aspects of Legal Theory'.

normative grounds) on a definition of law in 'flatly descriptive and morally neutral' terms. For such a definition attempts to sketch in rather broad and abstract terms (to be filled in later by supplemental, lower-level legal theory) the criteria of legal validity—or the truth conditions of propositions of law—in our legal practice (and perhaps, but not necessarily, practices distant from our own). It is clearly one thing to impose rigid positivist constraints on what can count as such criteria, restricting them to a canonical list of 'social facts'; but it is quite another thing, not at all required by stringent positivism at the level of content of these criteria, to impose such constraints on the kinds of arguments that may be advanced in favour of recognizing such criteria.[43] There is an inconsistency in Bentham's view only if it is assumed that he embraces the core assumption of Analytical Jurisprudence, viz. that jurisprudence must proceed by way of a priori analysis of legal concepts which can be sharply separated, for purposes of analysis, from the practical context within which they live. But it is clearly a mistake to attribute this assumption to Bentham. Furthermore, the assumption is highly implausible.

It is, of course, common ground that any theory which purports to give an account of the *nature* of law must remain faithful to 'the facts', and not substitute some new creation for them. But it is not agreed that these are metaphysical or logical 'facts' or even facts of linguistic practice (if we assume that linguistic facts are somehow divorced from the larger practice in which the language finds its home). These are general philosophical assumptions which jurisprudence need not accept, and in fact should view with scepticism.

Analytical Jurisprudence rests on a problematic philosophy of language. It mistakenly assumes that the concepts we use can be divorced from the language of everyday life in which they function. But language shapes thought, and language emerges from shared practices and patterns of meaningful human activity. It seems possible to abstract concepts from the practices in which they live because we find it possible to give more or less schematic definitions

---

[43] 'The [positivist] doctrine of the nature of law yields a test for identifying law the use of which requires no resort to moral or any other evaluative argument. But it does not follow that one can defend the doctrine of the nature of law itself without using evaluative (though not necessarily moral) arguments. Its justification is tied to an evaluative judgment about the relative importance of various features of social organizations and these reflect our moral and intellectual interests and concerns.' Raz, 'The Problem about the Nature of Law', 217–18.

of terms (analyses of concepts), definitions which may capture only a small part of the body of beliefs and attitudes which constitute the practice, and shape the concept. To develop richer and more detailed accounts and theories is not necessarily to engage in a process different in kind from giving a definition or analysis of the concept. It may, in fact, simply involve enriching and deepening our understanding of *the concept*.[44] Conceptual analysis is not sharply distinct from the enterprise of gaining an understanding of the practices and forms of life in which the concepts have their life.

I am not prepared here to defend this general thesis in the philosophy of language, but even if it is not true for language (and conceptual analysis) generally, it is true for the language of law and politics. General jurisprudence—reflection on the nature of law and adjudication—involves reflection on, and an attempt systematically to understand, our most general beliefs concerning our legal practice. It is the enterprise of giving determinate shape to the structuring beliefs and attitudes of our legal experience, or 'legal sensibility' to use Cliford Geertz's suggestive phrase.[45] But these beliefs and attitudes cannot without distortion be divorced from the larger practice of which they are a part and which gives them point and substance.

However, law *by design* concerns itself with matters of individual and community good which are of potentially highest priority and are constantly open to dispute—values, aims, and goals which are always open to redefinition and reassessment. It is not surprising, then, that the general structuring beliefs of our legal sensibility may themselves be controversial. Critics of the enterprise of normative jurisprudence are correct to point out that in order for there to be disagreement at the relatively more concrete level of judgments of the justice or wisdom of laws or even what laws there are, there must be common ground between disputants. But it is not necessary, and in this context it is highly unlikely, that what is shared are

---

44 Commenting on Mark Platts's notion of 'semantic depth' (*Ways of Meaning*, 262) Sabina Lovibond describes how conceptual analysis of this sort might proceed: 'We start . . . with a minimal, schematic understanding of the meaning of a moral term, such as might be captured in a dictionary definition; then, by exploring those aspects of life which moral terms pick out, we can *enrich* our understanding of those terms without it being the case that we ever come to mean something *different* by "courage" (for example) from what we meant at an earlier stage of the exploratory process' (*Realism and Imagination in Ethics*, 31–2).

45 C. Geertz, *Local Knowledge*, 175.

criteria for the proper use of the relevant concepts. For, because of the reciprocal influence of general and specific beliefs and judgments, often where there are disputes at the level of concrete judgments there will be disputes regarding these criteria as well. (Recall again Bentham's observation that 'no one entire thing is meant by a Law'—UC lxix. 86.) Disputants, however, do have common ground: the shared practice in which they participate, to which they are committed, and within which alone their dispute takes on meaning.

Jurisprudential theory, then, even when it appears to be engaged in conceptual analysis, is focused on the task of giving an account of legal institutions, and the practice and 'sensibility' that breathe life into them. This accounting can never limit itself to simple description. It is essentially a matter of *characterization* or interpretation. For these practices are not mere and mindless habits, or behavioural routines with no intrinsic significance to those who execute them. They are intelligible social enterprises with a certain, perhaps very complex, *meaning* or *point*. In fact, the law is not merely a device for regulating behaviour; it is a complex structure of discourse within which behaviour is *construed* (and on this construal action is taken and evaluations of it are formed). The context of law gives behaviour meaning; sense is made of it. And this constructive, interpretive power is rooted in the collective resources of the practice. Law is an '*Anschauung* in the market-place'.[46]

This must be refined: it may be *true* that law is merely an instrument for regulating social behaviour, but this is not a brute or 'objective' fact about law (even less a brute fact about law in *any* society or *any* culture). If the claim is true, it is true in virtue of a *social fact*, a fact about the point or function of law as viewed by its self-identified participants.[47]

We must note here two important features of intepretations or characterizations. As Charles Taylor has pointed out, simple descriptions can be accurate or inaccurate, and their inaccuracy can be shown by pointing to new or overlooked facts or evidence, but when characterizations fail they *distort* the reality they seek to interpret. And, after a point, no mere showing, or marshalling of more evidence, will settle a dispute regarding the truth of the characterization. That question will turn on the strength and plausibility

[46] Ibid.

[47] For a very helpful discussion of the distinction between 'objective' and 'social' facts see R. Brandom, 'Freedom and Constraint by Norms'.

of the sense, point, or meaning attributed to those facts. Thus, because they do not merely ascribe properties to objects, but instruct us about how to think about them, characterizations do not leave the phenomena unchanged.[48] In consequence, characterizations are always open to challenge.

Characterizations of legal practice are open to challenge for the further reason that the point or meaning attributed to the facts of the practice is inevitably tied up with moral or evaluative concerns which are fundamental, at least to participants in the practice. This is due to the fact, already noted, that the law by design concerns itself with individual and social interests, values, rights, and goals. Furthermore, law is typically appealed to in attempts to justify the organized use of coercion and the exercise of authority over persons in society.

But, then, it should be clear that no theory, even one which restricts itself to rather general and abstract characterizations of legal practice, or analyses of its structuring concepts, can be divorced from consideration of the aim, point, or function of the institutions of law without distortion of those institutions. And thus, no account of the nature of law can hope to advance our understanding of law and legal practice without relying at important points on normative considerations.

Note, this does not imply that a theory of the nature of law must show that the beliefs and attitudes of self-identified participants in the legal practice are in fact *justified*—for example, that they are correct in believing that appeals to law actually do justify official use of coercion, or that the aims or goals or tasks assigned to law are right and proper. It only requires that legal theorists frame their accounts of the nature of law in terms that take such participant beliefs into account and make them intelligible.[49]

[48] C. Taylor, 'Responsibility for Self', 286, 294–6. As Lon Fuller once wrote, 'In human affairs even what men mistakenly accept as real tends, by the very act of their acceptance to become real.' 'Positivism and Fidelity to Law', 631.

[49] Thus, general jurisprudential theory is inevitably *local*, at least in first approximation. Jurisprudential theories are first of all theories of *familiar*, that is local, legal practice (where 'local' may be understood to embrace an entire legal culture, not just a single jurisdiction). That is the home environment of the relevant concepts; they are inevitably shaped by this environment. Discussion of more distant legal practices is possible, but it will always involve *translation* of the idiom of that practice into our own. (See Brandom, 190–1.) The 'point' of that practice may not sharply mirror our views of *our* practice, but it will have to be constructed in terms of aims and values we can recognize as intelligible moral or political aims and values. (This, of course, does not require that we endorse them.)

And especially where the legal practice is our own, the choice between rival general theories of law, as Fuller once put it, is not 'between what we already have and striving after the unattainable', but 'between two kinds of striving'.[50] And, we could add, it is, at the same time, a choice between two (or more) ways of understanding what it is we already have. This, it seems to me, is the most profitable way of viewing the dispute between Bentham and the Common Law tradition. There is no incoherence involved in the jurisprudential enterprise as they conceived it. In fact, we only deceive ourselves if we think we can avoid the complications and 'messiness' of such a discussion by treating reflection on the nature of law on the model of the Analytical Jurists. The complications do not go away, they are merely silently ignored. Contemporary jurisprudential thought, an intrinsic part of the practice it seeks to characterize, is the child of its history and the history of the practice. We are, as Nietzsche reminds us, 'still burdened with those estimates of things that have their origin in the passions and loves of former centuries'.[51]

---

[50] Fuller, *Quest*, 12.
[51] F. Nietzsche, *The Gay Science*, para. 57.

Part III
Law, Utility, and Adjudication

10

The Judge as *Paterfamilias*

In short, the judge, as conceived by Bentham's doctrine, is a kind of
monarch isolated in his tribunal, delivering his sentences without
legal forms, and without any really efficacious control to prevent
eventual abuses of power, other than the purely moral control
exercised on him by public opinion.

Halévy, *Philosophic Radicalism.*

WE are now in a position to indicate more precisely the structure
of Bentham's general theory of law. At the foundation of this
theory is a normative account of the functions and natural limits of
law which itself rests on a more general social and political theory
structured by the principle of utility. Against this background two
complementary partial theories are developed: (*a*) a theory of *laws*,
consisting of (i) a strictly formal account of criteria of identification
of general propositions of law, as well as other concerns of universal jurisprudence, and (ii) a utilitarian theory of legislation (i.e. a
theory concerned with the *content*, not the form or structure of the
law); and (*b*) a theory of *adjudication* consisting of (i) a detailed
constitutional theory and theory of judicial procedure, and (ii) an
account of practical judgment in adjudication. The principle of
utility permeates this general theory. It not only determines the
general shape of the theory, but it also influences the substance of
the theories, and appears as the basic principle of rationality in
both the theory of legislation and the theory of adjudication.

After his radical critique of Common Law, both as a system of
laws and as a theory of adjudication, Bentham embarked on a
career-long attempt to produce an alternative which more adequately meets the criteria of his background utilitarian theory.
The basic outlines of the formal part of this theory of laws were
settled with the writing of *Of Laws in General* and the development
of the conceptual and technical machinery needed for an ideal
utilitarian code of laws. The theory of legislation was also settled in
outline reasonably early, although he spent most of his life working

out the details. But his theory of adjudication took a long time to develop. It is this latter part of the general theory which I shall discuss in this and the next two chapters.

Halévy's assessment of Bentham's late work on judicial procedure and organization quoted in the epigraph of this chapter[1] is sure to startle any one coming fresh from reading *Of Laws in General* or *A Comment on the Commentaries.* Yet this criticism is directed at a major strand in the complex fabric of Bentham's theory of adjudication. The picture of the judicial role one gets from Bentham's extensive writings on procedure and the structure of the judiciary is remarkably different from that which emerges from his writings on Blackstone and the Common Law. This is not to say that Bentham had two quite distinct, and possibly conflicting, conceptions of the judicial role, but rather that he highlighted different aspects of his conception according to his immediate needs. Nowhere do we find a complete, unified statement of his theory of adjudication. He left this task for others. As a result of this fact, focusing attention on any single discussion of adjudication in his corpus, to the exclusion of others, is likely to distort one's perception of the theory as a whole. One important source of such distortion is his powerful and relentless attack on judicial legislation. But if we can filter out for a moment that distorting light, important and otherwise easily overlooked details of Bentham's theory of adjudication emerge. This is the task of the present chapter.

Although Bentham recognized that any adequate theory of adjudication must be closely related to a theory of laws, he did not regard his theory of adjudication as merely a direct corollary of his positivist account of laws. He believed that even after the theory of laws is put on a firm and rational basis, work still remains to be done. In his view, the proper definition of the judicial role and a proper understanding of the nature, scope, and limits of judicial decision-making could only be achieved through attempting to solve central problems of the design of adjudicative institutions and procedures. The principle on which he based his construction of adjudicative institutions was drawn from his analysis of the defects of Common Law, especially his view that it is self-defeating to attempt to structure judicial decision-making by means of fixed rules in order to constrain arbitrariness and abuse of power (see 8.2

[1] E. Halévy, *The Growth of Philosophic Radicalism*, 403.

and 8.3). His basic assumption was that it is not by means of rules or principles *internal* to the decision process that limitations on judicial activity are most effectively imposed, but by means of structural, institutional constraints *external* to the decision process. Bentham came to this view quite early in his career, but it was not worked out in any detail until 1790 and did not receive full development until after the turn of the nineteenth century when he began work on his procedure and constitutional codes. We cannot hope, then, to construct a complete or faithful account of Bentham's views on adjudication unless we pay special attention to his procedural and constitutional writings.

10.1 PROCEDURES WITHOUT RULES

[J]ustice . . . like gold, may be bought too dear.

Bentham, *RJE*

Upon coming of age, Bentham turned away from the practice of law for which he had been trained to the task of producing a programme for its radical reformation. Immediately, he recognized the need for a theoretical framework within which to work out his programme. To the end of constructing this framework he set for himself two closely related philosophical tasks: (i) the articulation and defence of a general moral and political theory, and (ii) the articulation of a general conception of law. From the outset (in the years 1770–4) he held that the second task is defined by the fundamental question: What is *a* (single, comprehensive, intelligible) law?[2] Attempting to answer this question, Bentham sought to devise a suitable model for the analysis of law which made it possible to distinguish various sorts of laws in terms of their functions, and to relate them in some general and systematic way. Two problems especially occupied him at this juncture: (i) the clarification of the nature of civil law and the relationship between civil and penal laws, and (ii) clarification of the relationship between procedural (and later constitutional) law and the substantive laws of the system. On both of these problems one can find sketches in Bentham's earliest work, as well as throughout his corpus.

---

[2] See the earliest outline of his major 'Work' on legislation, which occupied almost all of his time during this early period of his life, UC xcvi. 73–5; see *IPML*, Concluding Note, 2.

The ends of adjective law

The distinction between procedural and substantive law gave Bentham much less trouble than that between civil and penal law (see above, 5.3). The design and principles of operation of legal procedure cannot be considered in isolation from the operation of the rest of the legal system of which they are a part, he argued. The principles of judicial procedure, then, are fixed by the functional relationship that the law of procedure bears to the rest of the law. 'A Procedure Code, fit to be invested with the form of the law,' he writes, 'could not be prepared otherwise than by and with reference to the codes of law, penal and non-penal' (*PJP, Bowring* ii, 5). Thus, substantive law is, according to Bentham, 'radical', 'primary', and 'principal'; whereas procedural law is 'subservient', 'accessory', and 'adjective' (UC xcvi. 74–5; UC lxiii. 51–3). It is 'adjective' in two respects. First, as the adjective is dependent on the noun for its intelligibility, so, adjective law is *dependent* on substantive law. Second, adjective law *modifies* substantive law. The law of procedure exists only for the sake of giving efficacy ('execution and effect') to substantive law.[3] But in doing so it tends to impose *conditions* on the execution of substantive law. It follows that adjective law is both a necessary instrument of, and a potential obstacle to, the execution of substantive law.

As accessory to substantive law, adjective is aimed at the same goal as substantive law: security. 'The object of an establishment for the administration of justice is to afford the people security, and the sense of security in as far as it depends upon the due execution of the laws' (UC li(b). 310). Since criminal law was uppermost in his mind in his early work, procedure was viewed as the means necessary to make legal punishment 'certain'.[4] The fundamental and 'direct' end of adjective law is said in this early formation to be securing the proper execution of the substantive law. But a tension emerges here. Bentham analyses this fundamental end into two different ends: (i) the 'primary' or 'original' end of securing the punishment of *all* violators of the law, and (ii) the 'collateral' end of ensuring that *only* the guilty are punished (UC l. 30, 36). The

---

[3] UC lxiii. 29; *PJP, Bowring* ii, 6. Bentham's arguments for this 'instrumentalist' thesis are discussed in detail in my essay 'The Principle of Utility and the Law of Procedure', 1397–1407.

[4] Some of Bentham's earliest work on procedural matters is lumped together with work on the definition of offences under the general heading of 'Certainty'. See, e.g., UC l. 28–160, dating from the period 1770–4.

primary end generates 'active' procedural regulations, he says, while the collateral end generates 'restrictive' ones. These two ends may conflict, since the best means of ensuring that all the guilty are punished may tend to increase the number of innocent punished.

In *OLG* Bentham develops a sophisticated theory of these 'restrictive' procedural laws, which he there calls 'anaetiosostic' ('innocent-protecting') laws (*OLG* XI. 25–7), as part of a larger theory of qualifying laws (or partial laws).[5] Such qualifying laws fall into two classes. *Exculpative* conditions, i.e. legal excuses, directly qualify principal penal laws by qualifying the description of the offence (*OLG* XI. 22). *Exemptive* conditions, in contrast, qualify the subsidiary punitory laws, i.e. those which, according to Bentham's doctrine, impose duties on officials (and define procedures and instruments for them) to carry out the threat of punishment contained in the principal penal law.

Anaetiosostic laws are *limitations*, a subclass of exemptive conditions. 'Exceptions' and 'limitations', the two subclasses of exemptive conditions, are defined relative to the scope of the reasons given for the rules they qualify. *Exceptions* to the rule arise when the primary reasons for the rule are overridden in the circumstances by countervailing reasons. In such a case, there may still be reasons to follow the rule, but they are overridden in the circumstances. The rule is not abandoned, but only restricted by introducing an exception to cover just such circumstances. *Limitations*, in contrast, define the scope of the reasons on which the rule rests for its justification. Where there is a rule-plus-limitation—e.g. 'no one, save the owner of the property, may freely make use of it'—the reasons justifying the qualified rule do not extend to an unqualified version of the rule. Thus, considerations justifying a limitation do not conflict with the rationale behind a rule, but rather are entailed by it. They conflict only with the unqualified rule. Limitations express the boundaries of the general rule as defined by its rationale.

Thus, anaetiosostic laws are restrictions of a general rule imposing a duty on officials to see that all the guilty are punished. They are not, however, restrictions on the rationale underlying the institution of punishment to provide the most efficient and cost-effective deterrence of socially harmful behaviour possible—the relevant

---

[5] For a fuller discussion of 'anaetiosostic laws', and especially for reasons to resist an indirect-utilitarian interpretation of them (*pace* J. Rawls, 'Two Concepts of Rules', 8), see my 'The Principle of Utility and the Law of Procedure', 1410–21.

harms being defined by the principal penal laws. In fact, Bentham holds, innocent-protecting laws are *required* by this underlying goal of efficient and cost-effective deterrence. For assurance must be given to the public that they are more likely to avoid bad treatment at the hands of the law by compliance with, than by violation of, the penal laws. Thus, in the name of utility-defined 'economical deterrence', a balance must be struck between the primary end of punishing the guilty and the collateral end of protecting the innocent. This, clearly, is a balance to be struck on the scale of the principle of utility. The legislator will, in wholesale fashion, strike this balance by creating general regulations and procedures, but, as we shall see shortly this does not preclude judicial fine-tuning, also by appeal to the principle of utility, in particular cases.[6]

Collateral ends and judicial balancing

Bentham recognized that formal legal proceedings have their own transaction costs. This creates another, and more pervasive, tension between adjective and substantive law.

Very early in his career Bentham became aware of the enormous delays, expense, frustration, and injustice caused by the complexity and technicality of Common Law procedure. He deplored the suffering caused by this 'wiglomeration' (as Dickens later would call it).[7] This system, of course, had been 'sanctified throughout the whole civilized world by the testimony of Montesquieu'.[8] It represented to many the most refined system of checks and balances for the protection of individual liberty known to Europe. Following Montesquieu, Blackstone boasted

In Turkey, . . . where little regard is shewn to the lives or fortunes of the subject, all causes are quickly decided: the basha, on a summary hearing, orders which party he pleases to be bastinadoed, and then sends them about their business. But in free states the trouble, expense, and delays of judicial proceedings are the price that every subject pays for his liberty . . . [T]he formalities of law increase, in proportion to the value which is set on

[6] See ibid. 1419–21.

[7] C. Dickens, *Bleak House*, ch. viii.

[8] Halévy, *Philosophic Radicalism*, 375. 'If you examine the formalities of justice with relation to the pains with which a citizen is able to get his goods returned to him, or to get satisfaction for some outrage, you will doubtless find too many of them. If you look at them in relation to the liberty and the security of the citizens you will often find them too few; and you will see that the pains, the expenses, the delays, even the dangers of justice are the price which every citizen pays for his liberty.' Montesquieu, *Esprit des Lois*, Bk. vi, ch. ii, quoted in Halévy, 379.

the honour, the fortune, the liberty, and the life of the subject (3 *Comm.* 423–4).

On this view, the very complexity and technicality of Common Law procedures protect the individual from arbitrary state action.

Bentham regarded this as nonsense, even if it echoed the venerated Montesquieu.[9] Worse than nonsense, such sentiments stood as a 'screen for corruption', camouflage for the oppression and rapacious fraud which the legal corporation ('Judge & Co.') perpetrated with impunity upon the people for centuries.[10] Complication, he insisted repeatedly, is 'the nursery of fraud' (*Bowring* x, 531).

His cynicism, however, did not lead Bentham to think that the costs of formal proceedings could be eliminated entirely (without eliminating the procedures). Inconveniences—the 'delay, vexation, and expense'—caused by legal proceedings, he believed, are unavoidable. He admitted that they have some salutary effects: they tend to discourage frivolous suits, for example. But these advantages are quickly outweighed by the opportunities they provide for the rich and powerful to harass and interfere with the lives of those unable to fight back (*PJP, Bowring* ii, 9). Such transaction costs, therefore, must be minimized.

Hence, to the 'positive' end of adjudication—securing the execution and effect of the substantive law—must be added a second set of ends, the 'negative' (or, shifting his terminology, 'collateral') ends of 'minimizing the evil, the hardship, in various shapes necessary to the accomplishment of the main specified end'.[11] This catalogue of ends, with the principle of utility lying close in the background, provides 'the foundations of the rationale of procedure' (*PJP, Bowring* ii, 19).

But these ends are in constant conflict:

The execution of the Law is more and more uncertain the greater the number of conditions of procedure, and the more difficult any of them is to fulfil: every fresh condition that is annext to it, creates an additional

---

9 Bentham relied heavily on Montesquieu in his 'Essay on the Influence of Place and Time in Matters of Legislation' (*Bowring* i, 169–95). But he was highly critical of his views on liberty and constitutional arrangements (see *CC* 123). Bentham traced Montesquieu's theoretical weaknesses to the fact that, despite being a 'fine gentleman, and a philosopher', he was 'before anything of all this . . . a lawyer' (*Bowring* viii, 481).

10 *Bowring* viii, 481; see also 478–81; *Bowring* ii, 169–79; *Bowring* v, 1–53.

11 *PJP, Bowring* ii, 8; see also 17–19, *Scotch Reform, Bowring* v, 8–16; *Justice Petition, Bowring* v, 446–7; *IRE, Bowring* vi, 10.

chance of failure . . . In one shape therefore there is no such condition but what tends to defeat the purposes of the law: what can never therefore be dispensed with is that in another shape it should have a tendency to promote them.[12]

Resolution of the conflict is made possible by the fact that each of the ends is reducible, in Bentham's view, to a species of utility. They bear the same relation to the principle of utility that the ends of the civil law—security, subsistence, etc.—do (see above, 5.3). The conflict between these ends is resolvable by translating their claims into utilities and disutilities and maximizing the net utility. But, then, as Bentham clearly points out, if the transaction costs of the adjudicative procedures necessary to execute some substantive law exceed the benefits of that law's being executed, then 'the price ought not to be paid: the law ought rather to remain unexecuted' (*RJE*, Bowring vii, 335).

Because the conflict between these two sets of ends is pervasive, Bentham insists that the fundamental principle of procedural design is *simplicity*. For this reason Bentham was from the outset attracted to a rather romanticized model of domestic governance. 'The transactions of the Courts of judication', he maintained in what may be among his earliest manuscripts, 'are nothing but the transactions of the Nursery formalized and extended . . .'[13] 'The simplest mode of jurisdiction is that which is exercised by the father of a family when employed in settling disputes or punishing the behaviour of his children' (UC lvii. 6). The directness and informality of family decision-making makes them most 'natural' and the best model and ideal for collective decision-making procedures.

Bentham's model of the 'domestic tribunal' clearly shaped his conception of adjudication. Bentham resisted the introduction of formalities into the process, and he sought to eliminate the possibility of dismissal of cases on procedural technicalities. The question of the validity of the proceedings must not be settled by technical rules. Rather, it must be left to the *judge* to decide on his assessment of what is best in the circumstances, in particular whether the aggrieved party was injured in such a way as to jeopardize the ability of the court to get at the truth. The party aggrieved by violation of procedural formalities should automatically have a cause of action

[12] UC lxix. 204; see also UC lxix. 121, 199; UC li(a). 1; *RJE*, Bowring vii, 335.
[13] UC lxx(a). 6. See also among Bentham's earliest writings UC lxix. 119, 121; and his use of the model of the domestic tribunal in his first attempts to develop a theory of legal evidence at UC xlvi. 2–4.

against the party who violates the rules, but no automatic invalidation of the proceedings (UC lxiii. 5). The proceedings are invalidated *only if*, in the judgment of the magistrate, the violation makes it impossible.to achieve the basic ends of adjudication.

This is just a special case of Bentham's more general strategy of assigning to the judge, rather than to fixed formal rules, the task of resolving the inevitable conflict amongst the various ends of adjudication. This conflict is to be resolved, upon each occasion, by the judge appealing to the principle of utility.

[T]hroughout the whole field of Judicial Procedure, conflict . . . has place between the *direct* ends of justice . . . and the *collateral* . . . and on which side shall be the claim to preference, will, *in each individual instance*, depend upon the circumstances of the *individual case* (*CC* 463, emphasis added).

Similarly in manuscript material headed 'Procedure Code' (1825) Bentham insists that at each stage in the progress of a case the judge must give the reasons or grounds for his decisions, and that these reasons consist of appeals to the ends of justice—in each case a balance being struck between the good achieved by serving the direct end and the evil of contravening the collateral ends, or vice versa (UC liv. 17–18). In another manuscript under the same heading, Bentham praises his 'natural' system of procedure on account of its *flexibility*; that is, 'the provision it makes for minimizing evil in each individual case: according to the quantity of evil reasonably to be expected in different cases, giving the preference sometimes to the direct, sometimes to the collateral ends of justice' (UC lvii. 251).

Thus, the two conflicting sets of ends which define the proper objectives of procedure simply mark out the most important species of utility and disutility which the judge must weigh in each particular case to determine the appropriate way to proceed. Rules have a place in this scheme, but they never impose absolute requirements on decision or action and the judge is empowered to make decisions which appeal directly to the principle of utility.

Bentham's attitude towards procedural rules and judicial balancing of utilities is well illustrated in his recommendations regarding standard rules for the admission and weighing of evidence. Here, again, his model is 'the domestic tribunal', as is clear already in his earliest sketches for his theory of evidence.[14] The 'technical system'

[14] See UC li(a). 1–35 (early 1770s). A more sophisticated attempt which goes a long way towards settling Bentham's basic principles dates from 1780 to 1785, UC xlvi. 1–55.

of Common Law, he maintained, has so distorted the fact-finding
process, with its byzantine collection of exclusions, privileges, presumptions, rules of competence, and formulas for weighing testimony, that eventual arrival at the truth in any case was at best a
happy accident. But, he argued, truth is the foundation of justice
and to exclude evidence is to deny justice. It is simply a mistake to
think that misdecision can be avoided by excluding false or misleading evidence. It is a mistake because fixing rules for the exclusion of evidence is more likely to cause misdecision on deceptive
evidence (*IRE*, *Bowring* vi, 87). The more rational and natural
course is to mimic the domestic tribunal. There all evidence is heard
and the 'judge' (*paterfamilias*) must use his own judgment and
common sense to weigh it for its probative value (UC xlvi. 2, 4).

In its broad outlines, Bentham's theory of evidence is a straightforward application of his general utilitarian theory of procedure
to the special case of evidence. All evidence is prima facie admiss-
ible, because it is necessary for achieving the direct end of justice:
rectitude of decision. However, 'evidence, even justice itself, like
gold, may be bought too dear'. And it 'always is bought too dear, if
bought at the expense [i.e. price] of a preponderant injustice' (*RJE*,
Bowring vii, 336). The fundamental rule of evidence is: 'Let in the
light of evidence . . . except where the letting in of such light is
attended with preponderant collateral inconvenience, in the shape
of vexation, expense, and delay' (ibid.).

Thus, not all evidence may be admitted, for there will be cases in
which the direct ends, as well as cases in which the collateral ends,
of justice will be disserved to such an extent that the overall cost
will outweigh the benefit of having the evidence available to the
court. In such cases 'the exclusion may be pronounced, and, according to the principle of utility ought to be pronounced proper,
legitimate' (ibid.).

Furthermore, the task of making these discriminations of overall
utility, according to Bentham, cannot be accomplished with general
rules of admissibility constructed by legislators. It can be successfully accomplished, in his view, only by empowering judges to
make decisions in particular cases by appeal to the principle of
utility.

In each individual instance, to weigh mischief on one side against mischief
on the other, where occasion calls for it, will be a task suitable to the station
of the judge. To provide powers adequate to the taking of it, and acting in

conformity to the result, will in every case be an attention suitable to the station of the legislator (ibid.).

The task and duty of the legislator, then, is to empower the judge effectively to do justice in particular cases. The task and duty of the judge is to see that justice is done in each case before him. This doctrine has two implications: (*a*) the judge must focus his attention on the case before him and its consequences alone. His station is not to make general rules, and so he is not to concern himself with future, yet unspecified, cases (*RJE*, *Bowring* vii, 345). Nor is he to guide his decision by appeal to precedent-setting decisions of his own or of other judges (ibid.) (*b*) In this matter, as in all matters of procedure, the 'justice' required is that determined by the principle of utility as the appropriate balance of the 'aggregate ends of justice'. This is a determination best left to the discretion—the informed, utilitarian judgment—of the judge.

Therefore, the best strategy for the legislator concerned to provide a structure of judicial procedure which successfully realizes the ends of justice is to refrain from imposing fixed rules for either the admission or the weighing of evidence. Instead he should (i) provide the judge with the appropriate powers to make the decisions required, (ii) set out clearly the fundamental ends for which the judge is to strive, and (iii) provide instruction for the judge regarding what, on the best available evidence, are likely to be the best means to achieving these ends. These instructions may take the form of a set, or even a code, of rules, but they must be understood not as authoritative peremptory imperatives, but as guide-lines offering instruction regarding the probative force of evidence.[15]

Halévy, commenting on Bentham's theory of evidence, says that we find here 'the familiar argument of the Utilitarian economists against all fixed regulations, which are in contradiction with the mobile and progressive nature of the human intelligence. General rules about evidence are condemned like commercial and industrial regulations, because they are blind.'[16] But this is precisely the opposite of Bentham's motivation. Rather than leaving the determination of 'particular (utilitarian) justice' to some 'invisible hand' —thereby hoping to achieve the utilitarian goal of maximal

---

[15] See, e.g., *RJE*, Bk. X, entitled 'Instructions to be delivered from the legislator to the judge, for the estimation of the probative force of evidence' (*Bowring* vii, 563–7). See also the parallel passage in *IRE*, *Bowring* vi, 151 (and 151–75 generally).

[16] Halévy, *Philosophic Radicalism*, 385.

happiness in the community through judicial indirection—Bentham insists that judges take the matter of doing justice directly in their own hands. It is not so much classical economic doctrine which Bentham reflects here as the attitudes and suspicions of the radical seventeenth-century reformers.[17]

10.2 ADJUDICATION ON THE DOMESTIC MODEL

State law and judicature is family law and judicature upon a large scale.

Bentham, UC xxx. 69.

'Justice is in itself simple', Bentham insisted. 'It is the same for one man as for another: it is only legislators who, by the advice of lawyers, have complicated it, and torn it into shreds' (*Bowring* iv, 334). And if justice itself is simple, the structures of law which are designed to deliver simple justice must themselves be simple. Domestic dispute settlement was, in his view, the 'simplest mode of jurisdiction' (UC lvii. 6). In the family, says Bentham, the father gets to the truth and renders his decision with a minimum of fuss, a maximum of direct participation of the disputing parties, and a maximum of justice. It is swift, inexpensive, open, and understandable; it operates simply on common sense. Because of this, no specialized art must be mastered, and no professional intermediaries are needed (*Justice Petition, Bowring* v, 438).

This model is 'natural', i.e. its virtues are immediately apparent to common sense, Bentham argues: furthermore it has been exemplified in familiar political institutions. Occasionally, he was moved to draw attention to the parallel between the 'domestic tribunal' and the legendary Turkish Cadi who, sitting in his gate, deals out fully particularized justice.[18] In his more petulant moments, he was inclined to defend this form of adjudication against what he regarded as the misguided 'liberal' attacks of the followers of Montesquieu; at least to defend it against the claim that it is inferior to

---

[17] See below, n. 22.

[18] 'The whole train of Adjective law is dispensed with in Despotic Government which comes nearest in its simplicity to the domestic. The Cade [sic] without form or precept takes cognizance of a complaint, and without delay of pleading or the intervention of official functions, issues his definitive command upon the spot' (UC lxix. 119). Bentham's language here is almost exactly that of Blackstone's at 3 *Comm.* 423–4 (see above, pp. 344–5), but the tone is exactly the opposite.

the justice meted out in English courts.[19] But this appeal to the figure of the Cadi was bound to fail as a rhetorical strategy; the Cadi was too deeply entrenched as a figure of political absurdity in the minds of the English public. In the political consciousness at the time, the Cadi represented both all that was arbitrary, irrational, and inscrutable in the Oriental mind, and the dangers of absolutism close to home. Fully aware of this, Bentham more frequently relied on the more powerful and familiar rhetorical strategy of appeal to the Saxon golden age.

Often he argued that the domestic model has been exemplified throughout the history of England—in isolated pockets after the Norman invasion, but in an exemplary way in the decentralized structure of manorial and hundreds courts in pre-Norman times.[20] Informal, inexpensive, accessible justice was available then; and pursuit of a cause required no professional assistance, he argued. But the Normans brought with them an unfamiliar and increasingly technical language. Legal rules and procedures became more formal and increasingly distant from the lives and common experience of the people. The Normans centralized the administration of justice replacing the old local judicatories with itinerant officials with very wide powers. From this arose the legal cartel and the artificial substantive law and adjudicative structure of Common Law.[21] The call to simplicity in adjudicative structures, Bentham insisted, is not a call for radical innovation, but rather a call for restoration of these ancient and effective institutions (*RJE, Bowring* vii, 598–9). This clearly echoes arguments of the Levellers and

[19] See 'Influence of Place and Time', *Bowring* i, 187–8 and the following MS passage not found in *Bowring*: 'By those who have nothing to give, a Cadi will not be bribed: those whom he knows nothing of he will have no motive to favour or to oppress. To those from his treatment of whom supposing it to be just, he has nothing to fear, nor supposing it to be unjust, to hope, he will have no motive to treat with more favour than is due to them, or with less. In this predicament lies the bulk of the poor: that is of the great body of the people. A Cadi then as far as his intelligence extends will generally do justice to the great body of the people. He will give the redress which is their due to those who come before him in the capacity of plaintiffs: he will give the protection that is their due to those who are brought before him in the capacity of defendants.

'Now the poor, that is the great body of the people, are precisely those to whom in civil matters the law of England has denied, most pertinaciously and absolutely denied, all protection and redress' (UC xcix, 178).

[20] *Justice Petition, Bowring* v, 448. Compare Bentham's use of this appeal to the Saxon golden age with Blackstone's use of it to legitimize existing Common Law institutions, 1 *Comm.* 30–2; 4 *Comm.* 407–43.

[21] *Justice Petition, Bowring* v, 448–9; *RJE, Bowring* vii, 598–9.

other radical reformers of the seventeenth century.[22] Bent on sweeping away the existing system of adjudication and replacing it with an egalitarian, decentralized, 'people's' justice, the Levellers argued that only with such reforms would the Norman yoke be thrown off and the nation returned to its traditions of Anglo-Saxon liberty. The rhetorical force of this appeal, which surely was not lost on Bentham, lay in the fact that it stood the Common Law myth on its head.[23]

How seriously did Bentham take these rhetorical appeals to a Saxon golden age? On the one hand, he was inclined to praise the Saxons for their 'liberalism' and to excoriate the Normans for their 'absolutism' (*Justice Petition, Bowring* v, 448); yet, on the other hand, sometimes he insisted that it is not the fact that the forms of summary justice he proposed represented ancient, lapsed traditions of the English people that gave them their legitimacy, but rather that it was their immanent rationality.[24] The latter, surely, is the more characteristic Benthamic position.

In any case, Bentham did not rest his case entirely on this mythology. He also took pains to point out that there existed in more recent history working examples of his domestic model—systems of dispute resolution which, he believed, worked admirably well. In his procedural writings, the litany of such institutions varies occasionally, but the following make regular appearances: (i) courts

---

[22] See B. Shapiro, 'Law Reform in Seventeenth Century England', and 'Codification of the Law in Seventeenth Century England'; also Pocock, *Ancient Constitution*, 125–7, and C. Hill, 'The Norman Yoke', *Democracy and the Labour Movement*. The two Shapiro essays illuminate the many parallels between the Levellers' programme of radical reform and Bentham's programme developed over a century later.

[23] Pocock: 'Both parties indeed looked to the past and laid emphasis on the rights of Englishmen in the past, but what the common lawyers described was the unbroken continuity between past and present, which alone gave justification to the present; while the radicals were talking of a golden age, a lost paradise in which Englishmen had enjoyed liberties that had been taken from them and must be restored' (*Ancient Constitution*, 126). Pocock's generalization fits Common Lawyers like Coke and probably Hale, but not Blackstone, who adopted a classic 'Norman yoke' position (Forbes, *Hume's Philosophical Politics*, 251–2). But this, in fact, makes the point in the text above even stronger, for Blackstone's view was that the Common Law worked itself pure, from the time of the Magna Carta to the Revolution, thereby lifting the Norman yoke from the Saxon free constitution. Bentham stands this rhetoric on its head.

[24] 'In point of fact, then, I mention it as a mere matter of accident, and in point of argument as no better than an argument *ad hominem*, that the system of procedure here proposed, happens to be, in its fundamental principles, not a novel, but an old one: and I give it for good, not *because* it is old, but *although* it happens to be so' (*RJE, Bowring* vii, 599).

martial of various sorts, (ii) local magistrates' courts and justices of the peace, (iii) courts of request or courts of conscience, designed to avoid the complication of Common Law and Chancery courts, dealing largely with small debts and claims,[25] (iv) courts of arbitration established by William III, and finally (v) Danish courts of reconciliation and their French equivalents.[26]

This is not the place to discuss the characteristics of each of these historical institutions in detail, but a few implications regarding Bentham's conception of adjudication can be drawn from his repeated mention of them. Although these institutions and forms of conflict resolution differ in important respects, it is apparent that they share some important properties. In each, an absolute minimum of procedural formality keeps the proceedings simple and inexpensive —a feature Bentham never fails to emphasize in contrast with the so-called 'technical' systems.[27] But what made this possible was the fact that the hearing was focused *by* the parties (i.e. without lawyers) on the dispute *between* the parties without reliance on a body of technical legal rules. When they were well designed, they excluded, or at least did not encourage, professional assistance and so were able to avoid highly technical discussion which distanced the eventual settlement of the case from the original dispute. Perhaps even more importantly, in all cases except for the penal procedures represented by the various forms of court martial, the objective was not the proper *execution* (administration) of some substantive law. Courts of conscience were so-called because they adjudicated disputes by appeal to shared principles of justice—principles of 'conscience'—without being bound to law. Courts of arbitration were informal arbitration arrangements established largely by agreement

[25] These courts were first established during the Tudor period as courts for poor suitors and became rivals of Common Law courts. See Holdsworth, *A History of English Law* I. 412–16, and Halévy, *Philosophic Radicalism*, 382. They were revived, though not without opposition, in the late seventeenth century in London, and in the next century in many large towns. They were officially recognized by the Act of 1846 (Holdsworth I. 190–1). In 1775 Bentham proposed to himself the task of drawing up a plan for revival of the old hundreds courts (UC clxix. 1). In various shapes, this project occupied his mind throughout his life and issued eventually (in 1829) in his proposal for what he called the 'Equity Dispatch Court' (*Bowring* iii, 297–431). See below, 12.2.

[26] One can find such lists, e.g., in *RJE, Bowring* vii, 321; *Scotch Reform, Bowring* v, 7; *IRE, Bowring* vi, 36; *CC* 485; *Bowring* iii, 299–300, 304; and UC lxxxi. 305–413.

[27] See esp. *Bowring* ii, 412; *Scotch Reform, Bowring* v, 7, 35; *RJE, Bowring* vii, 321 ff, 533; *IRE, Bowring* vi, 36; *Bowring* iii, 83, 299–300.

between the parties, in which the award was based on agreed principles, the formal structure of the law intervening only to enforce the award. Most important here, as Bentham notes, is that the decisions, though they had to be justified to the parties, did not have an effect on the substantive law in any way. The effect of the decisions was limited strictly to the particular parties. This is true also of the ancient Danish tradition of conciliation courts. Bentham's frequent mention of the Danish institution alerts us to a feature of his domestic model that is likely otherwise to escape our attention.[28]

In this romanticized version of the domestic community, Bentham pictured the activity of the *paterfamilias* going beyond issuing of even-handed justice (enforcing rights, punishing wrongs, and demanding reparations for injuries). An additional and sometimes overriding concern was that of maintaining, and where necessary restoring, harmony in the family circle (which included servants, day-labourers, etc.). Thus, the patriarch sometimes had to look beyond the particular, immediate wrongs or injuries complained of, and so beyond the particular dispute, between the parties, to the underlying causes of the dispute; and he had to attempt to deal directly with these underlying causes. He sought to settle the dispute and *reconcile* the parties, rather than merely to *decide* the particular issue dividing them. This function of conciliation played a central role in Bentham's (now rather broad) conception of 'adjudication'.

It should come as no surprise, then that Bentham was much attracted to ancient Saxon and Danish legal practice.[29] The Saxon conception of justice rested on compromise and mutual agreement which was then confirmed in judicial proceedings. This was true also of ancient Danish custom, but the Danes formally incorporated conciliation into their legal process in the late eighteenth century. Designed to provide a method for the resolution of private disputes less costly and complicated than formal litigation, these courts did

[28] At UC lxxxi. 261–3 Bentham links the reconciliation court idea to the domestic model of procedure. See also UC lxxxi. 251.

[29] On the customary practice of the Saxons and the Danes see G. W. Keeton, *The Norman Conquest and the Common Law*, 19, and D. Stenton, *English Justice between the Norman Conquest and the Great Charter*, 7–8, cited in Shapiro, 'Compromise and Litigation', 166. Christian VII, monarch of Denmark and Norway, officially established courts of reconciliation by edict in 1795. The law remained essentially in effect until 1919. See R. H. Smith, 'The Danish Conciliation System', 85–93, and G. H. Ostenfeld, 'Danish Courts of Conciliation', 747–8.

not attempt to adjudicate claims under law, but rather they sought to bring the parties together to achieve some accommodation or compromise. Only after a genuine attempt at reconciliation had been made and certified were the parties to a persistent conflict permitted to bring their dispute to a court of law.[30] Although he was sometimes critical of the institutional shape given to the idea of conciliation in the Danish (and to an extent French) legal system, Bentham wholeheartedly endorsed it.[31] In a critical discussion of the French Boards of Reconciliation, Bentham wrote in 1724:

If as here proposed the natural and domestic model of procedure had been employed as far as it could be carried, much more might have been done: but for what has been done no small praise and gratitude is due (UC lv. 59).

The French proposal failed to take the analogy with the domestic tribunal far enough. It set up *separate* courts to carry out the function of reconciliation. This violated Bentham's 'principle of universal competence' (a special case of his principle of simplicity), and so, in his view, invites abuse, expense, and delay. Here and elsewhere Bentham insisted on the merger of the functions of conciliation and ordinary adjudication in the competence of each judge (*Bowring* iv, 333–5; also *CC* 483).

Bentham integrated this idea of this conciliation into his proposals for procedural reform in his *Principles of Judicial Procedure*.[32] He notes at the outset that very often when a dispute arises between two parties, there is not merely a single wrong done or alleged, but a series of them suffered by both sides. For the judge to ignore this fact would be for him to fail to do justice between the parties.[33] Thus, the judge must take notice of all alleged

---

[30] Smith, 'Danish Conciliation System', 89.

[31] Bentham speaks warmly of the Scandinavian and French institutions at *Bowring* iii, 83, n. +; *CC* 483; UC li(a). 215; UC lv. 59; UC lxxxi. 219–22, 286–93, and 236–304 *passim*. He integrates the reconciliation function into the structure of judicial institutions in at least three of his major works on procedure. *Judicial Establishment in France*, *Bowring* iv, 319–20; *RJE*, *Bowring* vi, 366–7; and *PJP*, *Bowring* ii, 46–7. Amongst the papers relating to his work on the French National Assembly's proposals for reform of the judiciary (see *Bowring* iv, 287–406) is a rough essay, not published with the rest of his remarks, critical of the details of the French reconciliation court proposal. See UC li(a). 215–19.

[32] *Bowring* ii, 46–7. In this passage Bentham actually goes considerably further than he was willing to go in 1790. The MSS for this passage are dated 27 Jan. 1828; see UC lii(a). 307–9.

[33] 'In a case of this sort, if, on the occasion of the application made on one side, the judicial service due be rendered to the applicant, no notice being at the same time taken of any wrong done by him to the proposed defendant, justice would be rendered in appearance, in reality not' (*PJP*, *Bowring* ii, 46).

wrongs, and so must encourage all complaints to be brought into the open. This, says Bentham, will make it more likely that all feelings of ill will between the parties can be dealt with and the rift between them healed. In sharp contrast with usual English legal practice in which the objective of pre-trial procedure was to narrow the matters in dispute between the parties to fit the technical categories of formal pleading, Bentham's ideal procedure was designed to broaden the scope of the issues to be considered to include those which underlie the immediate symptomatic dispute which first brought the parties to court. Not every case would be ripe for this sort of treatment, according to Bentham, but it should be left up to the discretion of the judge to determine when reconciliation should be attempted and when strict adjudication under the law should be undertaken. Thus, he concludes,

> Upon the whole . . . two distinguishable courses may, on any such occasion, require to be taken—two distinguishable functions require to be exercised by the judge . . . 1st the conciliative; 2nd, the punitive.
> To the conciliative he will, to the best of his endeavour, give exercise in every case; to the punitive, at the charge of either or both, if, and in so far as, the circumstances of the individual case appear to him to require (*PJP, Bowring* ii, 47).

These two functions must be united in the single office of the judge, not in separate courts or offices, and only a system of 'natural' procedure can hope to achieve this merger of functions, Bentham argues. 'The increased faculty of extinguishing ill will and at the same time rendering complete justice, as between any two or any greater number of persons regarding themselves as wronged, is among the advantages possessed by the system of natural procedure in comparison of the system of technical procedure . . .' (ibid.). Far from regarding the functions of conciliation and adjudication as incompatible, Bentham maintained that they are complementary and that only when the functions are merged can the objective of 'rendering complete justice as between the parties' be fully achieved.

Without doubt, these considerations introduce a picture of the role and characteristic activities of the judge which is radically different from that suggested in Bentham's critical writings on Common Law adjudication and the general theory of law. The emphasis on informal hearing of the parties, the exclusive focus on the interests and injuries of the particular parties, the importance put on restoring harmony between disputing parties and, failing that, of particular justice as between parties—all this seems a far cry from judicial application of codes and statutes and subordination of the judge to the legislator. The judge's role is active and creative, rather than passive and mechanical. (Yet, it is worth noting, it is active in a way that does not involve *interpreting* statutory rules or code provisions, or even *making* rules for future cases.)

Can the two pictures of the role and characteristic activities of the judge, and the nature of judicial reasoning, be reconciled? I believe so. It is, in my view, the failure to see that these two apparently different pictures fit together that has undermined all previous accounts of Bentham's theory of adjudication. Most commentators focus on the model of the judge as the legislator's underworkman. This leaves no room for the dynamic and active functions Bentham insists on in his procedural writings. It also fails to understand the nature of his rejection of Common Law. Other critics, like Halévy, have stressed the dynamic account we have just considered. However, this view, though a useful corrective, leaves us as much in the dark about Bentham's theory of adjudication as the first. It entirely ignores that codification was a lifelong preoccupation of Bentham's and that the fact that a fully codified system of law is in force in a jurisdiction is bound to have an important impact on the nature and appropriate limits of judicial decision-making. Any adequate account of Bentham's mature theory of adjudication must attempt to make some sense of these two different sources of his views. I shall take up this task in the next two chapters.

11

Judicial Virtues and the Sanctions of Public Opinion

To give increase to the influence of sympathy at the expense of self-regard . . . is the constant and arduous task . . .

Bentham, *Constitutional Code.*

BENTHAM'S insistence on simplicity and flexibility in judicial procedure ruled out all fixed rules of procedure and evidence. Procedural rules may be set aside whenever utilitarian considerations warrant it. Bentham also insisted on a wide definition of the judicial role involving a broad grant of discretionary power to the judge. One might well ask at this point how the community is to be protected against the abuse of such wide powers. Since Bentham decisively rejected the standard method of binding judicial decision to fixed, pre-existing rules, it was incumbent on him to develop an adequate alternative. This alternative is to be found in his doctrine of publicity and the constitutional theory which gives that doctrine institutional expression. This chapter is devoted to a study of Bentham's basic principles of constitutional design as they apply to adjudication, and the relations between these principles and his psychology and general political theory.

11.1 JUDICIAL VIRTUES AND CONSTITUTIONAL STRUCTURES

. . . to connect the personal with the general interest. This union is the master principle . . .

Helvetius, *De l'Esprit.*

The only proper task of constitutional law, according to Bentham, is to define and distribute powers, duties, and responsibilities in the public domain. Constitutional law does not establish fundamental law—it does not set out broad declarations of basic civil, political, or social rights. In this respect Bentham's view of the task of constitutional law differs dramatically from the modern American conception. Bentham, of course, sharply and persistently criticized contemporary declarations of rights, and attempts to give them the status of fundamental law.[1] He believed that everything that a Bill of Rights may reasonably strive to do can be accomplished more directly and efficiently (and without the dangerous 'nonsense' of inalienable rights) with careful attention to constitutional structures designed to secure the community against misrule.[2]

The sole right and proper end of government, for Bentham, is the greatest happiness of the community (*CC* 5, 6). But it is criminal folly to expect 'the ruling few' to seek this end when it conflicts with their own self-interest. The tendency to misrule, to sacrifice the general good of the governed to sinister interest of the governors, is universal. The guiding aim of constitutional law, then, is 'to prevent the sinister sacrifice: leaving at the same time unimpaired, both the will and the power to perform whatsoever acts may be in the highest degree conducive to the only right and proper end of government' (*CC* 49). Security against misrule, and the proper exercise of official power will be guaranteed, he maintained, if 'official aptitude' is maximized. From the doctrine of official aptitudes we can extract a view about the sorts of dispositions (or, in an extended sense, 'virtues') which Bentham thought desirable in a judge.

Bentham distinguished three kinds of 'official aptitude'—the active, the intellectual, and the moral—all of which are required of the judge.[3] The active aptitude is the power or ability to act decisively on one's judgment.[4] The intellectual aptitude involves both appropriate knowledge and appropriate judgment on the basis of that knowledge.[5] However, the focal point of his doctrine is his notion of the *moral aptitude*. For in the absence of sufficient moral aptitude, the others are not simply useless, they are likely to be pernicious.[6]

---

[1] *Anarchical Fallacies, Bowring* ii, 489–534; *IPML*, Concluding Note, para. 27; *Pannomial Fragments, Bowring* iii, 218–21. See W. Twining, 'The Contemporary Significance of Bentham's *Anarchical Fallacies*', 315, and more generally, H. L. A. Hart, 'The United States', in his *Essays on Bentham*.

[2] *Securities Against Misrule, Bowring* viii, 557 and *passim*.

[3] The doctrine was framed in general terms to cover all government functionaries, but I will focus on its application to judges.

[4] See UC xcix. 17–19 (1780s) where Bentham locates sources of misrule in 'want of active talent', and 'want of judgment and firmness'.

[5] The 'cognoscitive' and 'judicative' aptitudes respectively; see *CC* 99, 200, 317.

[6] *PJP, Bowring* ii, 123; *CC* 45, 110; *Bowring* ii, 273. At one point Bentham even

In an early version of the doctrine, Bentham identified the moral aptitude with the virtue of probity (UC li(b). 377), but it is unclear what exactly he had in mind. He might have meant something quite general like 'righteousness' or 'right decision', or something more specific like 'impartiality'. To some extent this ambiguity persists throughout his writings. Occasionally, one finds the moral aptitude identified with the disposition to make right decisions according to existing law.[7] But we have already frequently seen that Bentham refused to define proper judicial decision-making simply in terms of strict adherence to existing law. Furthermore, one can find places in which Bentham speaks of rectitude of decision or judicial misdecision in which it is clear from the context that the standard he is using is the principle of utility. This is the case when he says in *Principles of Judicial Procedure* that moral aptitude fails in just that situation in which the judge 'is disposed by any cause to decide in a manner contrary to that which, in his eyes, is justice' (*Bowring* ii, 123).

On other occasions, he seems to link the moral aptitude with the negative virtue of impartiality, or 'freedom from bias'.[8] It is true that Bentham sought to create institutional structures which effectively rule out or block prejudice, interest, partial sympathies, and caprice. And this is just what he is discussing in these passages. But the moral aptitude is not *identified with* the absence of such biasing factors, rather these factors are *causes* of moral *in*aptitude—failure of moral aptitude. Moral aptitude itself is something more positive.

In his most frequent formulations of the doctrine, Bentham identifies the moral aptitude with the 'disposition to contribute, on all occasions and in all ways, to the great happiness of the greatest number' (*Bowring* ii, 273). '[B]y appropriate moral aptitude, understand the being in an adequate degree actuated and guided by the desire of securing to the greatest number in question, at all

suggests that the intellectual aptitude *depends* in some important way on the moral aptitude, but he never explains this claim. See UC li(b). 377. His view is no clearer in the passages of the published text corresponding to this manuscript (*Judicial Establishment, Bowring* iv, 360).

[7] 'As to the moral aptitude, my magistrates will have been engaged in the exclusive support of *right*—or at least of what the *legislature* has pronounced *right*—and the exclusive repression of *wrong*—or at least of what the *legislature* has pronounced *wrong*' (*Official Aptitude Maximized, Bowring* v, 338). F. Rosen attributes to Bentham the view that political virtue 'consists in obeying and carrying out rules and practices' defined by law and constitutional functions (*Bentham and Democracy*, 81). However, this view of Bentham's doctrine of judicial virtues is too narrow.

[8] *PJP, Bowring* ii, 129, 131–2, 123.

times, the greatest quantity . . . of happiness'.[9] The moral aptitude, then, in its positive form must be identified with the virtue or sentiment of benevolence (in its most extensive and enlightened form (*IPML* X. 36)). This has two important implications: (i) the moral aptitude is directed to the greatest happiness of the community; its object is defined by direct application of the principle of utility, and (ii) it is the disposition *to be moved* to do what one judges to be in the universal interest. It is not enough consistently to *act* in such a way as to maximize community welfare (regardless of the motive); for one's moral aptitude is well developed only if one acts *on the motive* of benevolence. Thus, the moral aptitude is directly linked to the motive (Bentham calls it a 'sanction') of *sympathy* (*CC* 192).

Viewed from the perspective of the doctrine of official aptitudes, the goal of constitutional design is to ensure that governors act as responsible and enlightened trustees of community well-being, and this is to be accomplished by maximizing the opportunity for governors to act decisively on the most enlightened and extensive benevolence. But a problem arises immediately: how are we to square this doctrine with the alleged psychological egoism[10] which underlies his political theory? Before he outlines and defends his constitutional theory, and the code which embodies it, Bentham states three foundational principles which are to guide construction of the theory, prominent among them is his 'self-preference principle' (*CC* 5-8). The basic problem of political theory, according to Bentham, is to reconcile the sole proper end of all government (the greatest happiness of the community) with the universal psychological fact that '[i]n the general tenor of life, in every human breast, self-regarding interest is predominant over all other interests put together' (*CC* 5).

According to the received interpretation of Bentham's constitutional theory (which has been standard at least since Halévy)[11]

---

[9] *CC* 97. See also *CC* 199-200 and somewhat more ambiguously *Plan of Parliamentary Reform, Bowring* iii, 359.

[10] Psychological egoism is the view that no human action is or could be motivated by considerations other than purely self-regarding concerns. Halévy attributes this view to Bentham (*Philosophic Radicalism*, 502-3), as does Plamenatz, *The English Utilitarians*, 82. This received interpretation is under serious attack in recent Bentham scholarship. See D. Lyons, *In the Interest of the Governed*, 66-9, and L. J. Hume, 'Revisionism in Bentham Studies', 6-7. But Professor Hart has very recently raised some doubts about this revisionist account of Bentham's psychology; see 'Introduction' to the paperback edition of *IPML* (1982), xlvi-xlix.

[11] Plamenatz, 82; Halévy, 403-6; G. Himmerlfarb, 'Bentham's Utopia: The National Charity Company', 84-5; Hart, 'The United States', in *Essays on Bentham*, 68.

Bentham borrowed a strategy common to eighteenth-century political theory, according to which institutional controls and checks were to be arranged so as to create an *artificial* harmony between the interests of the 'subject many' and the 'ruling few'.[12] The main device was the use of formal, legal (and, wherever possible, informal social) sanctions. This Bentham called his 'duty-and-interest-junction principle' and set it alongside the principle of utility and the thesis of self-preference as the third foundational element of his political theory. The core idea seems to have been to treat constitutional law on the model of criminal law. For, Bentham firmly believed, given the pervasive conflict between the interests of the ruling few and the subject many, rulers must be regarded as potential criminals poised to prey on the community. And the only way to prevent oppression and depredation is to subject officials to the control and 'punishment' of the people, thereby making it in the interest of the rulers to serve the good of the community.

But his strategy seems to depend directly on the assumption that officials are moved only by narrow self-interest. Does not this reliance on sanctions (the 'moral sanction' primarily) undermine Bentham's doctrine of official aptitudes? For if one acts out of fear of sanction one does not act out of sympathy or benevolence, and so moral aptitude seems to be unnecessary, as long as constitutional structures and the enforcement of them are effective.

Bentham, it seems, has allowed a contradiction to slip into the foundations of his political theory. But this is not our only problem, for this constitutional strategy also seems to threaten the theory of adjudication we have seen developing in Bentham's jurisprudential writings. For it appears to assume that the only available motivation for officials is that of narrowly defined self-interest and that contradicts the assumption, underlying the theory of adjudication as we have outlined it, that the principle of utility is not only a principle of right action, but is also the only proper judicial *decision principle.*

---

[12] This principle seems to have been advanced by Beccaria, Helvetius, Burke, Necker, Catherine, and Hume. See L. J. Hume, *Bentham and Bureaucracy*, 40. David Hume advances the principle in his essay 'That Politics May be Reduced to A Science': 'But a republican and free government would be an obvious absurdity if the particular checks and controls provided by the constitution had really no influence and made it not the interest even of bad men, to act for the public good. Such is the intention of these forms of government, and such is their real effect, where they are wisely constituted . . . ' in Hume, *Essays*, 14.

However, Bentham can be acquitted of this charge. In fact, his constitutional theory can be shown to be consistent with, and even to advance, the theory of adjudication we have already seen develop. This is the task of the present chapter. It calls for a closer look at some features of his political theory, and a more careful statement of both his underlying psychological theory and his constitutional strategy. I will argue that Bentham's psychology requires a reinterpretation of the strategy of the 'artificial identification of interests', and this reinterpretation eliminates all appearance of inconsistency between his theory of adjudication and his constitutional theory.

11.2   THE PEOPLE IS MY CAESAR

The eye of the public makes the statesman virtuous.

Bentham, *Commonplace Book*.

Bentham's strategy for protecting the community against official abuse of power was consciously developed in opposition to what he perceived to be the prevailing liberal theory of the constitution, associated with the work of Montesquieu. In Bentham's view, the system of checks and counterchecks on the exercise of official power was a method calculated to remove all effective power from officials and to make decisive action impossible. It was this paralysing of official action (useful in the context of tyrannical laws of the day) that, in Bentham's view, most attracted Montesquieu to the English constitution. As we have seen in the previous chapter, Bentham decisively rejected this method, because it violates his principle of simplicity and it is guaranteed to maximize the expense of government. But most importantly, in Bentham's view, it is simply irrational. With one hand power is granted to officials and with the other it is withdrawn. The power to do good is denied officials for fear that it will be used to do evil, with the result that neither good nor evil is done (UC li(a). 213).

Bentham is especially critical of the principle of the *independence* of the judiciary. Independence of the judiciary is tolerable only in a corrupt government; it is disastrous in a good one. A court dependent on no one 'is dependent on its own passions and caprice. Independence makes virtue as towards this or that man or body of men: but it is dependence that makes virtue as towards the body of the people.'[13] The only guarantee of probity and moral aptitude is judicial dependence upon, and full resonsibility to, the people. To prevent sinister interest, Bentham insisted, first, 'Minimize confidence' and, second,

[w]hile confidence is minimized, let not power be withheld. For security against breach of trust, the sole apt remedy is . . . not impotence, but constant responsibility, and as towards their creators—the authors of their political being—on every occasion, and at all times, the strictest and most absolute dependence.[14]

This dependence takes both a direct and an indirect form. Indirect dependence requires that the judiciary be subordinated to a superior within the governing body. This superior, of course, was the legislative branch of government for Bentham.[15] But control of judges also requires that the judiciary itself be structured so that individual judges are under the control of a superior. Judicial organization, then, calls for a hierarchy of authority and responsibility. Several times during his career Bentham turned to the task of drawing up a plan for judicial organization.[16]

Publicity: the soul of justice

But despite the importance of the institutional structure of the judiciary, in Bentham's view the key to control of official abuse of power lay in direct dependence of judges on the people. During his more radically democratic periods (early 1790s and again in the 1820s) this took the form of popular election and recall of judges. But always, from his earliest reflections on government, the foundation was tó be laid in strict adherence to the principle of *publicity*.

Political thinkers in the eighteenth century came to recognize the power of public opinion. It distributes praise and dishonour; it can

[13] UC li(a). 213; also see UC xxi. 309; UC cxxvii. 5; UC clxx. 183; UC cxxvi. 12.

[14] *CC* 62; also *Judicial Establishment, Bowring* iv, 362.

[15] On the nature of judicial subordination to the legislative branch of government see below, 12 and 13.1.

[16] The first, *Judicial Establishment in France*, appeared in 1790 in response to the first wave of revolutionary changes in France. See *Bowring* iv, 285–406 and UC li(a) and UC li(b). The second period was 1806–8 in which Bentham wrote *Scotch Reform* and *Court of Lords' Delegates*. See *Bowring* v, 1–60 and UC lxxxii. 43–264; UC lxxxix–xciv; UC cvi. 85–229; and UC clxvii. 1–213. The third phase, in the 1820s, brought together and developed his earlier work and incorporated it into his *Constitutional Code*, chs. XII–XXIV. This aspect of Bentham's theory of adjudication has been carefully discussed by L. J. Hume, *Bentham and Bureaucracy*, especially 2–5, 171–5, 216–19.

establish or ruin reputations. In the 1780s Necker noted that 'it is the ascendancy of public opinion that opposed more obstacles in France to the abuse of power than any other consideration whatsoever'.[17] Bentham echoed this sentiment in his *Essay on Political Tactics*—written for the French National Assembly in 1790: 'The public compose a tribunal, which is more powerful than all the other tribunals together' (*Bowring* ii, 310). Indeed, for Bentham, publicity has almost magical purifying powers:

Publicity is the very soul of justice. It is the keenest spur to exertion, and the surest of all guards against improbity. . . . It is through publicity alone that justice becomes the mother of security. By publicity, the temple of justice is converted into a school of the first order, where the most important branches of morality are enforced, by the most impressive means. . . . Without publicity, all other checks are fruitless; in comparison of publicity, all other checks are of small account.[18]

The public constitutes a kind of informal judicatory, a tribunal before which every official, judge, or person of public affairs must appear. (In his later writings this becomes the admittedly fictional 'Public Opinion Tribunal'.)[19] Thus, the judge, while conducting a trial, is himself on trial. 'Under the auspices of publicity, the cause in the court of law, and the appeal to the court of public opinion, are going on at the same time' (*Judicial Establishment, Bowring* iv, 316). In this way the impartiality, the probity, and in general the active, intellectual, and moral aptitudes of the judge are kept sharp. '[T]he eye of the public makes the statesman virtuous' (*Bowring* x, 145). When fully public, courts are teachers of morality for both the public and the judiciary. And only under such conditions does justice substantially contribute to security. For, according to Bentham, security is a function of the *public conviction* of order and justice (the 'appearance' of justice), not of its reality (*PJP, Bowring* ii, 21), and that conviction is most firmly embedded

[17] J. Necker, *A Treatise on the Administration of the Finances of France*, quoted in L. J. Hume, *Bentham and Bureaucracy*, 51.

[18] *Judicial Establishment, Bowring* iv, 316, 317; see also *PJP, Bowring* ii, 8; *Political Tactics, Bowring* ii, 310; *Security Against Misrule, Bowring* viii, 559; *Justice Petition, Bowring* v, 449; *Panopticon Papers, Bowring* iv, 128; UC li(b). 378.

[19] See, for example, *CC* 41–4, 155–60 and *Security Against Misrule, Bowring* viii, 561–72. The Public Opinion Tribunal (POT) is composed of members of the community regarded in respect of their capacity to assess each other's conduct and to express publicly such judgments (*CC* 41). Compare the ancient German tradition of the *Umstand*, M. Weber, *Law and Economy in Society*, 90–1.

in the public mind when it is *seen* that justice is regularly and consistently meted out by the courts.

Thus, all official deliberations, actions, and decisions must be subject to the critical scrutiny of the universal public, and the opinions of the public regarding official conduct must also be fully public (*Bowring* viii, 561). This is the heart of Bentham's notion of dependence—the principle to which he remained steadfastly committed throughout his career (when he was most sceptical of democratic political structures, as well as in his most radical democratic periods).[20] It is the key to his view of judicial *responsibility*, the essential guarantee of moral aptitude of the judiciary.

However, does not this dependence on the people put the judge at the mercy of 'every gust of passion which may overbear for a moment the reason of the people?' No, Bentham replies (in an almost Burkean fashion), because care has been taken to ensure that the judge is dependent not upon the opinion of the moment but on 'the opinion of their lives'. Not on 'their opinion in a storm', but on 'their opinion in fair weather'. Not on 'the opinion that succeeds it, when time and detection have condemned the lie of the day to silence'. This is the opinion not of a part of the community, or even of the majority of the moment, but rather the opinion 'of that majority which keeps the field and governs' (*Judicial Establishment, Bowring* iv, 362).

Despite his protestation to the contrary which immediately follows this passage,[21] Bentham here clearly reflects a worry about rule by the mob which gripped Burke, and much of the nineteenth century. But why does he believe that he has tapped the resources of this measured and enlightened public opinion, which 'unites all the wisdom and all the justice of the nation' (*Bowring* ii, 310)? The answer is not entirely clear. But it seems to rest ultimately in Bentham's deep conviction that the only thing to fear in rule by the people is rule by an unenlightened and aroused people manipulated by vested interests.[22] Factionalism and imprudence of the people at large is the product of inadequate publicity. Delusion is possible

[20] Bentham's changing attitude towards the French Revolution and his transition to democratic radicalism are carefully traced by J. R. Dinwiddy in 'Bentham's Transition to Political Radicalism 1809–10', and J. H. Burns, 'Bentham and the French Revolution'.

[21] 'I have not that horror of the people. I do not see in them that savage monster which their detractors dream of' (*Bowring* iv, 363).

[22] The 'People is my Caesar', a young Bentham grandly proclaims (1774–5). But he quickly adds: 'I appeal from the present Caesar to Caesar better informed' (*Bowring* x, 73).

only through explicit force, or through the removal from public cognizance of topics bearing on politics, morality, or religion (*CC* 43). The remedy to the risks of publicity lie not in restrictions on it, but in an even more resolute and comprehensive publicity and free flow of information about all matters of public concern. Sinister interest, in Bentham's view, is a pestilence which can survive only in the dark. An enlightened and informed public constantly sitting in judgment on officials and monitoring the influence of factional interest on their decisions and actions will not be dependent on sinister interest, but rather will act on their best judgment of the general interest.

This, of course, does not answer sufficiently the Burkean worry which Bentham seems to have harboured above. For why should we think that exposing official action and decisions to the critical scrutiny of the public opinion tribunal should transform the public as well as the officials? A clue to Bentham's reasons for believing this can be gathered from his notion of official responsibility, to which we now turn.

For Bentham 'responsibility' has a twofold significance. First, responsibility implies liability to sanction of some sort (*CC* 151). Frequently, Bentham distinguishes between the judge's legal or political responsibility and his moral responsibility; i.e. between his liability to legal sanctions ('punitional, satisfactional, and dislocational') and his liability to informal moral sanctions.[23] Although he believed that there was an important place for political or legal sanctions (in the form of either explicit punishment or the removal from office), Bentham held that these sanctions are difficult to administer fairly and efficiently against officials. The moral sanction, because informal and less drastic, is, in the case of judges, most effective, and need not be hedged about with efficiency-impairing safeguards.[24] It is the aim of full publicity of all judicial proceedings to mobilize public opinion and fully exploit the resources of the moral sanction. In a revealing passage in a manuscript on procedural matters from the 1780s, Bentham admits that, *in general*, the moral sanction is weaker and less reliable than the legal. But, he insists, the reverse is true in the case of controlling judicial activity.

Why [are] Courts of Justice in general required to be open? To prevent a Judge from failing on the side of inclination. To apply the force of the

---

[23] *PJP, Bowring* ii, 31; *CC* 50-1, 151-2.
[24] *CC* 198 n.*; *IRE, Bowring* vi, 24; *RJE, Bowring* vii, 326-7.

moral sanction to fix him to his duty. . . . In other cases the power of the
moral sanction is comparatively needless and besides that it is comparatively weak. Here it is supremely necessary and the force of it herculean . . .
[The] Judge is a man of honour: he has a rich fund of reputation to preserve
and to improve. Let the Courts be open, and their transactions public, then
whatever he does he does in the face of mankind (UC lvii. 9).

The informal sanction works well here, because the judge's sense of
professional integrity is at stake, and that, says Bentham, is a much
more powerful incentive to moral aptitude than threats of punishment, which are bound to lack credibility.

Accountability and the catechism of public reasons

'Responsibility' has a second important aspect, for Bentham,
which publicity is designed to secure: *accountability*. Not only must
all actions be open to public view, but also the judge is under strict
obligation to fully *justify* his decision and actions to the people.
'Responsibility', says Bentham, is 'the right which a subject has of
having the reasons publicly assigned and canvassed of every act of
power that is exerted over him.'[25] This is essential, according to
Bentham, if law and government are to be anything more than the
exercise of brute force and if obedience is to be anything more than
compliance out of blind fear. In this we have a central plank in
Bentham's political and jurisprudential platform.

The exercise of power is legitimate and beneficial, according to
Bentham, only if it seeks to direct behaviour through rational
persuasion. This legitimate 'influence of understanding on the
understanding' must be sharply distinguished from the prevalent
governing technique of the 'influence of the will on the will'.[26]
Government by the latter technique is unavoidably government by
sinister interest, Bentham held, because it is government that cannot operate in full public view. A rational, aware and informed
population would not willingly comply with its dictates. A paradigm case of such government—a microcosm of the evils Bentham
associates with government by will upon will—was the Church of
England.[27] The Church maintained its control only through either
explicit coercion of the unwilling, or delusion and irrational persua-

---

[25] *FG* IV. 24; see also *PJP*, *Bowring* ii, 32; *Lord Brougham Displayed*, *Bowring*
v, 556.

[26] UC cxxvi. 1 (see Mary Mack, *Jeremy Bentham*, 458); also *Bowring* iv, 539.

[27] Here I follow L. J. Hume's discussion of Bentham's *Church of Englandism
and its Catechism Examined* (London, 1818). See *Bentham and Bureaucracy*, 188.

sion of the willing. The result was that the unwilling are sentenced to perpetual insincerity, complying without conviction, and the willing are led into an irrational compliance due to the prostration of the understanding and the will.

Such a relationship between authorities and subjects is intolerable, for Bentham. It is incompatible with his view of a well-ordered political society, for the marks of such a society are rational obedience and free exercise of the understanding. Thus, Bentham argues,

the greatest advantage [of making all reasons for laws public] is that which results from conciliating the approbation of all minds, by satisfying the public judgment, and obtaining obedience to the laws; not from a passive principle of blind fear alone, but with the concurrence of the will also.[28]

Bentham's argument for this view of the well-ordered political society is twofold. First, subordination of one will to another is intrinsically intolerable. It represents a failure of the authorities to respect the humanity and rationality of citizens. 'Those who are able to convince men, will treat them like men; those who only command, avow their inability to convince', and thereby lose their right to command (*Bowring* i, 160). The only way to treat citizens 'like men' is to attempt to convince them of the desirability (utility) of the law or decision, that is, to address the understanding and not to dominate the will. Striking a surprisingly Kantian note, Bentham insists that only in this way is law consistent with human autonomy:

If the laws were founded upon reason, they would infuse themselves, so to speak, into the minds of the people: they would form part of the logic of the people; they would extend their influence over their moral nature: the code of public opinion would be formed by analogy upon the code of the laws, and by agreement between the man and the citizen; obedience to the laws would come to be hardly distinguishable from the feeling of liberty (*Bowring* i, 161).

Governed by rational laws, the rationale of which is plainly to be seen and understood by all, citizens would experience citizenship and its duties not as bondage but as freedom. Persons and citizens would be in harmony; obedience would be the natural response to the requirements of the law, an expression of freedom.

Secondly, addressing the understanding of citizens is instrumentally valuable in Bentham's view. It is a necessary condition of

[28] *Essay on Promulgation, Bowring* i, 161. 'Power gives existence to a law for the moment, but it is upon reason that it must depend for its stability' (*Bowring* iv, 310).

genuine political stability, and consequently a necessary condition of security and political liberty. For stability, security, and liberty depend on both punctual obedience *and* the most free and continual criticism (*FG*, Preface, p. 399).

From this Bentham draws one very important implication. Accountability of officials, and mobilization of the moral sanction, presuppose that it is possible to frame political justifications for official actions and decisions in terms that the people will be able to understand and critically assess. In his *Essay on Promulgation* which we have already quoted, Bentham makes very clear that it is not enough that officials give some account of their decisions. Because of its importance I quote the passage in full.

> I am so convinced of the necessity of this exposition of reasons, that I would not dispense with one of them at any price. To confide in what is called *a feeling of justice, a feeling of truth*, is a source of error. I have seen upon a thousand occasions, that the greatest mistakes are concealed in all those feelings which are not brought to the touchstone of examination. If this feeling, this first guide, the *avant courier* of the mind, be correct, it will always be possible to translate it into the language of reason. Pains and pleasures, as I have repeatedly shown, are the only sources of ideas in morals. These ideas may be rendered familiar to all the world. *The catechism of reasons is worthless, if it cannot be made the catechism of the people* (*Bowring* i, 163, emphasis added).

Bentham not only insists on the giving of reasons by officials for their actions and decisions, but more importantly he insists on their justifying these actions *to the people* in a public language they can understand, in which they can participate. The assertions judges make in support of their judgments, then, must themselves be open to critical assessment by the public. This requires a public, shared language of political morality. As we have seen, liberty and political stability require punctual rational obedience and free and unconstrained rational criticism. But this censure is effective, and liberty is secured, only if there is a shared political morality in terms of which official actions can be both justified and critically assessed.

For this purpose Bentham proposes the language of utility, i.e. the language of publicly detectable harms and rewards, pains, and pleasures.

> In morals, as in legislation, the *principle of utility* is that which holds up to view, as the only sources and tests of right and wrong, human suffering and enjoyment—pain and pleasure. It is by experience, and by that alone,

that the tendency of human conduct, in all its modifications, to give birth to pain and pleasure, is brought to view: it is by reference to experience, and to that standard alone, that the tendency of any such modifications to produce more pleasure than pain, and consequently to be *right*—or more pain than pleasure, and consequently to be *wrong*—is made known and demonstrated. *In this view of the matter, morality, as well as policy, is always matter of account.*[29]

Utility is the language of public accounting. According to Bentham, it is the practical language of all rational beings—only prejudice and superstition cloud its operation (*IPML* IV. 8). Regardless of how we first came to have our moral sentiments and notions of right and wrong, and regardless of how on reflection we attempt to justify them to ourselves in private, the only basis of justification of them 'in point of right . . . by a person addressing himself to the community' is the principle of utility (*IPML* II. 14 n. 1, p. 28).

Thus, in conjunction with a programme of public education, a constitution which makes fully public all judicial proceedings and requires full public justification of each judicial decision and action would, in Bentham's view, fully protect the public from abuse of the power they grant to judges (and the government generally) to wield in their behalf. The only hope for control of abuse of power which still leaves sufficient power in the hands of officials is to mobilize the moral sanction through full publicity, thereby maximizing the opportunity for the full and unobstructed exercise of the moral aptitudes of the judiciary.

This goes some way towards explaining Bentham's faith in publicity. For not only does it expose official conduct and decision-making to attack from the public, but it also converts the court (and the public forum in general) into a 'school of the first order'. The requirement of official accountability ensures that the people are treated as rational beings capable of governing their own actions in accord with their understanding. And it encourages them to participate in public life, and matters of concern to the community as a whole, on a basis that transcends private or parochial interests and focuses attention on the general good. For this reason Bentham thought that public opinion 'may err, [but] it is incorruptible' and 'it continually tends to be come enlightened'.[30]

---

[29] *RJE*, *Bowring* vi, 238, emphasis in the last sentence added. See also UC lxix. 6–7, 72–3; *Comment* 199.
[30] *Political Tactics*, *Bowring* ii, 310.

But why should participation in public judicial functions educate in this way? Because, Bentham argued, citizens come to see that they can successfully press concerns regarding their own good in this public forum only if their concerns are at the same time matters of general interest. Participation in public life, he believed, forces one to shift one's attention from purely private concerns to ends or interests which are component parts of the common interest. (In the language of Bentham's psychology to which we will turn in the next section, participation in public life trains up the semi-social motives and strengthens them over the purely self-regarding motives.)

This point is made most clearly in his discussion of the election of parliamentary representatives. It is the need for concerted collective action—for example, garnering a majority of votes for a favoured candidate—that forces a person to focus on issues of common concern around which he can rally others. These practical demands of collective action train up the moral aptitudes of electors and candidates alike, in Bentham's view.

The only interest of his, which an elector can expect to serve by the choice of an agent for this purpose [as parliamentary representative], is that which he has in common with all the rest. The only way in which, in quality of agent for this purpose, a man can expect to recommend himself to the good opinion and choice of the people in their quality of electors, is by appearing disposed to serve to his utmost this practically universal interest . . . (*CC* 98).

But this point can be generalized from the context of elections to the activities of the public opinion tribunal generally. For when sitting in judgment on the conduct of judges and other officials, the citizen's primary concern is to secure himself against oppression and depredation (*CC* 100). But this, he comes to recognize, is a 'public good', i.e. it is a good not only for him but also for the community as well (and to an extent, it is a good for him *because* it is a good for the community), *and* it can be achieved only through co-operative effort of a large part of the community.

In his endeavours to secure himself against depredation and oppression, each man finds all others in general disposed to become co-operators and supporters: for against depredation and oppression to his own prejudice, no man can find any means of security but such as cannot but afford the like security to other individuals in general (*CC* 100).

Thus, in the pursuit of common goods, interest is united with power in the people to good effect (*CC* 100). But if one were to seek some private good at the expense of the good of others, he could not hope to rally support. 'For the gratification of any sinister desire [i.e. purely private interest] at the expense of the universal interest, he cannot hope to find co-operation and support from any considerable number of his fellow-citizens' (*CC* 100, also *CC* 63). Thus, one comes to regard one's own good as a component of the common good. In this way, participation in public affairs focuses one's attention on goods which unite a community rather than on sinister interests or private goods which tend to divide it.

If Bentham's argument is persuasive here, it answers to some extent his concern about putting the power to rule the rulers in the hands of the people. For given full and complete publicity, he believed, the people would (in time if not immediately) become immune to manipulation, and would be fully capable of wise and prudent public judgment. '[I]n proportion as [the people become] more and more mature, [they become] more and more favorable to the universal interest' (*CC* 45, also *CC* 158). But it is still not clear how Bentham thought he could avoid having public assessment made on the basis of 'the opinion of the moment', or of the opinion of the *majority* of the moment. This Burkean worry is never fully answered. It is safe to say that as he progressed into his more radically democratic period in the early decades of the nineteenth century he tended to minimize the worry rather than attempt to answer it.

Democracy

Before we take up Bentham's psychological theory and its role in his theory of constitutional design, a few words should be said about Bentham's conception of democracy and its relationship to the principle of publicity which we have just considered.[31] In his most fully developed theory of government (worked out in the *Constitutional Code*) Bentham clearly embraced and tried to work out in detail a form of democratic theory. On this theory, sovereign power in the state is to be divided, according to function, into the Supreme Constitutive, the Supreme Legislative, and Supreme Operative (which includes both the executive and judicial functions).

[31] For a more general discussion (from which I depart at times) see F. Rosen, 'Jeremy Bentham and Democratic Theory', and *Bentham and Democracy*.

In the democratic state the Supreme Constitutive power lies with the entire people. But this is the only power wielded directly by the people. The policy- (and law-)forming and policy- (and law-) administering functions are performed by a bureaucratically structured and responsible government. The Constitutive power is exercised primarily through election and recall of representatives and government functionaries. The Supreme Constitutive answers the need in Bentham's theory of sovereignty for a body capable of investing the sovereign with legislative (and executive) power. Bentham's theory radically extends the scope of popular control, both by insisting on universal male suffrage, and by making parliamentary representatives and a large portion of the government bureaucracy (most importantly, most of the judiciary) subject to election and recall.

This is a radical departure from the halting moves towards democracy in early nineteenth-century England; yet in at least one respect Bentham's theory does not represent a fundamental radicalization of his political views as expressed already in, for example, the early *Fragment on Government*. For it represents no fundamental change in political theory, but a change in view concerning the expediency of certain methods or procedures for achieving political ends which remained constant throughout his career. This can be seen if we take a closer look at the tasks Bentham assigns to the people (the Supreme Constitutive) in his *Constitutional Code*.

Bentham did not restrict the activities of the constitutive authority to periodic elections, for he also gave to the 'public opinion tribunal' a crucial, though informal, role to play in the design of his democratic constitution. The POT was in Bentham's view broader than the electorate, not being limited to those with suffrage or even to persons living within the country. And the function of the POT was to be different: it was to perform an essentially *judicial* function. It was to sit in judgment on the conduct of all officials of government, and it was to express its judgments, on the streets and in the press. It was also 'empowered' to execute its judgments formally and legally through recall, but more often informally through exercise of the moral sanction, in extreme cases through resistance, non-co-operation and refusal of obedience, and ultimately subversive violence.[32]

---

[32] In addition to our earlier discussion of the POT's use of the moral sanction, see *Securities Against Misrule*, *Bowring* viii, 563 for a discussion of the more extreme forms of sanction available to the people.

But it is important to keep in mind that publicity and the POT are not, in Bentham's view, unique features of democratic polities. Indeed, Bentham held that the POT in some form or other exists in every society regardless of the form of government, though it is in a representative democracy that it is given freest rein and allowed fullest scope (*CC* 43). To the Moslem monarch of Tripoli he proposed full freedom of the press and the most extensive publicity of all official conduct and decision as the only remedy against misrule and abuse of power *short* of changing the form of government (to a representative democracy) (*Bowring* viii, 555–600). And already in his *Fragment on Government*, long before he toyed with the idea of popular democratic control of government, Bentham insisted on the fundamental principle of publicity and especially the requirement of providing reasons for all official actions (*FG* IV. 24). These requirements of publicity did not represent in Bentham's mind distinctively democratic devices; they were requirements of open and accountable government. The task of the POT was to constrain depredation and oppression of the many by the ruling few, and encourage the moral aptitudes of officials.[33] Publicity, from his very earliest reflections on political subjects till the *Constitutional Code*, was assigned an essentially judgmental function, holding government to public standards of official conduct.

This controlling function is neither abandoned nor expanded in Bentham's mature political theory. For even with the addition of the investitive and divestitive powers to the people's repertoire, the task is no different. 'In a representative democracy, take any one member of the community acting in the exercise of the supreme constitutive power. His desire is to afford to himself security against depredation and oppression . . .' (*CC* 100). Election (and removal) of representatives (and judges) is a further technique the people can use to ensure probity in legislation and adjudication. But the people do not *participate* in any substantial way in their own governance.

In the exercise of political power, whatsoever is done by the possessors of the supreme power must be done through agents: for as to actual governing,

---

[33] The main theme of *On the Liberty of the Press* (1821), *Bowring* ii, 275–97, is that freedom of the press is an essential check on the ruling few. It 'constitutes a controuling power, indispensibly necessary to the maintenance of good government' (*Bowring* ii, 279). The argument for full publicity is 'to constrain members of the assembly to perform their duty'. It also secures confidence of the people in the legislative measures adopted and ensures adequate information regarding the wishes of the people and other empirical information necessary for rational legislating. See *Bowring* ii, 310–11.

for this, it is admitted, the people are essentially unapt (*CC* 98). To the Constitutive Authority, it belongs, amongst other things, to depute and locate . . . the members composing the Legislative . . . and eventually . . . to dislocate them: but not to give direction, either *individual* or *specific*, to their measures . . . (*CC* 153).

This, Steintrager points out, is a surprisingly Burkean conception of representation.[34] They are not to take part in focusing policies or articulating a common conception of the good or of community. Democracy may be a vehicle for educating persons to take up a public point of view, and to abandon purely private interests for common ones, but in Bentham's polity there is no room for genuine public political debate over competing conceptions of what the common good consists in. Democracy is not a method of self-governing, for Bentham; it is a method—the most efficient method, he believed—of governmental *control*, holding government to the execution of a programme of public good which is already, at least in its broad outlines, settled by the dictates of the public language of politics: namely, the principle of utility and its code. Echoing de Tocqueville, J. S. Mill issues a timely warning against this tendency in Bentham's political theory—and in liberal theory generally: 'The spirit of a commercial people will be . . . essentially mean and slavish, whenever public spirit is not cultivated by an extensive participation of the people in the business of government in detail.'[35] There are resources within his doctrine of responsibility for development of a richer, more participatory conception of democracy, but Bentham never showed any inclination to exploit them.

11.3 SELF-PREFERENCE AND BENEVOLENCE

The general and standing bias of every man's nature is, therefore, towards . . . the social motives

Bentham, *IPML*.

From the discussion of the principle of publicity in Bentham's political theory it is clear that he put the heaviest burden of control of official abuse of power on an enlightened public's administration of the moral sanction. This, however, does not resolve the

---

[34] J. Steintrager, *Bentham*, 107.
[35] Mill, *Essays on Politics and Culture*, 244. See de Tocqueville, *Democracy in America*, V. 2, pt. 2, ch. 14.

difficulties noticed at the end of 11.1. In fact, it exacerbates them, for it closes off entirely the possibility of relieving the tension noted there by trying to explain away Bentham's reliance on the 'artificial identification of interests' strategy. Sanctions, whether legal or moral, are indispensable weapons in Bentham's war against official depredation and oppression.

We are still faced, then, with a conflict between his basic strategy of constitutional design, and the psychological assumptions on which it seems to rest, on the one hand, and his doctrine of official aptitudes (and more generally, the sovereignty of the principle of utility), on the other hand. This conflict can be resolved and the coherence of Bentham's constitutional and jurisprudential theories preserved, only if we abandon the standard understanding of both Bentham's egoism and his constitutional strategy. To prepare the ground for this reinterpretation we need to look briefly at Bentham's psychology.

There is no denying that Bentham sometimes expressed views which are difficult to distinguish from straightforward psychological egoism. For example, in 1822 he wrote, 'Man, from the very constitution of his nature, prefers his own happiness to that of all other sensitive beings put together,' adding that 'but for this self-preference, the species could not have had existence' (*Bowring* x, 80; *CC* 5-6). This truth, he believed, provided the clue to the labyrinth of politics, and with it he sought to construct a true and realistic constitutional theory. But such statements notwithstanding, Bentham never denied that human beings, and even government officials, are capable of being moved by sentiments of benevolence, sympathy, and disinterested concern for others.[36] Indeed, he insisted that 'were it not for the operation of this sanction [sympathy or benevolence], no small portion of the good, physical and moral, which has place in human affairs, would be an effect without a cause' (*Bowring* iii, 292). Bentham's use of the term 'sanction' to refer to the motive of sympathy or disinterested concern in the good of others is noteworthy. Some time after publishing his most widely known discussion of moral psychology, in his *Introduction to the Principles*, Bentham added to the well-known quartet of

---

[36] *Bowring* iv, 430-1, *Bowring* xi, 77 (1830s); *CC* 81 and UC xiv. 16, 88, 378 ff (1820s); UC cxi. 61-5 (1818); and *Bowring* x, 145; UC lxxxvii. 20-24, 27 (1780s). See also Steintrager, *Bentham*, 110; B. Parekh, 'Introduction' to *Jeremy Bentham Ten Critical Essays*, xiii; and R. Harrison, *Bentham*, 143.

sanctions to which human behaviour is subject—viz. the physical, legal, moral, and religious—a fifth, the sanction of sympathy.[37] But within the psychology of the *Introduction to the Principles* he already had sufficient grounds for doing so,[38] for he recognized four different classes of motives, each of which are operative as springs of human action.

Self-preferential motives, of course, are prominent in his theory, but Bentham's analysis of them is subtle. He distinguishes two classes of self-preferential motives. (*a*) The first is the class of purely self-regarding motives—including physical desire, desire for self-preservation, fear of bodily pain or injury, and (important for our purposes) pecuniary interest and love of power (*IPML* X. 34). These are desires for strictly private goods, which, because they ignore the good of others, can be sought at the expense of the universal or general interest. (*b*) The second class of self-preferential motives are 'semi-social' because they are both self-regarding and to some extent other-regarding ('social'). In this class he includes, e.g., the love of reputation and the desire of amity (*IPML* X. 34). These are semi-social because they incline one to act in ways that take the good of others into account in some essential way. In his early discussion of this class of motives Bentham seems to have in mind simply desires to benefit others in order to secure reciprocal benefits from them. Motives such as these arise from the recognition that one's own good is dependent on the goodwill, cooperation, and services of others such that it is in one's interest to cultivate their good: by promoting their good one lays up moral capital on which one can draw later.[39] In his later writings, how-

[37] *Nomography*, Bowring iii, 290–2. The importance Bentham assigned to the sympathetic sanction in his latter writings was noticed by contemporary readers. See, for example, W. M. Best, *A Treatise on the Principles of Evidence*, 13, commenting on the role of sympathy in Bentham's *Rationale of Judicial Evidence*.

[38] *IPML* V. 10–11, 26, 32; VI. 20–2; X. 25–6, 36–9; XI. 42; XVII. 7. It is not clear why Bentham did not include sympathy among the sanctions discussed at *IPML* III. A clue may be found at *IPML* XII. 8 and n. e where Bentham seems to regard the sanction of sympathy as a special case of the physical sanction. (On the link between talk of 'motives' and talk of 'sanctions' see *OLG* VI. 19.) But this does not explain why he did not seek to revise ch. III in the 1822 edn. of *IPML*. Bowring's edn. of *IPML* quotes in a footnote a letter from Bentham to Dumont dated 28 Oct. 1821: '*Sanctions.* Since the *Traites* others have been discovered. There are now, I. Human: 6 viz. (1) Physical (2) Retributive (3) Sympathetic (4) Antipathetic (5) Popular or moral (6) Political including legal and Administrative' Bowring i, 14 n. *.

[39] As we shall see in the next section, this is not an entirely accurate account of Bentham's view of the motive of love of reputation, at least to the extent that it is

ever, we get a quite different picture of the semi-social motives. (Perhaps this should be regarded as additional to, rather than replacing, the earlier conception.) The motive here is for the *common* good, or for public goods, in which one participates. In such cases, one's interest or good is a *component* of the general interest. We encountered this notion in our discussion of the educational function of the POT in 11.2, but Bentham did not restrict its operation to citizens. He also thought it was operative in government officials.

In the case of a public functionary, the *will* is on each occasion under the pressure of two opposite and conflicting interests: his fractional share in the universal interest, and his own particular and personal interest. The *former* is a fraction, and everywhere a small one—a partnership interest in a firm in which the partners are counted by millions: the *latter* is an integer: and the forces with which they act, are proportional. Still, be the fraction ever so small, action will be determined by it, if the integer be either taken out of the scales, or overbalanced (*CC* 49).

The motives in question here are desires for goods in which others in the community participate as well as oneself. Unlike purely private or personal goods, pursuit of these does not conflict with the interests of others.[40]

In addition to these self-regarding motives Bentham recognized two sorts of motives which *exclude* consideration of the interests of the agent entirely, viz. (*c*) *social* motives of benevolence and sympathy and (*d*) *dissocial* motives of malevolence, cruelty, and ill will (*IPML* X. 25–6, 34–5).

It is clear that Bentham believed that self-regarding motives are in some sense 'original' in human nature, but he believed that social motives have some place in every human breast and in general are more 'natural' than dissocial motives (*IPML* VI. 27). At the very least, Bentham thought, social motives govern and direct behaviour when private interest is silent. 'For in every man, be his disposition ever so depraved, the social motives are those which, wherever the self-regarding ones stand neuter, regulate and determine the general

linked to the moral sanction. The discussion here must be qualified by the discussion in 11.5, below.

[40] Obviously this needs qualification, for the 'public goods' in question might well be limited to only some portion of the community, and conflict between the interests of that partial community and the general good is still possible. However, Bentham was aware of this and could adjust his claims to take account of it.

tenor of his life' (*IPML* XI. 42). The social motives exert 'a gentle but constant force' on human actions which is capable, except in unusual circumstances, of restraining the dissocial motives. Occasionally Bentham makes much bolder claims, insisting that social motives are capable of restraining and overcoming even self-preferential motives.[41]

The relative strength of one sort of motive over others is largely a function of the circumstances—economic, social, and cultural—within which a person lives, thinks, and acts.[42] In a primitive and undeveloped society the life of a man is solitary, his wants are few and private and he is forced to satisfy them largely by his own efforts. His motivation is entirely focused on his own private good. In such a person,

scarce a trace of sympathetic affection is visible. . . . His time is divided between pursuit of food, enjoyment of means, and reckless apathy. At which of these three times should sympathetic affection find place in his breast? . . . While he is tortured by hunger, while he is . . . gorging himself, or while he is buried in sleep or in indolence?[43]

Human beings in such conditions have neither the economic security, the leisure, nor the opportunity to recognize and pursue goods common to a community. However, as material conditions improve, as society develops, as human wants increase and individuals become more interdependent, they come to recognize common interests and common goods. Each comes to develop interests in the well-being of others and of the community. Semi-social and even social motives—co-operation, reciprocity, sympathy, and benevolence—get a foothold. Sympathy which first is generated by self-regarding concerns gradually acquires status of its own.

[41] '[In] relation to all these several sources of action, two things have . . . been shown,—viz. that [the five sanctions] are each of them distinct from all the rest, and that they are all of them what are here termed sources of action; viz. motives, or sets of motives, derived in each of these five instances from so many different sources: to which may be added, that each of them is, according to circumstances, susceptible of such a degree of force as may prove sufficient, perhaps even the weakest of them, to enable it to overpower any one or more of the rest, i.e. to give determination to human conduct, even while all those others are operating in opposition to it' (*Nomography*, Bowring iii, 292–3). The 'weakest of them' refers to the sympathetic sanction.

[42] I follow B. Parekh, 'Introduction', xiv–xv.

[43] Parekh, xv, quoting Bentham from the MSS.

According to Bentham, the circumstances of life of the 'productive class' (largely the middle class and working-class élite) make it the truly beneficent class:

In the labouring—the productive class, life in its general tenor, is a life of beneficence: whatever maleficence has place forms the exception, and in comparison with the beneficence, those exceptions are extremely rare. By the produce of his labour, he procures his own subsistence, and contributes to that of the family to which he belongs . . . At the same time to an indefinite amount according to the nature of his employment, he contributes to the gratification of others in abundance (*CC* 62).

In the producing middle class all the conditions necessary for the cultivation of semi-social and social motives obtain. While working to meet his own needs the member of such a class produces for others; his subsistence and security depend on others and they on him. His producing for himself also produces for them. Thus, if social, economic, and cultural conditions are right, human beings are capable of a life of benevolence and service.

Contrast this glowing picture of the producing segment of what Bentham calls the 'democratical' class, with the other great social class he recognizes, the 'aristocratical' or 'ultra-opulent' class. Members of this class in general are dominated by strictly self-regarding motives. Though dependent on the services of others, they are in a position to *command* them and so they never have need to reciprocate. With no checks on their power, they tend to exercise it extravagantly. None of the factors which calls for recognition of the needs and interests of others and for the independence of individuals in the community is strong enough to call up substantial semi-social, let alone social, motives.[44]

At the other end of the economic ladder are the ultra-indigent. They too, being weak and powerless, and incapable of producing enough for themselves or contributing to the common good, can be

[44] See *CC* 61-2, 43-4; and *Securities Against Misrule, Bowring* viii, 569. Bentham believed that one can feel sympathy for the plight of another person only to the extent that one can conceive of or represent to oneself that experience. Thus one who has no direct experience of the life of those of lower station, those who literally have no idea what it's like to live the other's life, will find it difficult to drum up sympathy in appropriate circumstances. 'By, and in proportion to, sympathy of affection, a man is disposed to add to the enjoyments, and subtract from the sufferings of the objects of his sympathy. Proportioned to the correctness, clearness, and completeness of the *conception* a man has of those enjoyments and sufferings, (his degree of sensibility being given,) is the strength of the sympathy of affection with relation to those same objects of his sympathy' (*CC* 110).

expected to act only out of the narrowest self-interest. Indeed, in both such extreme social situations there is likely to be substantial weight thrown behind *dissocial* motives; both are likely to engage in depredation and oppression when given the opportunity: the rich— on a large scale, because there are few checks on their power, and they lack the capacity to conceive of the costs to their victims; the poor—on a small scale, because they have no economic security and are constant victims of depredation themselves.[45]

We must not make Bentham's social psychology to be more deterministic than it is. Although, in general, he believed it was rare for a member of the aristocratical class to act out of genuine benevolence or disinterested concern for the general good, he did not think this impossible. Putting the point paradoxically, he claimed that it is possible to be a member of the democratical class by choice or identification.

[T]o the aristocratical section belong all such individuals who, by hope of factitious honour, power, or wealth, are dependent on the members of the aristocratical section: to the democratical belong all those who, their self-regarding interest in any of these shapes notwithstanding, are listed on the democratical side by sympathy with the sufferings of those belonging to that section, or by antipathy towards this or that portion of the aristocratical section: belonging in reality to a side to which they are opposed in appearance (*CC* 46).

Thus, even for individuals who are by birth or fortune members of the privileged class, it is possible to identify with the sufferings of others, self-interest notwithstanding.

This is crucial for Bentham's theory, for, despite his enthusiasm for the producing middle class, he was convinced that most government functionaries and especially judges would be drawn from the educated and privileged classes. But if cultivation of other-regarding motives is not possible, then the task of instilling and encouraging the moral aptitude in judges would be impossible. However, even here he thought the problems lay in the structure of government and the tendency to heap 'factitious honour', opulence, and power on those who do nothing to deserve it except command great fortunes. Were the form of government to change, were government to be established free from 'extravasated factitious honour', the grand superiority of royal power, and general opulence, then

---

[45] *Bowring* viii, 569; *CC* 45, 61–2; Parekh, xviii.

'sympathy, and esteem, and thence free and spontaneous service in all its shapes, would attach itself to superiority in the scale of genuine moral virtue: of effective benevolence, in harmony and alliance with self-regarding prudence.'[46]

Thus, Bentham's doctrine seems to imply that since the scope and relative force of the various motives to which the human breast is subject are determined by social and other circumstances, and since these circumstances are within our collective control to some extent, it is possible to *arrange* the circumstances within which a person lives and works such that benevolence and semi-social motives can be cultivated and given an opportunity genuinely to determine action.[47] The fact that all human motivation has its origins in self-interest does not preclude the possibility of arranging things so that other-regarding motives can play a central role in determining human action. We might say, then, that the task of constitutional design is to block bias and partiality, to neutralize motives competing with the 'most extensive and enlightened benevolence', and to allow the moral aptitude to operate unobstructed. We can put the central problem of constitutional design again: how are we to prevent the influence of partial sympathies, limited social concerns, and strictly private interests, on judicial decision-making, and make way for the influence of universal sympathy?

11.4 STRATEGIC EGOISM

> It is therefore a just political maxim, that every man must be supposed a knave . . .
>
> Hume, *Essays.*

If the reading of Bentham's psychology in the previous section is correct, what explains his persistent use of the language of psychological egoism when he sets out the foundations of his political theory?

'Interest in its most enlarged sense'

We might look for an explanation in his special use of the term 'interest'. Bentham often maintained that man is never governed by

---

[46] *CC* 81; see also UC cxi. 61–5 and Steintrager, *Bentham*, 110.
[47] UC xv. 3–125; *CC* 192. See Rosen, *Bentham and Democracy*, 206–8; Steintrager, *Bentham*, 109; Long, *Bentham on Liberty*, 189–90; Parekh, 'Introduction', pp. xiv–xix.

anything but his own interest. However, in *Of Laws in General,* he notes that this truism is 'trite' and misleading.

This observation in a large and extensive sense of the word interest (as comprehending all sorts of motives) is indubitably true: but as indubitably false in any of the confined senses in which upon such an occasion the word *interest* is wont to be made use of (*OLG* VI. 19 n. p).

Thus, 'human beings are only motivated by self-interest' is true, says Bentham, only if included within the scope of 'interest' are all possible motives—other-regarding as well as self-regarding. This 'tautological' form of egoism is again mentioned in studies that formed the basis of his *Constitutional Code* late in his career.

Of action the sole efficient cause is interest, if interest be taken in its most enlarged sense, i.e. according to each man's perception of what, at the moment in question, is his most forcibly influencing interest: the interest determined by social sympathy and antipathy, as well as that which is of a purely self-regarding complexion, included (*CC* 46).

Thus, there is no contradiction involved in maintaining both that interest alone is the cause of all action, and that human beings can be moved as well by the prospect of good or ill for others as by prospects of their own good or ill. It is, surely, in this spirit that we must read the famous 'two sovereigns' passage in the *Introduction to the Principles* (I. 1). Here Bentham announces a *hedonistic* but not necessarily an egoistic, theory of motivation. But it is not surprising that commentators have confused his hedonism with psychological egoism, for Bentham himself was not always able to keep them straight.[48]

Mill was aware of the importance of this tautological form of egoism for Bentham's political and moral theory. 'That men's actions are always determined by their interests . . .' was a foundational principle of Bentham's theory of government, Mill noted.

[48] This seems to be the problem in his important discussion of motives at *IPML* X. 9–10. In the following passage Bentham seems to be expressing the view set out more clearly in the passages quoted above in the text, but his hedonism threatens to get in the way: A disinterested action is impossible, he says, because it is an action without a cause; when I act benevolently I act only because I find pleasure in helping the other person. '[T]he pleasure I feel in bestowing pleasure on my friend, whose pleasure is it but mine? The pain I feel at seeing my friend oppressed by pain, whose pain is it but mine? And if I feel no pleasure or felt no pain, where . . . would be my sympathy? [No man can] cast off his own skin, or jump out of it . . . the most disinterested of men is not less under the dominion of interest than the most interested' (*Deontology* I. 83–4, quoted in Parekh, 'Introduction', x).

But 'there is an ambiguity in this last expression; for . . . Bentham
gave the name of an interest to anything which a person likes, the
proposition may be understood to mean only this, that men's actions are always determined by their wishes.' Mill also recognized,
however, that Bentham and others were inclined to make illicit use
of this principle: for in the above sense, 'it would not bear out any
of the consequences which these writers drew from it; and the
word, therefore, in their political reasonings, must be understood
to mean (which is also the explanation they themselves, on such
occasions, gave it) what is commonly termed private or worldly
interest.'[49]

The problem, Mill pointed out, is that Bentham often shifts without warning from a statement of his tautological egoism to the
substantive, empirical claim that we must assume that all human
beings are driven by self-interest, or at least that all potential political rulers are so driven.[50] In this way Bentham sought illicitly to
gain plausibility for his substantive claim from the self-evidence of
the tautological statement.[51] Since Bentham was clearly aware of
the difference between these two statements of egoism, we cannot
adequately explain his insistence on the principle of self-preference
as a building-block of his constitutional theory by interpreting it
along lines suggested by his tautological egoism. We are left with
the task of explaining the egoism at the foundations of his theory of
the constitution and its role in his 'duty-and-interest-junction-
principle'.

Egoism as a political maxim

It is not difficult to reconcile Bentham's non-egoistic general moral
psychology with the apparently egoistic assumptions underlying his
political theory. The solution can be found in a maxim which Hume
advanced and which deeply influenced eighteenth- and nineteenth-
century British political thought. According to Hume, in politics,
'every man ought to be supposed a *knave*, and to have no other
end, in all his actions, than private interest'. He immediately owns

[49] J. S. Mill, *A System of Logic*, Bk. VI, ch. viii, *Collected Works* VIII. 890–2.

[50] This seems to be the case in *CC* 4–8 and *Bowring* x, 79–81.

[51] Macaulay pointed out a similar illicit move in James Mill's 'Essay on Govern-
ment', see Macaulay, 'Mill's Essay on Government: Utilitarian Logic and Politics',
Edinburgh Review (1829). The essays in the *Edinburgh Review* and *Westminster
Review* in which the debate over Mill's Essay was carried on are usefully collected in
J. Lively and J. Rees, *Utilitarian Logic and Politics*.

that 'it appears strange, that a maxim should be true in *politics* which is false in *fact*'. But this is explained, according to Hume, by the fact that men are generally more honest in their private than in their public lives, for usual restraints on self-interest (and sharply limited sympathies) are removed by the special circumstances of acting in parties and other corporate bodies.[52] Hume does not claim that this is a universal psychological truth, i.e. that no cases of selfless public behaviour can be found. But he insists it is true *in general*, and thus it is reasonable to assume that public figures will be guided by self-interest. John Stuart Mill expressed the central point well in his *System of Logic*:

[I]n politics we are for the most part concerned with the conduct, not of individual persons, but either of a series of persons (as a succession of kings) or a body or mass of persons, as a nation, an aristocracy, or a representative assembly. And whatever is true of a large majority of mankind, may without much error be taken for true of a succession of persons, considered as a whole, or of any collection of persons in which the act of the majority becomes the act of the whole body. Although, therefore, the maxim is sometimes expressed in a manner unnecessarily paradoxical, the consequences drawn from it will hold equally good if the assertion be limited as follows: A succession of persons, or the majority of any body of persons, will be governed in the bulk of their conduct by their personal interests.[53]

Furthermore, the extent to which self-interest, or other-regarding concerns, actually move people to act is determined, in part at least, by their situations or circumstances. In party politics, and in the context of political institutions, human beings can be expected to act largely from self-regarding motives or narrowly limited party-oriented sympathies. Thus, it would be unreasonable to expect political leaders in these circumstances to act out of natural goodwill or benevolence. The only safe assumption to make, when considering the design of political institutions, is that every man is a knave. Hume here is advancing not a general theory of motivation, or even a theory of political motivation, but a presumptive truth and, based on it, a strategic maxim reasonable for purposes of con-

---

[52] D. Hume, 'Of the Independence of Parliament', in *Essays*, 42. James Mill quotes this passage with approval in his *Fragment on Macintosh* and makes a great deal of the distinction between the private and public man in his theory of government. See Lively and Rees, *Utilitarian Logic*, 16. This echoes Bentham in his *Plan of Parliamentary Reform*, *Bowring* iii, 526–7 and *CC* 102–3.

[53] J. S. Mill, *A System of Logic*, 891–2.

structing the best and safest political institutions. Hume sets out what I shall call *strategic egoism*.

Bentham clearly adopted a similar strategic egoism for his political theory.[54] Very early in his career he wrote, by way of apology for checks he wished to impose on judges: 'In the choice of precautions against private interest in Judges I endeavour to find out such as would do against the worst of men: if they do against these *a fortiori* will they [do] against the best. The basis of all Jurisprudence is suspicion' (UC lxiii. 4).

Similarly, in a characteristic passage in his *Constitutional Code* Bentham insists on the prevalence of self-regard over sympathy and even the necessity of this for the survival of the species. He even goes so far as to say

[W]hatsoever evil it is possible for man to do for the advancement of his own private and personal interest . . . at the expense of the public interest, —that evil sooner or later, he will do, unless by some means or other, intentional or otherwise, he be prevented from doing it (*CC* 192).

But immediately in the next paragraph he makes clear the strategic character of this claim:

To the above rule suppose there is this or that exception: still, *with a view to practice*, there might as well be none: forasmuch as by no criterion will it be possible to distinguish the individuals in whose instance the exception has place, from those in whose instance the general rule has place . . . (*CC* 192, emphasis added).

Not only is it dangerous for us to rely on the goodwill and benevolent motives of most people, but even where such motives may in fact be reliable in individual cases, we have no way of isolating those cases. '[I]t is in what has place in the conduct on the part of the thousands, and not in what has place in the conduct of one in every thousand, that all rational and useful political arrangements will be grounded (*CC* 61; cf. *Bowring* viii, 381). In designing 'rational and useful political arrangements' we must be sceptical of all claims of the inherent natural benevolence and virtue of the rulers, especially under current forms of political organization resting as they do on 'opulence', 'extravasated factitious honour', and power concentrated in the aristocracy (*CC* 81). Power itself without sufficient checks on its abuse is corrupting, but power in the hands

---

[54] Rosen, *Bentham and Democracy*, 179–81; Harrison, *Bentham*, 144–5.

of the aristocracy can only be expected to be used for the narrowest of private ends. We have already seen that Bentham held that in general the extent to which individuals are capable of acting out of semi-social or social motives is a function of the economic, social, and cultural circumstances in which they live; and that the circumstances of the aristocracy typically breed self-regarding motives and seldom benevolence or sympathy.[55] Thus, with power in the hands of the aristocracy one can expect only depredation and oppression. There may have been specimens of persons who were 'no tyrants though bred up to tyranny', but, as Perronet Thompson said, speaking for Bentham, 'it would be as wise to recommend wolves for nurses at the Foundling, on the credit of Romulus and Remus, as to substitute the exception for the general fact, and advise mankind to take to trusting to arbitrary power on the credit of these specimens'.[56]

Thus, for the purposes of designing a structure within which ordinary human beings are given considerable power and influence over others, the only safe assumption to make is that 'every man is a knave', i.e. wherever there is an opportunity for limited sympathies, partial loyalties, or personal self-interest to influence human action, these are likely to do so, especially when the rulers are drawn from the opulent class. All attempts to encourage trust in the natural virtue of governors can be viewed only as attempts to disguise established techniques for class oppression.[57] No 'rational and useful political arrangements' can be constructed on such a basis, and so, as far as practice goes—as far as we are in the business

[55] J .S. Mill moderates this view, but only slightly: 'It is not true that the actions even of average rulers are wholly or anything approaching wholly, determined by their personal interest, or even by their own opinion of their personal interest. I do not speak of the influence of a sense of duty, or feelings of philanthropy, motives never to be mainly relied on, though (except in countries or during periods of great moral debasement) they influence almost all rulers in some degree, and some rulers in a very great degree. But I insist only on what is true of all rulers, viz. that the character and course of their actions is largely influenced (independently of personal calculation) by the habitual sentiments and feelings, the general modes of thinking and acting, which prevail throughout the community of which they are members, as well as by the feelings, habits and modes of thought which characterize the particular class in that community to which they themselves belong' (*System of Logic*, 891–2).

[56] Perronet Thompson, 'The Greatest Happiness Principle', *Westminster Review*, xxi (1829) in Lively and Rees, *Utilitarian Logic*, 135. This essay was written for the *Westminster Review* by Thompson based on an extensive manuscript prepared by Bentham; see UC xiv. 314–97.

[57] *CC* 61–2, 192 *Securities Against Misrule, Bowring* viii, 569.

of designing institutions of government—we must operate on the assumption of strategic egoism, the principle of self-preference.

Bentham's constitutional strategy: a reinterpretation

But this is not to say that the only motives available to officials, and so the only motivational resources constitutional theory can rely on, are self-regarding ones. Bentham argues that it is naïve and dangerous to ignore the extent of the influence of self-regarding motives, and so any rational political structure must take steps to block the influences of such motives when they conflict with what the general welfare requires. This still leaves open the possibility, however, that a fully adequate constitutional theory will exploit *all* the available motivational resources, including the available, though naturally weaker, social motives. For even in Bentham's boldest statement of the self-preference principle, he does not deny that sympathy or other social motives are capable of influencing human action. He only maintains that in circumstances of power, opulence, and factitious honour self-regarding considerations regularly predominate (*CC* 6, 41, 51, 81, 192). His view is little changed from that expressed almost fifty years earlier in the *Introduction to the Principles* (*IPML* XVII. 7). But since the relative strength of motives is to a considerable extent a function of the situation and circumstances within which deliberation, choice, and action take place, and since these situations and circumstances are capable of being manipulated, it may be possible to block the corrupting effects of power and position, and to liberate officials and judges to act on social motives.

This requires a reinterpretation of the constitutional strategy standardly attributed to Bentham. All those who have discussed Bentham's constitutional strategy have assumed that the means employed by the 'duty-and-interest-junction principle' is that of supplying motives for action, providing incentives directly appealing to the immediate self-interest of the individuals concerned.[58] The basic model is Bentham's understanding of the criminal law. As Hart put it, Bentham viewed the 'ruling few' as 'potential

[58] This is true of those who believe that Bentham held the view that conflict between the general good and individual interest (even long-range self-interest) is inevitable, like Hart ('Introduction', to *IPML* (1982), pp. xlvi–xlix); and of those, like Lyons (*In the Interest of the Governed*, ch. 4), who believe that Bentham held the view that in the long run there is a natural harmony between self-interest and the universal interest.

criminals perennially tempted to pursue their personal interests at the expense of the public. . . . Rulers therefore were to be regarded like potential robbers whom it was necessary always to suspect and always to subject to the control of the public'.[59] On this view, the sanction—fear of punishment either at the hands of the law or the people—motivates appropriate action.

But this is not an accurate representation of Bentham's strategy. The objective of skilful, rational institutional design is not always to make it maximally profitable, from an official's self-interested point of view, for the official to do his duty. Rather it is to construct institutions that cultivate and liberate the social motives. The objective is

[t]o give increase to the influence of sympathy at the expense of that of self-regard, and of sympathy for the greater number at the expense of sympathy for the lesser number—[this] is the constant and arduous task, as of every moralist, so of every legislator who deserves to be so (*CC* 192).

Bentham goes on to link this objective to the strategic egoism we noted above.

But, in regard to sympathy, the less the proportion of it is, the natural and actual existence of which he assumes as and for the basis of his arrangements, the greater will be the success of whatever endeavours he uses to give increase to it (*CC* 192).

The task of constitutional design is to bring what *is* (i.e. the natural dominance of self-preference over other motives) into accord with what *ought to be* (i.e. preference for the aggregate good) in official actions and decisions. There is, in Bentham's view, only one method by which to accomplish this, that is by 'destroying the influence and effect of whatever sinister interest the situation of the individual may expose him to the action of; this being accomplished, he will thereby be virtually divested of all such sinister interest' (*CC* 6-7). There are two ways in which the influence of sinister interest can be destroyed (*CC* 19). First, this can be accomplished by neutralizing it, opposing it with some contrary interest of equal force:

If this sinister force can by any means be prevented from becoming in that way effective, it must be by the operation of some counterforce, in addition to that opposed by his share in the universal interest: self-preference or

---

[59] Hart, 'The United States', in *Essays on Bentham*, 68.

sinister force the temptation, counterforce the sanction, antagonizing with one another (*CC* 50).

This technique alters the influence of sinister interest by affecting the will directly. The second strategy is to take away the power or opportunity to act on the interest in question. To deprive the desire of effect, deprive the person of the power to act on and fulfil the desire (*CC* 100), Bentham advises. Now with *some* strictly self-regarding desires—like hunger, thirst, and other simple corporeal desires—to deny them satisfaction is to increase their intensity. But other self-regarding desires—in particular, desires for money or power—are diminished in intensity, and even may eventually be extinguished, through denial of gratification. It is the latter class of desires, of course, that threaten abuse of power by officials.

But in the case of those desires which have for their object any such complex good as . . . *power* or *money*, in the quantities attached to political situations, the absence of the corresponding expectation is capable of keeping the desire in a state which is altogether void of efficiency, and even to the individual himself, for want of attention to what passes in his own mind imperceptible (*CC* 100).

'Thus it is', Bentham concludes, 'that the existence, not only of gratification, but even of desire itself, may depend on a union with power' (*CC* 100). This leaves the motivational void to be filled with proper, other-regarding motives.

[T]he only interest whereby his conduct can be determined, [then, is] his right and proper interest, that interest which consists in the share he has in the universal interest, which is the same thing as to say, that interest, which is in accordance with the universal, taken in the aggregate (*CC* 7).

Thus, Bentham's constitutional strategy was not to supply a self-interested motive on which officials are supposed to act. Rather, it was to neutralize, immobilize, and eventually destroy sinister, private interests and limited sympathies, and at the same time to cultivate and liberate the widest sympathy and concern for the common good (*Bowring* iii, 460–2, 539).

'Arbitrary power (or discretion), where it can do no wrong . . . (especially) going upon the interest of the whole people . . . does the greatest right . . . (and) makes a just judicatory.'[60] Harrington's

---

[60] J. Harrington, *A System of Politics* in *The Political Writings of James Harrington*, 25–6.

maxim sums up well Bentham's constitutional strategy. The most effective way to secure against corruption and abuse of power in government officials, and especially judges, is not to constrain them about by fixed and rigid rules, which deprive them of doing good, as well as evil, but rather to arrange the institutional context within which judicial action and deliberation take place such that only motives of concern for the general or common good have freedom to operate. This, plus guarantees for maximal intellectual and active aptitude, will ensure that utilitarianly best decisions will be made.

Hart argues that Bentham reconciled his utilitarianism with his egoistic psychology by regarding the principle of utility as the sole principle for the *evaluation* of actions as right or wrong, but denying it the status of a standard for the *guidance* of the conduct of individuals.[61] In support of this interpretation he quotes Bentham's claim that 'men in general embrace this principle [of utility] . . . if not for the ordering of their own actions, yet for the trying of their own actions, as well as of those of other men' (*IPML* I. 12). But we now have good reason to resist this interpretation of Bentham's theory, at least for the case of judges and other officials. Bentham surely allows that there may be persons who will only accept the principle of utility as a principle of evaluation and will never (perhaps never be able to) regard it as a standard for guidance of their own conduct. But this is neither universally true, nor is it, in Bentham's view, inevitable. It is true only in those social or institutional circumstances in which we cannot expect any motivation to be effective except self-regarding concerns. This may be true of *some* individuals and even perhaps of whole classes (the 'ultra-indigent', for example),[62] but it is not true of all individuals, nor need it be true of all officials and judges. Indeed, his constitutional theory is premissed on the belief that institutions can be constructed which will liberate other-regarding motivations such that the principle of utility can be a genuine principle of guidance as well as a principle for the evaluation of decisions and actions—an effective decision principle, not just a principle of right action.

We can conclude that there is no conflict between Bentham's psychology and his constitutional theory. As a practical matter, we must assume that, in the absence of devices to block the influence

---

61 Hart, 'Introduction' to *IPML* (1982) p. xlviii.
62 Parekh, 'Introduction', pp. xviii–xix.

of sinister interest, officials will be governed by their own private interest. But this strategic egoism is consistent with Bentham's essentially non-egoistic general theory of motivation and with his doctrine of official aptitudes. For the task of rationally designed political institutions is to clear the motivational field for other-regarding concerns. Bentham's constitutional theory, then, does not strictly speaking rest on a strategy of artificially identifying private with public interest. It rests, rather, on a much more complex psychological and institutional theory that seeks to substitute proper motivation according to official moral aptitude for sinister motivation. Thus, not only does Bentham's moral psychology *allow for* the possibility of motivationally effective other-regarding concerns, but his political theory explicitly *relies on* them. This goes a long way toward reconciling Bentham's political theory with his psychology, on the one hand, and his doctrine of official aptitudes and theory of adjudication, on the other. However, this still leaves us with a puzzle regarding Bentham's use of moral sanctions as the primary device for control of official abuse of power. If we can reconcile his doctrine of sanctions with his doctrine of official aptitudes, the coherence of Bentham's theory of adjudication will be preserved.

11.5 JUDICIAL VIRTUES AND THE MORAL SANCTION

> Honour is a great check upon mankind.
>
> Hume, *Essays.*

We noted earlier that the primary mechanism of enforcement in Bentham's constitutional theory is the moral, rather than the legal, sanction. Bentham's reliance on this sanction would appear to undermine the argument of the previous section and the doctrine of official aptitudes generally. For, understanding the moral sanction as simply an informal version of the legal sanction, the characteristic mode of operation of the moral sanction would be to supply external, self-regarding reasons for proper official behaviour. If this is correct, the actual principle ultimately guiding official deliberation would not be the principle of utility, but rather some version of egoism. But there are good reasons for resisting the analogy between the legal and moral sanctions. The argument cannot be conclusive, and it must be admitted at the outset that some of

Bentham's language, especially in his most general theoretical statements, seems to support the analogy. Nevertheless, the evidence against the analogy is persuasive, and reveals a side of Bentham's moral psychology and constitutional theory which is much subtler than his sometimes careless general pronouncements would lead a reader to believe.

Sanctions

To begin note that there are two central properties of the legal sanction model. (*a*) Legal sanctions are motives *supplied by* a party, or 'will', different from (external to) the agent in question. Punishment is a motive *added to* the directive from the lawgiver, and not internally or logically related to the rationale for the law or the reason why the commanded behaviour is desirable (*OLG* VI. 19). (*b*) The motive or reason supplied is entirely self-regarding—it involves the likelihood of some pain or deprivation to be suffered by the agent. Now, although these two properties are, according to Bentham, conceptually necessary for the *legal* sanction—conceptually linked to the notion of *law*—they are *not* conceptually necessary features of the notion of *sanction generally*, as Bentham used it. Bentham often uses the term 'sanction' to apply indifferently to *any* motives to which human beings are susceptible. Sanctions, in Bentham's use of the term, are simply motives identified according to their sources.[63]

Thus, the term 'sanction' is applied to reasons or motives for action that simply exist *naturally*, i.e. that obtain not through, or in virtue of, the will of some other person. This is true of both the *'physical'* and the *'sympathetic'* sanction.[64] If smoking causes cancer, then the prospect of cancer gives one a motive to stop smoking, and one's imprudence is, as it were, punished if one fails to stop. So too, the suffering of another person in whose welfare one is sympathetically interested, is the natural result of ('punishment for') failing to seize the opportunity to come to the aid of the person; or witnessing his suffering will move one to take steps to alleviate the suffering (*IPML* XII. 8 n. e). In each case it is false that the 'sanction' is *imposed* by some external will. Moreover, the motives in these cases *are* internally, logically related to the practical directives involved. The reason for the practical directive 'You

---

[63] *OLG* VI. 19; *Nomography, Bowring* iii, 290, 292.
[64] *IPML* III. 3; XII. 8; *OLG* VI. 19; *Bowring* iii, 291; *RJE, Bowring* vi, 262.

must stop smoking' is that, if you do not, you are likely to contract cancer; and the reason for the directive 'I must go to his aid' is that in doing so I will prevent or alleviate his suffering. Thus, the motivational field which Bentham is willing to cover with the term 'sanction' is very wide, far wider than ordinary usage permits. In many cases calling up such motives does not involve *supplying* additional reasons for doing something which one is otherwise indifferent to or even disinclined to do, but rather involves in pointing out reasons which the agent *already has* for acting in the prescribed way. The feature of *adding* motives is important for his concept of law, but it is not essential to his concept of a sanction.

Also, the sympathetic sanction differs from the others (the moral sanction, for the moment excepted) in another respect, for it is not primarily self-regarding (*Bowring* iii, 291-2). It is the evil to be suffered by *another* person that provides the 'sanction'. Bentham adds that the strength of this motive is *increased* by the fact that the other's suffering, in appropriate circumstances, causes suffering in one's own breast, but he insists that the sanction is *not constituted* by this suffering.[65]

A final note on Bentham's use of the term 'sanction': since the term refers not to *kinds* of motives but to *sources* of motives, it is possible that one or another of the several sanctions might bring together in some loose coalition *motives* of quite different kinds.[66] This, we shall see, is true of the moral sanction.

Consider now the moral sanction. This is a middle case, falling somewhere between the legal and the sympathetic sanction, and sharing features of both. Bentham's awareness of this fact is presupposed by much of his discussion of the moral sanction and the province of private morality, although his passion for a simple, unified account of morals and legislation often led him to ignore or understate it. Bentham's comments sometimes suggest a rather crude picture of the moral sanction as simply involving informal bad treatment at the hands of the public. But often Bentham draws a much more sophisticated picture. The moral sanction relies on the 'good or evil offices' of the public. The primary operative force is the goodwill, the good opinion, the esteem of others.[67] 'It is from

[65] *Bowring* iii, 291. On this point the *Nomography* discussion represents a development and sophistication of the earlier account of sympathy in *IPML* XII. 8 n. e., which treats sympathy simply as a special case of the physical sanction.

[66] See *RJE*, *Bowring* vi, 260-1.

[67] *CC* 41; *Plan of Parliamentary Reform*, *Bowring* iii, 543; *Nomography*, *Bowring* iii, 290; *IPML* X. 22.

the opinion expected to be on each occasion inwardly entertained by them, that the good is looked for' (*CC* 42).

This, of course, is still compatible with a view of the moral sanction as an externally imposed coercive measure, analogous to legal sanctions. But this reading misrepresents Bentham's view, for, according to Bentham, there is an important *internal* side to the moral sanction which alters the picture considerably. The moral sanction relies on a person's sense of honour, shame, or self-respect.[68] Bentham is most explicit about this when he considers persons holding public office. The sovereign, for example (as we saw in 7.3) is not bound by ordinary laws, but he is bound by *leges in principem* which are enforced by the moral sanction. Bentham recognizes that this brings together a rather large family of different motives. The fear of revolt and loss of control is one of them, but it lies in the background.[69] The primary motive is shame or a sense of dishonour felt by the sovereign, which is called up by the subjects' expression of discontent or dissatisfaction. But it is shame at the thought of violation of the *leges in principem* (UC xxxiii. 79 and UC cxlii. 212).

Similarly, the moral sanction is the most powerful source of motivation for judges, according to Bentham, because judges are men of honour, for whom their good name and reputation is an overriding concern (UC lvii. 9). This suggests that where the moral sanction is at work, the agent characteristically takes an 'internal attitude' towards the criticism—to use Hart's terminology.[70] That is, the agent sees criticism not simply as so much pain or inconvenience to avoid if possible, but as closely linked, in the case of judges, to his professional identity, and more generally to his sense of self-respect. In *Securities Against Misrule*, Bentham maintains that the moral sanction of public opinion works on officials, not as the legal sanction does, but in the way that children influence parental action (and thus, he thinks, control abuse of power), even though children are under the domination of their parents (*Bowring* viii, 561). It is by appeal to something like benevolent concern and internalized moral principles that the moral sanction works. For children cannot do much, themselves, to damage a parent's repu-

---

[68] *Comment* 69; *IPML* V. 7, X. 22; *IRE, Bowring* vi, 20.

[69] UC xxxiii. 79, quoted by J. Burns, 'Bentham on Sovereignty: an Exploration', 144. See also *Securities Against Misrule, Bowring* viii, 562.

[70] H. L. A. Hart, *Concept of Law*, 55–6, 86–8.

tation, or visit bad treatment on a parent. They can, however, appeal to a parent's sense of what is just or proper treatment, and appeal to a parent's sense of duty or responsibility as a parent. Such 'influence' calls up the prospect of pain, of course, but more on the analogy of the sympathetic sanction than of the legal sanction. The sanction is internally related to the practical demands on parental behaviour.

We find this view of the moral sanction already at work in Bentham's early *Comment on the Commentaries*. In a passage discussed earlier in 7.1, Bentham argues that even in the absence of explicit law a carrier is required to follow custom and make good lost or damaged goods entrusted to him—required, he claims, '[b]y considerations of what is called Natural justice enforced by the moral Sanction' (*Comment*, App. E, p. 334). But the relation between the sanction and the reason for the requirement to make good the losses is not merely external and contingent, as in the case of legal sanctions. Bentham holds that the carrier is inclined to follow custom here for fear of losing the goodwill of the community. It is clear, however, that the fear arises from the recognition that if he were to fail to make good the losses, the community would have *good reason* to think poorly of him.[71] Furthermore, the carrier recognizes that the same framework of mutual expectations (and ultimately the principle of utility) which justifies their sanctioning activity in response to his failure gives him reasons to make good the losses. This is not the standard sanction theory of obligation modelled after the law. There is here something *akin* to appeal to shared principles, principles which both justify, and provide motives for, the customary demands on behaviour, and which justify the sanctioning reactions on the part of the public when these demands are not met.

This account of the moral sanction fits well with the doctrine of publicity and the view of constant *responsibility* of officials to the public which we considered in 11.2. Bentham identified full

---

[71] 'Being entrusted with the goods, having that profit by them. . . . having it in their power to take care of them, and the owner no longer having it in his, it seemed reasonable that the Carrier should be answerable. The owner always expected it. The Carrier was sensible it was expected of him, and prepared himself accordingly. *It being reasonable [that] he should*, he had reason to think that if he did not, he should be thought to have acted unjustly, that in consequence he would be liable to lose in a certain degree the good will of his acquaintance . . .' (*Comment*, App. E, 334, emphasis added).

publicity and complete responsibility with mobilization of the moral sanction. Bentham's (perhaps rather naïve) view was that in this way public censure—guided by the principle of utility—would encourage officials, especially judges, better to apply that same standard to their actions and deliberations. It is for this reason that Bentham insisted that justification of official actions and decisions be attempted only in a language of political morality which is capable of being made fully public. In Bentham's view, the moral sanction of public opinion, though it may also include cruder aspects, at its heart involves appeal to this public language of political morality and to the judge's sense of honour in acting according to its dictates.

Moral sanctions and 'private deontology'

Although the focus of attention of this chapter has been on Bentham's doctrine of *official* virtues, and the formal institutional structures necessary to maximize their effect, nevertheless confirmation of the above interpretation of the moral sanction can be found in Bentham's account of 'private ethics', and I wish to look briefly at this doctrine before I close the book on the moral sanction.

Our focus for discussion is Chapter XVII of the *Introduction to the Principles*, where Bentham considers the relationship between public and private ethics. He maintains at the outset that they are both species of ethics, i.e. of 'the art of directing men's actions to the production of the greatest possible quantity of happiness, on the part of those whose interest is in view' (*IPML* XVII. 2). Public ethics is the art of government proper—the arts of legislation and administration; private ethics is the art of *self*-government (*IPML* XVII. 3). He goes on in paragraph 20 to say

Private ethics teaches how each man may dispose himself to pursue the course most conducive to his own happiness, by means of such motives as offer of themselves: the art of legislation . . . teaches how a multitude of men, composing a community, may be disposed to pursue that course which upon the whole is the most conducive to the happiness of the whole community, by means of motives to be applied by the legislator.

It is clear from this passage that private morality is a matter of self-direction, and not direction from informal community authorities. It is also true, though less clear from the passage, that the guiding principle is the principle of utility.[72] The moral sanction, it appears, has been entirely left out of the picture. But it has not been left out, as is clear in a parallel passage in *Of Laws in General*: 'To [private] ethics it belongs to ascertain the cases in which on the one hand the punishment, and on the other the reward of the moral sanction ought to apply: and to instruct a man how to avoid the one and obtain the other' (*OLG* XVII. iii. 4). The moral sanction is not to be understood as distinct from private ethics, according to Bentham, but as an important part of it. Private ethics, like public, is the art of *government*, the art of directing human action to the end of the greatest happiness of the community. Directing action, for Bentham, necessarily involves both setting out some desired course of action (issuing a command or prescription), and providing *motives* for pursuing that course of action. A practical directive for which there are no available motives for compliance seeks an effect without supplying a cause. The *art* of ethics, like the *art* of legislation, is concerned with techniques for motivating rational agents to do what is right; it is not a set of rules or principles defining right or proper conduct.[73] If the motives are not to come from external threats, they must come from some other source. The moral sanction will be among the sources.

Earlier in the chapter Bentham asked what motive can incline one to consult the happiness of others, i.e. to obey the dictates of probity and beneficence. He replied that self-interest is the most reliable, but it is not the only available motive, for 'there are no occasions in which a man has not some motives for consulting the happiness of other men' (*IPML* XVII. 7). These are either the 'purely social motive of sympathy or benevolence', or the 'semi-social motives of love of amity and love of reputation'. He argues that, in general, the legal sanction is best limited to securing compliance with the dictates of probity (non-maleficence), and that the dictates of beneficence are best (on utilitarian grounds) left to

---

[72] The first part of the passage provided Lyons with the strongest (and only direct) evidence for his 'differential' interpretation of the principle of utility, according to which the private agent, who governs only his own conduct, must be guided only by the principle of rational egoism. See *In the Interest of the Governed*, chs. 2, 4. But I will argue shortly that Bentham does not claim that the individual agent must follow some version of rational egoism. For other criticisms of Lyons's interpretation see L. J. Hume, 'Revisionism,' 9, J. Dinwiddy, 'Bentham on Private Ethics', F. Rosen, *Bentham and Democracy*, 203–6.

[73] See *CC* 192 quoted above, p. 390. Also see Hart, 'Introduction' to *IPML* (1982) pp. l–li; and generally, Dinwiddy, 'Bentham on Private Ethics'.

private ethics, i.e. to the motives of sympathy *and the moral sanction* (*IPML* X. 22).

Furthermore, he argues, in cases where the legal sanction would be unprofitable (i.e. cause, on the whole, greater suffering than it could prevent) the most the legislator can do is give encouragement and direction to the moral sanction, and *thereby* 'increase the efficacy of private ethics' (*IPML* XVII. 15). It is hard to deny, then, that Bentham believes the moral sanction to be not only an external enforcer of private ethics (as law is), but an essential part of it.

If this is so, then the self-directing aspect of private ethics forces us to view the moral sanction not only from the 'outside', as it were, but also from the 'inside'. It is only in this way that we can make sense of the passage from *Of Laws in General* just quoted (p. 399). Private ethics, says Bentham, teaches one how to determine when the moral sanction *ought* to apply. Now, if the moral sanction were viewed strictly on the model of the legal, as a special motive *added to* certain practical directives, then private ethics should instruct us how to ascertain in what cases the moral sanction *will* apply—not where it *ought* to apply. But it instructs us when it *ought* to apply, because the principle by which one's conduct is to be directed is the principle by which the moral sanction *is justified* in being applied, and the moral sanction involves first of all an appeal to this principle. This is not to deny that there is still an 'external' aspect of the moral sanction, or that it resembles in some ways the legal sanction. It is rather to assert that private ethics is social morality *viewed from within*—internalized. Thus, the moral sanction is a true middle case falling between the legal and the sympathetic sanction.

It falls between these two types of sanction in another way, which gives us a clue to what Bentham had in mind in that puzzling passage in Chapter XVII. 20 of the *Introduction* (see above, p. 398). There he said that private ethics involves directing a man to his own good. According to Lyons this implies that, unlike public ethics, the principle of private ethics is a form of rational egoism. This is an implausible reading for two reasons. First, in his later writings Bentham clearly includes beneficence and other-regarding ('social') motives in the repertoire of private ethics.[74] Second, the

---

[74] *Chrestomathia, Bowring* viii, 94. In his late 'Article on Utilitarianism' prepared for the *Westminster Review* (see n. 56), Bentham divides private morality into 'self-regarding prudence' and 'effectual benevolence', and further subdivides the

moral sanction involves the *semi*-social motives of honour, self-respect, concern for reputation, and what we might call professional integrity. Bentham often stresses the self-regarding side of these motives and standardly classifies them with the legal and physical sanctions. But at other times he plays down this self-regarding aspect (e.g. at *IPML* XVII. 19). Thus, he seems to have grasped, though uncertainly, an important insight. The motives to which the moral sanction appeals do indeed fall between pure self-regard and pure concern for others. They are non-self-regarding in that they are concerned with doing the right or honourable thing, and not with the advancement of one's own private good. But they have, to some extent (perhaps varying from person to person), a self-regarding character in that they appeal ultimately to one's sense of self-respect, one's conception of oneself as a good parent, just and honourable judge, or principled public official. Semi-social motives are just those, according to Bentham, which although other-directed, do not exclude from consideration the agent's own good. They are other-regarding, but not exclusively so.

Thus, if to private ethics it falls to direct a man to avoid the 'punishment' and seek the 'reward' of the moral sanction, then it involves directing a man to his *own* good in a wide sense of that term. And this is consistent with the basic *principle* of private ethics being none other than the principle of utility. Moreover, it is clear that we must not understand the moral sanction on the model of the legal sanction.

It is time to tie these remarks regarding Bentham's view of the moral sanction to his doctrine of official aptitudes and his strategy of constitutional design. Bentham seems to hold that, when they work properly, the motives of sympathy and the complex of motives constituting the moral sanction are closely linked (*IPML* X. 36-8). Ideally, they are guided by the same rational principle—the principle of utility. However, Bentham points out that neither necessarily conforms to the principle of utility. The dictates of utility are those of the most extensive, universal benevolence, but sympathy can be limited and partial (*IPML* X. 36). To this extent the moral

former into that which is purely self-regarding and that which is extra–regarding. (The latter concerns 'the feeling of other persons, on account and in consideration of the influence which those same feelings may have on those actions of the persons in question by which his own feelings—his own happiness may be affected.') See UC xiv. 380.

sanction instructs and guides the motive of sympathy. On the other hand, Bentham admits that the moral sanction is not always guided by the principle of utility (*IPML* X. 38). But, as we have already seen, he takes a very optimistic—actually quite naïve—view of this, at least in the context of his constitutional theory. Public opinion, he believes, will generally accord with the dictates of utility, and is tending to do so ever more consistently (*CC* 158). Putting aside questions of the plausibility of this view, it should be clear that if this is Bentham's view, then his reliance on the moral sanction does not jeopardize his definition of the moral aptitude ('the disposition to decide according to the dictates of the principle of utility'), and it further supports the alternative interpretation of Bentham's constitutional strategy which I advanced in the previous section. For the moral sanction can be viewed from two points of view: the internal and the external. From the external perspective, the moral sanction threatens dishonour, and the like, which provide (in Bentham's mind) a sufficient counterbalance to the prospect of individual gain at public expense through corruption and abuse of power (see *CC* 50). From the internal point of view, the moral sanction strengthens and corrects the sympathetic sanction. Both draw their guidance ultimately from the principle of utility.

12

Utilitarian Adjudication within
the Shadow of the Code

Discernment, or the art of judging of individual capacity, is a rare
quality, whose use it is impossible to supersede by general rules.

Bentham, *Rationale of Reward.*

I have traced separately the development of each of the central
elements of Bentham's theories of law and adjudication. It remains
for us to consider whether these elements can be stitched together
into a coherent and systematic theory.

12.1 UTILITARIAN ADJUDICATION:
OUTLINE OF THE THEORY

Bentham set out to construct a theory of adjudication which recon-
ciles the two fundamentally conflicting ends of certainty and flexibility in adjudication under law. Already early in his career the
basic principles of construction were fixed: security of expectations
must be maximized; and to this end he insisted on (i) the publicity
of all standards to be used in adjudication and full publicity of all
decisional processes, and (ii) the absolute subordination of the
judge to the legislator, which involves both restricting the exercise
of judicial discretion and blocking all forms of judicial lawmaking.
However, it is equally clear that he maintained steadfastly throughout his career the absolute sovereignty of the principle of utility.
These demands on law and adjudication seem to pull decisively in
opposite directions. Bentham struggled with this problem with
amazing persistence throughout his career. He experimented with
several different suggestions, but it was not until he had fully developed his procedural and constitutional theories that he felt reasonably satisfied with his solution.

Commentators and critics of Bentham's legal theory have never
done full justice to the complexity and intricacy of his theory of

adjudication. Either they stress his attacks on the arbitrariness and uncertainty of Common Law and maintain that his passion for codification and his principle of judicial subordination dictate a strictly mechanical theory of adjudication;[1] or they stress the broad definition of the role of the judge one finds in the later, largely procedural, writings and its grant of apparently unrestrained discretion to the judge, and consequently ignore the importance of the code in Bentham's theory of adjudication.[2] These misinterpretations arise from a failure to look carefully at the basic arguments Bentham directed against the Common Law. The close analysis of these arguments undertaken in Part II has made possible an understanding of the full scope of Bentham's theory.

As we saw in Chapters 6 and 8, the primary defect of Common Law, according to Bentham, lay in the fact that it could not adequately secure expectations. But Bentham soon became convinced that this could not be corrected simply by providing fixed and unalterable rules with which to constrain the alleged arbitrariness of judicial decision. Indeed, Bentham argued that inflexible rules in fact considerably increase the scope for arbitrariness of decision. (This is what I called, for Bentham, 'the paradox of inflexibility'.) The most striking feature of this argument is that, although it was thought by Bentham to apply with greatest force against a Common Law system governed by a principle of strict *stare decisis*, he also realized that it applies with considerable force against *any* system of fixed rules—even one designed according to the blueprint for codification drawn up in *Of Laws in General*. A fully systematic, comprehensive set of utilitarian codes are, for Bentham, absolutely essential for certainty and the security of expectations, but the codes alone cannot answer the needs of flexibility which Bentham felt so keenly. Room had to be made for a fully flexible, though completely public and responsible, system of adjudication under the code. The basic decision principle for *both* the construction of the code, and for adjudication under it, was to be the principle of utility.

Bentham sought to reconcile the conflicting ends of security and flexibility not by rejecting or severely modifying one or the other of

---

[1] This interpretation is suggested in the very useful paper by M. H. James, 'Bentham on the Individuation of Laws', 93–4; see also L. J. Hume, *Bentham and Bureaucracy*, 470–4.

[2] See, e.g., Halévy, *Philosophic Radicalism*, 403 and Rosenblum, *Bentham's Theory of the Modern State*, 96–7.

the conflicting principles, but rather by so defining the institutions of lawmaking and adjudicating (i.e. by restricting the jurisdictions of these institutions) that these principles no longer significantly conflict. The key to Bentham's solution lay in the interior of his arguments against Common Law adjudication. The basic problem with Common Law adjudication, argued Bentham, was not that judges made law, or from time to time set aside objectionable rules of law, but rather that they were forced to *make law in the process of adjudicating.* Security is possible, he insisted, only when the functions of lawmaking and of adjudicating particular cases under law are radically separated. But further, if they are in fact radically separated—and if appropriate constitutional and procedural safeguards are developed—not only is security best served, but so too is flexibility (and thus the principle of utility can be given its sovereign due). In basic outline, then, Bentham's complete theory of adjudication looks something like the following.

First, *all* lawmaking authority is ultimately to be located in the legislature. Laws are to be expressed in the form of a completely systematic, comprehensive code (or set of codes) on the pattern developed in *Of Laws in General.* The code must meet standards of publicity and simplicity, as well as completeness. Second, the judge's duty is to resolve all disputes that arise in the jurisdiction once the code is promulgated. He must, first, make every effort to resolve the conflict through mediation; and when (but only when) such efforts fail, or the net costs of a negotiated settlement are greater than the net costs of an imposed decision, the judge must decide on the merits of the case. Such decisions must be made ultimately by appeal to the balance of utilities in the particular case at hand. The judge will treat the code as a guide setting out the relevant (utilitarian) considerations to be taken into account, and indicating the most important expectation utilities, but he will not regard it as a set of fixed rules determining his decision in a mechanical way. Third, in no circumstances will any judicial decision be deemed to have precedential effect. The effect of the judge's resolution of the dispute is strictly limited to the case before him, and he is to consider only the utilities relevant to the decision in that particular case. Fourth, by maximizing *responsibility* of judges, abuse of this wide discretion is guarded against. Proper attention to the relevant utilitarian considerations—to the exclusion of bias and sinister interest—is focused by procedural and constitutional arrangements which maximize the publicity of decisions and the reasoning for them. Control of abuse rests heavily on the mobilization of the moral sanction. Fifth, judicial lawmaking (largely by way of interpretation or 'emendation' of the code) is to be permitted, but as an operation separate from adjudication of the case which gave rise to the question of interpretation, and only through the constitutionally defined 'emendation process' which gives the legislature formal veto power over any interpretation of the code. Thus, a case which raises a serious question of interpretation of the law must be treated in two distinct stages. First, the particular case is decided ultimately by application of the principle of utility to the peculiar features of the particular case; then the question of interpretation or alteration of the law is considered, apart from the details of the particular case, applying the principle of utility again, but this time asking whether the *rule* as it stands can be justified on utilitarian grounds, or whether some revision or alteration of the rule is called for.

A model of Bentham's theory of adjudication is provided by his theory of evidence and his view of the role of the judge in procedural matters generally. The judge, whether ruling on admission or weight of evidence or deciding some other procedural matter, must keep immediately in mind the direct and collateral 'ends of justice'. With the legislator's recommendations and instructions in mind (which might be contained in a procedure code or a set of instructions regarding reliability of evidence), the judge must weigh the utilities represented by these ends in each particular case and make his decision on the basis of the outcome of that weighing process. As always, the guiding and sole ultimate principle for the judge is the principle of utility. Furthermore, the judge is to consider only the case before him and the consequences of the decision in it; he is not to consider how his decision, if taken as precedent for future cases, would affect community welfare. The legislator, for his part, should provide the judge not with fixed rules, but with appropriate powers; he should set out fundamental ends, and include instructions, or the best evidence available, on the best means for achieving these ends. This model is familiar to us from our discussion in Chapter 10, above, and I shall argue here that Bentham did not limit it to procedural matters (e.g. evidence), but generalized it to cover adjudication of all disputes.

This, in outline, is Bentham's theory. Bentham's strategy was to maintain the principle of utility as the basic decision principle for both the lawmaking and the adjudicating functions. These functions are separable, according to Bentham, because importantly different utilitarian questions are raised in each and the utilitarian solution to the adjudicative problem may not be directly derivable from the utilitarian solution to the legislative (rule-making) problem. On this view, security of expectations is guaranteed primarily by a public, accessible, and comprehensive code of laws, and a (nearly) absolute proscription on judicial legislation. Any change in the basic ground rules in the community will emanate ultimately from a single source and only according to a fully public and accountable process. Correction and improvement of the code is possible, and the vast experience and knowledge of the day-to-day working of the code which judges acquire are harnessed in this process, but always subject to the will of the legislature. The full attention of the judge is focused on the dispute before him, and its resolution must be based solely on the utilities relevant to that case. (These will include not only the utilities and expectations of the parties, but also those of the whole community as well, but only as they are affected by this particular decision.) Constraint on the abuse of judicial power is provided in the only effective way available: through making the proceedings and the process of justification of judicial decisions fully public, thereby maximizing accountability.

Bentham's theory is surely unusual in the early nineteenth century. It combines in one account both (i) central elements of the codification movement (while rejecting the usual natural law theory on which it was grounded) and (ii) elements of the theory of equity. Unlike Blackstone, Bentham gave institutional expression to an essentially standard Aristotelian view of the role of equity (returning the rib of equity to the side of law from which it had been ripped by enterprising judges—*FG*, Preface, p. 395). Equitable correction does not always call for revision of the general rule of law in question. For even the best and most just of general rules may yield injustice in some particular cases. Burke expressed well the Aristotelian dictum which lies at the heart of Bentham's theory of adjudication: 'As no legislators can regard the minima of equity, a law may in some instances be a just subject of censure without

being at all an object of repeal.'³ Thus, there is a sharp difference
between utilitarian adjudication within the shadow of the law and
the 'correction' of the law it may call for in specific cases, on the
one hand, and legislative repeal, reform, or interpretation of the
law itself, on the other. These functions are kept separate, and
responsible performance of each secured, by denying adjudicative
corrective decisions precedential effect, by insisting on the absolute
publicity of all decisions, and by designing a special process for
'legislative' correction of the law by judges. Bentham believed that
in this way he had protected the people from the dangers always
posed by equity and the discretionary exercise of adjudicative
power. It is often said that we are destined to be ruled either by
fixed general rules, or by the arbitrary judgment of individuals (i.e.
by laws or by men). Bentham rejected this dilemma, by rejecting
the assumption on which it rests. In his view we are ruled well, and
genuine security is possible, only if we are ruled to the fullest extent
possible by *both*.

12.2   UTILITARIAN ADJUDICATION: PROTOTYPES

[I]n no case, on no occasion, . . . lay down inflexible rules.

Bentham, *PJP*.

Evidence provided in the previous chapters makes the above interpretation of Bentham's views on adjudication difficult to resist, but
there is direct evidence for it in some of Bentham's latest work on
adjudication and the structure of judicial institutions. In this
section I shall consider primarily Bentham's *Principles of Judicial
Procedure* and his *Equity Dispatch Court* papers. These works are
of special interest because in them judicial activity and the proper
grounds and limits of judicial decision-making are considered explicitly against the background of his larger work on the Constitutional Code⁴ and with the explicit assumption that the judge is
operating within a structure of substantive codes designed on his

³ Edmund Burke, *Tract on the Popery Laws, Works* VI. 317–18.
⁴ Some of the MS material for *PJP* dates from as early as 1802–3, but the bulk
was written in the years between 1823 and 1827 (?). See UC lii–lvii. The *Equity
Dispatch Court* papers were penned between May 1829 and March 1831 (see n. 11,
below). Much of the material for *Constitutional Code*, Bk. II, ch. XII ('Judiciary
Collectively') was written during this period (1823–8). In fact, there are repeated
references in *PJP* and the Dispatch Court papers to the cognate discussion in *CC*.

utilitarian blueprint. Thus, we have in these works a discussion of the role of the judge against the background of Bentham's fully developed views regarding both codification and the constitutional and procedural matters discussed in earlier chapters.

The Principles of Judicial Procedure

In Chapter 7 of *PJP* Bentham turns his attention to the form which the codewriter's directives to the judge should take. Echoing his attack on static Common Law rules, he insists that no rules be laid down which do not permit the judge to appeal to overriding utilitarian considerations if they present themselves in particular cases.

For minimizing evil, the main caution is, *in no case, on no occasion*, to lay down inflexible rules . . .

The pretence in this case is, the avoiding to place arbitrary power in the hands of the judge. But the good thus sought is illusory (*Bowring* ii, 31, emphasis added).

The aim of curbing abuse of power with fixed rules is illusory for two reasons, according to Bentham. First, it generates the same tensions between strict and liberal interpretation as does a regime of rigid *stare decisis* (*PJP, Bowring* ii, 32), and thus is likely to encourage *greater* arbitrariness and undermine public accountability ('the paradox of inflexibility'). Secondly, discretionary power in the hands of a judge, no matter how wide, is evil only in so far as its effect is to cause harm or evil of some sort to some assignable individuals, and that power can be used to benefit, as well as to harm. But, he insists, 'where an inflexible rule, as to quantity of anything, is laid down, the chances against its not producing evil in excess, are as infinity to one' (*PJP, Bowring* ii, 31).

The argument behind this second point is obscure, but perhaps the following captures the main thrust. It is not arbitrariness *in itself* that is objectionable, but only the actual suffering of individuals resulting from it; but the likelihood of misdecision, and its attendant suffering, he argues, is greater under a regime of fixed rules than under a regime of discretionary judicial decision-making. Uncharacteristically, Bentham seems to ignore here the general, systemic evil of alarm that would result from the widespread conviction that judicial decision-making is arbitrary. Or does he assume that such general concerns are provided for in other ways? The latter is more likely if we consider the comments about 'responsibility' discussed below. But if that is so, then he seems to be saying that the judge, considering each particular case on its own utilitarian terms, is much more likely to get the decision right than is some legislator attempting to get this case, and hundreds of others, right with just one rule. Rules constructed to cover an indefinite number of cases cannot avoid insensitivity to the special features of the cases that fall under them.[5] Perhaps, then, the task of the legislator is different from that of the judge. The judge must attempt to get the 'quantities' (the utilitarian balance) right in each case, but this is not the proper job of the legislator.

The abuse of judicial power cannot be combated effectively with fixed and inflexible rules; indeed 'the only effectual, or efficient security, is composed of responsibility: substantial, punitional, and dislocational responsibility, legal and moral' (*PJP, Bowring* ii, 31). And, he adds, precautions against abuse of power should not be taken in some substantive code of law, but in the procedure and constitutional codes, i.e. not in rules binding judicial decisions, but in the institutional arrangements within which they make their decisions. This, of course, invites us to introduce all the considerations discussed at length in the previous chapter. In particular, it links directly to the doctrine of official aptitudes and the principles of

---

[5] This does not make clear, yet, what exactly the problem is, according to Bentham. In a passage in *RJE*, parallel to that from *PJP* just quoted, he argues that no reliable general rules regarding the admission or assessment of evidence can be constructed either by judges or legislators. The reason is that 'the chances against right decision [are] . . . infinity to one. The ground of decision in each case will be, not the circumstances of that individual case, not the proportions between the quantities in that case, but the circumstances of, the proportions between, the quantities in some other case . . . in which they have but one chance against an infinity of chances for not being different from what they are in the case in hand' (*RJE, Bowring* vii, 345). No doubt this argument rests in part on Bentham's assumption that the assessment of evidence is radically situation-relative (a matter of 'instinctive' judgment—*RJE, Bowring* vi, 216). But since he uses the same argument with regard to other sorts of rules as well, it cannot draw much support from this special feature of evidential judgments. The above argument suggests that the problem is one of failure of vision on the part of the rule-maker—his exclusive focus being on the special features of a particular case without any appreciation for the variety of different cases to which the general rule will be made to apply. Misdecision is inevitable under such rules. This, however, is a puzzling argument, for it locates the defect not in *rules*, but in failures of rule-makers, and in failures which do not seem to be ineradicable. (Indeed, Bentham himself held that this sort of failure of vision was curable through taking up the code-writer's comprehensive view equipped with Bentham's general principles and method (see below, 12.3).) Elsewhere, we shall see, Bentham does pin the blame on *rules*: they are unavoidably 'under-and-over-inclusive', and so inevitably arbitrary. I will discuss this in detail in 13.1, below.

constitutional simplicity and publicity which are aimed at maximizing the 'moral aptitude' of judges.

In this connection Bentham mentions two 'remedies rendering inflexible rules needless': (i) the judge's 'obligation to rationalize', and (ii) the judge's 'sistitive and law emendative function'.[6] The second remedy, of course, refers to the procedure mentioned briefly in *Of Laws in General*, and set out in detail in the *Constitutional Code*.[7] The judge is empowered to alter the rule if it offends the general welfare and the problem can be remedied through correction of the rule.

The first remedy is explained further in the published text.

Of the several rules laid down in this code, there is not one that is meant to be regarded as inflexible: no one is there, from which, in case of necessity, the judge may not depart. But as often as he thus departs, the constituted authorities (the public opinion tribunal included) will be looking to him for the reason . . .

Every such reason, will consist in an indication of the evil which, in the individual case in question, would result from compliance with the rule: and with a proof, that by the aberration, either no evil in any shape has been produced, or none but what has been outweighed by concomitant good (*PJP*, *Bowring* ii, 32).

The judge is entirely accountable for every decision he makes under the law. And this accountability requires complete public justification for each decision in the public language available for such activity (i.e. in the language of the principle of utility). To fail to provide public justification in any case is considered by Bentham to be a violation of judicial duty.

The doctrine that arbitrary judicial power is most effectively curbed through publicity is familiar to us now. In *A Treatise on Judicial Evidence* he considers the objection that his rule-less theory of evidence grants judges too much arbitrary power, and replies that

in judicial matters, dangerous powers in the judges are those which they usurp in opposition to the law, rather than those which they receive from the law, and which they can exercise only under the eyes of the public that looks on them with distrust. The least formidable of all, are those

---

6 Headnote for the MS from which the text of sect. 5 of ch. vii of *PJP* (*Bowring* ii, 32) was taken (UC lii(a). 229). Here Bentham explicitly calls attention to the relevant chapters in his *Constitutional Code* concerning the judiciary.

7 *OLG* XIX. 6; *CC* Bk. II, ch. XII, sects. 20–1. See the Appendix to this chapter.

discretionary powers with which they are entrusted, only on the express condition of giving in every case, the reason why they use them. This check is sufficient, because it leaves their responsibility undiminished.[8]

'Publicity', he maintains a few pages earlier, 'is the preservative against anything arbitrary' (*Treatise on Judicial Evidence*, 231). Arbitrariness has, for Bentham, two defining features: (i) official action contrary to law, i.e. action *ultra vires*, and (ii) official action which is insufficiently public and thus insufficiently accountable. But, by granting the judiciary the constitutional power to make such decisions, and protecting against abuse through full public accountability of every exercise of the power, all plausible charges of arbitrariness levelled against the exercise of judicial discretion can be met.

Thus, Bentham's remarks in *The Principles of Judicial Procedure* (and the *Treatise on Judicial Evidence*) lend support to the interpretation of Bentham's view of adjudication set out in the previous section. But it might be objected that the works in question are explicitly concerned only with procedural matters, and thus generalization to substantive matters is unwarranted. This, I believe, is not a serious objection. First, two of the three examples Bentham uses in *The Principles of Judicial Procedure* to illustrate his point about the dangers of inflexible rules concern non-procedural matters. (One deals with the question of proper compensation, the other with sentencing.) This suggests strongly that Bentham did not believe his argument to be of only limited application. Second, this is consistent with a pattern one sees throughout Bentham's writings. His *general* reflections on adjudication tend to be found in his procedural or constitutional works in which the main question is one of the proper structure of judicial institutions. But consideration of this question prompts a discussion not only of the rules needed to structure the institution, but also of the role of rules in the decision-making process generally. Thus, there is no reason to regard his arguments as restricted to *procedural* rules, as if there were something especially problematic about them.[9] More-

---

[8] Bentham, *A Treatise on Judicial Evidence* (Dumont ed. 1825), 237. See also *IRE, Bowring* vi, 97 n, and Halévy, *Philosophic Radicalism*, 390.

[9] Also the objection assumes that Bentham's approach to adjective law was sharply different from his approach to substantive law, perhaps on the assumption that the former is 'lawyer's law' governing only the formal and artificial processes of forensic argument and proof and not governing directly the behaviour of ordinary citizens or affecting their lives outside of court. But this was not his view. In *Of*

over, the arguments Bentham develops against inflexible rules
governing judicial decisions are explicitly general in scope, applying
equally to substantive and adjective rules, and they reflect concerns
which we have traced throughout Bentham's writings. The main
outlines of these arguments were made clear already in early critical
discussions of Common Law, and were never restricted to adjective
law. But perhaps the strongest evidence that Bentham had in mind
judicial decision-making regarding substantive as well as procedural
matters can be found in his contemporaneous proposal for an ex-
perimental 'Equity Dispatch Court'.

The Equity Dispatch Court

A few remarks about Bentham's objectives in writing this piece are
necessary if we are to understand its importance for his theory.[10] By
the beginning of the nineteenth century the Court of Chancery had
abandoned its vocation as a court of appeal from the rigidity of
Common Law. It was a commonplace that its rules had become as
rigid as the Common Law it was designed to correct. Furthermore,
its procedure was so cumbersome and antiquated that it could not
handle the volume of cases brought before it. Enormous delays
were common and consequently the expense of having a case tried
in Chancery was very great. The situation became so grave that
Parliament became greatly concerned around 1824-5, and the drive
for some sort of relief gathered even greater momentum in the
period from 1827 to 1829. Bentham was keenly aware of these
problems and harboured hopes of seeing Brougham installed in the
post of Lord Chancellor. Bentham and Brougham were very close
in the years 1827-30, and Bentham pinned on Brougham all his
hopes for law reform, especially reform of Chancery, along utilitarian lines. Bentham seized this opportunity to bring to public

Laws in General Bentham insisted that the requirements of adjective law be treated
in the same way as substantive excuses and defences, as the precise definitions of
property, title, condition in life, etc., and as the careful definition of the offence
itself are treated, viz. as exceptions or limitations on the substantive law. The reason
for this was the fact that all such conditions affect the application of the substantive
law and thus affect ordinary citizen behaviour in similar ways. There is, then, in
Bentham's view, no sharp difference in kind of operation or effect between substantive law and adjective law, though there may be a difference in degree.

[10] I am indebted to Professor J. H. Burns for the historical background of
Bentham's writing of the papers relating to his proposal for an Equity Dispatch
Court. See Holdsworth, *A History of English Law* I, 442-5; and M. Shapiro,
Courts, 101-4.

attention, and to test on a limited scale, the procedural reforms he had advocated since the 1790s. The first suggestion of a scheme for an 'Equity Dispatch Court'—which would relieve the Chancery backlog and at the same time demonstrate the virtues of his procedural reforms—appeared in his *Justice Petition* (*Bowring* v, 437–545 (1829)). Bentham turned his full attention to this scheme in the spring of 1829.[11]

Bentham's objective was to replace the system of 'regular procedure', the corruption, injustice, and inefficiency of which was epitomized by Chancery procedure, with his utilitarian 'natural' system. This project recalls his work at the turn of the century in *Scotch Reform* and *The Court of Lords' Delegates*. The model for his 'natural' system, was the 'domestic tribunal'. Its primary virtue was its summary, and (according to Bentham) altogether rational, character. Not above using the rhetoric of his opponents when it served him, he cited as favourable precedent the old Saxon system of local judicatories (manorial and local hundreds courts), as well as the courts of arbitration established by William III.[12]

The main structural features are those outlined and defended at great length in his systematic work on procedural and constitutional arrangements which we considered in the preceding two chapters. The details need not concern us, although it should be pointed out that here, as in *PJP*, Bentham clearly had in mind his monumental work, the *Constitutional Code*. From many of Bentham's comments in this material it is clear that he is applying that general structure to the particular problem at hand, and in the process further developing his general theoretical structure.[13]

Let us focus on his discussion of judicial decision-making. Here his views are crystal clear and startlingly radical. (Or, rather, they would be startling if we had not been prepared for them by our earlier study of Bentham's attack on Common Law.) He addresses

[11] The Dispatch Court papers are published in *Bowring* iii, 296–431. The manuscripts are to be found in UC lxxxi. 94–167; UC cxiv. 221–92; and UC lxxxvi. 1–416. The earliest MSS date from March 1828, but he seems to have worked most on it through the summer, autumn, and winter 1829–30 and then intermittently throughout 1830 and early 1831. (He was still collecting materials for this project in early 1832, see UC lxxxvi. 111.) He left the project uncompleted. His *Equity Dispatch Court Proposal* (*Bowring* iii, 297–317) was originally published in 1830.

[12] *Bowring* iii, 304. See Shapiro, *Courts*, 70–4, and sources cited in Shapiro's ch. 2, n. 6. See above 10.2.

[13] This fact is especially important to keep in mind in trying to understand some otherwise recalcitrant passages in *CC* Bk. II, ch. XII. See Appendix to this chapter.

directly and clearly both the question of the standards which must guide adjudication and the procedure for authorized judicial legislation. His aim, he announces, is to provide the judge with 'strong and adequate powers' and to protect the use of that power with 'strong and adequate securities against abuse' (*Bowring* iii, 324). He charges the judge to decide every case ultimately by appeal to the principle of utility (or rather, to its deputy, the 'Disappointment Prevention Principle'). This discretion is to be constrained by (i) denial of all precedential effects of judicial decisions, and (ii) grants of special powers to alter or correct existing rules in accord with the 'emendation process' we mentioned above.

Bentham's basic principle is announced in a section entitled 'Grounds of Decision': 'So far as regards the matter of law, every decision of the Dispatch Court Judge will have for its ground the *non-disappointment principle*.'[14] This is the sole (ultimate) ground of decision.[15] The non-disappointment principle 'is the expression of the only reason or say justificative cause . . . which ought to be accepted as such' (UC lxxxi. 125).

On every occasion, in so far as benefit in any shape is the subject-matter of dispute, the question being, to which of a number of parties the possession, present or future, in whole or in part, shall be adjudged,—the manner in which for that purpose disposition will be made of it, is that by which, among all the *interessees* taken together, least disappointment will be produced.[16]

Thus no existing rules should figure in the grounds for decision *except in so far as* they affect expectations of the parties (and perhaps others). In property disputes, for example, 'the only purpose and use of the investigation respecting title is the ascertaining as far as can be ascertained on which side in case of loss disappointment would be least severe' (UC lxxxi. 96). The reasons for this, says Bentham, are obvious: to the extent that decisions in accord with the rules minimize disappointment, deciding on the basis of them is appropriate but needless, and to the extent that following them actually results in greater disappointment, they are objectionable, and following them clearly would be unacceptable. Thus,

[14] *Bowring* iii, 388, author's emphasis; see generally *Bowring* iii, 312–13, 388–90.
[15] *Bowring* iii, 312; also UC lxxxi. 100–2, 108, 124.
[16] *Bowring* iii, 388, emphasis added. Note the 'interessees' must include persons other than the parties to the dispute: see UC lxix. 238–9 and other references to Bentham's early MSS in 6.3, above.

'a much better chance for prevention of disappointment will be obtained, by aiming at that object *immediately*, than by aiming at it through so unconducive, and in every respect unapt a *medium*.'[17] Respect for legitimate expectations and minimization of disappointment are primary. The only question is whether this end should be sought directly or indirectly. Of course, Bentham insists that the only rational approach is the direct one.

Bentham's argument for the central role of the non-disappointment principle is twofold. First, he argues that upon reflection and after careful analysis all would agree that the non-disappointment principle expresses the core of truth in standard appeals to 'vested rights', 'natural justice', and the like.

By means of the non-disappointment principle,—by this means and no other, can any determinate import be annexed to the locution *vested rights*: take away from it this import, . . . none remains. . . . Where the idea in the mind, in so far as it is clear and determinate, is the idea of contrariety to the . . . *non-disappointment principle*, two expressions commonly employed are—*contrary to the first principles of justice*, and *contrary to every principle of justice*. Considered in themselves, these expressions are, both of them, nonsense.[18]

In so far as the notions of justice or vested rights have any intelligible content, that content is captured by the non-disappointment principle. The concern is to respect established and legitimate expectations, and the non-disappointment principle tells the judge what to do in the face of inevitably conflicting expectations. Moreover, Bentham maintains, this principle actually captures the practice of the *original* courts of equity (UC lxxxi. 109). In fashioning its remedies, an equity court sought to 'balance the equities'—that is, it sought a resolution which took into account the legitimate claims and potential burdens on each party.[19] It did so on the basis of the principle *aequum et bonum*. But, Bentham maintains, this 'original principle of Equity Courts . . . meant the non-disappointment principle or [it] was mere nonsense'. 'This', he says, 'is one of the few instances in which the principle of recurrence to original practice is consistent with the greatest happiness principle' (UC

---

[17] *Bowring* iii, 312. This argument is also suggested at UC lxxxi. 124–5; UC cxiv. 222; *Bowring* iii, 389; and *Lord Brougham Displayed*, *Bowring* v, 564.

[18] *Bowring* iii, 388 n. *, author's emphasis; see also *Bowring* iii, 312; UC cxiv. 222; UC lxxxi. 125.

[19] Shapiro, *Courts*, 85–6.

lxxxi. 109). The only difference, then, between the judge in an
original court of equity and the Dispatch Court Judge is that the
latter has a clearer conception of, and more self-consciously applies, the underlying principle (UC cxiv. 236).

Bentham clearly is returning to themes first announced in his
earliest manuscripts (see above, 5.1). There he identified justice
with concern for 'expectation utilities'; and he does so again here.
There also, we noted, he treated 'justice' as simply a species of
utility, and the principle of maximization of expectation utilities as
an application of the more general principle of utility. Here again
Bentham argues that the non-disappointment principle is 'the immediate lineal descendant' of the principle of utility (*Bowring* iii,
312). Thus, 'equity arrangements in as far as [they are] comformable to [the] greatest happiness principle are conformable to this
principle also.'[20] And, if decisions in this area conform to the greatest
happiness principle, no disappointment will result.

Bentham's argument is compressed here, but he is clearly relying
on arguments developed elsewhere[21] where he insists that the sole
ruling principle of all law is the principle of utility, but as this principle applies to matters of law, and especially matters of civil law
(property, contract, etc.), the principle of utility is largely, if not
exclusively, concerned with prevention of disappointment.

> Prevention of disappointment—this is the only justification in civil cases.
> This is the object of all arrangements for the security of property. This
> being admitted, why not in each instance give the Judge a direct power of
> giving such decisions? (UC lxxxi. 100).

The only proper foundation for the law is the principle of utility,
and since the non-disappointment principle is simply the principle of
utility applied to these matters of law, it surely is the only principle
to which judicial officers may or ought to refer in making their
decisions. All other rules are relevant, and reference to them is
permitted, only to the extent that they give evidence of relevant
utilities which the judge must consider in making his decision.[22]

---

[20] UC lxxxi. 124, also UC cxiv. 222.

[21] For example, see *Pannomial Fragments*, *Bowring* iii, 212 and BL Add. Mss
33,550, fos. 141, 144. See above, 5.1.

[22] Here Bentham also returns to (or perhaps rediscovers) another theme of his
early manuscripts. In the Dispatch Court Bill he describes the process of judicial
deliberation about expectations in precisely the terms he used in the 'Preparatory
Principles' MSS nearly sixty years earlier. (See UC lxix. 238–9 and other passages

At this point Bentham considers the objection that this is a very radical proposal. Allowing judges to set aside any rule which conflicts with the dictates of the principle of utility (through its deputy the non-disappointment principle), this scheme appears to threaten the very foundation of property and other vested rights. But Bentham replies that property and vested rights rest on established expectations, and it is precisely such expectations that he is most concerned about. But he admits that what is required in general for security of expectations may not coincide with what the non-disappointment principle would dictate in every particular case. Bentham does not shrink from this consequence. Rather, he introduces safeguards designed to protect the general security of expectations, while at the same time allowing for the flexibility required by case-by-case application of the principle of utility.

Bentham's strategy is twofold. First, judicial decisions are to be denied all precedential effect. 'To no decision or rule in force, or supposed so to be, in any other judicatory. . . . to no practice or *dictum* of any such judicatory, will the Dispatch Court Judge pay any regard.'[23] Thus, the effect of a decision is to be strictly limited to the parties in the case at hand, and is not to extend beyond their dispute (*Bowring* iii, 312). To the objection that the foundations of property will be shaken, Bentham replies in an early draft of the *Proposal*:

To no such security will any so much as the slightest shake be given. Parties affected by this change will be those, and those alone, who are parties to the suits to which the new course of procedure applies itself; . . . neither in the indirect way of precedent any more than in the direct way will the decrees, judgments, or other decisions pronounced . . . have any effect on any of the suits other than those to which it is applied in a direct way as above: everything that it does not specifically apply itself to, it will leave as it found it (UC lxxxvi. 412).

discussed in 6.3, above.) He argues that in order to determine whether disappointment would be caused by some arrangement under consideration 'the Judge will consider within himself, whether, if the case were his own, if that same arrangement took place, any such uneasy sensation as that expressed by the word disappointment would thereby have been produced in his breast'. And if the question concerns which of two competing arrangements is favoured by the non-disappointment principle, 'the Judge will consider within himself, by which of the two the greatest, by which the least, pain of disappointment would be produced . . . in his breast' (*Bowring* iii, 388).

23 *Bowring* iii, 389; see also UC lxxxi. 110, 124.

The effect of the judge's decision in a particular case will be strictly limited to the parties to the case at hand, just as arbitration decisions are, and will have no precedential force beyond that case. In respect of the precedential effect of judicial decisions under the Dispatch Court, he argues,

the matters will stand in this as it does and has always done in the case of ordinary arbitration. . . . [I]n no instance has the lot of the parties to any other suits been in any way affected by the arbitration: as little will they by any act done or directive laid down, on any occasion by the Dispatch Court (UC lxxxvi. 412).

Consider cases of judicial review of arbitrated disputes. Where the judge reviewing such decisions is content with the arbitrator's award even though it was contrary to law, his reason, says Bentham, is

that in such cases, the decision not being aggregated to the general fund of precedents, no uncertainty with relation to the rest of the stock, and the general principles and spirit of the mass of so stiled unwritten law would be the result (UC lxxxvi. 413).

Furthermore, Bentham adds, if such apprehension regarding 'the general course of the law' was not produced by the deviations of an 'unlearned individual' (i.e. lay arbitrator), it is even less likely to arise where the discretion is put in the hands of trained officials (UC lxxxvi. 413). Thus, in so far as the extent of the effect of a decision goes, decisions of this court are to be treated on a par with arbitrators' decisions.

In light of the fact that Bentham proposed the Dispatch Court not only as an *ad hoc* measure to clear up the backlog of Chancery business, but also (and much more fundamentally) as a trial-run for his mature theory of adjudication, this analogy to arbitration takes on great significance. It provides strong confirmation for the claims made earlier that (i) the activities of adjudicating and legislating (and even interpreting the law) are intended by Bentham to be kept sharply distinct, and (ii) that within the sphere of adjudication, wide discretion is given to appeal to considerations not explicitly provided for in the law. Furthermore, the analogy to arbitration fits very well Bentham's favoured model for all judicial activity, the 'domestic tribunal'.

But Bentham's strategy to protect general security and the expectations established by the general rules of law has a second aspect.

Judicial amendment or alteration of the general rules of law is possible, but only according to the carefully defined procedures of his 'emendation process'.[24] The most interesting feature of his discussion of this procedure here is that Bentham claims that the activities of the Dispatch Court Judge can serve as a test of his proposals in the *Constitutional Code* (*Bowring* iii, 389 n.∗).

Thus, we have clearly articulated in the Dispatch Court papers the core elements in Bentham's mature theory of adjudication. But again one might object that we cannot use the Dispatch Court as a model for Bentham's general theory of adjudication, because he intended it only as an *ad hoc* measure to correct the immediate problems faced by Chancery at the time. He was inclined, the objection might continue, to propose such radical measures because, for that limited purpose, radical measures alone would do the job. In particular, the proposal to treat the principle of utility as the only ultimate decision principle could only plausibly be suggested for an institution that had its history and theory completely shaped by the Aristotelian doctrine of equity.

This serious objection can be answered. First, a careful reading of sections I and II of the *Proposal* and the Preface of the *Bill* make it clear beyond doubt that Bentham in fact seized this particular opportunity to give a public test of the procedural theories which he had developed over the years. He insisted that the *'main and ultimate'* aim is 'to demonstrate by an appropriate experiment' the virtues of his procedural system to the public (*Bowring* iii, 322). The secondary aim was to provide relief for those caught in the traps of Chancery at the time.

He saw the proposed system as a 'preliminary and preparatory survey of the whole field of law, all-comprehensive' (*Bowring* iii, 324). There are clear indications throughout that Bentham did not see the account he developed as independent of his central theories of the constitution, procedure, or adjudication, but as specific developments and applications of them.[25] Furthermore, Bentham worried throughout about the radical appearance of his suggestions and tried at every opportunity to soften its impact, to make it appear less radical.[26] In light of this, it is unlikely that he would introduce

[24] *Bowring* iii, 311, 389 n. ∗, 367–74.

[25] See, for example, *Bowring* iii, 388 n. + where Bentham says that the present Bill is 'part of the pannomion'.

[26] See *Bowring* iii, 310 and the attempts he makes to avoid serious alienation of the lawyer class in *Bowring* iii, 325–7.

radical elements into his proposal unless he thought them absolutely central to the structure he wished to test.

Second, although it is true that Bentham made his proposals in the absence of fully developed substantive codes, this does not limit the scope of his proposals to the correction of Common Law (or equity) systems. He intended his account of the role of the judge to work in the same way within a system of utilitarian codes. It is quite clear that he intended the Equity Dispatch Court Bill itself and the judicial relationships defined by it to be a model for this ideal situation. He announced at the outset (*Bowring* iii, 300) that the structure of the Bill itself would have the form and structure of his only explicit attempt at a full-scale code: *The Constitutional Code.*[27]

Finally, it is not merely historical accident that Bentham chose to put his theories to the test in the place of an equity jurisdiction, for his theory can rightly be viewed as an attempt to take what was good and useful in the old (Aristotelian) theory of equity (on which, according to tradition, Chancery jurisdiction was founded), while screening out what he thought was bad. He wished to show how equity, properly structured and safeguarded, could be integrated into a system of law and adjudication that maximized *both* security and flexibility. It was not, then, merely political opportunism which attracted Bentham to the project of correcting the gross deficiencies of the Chancery court system.

12.3 COMPLETENESS AND THE CODE

With a good method, we go before events . . .

Bentham, *General Views of a Complete Code*

Bentham's theory, on my interpretation, allows judges considerable freedom to consult directly the principle of utility when deciding particular cases. This power is available to judges even when the

---

[27] It is worth noting that here, as in the discussion of a procedure code in *PJP* (*Bowring* ii, 28–32), the rules of the code take the form of *instructions*, guides for the judge, not inflexible rules. Bentham maintains that a proper code must include not only 'enactments', but also *examples* where necessary for explanation, *reasons* explaining and justifying the enactment, and finally *instructions* to the judge. The latter are required where 'in each individual case,—to enable him to do justice, by the adaptation of his decrees to each individual case,—the liberty allowed by such instructions may be necessary, instead of the obligation imposed by a set of general

law within which they work is an ideal, comprehensive, utilitarian code. But this suggests that either the judge is free to ignore the code at will, or that the code is composed of little more than broad general principles which must be applied in particular cases only with the help of the principle of utility.

Neither of these alternatives seems to square with Bentham's deeply held views regarding the comprehensive nature of a code of laws and of the role of the judge under such a code. Shirley Letwin, for example, has claimed that

against Blackstone [Bentham] argued that law rightly understood was the product of deliberate enactment by a legislative body, that it was possible, in the light of natural reason, to frame a body of law that could be universally applicable and *so complete that it would reduce the task of judge and jurist to the mechanical application of its terms.*[28]

She gives no textual support for this claim, however.[29] I suspect that it rests on a common understanding of Bentham's principle of judicial subordination. In light of the evidence we have considered in the last several chapters, in which Bentham soundly denounces mindless, mechanical methods of judicial decision making (whether

and *indiscriminating* enactments, applying alike to mutually different cases, such as require mutually different orders and decrees: for which cases accordingly one and the same enactment could not so well serve' (*Bowring* iii, 300). This, we shall see in the next section, is precisely how Bentham characterizes the central features of his codes in general.

[28] S. R. Letwin, *The Pursuit of Certainty*, 128, emphasis added. See also D. Alfange, Jr., 'Bentham and the Codification of Law', 71.

[29] The following passage from Bentham's 'Essay on Judicial Justice' (1807) *seems* to support this view. 'In the most perfect and most easily conceivable state of things the rule of action is, in all its branches, the expressly declared will of the person or persons possessing the supreme power or at any rate the legislative branch of the supreme power in the state.

'This declared will, how perfectly or how imperfectly soever conducive to the well fare [sic] of the community taken in the aggregage must to all practical purposes, so long as that obedience is manifested in which the supreme power is constituted, be taken for the standard of rectitude.

'This rule of action being thus declared—this standard of rectitude fixt, the function of the supreme judicial power or supreme judicature consists in the issuing of such particular orders or commands as are necessary to the causing of the conduct of several members of the community, in the character of subjects, to be kept on all occasions near as is possible to a state of perfect conformity to the standard of rectitude' (UC cvi. 162), quoted in L. J. Hume, *Bentham and Bureaucracy*, 170–1. But note that the *judicial* standard is *not* strictly to adhere to the law, but rather to decide in such a way as to cause citizens to conform *their* behaviour to the law. This is a difference Bentham would not overlook.

following precedent or applying statute law),[30] it is difficult to derive this conclusion from the doctrine of judicial subordination. Nevertheless, there is some evidence for this interpretation. For example, Bentham maintains, in *Lord Brougham Displayed* that the best rules of law are those the universal *conformity* to which will in *every case* yield the greatest happiness in the community.

The knowledge of what *law ought to be*—that is to say, of that rule of action, conformity to which will, on each occasion, be in the greatest degree possible contributory to the happiness of all persons interested—this is *indeed a science*. (*Bowring* v, 560, author's emphasis).

This suggests that the science of legislation is the science of discovering precise and detailed rules such that conforming to them will in each case maximize utility. And since law at its perfection 'is concise, intelligible, unambiguous, and in the hands of every man' (UC cxlii. 200), it seems to follow that Bentham's ideal code would be a set of laws so precisely framed and comprehensive that (i) no conflicts between rules would arise, and (ii) there would be absolutely no doubt in any particular case about any person's obligations or rights. Thus no occasion could arise for genuine dispute regarding any matters of law.[31]

This suggests a picture of the code as a very large, though systematically arranged, set of highly specific rules covering the entire field of human action. And this picture seems to be supported by Bentham's own description of the code in *Of Laws in General*, in which he set out the philosophical foundations of codification.

In a system thus constructed upon this plan, a man need but open the book in order to inform himself what the aspect borne by the law bears to every imaginable act that can come within the possible sphere of human agency; what acts it is his duty to perform for the sake of himself, his neighbour or the public: what acts he has a right to do, what other acts he has a right to have others perform for his advantage . . . In this one repository the whole system of the obligations which either he or any one else is subject to are recorded and displayed to view . . . (*OLG* XIX. 10).

[30] For example, *Justice Petition, Bowring* v, 472–3; UC cii. 120; UC lxxxi. 124–5; UC cxiv. 222; UC li(a). 31–2. See above, 6.3 and 8.2.
[31] 'The perfection of the law will be at its acme and the condition of mankind as far as depends upon the law will be at its optimum when [among other things] . . . the rights and duties of the various classes of subjects are so well defined by the civil code that there are no longer any controversies in which the question turns upon the point of law . . .' (UC cxlii. 200).

In a powerful metaphor he sums up his ideal of the completeness and comprehensiveness of the code:

In a map of the law executed upon such a plan there are no *terrae incognitae*, no blank spaces: nothing is at least omitted, nothing unprovided for: the vast and hitherto shapeless expanse of jurisprudence is collected and condensed into a compact sphere which the eye at a moment's warning can traverse in all imaginable directions (*OLG* XIX. 11).

Commenting on this passage in a careful and useful discussion of Bentham's doctrines of the completeness and unity of law, M. H. James argues that Bentham believed that the method he spelled out in his theory of fictions and analysis of law and the principles of individuation of law in *Of Laws in General* could yield a body of law of unprecedented clarity and comprehensiveness. Since, according to Bentham,

each law stands complete in itself, and provides comprehensive guidance within its sphere of application, it will never conflict with any other law. If the action in question appears to fall within the scope of more than one law, then the legal system stands in need of further clarification. Moreover, every class of acts is provided for, directly or indirectly, and the subject will have no difficulty in understanding where all his rights and obligations lie.[32]

As this ideal is approached, the need for interpretation is increasingly diminished, to the point where it withers away. 'The business of interpreting the law', says James, was 'to be reduced as far as possible to one of administering what is in principle a perfectly comprehensible body of laws.'

Thus far, James's interpretation is consistent with the account of Bentham's view of law and the judge's role in administering it for which I have been arguing. It begins to conflict with my reading of Bentham only when we take James's view a step further. Following Letwin we might claim that this comprehensiveness is achieved through including in the ideal code only *highly specific* rules which *themselves* sharply and precisely mark out in advance all obligations and rights, and which thereby block all judicial appeal to, or need for reliance on, the principle of utility (and its proxies). If this is Bentham's preferred conception of the code, then there is no room for judicial discretionary power, and we have reason to

---

[32] James, 'Individuation', 94.

reconsider the line of interpretation of Bentham's theory of adjudication which I have advanced.

However, there is nothing in the doctrine of completeness of law, on which the above passages from *Of Laws in General* are based, which requires this conception of the code. I shall argue that Bentham's conception of the nature of the ideal code is entirely consistent with the account of adjudication outlined in 12.1, above.

To begin, we should note that the conception of the code which Letwin suggests stresses only one side of Bentham's ideal of a comprehensive code. The central objective of codification, for Bentham, is to secure the certainty and accessibility of the law, to replace the indeterminate, ambiguous, uncertain, and inaccessible Common Law (which often was understandable only to trained professionals) with a clear, determinate, unambiguous, and systematic set of public codes which were available to all. This central objective, however, requires not only absolutely clear, unambiguous rules covering the entire field of action, but also conciseness, intelligibility, and in a word *simplicity*. Repeatedly, throughout his career, Bentham insisted that a primary virtue of law is its intelligibility to any citizen without the need of an intermediary. A good example of this can be found in the *Principles of the Civil Code*, in which he argues that the same effect of incoherence and inconsistency in a body of laws can be produced by complexity of the law:

Every man has his determinate measure of understanding: the more complex the law, the greater the number of those who cannot understand it. Hence it will be less known; it will have less hold upon men; it will not occur to their minds on the occasions on which it ought, or, what is still worse, it will deceive them, and give birth to false expectations. Both style and arrangement ought to be simple. The law should be a manual of instruction for every individual, and he ought to be able to consult it, under all his doubts, without requiring an interpreter (*Bowring* i, 324).

Echoing the Levellers of the previous century, Bentham's ideal called for 'every man [to be] his own lawyer'.[33] He prided himself on being the 'Luther of jurisprudence' and it was precisely at this point that his jurisprudential protestantism is most pronounced. Just as access to God was not to be mediated by priests, so too access to the law was not to be mediated by professional lawyers. It

---

[33] *Judicial Establishment, Bowring* iv, 318, 332; *RJE, Bowring* vii, 189. On the Levellers see B. Shapiro, 'Codification of the Laws in Seventeenth Century England', 449–50.

was essential to his programme of making law and government fully public (see 11.2) that law be made accessible to common sense, to the common reason of the people. Law must become the common property of the people, part of their folk-ways, Bentham argued.

A code formed upon these principles would not require schools for its explanation, would not require casuists to unravel its subtilties. It would speak a language familiar to everybody: each one might consult it at his need. It would be distinguished from all other books by its greater simplicity and clearness (*Bowring* iii, 209).

The code must be simple enough, Bentham continues, to function as an instruction book on civic virtue. It must be possible for a father to take it in hand and, without assistance, teach it to his children, thus giving 'to the precepts of private morality the force and dignity of public morals' (*Bowring* iii, 209).

Now, this latter suggestion appears dotty,[34] but the main idea is plausible, and one to which Bentham was deeply committed throughout his career. According to Bentham, full publicity is essential to rational obedience to established authority and it offers the only effective means of preventing exploitation of the weak and ignorant by those in power. In particular, the only way to break the power of the lawyer class was to break their monopoly on knowledge of the law. And this is possible only if the law is made simple enough so that each person bound by it can understand it and the rationale on which it rests.

---

[34] But Bentham was not alone in such views. Consider the following passage from a report on codification to the Massachusetts House of Representatives in 1836: 'Let the obsolete, unconstitutional, frivolous and iniquitous parts of the common law be abolished, and whatever is good and useful be passed into statute law, and a work will be accomplished, however imperfect it may at first be, which will be remembered for ages. The constitutions and the laws would then form a volume or two, written in concise, chaste, and elegant language, fit to be introduced into our common schools, and constitute the book of reading and study for the highest class. So that while our children shall be acquiring the rudiments of an English education, and learning to read, write and speak their mother tongue, they may at the same time be acquiring a knowledge of our forms of government, constitutions and laws. Liberty and popular government will then be placed on the broad foundation of knowledge and virtue . . .' (quoted in J. Honnold, ed., *The Life of the Law*, 103). This was written some twenty years after Bentham's attempts to convince the American people to 'throw off the yoke of the Common Law' and codify their laws (*Bowring* iv, 453–514). However, I am not aware of any influence Bentham's efforts had on the Commission of the Massachusetts legislature.

Thus, Bentham is committed not only to the principle of the completeness of law, but also to a radical idea of simplicity. However, it is not difficult to imagine that these two ideals may conflict. For if the code is to be completely precise, specific, and unambiguous, so that no two rules conflict and no justifiable exceptions are left out, the code will have to include a staggering number of very specific rules which would be difficult to grasp and hard to keep straight. This could never meet the criterion of simplicity. Bentham, it seems, is committed to inconsistent ideals.

Surely, it is possible that Bentham was committed to ideals incompatible in ways he did not fully realize. However, his theory of codification is subtler than we have yet been led to believe. Recognizing the tension between these two ideals, he sought a way of incorporating both consistently within his theory.

First, Bentham believed that the principle of utility itself introduced system and order into the body of law, and with these both completeness and simplicity. On his view, the principle of utility is the only rational practical principle; at the same time it is the only 'natural' or common-sense principle. Thus, it was easy (perhaps too easy) for him to maintain that 'The more conformable laws are to the principle of utility, the more simple will be their systematic arrangement. A system founded upon a single principle might be as simple in its form as in its foundation. It only is susceptible of a natural arrangement and a familiar nomenclature' (*Civil Code*, *Bowring* i, 324). That is, the code will be simple and accessible in virtue of being fully generated out of the principle of utility.[35]

The coherent, rational, 'natural' arrangement of the 'long winded and voluminous expressions of will' of the sovereign in a code of law (*OLG* XIV. 9) is, no doubt, a step toward intelligibility compared with the resolutely unsystematic body of Common Law. But this hardly yields the sort of simplicity that Bentham's jurisprudential protestantism seemed to call for. In fact, the connections between simplicity and completeness are closer, and go deeper into Bentham's conception of the structure and composition of the code, than we have yet seen.

---

[35] This seems to confirm Halévy's charge that Bentham shared with his century the tendency to confuse the rationally simple with what is intelligible to everyone immediately and without preliminary training (Halévy, *Philosophic Radicalism*, 78). But this criticism is not entirely fair, since Bentham's view of the unique suitability of the principle of utility for use as a rational principle of public and private morality goes much deeper, as we have seen in the preceding chapter.

In order to get a clear view of the outlines of this proposal for resolution we must take a closer look at Bentham's doctrines of the completeness and unity of the laws. Although a full discussion of the issues raised by Bentham's doctrines here would repay close study, it would take us too far afield. So I will only consider those features of the doctrines which will advance the argument here.

From the earliest point in his career Bentham was concerned with the question: what constitutes a single, complete, integral law? He sought in the concepts of completeness and individuality of *laws* a key to the nature and structure of *law*. It is probably this methodological point, more than any other feature of his approach to the analysis of law that sets his positivist legal theory off from its Common Law and natural law rivals. In these early attempts to clarify the notion of completeness two elements appear: (i) a focus on the act or offence to which the law is directed, and (ii) an attempt to embrace in a unitary structure all the necessary *parts* of a law (i.e. the directive, sanctional, expository, exceptive, and procedural 'parts'). In a very early manuscript he maintains that

A Law is complete [that is, completely expressed] when the act it prohibits . . . and the punishment for it . . . are so expressed as that, granting the act so described to have been done, no supposition can be framed, on which, according to the Will of the Legislator, the punishment in question, shall not take place.[36]

This suggests that a complete law is one which includes all the qualifications and exceptions that apply to the act which is the object of the law. This, we discover later, includes procedural constraints ('limitations') as well as recognized excuses and other exceptions narrowing the scope of the definitions of the act (see above, 10.1).

These early notions are clarified by *Of Laws in General* in the course of developing a full-scale analysis of completeness. There he carefully distinguishes the various parts of a law and spells out their logical relations. He articulates also his basic principle of individuation of laws: to each law there corresponds one and only one class of actions to which the will of the legislator is directed. Here also the earlier single concept of completeness is analysed into two components, *integrality* (or completeness in a narrow sense) and

---

[36] UC lxx(a). 8 (early 1770s); see also UC lxix. 87.

unity. A law is 'complete' in this narrow sense if it contains no *less* than one law (i.e. contains in it all the necessary parts of a law); whereas, a law is *unitary* if it contains no *more* than one law. These are two sides of the same coin. Completeness (and unity) are defined *relative to* the will of the legislator, actual or supposed. There is no such thing as absolute completeness (*OLG* XIV. 2). Among the ways in which a law can be incomplete is incompleteness *in design*: that is, relative to the end or will of the legislator, the class of actions is defined either too narrowly or too broadly. Of course, where the objective is to construct a utilitarian code, the principle which must guide the choice of the definition of the offense is the principle of utility. Bentham makes a similar point regarding the property of unity. The unity of a law is determined, he says, by the unity of the class of actions which it takes for its object. 'That system of provisions is one law which marks out one offence: that system of provisions is more than one law which does more than mark out one offence' (*OLG* XIV. 19). However, in Bentham's view the unity of a class of actions (i.e. the proper description of such a class) is not logically fixed; it can only be determined *relative to some* purpose or objective. Actions, he believed, are capable of being given an indefinite number of descriptions. Or as he puts it, 'classes of offences like any other classes of acts may be distinguished from one another *ad infinitum*'.[37] Thus, the unity of a law 'is not naturally determinable'. The definition of the class is to be determined, rather, by 'convenience'. In consequence, what might at one time be a *species* of act defined by the law, may at a later time be treated as a *genus*, its species being extended where it seems necessary to do so. Such further division may be required if a difference of treatment seems appropriate (for example, where a difference in punishment seems justified (*OLG* XIV. 19)). James maintains that 'It is the divisibility of acts which makes it possible for a code of laws to evolve over time in response to the needs of a community'.[38] Decisions in both kinds of cases are governed at least implicitly by the principle of utility; for, as we have seen several times before, it is a cardinal principle of Bentham's art of legislation that matters of form and structure, as well as content, in the code are to be governed by the principle of utility.

[37] *OLG* XIV. 19. The view is a direct product of his more general views on language and event descriptions. See above, 8.3 (The theory of fictions).

[38] James, 'Individuation', 109.

But now we have a way of bringing together the ideals of completeness and simplicity. For Bentham throughout his writings is keen to point out the disutility of complex rules. If rules of law are to perform the function of securing expectations and providing the framework for social co-operation, they must not be excessively complex. Also, complexity itself makes the law more difficult to understand and so makes it less accessible. Therefore, a good utilitarian legislator or code-writer must consider the utilities associated with simplicity when constructing the rules. That is, one of the criteria by which the completeness and unity of a law are determined is *simplicity itself*. Simplicity, then, is *not* an ideal *competing with* completeness (in the broad sense), but is in fact partially *constitutive of* completeness. Here the costs and benefits of simplicity must be weighed in, along with all the other relevant considerations, and a utilitarian balance struck. Thus, a body of law is complete if it is comprehensive and all its components are themselves complete. The degreee of specificity of the classes of actions defined by the laws will be determined by all relevant utilitarian considerations, among which, Bentham insists, will be simplicity.

But if this is true, then the ideal of completeness of the code is not likely to be that of a very large set of highly specific rules. It is much more likely that Bentham's ideal code will consist of a somewhat smaller number of quite general rules broadly defined. Bentham quite explicitly allows that the completeness of a law is not threatened by the fact that a judge is left to make a determination on his own regarding what might fall within the scope of a legally defined genus. For example, a judge may have to decide whether maize is to be regarded as falling within the scope of a law regulating the export of corn. If the law is silent on the matter, the judge may find it necessary to look to commercial practice to settle the issue. Nevertheless, Bentham maintains, 'the interpretation thus obtained may be considered as conclusive, without any disparagement to the completeness of the law' (*OLG* XIV. 4).

Bentham's code, then, seems to resemble the more recent European codes, provisions of which are fashioned around *grandes principes du droit*.[39] The French code, for example, provides rules,

---

[39] See M. Berger, 'Codification', 151. Llewellyn's so-called 'case-law code', the Uniform Commercial Code, seems to offer an even more extreme example. According to Gilmore, Llewellyn regarded the code as 'a statute whose principal function would be to abrogate obsolete rules, thus leaving the court free to improvise new

but they are very general and can be applied only through interpretation against the background of the tradition of Roman law. From the perspective of English and American lawyers, Shapiro points out, 'the French code offers many principles and few rules'.[40] His description of the German Civil Code is especially interesting for our purposes:

[It] is not so much a complete and detailed set of laws as an incredibly elaborate textbook about law. . . . Thus the German lawyer or judge seeking to resolve a legal problem does not usually expect to find a specific, concrete, legal rule directly applying to the situation at hand. Instead, he consults the texts from which he learned law, confident that he will find the general concepts, principles, and methodologies that will allow him to work out the correct solution to any legal problem that might arise. It is in this sense that the code is complete.[41]

Bentham's conception of the code and its completeness is closer to this model than to that attributed to Bentham by Letwin and most recent commentators.

For Bentham, the key to an adequate grasp of any part of human thought or action is systematic arrangement,[42] and system presupposes *rational method*,[43] and method guarantees both comprehensiveness and precision (*IRE, Bowring* vi, 7). In law, both in Common Law and statutory forms, what was lacking most was a rational, systematic structure. Even at their best, legislators simply respond to immediate needs or political pressures: the rules they create are characteristically governed by no rational plan. 'Laws have been made nearly in the same manner as the first towns were built. To look for a plan among these heaps of ordinances, would

rules to fit changing conditions and novel business practices'. G. Gilmore, *The Ages of American Law*, 85, see also 71; quoted in G. Calabresi, *A Common Law for the Age of Statutes*, 188.

[40] Shapiro, *Courts*, 134.

[41] Ibid. 135. Lon Fuller makes a similar observation: 'One of the best modern codes, the Swiss Code of Obligations, lays down very few rules and contents itself largely with charting the range of judicial discretion and with setting forth what might be called checklists for the judge to consult to make certain that he has overlooked no factor properly bearing on the exercise of his discretion' (L. Fuller, 'Forms and Limits of Adjudication', 100). As we shall see in the next chapter, this differs to some extent from Bentham's view of the provisions of his code—since he has a special role for genuine code rules to play—but it comes closer to his view than the picture sketched by Letwin at the opening of this section.

[42] See *Essay on Nomenclature, Bowring* vii, 63–128, and *Essay on Logic, Bowring* viii, 222.

[43] *IPML* XVI. 1 n. a, and XVI. 58 n. y[4]

be like searching for an order of architecture amidst the huts of a village' (*Essay on Promulgation, Bowring* i, 159). Bentham believed that he had done for jurisprudence and the art of legislation what Bacon had done for the natural sciences: 'The present [project] is an attempt to give to the art of legislation . . . something of the form of a science: to furnish it with a set of consistent principles and connected rules . . .' (UC xxvii. 165). He refined and carefully articulated the principle of utility,[44] and he developed logical techniques for analysis and classification of essential concepts ('fictional names').[45] These tools and techniques represented, in Bentham's mind, the *Novum Organum* of jurisprudence (*Bowring* iii, 285-95: 'Logical Arrangements, or Instruments of Invention and Discovery employed by Jeremy Bentham').

The code was not only to be constructed according to the principles of this method, it was to *embody the method*. Against those who complained that a complete and comprehensive code is simply impossible because it is impossible to foresee all the events we wish to regulate by law, Bentham replied with the enthusiasm of one who believes he had found the philosopher's stone,

I acknowledge that it is not possible to foresee them individually, but they may be foreseen in their species; . . . *With a good method, we go before events*, instead of following them; we govern them instead of being their sport. A narrow-minded and timid legislature waits till particular evils have arisen, before it prepares a remedy; an enlightened legislature foresees and prevents them by general precautions (*General View of a Complete Code of Laws, Bowring* iii, 205, emphasis added).

Rational method, not specificity, guarantees completeness and determinacy. '[B]e the occasion what it may, if *in specie*, the language cannot always be all-comprehensive . . . yet *in genere* it may always be: and, as every individual is contained within its

---

[44] The principle of utility defines the broad categories of harm which must be regulated, as well as the occasions for exceptions, limitations, and the like. Happiness is the end around which all offences are arranged (UC lxix. 166; *OLG*, App. B. 2; *Bowring* viii, 525).

[45] Bentham's logical method consists of (i) a method for the analysis of fictions and for their realistic definition, which relates them concretely and unambiguously to real entities, and (ii) a strategy for the systematic arrangement ('methodization') of these fictions, especially classes of events. These techniques, in Bentham's mind, insured comprehensiveness as well as clarity and perspicacity of the conceptual framework within which the principle of utility works. See *OLG*, App. B. 1; *Bowring* viii, 102-3; *IPML* XVI. 1 n. a.

species, so is every species within its genus (*Codification Proposal*, *Bowring* iv, 538).

Bentham's model of rational method and systematic arrangement is not geometry, but botany or natural history.[46] For the most natural system of classification of laws, Bentham counsels, go not to Coke or Hale or Blackstone, but to Linnaeus (UC lxiii. 71). Rational method involves, first, defining a fully comprehensive and realistic conceptual framework (i.e. one which is both most general and tied down to genuine real entities), one which takes in the entire field of human action.[47] Second, it requires principles of refinement and resolution of the more generic into the more specific. In a systematic arrangement on truly rational principles, the relations of any one part of the universe of discourse to all the rest are openly displayed (*OLG* XIX. 4). '[A] light kindled in one corner would shine at once to the whole universe . . .'[48] From any part of the arrangement one can move to any other part by rational and perspicuous steps. Also from generic concepts and general principles one can trace out all specific duties, right, and other legal consequences. These specifics, though part of the universe of law, are not part of the code, any more than are the particular commands of a father, husband, or guardian (*OLG* XIV. 31–3, and I. 6). Or, rather, both are included in the code, albeit *implicitly* rather than *explicitly*.

In its *method*, then, lies the completeness of the code. The legislator/code-writer, equipped with Bentham's method, can survey the entire field of human conduct, like Moses on Mt Pisgah.[49] From this vantage-point he may draw up a map of the entire region for those, citizens and officials alike, who must traverse it. It is in this sense that the map of the law executed upon the plan articulated in the *Introduction to the Principles* and *Of Laws in General* leaves 'no *terrae incognitae*'. '[T]he vast and hitherto shapeless expanse of jurisprudence is collected and condensed into a compact sphere which the eye at a moment's warning can traverse in all

[46] UC lxiii. 68–9; UC xlvi. 96; UC xxvii. 103–4.

[47] After a little reflection, Bentham says, we should be able to see that by 'words such as *state of things, events, things immoveable, things moveable, action, forbearance, misdeed, obligation, command, prohibition, permission, condition, right, punishment, reward*—by these, with the addition of a few others, not only has the whole field of legislation, but the whole field of possible thought and action, been covered' (*Codification Proposal, Bowring* iv, 538 n. *).

[48] UC lxiii. 74; see also *Chrestomathia, Bowring* viii, 65, 106.

[49] UC cxlii. 200; see also *Bowring* i, 194 and UC xxvii. 165, 123.

imaginable directions' (*OLG* XIX. 11). All will be provided for, not *in specie*, but *in genera*. The code is a map, a schematic representation of the legal landscape, it is not the landscape itself. Nevertheless, thinks Bentham, armed with this map and a firm grasp of the rational principles on which it was constructed, any citizen or judge can trace out from the code 'the aspect borne by the law' regarding any 'imaginable act that can come within the possible sphere of human agency' (*OLG* XIX. 10) confident that the result is the same as any other intelligent inquirer would achieve. The key principle of the method, of course, is the principle of utility. And so, far from blocking judicial appeal to the principle of utility with highly specific legal rules, Bentham's theory of codification explicitly calls for judicial use of the principle as a key component in the rational method for adjudication under the code.

Appendix
Judicial Amendment of the Code

Perhaps out of an abundance of caution I wish to consider one last problem for the above interpretation of Bentham's theory of adjudication. The problem arises from Bentham's discussion of the detailed procedure he developed for judicial alteration (interpretation or amendment) of the code which he called the 'emendation process'. This procedure is discussed in some form on at least thirteen occasions in his writings from the early 1770s to 1831.[50] On all but five of these occasions, Bentham concerns himself exclusively with the procedure for amending the law, without making any mention of the judge's disposition of the case before him that occasioned the alteration or amendment. On two occasions, however, he does concern himself in detail with the judge's decision in the case before him as well. The relevant discussions here are those in the papers relating to his *Judicial Establishment* and to his *Constitutional Code*. It is also in these discussions that the problem for the above interpretation of Bentham's view arises. It

---

[50] From the 1770s: UC lxiii. 4; 'Preparatory Principles', UC lxix. 200; *Comment* I. 9, 90–7. From the 1780s: *OLG* XIX. 6; *General View*, *Bowring* iii, 209 and UC c. 90–3. From the 1790s: *Judicial Establishment*, *Bowring* iv, 310–14, 340–2 and UC li(a). 220. From post 1800s: *RJE*, *Bowring* vii, 312–14; *PJP*, *Bowring* ii, 27, 29, 32 (1825); *CC* 504–14 and UC xlii(b). 412–90 (1823–5); BL Add. MSS 33,549, fo. 66 (1827), *Justice Petition*, *Bowring* v, 500 (1829); 'Procedure Code' MSS UC liii. 250–1 (1827); *Equity Dispatch Court* papers, *Bowring* iii, 311, 388–9 and UC lxxxvi. 23, 38, 41, 42, 45–8 (1829).

would be easy to dismiss the problem as insignificant, since it appears in only these two discussions, but the two works are of such great importance in Bentham's career, that they cannot be dismissed. They represent two occasions on which Bentham attempted to sum up and state as clearly as he could his views on adjudication and judicial establishment generally.[51]

The problem is that, in addition to the circumscribed power to amend the existing law—with the tacit consent of the legislature—Bentham also introduces another judicial function which he calls the 'suspensive power' (*Judicial Establishment*) or 'sistitive function' (*CC*). Ignoring slight differences of detail, the main idea is that the judge in exercising this power simply suspends execution of the existing law—which is under consideration for alteration or amendment—*until* the legislature decides regarding (or consents through its silence to) the alteration proposed by the judge. The judge is empowered, and apparently required, to secure the expectations of the parties (and take whatever other steps are necessary to avoid injustice to either party) while the legislature considers the amendment. Furthermore the decision of the legislature will not only affect the law or provision of the code but also will apply to the case which occasioned the proposed amendment. The judge apparently has no power to decide the case before him, but must wait on the decision from the legislature, and the decision of the legislature automatically determines the disposition of the particular case before the court. This, of course, would pose a challenge to my interpretation of Bentham's view of adjudication. For on this view the judge appears to be justified in *questioning* the application of the law to a particular case (on utilitarian grounds) *only when* there is apparent utilitarian justification for *alteration* of the law. Moreover, the power to decide even particular cases according to the principle of utility is taken from the judge and placed in the hands of the legislature.

It is possible, I believe, to blunt the force of this objection to my interpretation, although it is difficult to square these discussions of the suspensive power of judges entirely with what I think is Bentham's dominant view. I shall consider each of these works separately.

Judicial Establishment was written as an extended critical treatment of the (1790) draft for a new judicial establishment in Revolutionary France proposed by the National Assembly. It was intended as a sympathetic critique working *within* the basic structure proposed by the National Assembly's Committee, but seeking to correct its main defects. Although Bentham stood by this document for thirty years, there is some doubt about the extent to which Bentham himself felt committed to some of the

[51] *Judicial Establishment* remained in Bentham's own view the most complete statement of his procedural views until his writing of the relevant portions of the *Constitutional Code*. See Bentham's letter to Senor Mora, 19 Sept. 1820, BL Add. MSS 33,551, fos. 1–13, esp. fos. 3–5.

details of the programme.[52] Bentham's view of the role of the judge in this document is in many ways very 'conservative', giving little evidence, in the more visible portions of it, of his view of the importance of flexibility in adjudication which he had expressed frequently earlier and elsewhere. This is particularly true of his discussion of the emendation process. In the initial discussions of judicial interpretation, and constraints on the exercise of judicial power (*Bowring* iv, 310–14), he seems to give judges absolutely no flexibility, viewing them entirely as administrative subordinates of the legislature. However, much later in a long footnote (342 n), he argues (directly contrary to the view expressed earlier) that the decisions of the legislature's Committee of Revision should have only *prospective* effect, for otherwise that committee will become a *de facto* court of appeal without the appropriate resources of such a court.[53]

There are, then, even in this document, hints of a more radical doctrine of adjudication. But what kept Bentham from expressing that doctrine more explicitly? Two things, I think, (i) he was working within the political realities of Revolutionary France, and at that time there was no more hated institution of the *ancien régime* than the French judiciary (Parlement); and (ii) he had not yet worked out all the details of his theory of adjudication— the important principles of constitutional design had not been clearly worked out until the 1820s. His theory of adjudication had not yet matured. In light of these factors, it would be unwise to put great weight on this one particular aspect of Bentham's views and so it does not pose a great problem for my interpretation.

The *Constitutional Code* poses more difficult problems to deal with, for in this work we have Bentham's most explicit, well-developed, and internally self-consistent statement of the processes and powers of judicial interpretation and code amendment. He takes great pains to structure the

---

[52] In the letter to Mora cited in n. 51, Bentham reveals that some details, especially the matter of the popular election of judges, he included largely because he recognized that they were politically essential to the adoption of the scheme in the political climate at the time.

[53] At *Bowring* iv, 342 he argues that a committee of revision should oversee the interpretation of the laws by the courts and 'report such as appear to have erred from the mark, that their influence, *as to the future*, may be stopped . . .' (emphasis in the original). Then he refers to the earlier discussion of suspensive power. He spells out what he means more clearly in a footnote to this passage: 'I say, *as to the future*: to extend the effect of the interpretation to the past, would be to turn the legislative assembly into a court of appeal, and the time of the legislature would be consumed in judicature. In the one way, the only cases about which the legislature will be occupied, will be those in which the interpretation given in the courts below has appeared erroneous in the eyes of the *committee*: in the other way, the legislature would be troubled with all the cases in which the *unsuccessful party* thought it erroneous, or for the purpose of delay found his account in pretending to think it so.'

lawmaking power of the judiciary so that the basic principle of judicial subordination to the legislature is maximally served. It is evident that Bentham took the statement (developed largely between 1823 and 1825) to be definitive.[54]

The details of his scheme are not important for our purposes, the main idea is that in addition to the 'eventually-emendative' function of the judge, whereby the judge is empowered to propose amendments to the Legislative Minister, Bentham defines a 'sistitive' function. The reason for introducing this function is to give the judge the power to take steps necessary to prevent injustice or disappointment in the particular cases which occasion proposals for amendment of the law. In particular, it is power to suspend execution of an applicable valid law until the status of the proposed amendment to that law is determined.

> Of an amendment proposed by a Judge a natural object will be prevention of injustice, no matter in what shape. Should it so happen to a Judge to be applied to for giving execution and effect to a law. . . . besides proposing an appropriate amendment, he may stop and is expected to stop the giving of such execution and effect to it.[55]

It would be absurd, says Bentham, if relief from a bad, or poorly drafted, law were given to persons in the future but none to the party whose plight first draws attention to the defect in the law (UC xlii(b). 483).

This power is exercised as follows: the judge issues three decrees, one giving execution to the law as it stands, one giving execution to the law as amended, and one suspending the first two 'until the will of the legislature has been made known'.[56] Thus it appears that the effect of judicial creativity on the instant case depends entirely on the expressed or tacit will of the legislature.

It is very tempting to interpret this account of the 'sistitive' function in such a way as to imply that the judge is denied the power in *any* case to appeal directly to the principle of utility to determine the case before him, i.e. as an assertion of an extreme form of judicial subordination to the legislature and an explicit denial of the radical view of adjudication I have argued for earlier. But such an interpretation would be difficult to advance without strong textual evidence to support it, because it would involve attributing a view of adjudication to Bentham which he explicitly rejects in other works contemporaneous with, or written shortly after, the relevant sections of the *Constitutional Code*—in particular, the views expressed in the materials discussed in 12.2 from *Principles of Judicial Procedure* and

---

[54] In several other works on related topics written after this chapter was composed he refers to the relevant sections Bk. II, ch. XII, sects. 19–23. See, e.g., *PJP*, *Bowring* ii, 32; *Bowring* iii, 389; *Bowring* v, 564–5.

[55] UC xliii(b). 430; see also UC xliii(b). 427 and *CC* 508.

[56] UC xliii(b). 430; see also *CC* 508.

the *Equity Dispatch Court* papers.[57] This is especially puzzling because in these passages Bentham explicitly refers to these sections of the *Constitutional Code*. A more plausible interpretation would seek to find some way to make compatible these apparently incompatible views of the judge's role and limits on his judicial activity. I shall attempt such an interpretation.

First, it must be noted that the portion of the *Constitutional Code* we are here concerned with was never completed by Bentham. In fact, he returned to it repeatedly between 1823 and 1826 and there is evidence that he was working on it as late as May of 1828 (see UC xlii(b). 423–5). During this same period (especially 1824–5) Bentham wrote most of the manuscript for his *Principles of Judicial Procedure*. Indeed, many of the manuscript folios headed 'Procedure'—some of which are included in *Principles of Judicial Procedure*—are also headed 'CC' (*Constitutional Code*); sometimes the 'CC' is lined out, sometimes 'Procedure' is lined out, sometimes both stand together heading the MS pages.[58] It is quite clear that while working on the details of the *Constitutional Code* he was also at work on other aspects of his theory of adjudication. *Principles of Judicial Procedure* (*Bowring* ii, 32) is the clearest example. For here, after arguing against inflexible rules and in favour of considerable judicial discretion, Bentham states that the protection against the abuse of this power is to be found in the constraints on judicial lawmaking outlined in the *Constitutional Code*, Book II, Chapter XII, especially the Judge's sistitive and emendative functions (UC lii(a). 229). Bentham's slightly later works on similar themes, especially the *Equity Dispatch Court* papers, in which a very radical view of judicial activity is advanced, are also similarly linked.

We can conclude from this evidence that Bentham did not see these works as *conflicting with* the *Constitutional Code*, but importantly *supplementing it*. A more plausible interpretation is that Bentham did not believe that his *Constitutional Code* expressed his *entire* theory of adjudication, but rather limited the Code to constraints on judicial legislation, and definition of procedures for judicial amendment of the law. Along with these procedures, he assigned powers for provisional treatment of the particular cases that give rise to the need for interpretation. That is, on most occasions in which Bentham speaks of the emendative function of the judge, he is concerned only with the problem of defining proper channels for judicial *legislation*, and not with adjudication proper. I suggest that the discussion of the sistitive power in the *Constitutional Code* must be viewed in the same way. The question of a special sort of power to handle particular cases comes up in this context because special problems arise. The judge, then, is given the *power* to suspend execution of the law—the power not to decide

---

[57] See also *Bowring* v, 564–5 and *Bankruptcy Court Bill, Bowring* v, 579–80.
[58] See, e.g., UC lii(a). 31–52; UC liii. 14–23; UC lv. 315–21.

—if he thinks this is warranted by considerations of utility.[59] Thus, the sistitive power of the judge does not impose a constraint on the judge, but rather provides him with another possible *option* when faced with a case in which simple application of the law would appear to bring about a less than optimal result. The judge may decide to set aside the law, making his decision by direct appeal to the principle of utility, *or* he may decide to submit a proposal for amendment to the legislature. If he chooses that latter course, he must decide *further* whether, on utilitarian grounds, he ought to decide the present case (either in accord with the existing law, or with the law as he thinks it should be amended) or to suspend decision until the legislature has decided.

This interpretation has the further virtue of preserving intact the distinction between the function of lawmaking and adjudication which, we have seen, Bentham took to be fundamental. The alternative interpretation of the sistitive function, which insists that all judicial creative activity must be overseen by the legislature, violates this very principle—not by allowing legislation in the process of *adjudication*, but rather in allowing *adjudication* (decision of the particular case by the legislature) in the process of *legislation*. This is precisely the objection Bentham himself raised against giving the legislature power to decide particular cases in his discussion in *Judicial Establishment*.

[59] The fact that Bentham views the sistitive function as a *discretionary* power, and not imposing a *duty* on the judge whenever he submits a proposal for amendment of the code is clear from *CC* 533 and UC liii. 250-1. That this discretion is to be guided by the principle of utility is clear from *CC* 509 and UC xlii(b). 432, 483.

13

The Coherence of Bentham's
Theory of Law

IN 9.4 we considered the coherence of Bentham's jurisprudential method. But, since we did not yet have available to us Bentham's mature theory of adjudication, we could not assess the general theory of law he developed using this method. In this chapter I want to consider again the question of the coherence of Bentham's theory. But I will here take up only two issues: (i) the compatibility of Bentham's utilitarian theory of adjudication with his positivist theory of laws, and (ii) the plausibility of his theory of adjudication. I shall leave for another occasion the important questions raised by the intense debate between Common Law and positivist traditions which we have traced in this study. In particular, I will leave for detailed consideration on another occasion questions regarding the nature and fundamental tasks of law, and the conceptions of community and of collective rationality on which the competing theories of law seemed to rest.

13.1 LAW IN THE COURTS AND LAW IN THE MARKET-PLACE

In truth, this code will rather be a set of authentic *instructions* for the judges, than a collection of peremptory ordinances.

Bentham, *Letter to Citizens of U.S.*

Considering the logical structure of Bentham's ideal code in 12.3, we found a certain kinship between Bentham's conception of the code and recent European codification efforts. On this model, the code consists of relatively general rules requiring a significant amount of judicial prudence for proper application. But the case for reconciling Bentham's general reflections on law and codification with his apparent direct-utilitarian approach to adjudication need not rest on these arguments about the relative generality or specificity of code provisions. For even in Bentham's mind this issue was largely a tactical one, settled by determining how practically to guarantee that the basic tasks of law and adjudication will be maximally served. A central question is, rather, how to characterize the fundamental relationship between the judge and the code. What role must the code play in judicial deliberation, and more generally, what is the nature of judicial subordination to the legislator and the code?

A central thesis of this book has been that Bentham, from the very outset of his career, was committed to the principle of utility as the sovereign *decision principle* in all areas of practical life, including adjudication. Thus, judges must never regard established rules (even ideal, utilitarian, codified rules) as absolutely conclusive determinants of decision. Judicial decision-making under fixed and inflexible rules is mindless and mechanical, according to Bentham. It is the product of a strategy of *manipulation*—manipulation of the will of the judge by the will of the legislator. In its place Bentham insisted on a strategy of guidance of the rational understanding of the judge, dealing with the details of the day-to-day operations of social life, by the understanding of the legislator who is alone able to take a commanding view of the whole field of human social interaction. Proper adjudicative decision-making must, then, be guided by existing established legal standards, and the more so the more determinate, perspicuous, and publicly known the rules are. But they guide judgment only against the background and under the continual superintendence of the principle of utility. Whatever subordination of the judge to the legislator meant for Bentham, it is clear that it did not mean that judges are duty bound to apply fixed rules handed down by the legislator to specific cases without appeal to relevant (utilitarian) moral-political considerations. In Bentham's view, proper adjudication under even the best law essentially relies on judicial appeal to moral and political considerations as defined by the principle of utility.

However, this direct-utilitarian theory of adjudication threatens to undermine his general theory of law at a more fundamental level. It appears to challenge structurally essential tenets of his legal *positivism* on which his view of codification rests. How does Bentham propose to reconcile his positivism and his direct-utilitarian theory of adjudication? Consideration of the answer to this question will underscore a feature of Bentham's conception of law which we noticed already in 9.3 and which distinguishes his positivism from both earlier and more recent versions of the doctrine.

The role of legal formalities

Consider again Bentham's positivist theory of laws. To begin, we must note that the debate over the relative generality or specificity of the components of Bentham's ideal code rested on a mistaken assumption. Defenders of the standard interpretation of Bentham's conception of the code assumed that a high degree of specificity of code rules is required by Bentham's insistence on *determinacy* and incontestability of legal standards. But this is not so. The relative determinacy or indeterminacy of legal standards is not strictly a function of their relative specificity or generality. It is a function rather of the public accessibility and clarity of the properties used to define the class of actions or subjects or objects of the standards. Quite general rules can be perfectly determinate; take, for example, the rule that defines legal majority at the age of sixteen. There may be some dispute over whether Bentham favoured relatively more general or relatively more specific standards for his code, but it is beyond doubt that standards, if they are to qualify as legal, must be determinate and publicly accessible, according to Bentham.

Some have challenged Professor Dworkin's claim that legal positivism is committed to the 'model of rules',[1] but surely Bentham's theory of laws is a good fit, if any positivist theory is. According to Dworkin, positivist legal standards take the form of 'rules' rather than 'principles'. To assess this claim about Bentham's theory, we need to be a bit more precise about the terminology used. Dworkin says that rules are standards which apply in an 'all-or-nothing' fashion. That is, either a subject or action falls within the scope of the rule, and so one must follow it (or one must be treated in accord with its dictates), or the subject or action falls outside its scope and it need not play any role in deliberation whatsoever. In contrast, principles have a dimension of weight. They set out considerations which count in favour of a decision, but they may be met by competing considerations of greater weight, in which case, although the principles apply, they may not rationally determine a decision in the direction in which they point.

---

[1] R. Dworkin, *Taking Rights Seriously*, ch. 2. Jules Coleman among others challenges Dworkin's characterization of legal positivism; see 'Negative and Positive Positivism'.

Despite its surface simplicity, the Dworkinian distinction marries three logically distinct, though perhaps related, contrasts between kinds of standards. (I shall leave open the question whether these contrasts in fact correspond in each case to the distinction between rules and principles.) First, 'rules', on this view, tend to have relatively precise or determinate boundaries, usually because they are defined in terms of publicly accessible, morally neutral, empirical facts. 'Principles', in contrast, are much less determinate, in large part because they are formulated in terms of normatively substantive concepts which often admit of different and conflicting conceptions. Thus, rules are, in one sense of the term, 'formal', whereas principles are 'substantive'. This is not to say that rules lack substance and need to be supplemented with other standards before they can be applied to particular situations. Rather, the substantive ends or objectives to which rules are directed (or on which they are grounded) are not part of the rules themselves. The conditions for application of the rules are defined in terms of certain empirical facts on the assumption that they bear some rational relationship to the achievement of the substantive aims or values in question. Principles, on the other hand, are formulated in terms of substantive aims or values.

But rules and principles differ in a second respect. Formal rules, because of their 'arbitrariness', or content neutrality, are dispositive of practical issues in virtue of their *formal authority* (for example their being validly enacted by a duly recognized, authorized legislative body), whereas principles, in general, make their claim upon our consideration in virtue of their own *merits* or *reasonableness*. Thus, on this view, the existence and validity of rules is always and necessarily a matter of formal pedigree, whereas principles recommend themselves to us by appeal to broader principles of morality or practical reason.[2] We may sum up these two features of rules, in contrast to principles, by saying that both the existence and the validity of rules *and* their content and identity are determined formally by appeal to morally neutral, publicly accessible criteria.

---

[2] It would be a mistake to conclude, as Dworkin seems to do, that this precludes principles from ever resting on formal, pedigree authority. First, because it is possible for there to be *un*reasonable principles which nevertheless may make some claim on judges despite their unreasonableness. The claim would arise from such formal sources of authority. Second, there is nothing standing in the way of formal recognition of reasonable principles. See J. Raz, 'Legal Principles and the Limits of Law', 823–54 and Postema, 'Co-ordination and Convention', 177.

Dworkin's contrast between the 'all-or-nothing' property of rules and the 'dimension of weight' of principles suggests a third important difference between rules and other standards. Rules are, in a way, 'peremptory'.[3] When they apply, they tend to direct a decision, or action on such a decision, *to the exclusion* of deliberation or debate over the merits of the action involved. In this respect, rules are 'exclusionary', and principles are not. Principles present a case for decision going in a certain direction, but do not seek to screen out other potentially competing considerations. This factor, I believe, and not the relative clarity or determinateness of the standard, accounts for rules appearing to apply in an 'all-or-nothing' fashion.

Return now to Bentham's positivist view of the nature of legal standards. Clearly, Bentham's legal standards meet the first two conditions of the model of rules. Legal standards, for Bentham, are formal, not substantive; they draw lines rather than spell out relevant considerations. This is because they must be defined in terms of publicly accessible, morally neutral, determinate empirical facts. To perform well the function of laws legal standards must be incontestable across most of the area of their application. Furthermore, the authenticity or validity of such rules must also be a formally determinable matter. The criteria of validity must, on Bentham's view, be defined, again, in terms of publicly accessible, morally neutral, social facts—facts of origin and pedigree. And these requirements of his general positivist theory of laws are incorporated into his command—or 'imperational'—theory of law. This underlying doctrine also motivates the more specific requirements he imposes on the formal shape and structure of law: that they must take a written form, in determinate language, for example, and that their creation and periodic amendment must issue from some central and publicly known source, and the like.

However, there is good reason to doubt whether Bentham's conception of legal standards embraces the third component of the model of rules. Indeed, as we have seen in 9.3, Bentham's positivism does not maintain that legal standards are 'peremptory'. His is a unique form of positivism which not only can be consistently combined with a direct-utilitarian theory of practical reasoning, but which in fact is required by it.

---

[3] H. L. A. Hart, *Essays on Bentham*, 252–4; Raz, *Practical Reason and Norms*, 35–48. See above, 9.3.

We have a wealth of material to draw from in the previous chapters to establish Bentham's general philosophical view on the role and character of legal rules, but they are usefully summarized, and precisely focused on the question with which we are now concerned, in his discussion of 'preappointed evidence'—that species of 'evidence' preserved for the court by formal requirements on legal transactions. According to Bentham, the need for such formalities arises primarily in three broad areas: (i) authentication of legally operative facts (e.g. records of births, deaths, etc.); (ii) authentication of contracts, conveyances, wills, and other legal transactions both private and public; and (iii) authentication of the products of general lawmaking.[4] From one perspective, the first of these categories is concerned with matters of fact and the latter two with matters of law (individual or particular laws, and general legislation). But from a more general jurisprudential perspective, Bentham insists, they all regard matters of fact, albeit facts of quite different sorts.[5] The 'formation of an obligatory rule of action, whether law or legalized contract', he writes, 'is itself a matter of fact to be established by evidence, as well as the existence of those legally operative facts which derive their operation from laws and legalized contracts' (*RJE, Bowring* vi, 509 n. ∗).

The use of formalities in each of these areas is very important for utilitarian reasons. Consider private (particular) 'laws', for example, contracts, titles, deeds of trust, and the like. Formalities are needed here because they guarantee certainty and public knowledge of both the existence and the content ('import') of the legal instruments or rules (*RJE, Bowring* vi, 511, 513, 551). They ensure the authenticity of the laws and prevent fraud, unfair reliance, and disappointment. Clearly the primary objective of introducing requirements of formal validation, in Bentham's view, is 'anti-litigious', i.e. they are designed to give effect to the desires and wills of the parties involved, and to secure smooth interaction among citizens outside of court. But also where litigation does arise, they make resolution of the dispute as fair and efficient as possible.

This, of course, is familiar ground. The arguments relied on here are Bentham's standard utilitarian arguments for the formal characteristics of law which we have canvassed several times before.[6]

---

[4] *RJE, Bowring* vi, 509; *IRE, Bowring* vi, 62–3.

[5] See *RJE, Bowring* vi, 509 and n. + and generally *OLG* IX.

[6] Indeed, at *RJE, Bowring* vi, 551–3 where Bentham is concerned with the need for formalities in law, he repeats many of the now familiar charges against the uncertainty and indeterminacy of Common Law.

The interest in this part of Bentham's discussion of pre-appointed evidence comes in his coupling of these familiar claims about the merits of positivist rules with a clear statement of the attitude which *judges* must take toward such rules.

Bentham insists that, despite the great value and utility of formalities in private transactions, they must never be regarded by the judge as entirely dispositive of the question at the centre of the judge's proper concern, viz. the authenticity of the instrument and the expectations associated with it. Such judgments are only 'probabilized' by the fact that the formal conditions have (or have not) been met; they are not thereby conclusively settled (*RJE, Bowring* vi, 523–4). Bentham repeatedly and vigorously denounced the Common Law practice of nullification, whereby a legal instrument is declared void or invalid and hence unenforceable simply for failing to meet formal conditions defined by law. This method, he argued, is unconscienably harsh, unjust, and, from a utilitarian point of view, irrational. For where there is reason to regard the instrument or transaction as spurious or unfair, the requirement is simply useless, but where there is no such reason the result is injust. The method of nullification is too blunt an instrument to achieve the objective which the formal rules were introduced to achieve. They either fail to give effect to formally inadequate but genuine arrangements, or they give effect to arrangements which, although they meet formal conditions, fail on substantive grounds.

In a rational, utilitarian system of law attention must always be paid to the utilitarian considerations which call for respect for formalities. Consider contract formalities, for example. Bentham writes,

it is only to the prevention of unfairness and spuriousness, and thence, and thus far only, to the prevention of mischievous effects, considered as liable to take their rise in contracts, that *formalities*, in so far as in the institution of them the principle of utility has been taken for the guide, have been directed (*IRE, Bowring* vi, 64, author's emphasis).

Spurious or unfair contracts are to be denied their intended effect only when giving them effect 'would to a preponderant amount be productive of mischievous consequences' (ibid.).

The basic problem here again is that of the inevitable over- or under-inclusiveness of legal rules. Formalities in general do a reasonably good job of separating unfair, inauthentic legal instruments and transactions from fair and authentic ones, and in this way they focus the attention of the judge on the locus of legitimate expectations. But they cannot capture all and only such instruments or transactions, with the result that simply following the formalities will lead to misdecision in many cases. More generally, rules are often introduced in order to make phenomena clear and determinate which are, at least from the point of view of the public, often fuzzy and indeterminate. But rules achieve clarity, certainty, and determinateness, at the price of including either more or fewer cases in the legal categories defined by the rules than the rationale underlying the rule calls for. 'Discernment or the art of judging of individual capacity', Bentham writes, 'is a rare quality, whose use it is impossible to supercede by general rules' (*Bowring* ii, 195).

Bentham's solution, however, was not to abandon all formalities. That would entail losing all the utilitarian advantages which they bring with them. Rather, he insisted that the judge must be instructed to be sensitive to the underlying objectives of the rules defining the formal conditions and must be empowered to disregard the conditions where the balance of utilities (expectation utilities largely) warrants.

[I]f in any case, and in any particular, either in the instance of an unfair contract, or in the instance of a spurious instrument of contract in the event of its being carried into effect, the balance would, upon the whole—the aggregate interest of the whole community being taken into the account— be on the side—not of mischief, but of advantage; this being supposed, no sufficient reason for refusing to give effect to it would have place: on the contrary, the reason for giving effect to it would, by the supposition, predominate or stand alone (*IRE, Bowring* vi, 64).

Thus, the rules defining formal conditions for contracts, conveyances and other legal instruments, must not be regarded as conclusive, settling in a peremptory fashion the question of the authenticity of the instrument. Rather, they provide strong *presumptive* evidence of the authenticity of the instrument (and thus presumptive evidence of the locus of legitimate expectations). This presumption can be defeated in particular cases, and when it is defeated, the judge must decide on the basis of his assessment of the overall balance of utilities.

Bentham clearly intends his account of formalities in private law to apply to legislation in general (*RJE, Bowring* vi, 509). The analogy is clear: 'positivist' formalities are essential for the clarity and authenticity of laws. Like private legal instruments, they guarantee certainty and public knowledge of the existence, authenticity, and content of the legal standards. But since legal standards are always subject to the defects of over- or under-inclusiveness, such fixed and determinate rules must never themselves conclusively determine judicial decision-making. The judge must regard them as presumptive of the will of the lawmaker, that is, there is a strong presumption that following the rule will in normal cases achieve the end at which the rule is aimed. But this is not to say that legal standards are mere rules of thumb, setting out the usually most efficient ways of achieving desirable utilitarian social goals. They play a larger and more important role in the practical reasoning of citizens, and this must be recognized by the judge. For these rules, in Bentham's view, focus expectations due to their publicity and determinacy. The rules permit him, then, to chart with some confidence the range of utilities, especially expectation utilities, which must ultimately determine his decision. The rules themselves, however, provide no peremptory reasons for judicial decisions. On Bentham's account, they do not exclude from judicial deliberation otherwise relevant (utilitarian) considerations. They merely provide a reasonably accurate guide to the most important such relevant considerations. Responsible adjudication is always capable of penetrating through the veil of the rules to the underlying rationales and grounding concerns, and the best such decisions are those which in each case accord with the overall balance of such considerations.

The two faces of utilitarian positivist law

The key to Bentham's marriage of positivism with his direct-utilitarian theory of adjudication is his sharp distinction between the social tasks of laws (more specifically, the code) and of adjudication in the shadow of such laws. The fundamental task of laws is to define and maintain a secure framework for social interaction. Certainty, stability, and efficiency are its primary virtues. Its primary tools are formal rules, both the existence and import of which are fixed and determinate and which are arranged according to a natural and rational system. The primary task of adjudication is fine-tuning that system in so far as it applies to particular cases that come before the court. In this way it guarantees flexibility and adjustment to the variety of changing circumstances characteristic of modern social life and interaction, a task which the rules themselves cannot do without jeopardizing their effectiveness as guarantors of certainty and predictability. Bentham's solution is an institutional and functional one. The two opposed elements in his general theory of law are reconciled by assigning responsibility for the different tasks to different institutions.[7]

Bentham's view of laws (the code), then, is one of a largely static system of quite general standards which define a comprehensive formal framework for social interaction. It is comprehensive, not in the sense that it attempts to regulate in detail each specific situation, but rather, in the sense that it provides the structure within which all private decisions and forms of interaction can take place on a rational, well co-ordinated and efficient basis. It defines and establishes with reasonable certainty the boundaries within which individual decisions can be made. This requires that the framework be stable, even static, as well as relatively simple and publicly accessible. It cannot maintain its stability if it attempts to regulate each situation or transaction directly, and so its provisions must be generic. The dynamic features of social life and interaction are accounted for on this view, not within the structure of the law/code itself, but through private and individual adjustment within the generic framework of the code according to the methodological principles on which the code itself is based. Since the rules of the game have been worked out with sufficient clarity, the private parties can take changes in their particular situations into account in the way in which they manipulate (their) rights.

Adjustment is not left entirely to the market-place on Bentham's account, however; for the courts are involved in this adjustment as well. But, here again, the adjustments will not be made in the *law* (except in special circumstances). Denial of all precedential effect of judicial decisions is designed by Bentham to restrict the legal effect of adjudicative adjustment or fine-tuning of the legal structure to the parties appearing before the court.

In light of these different functions, Bentham's code appears Janus-faced. It presents different aspects depending on whether one views it from the market-place or from the bench. In neither case do the standards of law take on a fully peremptory character, but in the market-place their formal character is more prominent. For in that context, Bentham seems to hold, the primary concern is efficient co-ordination of social interaction, and since public,

---

[7] In this respect, ironically, Bentham follows the example of the development of English law which (in its early stages at least) assigned the task of 'law' to Common Law courts and the task of 'equity' to Chancery.

determinate, and stable rules focus expectations, they will play a central role in practical deliberation. But in the court the formal legal standards take on a quite different character. The court does not face the pressure of *prospective* co-ordination. It is able to assess the situation between the parties retrospectively. This difference emerges clearly from Bentham's discussion of the importance of attaching reasons to the laws promulgated in the code.

Throughout his writings Bentham insists that it is not enough for the legislator to promulgate good laws which are in fact grounded in good (utilitarian) reasons. A good code must in addition supply, and integrate directly into the code, the reasons for the laws promulgated.[8] The reason for this remarkable requirement is his familiar aim to substitute for 'the primeval barbarism' of rule by power (of *will* addressed to *will*) a regime in which as far as possible *understanding* is addressed to *understanding*.[9] He sought to replace the manipulation of the people by the arbitrary will of judge and lawgiver with the enlightened direction of behaviour by appeal to considerations of reason and utility themselves. However, this common project takes on a quite different character depending on whether the party addressed by the lawgiver, or (more impersonally) by the code, is a private citizen or a judge.

We saw in 11.2 that law, if it is to address human beings in a manner appropriate to them, i.e. if it is to command respect and rational, willing obedience, must address the understanding with reasons for the laws it promulgates. Nevertheless, the needs of the market-place call for *formal* rules which are public, determinate, and stable, if they are adequately to perform their function of focusing expectations and providing security. This we learned already in 5.1 and Chapter 6, in the discussion of Bentham's early theory of justice and adjudication. Thus, the code must be *accompanied by* a full 'commentary of reasons' for the benefit of citizens governed by that law, although that commentary can never replace those laws. This is one prominent countenance of the code.

The code presents a quite different face to the judge. Again, the commentary of reasons is of central importance. But the reasons now have a different function according to Bentham: they provide a 'compass' for the judge who is 'well-disposed', indicating the

[8] See *Essay on Promulgation*, *Bowring* i, 159–63; also *Bowring* iv, 492; *Bowring* iii, 300; *Bowring* viii, 491; *PJP*, *Bowring* ii, 28–32; and generally the structure of the *Constitutional Code*, *Bowring* ix.

[9] *RJE*, *Bowring* vi, 524, n. *, 563–4, and *Bowring* i, 160.

appropriate path for decision where there is doubt or ambiguity in the formulation of the rules of the code, as well as a 'barrier' for those 'ill-disposed', thus preventing deviation from the right (utilitarian) path, and a 'support' to the well-disposed judge who is, nevertheless, 'subjected to accusation at the hands of part of his fellow-citizens . . . to justify him in the sight of the whole'.[10] From the perspective of the bench the reasons behind the laws play a more fundamental role than the rules of law do. The rules have a presumptive character, both because they are formed by the legislator to cover the majority of cases (and so, presumably, indicate the path along which utility is likely to travel), and because, if the rules function as Bentham believes they will, they will focus expectations. But these are presumptive guides, not peremptory rules of decision. For the legislator to issue such peremptory rules would be to attempt to manipulate the will of the judge. The aim, rather, must be to guide the understanding of the judge. The appropriate language of the code addressed to the bench is not that of fixed rules or coercive mandates or directives, but that of 'instructions' or guides.[11]

This conception of the code, its rules and its commentary of reasons, as viewed from the bench, is lucidly stated in the following comments of Dumont on Bentham's penal code, comments which Bentham himself quotes with approval in an open letter addressed 'to the citizens of the United States' advocating his scheme of codification.

In truth, this code will rather be a set of authentic *instructions* for the judges, than a collection of peremptory ordinances. A greater latitude of discretion will be left to them than was ever left by any code: yet their path being everywhere chalked out for them, as it were between two parallel lines, no power that can be called *arbitrary* is left to them in any part of it.

In the code itself they will behold all the *considerations* capable of affording proper *grounds* for their decision: and, on each occasion, it is to the *text of the law* that, in justification of such applications as, on that occasion, they think fit to make of those same grounds they will all along make reference . . . (*Bowring* iv, 479, author's emphasis).

The code, on this view, is not to be conceived by the judge *from his point of view*, as a series of fixed rules ('peremptory ordinances'), but as a set of considerations relevant to decision of matters that

---

10 *Bowring* iv, 492; see also *Bowring* i, 161.
11 *RJE, Bowring* vi, 563–4; *Bowring* iii, 300. Compare *Bowring* iv, 538–9.

come before him. These rules mark out the *parameters* of judicial decision, they do not, themselves, determine any decision. And lying behind them, always, is the principle of utility. This strategy, in Bentham's view, has the advantage of freeing the full rational faculties of the judge from the shackles of fixed rules which are inevitably inadequate to the complexity of particular situations, thereby eliminating the mindless, and mechanical adjudication characteristic of one half of the Common Law judiciary, while at the same time avoiding entirely the accompanying self-willed, arbitrary, and unaccountable adjudication characteristic of the other half.

Thus, we are forced again to the conclusion that Bentham's positivism has a very special character. Although it embraces many of the properties of the model of rules, it rejects the crucial claim that legal standards supply a special sort of peremptory reason for action (at least for officials, and apparently for ordinary citizens as well). In this important respect Bentham's positivist jurisprudence not only differs from more recent positivist theories (for example, Hart's),[12] but it also rejects an important assumption about the nature of authority and law running through British legal theory from Hobbes (and Hale) through Hume.[13]

We also must revise the standard understanding of Bentham's doctrine of judicial 'subordination' to the sovereign legislator and the sovereign's code. This is a subordination of understanding to understanding designed to liberate the rational faculties of the judge—a functional subordination of clearly defined tasks and broadly defined powers the exercise of which is guided by utilitarian standards and is constantly accountable to the people in whose name and for whose welfare the power is exercised. This is a distinctively direct-utilitarian theory of adjudication, yet it is compatible with Bentham's utility-inspired positivism. The theory of adjudication cannot be deduced simply from his positivism, nor can the theory of law be deduced logically from his theory of adjudication. They form an organic whole with the theory of citizen compliance and the broader moral-social-political theory into which they are embedded.

[12] For the clearest statement of his views on this matter see Hart, *Essays on Bentham*, 17–20, 143–61, 243–68.

[13] And reiterated in contemporary positivist jurisprudence. See, in addition to Hart's work mentioned in n. 12, Raz, *The Authority of Law*, chs. 1–3, 'Authority, Law, and Morality', and 'Authority and Justification'.

13.2 CRITIQUE OF BENTHAM'S THEORY OF ADJUDICATION

[T]hey continue to multiply laws, . . . as if they could remove every possible ground of dispute, and were secure in their rights, merely by having put them in writing.

A. Ferguson, *Essay on the History of Civil Society.*

Bentham devised a unique and sophisticated theory of law and adjudication. Its most striking feature is its attempt to unite a positivist account of the nature of laws—laws regarded as conventionally defined and identified formal rules—with an uncompromising direct-utilitarian theory of adjudication in which those rules and other institutional facts of legal practice have only strategic significance and do not themselves peremptorily direct judicial decisions. This theory faces a number of problems, some of them quite serious. This is not the place for a full-scale critique of Bentham's complex theory. I shall only consider two groups of criticisms, one internal and one external to Bentham's project. I begin with a set of problems internal to Bentham's theory. In particular, I shall argue that Bentham's theories of law and adjudication, far from fitting together into an organic unity as he supposes, are in fact in deep conflict, and the general theory of law which seeks to unite them is self-defeating.

The paradox of utilitarian positivist adjudication

We saw in 13.1 that the key device by which Bentham sought to reconcile his positivist theory of laws and his utilitarian theory of adjudication was the sharp functional distinction between law and adjudication. To the former was assigned the task of wholesale structuring and co-ordinating of social interaction, creating a stable and fully public framework of rules around which expectations could focus. To the latter was assigned the task of fine-tuning this structure, adjusting it to the near unique circumstances of private individuals. But the delicate balance of security and flexibility, of social order and private judgment, that Bentham tried to achieve on the point of this functional distinction is seriously threatened by tensions deep within the theory.

Bentham's strategy was to shift the focus of public expectations from the practice of the courts to a comprehensive code of laws consisting of fully public and formally identifiable legal directives. Now, this code can serve the purpose of securing expectations and co-ordinating social interaction only so long as citizens are convinced, and have good reason to believe that others are convinced, that the laws on the books correspond closely to the laws applied and enforced by the courts. 'There is real incentive to orient this conduct in accordance with the announced rules only if the same rules are used to assess conduct when a dispute arises, as could reasonably have been expected at the time the decisions to act were made.'[14] Of course, as long as the courts make decisions in accord with the law, it would seem, there would be no problem.

However, on Bentham's view judges are not bound to adhere strictly to this code. They are encouraged to give the utilitarianly best judgment in every case, taking into account the important role of the code of focusing expectations. And Bentham seems to believe that there will be a significant number of occasions on which deviation from the line marked out by pre-established law will be justified òn utilitarian grounds, especially when the judge's attention need focus only on the consequences of his particular decision. Problems arise for Bentham, however, if these deviations from the code become matters of public knowledge. And, because of the extensive (and, for his scheme, absolutely necessary) publicity of the activity of the courts, and of public justification of judicial decisions, they inevitably will become public knowledge. It appears, then, that Bentham's strategy must fail, for no matter how well *initially* public expectations are fixed on the code, they will inevitably shift back to focus on the activities of the courts and the patterns that emerge from them. The attempt formally to deny precedential effect to judicial decisions will be futile. A system of precedent-based case-law will inevitably arise, and its force and importance will not be diminished by the fact that its legitimacy cannot be recognized officially in theory.[15] Bentham's mature theory of laws and adjudication, it appears, is self-defeating: constraints essential for its success in fact make success impossible.

Bentham is not without resources for rebuttal at this point. First of all, he can legitimately point out that effective co-ordination

[14] P. Weiler, 'Legal Values and Judicial Decision Making', quoted in R. Sartorius, *Individual Conduct and Social Norms*, 179.
[15] This, of course, has been the experience of European code-based systems, especially the French.

does not require absolutely universal compliance with the public rules. Necessary only is that degree of compliance which makes it more reasonable than not for most people to expect compliance with it and to act on that expectation. To see this take a simple system of rules the main function of which is co-ordination, say traffice signals on city streets. It is reasonable to expect others to comply, and to act on this expectation, even though we all know that some persons may legitimately ignore them. The class of legitimate exceptions includes not only recognizable emergency vehicles, but also in some cases private vehicles whose right to ignore the traffic rules is not public knowledge at the time (these vehicles do not carry the customary special markings of emergency vehicles). Despite this, and despite the fact that it is known that some drivers illegitimately violate the rules, it is still reasonable in most cases to orient our driving to those rules rather than to some alternative set.

Moreover, two features of Bentham's system further encourage public focus of attention on the code. (*a*) Bentham would argue that the rules of the code are not arbitrary, reasonable to follow *only* because they seem to *work* (i.e. co-ordinate social interaction). They are, and should be known to be, good, reasonable, and appropriate laws. So there usually will be strong reason to comply with the rules *apart* from considerations of co-ordination. (*b*) The enforced isolation of the courts—the requirement that judges treat each case solely on its merits without regard to other cases—ensures that there will be no pressure to conform to the patterns of decisional behaviour exhibited in other jurisdictions, on the contrary, there is pressure to ignore such behaviour. Thus, Bentham might argue, whatever deviations from the code there may be will not exhibit the sort of reasonable coherence required to focus attention away from the more reasonable and public code.[16]

Bentham's arguments are subtle and sound, as far as they go. But they do not fully deflect the initial objection to his theory of adjudication. He seems to have overlooked two important features of adjudication which strengthen the paradox facing his theory. First, he overlooks the extensive *interdependence* of the public and

---

[16] Bentham frequently suggests this line of argument. For example he regarded the saving grace of English juries, in comparison with decisions by corrupt judges, to lie in the fact that jury decisions were denied all public, precedential effect. The result was that, no matter how bad the decision was, it could not extend its corrupting influence beyond the particular case. See *IRE, Bowring* vi, 52–3.

the courts when it comes to interpreting and applying the law (although he was keenly aware of this in his early reflections on Common Law adjudication). The problem arises from the fact that all language—and especially language used instrumentally to achieve social goals, for example statutory or code language—has meaning only within a context of interpretation. The interpretation some persons give to statutory language depends heavily upon the interpretation they expect other relevant persons to give to it. Bentham clearly recognized that this is true of interpretations of *customary* practice, but he seems to have thought it could be avoided through the use of clearly defined language regimented to its plan meaning. But the 'plain meaning' of words is plain only relative to certain conventions of interpretation of those words, and those conventions are constantly influenced by the interpretations carried out by reference to them.

Bentham required that judges take into account the public's interpretation of code provisions, at least to the extent of recognizing how those interpretations shape public expectations. But he failed to recognize that the interpretations citizens are likely to give of the law depend on their expectations regarding the interpretations the courts will give to them. These interpretations could be ignored if the courts' interpretations had no consequences for citizens who followed their own understanding of the law, or if the courts' actions were not generally known by the public and if their interpretations were inaccessible to it. But, of course, in Bentham's scheme neither of these conditions is met. Judicial proceedings, decisions, and the grounds for them, all *must* be fully public and thus will inevitably be matters of public knowledge. It will also be public knowledge that the courts are not *bound* to follow the code, but are bound only to decide on their best judgment of its spirit, as indicated by the rationale that accompanies it. But if this is so, then the more prudent course for citizens to follow would be to focus on judicial interpretations of that rationale than on the explicit formal language of the code. Or, rather, judicial understanding of the underlying aims and objectives of the law will be an important part of the context of interpretation of the code. Citizens ignore it at their peril, even in their daily interactions with other citizens on matters that never get to court. Given publicity of judicial proceedings, the code *cannot* turn one face to the market-place and another to the bench, as Bentham requires.

Thus, even if we do not consider the effect of official deviations from expected applications of the law, there are strong pressures for citizens to pay attention to the practices of adjudicative institutions. For what the courts *do* has an important (though not necessarily decisive) impact on what the law *is* and what it requires, and not just on whether it is followed or not, i.e. it has an impact on the *content* of the law and not just on the likelihood of its being enforced.

Bentham has also overlooked a second force active in the process of adjudication: the demand for coherence. This is, ultimately, a moral demand, a requirement of fairness or perhaps 'integrity'—as Dworkin has recently suggested.[17] But I want to consider it here from a different angle, as a necessary condition of the acceptance or perceived legitimacy of the system of adjudication.

Informal, private dispute resolution arrangements, even forms of private arbitration within the context of a body of formal law, depend for their legitimacy on the voluntary submission of the parties to the process and its outcomes. These outcomes are likely to be judged fair or unfair largely on the basis of the parties' assessment of the fairness of the particular proceedings, and the merits of the particular cases submitted to it. The fact that different outcomes were achieved in other private cases may have little effect on the parties' sense of the fairness of the settlement in their case.[18]

But the situation would be different within Bentham's structure of conciliation-cum-adjudication. The institutions are not strictly voluntary, and the presiding official will inevitably be viewed, not as an agent of the parties, but as an official speaking for the community and its laws. This will be true even at the conciliation stage. Conciliation will inevitably be carried on under the shadow of the

---

[17] Suggested in an unpublished manuscript which Professor Dworkin kindly allowed me to read.

[18] I am granting this much to Bentham, although there is strong empirical evidence to the contrary. Informal systems of arbitration and mediation, operating, in theory at least, independently of the legal system, are subject to strong pressures to recognize precedent. One observer notes that 'there are strong pressures in labor arbitration within the context of a collective bargaining agreement toward developing a body of precedent guiding management in administering the contract, guiding unions in deciding which cases to bring to arbitration and guiding arbitration in making future decisions. Theoretically, the doctrine of *stare decisis* does not apply in labor arbitration, but in fact arbitrators follow precedent as carefully as courts do.' (J. Getwin, 'Labor Arbitration and Dispute Resolution', 920 n. 18. See also M. Eisenberg, 'Private Ordering through Negotiation', 650–21; L. Fuller, 'Collective, Bargaining and the Arbitrator', 3–46, and 'Forms and Limits of Adjudication', 86–124.)

law and whatever legitimacy the mediating judge has will be a consequence of his ability to impose a settlement at the adjudicative stage.[19] This, in itself, is no matter for concern. But the consequence is that the legitimacy of the process will be entirely a function of the legitimacy of the law and legal system as a whole, and not at all, as in more informal mediating or arbitration settings, a function of the parties' voluntary consent. This is likely to generate substantial pressures for consistency of judicial decisions over time and among different courts in the legal system. In the absence of voluntary submission, and given the inevitable public focus of the proceedings, the parties are more likely to focus their assessments of the fairness of the process on the appropriateness of the outcomes and demand that *comparative* justice be done. This tendency is strengthened by the publicity of the proceedings which Bentham requires.

Thus, again, there are pressures within the structure of adjudication forcing citizens to focus attention away from the code and onto the activities of the courts. Now one might think that the solution, from Bentham's point of view, is simply to instruct the judges to adhere strictly to the code. The argument, in fact, would be very similar to his argument for a strict regime of *stare decisis*. However, there are several problems with this solution.

First, it seems to fall prey to the 'paradox of inflexibility' which undermined any Common Law scheme on Bentham's view. The only difference between the present scheme and his revisionist Common Law theory (Chapter 6) is that the law is initially formulated in a set of comprehensive codes. But Bentham clearly believed that the code cannot do the job of legal ordering alone. The demands for 'flexibility' are not met by his code even in its most ideal form. Thus, if the 'paradox of inflexibility' is a powerful argument against Common Law adjudication, it is equally powerful against this solution.

Second, it is not clear that this solution is available to Bentham. The argument for it calls for reflection on the *cumulative* effects of judicial decision-making not bound to strict adherence to the code. But Bentham has designed the institutions of adjudication in such a way that these considerations will not be given full and adequate consideration by officials themselves. They will appear, from the

---

[19] See generally M. Shapiro, 'Compromise and Litigation', 163–75, and *Courts*, ch. 1.

point of view of officials within the system, as 'externalities'. But, then, the instruction to consider them can only come from the outside, as a constraint imposed on the process of judicial deliberation, requiring officials to regard the code provisions as peremptory. But, of course, this is inconsistent with the spirit of Bentham's entire enterprise. It appears, then, that he can only save his scheme of adjudication by abandoning his most powerful motivation for proposing it.

Bentham's theory of adjudication, then, is practically self-defeating. It is not practically feasible to separate functionally the demands for coherence and consistency of the law, on the one hand, and the demands of 'flexibility', on the other. The fault of Bentham's theory lies, in part, in his mistaken belief that through regimentation of language we can avoid the need to appeal to a shared context of interpretation. But the fault lies also in his failure to realize that the demand for coherence must be met not merely for strategic reasons of securing adequate co-ordination of social interaction, but also for a deeper reason of securing the legitimacy of the legal system. The requirement of coherence is not only a strategic demand, it is a moral one. But it is a moral demand independent of 'outcome' justice, and consequently it can conflict with it. This conflict is an inevitable element of public adjudication. It cannot be eliminated by separating the contending values or virtues functionally. The value of Bentham's theory of adjudication lies not in his successful treatment of this problem, but in his having brought this problem to our attention.

The privatizing of adjudication

Bentham's theories of law and adjudication, I have argued, cannot achieve the aims of the jurisprudential project he set for himself. In these concluding pages I want to suggest briefly why this project itself is fundamentally mistaken. The arguments here can only be sketchy and to an extent they presuppose a conception of the nature and tasks of law which needs to be more fully articulated and defended. But that is a task for another occasion.

Bentham's proposals for accessible, informal, quick, inexpensive, and participatory dispute resolution have much in common with proposals from many radical groups throughout history.[20] But

---

[20] For a discussion of seventeenth century radical proposals see B. Shapiro, 'Law Reform in Seventeenth Century England'. An entire issue of the *Yale Law Journal*

there are also some very important differences. Like the proposals of many radical groups, the Levellers for example, Bentham's proposal has a distinctly populist motivation. The aim is to take the law out of the hands of the ruling class and its professional servants and put it directly in the hands of the people. But Bentham's proposals do not share two other objectives often associated with these calls for informal, 'people's' justice: the interest in decentralization of social and legal power and the interest in politicizing the mechanisms of justice.

Bentham was never sceptical of centralized power, and the scheme of popular justice he devised, though designed to be accessible to all the people (or at least to all members of the middle class), is still carefully structured around a strongly centralized power. It is a scheme of local, but not decentralized justice. Furthermore, it should now be clear that Bentham radically privatized the institutions of justice and adjudication, a tendency already gaining strength in the English legal practice of his day.

In Bentham's scheme, the focus of 'adjudication'—or perhaps more accurately of official administration under the law—is entirely on the particular disputes of private individuals. This is a product of several features of Bentham's proposed judicial institutions. First, every effort must be made by the 'judge' to resolve conflicts between the parties through mediation before he may bring the dispute to the more formal trial stage. The judge is not only empowered but also under obligation to act as mediator, with the sole objective of bringing the parties to some resolution of their dispute. There is no recognized public interest in this process, and it may be carried on in private whenever necessary. Second, there is no sharp differentiation between the conciliation and adjudication stages of the process. The two are continuous and the same person who acts as conciliator is authorized to adjudicate. The result, again, is that the focus even at the adjudicative stage is entirely on the interests of the parties. Bentham does not deny that there may be consequences of the judge's decisions for third parties. Yet, when he discusses the kind of deliberation the judge would engage in at this stage, he often overlooks those considerations. I suspect this is because he believed they

(v. 82, no. 5, 1979) is devoted to extensive discussion of contemporary advocacy of alternatives to formal legal institutions for dispute resolution. See also J. S. Auerbach, *Justice Without Law?*

would not in fact play a very important role in judicial deliberations.

Third, since the system is set up to eliminate all precedential effects of the decision, the judge must concern himself *only* with the features of the instant case and may pay no attention either to past cases or to potential future cases. Thus, where there are relevant consequences for third parties to be considered, Bentham arranges it so that judicial attention is focused only on the consequences of the particular decision, and not on the potential consequences of the establishment of a general rule. Finally, in light of this denial of the precedential effect of judicial decisions, and the pervasive concentration on the prevention of disappointment of expectations, there seems to be no reason at all for adjudicative decisions, even if imposed on the parties, to take the form of determination of rights. The law, and the 'entitlements' it defines, guide but do not determine proper judicial decision in such cases. The judge is empowered to work out solutions tailored to the specific features of the dispute between the parties.

One might say, then, that Bentham sought the withering away not only of judicial *interpretation* of the law but also of *adjudication* itself. For the essentially public process of adjudication is replaced by what amounts to a system of private conciliation-cum-arbitration within the context of law. The public law-integrating and law-mediating functions of the courts are entirely absent from this conception of adjudication. No longer is there any institutional means, or incentive for parties affected by controversial exercises of governmental power, to argue their claims by appeal to principles implied by existing practices, except in so far as they can argue that their own *expectations* have been defeated in some specific and demonstrable way. Despite the constant presence of the public in the form of the 'public opinion tribunal', there is no vehicle for the parties, acting in the name of the public, to force consideration and public justification of the substantive objectives underlying the laws and governmental policies.[21] Nor is there any way to force the government or the community at large to take seriously commitments to principles implicit in their long-standing practices and institutions unless those commitments are already made explicit in formally recognized law.[22]

---

[21] A function of adjudication, the importance of which Fuller rightly stressed. See his 'Forms and Limits of Adjudication'.

[22] This, of course, is a major theme of Dworkin's criticism of positivism (see,

462 *Law, Utility, and Adjudication*

Not only is this mechanism for public control of power lost, but so too is a powerful forum for the public articulation of shared purposes and principles. In 11.2 we noted the important role that Bentham assigned to publicity and the public opinion tribunal. But the aim of these devices, as of his democratic proposals generally, was to maximize accountability of those in power. It was not to increase the level of public participation in community governance. The public plays a passive judgmental and enforcement role, not an active, policy-affecting, participatory role in government. There is no room in his theory of adjudication, or indeed in his theory of law generally, for public debate over matters of justice, of common good, or the kind of community we wish to be.

This, however, is a result not only of Bentham's theory of adjudication, but it is the intended result of his entire general theory of law. Following the established pattern of British legal theory, Bentham's reflections on the nature and basic tasks of law started from the perceived need to establish order in a social context characterized by dissensus over fundamental moral and political issues. Recall, Common Law theory sought to establish this order by putting into the hands of the judiciary the authority to uncover and articulate the 'deeper' coherence and consensus lying behind the surface anarchy of private judgment. Hobbes, in contrast, called for investing full authority in the 'natural reason' of the sovereign to meet this crisis. Both sought to establish order by denying the competence of individual rational judgment in the public arena.

Bentham decisively rejected both strategies because of their authoritarian tendencies. He struggled to work out an alternative solution to the same problem which preserved the sovereignty of individual rational judgment. But his strategy was, in effect, to define substantive political conflict out of existence. First, he relegated all disagreement that could not be reduced to conflicts of individual interests (themselves translatable into conflicts of utility) to the irrational influence of 'the principle of sympathy and antipathy'. Second, he sought through his comprehensive code to define all social situations, at least in genus, such that all remaining conflict could only be regarded as matters of minor adjustment of the basic balance of utilities struck by the code.

e.g., *Taking Rights Seriously*, ch. 3), although it applies to Bentham's theory of adjudication for quite different reasons than those Dworkin sets out.

Law, on this model (which, in this respect, represents only a refinement of the basic tendency of positivist legal theory), is a political debate *stopper*, a technique for either preventing disputes from arising or taking public form at all, or for enforcing and executing the results of political debate carried on in other forums[23] (and, in Bentham's theory, debate carried on at a different time, viz. at the establishment of the code). The aim of law, according to the British legal theory, from Coke to Bentham (and beyond to the present) was, in Hume's words, 'to cut off all occasion of discord and contention' (*Treatise* 502).

But the futility of this strategy was observed already in the late eighteenth century by Adam Ferguson: '[T]hey continue to multiply laws, and to accumulate volumes,' he observes, 'as if they could remove every possible ground of dispute, and were secure of their rights, merely by having put them in writing.' But, he continues, it 'is not in mere laws, after all, that we are to look for the securities to justice, but in the powers by which those laws have been obtained, and without whose constant support they must fall to disuse.'[24] And these 'powers' include fundamentally a vigorous public spirit.[25]

The formal rules are capable of achieving their executive effect only if there is a context of interpretation actively utilized by those subject to them. Even if we restrict the task of law to co-ordination of social interaction, Bentham cannot expect the whole burden of this task to be carried by the rules themselves. The rules can serve this function only if those subject to them regard the rules not as final result of co-operative action and reasoning, but as the starting-point for it.[26]

Moreover, Bentham's identification of law with the execution of *already achieved* agreement or consensus fails to give place in the general theory of law for the much more substantial contributions to social order and public life made by law through providing the materials and public context for the forging and reforging of consensus. Common Law theory refused to identify law with a set of formally defined and identified rules. Instead, it insisted on viewing

---

[23] Joseph Raz, for example, has recently argued that law must be identified with the 'executive' rather than the 'deliberative' stage of practical reasoning. See, e.g., *Concept of a Legal System*, 2nd edn., 213–16.

[24] A Ferguson, *Essay*, 165–6; see also 263–4.

[25] Ibid. 220–2.

[26] See D. Regan, *Utilitarian Co-operation*, esp. 208–9.

law as the matrix within which the public life of the community was lived. Ironically, its mistake, like that of Bentham, was to identify law with consensus already achieved. This tendency of both the positivist and Common Law traditions to identify law with the product of consensus is unfortunate. As Clifford Geertz has observed, such a conception of law 'not only leaves law the most powerful where the least needed, a sprinkler system that turns off when the fire gets too hot, but more importantly, leaves it . . . wholly marginal to the main disturbances of modern life.'[27]

But it is in the nature of *living* traditions and practices for their principles and aims, even the most fundamental ones, to be open to reassessment and rearticulation—and not just by an officially recognized, technically trained professional élite. With this in mind we can, perhaps, borrow a notion from Common Law theory without fear of surrendering to its authoritarian tendencies. A major failure of Bentham's positivist theory of law, I believe, lies in its inability to recognize the capacity of the tradition of legal practice to provide both a *matrix of* and *forum for* the continual forging and reforging of consensus on fundamental public and essentially political questions. Rousseau was right to point out that there is 'a universal justice emanating from reason alone . . . But if we knew how to receive it from on high we would need neither government nor laws.' Thus, we need 'conventions and laws to combine rights with duties and to bring justice back to its object'.[28] But these conventions are not accomplished facts waiting to be discovered, they are continually being constructed and reconstructed from the materials and within the matrix of law. Law on this view does not strive to block political debate, or regiment it, or relegate it to conflict of private interest. It rather provides the forum and language in which the debate can be carried on publicly, i.e. in public, by the public, on public grounds. Legal justice is never likely to match ideal justice because it is always the product of a temporary public consensus. What makes it attractive (or, if you will, normative) is that it is a consensus, a public expression of the values of the community at the time. What makes it tolerable is that it is temporary and always open to challenge and reformulation.

[27] *Local Knowledge*, 217.
[28] *Social Contract*, Bk. II, ch. vi.

Bibliography

PRIMARY WORKS

Bentham's Works

Bentham Manuscripts in the University College, London Library.

Bentham Manuscripts in the British Library, Add. MSS.

Bentham's Political Thought, ed. B. Parekh, London, 1973.

The Collected Works of Jeremy Bentham, general eds. J. H. Burns, J. R. Dinwiddy, F. Rosen, London and Oxford 1968– (in progress): *A Comment on the Commentaries and A Fragment on Government*, eds. J. H. Burns and H. L. A. Hart, London, 1977.

Constitutional Code, vol. I, eds. F. Rosen and J. H. Burns, Oxford, 1983.

The Correspondence of Jeremy Bentham, 1752–1780, ed. T. L. S. Sprigge, 2 vols., London, 1968.

The Correspondence of Jeremy Bentham, 1781–1788, ed. I. Christie, London, 1971.

The Correspondence of Jeremy Bentham, 1788–1797, ed. A. T. Milne, 2 vols., London, 1981.

An Introduction to the Principles of Morals and Legislation, eds. J. H. Burns and H. L. A. Hart, London, 1970. New introduction by H. L. A. Hart, New York, 1982.

Of Laws in General, ed. H. L. A. Hart, London, 1970.

On the Influence of Place and Time in Matters of Legislation and Of Indirect Legislation, eds. C. Bahmueller and H. Wieting, Jr., Oxford, 1986.

A Fragment on Government, ed. F. C. Montague, Oxford, 1891.

Jeremy Bentham's Economic Writings, ed. W. Stark, 3 vols., London, 1952–4.

A Treatise on Judicial Evidence, ed. E. Dumont, London, 1825.

The Works of Jeremy Bentham, ed. J. Bowring, 11 vols., Edinburgh, 1838–43.

Other Primary Works

Aquinas, St Thomas, *Selected Political Writings*, ed. A. P. D'Entreves, Oxford, 1959.

—— *Summa Theologiae*, Blackfriars edn., 60 vols., New York, 1964–75.

466   Bibliography

Law and Political Theory (*ST* 1a2ae. 90–7; vol. 28), trans. and notes
T. Gilby OP, New York, 1966.

Justice, (*ST* 2a2ae. 57–62; vol. 37), trans. and notes T. Gilby OP, New
York, 1975.

Injustice, (*ST* 2a2ae. 63–79; vol. 38), trans. and notes M. Lefebure OP,
New York, 1975.

Blackstone, W., *Commentaries on the Law of England*, 4 vols., Oxford,
1767.

Hale, Sir M., *Considerations Touching the Amendment or Alteration of
Laws* (1665), published in F. Hargrave, *A Collection of Tracts Relating
to the Law of England*, vol. 1 (1787), portions reprinted in E. Howard,
Matthew Hale, ch. xv.

—— *A History of the Common Law*, 3rd edn., ed. C. M. Gray, Chicago,
1971.

—— 'Preface to Rolle's Abridgment', *Collectanea Juridica*, vol. 1, eds.
E. and R. Brooke, London, 1791.

—— 'Reflections by the Lrd. Chiefe Justice Hale on Mr. Hobbes His
Dialogue of the Lawe', in W. Holdsworth, *A History of English Law*,
7th edn., London, 1956, vol. 1, pp. 499–513.

Hobbes, T., *Behemoth*, ed. W. Molesworth, New York, n.d.

—— *De Cive*, in *Man and Citizen*, ed. B. Gert, New York, 1972. Cited by
chapter and section.

—— *A Dialogue between a Philosopher and a Student of the Common
Laws*, ed. J. Cropsey, Chicago, 1971.

—— *The English Works of Thomas Hobbes*, ed. W. Molesworth, 11 vols.,
London, 1840.

The Elements of Law (*De Corpore Politico*), vol. IV. Cited by part,
chapter, and section.

Human Nature, vol. IV. Cited by chapter and section.

Questions Concerning Liberty, Necessity, and Chance, vol. V.

—— *De Hommine*, trans. T. S. K. Scott-Craig and C. T. Wood, *Man
and Citizen*, ed. B. Gert, New York, 1972. Cited by chapter and section.

—— *Leviathan*, ed. C. B. Macpherson, Baltimore, 1968. Cited by chapter
and page (this edn.).

Hume, D., *A Dissertation on the Passions*, in *Essays: Moral, Political
and Literary*, vol. II, eds. T. H. Green and T. H. Grose, London,
1898.

—— *Enquiries*, ed. L. A. Selby-Bigge, 3rd edn., revised by P. H. Nidditch,
Oxford, 1975; includes *An Enquiry Concerning Human Understand-
ing* (*Enquiry* I), *An Enquiry Concerning the Principles of Morals*
(*Enquiry* II), and *A Dialogue*.

—— *Essays: Moral, Political and Literary*, Oxford, 1963.

—— *The History of England from the Invasion of Julius Caesar to The Revolution in 1688*, Indianapolis, 1983-5.

—— *A Treatise of Human Nature*, ed. L. A. Selby-Bigge, 2nd edn., revised by P. H. Nidditch, Oxford, 1978.

OTHER BOOKS AND ARTICLES

Alfange, D., Jr., 'Bentham and the Codification of Law', *Cornell Law Review*, 55 (1969), 58-77.

Ardal, P. S., 'Convention and Value', *David Hume: Bicentenary Papers*, ed. G. P. Morice, Edinburgh, 1977, 51-68.

Atiyah, P. S., *Promises, Morals, and Law*, Oxford, 1981.

Auerbach, J. S., *Justice Without Law?* Oxford, 1982.

Austin, J., *The Province of Jurisprudence Determined*, ed. H. L. A. Hart, London, 1955.

Ayer, A. J., 'The Principle of Utility', *Jeremy Bentham and the Law*, ed. G. W. Keeton and G. Schwarzenberger, London, 1948, 245-59.

Bacon, F., *Francis Bacon's Essays*, ed. O. Smeaton, London, 1906.

Baier, A. 'Helping Hume to "Complete the Union" ', *Philosophy and Phenomenological Research*, 41 (1980), 167-86.

—— 'Hume on Fixing and Adjusting in Nature and Artifice' (unpublished MS).

—— 'Hume on Truth and Superstition' (unpublished MS).

—— 'Promises, Promises, Promises', in A. Baier, *Postures of the Mind*, Minneapolis, 1985.

Baumgardt, D., *Bentham and the Ethics of Today*, Princeton, 1952.

Berger, M., 'Codification', *Perspectives in Jurisprudence*, ed. E. Attwool, Glasgow, 1977, 142-59.

Best, W. M., *A Treatise on the Principles of Evidence*, London, 1849, republished New York, 1978.

Bickel, A., *The Morality of Consent*, New Haven, 1975.

Brandom, R., 'Freedom and Constraint by Norms', *American Philosophical Quarterly*, 16 (1979), 187-96.

Bromwich, D., *The Mind of a Critic*, Oxford, 1983.

Burke, E., *Reflections on the Revolution in France*, ed. C. C. O'Brian, New York, 1969.

—— *Works*, Boston, 1866.

Burns, J. H., 'Bentham and the French Revolution', *The Transactions of the Royal Historical Society*, 5th series, 16 (1966), 95-114.

—— 'Bentham on Sovereignty: An Exploration', *Bentham and Legal Theory*, ed. M. H. James, Belfast, 1974, 133-50.

—— *The Fabric of Felicity: The Legislator and the Human Condition*, London, 1967.

Calabresi, G., *A Common Law for the Age of Statutes*, Cambridge, Mass., 1982.

Charron, W., 'Convention, Games of Strategy, and Hume's Philosophy of Law and Government', *American Philosophical Quarterly*, 17 (1980), 327-34.

Coleman, J., 'Negative and Positive Positivism', *Journal of Legal Studies*, 11 (1982), 139-64.

Cross, R., *Precedent in English Law*, 3rd edn., Oxford, 1977.

Dickinson, H. T., *Liberty and Property: Political Ideology in Eighteenth Century Britain*, London, 1977.

Dinwiddy, J. R., 'Bentham on Private Ethics and the Principle of Utility', *Revue Internationale de Philosophie*, no. 141 (1982), 278-300.

—— 'Bentham's Transition to Political Radicalism, 1809-10', *Journal of the History of Ideas*, 36 (1975), 683-700.

Durkheim, E., *The Division of Labor*, New York, 1964.

Dworkin, R., 'Law as Interpretation', *Texas Law Review*, 60 (1982), 527-50.

—— ' "Natural" Law Revisited', *University of Florida Law Review*, 34 (1982), 165-88.

—— *Taking Rights Seriously*, Cambridge, Mass., 1978.

Eisenberg, M., 'Private Ordering through Negotiation: Dispute-Settlement and Rule Making', *Harvard Law Review*, 89 (1976), 637-81.

Elster, J., *Ulysees and the Sirens: Studies in Rationality and Irrationality*, Cambridge, England, 1979.

Ely, J., *Democracy and Distrust*, Cambridge, Mass., 1980.

Epstein, R., 'The Static Conception of the Common Law', *Journal of Legal Studies*, 9 (1980), 253-75.

Ferguson, A., *An Essay on the History of Civil Society*, ed. D. Forbes, Edinburgh, 1966.

—— *Principles of Moral and Political Science* (1792), reprinted New York, 1978.

Finnis, J., *Natural Law and Natural Rights*, Oxford, 1979.

Forbes, D., *Hume's Philosophical Politics*, New York, 1975.

Fried, C., 'The Artificial Reason of the Law, or: What Lawyers Know', *Texas Law Review*, 60 (1981), 35-58.

Friedman, B., 'An Introduction to Mill's Theory of Authority', *Mill: A Collection of Critical Essays*, ed. J. B. Schneewind, New York, 1968, 379-425.

Fuller, L. L., 'Collective Bargaining and the Arbitrator', *Wisconsin Law Review* (1963), 3-46.

—— 'The Forms and Limits of Adjudication', *The Principles of Order: Selected Essays of Lon L. Fuller*, ed. K. I. Winston, Durham, North Carolina, 1981, 86-124.

—— 'Human Interaction and the Law', *Principles of Order: Selected Essays of Lon L. Fuller*, ed. K. I. Winston, Durham, North Carolina, 1981, 211–46.

—— *The Law in Quest of Itself*, Boston, 1966.

—— *The Morality of Law* (revised edn.), New Haven, 1969.

—— 'Positivism and Fidelity To Law: A Reply To Professor Hart', *Harvard Law Review*, 71 (1958), 593–672.

Gadamer, H. G., *Philosophical Hermeneutics*, Berkeley, 1976.

—— 'The Problem of Historical Consciousness', *Interpretive Social Science: A Reader*, eds. P. Rabinow and W. Sullivan, Berkeley, 1979, 103–60.

—— *Wahrheit und Methode* (4th edn.), Tubingen, 1975.

Gans, C., 'The Normativity of Law and its Co-ordinative Function', *Israel Law Review*, 16 (1981), 333–49.

Gauthier, D., 'David Hume: Contractarian', *Philosophical Review*, 88 (1979), 3–38.

—— *The Logic of the Leviathan*, Oxford, 1969.

—— 'Thomas Hobbes: Moral Theorist', *Journal of Philosophy*, 76 (1979), 547–59.

—— 'Three Against Justice: The Foole, the Sensible Knave, and the Lydian Shepherd', *Midwest Studies in Philosophy VII: Social and Political Philosophy*, eds. P. A. French, T. E. Uehling, H. F. Wettstein, Minneapolis, 1982, 11–29.

Gay, P., *The Enlightenment: An Interpretation, Vol. I: The Rise of Modern Paganism*, London, 1967.

Geertz, C., *The Interpretation of Cultures*, New York, 1973.

—— *Local Knowledge: Further Essays in Interpretive Anthropology*, New York, 1983.

Getwin, J., 'Labor Arbitration and Dispute Resolution', *Yale Law Journal*, 88 (1979), 916–49.

Gilbert, M., 'Game Theory and *Convention*', *Synthese*, 46 (1981), 41–93.

—— 'Some Limitations of Rationality', symposium paper, American Philosophical Association, Dec. 1983, abstract in *Journal of Philosophy*, 80 (1983), 615.

—— 'Some Notes on the Concept of Social Convention', *New Literary History*, 14 (1983), 225–51.

Goldworth, A., 'The Meaning of Bentham's Greatest Happiness Principle', *Journal of the History of Philosophy*, 7 (1969), 315–21.

Graveson, R., 'The Restless Spirit of English Law', *Jeremy Bentham and the Law*, eds. G. Keeton and G. Schwarzenberger, London, 1948, 101–21.

Gray, J. C., *The Nature and Sources of Law*, 2nd edn., New York, 1972.

Haakonssen, K., *The Science of a Legislator: The Natural Jurisprudence of David Hume and Adam Smith*, Cambridge, England, 1981.

Hacker, P. M. S., 'Sanction Theories of Duties', *Oxford Essays in Jurisprudence*, 2nd series, ed. A. W. B. Simpson, Oxford, 1973.

Halévy, E., *La Formation du Radicalisme Philosophique*, 3 vols., Paris, 1901-4, translated as *The Growth of Philosophic Radicalism*, trans. M. Moriss, London, 1928, 1972.

Hardin, R., *Collective Action*, Baltimore, 1982.

Hare, R., *Freedom and Reason*, Oxford, 1963.

Harrington, J., *The Political Writings of James Harrington*, ed. C. Blitzer, New York, 1955.

Harrison, J., *Hume's Theory of Justice*, Oxford, 1981.

Harrison, R., *Bentham*, London, 1983.

Hart, H. L. A., *The Concept of Law*, Oxford, 1961.

—— *Essays on Bentham: Jurisprudence and Political Theory*, Oxford, 1982.

—— *Essays on Jurisprudence and Philosophy*, Oxford, 1983.

Hay, D., 'Property, Authority, and the Criminal Law', *Albion's Fatal Tree*, eds. D. Hay *et al.*, New York, 1975, 17-63.

Hayek, F. A., *The Constitution of Liberty*, Chicago, 1960.

—— *Law, Legislation, and Liberty, vol. 1: Rules and Order*, Chicago, 1973.

Hazlitt, W., *Political Essays, Complete Works of William Hazlitt*, London, 1932, v. 7.

—— *The Spirit of the Age*, London, 1947.

Hegel, G. W. F., *The Phenomenology of Spirit*, tr. A. V. Miller, Oxford, 1977

Helvetius, C., *De l'esprit: or Essay on the Mind and its Several Faculties*, London, 1959.

Hendel, C. W., *Studies in the Philosophy of David Hume*, Indianapolis, 1963.

Hill, C., *Intellectual Origins of the English Revolution*, Oxford, 1965.

—— 'The Norman Yoke', C. Hill, *Democracy and the Labour Movement*, London, 1954.

—— *Some Intellectual Consequences of the English Revolution*, Madison, Wisc., 1980.

Himmelfarb, G., 'Bentham's Utopia: The National Charity Company', *Journal of British Studies*, 10 (1970), 80-125.

Hirschman, A. O., *The Passions and the Interests: Political Arguments for Capitalism before Its Triumph*, Princeton, 1977.

Home, H., Lord Kames, *Essays on Several Subjects of Law*, Edinburgh, 1732.

—— Lord Kames, *Historical Law Tracts*, 2nd edn., Edinburgh, 1761.

Honnold, J., ed., *The Life of the Law*, New York, 1964.

Howard, E., *Matthew Hale*, London, 1972.

Hume, L. J., *Bentham and Bureaucracy*, Cambridge, England, 1981.

—— 'The Political Functions of Bentham's Theory of Fictions', *The Bentham Newsletter*, 3 (May 1979), 18–27.

—— 'Revisionism in Bentham Studies', *The Bentham Newsletter*, 1 (1978), 3–20.

Jaffe, L., *Judicial Control of Administrative Action*, Boston, 1965.

James, M. H., *Bentham and Legal Theory*, Belfast, 1974, reprinted from *Northern Ireland Legal Quarterly*, 24 (1973).

—— 'Bentham on the Individuation of Laws', *Bentham and Legal Theory*, ed. M. H. James, Belfast, 1974, 91–116.

Jenkins, I., *Social Order and the Limits of Law*, Princeton, 1980.

Jolowicz, H. F., *Lectures on Jurisprudence*, London, 1963.

Jones, P., 'Strains in Hume and Wittgenstein', *Hume: A Re-evaluation*, eds. D. W. Livingston and J. T. King, New York, 1976, 191–209.

Kant, I., 'What is Enlightenment?' *On History*, ed. L. W. Beck, Indianapolis, 1963.

Kavka, G. S., 'Hobbes's War of All Against All', *Ethics*, 93 (1983), 291–310.

—— 'Two Solutions to the Paradox of Revolution', *Midwest Studies in Philosophy VII: Social and Political Philosophy*, eds. P. French, T. E. Uehling, and H. K. Wettstein, Minneapolis, 1982, 455–72.

Keeton, G. W., *The Norman Conquest and the Common Law*, New York, 1960.

Kirk, R., 'Burke and the Philosophy of Prescription', *Journal of the History of Ideas*, 14 (1953), 365–80.

Knafla, L. W., *Law and Politics in Jacobean England*, New York, 1977.

Kripke, S., *Wittgenstein On Rules and Private Language*, Cambridge, Mass., 1982.

Lehmann, W. C., *Henry Home, Lord Kames, and the Scottish Enlightenment*, The Hague, 1971.

Letwin, S., *The Pursuit of Certainty*, Cambridge, England, 1965.

Lewis, D., *Convention: A Philosophical Study*, Cambridge, Mass., 1969.

Lieberman, D., 'The Province of Legislation Determined: Legal Theory in Eighteenth Century Britain', Ph.D. dissertation, University College, London, 1980.

Lively, J. and Rees, J., eds., *Utilitarian Logic and Politics*, Oxford, 1978.

Long, D., *Bentham on Liberty: Bentham's Idea of Liberty in Relation to His Utilitarianism*, Toronto, 1977.

Lovibond, S., *Realism and Imagination in Ethics*, Minneapolis, 1983.

Lucas, J., *On Justice*, Oxford, 1980.

—— 'The Phenomenon of Law', *Law, Morality, and Society: Essays in Honour of H. L. A. Hart*, eds. P. M. S. Hacker and J. Raz, Oxford, 1977, 85–98.

Lucas, P., 'On Edmund Burke's Doctrine of Prescription: or An Appeal

472 Bibliography

from the New to the Old Lawyers', *The Historical Journal*, 11 (1968), 35-63.

Lyons, D., 'Benevolence and Justice in Mill', *The Limits of Utilitarianism*, eds. H. B. Miller and W. H. Williams, Minneapolis, 1982, 42-70.

—— 'Founders and Foundations of Legal Positivism', *Michigan Law Review*, 82 (1984), 722-39.

—— 'Human Rights and General Welfare', *Philosophy and Public Affairs*, 6 (1977), 113-29.

—— *In the Interest of the Governed*, Oxford, 1973.

—— 'Mill's Theory of Justice', *Values and Morals*, eds. A. I. Goldman and J. Kim, Dordrecht, 1978.

—— 'Moral Aspects of Legal Theory', *Midwest Studies in Philosophy*, VII: *Social and Political Philosophy*, eds. P. A. French, T. E. Uehling, and H. K. Wettstein, Minneapolis, 1982, 223-54.

—— 'Utility and Rights', *Nomos XXIV: Ethics, Economics, and the Law*, New York, 1982, 107-38.

Macaulay, T. B., *History of England*, London, 1855-6.

MacCormick, D. N., *H. L. A. Hart*, Stanford, 1981.

—— *Legal Reasoning and Legal Theory*, Oxford, 1978.

McNeilly, F. S., *The Anatomy of Leviathan*, New York, 1968.

Mack, M., *Jeremy Bentham: An Odyssey of Ideas 1748-1792*, London, 1962.

Maine, H. S., *Ancient Law*, New York, 1917.

—— *The Early History of Institutions*, London, 1875.

—— *Popular Government*, Indianapolis, 1976.

Marx, K., *Capital*, vol. 1, 3rd edn., trs. Moore and Aveling, Moscow, 1970.

Mill, J. S., 'Austin on Jurisprudence', *Dissertations and Discussions*, vol. 3, London, 1874, 206-74.

—— 'Bentham', reprinted in *Jeremy Bentham*, ed. B. Parekh, London, 1974, 1-40.

—— *The Collected Works of John Stuart Mill*, ed. J. M. Robson *et al.*, 21 vols., Toronto, 1963-84.

A System of Logic, vol. VIII, Toronto, 1974.

Essays on Ethics, Religion and Society, vol. X, Toronto, 1969.

Essays on Politics and Society, vol. XIX, Toronto, 1977.

—— *Early Draft of J. S. Mill's Autobiography*, ed. J. Stillinger, Urbana, Ill., 1961.

—— *Essays on Politics and Culture*, ed. G. Himmelfarb, New York, 1982.

Miller, D., *Philosophy and Ideology in Hume's Political Philosophy*, Oxford, 1982.

Milne, A. J. M., 'Bentham's Principle of Utility and Legal Philosophy', *Bentham and Legal Theory*, ed. M. H. James, Belfast, 1974, 9-38.

Milsom, S. F. C., *Historical Foundations of the Common Law*, London, 1969.

Montesquieu, C., *The Spirit of the Laws*, Worcester, Mass., 1802.

Mossner, E. C., *The Life of David Hume*, 2nd edn., Oxford, 1980.

Munzer, S. R., 'A Theory of Retroactive Legislation', *Texas Law Review*, 61 (1982), 425–80.

Nietzsche, F., *The Gay Science*, trs. W. Kaufman, New York, 1974.

Norton, D. F., *David Hume: Common Sense Moralist and Sceptical Metaphysician*, Princeton, 1982.

Nozick, R., *Anarchy, State, and Utopia*, New York, 1974.

Oakeshott, M., *Rationalism in Politics*, London, 1962.

Olivecrona, K., 'The Will of the Sovereign: Some Reflections on Bentham's Concept of "a Law" ', *American Journal of Jurisprudence*, 20 (1975), 95–110.

Ostenfeld, J. H., 'Danish Courts of Conciliation', *American Bar Association Journal*, 9 (1923), 747–8.

Paley, W., *The Principles of Moral and Political Philosophy*, London, 1785.

Parekh, B., *Jeremy Bentham: Ten Critical Essays*, London, 1974.

Peirce, C. S., *The Philosophical Writings of Peirce*, ed., J. Buchler, New York, 1975.

Platts, M., *Ways of Meaning: and Introduction to a Philosophy of Language*, London, 1979.

Plucknett, T. F. T., *A Concise History of the Common Law*, 2nd edn., Rochester, NY, 1936.

Pocock, J. A. G., *The Ancient Constitution and the Feudal Law*, Cambridge, England, 1957.

—— 'Burke and the Ancient Constitution', in J. A. G. Pocock, *Politics, Language, and Time*, New York, 1971.

Posner, R., 'Blackstone and Bentham', *Journal of Law and Economics*, 19 (1976), 569–606.

Postema, G. J., 'Bentham and Dworkin on Positivism and Adjudication', *Social Theory and Practice*, 5 (1980), 347–76.

—— 'Co-ordination and Convention at the Foundations of Law', *Journal of Legal Studies*, 11 (1982), 165–203.

—— 'The Expositor, the Censor, and the Common Law', *Canadian Journal of Philosophy*, 9 (1979), 643–70.

—— 'Facts, Fictions, and Law: Bentham on the Foundations of Evidence', *Archiv fur Rechts- und Socialphilosophie*, Beiheft no. 16, *Facts in Law*, ed. W. Twining, Wiesbaden, 1983, 37–64.

—— 'The Normativity of Law' (forthcoming).

—— 'Nozick on Liberty, Compensation, and the Individual's Right to Punish', *Social Theory and Practice*, 6 (1980), 311–37.

—— 'The Principle of Utility and the Law of Procedure: Bentham's Theory of Adjudication', *Georgia Law Review*, 11 (1977), 1393–1424.

Putnam, H., *Reason, Truth, and History*, Cambridge, England, 1981.

474 *Bibliography*

Rabinow, P. and Sullivan, W. M., *Interpretive Social Science: A Reader*, Berkeley, Calif., 1979.

Radzinowicz, L., *A History of English Criminal Law and Its Administration From 1750*, 4 vols., London, 1948–68.

Raphael, D. D., 'Hume and Adam Smith on Justice and Utility', *Proceedings of the Aristotelian Society, 1972–3*, 87–103.

Rawls, J., *A Theory of Justice*, Cambridge, Mass., 1971.

—— 'Two Concepts of Rules', *Philosophical Review*, 64 (1955), 3–32.

Raz, J., 'Authority and Justification', *Philosophy and Public Affairs*, 14 (1985), 3–29.

—— 'Authority, Law, and Morality', *Monist*, 68 (1985), 295–324.

—— *The Authority of Law*, Oxford, 1979.

—— *The Concept of a Legal System*, 2nd edn., Oxford, 1980.

—— 'Legal Principles and the Limits of Law', *Yale Law Review*, 81 (1972), 823–54.

—— 'On the Functions of Law', *Oxford Essays in Jurisprudence, 2nd Series*, ed. A. W. B. Simpson, Oxford, 1973, 278–304.

—— *Practical Reason and Norms*, London, 1975.

—— 'The Problem about the Nature of Law', *University of Western Ontario Law Review*, 21 (1983), 203–18.

Regan, D., *Utilitarianism and Co-operation*, Oxford, 1980.

Reich, C., 'The New Property', *Yale Law Journal*, 73 (1964), 733–87.

Rosen, F., 'Jeremy Bentham and Democratic Theory', *The Bentham Newsletter*, 3 (1979), 46–61.

—— *Jeremy Bentham and Representative Democracy*, Oxford, 1983.

Rosenberg, J. F., *Linguistic Representation*, Dordrecht, 1975.

Rosenblum, N., *Bentham's Theory of the Modern State*, Cambridge, Mass., 1978.

Rousseau, J.-J., *Social Contract*, tr. J. R. Masters, ed. R. D. Masters, New York, 1978.

Salmond, J., *Jurisprudence*, 11th edn., ed. G. Williams, London, 1957.

Sartorius, R., *Individual Conduct and Social Norms*, Encino, Calif., 1975.

Scheffler, I., 'Ritual and Reference', *Synthese*, 46 (1981), 421–37.

Schelling, T., *Micromotives and Macrobehavior*, New York, 1978.

—— *The Strategy of Conflict*, Oxford, 1960.

Schutz, A., 'The Problem of Social Reality', *Collected Papers*, The Hague, 1962, vol. 1.

Shapiro, B., 'Codification of the Law in Seventeenth Century England', *Wisconsin Law Review* (1974), 428–65.

—— 'Law Reform in Seventeenth Century England', *American Journal of Legal History*, 19 (1975), 280–312.

Shapiro, M., 'Compromise and Litigation', *Nomos XXI: Compromise*, eds. J. R. Pennock and J. Chapman, New York, 1979.

—— *Courts: A Comparative and Political Analysis*, Chicago, 1981.

Shwayder, D., *The Stratification of Behaviour*, London, 1965.

Simpson, A. W. B., 'The Common Law and Legal Theory', *Oxford Essays in Jurisprudence, 2nd Series*, Oxford, 1973, 77–99.

Smith, A., *Lectures on Jurisprudence*, eds. R. L. Meek, D. D. Raphael, and P. G. Stein, Oxford, 1978.

Smith, R. H., 'The Danish Conciliation System', *American Judicature Society* (1927), 85–93.

Stearns, J. B., 'Bentham on Public and Private Ethics', *Canadian Journal of Philosophy*, 5 (1975), 583–94.

Stein, P., 'Adam Smith's Jurisprudence—Between Morality and Economics', *Cornell Law Review*, 64 (1979), 621–38.

—— 'Law and Society in Eighteenth-Century Scottish Thought', *Scotland in the Age of Improvement*, eds. N. T. Phillipson and R. Mitchison, Edinburgh, 1970.

Steintrager, J., *Bentham*, Ithaca, NY, 1977.

Stenton, D., *English Justice Between the Norman Conquest and the Great Charter*, Philadelphia, 1964.

Stone, R., 'Ratiocination not Rationalisation', *Mind*, 74 (1965), 463–82.

Stroud, B., *Hume*, London, 1977.

Taylor, C., 'Responsibility for Self', *Identities of Persons*, ed. A. O. Rorty, Berkeley, 1976.

Thompson, E. P., *The Making of the English Working Class*, New York, 1966.

—— *Whigs and Hunters*, New York, 1975.

Tuck, R., *Natural Rights Theories: Their Origin and Development*, Cambridge, England, 1979.

Twining, W. L., 'The Contemporary Significance of Bentham's *Anarchical Fallacies*', *Archiv fur Rechts- und Socialphilosophie*, 41 (1975), 325–56.

—— 'Rule-Scepticism and Fact-Scepticism in Bentham's Theory of Evidence', *Archive fur Rechts- und Socialphilosophie*, Beiheft no. 16, *Facts in Law*, ed. W. L. Twining, Wiesbaden, 1983, 65–84.

Ullmann-Margalit, E., *The Emergence of Norms*, Oxford, 1977.

Voltaire, F. M., *Oeuvres complètes de Voltaire*, ed. L. Moland, *Dictionaire philosophique*, Paris, 1977–85.

Wasserstrom, R., *The Judicial Decision*, Stanford, 1961.

Weber, M., *Law and Economy in Society*, trs. E. Shils and M. Rheinstein, New York, 1954.

Wittgenstein, L., *Philosophical Investigations*, tr. G. E. M. Anscombe, Oxford, 1953.

—— *On Certainty*, eds. G. E. M. Anscombe and G. H. von Wright, trs. D. Paul and G. E. M. Anscombe, Oxford, 1969.

Wolin, S., 'Hume and Conservatism', *Hume: A Re-Evaluation*, eds. D. W. Livingston and J. T. King, New York, 1976.

Yale, D. E. C., 'Hale and Hobbes on Law, Legislation, and the Sovereign', *Cambridge Law Journal*, 31 (1972), 121–56.

Yale Law Journal, 88 (1977), 905–1104 (Dispute Resolution Issue).

Index of Names

Adorno, T., 95n
Alfange, D. Jr., 422n, 467
Aquinas, St Thomas, 40–6, 59, 78,
109, 138n, 465–6
Ardal, P. S., 467
Aristotle, 43n, 70n
Ashburton, Lord, 307, 312
Atiyah, P. S., 467
Attwool, E., 467
Auerbach, J. S., 460n, 467
Austin, J., 165n, 179, 210, 230, 235,
246, 252, 302, 327–8, 330, 467

Bacon, F., 11n, 30, 33n, 60n, 199,
432, 467
Bahmueller, C., 465
Baier, A., 85, 92n, 95n, 99, 104n,
108n, 111n, 112n, 118, 122n, 142n,
467
Baumgardt, D., 266n, 312n, 467
Beccaria, C., 307, 362n
Bentham, J., 81, 82, 89n, 104, 107–8,
124n, 134–6, 143, 147–464 passim.,
467
Berger, M. 430n, 467
Best, W. M., 378n, 467
Bickel, A., 7n, 467
Blackstone, Sir W., 4, 5, 7, 9–19, 23,
29, 32–4, 36–7, 62n, 63, 67n, 68,
72–4, 81, 89, 153, 165, 180n, 192,
194–5, 197, 198n, 210, 221n, 227,
250, 265–6, 268, 271, 274, 290, 293–4,
298, 305, 310–12, 329, 340, 344,
350n, 351n, 352n, 422, 433, 466
Bowring, Sir J., 465
Bracton, 31
Bramhall, Bishop, 49, 58
Brandeis, L., 196n
Brandom, R., 75n, 334n, 335n, 467
Bromwich, D., 467
Brougham, H. P., 1st Baron Brougham
and Vaux, 413
Burke, E., 13n, 17n, 23, 29, 33, 61n,
66–8, 72n, 74n, 77n, 81, 99, 191,
362n, 366, 407–8, 467

Burns, J. H., 234, 251n, 252n, 366n,
396n, 413n, 465, 467

Calabresi, G., 11n, 74n, 431n, 468
Camden, Lord, 285
Carter, J. C., 19
Cavell, S., 74n, 116, 117n
Charron, W., 468
Cicero, 41
Coke, Sir E., 3n, 6–7, 9, 15, 19, 20–2,
30, 33, 46–8, 55, 59–61, 64, 66, 67,
81, 89, 210, 271n, 307, 352n, 433, 463
Coleman, J., 231n, 330, 468
Cropsey, J., 46n, 60n, 466
Cross, Sir R., 195n, 468

Davies, Sir J., 4, 64n, 73n
D'Entreves, A. P., 41n, 465
Devlin, Lord, 38n
Dickens, C., 344
Dickinson, H. T., 29n, 264n, 265n, 468
Dinwiddy, J. R., 366n, 399n, 465, 468
Dumont, E., 378n, 451, 465
Durkheim, E., vii, 23n, 468
Dworkin, R., 38, 213n, 331n, 442–4,
447, 461–2n, 468

Edward I, 15n, 17n, 89n
Eisenberg, M., 457n, 468
Ellsmere, Lord, 11n
Elster, J., 468
Ely, J., 269n, 468
Epstein, R., 468

Ferguson, A., 93n, 97n, 104n, 119n,
453, 463, 468
Filmer, R., 235
Finnis, J., 43n, 468
Forbes, D., 29, 86n, 87n, 89n, 92n, 95,
96n, 97n, 352n, 468
Fortescue, J., 3n
Fried, C., 31, 468
Friedman, B., 165n, 327n, 468
Fuller, L. L., 71n, 127n, 168, 328, 329n,
335n, 336, 431n, 457n, 461n, 468

Index of Subjects

and complexity of law and legal procedures, 274, 344–5, 350–1
individual, 162–6
negative, 170–1
and public justification of laws and decisions, 369–70
Logic of the will, 179–80

Mediation, 405, 460
Motives
dissocial, 379–80, 382
effect of social conditions on relative strength of, 185–6, 380–3
integrity, 396, 398
and sanctions, 394–5
and self-government, 399
self-regarding, 372, 378–9, 381, 383, 388
semi-social 372, 378–9, 381, 399, 401
social, 379–83, 388, 399–401

Natural Law, laws of nature, 40–6, 244–5
Bentham on, 269–70, 284, 293
in Common Law theory, 30–8, 62, 68–9, 269–70
and criteria of validity, 247–9, 293–4
Hobbes on, 51, 59
Hume on, 88n, 123n
and public expectations, 248
Natural rights, see Rights

Obedience
Hobbes on, 59
Common Law on, 78–9
Bentham on, 275, 277, 294, 309, 312, 316–17, 319, 326, 368–70
Offences, 176, 178, 193
Ontology, see Fiction(s)

Paradox of inflexibility, 48n, 279–86, 404, 409, 458
Parliamentary sovereignty, see Sovereignty, parliamentary
Penal Law
in eighteenth century England, 264–6
(see also Civil v. penal law)
Positivism, legal, vii, ix, 39, 218, 230–2, 262, 290, 295–301, 302–36, 463–4
its ahistorical character, 329
conception of community 314–15
and conceptual revisionism, 311–13, 318–29, 331

and empiricist ontology, 296–301
historical relativity of, 310, 312–13, 329–30
and model of rules, 314–15, 442, 444, 447–8, 452, 463–4
and modern state, 218
morally neutral definitions of legal terms 303, 332
and rights, 321
theory of law v. theory of laws, 303, 339
utilitarian, 301–36
—and natural law theory compared, 302–3
—coherence of, 302–3, 330–6
and utilitarian adjudication, 440, 447–8, 452
(see also Sovereignty)
Power(s), 179–80, 232–4, 258
of imperation, 232–3
investitive, 234, 258
Precedent, 11, 47–8, 67, 131–2, 193–200, 211, 215, 278–9, 282–3, 286, 349, 405–6, 408, 415, 418–19, 449, 454, 461
in arbitration, 457n
and effects of jury decisions, 455n
Prejudice and prepossessions, 67, 98–9, 116, 133
Prescription, 88n, 120, 127
Princeps, 40, 42, 45–6
Principle of utility (see also Greatest happiness)
in adjudication, 198–200, 203–7, 210–17, 404–7, 411, 415–18, 435, 439, 441, 447–8, 452
in Bentham's theory of law, 307, 318, 326–8, 339
in Bentham's theory of procedure, 344, 346
a common-sense principle, 427
and completeness of law, 429
in constitutional theory, 362
and disappointment prevention principle, 159, 415–17
and formal rules, 445, 446, 451–2
and moral sanction, 401–2
as principle for evaluating actions, 392
and private ethics, 399, 401
and public opinion, 153–4, 203–6, 244, 248, 402
and simplicity, 427, 430